NASM's
Essentials of
Sports Performance
Training

Micheal A. Clark, DPT, MS, PES, CES
CEO
National Academy of Sports Medicine
Calabasas, CA

Scott C. Lucett, MS, PES, CES, NASM – CPT
Director of Education
National Academy of Sports Medicine,
Calabasas, CA

Wolters Kluwer | Lippincott Williams & Wilkins
Health

Philadelphia • Baltimore • New York • London
Buenos Aires • Hong Kong • Sydney • Tokyo

Acquisitions Editor: Emily Lupash
Product Manager: Andrea Klingler
Marketing Manager: Christen Murphy
Designer: Teresa Mallon
Compositor: Aptara Corporation

First Edition

Copyright © 2010 Lippincott Williams & Wilkins, a Wolters Kluwer business

351 West Camden Street
Baltimore, MD 21201

530 Walnut Street
Philadelphia, PA 19106

Printed in China

9 8 7 6 5 4 3 2 1

Library of Congress Cataloging-in-Publication Data

Clark, Micheal.
  NASM's essentials of sports performance training / Micheal A. Clark, Scott C. Lucett.
    p. ; cm.
  Includes bibliographical references and index.
  ISBN 978-0-7817-6803-0 (alk. paper)
  1. Physical education and training. 2. Sports medicine. I. Lucett, Scott. II. Kirkendall, Donald T.
  III. National Academy of Sports Medicine. IV. Title. V. Title: Essentials of sports performance training.
  [DNLM: 1. Athletic Performance. 2. Athletic Injuries—prevention & control. 3. Sports Medicine—methods. QT 260 C594n 2010]
  GV341.C5557 2010
  613.7'11—dc22

                                                                                              2009015994

DISCLAIMER

Care has been taken to confirm the accuracy of the information present and to describe generally accepted practices. However, the authors, editors, and publisher are not responsible for errors or omissions or for any consequences from application of the information in this book and make no warranty, expressed or implied, with respect to the currency, completeness, or accuracy of the contents of the publication. Application of this information in a particular situation remains the professional responsibility of the practitioner; the clinical treatments described and recommended may not be considered absolute and universal recommendations.

The authors, editors, and publisher have exerted every effort to ensure that drug selection and dosage set forth in this text are in accordance with the current recommendations and practice at the time of publication. However, in view of ongoing research, changes in government regulations, and the constant flow of information relating to drug therapy and drug reactions, the reader is urged to check the package insert for each drug for any change in indications and dosage and for added warnings and precautions. This is particularly important when the recommended agent is a new or infrequently employed drug.

Some drugs and medical devices presented in this publication have Food and Drug Administration (FDA) clearance for limited use in restricted research settings. It is the responsibility of the health care provider to ascertain the FDA status of each drug or device planned for use in their clinical practice.

To purchase additional copies of this book, call our customer service department at **(800) 638-3030** or fax orders to **(301) 223-2320**. International customers should call **(301) 223-2300**.

Visit Lippincott Williams & Wilkins on the Internet: **http://www.lww.com**. Lippincott Williams & Wilkins customer service representatives are available from 8:30 am to 6:00 pm, EST.

NASM's Essentials of Sports Performance Training Mission

To help athletes accomplish their sports performance goals.

National Academy of Sports Medicine Code of Professional Conduct

Introduction

The following code of conduct is designed to assist certified and non-certified members of the National Academy of Sports Medicine (NASM) to uphold (both as individuals and as an industry) the highest levels of professional and ethical conduct. This Code of Professional Conduct reflects the level of commitment and integrity necessary to ensure that all NASM members provide the highest level of service and respect for all colleagues, allied professionals, and the general public.

Professionalism

Each certified or non-certified member must provide optimal professional service and demonstrate excellent client care in his/her practice. Each member must:

1. Abide fully by the NASM Code of Professional Conduct.
2. Conduct themselves in a manner that merits the respect of the public, other colleagues, and NASM.
3. Treat each colleague and client with the utmost respect and dignity.
4. Not make false or derogatory assumptions concerning the practices of colleagues and clients.
5. Use appropriate professional communication in all verbal, non-verbal, and written transactions.
6. Provide and maintain an environment that ensures client safety that, at minimum, requires that the certified or non-certified member must:
   a. Not diagnose or treat illness or injury (except for basic first aid) unless the certified or non-certified member is legally licensed to do so and is working in that capacity, at that time.
   b. Not train clients with a diagnosed health condition unless the certified or non-certified member has been specifically trained to do so, is following procedures prescribed and supervised by a valid licensed medical professional, or unless the certified or non-certified member is legally licensed to do so and is working in that capacity at that time.
   c. Not begin to train a client prior to receiving and reviewing a current health-history questionnaire signed by the client.
   d. Hold a current cardiopulmonary resuscitation (CPR) and automated external defibrillator (AED) certification at all times.
7. Refer the client to the appropriate medical practitioner when, at minimum, the certified or non-certified member:
   a. Becomes aware of any change in the client's health status or medication.
   b. Becomes aware of an undiagnosed illness, injury, or risk factor.
   c. Becomes aware of any unusual pain and/or discomfort experienced by the client during the course the training session that warrants professional care after the session has been discontinued and assessed.

8. Refer the client to other healthcare professionals when nutritional and supplemental advice is requested, unless the certified or non-certified member has been specifically trained to do so or holds a credential to do so and is acting in that capacity at the time
9. Maintain a level of personal hygiene appropriate for a health and fitness setting.
10. Wear clothing that is clean, modest, and professional.
11. Remain in good standing and maintain current certification status by acquiring all necessary continuing-education requirements (see NASM Re-certification Information).

Confidentiality

Each certified and non-certified member must respect the confidentiality of all client information. In his/her professional role, the certified or non-certified member:

1. Protect the client's confidentiality in conversations, advertisements and any other arena, unless otherwise agreed upon by the client in writing, or due to medical and/or legal necessity.
2. Protect the interest of clients who are minors by law, or who are unable to give voluntary consent, by securing the legal permission of the appropriate third party or guardian.
3. Store and dispose of client records in a secure manner.

Legal and Ethical

Each certified or non-certified member must comply with all legal requirements within the applicable jurisdiction. In his/her professional role, the certified or non-certified member must:

1. Obey all local, state, federal, and providence laws.
2. Accept complete responsibility for his/her actions.
3. Maintain accurate and truthful records.
4. Respect and uphold all existing publishing and copyright laws.

Business Practice

Each certified or non-certified member must practice with honesty, integrity, and lawfulness. In his/her professional role, the certified or non-certified member must:

1. Maintain adequate liability insurance.
2. Maintain adequate and truthful progress notes for each client.
3. Accurately and truthfully inform the public of services rendered.
4. Honestly and truthfully represent all professional qualifications and affiliations.
5. Advertise in a manner that is honest, dignified, and representative of services that can be delivered without the use of provocative and/or sexual language and/or pictures.
6. Maintain accurate financial, contract, appointment, and tax records including original receipts for a minimum of four years.
7. Comply with all local, state, federal, and providence laws regarding sexual harassment.

NASM expects each member to uphold the Code of Professional Conduct in its entirety. Failure to comply with the NASM Code of Professional Conduct may result in disciplinary actions including but not limited to suspension or termination of membership and/or certification. NASM will not certify any individual who has previously been convicted of a felony or misdemeanor. All members are obligated to report any unethical behavior or violation of the Code of Professional Conduct by other NASM members.

Preface

The NASM Optimum Performance Training (OPT™) model has been a facet in the performance training arena for years and as such, has benefited many professionals and top-notch athletes along the way. From top-level executives owning and managing professional teams, to the athletes themselves, the reach of the OPT™ model is beyond compare as noted by the following friends of NASM, who have been instrumental in the success of the best performance and injury prevention training system in the field.

"NASM OPT-Training is a huge benefit. It has a cumulative effect on your body. If your body is more receptive every night, it's going to help you over the long term."

—*Steve Nash, Phoenix Suns, Two-Time NBA MVP*

"As an organization we strive to provide the highest benchmarks for our athletes to reach and we expect no less of our staff and sports medicine partners. NASM has reached beyond our organization's expectations and delivered on providing the best quality programming and training techniques to keep our athletes healthy and ready to perform at their peak. This helps our team focus more on the task at hand and less about potential injuries during the season."

—*Jim Ramsay, Head Athletic Trainer, New York Rangers*

"Proper preparation off the court keeps athletes performing at peak levels, which is critical in professional sports. NASM understands this and has created the most effective integrated performance training systems based on years of research and experience."

—*Bryan Colangelo, President and General Manager, Toronto Raptors*

"NASM's innovative approach to performance training through specialized programming has shown in the health, fitness and prepared of each athlete NASM has worked with."

—*Dr. Craig Phelps, Team Physician, Phoenix Suns*

"The importance of injury prevention within professional sports is beyond measure. With NASM's systematic and integrated training system, I feel confident that our players will not only have decreased injury rates, but perform at higher levels. The uniqueness of the programming schemes is unparalleled throughout the strength and conditioning field."

—*Mike D'Antoni, Head Coach, New York Knicks*

"I've always sought out the best technology in my sport to enhance my career. Getting together with NASM has been a perfect fit for me because it's about one thing, always getting better and never being complacent. This is a common vision that NASM and I have. My biggest asset is my durability and I attribute my ability to stay healthy over the course of 9 seasons in the Major Leagues to NASM and the techniques it's incorporated in its programs. What sets NASM apart from the rest for me is the willingness to constantly adapt the programs and techniques to the latest technology that's come about from the most up to date studies and research. NASM has never hesitated to upgrade their programs constantly to coincide with the latest and greatest technology in this field. I am an NASM advocate for life and look forward to seeing how and where this visionary company will go."

—*Barry Zito, San Francisco Giants, Cy Young Award Winner, MLB All-Star*

"The health and wellness of professional athletes has an intangible value—sickness or injury can devastate an organization, team and athlete. As a medical professional, I understand the importance of keeping each athlete healthy and I rely on the best science and techniques to do just that. NASM's unique programming model and integrated training techniques exemplify their commitment to cutting-edge performance training methods. Too often we dedicate our resources to rehabilitating an athlete and neglect to focus on injury prevention, but NASM's programs combine the latest science, research and clinical applications available to help athletes reduce injuries and reach their performance potential. NASM's evidence-based approach systematically progresses athletes through a solid foundation punctuated with preventative measures and works to ensure a physically sound athlete throughout their career."

—Dr. Thomas Carter, Team Physician, Phoenix Suns and Emeritus Head of Orthopedic Surgery, Arizona State University

"Over my 10 years in professional athletics as a strength and conditioning professional I have found a scientifically based systematic approach to performance training ideal for the professional athlete. The research based OPT model by the National Academy of Sports Medicine has been the driving force behind the implementation of this approach in athletics today. I would highly recommend the utilization of NASM's scientific based approach to performance training for all athletes, conditioning coaches, medical professionals and fitness practitioners in their pursuit of excellence in sport today."

—Sean Cochran, former strength and conditioning coach, San Diego Padres, current strength and conditioning coach on the PGA Tour

"For competitive athletes, resistance training is a means to an end. It is supplemental to the technical practice of the actual sport. If this training does not result in improved sport performance then it is irrelevant how much weight the athlete was able to lift or how many reps they were able to perform or how much muscle mass they have added to their frame. Even more importantly, the strength/power/speed that the athlete develops in the off-season can only be enjoyed during the season if the athlete is able to stay healthy. If you can't compete due to injury then what good is your new-found strength or muscle?

The real secret to optimum sport performance through training lies in the application of a comprehensive and evidence based approach. The integrated OPT model fits this description and is a system that will arm the personal trainer or strength coach with a solid protocol to use as a foundation for their programming. This program will allow the trainer to implement safe and effective programs that will enhance an athlete's performance."

—Matt Nichol, Strength Coach, Toronto Maple Leafs

"Being a professional athlete means I make a living with my body. I need it performing at the highest levels every second I am on the court. I rely on NASM's system of performance training to make sure I am playing at peak levels every game, every play."

—Emeka Okafor, Charlotte Bobcats

"NASM has been instrumental in my continuing education over the past 8 years. The OPT™ model and the Performance Enhancement Specialist credential allow me to strategically and systematically address the musculoskeletal issues that my players present on a daily basis. The approach also allows me to educate my athletes and let them take an active part in their performance enhancement, rehabilitation, and injury prevention."

—Casey Smith, Head Athletic Trainer, Dallas Mavericks

Letter from the CEO

I applaud you on your dedication to helping athletes achieve the height of their physical skill, and thank you for entrusting the National Academy of Sports Medicine (NASM) with your education.

By following the techniques in this book, *NASM's Essentials of Sports Performance Training*, you will gain the information, insight, and inspiration you need to impact the athletic world as a Sports Performance Professional.

Since 1987, NASM has been the leading authority in certification, continuing education, solutions, and tools for Health and Fitness, Sports Performance, and Sports Medicine Professionals. Our systematic and scientific approach to both fitness and performance continues to raise the bar as the "gold standard" in the industry. Today, we serve as the global authority in more than 80 countries, serving more than 100,000 members! Tomorrow, our possibilities are endless.

The performance industry is prime for a convergence of the latest science with cutting-edge technological solutions for maximizing the human potential. With the advances in research and application techniques, performance training will shift upward, drawing on traditional approaches while embracing new ideologies for enhancing the abilities of athletes. These industry shifts will continue to provide unlimited opportunities for you as an elite NASM professional.

Today's athlete has an increasingly high level of expectations. They demand the best and the brightest who can provide unparalleled results. To meet these expectations and better deliver quality, innovation, and evidence-based performance enhancement solutions to the world, NASM has developed new and exciting solutions with best-in-class partners from the education, healthcare, sports and entertainment, and technology industries. With the help of our best-in-class partnerships—and top professionals like you—we will continue to live up to the expectations placed upon us and strive to raise the bar in our pursuit of excellence!

Innovation is important in performance and the new NASM reflects our ability to stay ground-breaking in an ever-evolving world. Amidst all of the change, we will always stay true to our mission and values: delivering evidence-based solutions driven by excellence, innovation, and results. This is essential to our long-term success as a company, and to your individual career success as a Sports Performance Professional.

Scientific research and techniques also continue to advance and, as a result, you must remain on the cutting edge in order to remain competitive. The NASM education continuum—certification, specializations, continuing and higher education—is based on a foundation of comprehensive, scientific research supported by leading institutes and universities. As a result, NASM offers scientifically-validated education, evidence-based solutions and user-friendly tools that can be applied immediately.

The tools and solutions in the Optimum Performance Training™ (OPT) methodology help put science into practice to create amazing results for athletes. OPT™ is an innovative, systematic approach, used by thousands of Sports Performance Professionals and athletes worldwide. NASM's techniques work, creating a dramatic difference in training programs and their results.

One of the most influential people of the twentieth century told us "a life is not important except for the impact it has on other lives."[1] For us as Sports Performance Professionals in the twenty-first century, the truth behind this wisdom has never been greater.

The road to athletic achievement requires more than one approach. Competitive athletes need comprehensive nutritional strategies, practice in sports psychology and a systematic training process that focuses on the needs of the individual athlete as well as the sport. NASM's education, solutions, and tools can positively impact the sports world by engaging athletes in practical, customized, evidence-based exercise.

---

1. Jackie Robinson, Hall of Fame baseball player and civil rights leader (1919–1972).

The evolution of performance is upon us, and the potential for you and your athletes to achieve the pinnacle of your careers lies in front of you. With that, I welcome you to the NASM community of Sports Performance Professionals. If you ever need assistance from one of our subject matter experts, or simply want to learn more about our new partnerships and evidence-based health and fitness solutions, please call us at 800-460-NASM or visit us online at http://www.nasm.org.

We look forward to working with you to impact the performance world. Now let's go out together and empower our athletes to achieve their potential!

MICHEAL A. CLARK, DPT, MS, PES, CES
CEO

New Content

Based upon feedback from past students and Sports Performance Professionals, this new textbook includes several new updates in comparison to the previous performance enhancement materials:

1. **Streamlined OPT™ Model**—The OPT™ model has been simplified to include six of the most commonly used phases of training for sports performance goals, versus the previous seven-phase model. The one phase of training that is no longer included in this performance version of the model, Corrective Exercise Training, is a specialized form of training that would be used for athletes who've come off an injury and *prepares* the athlete to enter into the OPT™ model. This form of training is covered exclusively in NASM's Corrective Exercise Specialist course.

2. **Revised Model Nomenclature**—We've also renamed the phases so it is easier to understand the exact function and desired adaptation for that phase of training.

3. **Additional Chapters**—This textbook includes several new chapters not included in the previous performance enhancement materials. These additional chapter topics will assist in creating a more well-rounded Sports Performance Professional and thus in creating more value in you as a professional. These additional chapters include:
   1. Cardiorespiratory Training for Performance Enhancement
   2. Olympic Lifting for Performance Enhancement
   3. Current Concepts in Injury Prevention and Reconditioning
   4. Ergogenic Aids
   5. Sports Psychology

4. **Updated Chapter Content**—All of the chapter topics in this textbook have been updated to include new information and the most up-to-date research provided and reviewed by some of the most well-respected Sports Performance Professionals in the industry. Some of the new content update highlights include:
   1. Over 30 different performance assessments measuring movement efficiency, stability, strength, muscular endurance, cardiorespiratory efficiency, speed, agility, quickness, and power.
   2. Sports-specific assessments, programming strategies, and example programs for the below sports:
      1. Football
      2. Baseball
      3. Basketball
      4. Soccer
      5. Hockey
      6. Golf
   3. A greatly improved Speed, Agility, and Quickness (SAQ) chapter with nearly 40 different SAQ drills
   4. Almost 400 exercises in the categories of flexibility, core, balance, plyometrics, speed, agility, quickness, and resistance training.

5. **Glossary of Terms**—We've also updated our Glossary of Terms to include a larger number of terms and definitions and added an index for easy navigation when searching for topics, concepts, or programming strategies.

Pedagogical Features

The new textbook comes with a variety of new educational features. These features include:
- New illustrations that visually bring principles and concepts to life
- Updated tables that summarize additional information not included in the body of the text
- New anatomical images that clearly identify important structures of the nervous, musculoskeletal, and cardiorespiratory systems
- Time Out and Key Term sidebars to highlight important principles and concepts
- End-of-chapter summaries for quick-hitting chapter highlights
- Updated exercise photos that show proper execution and progression variety.

Additional Resources

NASM'S Essentials of Sports Performance Training includes additional resources for both instructors and students that are available on the book's companion website at thePoint.lww.com/NASMPES.

Instructor Resources

Approved adopting instructors will be given access to the following additional resources:
- Answer key to lab-based activities
- Image bank
- Brownstone test generator
- PowerPoint presentations
- WebCT- and Blackboard-ready cartridges

Student Resources

- Video clips
- Quiz bank
- Lab-based activities
- Features about Cardiopulmonary Resuscitation (CPR), Administering First Aid, and AED (Automated External Defibrillators)

In addition, purchasers of the text can access the searchable Full Text On-line by going to the *NASM's Essentials of Sports Performance Training* website at http://thePoint.lww.com. See the inside front cover of this text for more details, including the passcode you will need to gain access to the website.

Contributors

Mike Bahn, MS, PES, CSCS
Strength and Conditioning Coordinator
Phoenix Coyotes

Michelle C. Boling, PhD, ATC
Assistant Professor
Department of Athletic Training &
    Physical Therapy
Brooks College of Health
University of North Florida

Cathleen N. Brown, PhD, ATC
Department of Kinesiology
University of Georgia

Joe Carbone, MS, CSCS
Sports Performance Director, Velocity SP
Former Strength & Conditioning Coach
Los Angeles Lakers

Micheal A. Clark, DPT, MS, PES, CES
CEO
National Academy of Sports Medicine

John Cone, MS, CSCS
Cone Fitness Training & Consulting LLC

Michael Gervais, PhD
CEO, Director of Performance
    Psychology
Pinnacle Performance Center, Inc.

Benjamin Goerger, MS, ATC
Department of Exercise and Sport
    Science
University of North Carolina at Chapel
    Hill

Jennifer E. Ketterly, MS, RD
Campus Health Services Sports Medicine
    & Department of Athletics
University of North Carolina at Chapel
    Hill

Brett Klika, CSCS
Director of Athletic Performance
Fitness Quest 10

Scott C. Lucett, MS, PES, CES, NASM–CPT
Director of Education
National Academy of Sports Medicine

Joseph B. Myers, PhD, ATC
Assistant Professor
Department of Exercise and Sport
    Science
University of North Carolina at Chapel
    Hill

Darin A. Padua, PhD, ATC
Associate Professor
Director, Sports Medicine Research
    Laboratory
Department of Exercise and Sport
    Science
University of North Carolina at Chapel Hill

Peter Papadogiannis, PhD
Senior Research Associate
Multi-Health Systems Inc.

Erik Phillips, ATC-L, PES, CES
Head Strength & Conditioning Coach/
    Asst Athletic Trainer
Phoenix Suns

Ben Potenziano, M.Ed, LATC, CES
Strength and Conditioning
  Coordinator
San Francisco Giants

Paul Robbins, MS
Metabolic Specialist
Athletes Performance

Cedric Smith
Strength and Conditioning Coach
Kansas City Chiefs

Bob Takano, CSCS
Member
USA Weightlifting Hall of Fame

Chuck Thigpen, PT, PhD, ATC
Assistant Professor
Department of Athletic Training &
  Physical Therapy
Brooks College of Health
University of North Florida

C. Alan Titchenal, PhD, CNS
Associate Professor
Human Nutrition, Food and Animal
  Sciences
University of Hawaii at Manoa

Tyler Wallace, PES, CES
Vice President of Product Development
National Academy of Sports Medicine

Reviewers

Todd Durkin, MA, CSCS, NCTMB
Owner & Performance Coach, Fitness
  Quest 10 & Todd Durkin Enterprises
Head, Under Armour Performance
  Training Council

Kevin Guskiewicz, PhD, ATC
Professor and Chair
Department of Exercise and Sports
  Science
University of North Carolina at Chapel
  Hill

Marjorie A. King, PhD, ATC, PT
Director of Graduate Athletic Training
  Education
Plymouth State University

Gay Riley, MS, RD, CCN
Founder of netnutritionist.com

Matthew Rhea, PhD
Director of Human Movement MS
  Program
Arizona School of Health Sciences

Acknowledgments

We would like to thank our photographer, Ben Bercovici, President of In Sync Production (Calabasas, CA), and his talented staff: Mark Mardoyan, Dave Whittaker, Justin Duquette, Dan Mardoyan, Francisco Gonzales, Donald Bogner, Robert Bunce, Arpee Markarian, Jeff Sterling, Susan Bercovici, and Joshua Bobrove.

A special acknowledgment goes out to our models, who made all of these exercises look easy: Christine Silva, Steven McDougal, Joey Metz, Rian Chab, Jessica Kern, Geoff Etherson, Monica Munson, Harold Spencer, Alexis Weatherspoon, Golden Goodwin, and Sean Brown.

Finally, a special thank you to Jim Benkert, who coordinated our shoot at Westlake High School (Westlake Village, CA). Photos were also taken at the NASM Headquarters in Calabasas, CA.

Contents

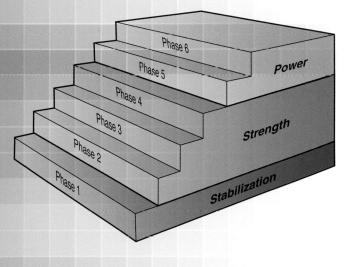

SECTION I

Principles and Concepts of Human Movement Science

CHAPTER I

Essentials of Integrated Training

UPON COMPLETION OF THIS CHAPTER, YOU WILL BE ABLE TO:

Define integrated training.

Describe the principles of integrated training.

Define the components, scientific rationale, and evidence for integrated training.

Introduction

Integrated Training
A comprehensive approach that attempts to improve all components necessary for an athlete to perform at the highest level and prevent injury.

Neuromuscular Efficiency
The ability of the human movement system to allow agonists, antagonists, synergists, and stabilizers to work synergistically to produce force, reduce force, and dynamically stabilize the entire human movement system (1,2). This process helps to maintain optimal length-tension relationships, force-couple relationships, and arthrokinematics.

Sports Performance Professionals need to follow a comprehensive, systematic, and integrated training approach to help athletes achieve their desired performance goals. To bridge the ever widening gap between science and practical application, a full understanding of the structure and function of the human movement system is needed to stay on the cutting edge of research, sports science, and practical application.

Function is an integrated, multiplanar movement that involves acceleration, deceleration, and stabilization (1). **Integrated training** is a comprehensive approach that attempts to improve all components necessary for an athlete to perform at the highest level and prevent injury. Integrated training does this by focusing on developing **functional strength** and **neuromuscular efficiency**. Functional strength is the ability of the neuromusculoskeletal system to efficiently and effectively produce force, reduce force, and dynamically stabilize the entire human movement system during functional movements (2–4). Neuromuscular efficiency is the ability of the central nervous system (CNS) to allow agonists, antagonists, synergists, and stabilizers to work interdependently during dynamic athletic activities (2,4–6).

Traditional strength and conditioning programs primarily focus on absolute or maximum strength gains in isolated muscles (chiefly the prime movers), throughout single planes of motion (1). Functional athletic activities are, however, multiplanar and require acceleration, deceleration, and dynamic stabilization (1,7–13). Although some functional movements may appear to be single-plane dominant (e.g., sprinting), dynamic stabilization in other planes is required for optimal neuromuscular efficiency and performance (8,11). Sports Performance Professionals must make a fundamental paradigm shift when they recognize that functional athletic movements require a highly complex and integrated training system. This paradigm shift directs training toward the entire human movement system through all planes of motion by establishing high levels of functional strength and neuromuscular

Functional Strength
The ability of the neuro-muscular system to contract eccentrically, isometrically and concentrically in all three planes of motion.

efficiency. To do this, the Sports Performance Professional will design training programs that integrate flexibility, core, balance, plyometric, speed/agility/quickness, resistance, and sport specific cardiorespiratory training (1,14–16).

Integrated Training Principles

UTILIZATION OF THE STRETCH-SHORTENING CYCLE

An important factor in athletic performance is explosive force. Sports that require sprinting, cutting, jumping, and throwing rely heavily on integrating speed, strength, and power of an athlete (16–20). Specific exercises can increase power output and explosiveness by training muscles to do more work in a shorter amount of time (17,21–24). This occurs by utilizing the **stretch-shortening cycle**, which occurs when an activated muscle transitions from an eccentric contraction (deceleration) to a rapid concentric contraction (acceleration) (25–28). The rapid eccentric contraction creates a stretch reflex storing potential energy that is used to produce a concentric contraction more forceful than could otherwise be generated by the resting muscle (17,29). The shorter the amount of time between the eccentric and the concentric contraction, the greater the potential energy stored and used for a more concentric force production (16,25–27,30,31). Stabilization strength, core strength, and neuromuscular efficiency may help to control the time between the eccentric and the concentric contraction (1). When eccentric strength, neuromuscular efficiency, and stabilization strength are optimized, your athletes will realize greater concentric force production without an increase in hypertrophy (morphological changes) (15–17,32,33). After you fully understand this concept, you will advise your athletes to make use of exercises that maximize the stretch-shortening cycle that will make up a larger portion of your athlete's integrated sports performance program (8,14–17,32,34–36).

Stretch-Shortening Cycle
An active stretch (eccentric contraction) of a muscle followed by an immediate shortening (concentric contraction) of that same muscle.

UTILIZATION OF THE INTEGRATED TRAINING CONTINUUM

Most strength and conditioning programs focus on isolated, uniplanar exercises to maximize absolute strength gains and hypertrophy. However, the central nervous system (CNS) is designed to optimize the selection of muscle synergies to perform integrated movement patterns in all three planes of motion (4,7,9–11). Therefore, if the human movement system is designed to move in all three planes of motion as an interdependent unit, isolated training does little to improve overall athletic performance. The athlete who applies an integrated functional approach to training will develop high levels of dynamic flexibility, core strength, neuromuscular control, power, speed/agility/quickness, and functional strength (14–17,32–36,38–47). In addition, your athlete may develop similar, or even greater, levels of hypertrophy following improved motor unit recruitment. Training that exploits integrated, functional movement patterns targets synergistic muscles to regulate isometric, concentric, and eccentric force while dynamically stabilizing the entire human movement system in all three planes of motion. This creates maximal motor unit recruitment and facilitates a greater overall training response (44,47).

TRAINING IN ALL PLANES OF MOTION

Every athletic activity occurs in all three planes of motion (Fig. 1.1): sagittal, frontal (or coronal), and transverse (5,7,8,10–13). The majority of traditional strength and conditioning exercises occur in the sagittal plane with the primary emphasis on concentric force production. An athletic activity may appear to be dominant in one plane (e.g., sprinting), but movements in the other two planes of motion must be controlled for effective performance (8,9,11). If a muscle is dominant in primarily one plane (e.g., gluteus medius in the frontal plane, quadriceps in the sagittal plane, and external obliques in the transverse plane), then you must develop a multiplanar training program. Only then will you be able to efficiently and effectively prepare your athletes for their athletic activities and injury prevention because many athletic injuries occur in the frontal and transverse plane (7,8,10,12,15,48,49). Training only in the sagittal plane will not effectively prepare your athlete's muscles that are dominant in the frontal and transverse plane (8,9,50,51).

TRAINING WITH OPTIMUM POSTURE

Posture is a dynamic controlling quality. Optimum alignment of each segment of the human movement system is a cornerstone to any functional sports performance program. If one component of the human movement system is out of alignment, other components will have

Frontal
plane

Sagittal
plane

Transverse
plane

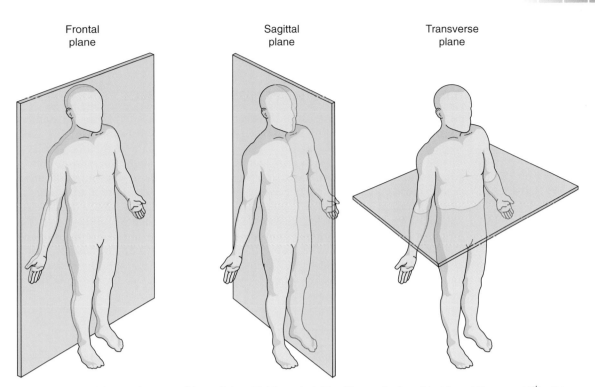

FIGURE 1.1 Planes of motion. (From Cohen BJ. Memmler's The Human Body in Health and Disease, 10ᵗʰ edition. Baltimore: Lippincott Williams & Wilkins; 2007.)

to compensate for decreasing neuromuscular efficiency, which increases the chance of injury (2,3,8,9,13,48,49,52–60). Poor posture during training can lead to muscle imbalances, joint dysfunctions, and impairment of human movement (60).

Training with proper posture ensures optimum results and decreases the risk of developing muscle imbalances, joint dysfunctions, and tissue overload (Fig. 1.2). Allowing an athlete to perform exercises with poor lumbar posture may result in the development of muscle imbalances

FIGURE 1.2 Training with optimum posture.

and possible injury (4,43,58,59,61). A functional, integrated training program of the entire human movement system ensures maintenance of structural integrity while requiring your athlete to perform exercises correctly with proper postural control.

TRAINING FOR OPTIMUM MUSCLE BALANCE

Altered Reciprocal Inhibition

When a tight muscle, for example, the psoas, causes decreased neural drive to its functional antagonist (gluteus maximus).

Synergistic Dominance

When synergists compensate for a weak or inhibited prime mover in an attempt to maintain force production and functional movement patterns.

Muscles function optimally from an ideal predetermined length, thus an optimum length-tension relationship (5). The muscle's length-tension relationship is altered when a muscle is stimulated at a length less than or greater than this optimal length effectively altering force-couple relationships and joint kinematics (3,56,60). Subtle changes in posture, pattern overload, injury, and decreased neuromuscular efficiency can alter the resting length of muscle that can lead to muscle imbalances. Muscle overactivity, adaptive muscle shortening or both can cause **altered reciprocal inhibition** and **synergistic dominance** (2,8,9,54–56,62–64). Altered reciprocal inhibition results in decreased force production by the prime mover and leads to compensation by the synergists (synergistic dominance) (2,65). Synergistic dominance leads to altered movement patterns and decreased neuromuscular control (2,7,8,12,55,60). Therefore, all sports performance programs should be well planned and executed to ensure the development of optimum muscle balance. In turn, this will ensure maintenance of the structural integrity of the entire human movement system.

TRAINING FOR OPTIMUM MUSCLE FUNCTION

It is imperative that today's Sports Performance Professional understands human movement science. The greater your understanding of human movement science, the more effective the performance enhancement and injury prevention programs you design will be. As mentioned before, muscles function eccentrically, isometrically, and concentrically in all three planes of motion (5). Movement is a complex event orchestrated by the CNS. The CNS executes pre-programmed patterns of movements that can be modified in response to gravity, ground reaction forces, and momentum that must be trained accordingly. For example, CNS control allows the gluteus maximus to work *eccentrically* to decelerate hip flexion, internal rotation, adduction, and tibial internal rotation (through its attachment to the iliotibial band), *isometrically* to stabilize the SI joint, and *concentrically* to extend and externally rotate the hip (5). The typical way to strengthen the gluteus maximus is to have the athlete perform sagittal plane hip flexion/extension exercises (squats, lunges, step ups, etc.) with little attention to transverse plane, eccentric function, or the stabilization function of the gluteus maximus. Remember that while muscles can have some anatomical individuality, they lack functional individuality.

An integrated sports performance training program will focus on multiplanar training (sagittal, frontal, and transverse) while activating the entire spectrum of muscle contraction (eccentric, isometric, and concentric) using multiple modalities (free weights, dumbbells, cables, machines, tubing, medicine balls, etc.) incorporating flexibility, core, balance, plyometrics, speed, agility, quickness, integrated resistance training, and sports specific conditioning to efficiently and effectively prepare athletes for optimal performance and injury prevention.

Components of an Integrated Sports Performance Program

FLEXIBILITY TRAINING

Flexibility

The ability of the human movement system to have optimum range of motion (ROM) as well as neuromuscular control throughout that ROM in order to prevent injury and enhance functional efficiency.

Muscle imbalances and poor **flexibility** may decrease performance and increase the risk of injury (33,46,52,61,66). Because static, active, and dynamic stretching all can be effective for improving range of motion (ROM) (39,67–70,77,78), this complete continuum of flexibility training should be incorporated into a comprehensive training program in order to develop optimum functional range of motion and neuromuscular efficiency.

CARDIORESPIRATORY TRAINING

Of the various components that comprise the total physical fitness program of an athlete, cardiorespiratory endurance, while being probably the most studied, is probably the most misunderstood and underrated. Athletes often fail to understand why building a base is so important to their total training program. Without a proper aerobic base, fatigue leads to a reduction in an

TIME OUT
Components of an Integrated Sports Performance Program

- Flexibility Training
- Cardiorespiratory Training
- Core Training
- Balance Training
- Plyometrics Training
- Speed, Agility, and Quickness Training
- Integrated, Multiplanar Resistance Training
- Sports Specific Conditioning

athlete's performance, increasing the risk of injury. Although Sports Performance Professionals must be creative in designing cardiorespiratory training experiences for current programs, athletes need to know how to start a safe program that will improve endurance, avoid overtraining, and minimize the risk for injury.

CORE TRAINING

Core training is the foundation from which a progressive sports performance program is built. Many athletes have developed the strength, power, and endurance in their prime movers, but many neglect to develop adequate neuromuscular control, strength, power, and endurance in their core (43,54,55,59,62–64,71–76). Core training is a systematic and progressive approach to develop muscle balance, neuromuscular efficiency, strength, power, and endurance in the core musculature (1,50,73–76). The core has to function optimally to fully harness the strength and power of the prime movers. A stable, strong, and reactively efficient core should be a cornerstone in all integrated sports performance and injury prevention programs (73,74,76).

BALANCE TRAINING

Balance training is the systematic and progressive training process designed to develop neuromuscular efficiency. Balance training, in a proprioceptively enriched environment (e.g., $^1/_2$-foam roll, Airex pad, BOSU ball, etc.), stimulates neuromuscular adaptations (recruiting the right muscles to work at the right time with the right amount of force for the desired outcome), leading to improved intramuscular and intermuscular coordination. Intramuscular coordination is the ability of the CNS to improve motor unit recruitment, rate coding, and synchronization within an individual muscle. Intermuscular coordination is the ability of the entire human movement system and each muscular subsystem to work interdependently to improve movement efficiency—another CNS function. Improved intra- and intermuscular efficiency will yield greater recruitment of the agonist musculature and less inhibition (interference) from the antagonist musculature. This will result in greater force production (19,38,45,80–82) and injury prevention (8,14–16,32,34–36,40,83,84).

PLYOMETRIC TRAINING

Enhanced athletic performance is related to the rate of force production (17) that is regulated by the CNS. The demands of training should occur at speeds that will be encountered during functional activities (25) so that the system learns just how rapidly force production will be required. This means that the human movement system will only move within a defined range of speeds set by the CNS (25). Most human movement involves the stretch-shortening cycle where deceleration (stretch) transitions to acceleration (shortening). The human movement system must react quickly following an eccentric contraction to produce a concentric contraction and impart the necessary force and acceleration in the proper direction (32). Plyometric training overloads the stretch-shortening cycle (e.g., box jumps, squat jumps, hops, etc.)

TIME OUT
The Core

The core is considered as the lumbo-pelvic-hip complex that operates as an integrated functional unit providing intersegmental stability, deceleration, and force production during athletic activities.

to enhance neuromuscular efficiency, rate of force production, and reduce neuromuscular inhibition by stimulating the proprioceptive mechanisms and elastic properties of the human movement system (32).

SPEED, AGILITY, AND QUICKNESS TRAINING

As mentioned earlier, human movement occurs in all planes of motion at varying speeds in response to multiple stimuli. The ability to change speed and direction of movement, and appropriately react to all given stimuli is often the difference between injury and safety, success or failure (42,61,84). Improving speed, change of direction, and reaction time is possible through proper training strategies (41). These strategies have come to be known as speed, agility, and quickness, or SAQ, training. Each of these abilities is an independent quality, yet is related and dependent on the other to optimize human function.

Integrated, Multiplanar Resistance Training

Strength
The ability of the neuro-muscular system to exert force against resistance.

The world of sports performance and injury prevention is changing drastically. Athletes are bigger, faster, stronger, and leaner than ever before. **Strength** is one of the most important training components for athletic performance. There are many types of strength, including maximal strength, relative strength, strength endurance, speed strength, stabilization strength, and functional strength (1,86,87).

An integrated resistance training program makes use of the principles of integrated training (discussed previously in this chapter) to develop a comprehensive sports performance program that will ensure each individual athlete will achieve their optimum performance and reduce the risk of injury. The scientific rationale for integrated resistance training and the NASM evidence-based application guidelines will be discussed in Chapter 10.

Integrated Sports Performance Training

The goal of a sports performance training program is to prevent injury, decrease body fat, increase lean muscle mass, and increase athletic performance measures that include flexibility, core function, balance, power, speed, agility, quickness, strength, and sport-specific cardiorespiratory efficiency. When designing an integrated sports performance program, the Sports Performance Professional should perform a comprehensive sports performance assessment. This will be addressed in much greater detail in Section 3: Human Performance Testing and Evaluation.

All sports performance programs should, above all, be safe. Choosing the components of a program requires careful selection of activities that meet specific criteria (Table 1.1). A program should be progressive, proprioceptively challenging, stress multiple planes of motion, integrate multiple joints when possible, challenge the entire contraction velocity spectrum (slow, fast, explosive), and be as sports specific as possible.

The Sports Performance Professional should follow a progressive, systematic, functional continuum to allow optimum performance adaptations. The following are key concepts for proper exercise progression: slow to fast, simple to complex, known to unknown, low force to high force, eyes open to eyes closed, static to dynamic, and correct execution of increased repetitions, sets, and intensity (Table 1.2).

TABLE 1.1
Exercise Selection Criteria
• Safe
• Challenging
• Progressive
• Systematic (integrated functional continuum)
• Proprioceptively enriched
• Activity specific

TABLE 1.2
Exercise Progression Continuum
• Slow to Fast
• Known to Unknown
• Stable > Controlled > Dynamic Functional Movement
• Low Force to High Force
• Correct Execution to Increased Intensity

TABLE 1.3

Integrated Training Variables

Plane of Motion	Body Position	Base of Support	Lower Extremity Symmetry	Upper Extremity Symmetry	External Resistance	Balance Modality
• Sagittal • Frontal • Transverse • Combination	• Supine • Prone • Side-lying • Sitting • Kneeling • Half-kneeling • Double-leg standing • Staggered stance standing • Single-leg standing	• Bench • Stability ball • Balance modality • Other	• 2 leg, stable • Staggered stance, stable • 1 leg, stable • 2 leg, unstable • Staggered stance, unstable • 1 leg, unstable	• 2 arm • Alternate arms • 1 arm • 1 arm with rotation	• Barbell • Dumbbell • Cable machines • Tubing • Medicine balls • Power balls • Bodyblade • Other	• Floor • Sport beam • 1/2-foam roll • Reebok Core Board • Airex Pad • Dyna Disc • BOSU Balance Trainer • Proprio Shoes • Sand

The goal of an integrated sports performance program should be to develop optimum levels of functional strength and dynamic stabilization. Neural adaptations become a significant focus of the program instead of striving solely for absolute strength gains. Increasing the proprioceptive demands in a multisensory environment (e.g., Bodyblade, stability ball, 1/2 foam roll, Airex pad, Dyna disc) becomes as important as increasing the external resistance (Table 1.3).

The concept of quality before quantity of training should be emphasized. You must be concerned with the sensory information that is stimulating your athlete's CNS. If your athletes train with poor technique and poor neuromuscular control, they will develop poor motor patterns and poor stabilization. Therefore, your athlete's program should focus on the functional continuum (Table 1.4). To determine if your program is functional, answer the following questions: Is it progressive? Is it systematic? Is it sports-specific? Is it integrated? Is it proprioceptively challenging? Is it based on functional anatomy and evidence-based practices?

TABLE 1.4

Functional Continuum

- Multiplanar (3 planes of motion)
- Multidimensional
- Use the entire muscle-contraction spectrum
- Use the entire contraction-velocity spectrum
- Manipulate all acute training variables (sets, repetitions, intensity, rest intervals, frequency, and duration)

Applied Integrated Sports Performance Training

As mentioned before, Integrated Sports Performance Training is a concept that applies all forms of training in an integrated fashion, such as flexibility training, cardiorespiratory training, balance training, core training, plyometric training, speed, agility and quickness training, and integrated resistance training in a progressive system. This system, developed by NASM, is termed the *Optimum Performance Training™ (OPT™) model.*

The OPT™ model is a process of programming that systematically progresses any athlete to any performance goal. As depicted in Figure 1.3, the OPT™ model is built upon a foundation of Stabilization training principles. With the acquisition of proper levels of stabilization, an athlete can then progress into the Strength stage of the training model. As the athlete obtains ample amounts of strength, they progress into the Power stage of the training model.

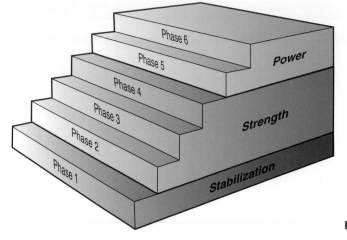

FIGURE 1.3 The OPT™ Model.

SCIENTIFIC RATIONALE FOR THE OPT™ MODEL

As mentioned earlier, the OPT™ model is divided into three different stages. These include: Stabilization, Strength, and Power. Each stage is built upon and dependent on the prior stage. Within each stage, there exists specific phases of training that progress an athlete through the model:

- Phase 1: Stabilization Endurance Training
- Phase 2: Strength Endurance Training
- Phase 3: Hypertrophy Training
- Phase 4: Maximal Strength Training
- Phase 5: Power Training
- Phase 6: Maximal Power Training

It is imperative that the Sports Performance Professional understands the scientific rationale behind each stage in order to properly utilize the OPT™ model. We will also be referring back to this model throughout the text to show how the components of an integrated sports performance training program are incorporated into this training system.

STABILIZATION STAGE OF TRAINING

The Stabilization stage consists of one phase of training, Stabilization Endurance Training. The main focus of Stabilization Endurance Training is to increase stabilization strength (the ability of the stabilizing muscles to provide dynamic joint stabilization and postural equilibrium during functional activities) and develop optimal communication between one's nervous system and muscular system (neuromuscular efficiency).

The progression for this phase of training is proprioceptively based. This means that difficulty is increased by introducing more challenge to the balance and stabilization systems of the body versus simply increasing the load.

Stabilization training must be done prior to advancing into the Strength and Power stages as research has shown that inefficient stabilization can lead to altered force production in muscles, increased stress at the joints, tissue overload, and eventual injury (2,43,63). This stage essentially prepares the athlete's structure to engage in more demanding exercise by correcting muscle imbalances, increasing flexibility and extensibility of the muscles as well as increasing the joint and postural stabilization mechanisms.

STRENGTH STAGE OF TRAINING

The Strength stage of training follows the successful completion of the Stabilization stage. The emphasis in this stage is to enhance stabilization strength while increasing prime mover strength. This is also the stage of training an athlete will progress to if their goals are muscle growth (hypertrophy) or maximal strength (lifting heavy loads). This stage of training consists of three phases of training: Strength Endurance Training, Hypertrophy Training, and Maximal Strength Training.

The goal of Strength Endurance Training is to enhance stabilization strength and endurance while increasing prime mover strength. These two adaptations are accomplished by performing two exercises with similar joint dynamics in a "superset" manner (back-to-back without rest). One exercise is more traditional and performed in a more stable environment (e.g., a bench press), whereas the other is an integrated exercise performed in a less stable environment (e.g., a stability ball push up). The principle behind this method is to work the prime movers predominantly with the first exercise to elicit prime mover strength. By immediately following with an exercise that challenges the stabilizers, neuromuscular and postural stabilization endurance and dynamic joint stabilization are enhanced.

Other phases of the Strength stage are Hypertrophy Training for the goal of maximal muscle hypertrophy and Maximal Strength Training for the goal of increasing maximal prime mover strength.

POWER STAGE OF TRAINING

The Power stage of the OPT™ model emphasizes the development of speed and power. The speed and power with which athletes can produce muscular actions determine successful performance in most sports. This stage of training is necessary to enhance the speed spectrum that the body is allowed to operate within. The speed with which muscles are able to exert force is dictated by the neuromuscular system. Therefore, the body will only be able to move within a set range of speed that is determined by the nervous system (88). This is achieved through two phases of training termed *Power Training* and *Maximal Power Training*.

The premise behind Power Training is the supersetting of a more traditional strength exercise (e.g., barbell squats) supersetted with a plyometric/power exercise of similar joint dynamics (e.g., squat jumps). This is to enhance prime mover strength while also improving the rate of force production (how quickly a muscle can generate force).

Utilization of Maximal Power Training is the next progression to produce maximal acceleration and rate of force production. This phase of training is typically reserved for high-level athletes who require maximal levels of power.

Each of the phases of the OPT™ model and their application will be covered in greater detail in Chapter 12 of the textbook.

SUMMARY

Programming for today's athlete must address factors such as appropriate forms of flexibility, increasing stabilization strength and endurance, and training in a multiplanar environment. All of these forms of training have been specifically designed to follow physiological principles of the human movement system to provide a systematic progression to training (OPT™ model), minimizing injury and maximizing the athlete's results.

REFERENCES

1. Clark MA. Integrated Training for the New Millennium. Thousand Oaks: National Academy of Sports Medicine; 2000.
2. Edgerton VR, Wolf SL, Levendowski DJ, et al. Theoretical basis for patterning EMG amplitudes to assess muscle dysfunction. *Med Sci Sports Exerc* 1996;28:744–51.
3. Panjabi MM. The stabilizing system of the spine. Part I. Function, dysfunction, adaptation, and enhancement. *J Spinal Disord* 1992;5:383–89; discussion 397.
4. Sahrmann S. Diagnosis and Treatment of Movement Impairment Syndromes. St. Louis: Mosby; 2002.
5. Newmann D. Kinesiology of the Musculoskeletal System: Foundations for Physical Rehabilitation. St. Louis: CV Mosby; 2002.
6. Porterfield JA. Mechanical Low Back Pain: Perspectives in Functional Anatomy. Philadelphia: WB Saunders; 1991.
7. Ford KR, Myer GD, Hewett TE. Valgus knee motion during landing in high school female and male basketball players. *Med Sci Sports Exerc* 2003;35:1745–750.
8. Fredericson M, Cookingham CL, Chaudhari AM, et al. Hip abductor weakness in distance runners with iliotibial band syndrome. *Clin J Sports Med* 2000;10:169–75.
9. Ireland ML, Willson JD, Ballantyne BT, et al. Hip strength in females with and without patellofemoral pain. *J Orthop Sports Phys Ther* 2003;33:671–76.
10. Lee TQ, Yang BY, Sandusky MD, et al. The effects of tibial rotation on the patellofemoral joint: assessment of the changes in in situ strain in the peripatellar retinaculum and the patellofemoral contact pressures and areas. *J Rehabil Res Dev* 2001;38:463–69.
11. McClay I, Manal K. Three-dimensional kinetic analysis of running: significance of secondary planes of motion. *Med Sci Sports Exerc* 1999;31:1629–637.
12. Nyland J, Smith S, Beickman K, et al. Frontal plane knee angle affects dynamic postural control strategy during unilateral stance. *Med Sci Sports Exerc* 2002;34:1150–157.
13. Powers CM. The influence of altered lower-extremity kinematics on patellofemoral joint dysfunction: a theoretical perspective. *J Orthop Sports Phys Ther* 2003;33:639–46.
14. Caraffa A, Cerulli G, Projetti M, et al. Prevention of anterior cruciate ligament injuries in soccer. A prospective controlled study of proprioceptive training. *Knee Surg Sports Traumatol Arthrosc* 1996;4:19–21.

15. Hewett TE, Lindenfeld TN, Riccobene JV, et al. The effect of neuromuscular training on the incidence of knee injury in female athletes. A prospective study. *Am J Sports Med* 1999;27:699–706.

16. Hewett TE, Stroupe AL, Nance TA, et al. Plyometric training in female athletes. Decreased impact forces and increased hamstring torques. *Am J Sports Med* 1996;24:765–73.

17. Luebbers PE, Potteiger JA, Hulver MW, et al. Effects of plyometric training and recovery on vertical jump performance and anaerobic power. *J Strength Cond Res* 2003;17:704–09.

18. Adams K, O'Shea JP, O'Shea KL, et al. The effect of six weeks of squat, plyometric and squat-plyometric training on power production. *J Appl Sport Sci Res* 1992;6:36–41.

19. Baker D. Improving vertical jump performance through general, special and specific strength training: a brief review. *J Strength Cond Res* 1996;10:131–36.

20. Gehri DJ, Ricard MD, Kleiner DM, Kirkendall DT. A comparison of plyometric training techniques for improving vertical jump ability and energy production. *J Strength Cond Res* 1998;12:85–9.

21. Rimmer E, Sleivert G. Effects of a plyometrics intervention program on sprint performance. *J Strength Cond Res* 2000;14:295–301.

22. Holcomb WR, Lander JE, Rutland RM, et al. The effectiveness of a modified plyometric program on power and the vertical jump. *J Strength Cond Res* 1996;10:89–92.

23. Wilson GD, Murphy AJ, Giorgi A. Weight and plyometric training: effects on eccentric and concentric force production. *Can J Appl Physiol* 1996;21:301–15.

24. Wilson GJ, Newton RU, Murphy AJ, et al. The optimal training load for the development of dynamic athletic performance. *Med Sci Sports Exerc* 1993;25:1279–286.

25. Chmielewski TL, Hurd WJ, Rudolph KS, et al. Perturbation training improves knee kinematics and reduces muscle co-contraction after complete unilateral anterior cruciate ligament rupture. *Phys Ther* 2005;85:740–49.

26. Bosco C, Komi PV, Ito A. Prestretch potentiation of human skeletal muscle during ballistic movement. *Acta Physiol Scand* 1981;111:135–40.

27. Bosco C, Viitasalo JT, Komi PV, et al. Combined effect of elastic energy and myoelectrical potentiation during stretch-shortening cycle exercise. *Acta Physiol Scand* 1982;114:557–65.

28. Rassier DE, Herzog W. Force enhancement and relaxation rates after stretch of activated muscle fibres. *Proc Biol Sci* 2005;272:475–80.

29. Potteiger JA, Lockwood RH, Haub MD, et al. Muscle power and fiber characteristics in human skeletal muscle. *J Strength Cond Res* 1999;13:275–79.

30. Clutch D, Wilton M, McGown C, et al. The effect of depth jumps and weight training on leg strength and vertical jump. *Res Q* 1983;54:5–10.

31. Wagner DR, Kocak MS. A multivariate approach to assessing anaerobic power following a plyometric training program. *J Strength Cond Res* 1997;11:251–55.

32. Chimera NJ, Swanik KA, Swanik CB, et al. Effects of plyometric training on muscle-activation strategies and performance in female athletes. *J Athl Train* 2004;39:24–31.

33. Sherry MA, Best TM. A comparison of 2 rehabilitation programs in the treatment of acute hamstring strains. *J Orthop Sports Phys Ther* 2004;34:116–25.

34. Junge A, Rosch D, Peterson L, et al. Prevention of soccer injuries: a prospective intervention study in youth amateur players. *Am J Sports Med* 2002;30:652–59.

35. Mandelbaum BR, Silvers HJ, Watanabe DS, et al. Effectiveness of a neuromuscular and proprioceptive training program in preventing the incidence of ACL injuries in female athletes: a 2-year follow-up. *Am J Sports Med* 2005;33:1003–10.

36. Paterno MV, Myer GD, Ford KR, et al. Neuromuscular training improves single-limb stability in young female athletes. *J Orthop Sports Phys Ther* 2004;34:305–16.

37. Bergmark A. Stability of the lumbar spine. A study in mechanical engineering. *Acta Orthop Scand Suppl* 1989;230:1–54.

38. Hahn S, Stanforth D, Stanforth PR, et al. A 10-week training study comparing resist-a-ball and traditional trunk training. *Med Sci Sports Exerc* 1998;30:S199.

39. Hanten WP, Olson SL, Butts NL, et al. Effectiveness of a home program of ischemic pressure followed by sustained stretch for treatment of myofascial trigger points. *Phys Ther* 2000;80:997–1003.

40. Kovacs EJ, Birmingham TB, Forwell L, et al. Effect of training on postural control in figure skaters: a randomized controlled trial of neuromuscular versus basic off-ice training programs. *Clin J Sport Med* 2004;14:215–24.

41. Mills J, Taunton JE. The effect of spinal stabilization training on spinal mobility, vertical jump, agility and balance. *Med Sci Sports Exerc* 2003;35:S323.

42. Nadler SF, Malanga GA, Bartoli LA, et al. Hip muscle imbalance and low back pain in athletes: influence of core strengthening. *Med Sci Sports Exerc* 2002;34:9–16.

43. O'Sullivan PB, Twomey L, Allison GT. Altered abdominal muscle recruitment in patients with chronic back pain following a specific exercise intervention. *J Orthop Sports Phys Ther* 1998;27:114–24.

44. Vera-Garcia FJ, Grenier SG, McGill SM. Abdominal muscle response during curl-ups on both stable and labile surfaces. *Phys Ther* 2000;80:564–69.

45. Cosio-Lima LM, Reynolds KL, Winter C, et al. Effects of physio-ball and conventional floor exercises on early phase adaptations in back and abdominal core stability and balance in women. *J Strength Cond Res* 2003;17:721–25.

46. Witvrouw E, Danneels L, Asselman P, et al. Muscle flexibility as a risk factor for developing muscle injuries in male professional soccer players. A prospective study. *Am J Sports Med* 2003;31:41–6.

47. Thompson CJ, Cobb KM, Blackwell J. Functional training improves club head speed and functional fitness in older golfers. *J Strength Cond Res* 2007;21:131–37.

48. Beckman SM, Buchanan TS. Ankle inversion injury and hypermobility: effect on hip and ankle muscle electromyography onset latency. *Arch Phys Med Rehabil* 1995;76:1138–143.
49. Bullock-Saxton JE. Local sensation changes and altered hip muscle function following severe ankle sprain. *Physical Therapy* 1994;74:17–28.
50. Willson JD, Dougherty CP, Ireland ML, et al. Core stability and its relationship to lower extremity function and injury. *J Am Acad Orthop Surg* 2005;13:316–25.
51. Willson JD, Ireland ML, Davis I. Core strength and lower extremity alignment during single leg squats. *Med Sci Sports Exerc* 2006;38:945–52.
52. Cibulka MT, Sinacore DR, Cromer GS, et al. Unilateral hip rotation range of motion asymmetry in patients with sacroiliac joint regional pain. *Spine* 1998;23:1009–1015.
53. Denegar CR, Hertel J, Fonseca J. The effect of lateral ankle sprain on dorsiflexion range of motion, posterior talar glide, and joint laxity. *J Orthop Sports Phys Ther* 2002;32:166–73.
54. Hides JA, Stokes MJ, Saide M, et al. Evidence of lumbar multifidus muscle wasting ipsilateral to symptoms in patients with acute/subacute low back pain. *Spine* 1994;19:165–72.
55. Hungerford BP, Gilleard WP, Hodges PP. Evidence of altered lumbopelvic muscle recruitment in the presence of sacroiliac joint pain. *Spine* 2003; 28:1593–600.
56. Janda V. Muscles, Central Nervous System Regulation and Back Problems. New York: Plenum Press; 1978.
57. Nicholas JA, Marino M. The relationship of injuries of the leg, foot, and ankle to proximal thigh strength in athletes. *Foot Ankle* 1987;7:218–28.
58. O'Sullivan PB, Phyty GD, Twomey LT, et al. Evaluation of specific stabilizing exercise in the treatment of chronic low back pain with radiologic diagnosis of spondylolysis or spondylolisthesis. *Spine* 1997;22:2959–967.
59. Richardson CA, Snijders CJ, Hides JA, et al. The relation between the transverse abdominis muscle, sacroiliac joint mechanics and low back pain. *Spine* 2002;27:399–405.
60. Sahrmann SA. Posture and muscle imbalance. Faulty lumbo-pelvic alignment and associated musculoskeletal pain syndromes. *Orthop Div Rev-Can Phys Ther* 1992;12:13–20.
61. Nadler SF, Malanga GA, Feinberg JH, et al. Functional performance deficits in athletes with previous lower extremity injury. *Clin J Sport Med* 2002;12:73–8.
62. Hodges P, Richardson C, Jull G. Evaluation of the relationship between laboratory and clinical tests of transversus abdominis function. *Physiother Res Int* 1996;1:30–40.
63. Hodges PW, Richardson CA. Inefficient muscular stabilization of the lumbar spine associated with low back pain. A motor control evaluation of transversus abdominis. *Spine* 1996;21:2640–650.
64. Hodges PW, Richardson CA. Contraction of the abdominal muscles associated with movement of the lower limb. *Phys Ther* 1997;77:132–42.
65. Sherrington CS. Flexion-reflex of the limb, crossed extension-reflex, and reflex stepping and standing. *J Physiol* 1910;40:28–121.
66. Knapik JJ, Bauman CL, Jones BH, et al. Preseason strength and flexibility imbalances associated with athletic injuries in female collegiate athletes. *Am J Sports Med* 1991;19:76–81.
67. Davis DS, Ashby PE, McCale KL, et al. The effectiveness of 3 stretching techniques on hamstring flexibility using consistent stretching parameters. *J Strength Cond Res* 2005;19:27–32.
68. Kokkonen J, Nelson AG, Eldredge C, et al. Chronic static stretching improves exercise performance. *Med Sci Sports Exerc* 2007;39:1825–831.
69. Shrier I. Meta-analysis on pre-exercise stretching (letter). *Med Sci Sports Exerc* 2004;36:1832.
70. Winters MV, Blake CG, Trost JS, et al. Passive versus active stretching of hip flexor muscles in subjects with limited hip extension: a randomized clinical trial. *Phys Ther* 2004;84:800–07.
71. McGill SM. Low back stability: from formal description to issues for performance and rehabilitation. *Exerc Sport Sci Rev* 2001;29:26–31.
72. McGill SM, Cholewicki J. Biomechanical basis for stability: an explanation to enhance clinical utility. *J Orthop Sports Phys Ther* 2001;31:96–100.
73. Barr KP, Griggs M, Cadby T. Lumbar stabilization: core concepts and current literature, Part 1. *Am J Phys Med Rehabil* 2005;84:473–80.
74. Barr KP, Griggs M, Cadby T. Lumbar stabilization: a review of core concepts and current literature, part 2. *Am J Phys Med Rehabil* 2007;86:72–80.
75. Sherry M, Best T, Heiderscheit B. The core: where are we and where are we going? *Clin J Sport Med* 2005;15:1–2.
76. Heiderscheit B, Sherry M. What Effect Do Core Strength and Stability Have on Injury Prevention? In: MacAuley D., Best T. Evidence-Based Sports Medicine, 2nd ed. Malden, MA: Blackwell Publishing; 2007. p 59–72.
77. Behm DG, Bambury A, Cahill F, et al. Effect of acute static stretching on force, balance, reaction time, and movement time. *Med Sci Sports Exerc* 2004;36:1397–402.
78. Blackburn JT, Padua DA, Riemann BL, et al. The relationships between active extensibility, and passive and active stiffness of the knee flexors. *J Electromyogr Kinesiology* 2004;14:683–91.
79. Blackburn JT, Hirth CJ, Guskiewicz KM. Exercise sandals improve lower extremity electromyographic activity during functional activities. *J Athl Train* 2003; 38:198–203.
80. Myer GD, Ford KR, Brent JL, et al. The effects of plyometric vs. dynamic stabilization and balance training on power, balance, and landing force in female athletes. *J Strength Cond Res* 2006; 20:345–53.
81. Yaggie JA, Campbell BM. Effects of balance training on selected skills. *J Strength Cond Res* 2006;20:422–28.

82. Bruhn S, Kullmann N, Gollhofer A. The effects of a sensorimotor training and a strength training on postural stabilisation, maximum isometric contraction and jump performance. *Int J Sports Med* 2004; 25:56–60.

83. Etty Griffin LY. Neuromuscular training and injury prevention in sports. *Clin Orthopaed Related Res* 2003;409:53–60.

84. Padua DA, Marshall SW. Evidence supporting ACL-injury-prevention exercise programs: a review of the literature. *Athletic Therapy Today* 2006;11:11–23.

85. Kraemer WJ, Nindl BC, Ratamess NA, et al. Changes in muscle hypertrophy in women with periodized resistance training. *Med Sci Sports Exercise* 2004;36:697–708.

86. Kraemer WJ, Ratamess NA. Fundamentals of resistance training: progression and exercise prescription. *Med Sci Sports Exerc* 2004;36:674–88.

87. Bird SP, Tarpenning KM, Marino FE. Designing resistance training programmes to enhance muscular fitness: a review of the acute programme variables. *Sports Med* 2005;35:841–51.

88. Voight M, Draovitch P: Plyometrics. In: Albert M. Eccentric Muscle Training in Sports and Orthopedics. New York: Churchill Livingstone; 1991. p 45–73.

CHAPTER 2

Introduction to Human Movement Science

Introduction

Human movement science is the study of how the human movement system (HMS) functions in an interdependent, interrelated scheme. The HMS consists of the muscular system (functional anatomy), skeletal system (functional biomechanics), and the nervous system (motor behavior) (1–3) (Fig. 2.1). Although they seem separate, each system and its components must collaborate to form interdependent links. In turn, this entire interdependent system must be aware of its relationship to internal and external environments while gathering necessary information to produce the appropriate movement patterns. This process ensures optimum functioning of the HMS and optimum human movement in sports. This chapter will review the pertinent aspects of each component of the HMS as it relates to integrated sports performance training.

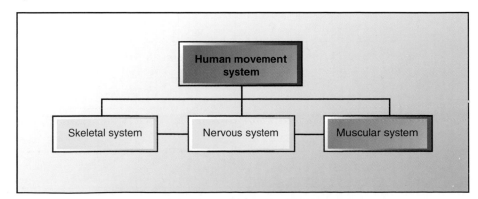

FIGURE 2.1 Components of the Human Movement System.

15

Biomechanics

Biomechanics
A study that uses principles of physics to quantitatively study how forces interact within a living body.

Biomechanics applies the principles of physics to quantitatively study how forces interact within a living body (4–7). For purposes of this text, the specific focus will be on the motions that the HMS produces and the forces that act upon it in order to present a basic understanding of anatomical terminology, planes of motion, joint motions, muscle action, force-couples, leverage, and basic muscle mechanics.

ANATOMICAL TERMINOLOGY

All professions have language that is specific to their needs. The Sports Performance Professional needs to understand the basic anatomical terminology for effective communication.

PLANES OF MOTION, AXES, AND COMBINED JOINT MOTIONS

Human movement occurs in three dimensions and is universally discussed in a system of planes and axes (Fig. 2.2). Three imaginary planes are positioned through the body at right angles so they intersect at the body's center of mass. These planes are termed the *sagittal, frontal,* and *transverse* planes. Movement is said to occur predominantly in a specific plane when that movement occurs along or parallel to the plane. Although movements can be dominant in one plane, no motion occurs strictly in one plane of motion. Movement in a plane occurs around an axis running perpendicular to that plane—much like the axle that a car wheel revolves around. This is known as joint motion. Joint motions are termed for their action in each of the three planes of motion (Table 2.1).

THE SAGITTAL PLANE
The sagittal plane bisects the body into right and left halves. Sagittal plane motion occurs around a frontal axis (4,5,8). Movements in the sagittal plane include flexion and extension.

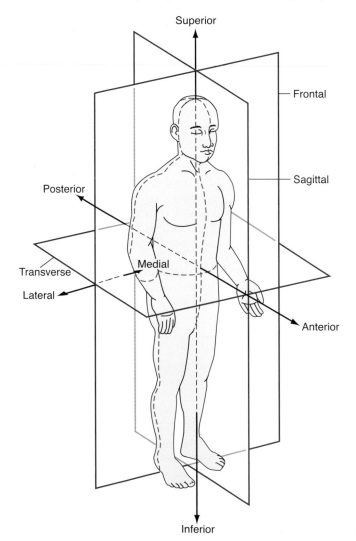

FIGURE 2.2 Planes of Motion.

TABLE 2.1

Examples of Planes of Motion, Motions and Axes

Plane	Motion	Axis	Example
Sagittal	Flexion/Extension	Coronal	• Bicep Curls • Tricep Pushdowns • Squats • Front Lunges • Calf Raises • Walking • Running • Vertical Jumping • Climbing Stairs
Frontal	Adduction/Abduction Lateral Flexion Eversion/Inversion	Anterior-Posterior	• Side Lateral Raises • Side Lunges • Side Shuffling
Transverse	Internal/External Rotation Left/Right Spinal Rotation Horizontal Adduction/Abduction	Longitudinal	• Cable Rotations • Turning Lunges • Throwing • Golfing • Swinging a Bat

Flexion occurs when the relative angle between two adjacent segments decreases (5,9). Extension occurs when the relative angle between two adjacent segments increases (5,9) (Fig. 2.3). Flexion and extension occur in many joints in the body including vertebral, shoulder, elbow, wrist, hip, knee, foot, and hand (Fig. 2.3). The ankle is unique and has special terms from movement in the sagittal plane. At the ankle, "flexion" is more accurately termed *dorsiflexion* and "extension" is referred to as *plantarflexion* (4,5,9). Examples of predominantly sagittal plane movements include bicep curls, triceps pushdowns, squats, front lunges, calf raises, walking, running, and climbing stairs (Table 2.1).

THE FRONTAL PLANE
The frontal plane bisects the body into front and back halves with frontal plane motion occurring around an anterior-posterior axis (4,5,9). Movements in the frontal plane include abduction and adduction of the limbs (relative to the trunk), lateral flexion in the spine and eversion and inversion of the foot and ankle complex (4,5,8,9). Abduction is a movement away from the midline of the body or, similar to extension, an increase in the angle between two adjoining segments only in the frontal plane (4,5,8,9) (Fig. 2.4). Adduction is a movement of the segment toward the midline of the body or, like flexion, a decrease in the angle between two adjoining segments only in the frontal plane (4,5,8,9) (Fig. 2.4). Lateral flexion is the bending of the spine (cervical, thoracic, lumbar) from side to side or simply side-bending (4,5). Eversion and inversion relate specifically to the movement of the calcaneus and tarsals in the frontal plane during functional movements of pronation and supination (discussed later) (4,5,8,9). Examples of frontal plane movements include side lateral raises, side lunges, and side shuffling (Table 2.1).

THE TRANSVERSE PLANE
The transverse plane bisects the body to create upper and lower halves. Transverse plane motion occurs around a longitudinal or a vertical axis (4,5,8). Movements in the transverse plane include internal rotation and external rotation for the limbs, right and left rotation for the head and trunk, and radioulnar pronation and supination (4,5,8) (Fig. 2.5). The transverse plane motion of the foot is termed *abduction* (toes pointing outward, externally rotated) and *adduction* (toes pointing inward, internally rotated) (5). Examples of transverse plane movements include cable rotations, turning lunges, throwing a ball, and swinging a bat (Table 2.1).

COMBINED JOINT MOTIONS
During athletic movements, the body must maintain its center of gravity aligned over a constantly changing base of support. If a change in alignment occurs at one joint, changes in alignment of other joints must occur. For example, when an athlete stands and rotates his femur inward, then outward, you will notice obligatory effects from the subtalar joint to the pelvis. When the femur is turned inward (femoral internal rotation), total kinetic chain pronation occurs at the subtalar joint, knee joint, and the lumbo-pelvic-hip complex. When the femur is turned outward (femoral external rotation), total kinetic chain supination occurs.

FIGURE 2.3 FLEXION/EXTENSION MOVEMENTS. **(A)** Shoulder flexion. **(B)** Shoulder extension. **(C)** Hip flexion. **(D)** Hip extension. **(E)** Spinal flexion. **(F)** Spinal extension. **(G)** Elbow flexion. **(H)** Elbow extension. **(I)** Knee flexion. **(J)** Knee extension. **(K)** Plantar flexion. **(L)** Dorsiflexion.

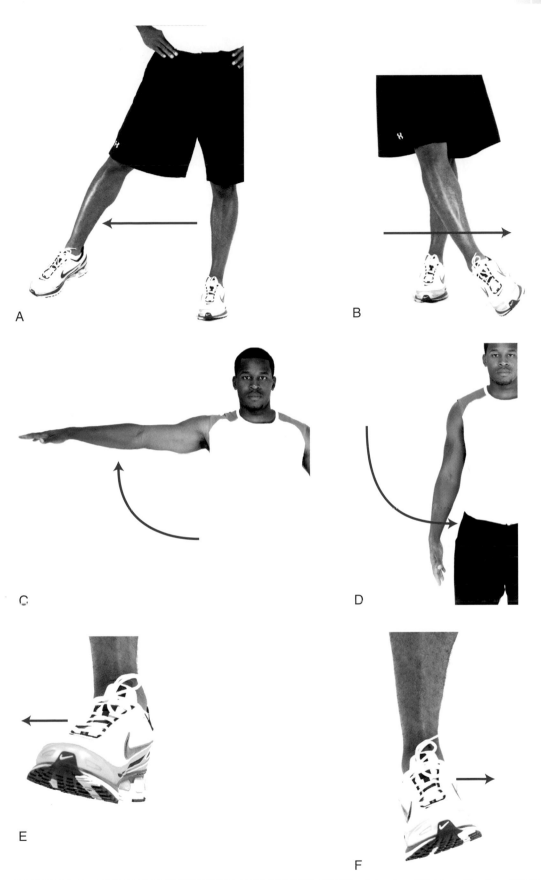

FIGURE 2.4   ADDUCTION/ABDUCTION MOVEMENTS. **(A)** Hip abduction. **(B)** Hip adduction. **(C)** Shoulder abduction. **(D)** Shoulder adduction. **(E)** Eversion. **(F)** Inversion.

A

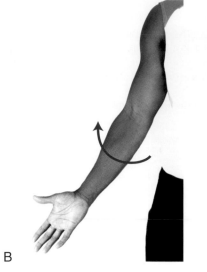

B

C

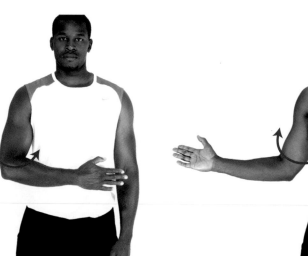

D

E

F

G

FIGURE 2.5 ROTATIONAL MOVEMENTS. **(A)** Spinal rotation. **(B)** Radioulnar supination. **(C)** Radioulnar pronation. **(D)** Shoulder internal rotation. **(E)** Shoulder external rotation. **(F)** Hip internal rotation. **(G)** Hip external rotation.

Even though a joint has a predominant plane of movement, all freely moveable joints can display some movement in all three planes of motion. Functional, multiplanar biomechanics can be simplified into pronation and supination (10); the key word being simplified. In reality, pronation is a multiplanar, synchronized joint motion that occurs with eccentric muscle function. Thus, supination is also a multiplanar, synchronized joint motion that occurs with concentric muscle function (Table 2.2).

TABLE 2.2

Pronation and Supination

During Pronation	
The foot	Dorsiflexes, everts, abducts
The ankle	Dorsiflexes, everts, abducts
The knee	Flexes, adducts, internally rotates
The hip	Flexes, adducts, internally rotates
During Supination	
The foot	Plantar flexes, inverts, adducts
The ankle	Plantar flexes, inverts, adducts
The knee	Extends, abducts, externally rotates
The hip	Extends, abducts, externally rotates

The gait cycle will be used to briefly describe functional biomechanics to show the interdependence of joint and muscle actions on each other (11,12). During the initial contact phase of gait, the subtalar joint pronates creating obligatory internal rotation of the tibia, femur, and pelvis. At midstance, the subtalar joint supinates leading to obligatory external rotation of the tibia, femur, and pelvis. The Sports Performance Professional should remember that these linkages are bidirectional. For example, pelvic motion can create lower extremity motion and lower extremity motion can create pelvic motion (10,13).

Poor control of pronation decreases the ability to eccentrically decelerate multisegmental motion that can lead to muscle imbalances, joint dysfunction, and injury. Poor production of supination decreases the ability of the HMS to concentrically produce the appropriate force for push-off that can lead to synergistic dominance. During functional movement patterns, almost every muscle has the same synergistic function: to eccentrically decelerate pronation or to concentrically accelerate supination. When an articular structure is out of alignment, abnormal distorting forces are placed on the articular surfaces. Poor alignment also changes the mechanical function of muscle and force-couple relationships of all of the muscles that cross that joint. This leads to altered movement patterns, altered reciprocal inhibition, synergistic dominance, and ultimately, decreased neuromuscular efficiency—concepts that will be developed throughout this book.

MUSCLE ACTIONS

Muscles produce tension through a variety of means to effectively manipulate gravity, ground reaction forces, momentum, and external resistance. There are three different muscle actions (Table 2.3):
- Eccentric
- Isometric
- Concentric

TABLE 2.3

Muscle Action Spectrum

Concentric	Developing tension while a muscle is shortening; when developed tension overcomes resistive force
Eccentric	Developing tension while a muscle is lengthening; when resistive force overcomes developed tension
Isometric	When the contractile force is equal to the resistive force

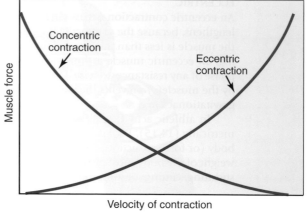

FIGURE 2.8 Force-Velocity Curves.

affect other joints, a change in joint angle can affect the tension produced by muscles that surround the joint. If muscle length is altered as a result of misalignment (i.e., poor posture), then tension development will be reduced and the muscle will be unable to generate proper force for efficient movement. With movement at one joint being interdependent on movement or preparation for movement of other joints, any dysfunction in the chain of events producing movement will have direct effects elsewhere (2,10).

FORCE-VELOCITY CURVE

The force-velocity curve refers to the relationship of muscle's ability to produce tension at differing shortening velocities. This hyperbolic relationship (Fig. 2.8) shows that as the velocity of a concentric contraction increases, the developed tension decreases. The velocity of shortening appears to be related to the maximum rate at which the cross bridges can cycle and can be influenced by the external load (17). Conversely, with eccentric muscle action, as the velocity of muscle action increases the ability to develop force increases. This is believed to be the result of the use of the elastic component of the connective tissue surrounding and within the muscle (1,4–6,16–18).

Muscles produce a force that is transmitted to bones through elastic and connective tissues (tendons). Because muscles are recruited as groups, many muscles will transmit force onto their respective bones, creating movement at the joints (1,5,8). This synergistic action of muscles to produce movement around a joint is also known as a force-couple (1,5,8) (Fig. 2.9). Muscles in a force-couple provide divergent tension to the bone or bones to which they attach. Because each muscle has different attachment sites and lever systems, the tension at different angles creates a different force on that joint. The motion that results from these forces is dependent upon the structure of the joint, intrinsic properties of each fiber, and the collective pull of each muscle involved.

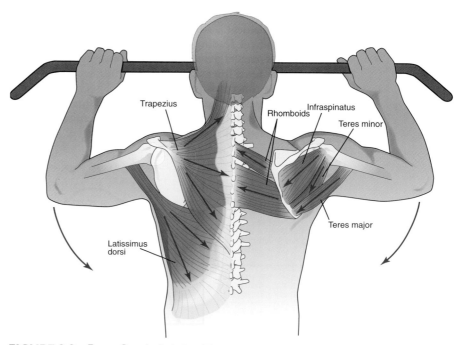

FIGURE 2.9 Force-Couple Relationships.

In reality, however, every movement we produce must involve all muscle actions (eccentric, isometric, concentric) and functions (agonists, synergists, stabilizers, and antagonists) to ensure proper joint motion as well as minimize unwanted motion. Therefore, all muscles that work together for the production of proper movement are working in a force-couple (1,5,8). Proper force-couple relationships are needed so that the HMS moves in the desired manner. This can only happen if the muscles are at the optimal length-tension relationships and the joints have proper arthrokinematics (or joint motion). Collectively, optimal length-tension relationships, force-couple relationships and arthrokinematics produce ideal sensorimotor integration and ultimately proper and efficient movement (2,3) (Figs. 2.10 and 2.11).

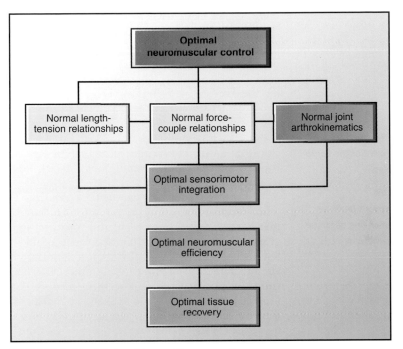

FIGURE 2.10   Efficient Human Movement System.

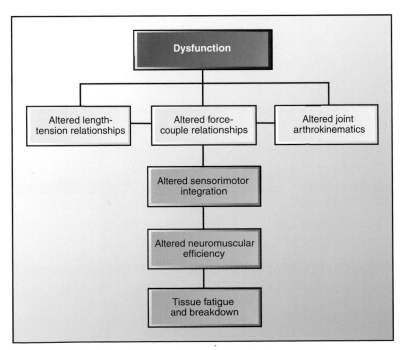

FIGURE 2.11   Human Movement System Dysfunction.

TABLE 2.4

Classes of Levers

Class	Common Example	Body Example
I	Teeter-totter	Flexion-extension of the head
II	Wheelbarrow	Dorsiflexion—rising up on tiptoes
III	Lifting a shovel	Forearm flexion

MUSCULAR LEVERAGE AND ARTHROKINEMATICS

The amount of force that the HMS can produce is not only dependent upon motor unit recruitment and muscle size, but also on the lever system of the joint (1,4). A level system is composed of some force (muscles), a resistance (load to be moved), lever arms (bones), and a fulcrum (the pivot point). Three classes of levers are present in the body (Table 2.4). A class I lever has the fulcrum between the force and the load. A class II lever has the load between the force and the fulcrum. Class III levers, the most common in the body, has the pull between the load and the fulcrum. See Table 2.4 for common examples and examples in the body.

In the HMS, the bones act as lever arms that move a load from the force applied by the muscles. This movement around an axis can be termed **rotary motion** and implies that the levers (bones) rotate around the axis (joints) (4,5,9). This "turning" effect of the joint is often referred to as **torque** (Fig. 2.12 A,B,C) (10,19).

In resistance training, torque (distance from the load to the center of the axis of rotation × the force) is applied so we can move our joints. Because the neuromuscular system is ultimately responsible for manipulating force, the amount of leverage the HMS will have (for any given movement) depends on the leverage of the muscles in relation to the resistance. The difference between the distance that the weight is from the center of the joint, and the muscle's attachment and line of pull (direction through which tension is applied through the tendon) is from the joint will determine the efficiency that the muscles manipulate the movement (1,4,5,9). Because we cannot alter the attachment sites or the line of pull of our muscles through the tendon, the easiest way to alter the amount of torque generated at a joint is to move the resistance. In other words, the closer the weight is to the point of rotation (the joint), the less torque it creates. The farther away the weight is from the point of rotation, the more torque it creates.

For example, to hold a dumbbell straight out to the side at arm's length (shoulder abduction), the weight may be approximately 24 inches from the center of the shoulder joint (Fig. 2.13). The prime mover for shoulder abduction is the deltoid muscle. Let's say its attachment is approximately two inches from the joint center. That is a disparity of 22 inches (or roughly 12 times the difference). If the weight is moved closer to the joint center, let's say to the elbow, the resistance is only approximately 12 inches from the joint center. Now the difference is only 10 inches or 5 times greater. Essentially, the torque required to hold the weight was reduced by half. Many people performing side lateral raises with dumbbells

---

![Rotary Motion icon] **Rotary Motion**
Movement of the bones around the joints.

![Torque icon] **Torque**
A force that produces rotation. Common unit of torque is the Newton-Meter or N.m.

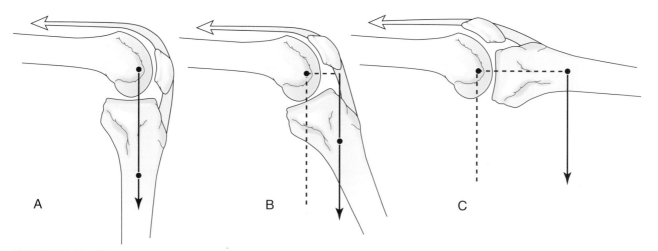

A   B   C

FIGURE 2.12   Torque.

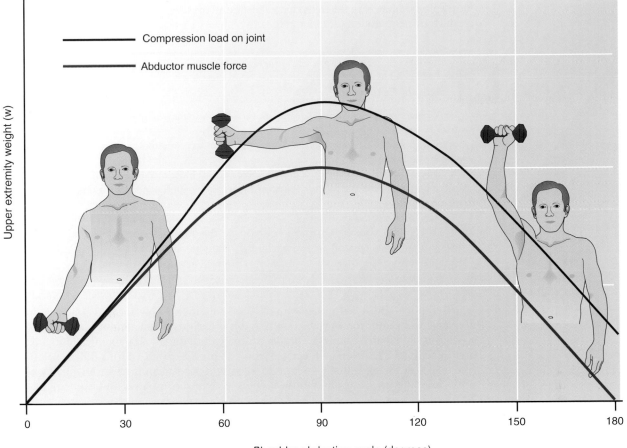

FIGURE 2.13   Load and Torque Relationship.

(laterally raising dumbbells to the side) do this inadvertently by flexing their elbow, bringing the weight closer to the shoulder joint and effectively reducing the required torque. Sports Performance Professionals can use this principle as a regression for exercises that are too demanding, which reduces the torque placed on the HMS, or as a progression to increase the torque and place a greater demand on the HMS.

Functional Anatomy

Traditionally, anatomy has been taught in isolated and fragmented components. The traditional approach mapped the body, provided simplistic answers about the structures, and categorized each component. Looking at each muscle as an isolated structure fails to answer complex questions such as, "How does the human movement system function as an integrated system?" Or even more simply, "What do our muscles do when we move during sports?" The everyday functioning of the human body is an integrated and multidimensional system, not a series of isolated, independent pieces. Over the last 25 years, traditional sports performance training has focused on training specific body parts, often in single, fixed planes of motion. The new paradigm is to present anatomy from a functional, integrated perspective. The Sports Performance Professional armed with a thorough understanding of functional anatomy will be better-equipped to select exercises and design programs.

Whereas muscles have the ability to dominate a certain plane of motion, the central nervous system optimizes the selection of muscle synergies (1,20–25), not simply the selection of individual muscles. The central nervous system coordinates deceleration, stabilization, and acceleration at every joint in the HMS in all three planes of motion. Muscles must also react proprioceptively to gravity, momentum, ground reaction forces, and forces created by other functioning muscles. Depending on the load, the direction of resistance, body position, and the movement being performed, muscles will participate as an agonist, antagonist, synergist, and/or a stabilizer. Although they may have different characteristics, all muscles work in concert with one another to produce efficient motion (1,23,24,26,27).

TIME OUT
Muscle Category

Agonists: muscles that act as prime movers. For example, the gluteus maximus is the prime mover for hip extension.

Antagonists: muscles that act in direct opposition to prime movers. For example, the psoas is antagonistic to the gluteus maximus.

Synergists: muscles that assist prime movers during functional movement patterns. For example, the hamstring and the erector spinae are synergistic with the gluteus maximus during hip extension.

Stabilizers: muscles that support or stabilize the body while the prime movers and the synergists perform the movement patterns. For example, the transverse abdominus, internal oblique, multifidus, and deep erector spinae stabilize the lumbo-pelvic-hip complex (LPHC) during functional movements while the prime movers perform functional activities.

Traditional sports performance training and conditioning has focused almost exclusively on uniplanar, concentric force production. But this is a shortsighted approach as muscles function synergistically in force-couples to produce force, reduce force, and dynamically stabilize the entire HMS. Muscles function in integrated groups to provide control during functional movements (5,8,9,28). Realizing this allows one to view muscles functioning in all planes of motion throughout the full spectrum of muscle action (eccentric, concentric, and isometric).

CURRENT CONCEPTS IN FUNCTIONAL ANATOMY

It has been proposed that there are two distinct, yet interdependent, muscular systems that enable our bodies to maintain proper stabilization and ensure efficient distribution of forces for the production of movement (28,30). Muscles that are located more centrally to the spine provide intersegmental stability (support from vertebrae to vertebrae), whereas the more lateral muscles support the spine as a whole (30). Bergmark (28) categorized these different systems with relation to the trunk into local and global muscular systems.

JOINT SUPPORT SYSTEM

THE LOCAL MUSCULAR SYSTEM (STABILIZATION SYSTEM)
The local muscular system consists of muscles that are predominantly involved in joint support or stabilization (3,28,30,31). It is important to note, however, that joint support systems are not confined to the spine and are evident in peripheral joints as well. Joint support systems consist of muscles that are not movement specific, rather they provide stability to allow movement of a joint. They usually are located in close proximity to the joint with a broad spectrum of attachments to the joint's passive elements that make them ideal for increasing joint stiffness and stability (3,31). A common example of a peripheral joint support system is the rotator cuff that provides dynamic stabilization for the humeral head in relation to the glenoid fossa (32). Other joint support systems include the posterior fibers of the gluteus medius and the external rotators of the hip that provide pelvofemoral stabilization (1,36–39) and the oblique fibers of the vastus medialis that provides patellar stabilization at the knee (1,40,41).

The joint support system of the core, or LPHC, includes muscles that either originate or insert (or both) into the lumbar spine (28,31). The major muscles include the transverse abdominis (TA), multifidus, internal oblique, diaphragm, and the muscles of the pelvic floor (13,28,30,31). Stabilization of the LPHC will be discussed in more detail in Chapter 6 on core training.

THE GLOBAL MUSCULAR SYSTEMS (MOVEMENT SYSTEMS)
The global muscular systems are responsible predominantly for movement and consist of more superficial musculature that originate from the pelvis to the rib cage, the lower extremities, or both (1,23,24,28,30,31,42). Some of these major muscles include the rectus abdominis, external obliques, erector spinae, hamstrings, gluteus maximus, latissimus dorsi, adductors, hamstrings, quadriceps, and gastrocnemius. The movement system muscles are predominantly larger and associated with movement of the trunk and limbs that equalizes external loads placed upon the body. These muscles are also important in transferring and absorbing forces from the upper and lower extremities to the pelvis. The movement system muscles have been broken down and

described as force-couples working in four distinct subsystems (1,29,43,44): the deep longitudinal, posterior oblique, anterior oblique, and lateral subsystems. This distinction allows for an easier description and review of functional anatomy. It is crucial for Sports Performance Professionals to think of these subsystems operating as an integrated functional unit. Remember, the central nervous system optimizes the selection of muscle synergies, not isolated muscles (23,24,45,46).

THE DEEP LONGITUDINAL SUBSYSTEM (DLS)

The major soft tissue contributors to the DLS are the erector spinae, thoracolumbar fascia, sacrotuberous ligament, biceps femoris, and peroneus longus (Fig. 2.14). Some experts suggest that the DLS provides a longitudinal means of reciprocal force transmission from the trunk to the ground (13,23,24,43,44). As illustrated in Figure 2.14, the long head of the biceps femoris attaches in part to the sacrotuberous ligament at the ischium. The sacrotuberous ligament in turn attaches from the ischium to the sacrum. The erector spinae attaches from the sacrum and ilium up the ribs to the cervical spine. Thus, activation of the biceps femoris increases tension in the sacrotuberous ligament, which in turn transmits force across the sacrum stabilizing the sacroiliac joint (SIJ), then up the trunk through the erector spinae (43,44) (Fig. 2.14).

As illustrated in Figure 2.14, this transference of force is apparent during normal gait or running. Prior to heel strike, the biceps femoris activates to eccentrically decelerate hip flexion and knee extension. Just after heel strike, the biceps femoris is further loaded through the lower leg via posterior movement of the fibula. This tension from the lower leg, up through the biceps

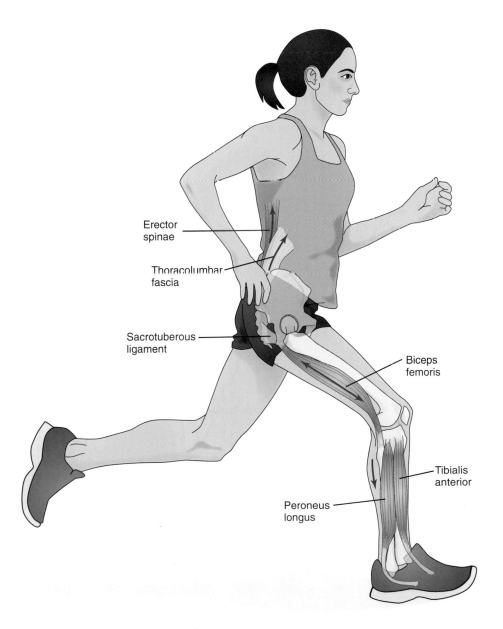

FIGURE 2.14   Deep Longitudinal System.

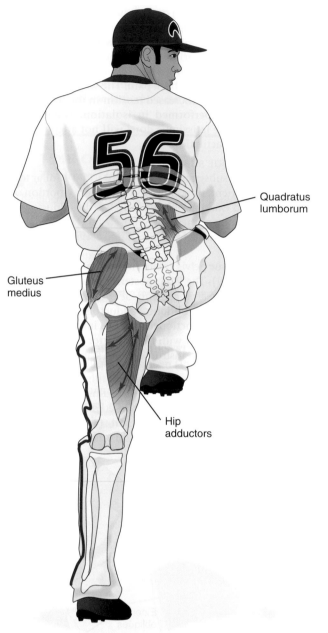

Quadratus
lumborum

Gluteus
medius

Hip
adductors

FIGURE 2.17 Lateral Subsystem.

stability (10,50). Figure 2.17 shows how the ipsilateral gluteus medius, and adductors combine with the contralateral quadratus lumborum to control the pelvis and femur in the frontal plane during single-leg functional movements, such as in gait, lunges, or throwing a pitch (42). Dysfunction in the LS is evident during increased pronation (flexion, internal rotation, and adduction) of the knee, hip, feet, or all three during functional activities (10). Unwanted frontal plane movement is characterized by decreased strength and neuromuscular control in the LS (10,50–52).

The description of these four subsystems has been simplified, but realize that the human body simultaneously coordinates these subsystems during athletic activity. Each subsystem individually and collectively contributes to the production of efficient athletic movement by accelerating, decelerating, and dynamically stabilizing the HMS during motion.

FUNCTIONAL ANATOMY OF THE MAJOR MUSCLES

The traditional, simplistic explanation of skeletal muscles is that they work concentrically and predominantly in one plane of motion. However, as mentioned earlier, muscles should be viewed as functioning in all planes of motion, and throughout the full muscle action spectrum. The following section lists attachments and innervations, as well as the isolated and integrated functions of the major muscles of the HMS (1,6,53).

Leg Complex

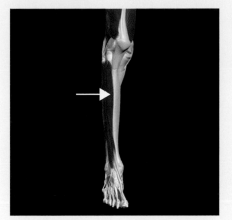

ANTERIOR TIBIALIS

ORIGIN
- Lateral condyle and proximal two-thirds of the lateral surface of the tibia

INSERTION
- Medial and plantar aspects of the medial cuneiform and the base of the first metatarsal

ISOLATED FUNCTION

Concentric Action
- Ankle dorsiflexion and inversion

INTEGRATED FUNCTION

Eccentric Action
- Ankle plantar flexion and eversion

Isometric Action
- Stabilizes the arch of the foot

INNERVATION
- Deep peroneal nerve

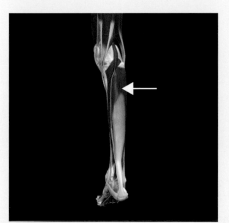

POSTERIOR TIBIALIS

ORIGIN
- Proximal two-thirds of posterior surface of the tibia and fibula

INSERTION
- Every tarsal bone (naviular, cuneiform, cuboid) but the talus plus the bases of the second through the fourth metatarsal bones. The main insertion is on the navicular tuberosity and the medial cuneiform bone

ISOLATED FUNCTION

Concentric Action
- Ankle plantar flexion and inversion of the foot

INTEGRATED FUNCTION

Eccentric Action
- Ankle dorsiflexion and eversion

Isometric Action
- Stabilizes the arch of the foot

INNERVATION
- Tibial nerve

SOLEUS

ORIGIN
- Posterior surface of the fibular head and proximal one-third of its shaft and from the posterior side of the tibia

INSERTION
- Calcaneus via the Achilles tendon

ISOLATED FUNCTION

Concentric Action
- Accelerates plantar flexion

INTEGRATED FUNCTION

Eccentric Action
- Decelerates ankle dorsiflexion

Isometric Action
- Stabilizes the foot and ankle complex

INNERVATION
- Tibial nerve

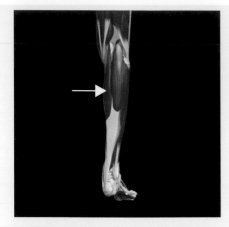

GASTROCNEMIUS

ORIGIN
- Posterior aspect of the lateral and medial femoral condyles

INSERTION
- Calcaneus via the Achilles tendon

ISOLATED FUNCTION

Concentric Action
- Accelerates plantar flexion

INTEGRATED FUNCTION

Eccentric Action
- Decelerates ankle dorsiflexion

Isometric Action
- Isometrically stabilizes the foot and ankle complex

INNERVATION
- Tibial nerve

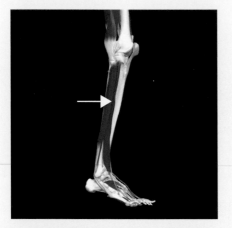

PERONEUS LONGUS

ORIGIN
- Lateral condyle of tibia, head and proximal two-thirds of the lateral surface of the fibula

INSERTION
- Lateral surface of the medial cuneiform and lateral side of the base of the first metatarsal

ISOLATED FUNCTION

Concentric Action
- Plantar flexes and everts the foot

INTEGRATED FUNCTION

Eccentric Action
- Decelerates ankle dorsiflexion and inversion

Isometric Action
- Stabilizes the foot and ankle complex

INNERVATION
- Superficial peroneal nerve

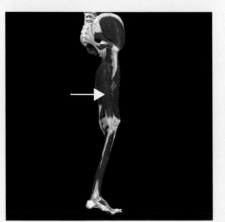

BICEPS FEMORIS-LONG HEAD

ORIGIN
- Ischial tuberosity of the pelvis, part of the sacrotuberous ligament

INSERTION
- Head of the fibula

ISOLATED FUNCTION

Concentric Action
- Accelerates knee flexion and hip extension, tibial external rotation

INTEGRATED FUNCTION

Eccentric Action
- Decelerates knee extension, hip flexion, and tibial internal rotation

Isometric Action
- Stabilizes the lumbo-pelvic-hip complex and knee

INNERVATION
- Tibial nerve

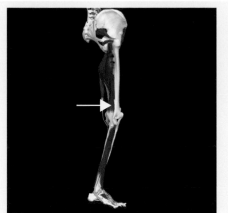

BICEPS FEMORIS-SHORT HEAD

ORIGIN
- Lower one-third of the posterior aspect of the femur

INSERTION
- Head of the fibula

ISOLATED FUNCTION

Concentric Action
- Accelerates knee flexion and tibial external rotation

INTEGRATED FUNCTION

Eccentric Action
- Decelerates knee extension and tibial internal rotation

Isometric Action
- Stabilizes the knee

INNERVATION
- Common peroneal nerve

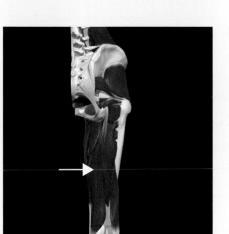

SEMIMEMBRANOSUS

ORIGIN
- Ischial tuberosity of the pelvis

INSERTION
- Posterior aspect of the medial tibial condyle of the tibia

ISOLATED FUNCTION

Concentric Action
- Accelerates knee flexion, hip extension and tibial internal rotation

INTEGRATED FUNCTION

Eccentric Action
- Decelerates knee extension, hip flexion and tibial external rotation

Isometric Action
- Stabilizes the lumbo-pelvic-hip complex and knee

INNERVATION
- Tibial nerve

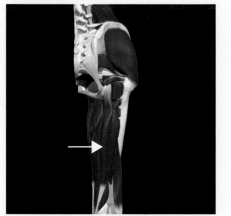

SEMITENDINOSUS

ORIGIN
- Ischial tuberosity of the pelvis and part of the sacrotuberous ligament

INSERTION
- Proximal aspect of the medial tibial condyle of the tibia (pes anserine)

ISOLATED FUNCTION

Concentric Action
- Accelerates knee flexion, hip extension and tibial internal rotation

INTEGRATED FUNCTION

Eccentric Action
- Decelerates knee extension, hip flexion and tibial external rotation

Isometric Action
- Stabilizes the lumbo-pelvic-hip complex and knee

INNERVATION
- Tibial nerve

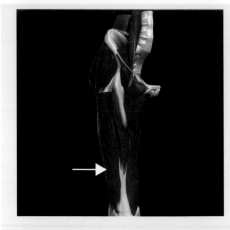

VASTUS LATERALIS

ORIGIN
- Anterior and inferior border of the greater trochanter, lateral region of the gluteal tuberosity, lateral lip of the linea aspera of the femur

INSERTION
- Base of patella and tibial tuberosity of the tibia

ISOLATED FUNCTION

Concentric Action
- Accelerates knee extension

INTEGRATED FUNCTION

Eccentric Action
- Decelerates knee flexion

Isometric Action
- Stabilizes the knee

INNERVATION
- Femoral nerve

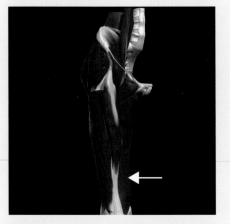

VASTUS MEDIALIS

ORIGIN
- Lower region of intertrochanteric line, medial lip of linea aspera, proximal medial supracondylar line of the femur

INSERTION
- Base of patella, tibial tuberosity of the tibia

ISOLATED FUNCTION

Concentric Action
- Accelerates knee extension

INTEGRATED FUNCTION

Eccentric Action
- Decelerates knee flexion

Isometric Action
- Stabilizes the knee

INNERVATION
- Femoral nerve

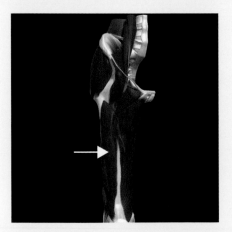

VASTUS INTERMEDIUS

ORIGIN
- Anterior-lateral regions of the upper two-thirds of the femur

INSERTION
- Base of patella, tibial tuberosity of the tibia

ISOLATED FUNCTION

Concentric Action
- Accelerates knee extension

INTEGRATED FUNCTION

Eccentric Action
- Decelerates knee flexion

Isometric Action
- Stabilizes the knee

INNERVATION
- Femoral nerve

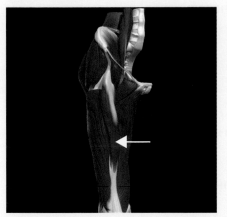

RECTUS FEMORIS

ORIGIN
- Anterior-inferior iliac spine of the pelvis

INSERTION
- Base of patella, tibial tuberosity of the tibia

ISOLATED FUNCTION

Concentric Action
- Accelerates knee extension and hip flexion

INTEGRATED FUNCTION

Eccentric Action
- Decelerates knee flexion and hip extension

Isometric Action
- Stabilizes the lumbo-pelvic-hip complex and knee

INNERVATION
- Femoral nerve

Hip Complex

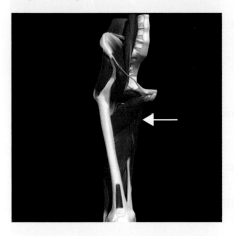

ADDUCTOR LONGUS

ORIGIN
- Anterior surface of the inferior pubic ramus of the pelvis

INSERTION
- Proximal one-third of the linea aspera of the femur

ISOLATED FUNCTION

Concentric Action
- Accelerates hip adduction, flexion and internal rotation

INTEGRATED FUNCTION

Eccentric Action
- Decelerates hip abduction, extension and external rotation

Isometric Action
- Stabilizes the lumbo-pelvic-hip complex

INNERVATION
- Obturator nerve

ADDUCTOR MAGNUS, ANTERIOR FIBERS

ORIGIN
- Ischial ramus of the pelvis

INSERTION
- Linea aspera of the femur

ISOLATED FUNCTION

Concentric Action
- Accelerates hip adduction, flexion and internal rotation

INTEGRATED FUNCTION

Eccentric Action
- Decelerates hip abduction, extension and external rotation

Isometric Action
- Stabilizes the lumbo-pelvic-hip complex

INNERVATION
- Obturator nerve

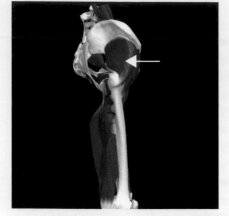

GLUTEUS MINIMUS

ORIGIN
* Ilium between the anterior and inferior gluteal line

INSERTION
* Greater trochanter of the femur

ISOLATED FUNCTION

Concentric Action
* Accelerates hip abduction, flexion, and internal rotation

INTEGRATED FUNCTION

Eccentric Action
* Decelerates frontal plane hip adduction, extension, and external rotation

Isometric Action
* Stabilizes the lumbo-pelvic-hip complex

INNERVATION
* Superior gluteal nerve

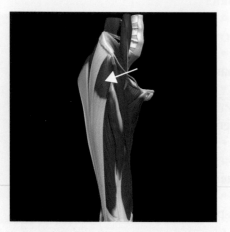

TENSOR FASCIA LATAE

ORIGIN
* Outer surface of the iliac crest just posterior to the anterior-superior iliac spine of the pelvis

INSERTION
* Proximal one-third of the iliotibial band

ISOLATED FUNCTION

Concentric Action
* Accelerates hip flexion, abduction and internal rotation

INTEGRATED FUNCTION

Eccentric Action
* Decelerates hip extension, adduction and external rotation

Isometric Action
* Stabilizes the lumbo-pelvic-hip complex

INNERVATION
* Superior gluteal nerve

GLUTEUS MAXIMUS

ORIGIN
* Outer ilium, posterior side of sacrum and coccyx and part of the sacro-tuberous and posterior sacroiliac ligament

INSERTION
* Gluteal tuberosity of the femur and iliotibial tract

ISOLATED FUNCTION

Concentric Action
* Accelerates hip extension and external rotation

INTEGRATED FUNCTION

Eccentric Action
* Decelerates hip flexion, internal rotation, and tibial internal rotation via the iliotibial band

Isometric Action
* Stabilizes the lumbo-pelvic-hip complex

INNERVATION
* Inferior gluteal nerve

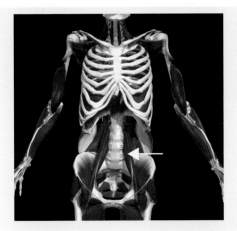

PSOAS

ORIGIN
- Transverse processes and lateral bodies of the last thoracic and all lumbar vertebrae including intervertebral discs

INSERTION
- Lesser trochanter of the femur

ISOLATED FUNCTION

Concentric Action
- Accelerates hip flexion and external rotation, extends and rotates lumbar spine

INTEGRATED FUNCTION

Eccentric Action
- Decelerates hip internal rotation and decelerates hip extension

Isometric Action
- Stabilizes the lumbo-pelvic-hip complex

INNERVATION
- Spinal nerve branches of L2-L4

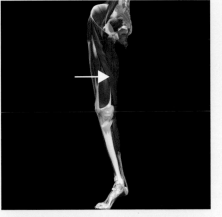

SARTORIUS

ORIGIN
- Anterior-superior iliac spine of the pelvis

INSERTION
- Proximal medial surface of the tibia

ISOLATED FUNCTION

Concentric Action
- Accelerates hip flexion, external rotation and abduction, accelerates knee flexion and internal rotation

INTEGRATED FUNCTION

Eccentric Action
- Decelerates hip extension, external rotation, knee extension and external rotation

Isometric Action
- Stabilizes the lumbo-pelvic-hip complex and knee

INNERVATION
- Femoral nerve

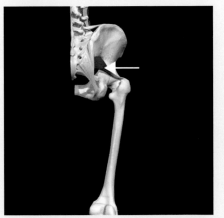

PIRIFORMIS

ORIGIN
- Anterior surface of the sacrum

INSERTION
- The greater trochanter of the femur

ISOLATED FUNCTION

Concentric Action
- Accelerates hip external rotation, abduction and extension

INTEGRATED FUNCTION

Eccentric Action
- Decelerates hip internal rotation, adduction and flexion

Isometric Action
- Stabilizes the hip and sacroiliac joints

INNERVATION
- Sciatic nerve

Abdominal Musculature

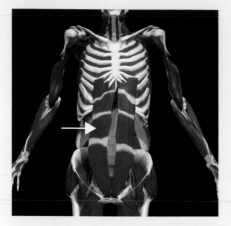

RECTUS ABDOMINUS

ORIGIN
- Pubic symphysis of the pelvis

INSERTION
- Ribs 5-7

ISOLATED FUNCTION

Concentric Action
- Spinal flexion, lateral flexion and rotation

INTEGRATED FUNCTION

Eccentric Action
- Spinal extension, lateral flexion and rotation

Isometric Action
- Stabilizes the lumbo-pelvic-hip complex

INNERVATION
- Intercostal nerve T7-T12

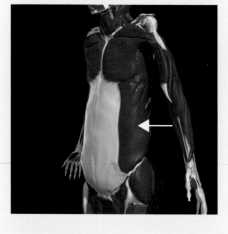

EXTERNAL OBLIQUE

ORIGIN
- External surface of ribs 4-12

INSERTION
- Anterior iliac crest of the pelvis, linea alba and contralateral rectus sheaths

ISOLATED FUNCTION

Concentric Action
- Spinal flexion, lateral flexion and contralateral rotation

INTEGRATED FUNCTION

Eccentric Action
- Spinal extension, lateral flexion and rotation

Isometric Action
- Stabilizes the lumbo-pelvic-hip complex

INNERVATION
- Intercostal nerves (T8-T12), iliohypogastric (L1), ilioinguinal (L1)

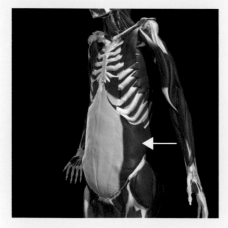

INTERNAL OBLIQUE

ORIGIN
- Anterior two-thirds of the iliac crest of the pelvis and thoracolumbar fascia

INSERTION
- Ribs 9-12, linea alba and contralateral rectus sheaths

ISOLATED FUNCTION

Concentric Action
- Spinal flexion (bilateral), lateral flexion and ipsilateral rotation

INTEGRATED FUNCTION

Eccentric Action
- Spinal extension, rotation and lateral flexion

Isometric Action
- Stabilizes the lumbo-pelvic-hip complex

INNERVATION
- Intercostal nerves (T8-T12), iliohypogastric (L1), ilioinguinal (L1)

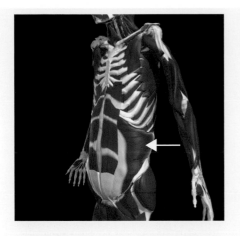

TRANSVERSE ABDOMINUS

ORIGIN
- Ribs 7-12, anterior two-thirds of the iliac crest of the pelvis and thoracolumbar fascia

INSERTION
- Lineae alba and contralateral rectus sheaths

ISOLATED FUNCTION

Concentric Action
- Increases intra-abdominal pressure. Supports the abdominal viscera.

INTEGRATED FUNCTION

Isometric Action
- Synergistically with the internal oblique, multifidus and deep erector spinae to stabilize the lumbo-pelvic-hip complex

INNERVATION
- Intercostal nerves (T7-T12), iliohypogastric (L1), ilioinguinal (L1)

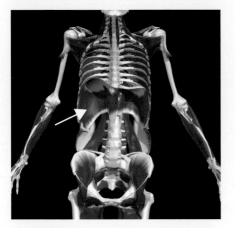

DIAPHRAGM

ORIGIN
- Costal part: inner surfaces of the cartilages and adjacent bony regions of ribs 6-12. Sternal part: posterior side of the xiphoid process. Crural (lumbar) part: (1) two aponeurotic arches covering the external surfaces of the quadratus lumborum and psoas major; (2) right and left crus, originating from the bodies of L1-L3 and their intervertebral discs

INSERTION
- Central tendon

ISOLATED FUNCTION

Concentric Action
- Pulls the central tendon inferiorly, increasing the volume in the thoracic cavity

INTEGRATED FUNCTION

Isometric Action
- Stabilization of the lumbo-pelvic-hip complex

INNERVATION
- Phrenic nerve (C3-C5)

Back Musculature

SUPERFICIAL ERECTOR SPINAE

ORIGIN
- Common origin: iliac crest of the pelvis, sacrum, spinous and transverse processes of T1-L5

ILIOCOSTALIS: LUMBORUM DIVISION

ORIGIN
- Common origin

INSERTION
- Inferior border of ribs 7-12

ISOLATED FUNCTION

Concentric Action
- Spinal extension, rotation and lateral flexion

INTEGRATED FUNCTION

Eccentric Action
- Spinal flexion, rotation and lateral flexion

Isometric Action
- Stabilizes the spine during functional movements

INNERVATION
- Dorsal rami of thoracic and lumbar nerves

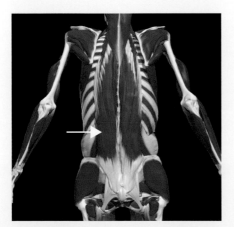

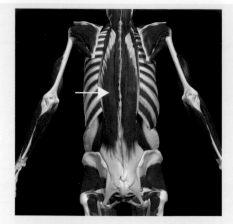

ILIOCOSTALIS: THORACIS DIVISION

ORIGIN
- Common origin

INSERTION
- Superior border of ribs 1-6

ISOLATED FUNCTION

Concentric Action
- Spinal extension, rotation and lateral flexion

INTEGRATED FUNCTION

Eccentric Action
- Spinal flexion, rotation and lateral flexion

Isometric Action
- Stabilizes the spine during functional movements

INNERVATION
- Dorsal rami of thoracic nerves

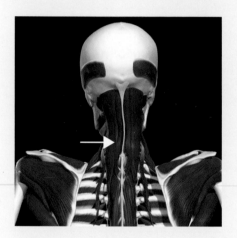

ILIOCOSTALIS: CERVICUS DIVISION

ORIGIN
- Common origin

INSERTION
- Transverse process of C4-C6

ISOLATED FUNCTION

Concentric Action
- Spinal extension, rotation and lateral flexion

INTEGRATED FUNCTION

Eccentric Action
- Spinal flexion, rotation and lateral flexion.

Isometric Action
- Stabilizes the spine during functional movements

INNERVATION
- Dorsal rami of thoracic nerves

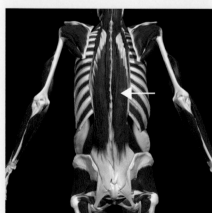

LONGISSIMUS: THORACIS DIVISION

ORIGIN
- Common origin

INSERTION
- Transverse process T1-T12; Ribs 2-12

ISOLATED FUNCTION

Concentric Action
- Spinal extension, rotation and lateral flexion

INTEGRATED FUNCTION

Eccentric Action
- Spinal flexion, rotation and lateral flexion

Isometric Action
- Stabilizes the spine during functional movements

INNERVATION
- Dorsal rami of thoracic and lumbar nerves

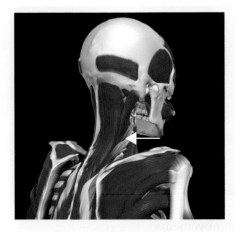

LONGISSIMUS: CERVICUS DIVISION

ORIGIN
- Common origin

INSERTION
- Transverse process of C6-C2

ISOLATED FUNCTION

Concentric Action
- Spinal extension, rotation and lateral flexion

INTEGRATED FUNCTION

Eccentric Action
- Spinal flexion, rotation and lateral flexion

Isometric Action
- Stabilizes the spine during functional movements

INNERVATION
- Dorsal rami of cervical nerves

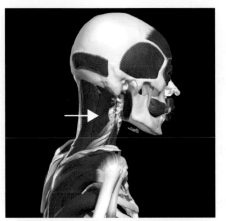

LONGISSIMUS: CAPITIS DIVISION

ORIGIN
- Common origin

INSERTION
- Mastoid process of the skull

ISOLATED FUNCTION

Concentric Action
- Spinal extension, rotation and lateral flexion

INTEGRATED FUNCTION

Eccentric Action
- Spinal flexion, rotation and lateral flexion

Isometric Action
- Stabilizes the spine during functional movements

INNERVATION
- Dorsal rami of cervical nerves

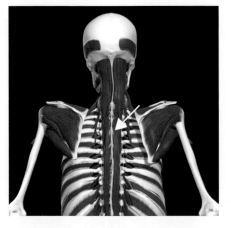

SPINALIS: THORACIS DIVISION

ORIGIN
- Common origin

INSERTION
- Spinous process of T7-T4

ISOLATED FUNCTION

Concentric Action
- Spinal extension, rotation and lateral flexion

INTEGRATED FUNCTION

Eccentric Action
- Spinal flexion, rotation and lateral flexion

Isometric Action
- Stabilizes the spine during functional movements

INNERVATION
- Dorsal rami of thoracic nerves

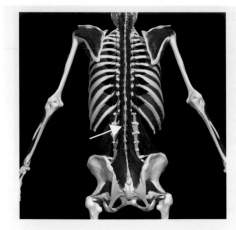

MULTIFIDUS

ORIGIN
- Posterior aspect of the sacrum; Processes of the lumbar, thoracic and cervical spine

INSERTION
- Spinous processes 1 to 4 segments above the origin

ISOLATED FUNCTION

Concentric Action
- Spinal extension and contralateral rotation

INTEGRATED FUNCTION

Eccentric Action
- Spinal flexion and rotation

Isometric Action
- Stabilizes the spine

INNERVATION
- Corresponding spinal nerves

Shoulder Musculature

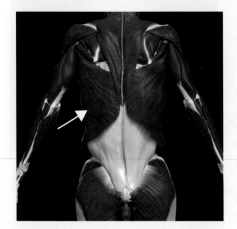

LATISSIMUS DORSI

ORIGIN
- Spinous processes of T7-T12 ; Iliac crest of the pelvis; Thoracolumbar fascia; Ribs 9-12

INSERTION
- Inferior angle of the scapula; Intertubecular groove of the humerus

ISOLATED FUNCTION

Concentric Action
- Shoulder extension, adduction and internal rotation

INTEGRATED FUNCTION

Eccentric Action
- Shoulder flexion, abduction and external rotation and spinal flexion

Isometric Action
- Stabilizes the lumbo-pelvic-hip complex and shoulder

INNERVATION
- Thoracodorsal nerve (C6-C8)

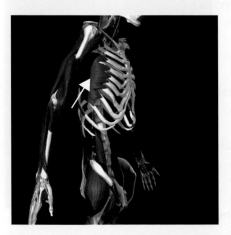

SERRATUS ANTERIOR

ORIGIN
- Ribs 4-12

INSERTION
- Medial border of the scapula

ISOLATED FUNCTION

Concentric Action
- Scapular protraction

INTEGRATED FUNCTION

Eccentric Action
- Scapular retraction

Isometric Action
- Stabilizes the scapula

INNERVATION
- Long thoracic nerve (C5-C7)

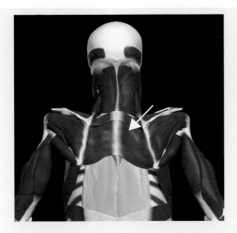

RHOMBOIDS

ORIGIN
- Spinous processes of C7-T5

INSERTION
- Medial border of the scapula

ISOLATED FUNCTION

Concentric Action
- Produces scapular retraction and downward rotation

INTEGRATED FUNCTION

Eccentric Action
- Scapular protraction and upward rotation

Isometric Action
- Stabilizes the scapula

INNERVATION
- Dorsal scapular nerve (C4-C5)

LOWER TRAPEZIUS

ORIGIN
- Spinous processes of T6-T12

INSERTION
- Spine of the scapula

ISOLATED FUNCTION

Concentric Action
- Scapular depression

INTEGRATED FUNCTION

Eccentric Action
- Scapular elevation

Isometric Action
- Stabilizes the scapula

INNERVATION
- Ventral rami C2-C4

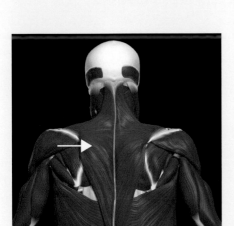

MIDDLE TRAPEZIUS

ORIGIN
- Spinous processes of T1-T5

INSERTION
- Acromion process of the scapula; Superior aspect of the spine of the scapula

ISOLATED FUNCTION

Concentric Action
- Scapular retraction

INTEGRATED FUNCTION

Eccentric Action
- Scapular protraction and elevation

Isometric Action
- Stabilizes scapula

INNERVATION
- Cranial nerve XI, ventral rami C2-C4

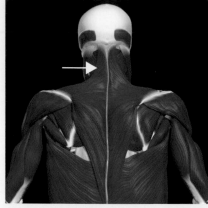

UPPER TRAPEZIUS

ORIGIN
- External occipital protuberance of the skull; Spinous process of C7

INSERTION
- Lateral third of the clavicle; Acromion process of the scapula

ISOLATED FUNCTION

Concentric Action
- Cervical extension, lateral flexion and rotation; scapular elevation

INTEGRATED FUNCTION

Eccentric Action
- Cervical flexion, lateral flexion, rotation, scapular depression

Isometric Action
- Stabilizes the cervical spine and scapula, stabilizes the medial border of the scapula creating a stable base for the prime movers during scapular abduction and upward rotation

INNERVATION
- Cranial nerve XI, ventral rami C2-C4

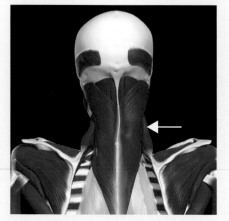

LEVATOR SCAPULAE

ORIGIN
- Transverse processes of C1-C4

INSERTION
- Superior vertebral border of the scapulae

ISOLATED FUNCTION

Concentric Action
- Cervical extension, lateral flexion and ipsilateral rotation when the scapulae is anchored; Assists in elevation and downward rotation of the scapulae

INTEGRATED FUNCTION

Eccentric Action
- Cervical flexion, contralateral cervical rotation, lateral flexion, scapular depression and upward rotation when the neck is stabilized

Isometric Action
- Stabilizes the cervical spine and scapulae

INNERVATION
- Cranial nerve XI, ventral rami C2-C4

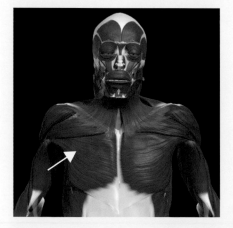

PECTORALIS MAJOR

ORIGIN
- Anterior surface of the clavicle; Anterior surface of the sternum, cartilage of ribs 1-7

INSERTION
- Greater tubercle of the humerus

ISOLATED FUNCTION

Concentric Action
- Shoulder flexion (clavicular fibers), horizontal adduction and internal rotation

INTEGRATED FUNCTION

Eccentric Action
- Shoulder extension horizontal abduction and external rotation

Isometric Action
- Stabilizes the shoulder girdle

INNERVATION
- Medial and lateral pectoral nerve (C5-C7)

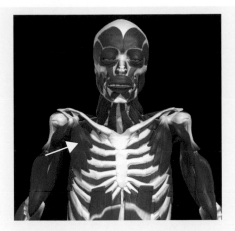

PECTORALIS MINOR

ORIGIN
- Ribs 3-5

INSERTION
- Coracoid process of the scapula

ISOLATED FUNCTION

Concentric Action
- Protracts the scapula

INTEGRATED FUNCTION

Eccentric Action
- Scapular retraction

Isometric Action
- Stabilizes the shoulder girdle

INNERVATION
- Medial pectoral nerve (C6-T1)

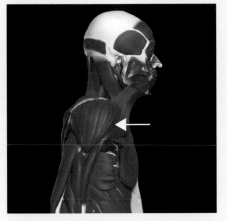

ANTERIOR DELTOID

ORIGIN
- Lateral third of the clavicle

INSERTION
- Deltoid tuberosity of the humerus

ISOLATED FUNCTION

Concentric Action
- Shoulder flexion and internal rotation

INTEGRATED FUNCTION

Eccentric Action
- Shoulder extension and external rotation

Isometric Action
- Stabilizes the shoulder girdle

INNERVATION
- Axillary nerve (C5-C6)

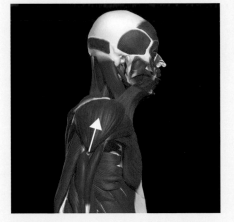

MEDIAL DELTOID

ORIGIN
- Acromion process of the scapula

INSERTION
- Deltoid tuberosity of the humerus

ISOLATED FUNCTION

Concentric Action
- Shoulder abduction

INTEGRATED FUNCTION

Eccentric Action
- Shoulder adduction

Isometric Action
- Stabilizes the shoulder girdle

INNERVATION
- Axillary nerve (C5-C6)

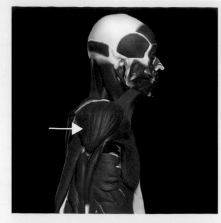

POSTERIOR DELTOID

ORIGIN
- Spine of the scapula

INSERTION
- Deltoid tuberosity of the humerus

ISOLATED FUNCTION

Concentric Action
- Shoulder extension and external rotation

INTEGRATED FUNCTION

Eccentric Action
- Shoulder flexion and internal rotation

Isometric Action
- Stabilizes the shoulder girdle

INNERVATION
- Axillary nerve (C5-C6)

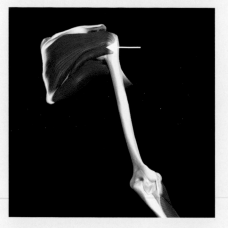

TERES MINOR

ORIGIN
- Lateral border of the scapula

INSERTION
- Greater tubercle of the humerus

ISOLATED FUNCTION

Concentric Action
- Shoulder external rotation

INTEGRATED FUNCTION

Eccentric Action
- Shoulder internal rotation

Isometric Action
- Stabilizes the shoulder girdle

INNERVATION
- Axillary nerve (C5-C6)

INFRASPINATUS

ORIGIN
- Infraspinous fossa of the scapula

INSERTION
- Middle facet of the greater tubercle of the humerus

ISOLATED FUNCTION

Concentric Action
- Shoulder external rotation

INTEGRATED FUNCTION

Eccentric Action
- Shoulder internal rotation

Isometric Action
- Stabilizes the shoulder girdle

INNERVATION
- Suprascapular nerve (C5-C6)

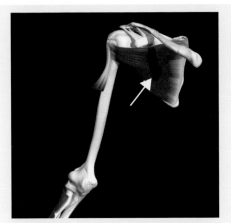

SUBSCAPULARIS

ORIGIN
- Subscapular fossa of the scapula

INSERTION
- Lesser tubercle of the humerus

ISOLATED FUNCTION

Concentric Action
- Shoulder internal rotation

INTEGRATED FUNCTION

Eccentric Action
- Shoulder external rotation

Isometric Action
- Stabilizes the shoulder girdle

INNERVATION
- Upper and lower subscapular nerve (C5-C6)

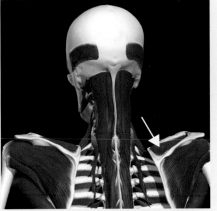

SUPRASPINATUS

ORIGIN
- Supraspinous fossa of the scapula

INSERTION
- Superior facet of the greater tubercle of the humerus

ISOLATED FUNCTION

Concentric Action
- Abduction of the arm

INTEGRATED FUNCTION

Eccentric Action
- Adduction of the arm

Isometric Action
- Stabilizes the shoulder girdle

INNERVATION
- Suprascapular nerve (C5-C6)

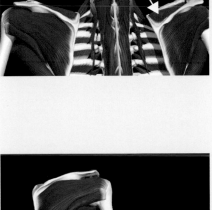
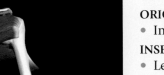

TERES MAJOR

ORIGIN
- Inferior angle of the scapula

INSERTION
- Lesser tubercle of the humerus

ISOLATED FUNCTION

Concentric Action
- Shoulder internal rotation, adduction and extension

INTEGRATED FUNCTION

Eccentric Action
- Shoulder external rotation, abduction and flexion

Isometric Action
- Stabilizes the shoulder girdle

INNERVATION
- Subscapular nerve (C5-C6)

Arm Musculature

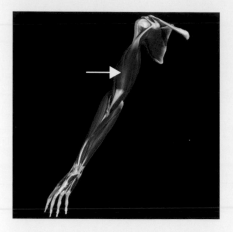

BICEPS BRACHII

ORIGIN
- Short head: Corocoid process; Long head: Tubercle above glenoid cavity on the humerus

INSERTION
- Radial tuberosity of the radius

ISOLATED FUNCTION

Concentric Action
- Elbow flexion, supination of the radioulnar joint, shoulder flexion

INTEGRATED FUNCTION

Eccentric Action
- Elbow extension, pronation of the radioulnar joint, shoulder extension

Isometric Action
- Stabilizes the elbow and shoulder girdle

INNERVATION
- Axillary nerve

TRICEPS BRACHII

ORIGIN
- Long head: Infraglenoid tubercle of the scapula; Short head: Posterior humerus; Medial head: posterior humerus

INSERTION
- Olecranon process of the ulna

ISOLATED FUNCTION

Concentric Action
- Elbow extension, shoulder extension

INTEGRATED FUNCTION

Eccentric Action
- Elbow flexion, shoulder flexion

Isometric Action
- Stabilizes the elbow and shoulder girdle

INNERVATION
- Radial nerve

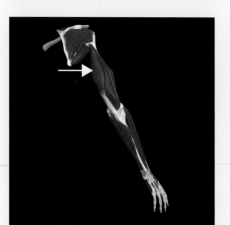

BRACHIALIS

ORIGIN
- Humerus

INSERTION
- Coronoid process of ulna

ISOLATED FUNCTION

Concentric Action
- Flexes elbow

INTEGRATED FUNCTION

Eccentric Action
- Elbow extension

Isometric Action
- Stabilizes the elbow

INNERVATION
- Musculocutaneous, radial nerve

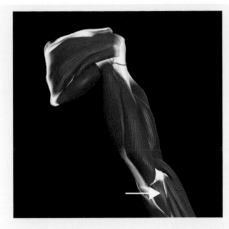

ANCONEUS

ORIGIN
- Lateral epicondyle of humerus

INSERTION
- Olecranon process, posterior ulna

ISOLATED FUNCTION

Concentric Action
- Extends elbow

INTEGRATED FUNCTION

Eccentric Action
- Elbow flexion

Isometric Action
- Stabilizes the elbow

INNERVATION
- Radial nerve

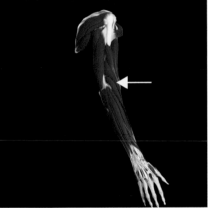
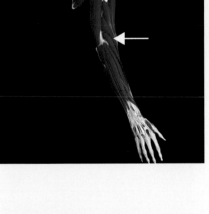

BRACHIORADIALIS

ORIGIN
- Lateral supracondylar ridge of humerus

INSERTION
- Styloid process of radius

ISOLATED FUNCTION

Concentric Action
- Flexes elbow

INTEGRATED FUNCTION

Eccentric Action
- Elbow extension

Isometric Action
- Stabilizes the elbow

INNERVATION
- Radial nerve

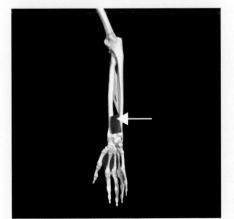

PRONATOR QUADRATUS

ORIGIN
- Distal ulna

INSERTION
- Distal radius

ISOLATED FUNCTION

Concentric Action
- Pronates forearm

INTEGRATED FUNCTION

Eccentric Action
- Forearm supination

Isometric Action
- Stabilizes distal radioulnar joint

INNERVATION
- Anterior interosseus nerve

PRONATOR TERES

ORIGIN
- Medial epicondyle of humerus, coronoid process of ulna

INSERTION
- Radius

ISOLATED FUNCTION

Concentric Action
- Pronates forearm

INTEGRATED FUNCTION

Eccentric Action
- Forearm supination

Isometric Action
- Stabilizes proximal radioulnar joint and elbow

INNERVATION
- Median nerve

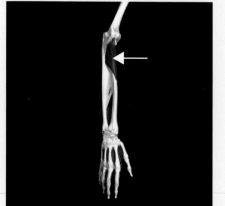

SUPINATOR

ORIGIN
- Lateral epicondyle of humerus

INSERTION
- Radius

ISOLATED FUNCTION

Concentric Action
- Supinates forearm

INTEGRATED FUNCTION

Eccentric Action
- Forearm pronation

Isometric Action
- Stabilizes proximal radioulnar joint and elbow

INNERVATION
- Radial nerve

Neck Musculature

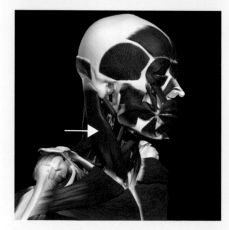

STERNOCLEIDOMASTOID

ORIGIN
- Sternal head: Top of Maubrium of the sternum; Clavicular head: Medial one-third of the clavicle

INSERTION
- Mastoid process, lateral superior nuchal line of the occiput of the skull

ISOLATED FUNCTION

Concentric Action
- Cervical flexion, rotation and lateral flexion

INTEGRATED FUNCTION

Eccentric Action
- Cervical extension, rotation and lateral flexion

Isometric Action
- Stabilizes the cervical spine and acromioclavicular joint

INNERVATION
- Lower subscapular nerve (C6-C7)

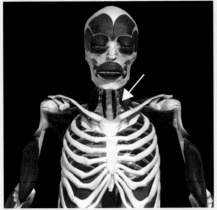

SCALENES

ORIGIN
- Transverse processes of C3-C7

INSERTION
- First and second ribs

ISOLATED FUNCTION

Concentric Action
- Cervical flexion, rotation and lateral flexion; Assists rib elevation during inhalation

INTEGRATED FUNCTION

Eccentric Action
- Cervical extension, rotation and lateral flexion

Isometric Action
- Stabilizes the cervical spine

INNERVATION
- Lower subscapular nerve (C6-C7)

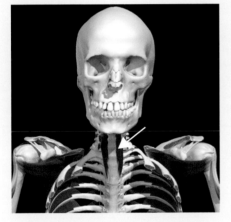

LONGUS COLLI

ORIGIN
- Anterior portion of T1-T3

INSERTION
- Anterior and lateral C1

ISOLATED FUNCTION

Concentric Action
- Cervical flexion, lateral flexion and ipsilateral rotation

INTEGRATED FUNCTION

Eccentric Action
- Cervical extension, lateral flexion and contralateral rotation

Isometric Action
- Stabilizes the cervical spine

INNERVATION
- Lower subscapular nerve (C6-C7)

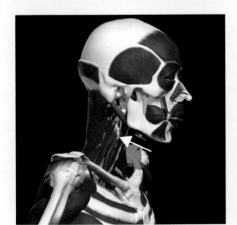

LONGUS CAPITUS

ORIGIN
- Transverse processes of C3-C6

INSERTION
- Inferior occipital bone

ISOLATED FUNCTION

Concentric Action
- Cervical flexion and lateral flexion

INTEGRATED FUNCTION

Eccentric Action
- Cervical extension

Isometric Action
- Stabilizes the cervical spine

INNERVATION
- Lower subscapular nerve (C6-C7)

A review of the actions within this section of pertinent skeletal muscles should make it clear that muscles function in all three planes of motion (sagittal, frontal, and transverse) using the entire spectrum of muscle actions (eccentric, isometric, and concentric). In addition, the section shows which muscles work synergistically with each other to produce force, stabilize the body, reduce force, or all three.

Sports performance exercise programs become more specific when there is a broader understanding of functional anatomy. A limited understanding of the synergistic functions of the HMS in all three planes of motion can lead to a lack of optimum performance, the potential of developing muscle imbalances, and injury.

Motor Behavior

 Motor Behavior
Motor response to internal and external environmental stimuli.

 Motor Control
How the central nervous system integrates internal and external sensory information with previous experiences to produce a motor response.

 Motor Learning
Integration of motor control processes through practice and experience, leading to a relatively permanent change in the capacity to produce skilled movements.

 Motor Development
The change in motor behavior over time throughout the lifespan.

The functional anatomy and biomechanics portions of this chapter present information about how the different parts of the HMS operate as a synergistic, integrated functional unit in all three planes of motion. This is accomplished and retained using the concept of motor behavior. **Motor behavior** is the HMS's response to internal and external environmental stimuli. The study of motor behavior examines the manner by which the nervous, skeletal, and muscular systems interact to produce skilled movement using sensory information from internal and external environments.

Motor behavior is the collective study of motor control, motor learning, and motor development (13,54) (Fig. 2.18). **Motor control** is the study of posture and movements with the involved structures and mechanisms used by the central nervous system to assimilate and integrate sensory information with previous experiences (45,46). Motor control is concerned with what central nervous system structures are involved with motor behavior to produce movement (46). **Motor learning** is the utilization of these processes through practice and experience, leading to a relatively permanent change in one's capacity to produce skilled movements (21). Finally, **motor development** is defined as the change in motor behavior over time throughout the lifespan (55). For the purposes of this text, we will confine this section to a brief discussion of motor control and motor learning.

MOTOR CONTROL

To move in an organized and efficient manner, the HMS must exhibit precise control over its collective segments. This segmental control is an integrated process involving neural, skeletal, and muscular components to produce appropriate motor responses. This process (and the study of these movements) is known as motor control and focuses on the involved structures and mechanisms used by the central nervous system to integrate internal and external sensory information with previous experiences to produce a skilled motor response. Essentially, motor control is concerned with the neural structures that are involved with motor behavior and how they produce movement (13,23,24,46).

One of the most important concepts in motor control and motor learning is how the central nervous system incorporates the information it receives to produce, refine, manipulate, and remember a movement pattern. The best place to start is with sensory information followed by proprioception, muscle synergies, and sensorimotor integration.

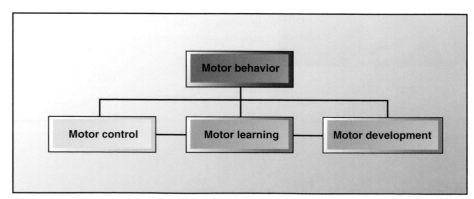

FIGURE 2.18   Components of Motor Behavior.

SENSORY INFORMATION

Sensory information is the data that the central nervous system receives from sensory receptors to determine such things as the body's position in space, limb orientation, as well as information to the environment, temperature, and texture, for example (45,46). This information allows the central nervous system to monitor the internal and external environments in order to modify motor behavior using adjustments ranging from simple reflexes to intricate movement patterns.

Sensory information is essential in protecting the body from harm. It also provides feedback about movement to acquire and refine new skills through sensory sensations and perceptions. A sensation is a process whereby sensory information is received by the receptor and transferred to the spinal cord for either reflexive motor behavior, to higher cortical areas for processing, or both (45,46). Perception is the integration of sensory information with past experiences or memories (56).

The body uses sensory information in three ways:

1. Sensory information provides information about the body's spatial orientation to the environment and itself before, during, and after movement.
2. It assists in planning and manipulating movement action plans. This may occur at the spinal level in the form of a reflex or at the cerebellum to compare the intended outcome with the actual performance.
3. Sensory information facilitates learning new skills as well as relearning existing movement patterns that may have become dysfunctional (45,46).

PROPRIOCEPTION

Proprioception
The cumulative neural input from sensory afferents to the central nervous system.

Proprioception is one form of sensory (afferent) information that uses mechanoreceptors (from cutaneous, muscle, tendon, and joint receptors) to provide information about static and dynamic positions, movements, and sensations related to muscle force and movement (45). Lephart (54) defines **proprioception** as the cumulative neural input from sensory afferents to the central nervous system. This vital information ensures optimum motor behavior and neuromuscular efficiency (21,57). This afferent information is delivered to different levels of motor control within the central nervous system to use in monitoring and manipulating movement (54).

Proprioception is altered following injury (58–60). With many of the receptors being located in and around joints, any joint injury will likely also damage proprioceptive components that could be compromised for some time following an injury. When one considers that 85% of our population experiences low-back pain, or the estimated 80,000 to 100,000+ anterior cruciate ligament (ACL) injuries annually, or the more than 2 million ankle sprains, today's athlete may have altered proprioception due to past injuries. A thorough rehabilitation program following a musculoskeletal injury normally will contain a proprioceptive component. Much of our movement is supported by the global muscular system reinforcing the need for core and balance training to enhance one's proprioceptive capabilities, increase postural control, and decrease tissue overload (52,61,62).

MUSCLE SYNERGIES

One of the most important concepts in motor control is that the central nervous system recruits muscles in groups or synergies (1,21,26). This simplifies movement by allowing muscles to operate as a functional unit (1,5). Through practice of proper movement patterns and technique, these synergies become more fluent and automated (Table 2.5).

SENSORIMOTOR INTEGRATION

Sensorimotor Integration

The ability of the central nervous system to gather and interpret sensory information to execute the proper motor response.

Sensorimotor integration is the ability for the central nervous system to gather and interpret sensory information to execute the proper motor response (23,24,46,53,64). Sensorimotor integration is only as effective as the quality of the incoming sensory information (21,63). An athlete who trains with improper form delivers improper sensory information to the central nervous system, which can lead to movement compensation and potential injury. Thus, proper programs need to be designed to train and to reinforce correct technique. For example, the athlete who consistently performs a squat with an arched lower back and adducted femur will alter the length-tension relationships of muscles, alter the force-couple relationships, and alter arthrokinematics. This can ultimately lead to back, knee, and hamstring problems (52,65–69).

MOTOR LEARNING

Motor learning is the integration of these motor control processes through practice and experience, leading to a relatively permanent change in the capacity to produce skilled movements (21,46). At its most basic, the study of motor learning looks at how movements are learned and retained for future use. Proper practice and experience will lead to a permanent change in an athlete's ability to perform skilled movements effectively. For this to occur, feedback is necessary to ensure optimal development of these skilled movements.

TABLE 2.5		
Muscle Synergies		
	Bench Press	**Squats**
Prime Mover	Pectoralis Major	Quadriceps Gluteus Maximus
Synergists	Anterior Deltoid Triceps	Hamstrings Adductor Magnus
Stabilizers	Rotator Cuff	Lower Extremity Musculature • Flexor Hallicus Longus • Posterior Tibialis • Anterior Tibialis • Soleus • Gastrocnemius Lumbo-Pelvic-Hip Complex • Adductor Longus • Adductor Brevis • Transverse Abdominus • Gluteus Medius Scapular Stabilizers • Trapezius • Rhomboids Cervical Stabilizers

FEEDBACK

Feedback

Internal feedback: sensory information provided by the body via length-tension relationships, force-couple relationships, and arthrokinematics to monitor movement and the environment.

External feedback: information provided by some external source.

Feedback is the utilization of sensory information and sensorimotor integration to aid in the development of permanent neural representations of motor patterns for efficient movement. This is achieved through internal (or sensory) feedback and external (or augmented) feedback (13,46,63).

INTERNAL FEEDBACK

Internal (or sensory) feedback is the process by which sensory information is used by the body via length-tension relationships, force-couple relationships, and arthrokinematics to monitor movement and the environment. Internal feedback acts as a guide, steering the HMS to the proper force, speed, and amplitude of movement patterns. Proper form during movement ensures that the incoming internal (sensory) feedback is the correct information allowing for optimal sensorimotor integration for ideal structural and functional efficiency (21).

EXTERNAL FEEDBACK

External (or augmented) feedback is information provided by some external source, for example, a Sports Performance Professional, videotape, mirror, or heart rate monitor. This information is used to supplement internal feedback (46,63). External feedback provides another source of information that allows for the athlete to associate the outcome of the achieved movement pattern ("good" or "bad") with what is felt internally.

Knowledge of Results

Feedback used after the completion of a movement, to help inform the athlete about the outcome of his performance.

Two major forms of external feedback are **knowledge of results** and **knowledge of performance** (21). Knowledge of results is used after the completion of a movement to inform the athlete about the outcome of their performance. This can come from the Sports Performance Professional, the athlete, or some technological means. The Sports Performance Professional might inform the athlete that their squats were "good" and ask the athlete if they could "feel" or "see" their form. By getting your athletes involved with knowledge of results, they increase their own awareness and augment their impressions with multiple forms of feedback. This can be done after each repetition, after a few repetitions, or once the set is completed. As the athlete becomes more familiar with the desired movement technique, knowledge of results from the Sports Performance Professional should be given less frequently. This improves neuromuscular efficiency (63).

Knowledge of Performance

Feedback that provides information about the quality of the movement during exercise.

Knowledge of performance provides information about the quality of the movement. An example would be noticing that, during a squat, the athlete's feet were externally rotated, the femurs were excessively adducting, and then, asking if the athlete felt or saw anything different about those reps. Or, to get younger athletes, especially girls in team sports, to absorb the shock of landing from a jump (and not land with extended knees that places the ACL in a precarious position), tell them to listen to the impact and land quietly, effectively teaching the athlete to absorb the shock of landing. These examples get the athlete involved in his/her own sensory process. Such feedback will be given less frequently as the athlete becomes more proficient (63).

These forms of external feedback identify performance errors. This feedback is also an important component in motivation. Further, feedback gives the athlete supplemental sensory input to help create an awareness of the desired action (21). It is important to state, however, that an athlete must not become too dependent on external feedback, especially from the Sports Performance Professional, as this may detract from the athlete's own responsiveness to internal sensory input (21,46). This could alter sensorimotor integration and affect the learning by the athlete and the ultimate performance of new and skilled movement.

SUMMARY

In summary, each component of the HMS is interdependent. The HMS must work interdependently to gather information from internal and external environments to create, learn, and refine movements (or motor behavior) through proprioception, sensorimotor integration, and muscle synergies necessary to create efficient movement (motor control). Then, repeated practice, and incorporating internal and external feedback allows this efficient movement to be reproduced (motor learning).

REFERENCES

1. Newmann D. Kinesiology of the Musculoskeletal System; Foundations for Physical Rehabilitation. St. Louis: Mosby; 2002.
2. Sahrmann S. Diagnosis and Treatment of Movement Impairment Syndromes. St. Louis: Mosby; 2002.
3. Panjabi MM. The stabilizing system of the spine. Part I. Function, dysfunction, adaptation, and enhancement. *J Spinal Disord* 1992;5:383–89; discussion 397.
4. Hamill J, Knutzen KM. Biomechanical Basis of Human Movement, 2nd ed. Philadelphia: Lippincott Williams & Wilkins; 2003.
5. Levangle PK, Norkin CC. Joint Structure and Function: A Comprehensive Analysis, 3rd ed. Philadelphia: FA Davis Company; 2001.
6. Watkins J. Structure and Function of the Musculoskeletal System. Champaign, IL: Human Kinetics; 1999.
7. Nordin M, Frankel VH. Basic Biomechanics of the Musculoskeletal System, 3rd ed. Philadelphia: Lippincott Williams & Wilkins; 2001.
8. Kendall FP, McCreary EK, Provance PG. Muscles Testing and Function with Posture and Pain, 5th ed. Baltimore: Lippincott Williams & Wilkins; 2005.
9. Luttgens K, Hamilton N. Kinesiology: Scientific Basis of Human Motion, 9th ed. Dubuque, IA: Brown & Benchmark Publishers; 1997.
10. Powers SK. Exercise Physiology: Theory and Application to Fitness and Performance. Dubuque, IA: McGraw Hill; 2000.
11. Inman VT, Ralston HJ, Todd F. Human Walking. Baltimore: Williams & Wilkins; 1981.
12. Innes KA. The Effect of Gait on Extremity Evaluation. In: Hammer WI. Functional Soft Tissue Examination and Treatment by Manual Methods, 2nd ed. Gaithsburg, MD: Aspen Publishers, Inc; 1999.
13. Schmidt RA, Lee TD. Motor Control and Learning: A Behavioral Emphasis, 3rd ed. Champaign, IL: Human Kinetics; 1999.
14. Basmajian J: Muscles Alive: Their Functions Revealed by EMG, 5th ed. Baltimore: Williams & Wilkins; 1985.
15. Clark MA. Integrated Core Stabilization Training. Thousand Oaks, CA: National Academy of Sports Medicine; 2000.
16. Aidley DJ. Physiology of Excitable Cells. Cambridge: Cambridge University Press; 1971.
17. Katz AM. Physiology of the Heart. Philadelphia: Lippincott Williams & Wilkins; 2006.
18. Vander A, Sherman J, Luciano D. Human Physiology: The Mechanisms of Body Function, 8th ed. New York: McGraw-Hill; 2001.
19. McArdle WD, Katch FI, Katch VL. Exercise Physiology: Energy, Nutrition and Human Performance. Philadelphia: Lippincott Williams & Wilkins; 2007.
20. McClay I, Manal K. Three-dimensional kinetic analysis of running: significance of secondary planes of motion. *Med Sci Sports Exerc* Nov 1999;31:1629–637.
21. Schmidt RA, Wrisberg CA. Motor Learning and Performance, 2nd ed. Champaign, IL: Human Kinetics; 2000.
22. Nyland J, Smith S, Beickman K et al. Frontal plane knee angle affects dynamic postural control strategy during unilateral stance. *Med Sci Sports Exerc* 2002;34:1150–157.
23. Coker CA. Motor Learning and Control for Practitioners. Boston: McGraw-Hill; 2004.
24. Magill RA. Motor Learning and Control: Concepts and Applications. Boston: McGraw-Hill; 2007.
25. Grigg P. Peripheral neural mechanisms in proprioception. *J Sport Rehab* 1994;3:2–17.
26. Edgerton VR, Wolf SL, Levendowski DJ et al. Theoretical basis for patterning EMG amplitudes to assess muscle dysfunction. *Med Sci Sports Exerc* June 1996;28:744–51.
27. Lieber RL. Skeletal Muscle Structure and Function: Implications for Rehabilitation. Baltimore: Lippincott Williams & Wilkins; 2002.

28. Bergmark A. Stability of the lumbar spine. A study in mechanical engineering. *Acta Ortho Scand* 1989;230(suppl):20–4.

29. Mooney V. Sacroiliac Joint Dysfunction. In: Vleeming A, Mooney V, Dorman T et al. Movement, Stability and Low Back Pain. London: Churchill Livingstone; 1997.

30. Crisco JJ, Panjabi MM. The intersegmental and multisegmental muscles of the spine: a biomechanical model comparing lateral stabilizing potential. *Spine* 1991;7:793–99.

31. Richardson C, Jull G, Hodges P et al. Therapeutic Exercise for Spinal Segmental Stabilization in Low Back Pain. London: Churchill Livingstone; 1999.

32. Culham LC, Peat M. Functional anatomy of the shoulder complex. *J Ortho Sports Phys Ther* 1993; 18:342–50.

33. Wilk KE, Reinold MM, Dugas JR et al. Current concepts in the recognition and treatment of superior labral (SLAP) lesions. *J Orthop Sports Phys Ther* 2005;35:273–91.

34. Millett PJ, Wilcox RB 3rd, O'Holleran JD et al. Rehabilitation of the rotator cuff: an evaluation-based approach. *J Am Acad Orthop Surg* 2006;14:599–609.

35. Kibler WB, Chandler TJ, Shapiro R et al. Muscle activation in coupled scapulohumeral motions in the high performance tennis serve. *Br J Sports Med.* 2007;41:745–49.

36. Gottschalk F, Kourosh S, Leveau B. The functional anatomy of tensor fascia latae and gluteus medius and minimus. *J Anat* 1989;166:179–89.

37. Anderson FC, Pandy MG. Individual muscle contributions to support in normal walking. *Gait Posture* 2003;17:159–69.

38. Hossain M, Nokes LD. A model of dynamic sacroiliac joint instability from malrecruitment of gluteus maximus and biceps femoris muscles resulting in low back pain. *Med Hypotheses* 2005;65:278–81.

39. Liu MQ, Anderson FC, Pandy MG et al. Muscles that support the body also modulate forward progression during walking. *J Biomech* 2006;39:2623–630.

40. Lieb FJ, Perry J. Quadriceps Function. *J Bone Joint Surg* 1971;50A:1535–548.

41. Toumi H, Poumarat G, Benjamin M et al. New insights into the function of the vastus medialis with clinical implications. *Med Sci Sports Exerc* 2007;39:1153–159.

42. Lee D. Instability of the Sacroiliac Joint and the Consequences for Gait. In: Vleeming A, Mooney V, Dorman T et al. Movement, Stability and Low Back Pain. London: Churchill Livingstone; 1997.

43. Gracovetsky SA. Linking the Spinal Engine with the Legs: A Theory of Human Gait. In: Vleeming A, Mooney V, Dorman T et al. Movement, Stability and Low Back Pain. London: Churchill Livingstone; 1997.

44. Vleeming A, Snijders CJ, Stoeckart R et al. The Role of the Sacroiliac Joints in Coupling Between Spine, Pelvis, Legs and Arms. In Vleeming A, Mooney V, Dorman T et al. Movement, Stability and Low Back Pain. London: Churchill Livingstone; 1997.

45. Newton RA. Neural Systems Underlying Motor Control. In: Montgomery PC, Connoly BH. Motor Control and Physical Therapy: Theoretical Framework and Practical Applications. Hixson, TN: Chattanooga Group, Inc; 1991.

46. Rose DJ. A Multi-level Approach to the Study of Motor Control and Learning. Needham Heights, MA: Allyn & Bacon; 1997.

47. Vleeming A, Mooney V, Dorman T et al (eds). Movement, Stability and Low Back Pain. London: Churchill Livingstone; 1997.

48. Snijders CJ, Vleeming A, Stoeckart R et al. Biomechanics of the Interface Between Spine and Pelvis in Different Postures. In: Vleeming A, Mooney V, Dorman T et al. Movement, Stability and Low Back Pain. London: Churchill Livingstone; 1997.

49. Okamoto T, Okamoto K. Development of Gait by Electromyography: Application to Gait Analysis and Evaluation. Osaka, Japan: Walking Development Group; 2007.

50. Fredericson M, Cookingham CL, Chaudhari AM et al. Hip abductor weakness in distance runners with iliotibial band syndrome. *Clin J Sport Med* 2000;10:169–75.

51. Ireland ML, Wilson JD, Ballantyne BT et al. Hip strength in females with and without patellofemoral pain. *J Orthop Sports Phys Ther* 2003;33:671–76.

52. Hewett TE, Lindenfeld TN, Riccobene JV et al. The effect of neuromuscular training on the incidence of knee injury in female athletes. A prospective study. *Am J Sports Med.* 1999;27:699–706.

53. Seeley RR, Stephans TD, Tate P. Anatomy and Physiology, 6th ed. Boston: McGraw Hill; 2003.

54. Lephart SM, Fu FH (eds). Proprioception and Neuromuscular Control in Joint Stability. Champaign, IL: Human Kinetics; 2000.

55. Gabbard C. Lifelong Motor Development. San Francisco: Pearson Benjamin Cummings; 2008.

56. Sage GH. Introduction to Motor Behavior: A Neuropsychological Approach, 3rd ed. Dubuque, IA: WC Brown; 1984.

57. Ghez C. The Control of Movement. In: Kandel E, Schwartz J, Jessel T. Principles of Neuroscience. New York: Elsevier Science; 1991.

58. Brown CN, Mynark R. Balance deficits in recreational athletes with chronic ankle instability. *J Athl Train* 2007;42:367–73.

59. Solomonow M, Barratta R, Zhou BH. The synergistic action of the anterior cruciate ligament and thigh muscles in maintaining joint stability. *Am J Sports Med* 1987;15:207–13.

60. Uremović M, Cvijetić S, Pasić MB et al. Impairment of proprioception after whiplash injury. *Coll Antropol* 2007;31:823–27.

61. Paterno MV, Myer GD, Ford KR et al. Neuromuscular training improves single-limb stability in young female athletes. *J Orthop Sports Phys Ther* 2004;34:305–16.

62. Chmielewski TL, Hurd WJ, Rudolph KS et al. Perturbation training improves knee kinematics and reduces muscle co-contraction after complete unilateral anterior cruciate ligament rupture. *Phys Ther* Aug 2005;85:740–49.

63. Swinnen SP. Information Feedback for Motor Skill Learning: A Review. In: Zelaznik HN. Advances in Motor Learning and Control. Champaign, IL: Human Kinetics; 1996.

64. Biedert RM. Contribution of the Three Levels of Nervous System Motor Control: Spinal Cord, Lower Brain, Cerebral Cortex. In: Lephart SM, Fu FH. Proprioception and Neuromuscular Control in Joint Stability. Champaign, IL: Human Kinetics; 2000.

65. Ford KR, Myer GD, Hewett TE. Valgus knee motion during landing in high school female and male basketball players. *Med Sci Sports Exerc* 2003;35:1745–750.

66. Nadler SF, Malanga GA, Bartoli LA et al. Hip muscle imbalance and low back pain in athletes: influence of core strengthening. *Med Sci Sports Exerc* 2002a;34:9–16.

67. Nadler SF, Malanga GA, Feinberg JH et al. Functional performance deficits in athletes with previous lower extremity injury. *Clin J Sport Med* 2002b;12:73–8.

68. Bullock-Saxton JE. Local sensation changes and altered hip muscle function following severe ankle sprain. *Physical Therapy* 1994;74:17–28.

69. Knapik JJ, Bauman CL, Jones BH et al. Preseason strength and flexibility imbalances associated with athletic injuries in female collegiate athletes. *Am J Sports Med* 1991;19:76–81.

CHAPTER 3

Sports Performance Testing

UPON COMPLETION OF THIS CHAPTER, YOU WILL BE ABLE TO:

Explain the components and function of an integrated sports performance assessment.

Ask appropriate general and medical questions to gather subjective information from your athletes.

Perform a systematic assessment to obtain objective information about your athletes.

Introduction

Designing an individualized sports performance program can only be properly accomplished by having an understanding of an athlete's goals, needs, and abilities. This entails knowing what the athlete wants to gain from a training program, what the athlete needs from this program to successfully accomplish a personal goal(s), and the athlete's capability in (structurally and functionally) performing the required tasks within an integrated program. The information necessary to create the right program for a specific athlete (or group of athletes) comes through proper sports performance testing. The remainder of this chapter will focus on specific sports performance tests.

DEFINITION OF SPORTS PERFORMANCE TESTING

Sports performance testing is a systematic approach to problem solving that provides the Sports Performance Professional with a basis for making educated decisions about exercise and acute variable selection. A systematic schedule of assessments provides an ongoing source of information in order to modify training and progress an athlete through an integrated training program. Such assessments allow continual monitoring of an athlete's needs, functional capabilities, and physiological effects of exercise, enabling the athlete to realize the full benefit of an individualized training program.

It is important to understand that sports performance testing is not designed to diagnose any condition, but rather to observe each athlete's individual structural and functional status. Furthermore, the sports performance assessment presented by NASM is not intended to replace a medical examination. Athletes who exhibit extreme difficulty or pain with any observation or exercise should be referred to their personal physician or qualified health-care provider to identify any underlying cause.

INFORMATION PROVIDED BY A SPORTS PERFORMANCE ASSESSMENT

The assessment provides the Sports Performance Professional with a three-dimensional representation of the athlete, offering insights into the athlete's past, present, and perhaps their future. The assessment covers information regarding the athlete's cardiorespiratory fitness, strength, power, and movement abilities as well as past and present medical history. Essentially, the assessment offers a view of the current structure and function of an athlete.

A fundamental representation of an athlete's goals, needs, and status can be created through the sports performance assessment. From this profile of status, needs, and goals, an integrated sports performance program is individualized specifically for each athlete. When conducting these assessments, it is essential to utilize a variety of observation methods in order to obtain a balanced overview of an athlete (Fig. 3.1).

Types of Subjective Information Provided in a Sports Performance Assessment

The first step in the sports performance assessment is the athlete's personal medical history.

READINESS FOR ACTIVITY

Gathering personal background information about an athlete can be very valuable in gaining an understanding of the athlete's physical condition and can also provide insight into what types of imbalances they may exhibit. One of the easiest methods for gathering this information is through the Physical Activity Readiness Questionnaire (PAR-Q) (Fig. 3.2), which was designed to help determine if a person is ready to undertake low-to-moderate-to-high activity levels (1). Furthermore, it aids in identifying people for whom certain activities may not be appropriate or who may need further medical attention.

The PAR-Q is directed toward detecting any possible cardiorespiratory dysfunction, such as coronary heart disease, and is a good beginning point for gathering personal background information concerning an athlete's cardiorespiratory function. However, it is only one component of a thorough sports performance assessment. Although this information is extremely important, asking other questions can provide additional information about an athlete. This includes questions about an athlete's medical history.

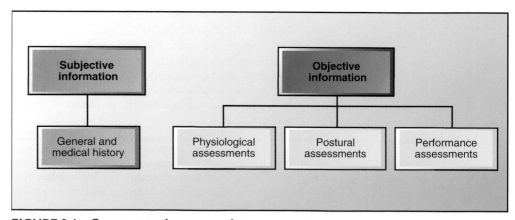

FIGURE 3.1 Components of a sports performance assessment.

	Questions	Yes	No
1	Has your doctor ever said that you have a heart condition and that you should only perform physical activity recommended by a doctor?	☐	☐
2	Do you feel pain in your chest when you perform physical activity?	☐	☐
3	In the past month, have you had chest pain when you were not performing any physical activity?	☐	☐
4	Do you lose your balance because of dizziness or do you ever lose consciousness?	☐	☐
5	Do you have a bone or joint problem that could be made worse by a change in your physical activity?	☐	☐
6	Is your doctor currently prescribing any medication for your blood pressure or for a heart condition?	☐	☐
7	Do you know of <u>any</u> other reason why you should not engage in physical activity?	☐	☐

If you have answered "Yes" to one or more of the above questions, consult your physician <u>before</u> engaging in physical activity. Tell your physician which questions you answered "Yes" to. After a medical evaluation, seek advice from your physician on what type of activity is suitable for your current condition.

FIGURE 3.2 Sample Physical Activity Readiness Questionnaire (PAR-Q).

MEDICAL HISTORY

The medical history (Fig. 3.3) is absolutely crucial. Not only does it provide information about any life-threatening chronic diseases (such as coronary heart disease, high blood pressure, diabetes, etc.), it also provides information about the structure and function of the athlete by uncovering important information such as past injuries, surgeries, imbalances, and chronic conditions.

PAST INJURIES

Inquiring about an athlete's past injuries can illuminate possible dysfunctions. One of the best predictors of future injuries is past injury; an athlete with a previously strained hamstring is 6 to 8 times more likely to suffer another strain. There is a vast array of research that has demonstrated the effects of past injuries and the function of the human movement system. Beyond the risk

	Questions	Yes	No
1	Have you ever had any pain or injuries (ankle, knee, hip, back, shoulder, etc.)? (If yes, please explain.) _____ _____	☐	☐
2	Have you ever had any surgeries? (If yes, please explain.) _____ _____	☐	☐
3	Has a medical doctor ever diagnosed you with a chronic disease, such as coronary heart disease, coronary artery disease, hypertension (high blood pressure), high cholesterol or diabetes? (If yes, please explain.) _____ _____	☐	☐
4	Are you currently taking any medication? (If yes, please explain.) _____ _____	☐	☐

FIGURE 3.3 Sample questions: athlete's medical history.

PHYSIOLOGICAL ASSESSMENTS

Physiological assessments provide valuable information regarding the status of the athlete's overall health. Regular assessment of an athlete's resting heart rate, blood pressure, body fat, circumferences, and body mass index provide constructive information in designing an athlete's conditioning program.

HEART RATE

The resting heart rate can be taken at the base of the thumb (radial pulse; the preferred location) or on the neck to the side of the windpipe (carotid pulse; use with caution). It is best to teach athletes how to measure their resting heart rate upon rising in the morning. Instruct them to test their RHR three mornings in a row and average the three readings.

RADIAL PULSE

To find the radial pulse, lightly place two fingers along the arm in line and just above (proximal to) the thumb (Fig. 3.4). After the pulse is felt, count the pulses for 30 seconds and multiply by two (the first beat counted is zero). Record the 60-second pulse rate and average over 3 days. Points to consider:
- The touch should be gentle.
- The test must be taken when the athlete is calm.
- All three tests must be taken the same time and surrounding conditions to ensure accuracy.

CAROTID PULSE

To find the carotid pulse, lightly place two fingers diagonally on the neck, just to the side of the larynx (Fig. 3.5). After the pulse is felt, count the pulses for 30 seconds and multiply by two. Record the 60-second pulse rate and average over 3 days. Points to consider:
- The touch should be gentle.
  - Excessive pressure can decrease heart rate and blood pressure leading to an inaccurate reading, possible dizziness, and fainting.
- The test must be taken when the athlete is calm.
- All three tests should be taken the same time and surrounding conditions to ensure accuracy.

RESTING HEART RATE

Resting heart rates can vary between and within individuals. However, on average, the resting heart rate is 70 beats per minute for a man and 75 beats per minute for a woman. Resting heart

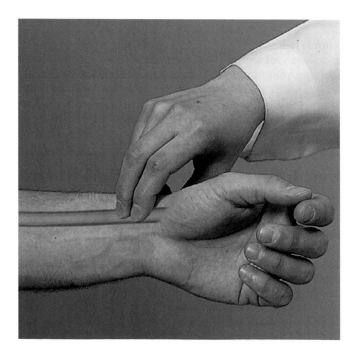

FIGURE 3.4 Radial pulse.

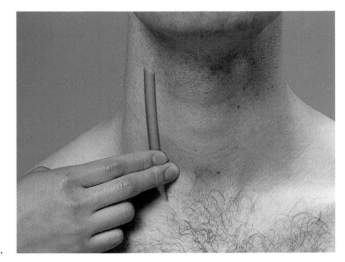

FIGURE 3.5   Carotid pulse.

rates become lower as fitness improves and impressively low pulse rates can be seen in endurance athletes. Having a stable assessment of resting heart rate may be helpful in monitoring training status. If the resting pulse rate continues to decline, it might be safe to assume that fitness is improving. A steady climb in pulse rate may be indicative of the overtraining syndrome (29,30).

TRAINING HEART RATE ZONES

The Sports Performance Professional can also calculate the training heart rate zone in which an athlete should perform cardiorespiratory exercise. There are many ways to determine heart rate zones. Create heart rate zones by first estimating the athlete's maximum heart rate by subtracting the athlete's age from the number 220 (220 – age). Second, multiply the estimated maximum heart rate by the appropriate intensity (65–90%) in which the athlete should work while performing cardiorespiratory exercise.

Zone One	Maximum Heart Rate × 0.65
	Maximum Heart Rate × 0.75
Zone Two	Maximum Heart Rate × 0.80
	Maximum Heart Rate × 0.85
Zone Three	Maximum Heart Rate × 0.86
	Maximum Heart Rate × 0.90

The heart rate zone numbers should be combined with the various cardiorespiratory assessments (discussed later in this chapter) in order to establish the appropriate heart rate zone the athlete will start in. This calculation is a crude average that will most likely have to be modified. Intensity levels may need to be lowered (to 40–55% of maximum), depending on the age and physical condition of the athlete.

BLOOD PRESSURE

Blood pressure measurements consist of systolic and diastolic readings. The systolic reading (top number) reflects the pressure produced by the heart as it pumps blood to the body. Normal systolic pressure ranges from 120 millimeters of mercury (mm Hg) to 130 mm Hg. The diastolic blood pressure (lower number) signifies the minimum pressure within the arteries through a full cardiac cycle. Normal diastolic pressure ranges from 80 mm Hg to 85 mm Hg.

BLOOD PRESSURE TESTING

Blood pressure is measured using a sphygmomanometer, which consists of an inflatable cuff, a pressure meter with an inflation bulb/valve and a stethoscope (this can also be done using a digital device). To record blood pressure, instruct the athlete to assume a comfortable seated position and place the appropriate size cuff on the athlete, just above the elbow (Fig. 3.6). Next, rest the arm on a supported chair (or support the arm using your own arm. If done while

TIME OUT
Body Composition and the Heavy Athlete

Assessing one's body fat using skin-fold calipers can be a sensitive situation, particularly for very overweight individuals. The accuracy of the skin-fold measurements in these situations typically decreases; thus, it would be more appropriate not to use this method for assessing body fat. Instead, use bioelectrical impedance (if available), circumference measurements, scale weight, or even how clothes fit to evaluate one's weight-loss/body fat reduction progress.

This formula was chosen for its simple four-site upper body measurement process. All measurements are done on the right side of the body unless there are specific reasons to use the left (like scars from large burns, for example). The Durnin formula's four sites of skin-fold measurement are as follows:

1. *Biceps:* A vertical fold on the front of the right arm over the biceps muscle, halfway between the shoulder and the elbow (Fig. 3.7).
2. *Triceps:* A vertical fold on the back of the upper arm with the arm relaxed and held freely at the side. This skin fold should also be taken halfway between the shoulder and the elbow (Fig. 3.8). The midpoint is best found with the arm flexed. After the site is found, the athlete lets the extended arm hang while you keep your fingers on the site. This one is easy to measure improperly. You *must* be on the posterior aspect and halfway down the arm. For practice, take this measurement an inch medial, lateral, proximal, and distal of the correct site and notice the differences. To ensure you get just the fat and not the underlying triceps, have the athlete gently extend their elbow against a resistance (like your leg) while you hold the skin fold. Any muscle in the skin fold will pop out from your fingertips.
3. *Subscapular:* A 45-degree angle fold of 1 to 2 cm, below the inferior angle of the scapula (Fig. 3.9). If you have trouble finding the landmark, have the athlete touch the center of the back with the right arm. The scapula will "wing" out easily showing the inferior angle. Manually locate the angle and have the athlete return their arm to their side before taking the measurement.
4. *Iliac Crest:* A 45-degree angle fold, taken just above the iliac crest at the anterior axillary line (Fig. 3.10).

Take the measurements in triplicate. Obtain measurements from each site before repeating, and then average either all three or the two closest measurements if one measurement is remarkably different. Then, add these averages of the four sites (most calipers measure in millimeters) and

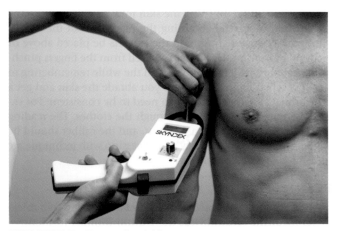

FIGURE 3.7 Biceps skin fold.

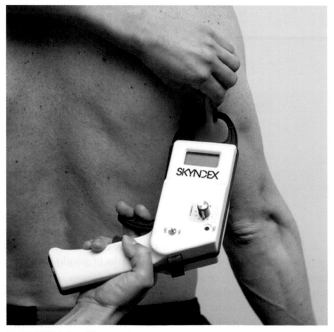

FIGURE 3.8 Triceps skin fold.

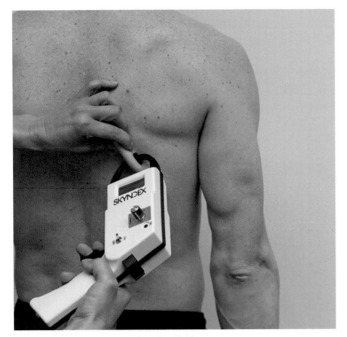

FIGURE 3.9   Subscapular skin fold.

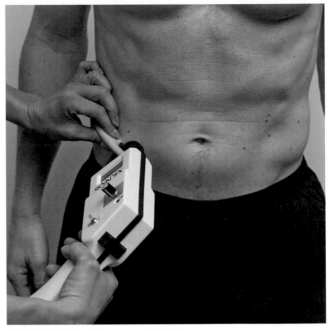

FIGURE 3.10   Iliac crest skin fold.

find the appropriate gender and age category for the body composition based on the Durnin/ Wormersley Body Fat Percentage Calculation table (Table 3.3).

As mentioned earlier, another benefit to assessing one's body fat is the ability to determine approximately how much of an athlete's scale weight comes from body fat and how much from lean body mass (bone, muscle, and organ weight; everything but fat). This becomes very useful when it comes time to reassess the athlete because it allows you to determine how fat mass and lean body mass has changed as a result of training. To calculate one's fat mass and lean body mass:

1) Body fat % × scale weight = fat mass

2) Scale weight − fat mass = lean body mass

For example, a 25-year-old, 130-pound female athlete whose sum of four skin folds equals 55 mm (refer to Table 3.3) carries an estimated 28% of her body weight as fat. To determine her pounds of fat and lean mass:

1) 0.28 (body fat %) × 130 (scale weight) = 36 pounds of body fat

2) 130 (scale weight) − 36 (pounds of body fat) = 94 pounds of lean body mass

If she wants to lose weight, use this information to give a realistic estimate of a goal weight. First, determine an appropriate (and attainable) percentage of body fat. Then divide her lean mass by 1 minus the goal percentage. For example, you might suggest that this athlete might want to try to lose weight so that she carries 24% of her body weight as fat. Thus, divide her lean mass by 0.76 (1 − 0.24):

Goal weight = 94/0.76 = 124 pounds

The assumption of this method is that all weight is lost as fat with no changes in lean body mass. If muscle mass changes, it is best to remeasure, but this method gives reasonable goals for weight loss, especially in athletes doing aerobic conditioning.

Age is a factor. If that female with the same sum of the four skin folds was not 25, but instead was 45, Table 3.3 shows that her percent fat would be 32%. Consider an 18-year-old male wrestler who weighs 140 pounds and wants to wrestle at 130 pounds, because he cannot beat his competition at the 140- or 135-pound weight classes. Suppose his sum of four skin folds was 20 mm (already pretty lean). Table 3.3 indicates this athlete to be carrying about 8% of his mass as fat. This means he is 11 pounds of fat and 129 pounds of lean body mass. For him to lose body fat to reach the 130-pound weight class would mean he would have to lose *all* but one pound of fat, which is not going to happen. To make weight, he would probably have to starve off some muscle mass as well as dehydrate, both of which will impair performance. Imagine his chances against an equally skilled opponent who has not starved or dehydrated to make weight.

TABLE 3.3

Durnin/Wormersley Body Fat Percentage Calculation

Sum of Folds	Males <19	Males 20–29	Males 30–39	Males 40–49	Males >50	Females <19	Females 20–29	Females 30–39	Females 40–49	Females >50
5	−7.23	−7.61	−1.70	−5.28	−6.87	−2.69	−3.97	0.77	3.91	4.84
10	0.41	0.04	5.05	3.30	2.63	5.72	4.88	8.72	11.71	13.10
15	5.00	4.64	9.09	8.47	8.38	10.78	10.22	13.50	16.40	18.07
20	8.32	7.96	12.00	12.22	12.55	14.44	14.08	16.95	19.78	21.67
25	10.92	10.57	14.29	15.16	15.84	17.33	17.13	19.66	22.44	24.49
30	13.07	12.73	16.17	17.60	18.56	19.71	19.64	21.90	24.64	26.83
35	14.91	14.56	17.77	19.68	20.88	21.74	21.79	23.81	26.51	28.82
40	16.51	16.17	19.17	21.49	22.92	23.51	23.67	25.48	28.14	30.56
45	17.93	17.59	20.41	23.11	24.72	25.09	25.34	26.96	29.59	32.10
50	19.21	18.87	21.53	24.56	26.35	26.51	26.84	28.30	30.90	33.49
55	20.37	20.04	22.54	25.88	27.83	27.80	28.21	29.51	32.09	34.75
60	21.44	21.11	23.47	27.09	29.20	28.98	29.46	30.62	33.17	35.91
65	22.42	22.09	24.33	28.22	30.45	30.08	30.62	31.65	34.18	36.99
70	23.34	23.01	25.13	29.26	31.63	31.10	31.70	32.60	35.11	37.98
75	24.20	23.87	25.87	30.23	32.72	32.05	32.71	33.49	35.99	38.91
80	25.00	24.67	26.57	31.15	33.75	32.94	33.66	34.33	36.81	39.79
85	25.76	25.43	27.23	32.01	34.72	33.78	34.55	35.12	37.58	40.61
90	26.47	26.15	27.85	32.83	35.64	34.58	35.40	35.87	38.31	41.39
95	27.15	26.83	28.44	33.61	36.52	35.34	36.20	36.58	39.00	42.13
100	27.80	27.48	29.00	34.34	37.35	36.06	36.97	37.25	39.66	42.84
105	28.42	28.09	29.54	35.05	38.14	36.74	37.69	37.90	40.29	43.51
110	29.00	28.68	30.05	35.72	38.90	37.40	38.39	38.51	40.89	44.15
115	29.57	29.25	30.54	36.37	39.63	38.03	39.06	39.10	41.47	44.76
120	30.11	29.79	31.01	36.99	40.33	38.63	39.70	39.66	42.02	45.36
125	30.63	30.31	31.46	37.58	41.00	39.21	40.32	40.21	42.55	45.92
130	31.13	30.82	31.89	38.15	41.65	39.77	40.91	40.73	43.06	46.47
135	31.62	31.30	32.31	38.71	42.27	40.31	41.48	41.24	43.56	47.00
140	32.08	31.77	32.71	39.24	42.87	40.83	42.04	41.72	44.03	47.51
145	32.53	32.22	33.11	39.76	43.46	41.34	42.57	42.19	44.49	48.00
150	32.97	32.66	33.48	40.26	44.02	41.82	43.09	42.65	44.94	48.47
155	33.39	33.08	33.85	40.74	44.57	42.29	43.59	43.09	45.37	48.93
160	33.80	33.49	34.20	41.21	45.10	42.75	44.08	43.52	45.79	49.38
165	34.20	33.89	34.55	41.67	45.62	43.20	44.55	43.94	46.20	49.82
170	34.59	34.28	34.88	42.11	46.12	43.63	45.01	44.34	46.59	50.24
175	34.97	34.66	35.21	42.54	46.61	44.05	45.46	44.73	46.97	50.65
180	35.33	35.02	35.53	42.96	47.08	44.46	45.89	45.12	47.35	51.05
185	35.69	35.38	35.83	43.37	47.54	44.86	46.32	45.49	47.71	51.44
190	36.04	35.73	36.13	43.77	48.00	45.25	46.73	45.85	48.07	51.82
195	36.38	36.07	36.43	44.16	48.44	45.63	47.14	46.21	48.41	52.19
200	36.71	36.40	36.71	44.54	48.87	46.00	47.53	46.55	48.75	52.55

TABLE 3.4		
Typical Ranges of Body Fat Percentage of Athletes		
Sport	**Men (%)**	**Women (%)**
Aesthetic sports (gymnastics, diving, figure skating)	<7	<15
Baseball/softball	11–13	21–25
Basketball—centers	11–13	19–20
Basketball—guards/forward	8–10	16–18
Bodybuilders	<7	<15
Canoe/kayak	11–13	19–20
Cross country runner	<7	<15
Decathlon	8–10	16–18
Discus	14–17	21–25
Downhill skiing	11–13	19–20
Football—lineman	18–22	
Football—quarterbacks, linebackers, kickers	14–17	
Heptathlon	8–10	16–18
Hockey	14–17	21–25
Jockeys	14–17	21–25
Power lifting	14–17	21–25
Racquetball	8–10	16–18
Rowing	8–10	16–18
Shot put	18–22	26–30
Soccer	8–10	16–18
Speed skating	11–13	19–20
Tennis	14–17	21–25
Volleyball	14–17	21–25
Weightlifters (Olympic)	11–13	19–20
Wrestling	<7	

Modified from Nieman D. Fitness and Sports Medicine. Palo Alto, CA: Bull Publishing; 1995.

In addition, race is a factor and specific body composition equations have been developed for Japanese, American Indians, blacks, whites, and Hispanics. See Table 3.4 for comparison of body fat percentages in various athletes (32).

CIRCUMFERENCE MEASUREMENTS

Circumference measurements can also be another source of feedback used with athletes who have the goal of altering body composition. They are designed to assess girth changes in the body. The most important factor to consider when taking circumference measurements is consistency. Also make sure the tape measure is taut and horizontal around the area that is being measured. You must be consistent in how taut the tape is pulled to avoid compressing the underlying tissue. Take measurements in front of a floor-length mirror to confirm the tape is indeed horizontal.

1. *Neck:* Level with the Adam's apple (Fig. 3.11)
2. *Chest:* Across the nipple line (Fig. 3.12)
3. *Waist:* Measure at the narrowest point of the waist, below the rib cage and just above the iliac crest (top of the hipbones). If there is no apparent narrowing of the waist, measure at the naval (Fig. 3.13).
4. *Hip:* With feet together, measure circumference at the widest portion of the buttocks (Fig. 3.14).
5. *Thigh:* Measured 10 inches above the top of the patella (Fig. 3.15).

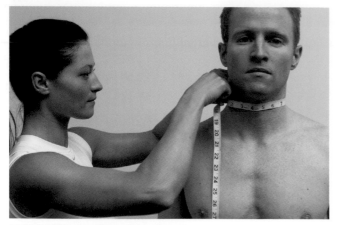

FIGURE 3.11 Neck circumference.

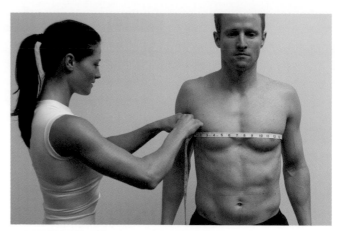

FIGURE 3.12 Chest circumference.

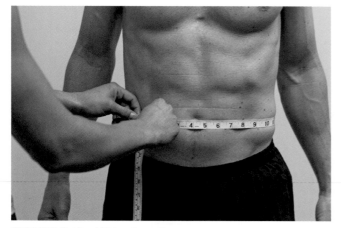

FIGURE 3.13 Waist circumference.

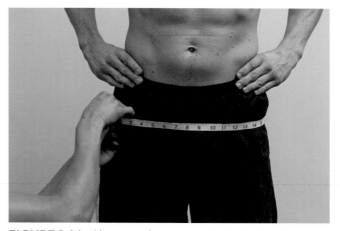

FIGURE 3.14 Hip circumference.

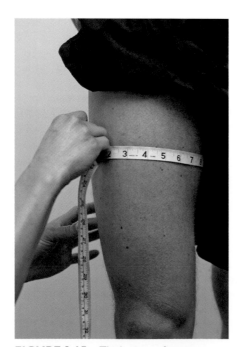

FIGURE 3.15 Thigh circumference.

FIGURE 3.16 Calf circumference.

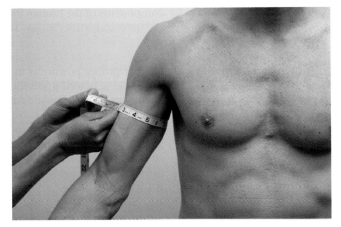

FIGURE 3.17 Biceps circumference.

6. *Calves:* At the maximal calf circumference between the ankle and the knee (Fig. 3.16).
7. *Upper arm:* At the maximal circumference of the biceps, measure with arm extended, palm facing forward (Fig. 3.17).

BODY MASS INDEX

Although this assessment is not designed to assess body fat, the body mass index (BMI) is a quick and easy method for determining if your athlete's weight is appropriate for their height, but is not without its limitations (33). To assess weight relative to height, divide body weight (in kilograms) by height (in meters squared). BMI is reported as kg/m^2.

It has been shown that obesity-related health problems increase when a person's BMI exceeds 25. The obesity classifications using BMI are the following:

- Mild = 25–30
- Moderate = 30–35
- Severe >35

A limitation in using BMI is that athletes with a lot of muscle mass and low body fat can have a BMI over 25, a common situation with males who play football, lift weights, or are body builders. See Table 3.5 for some examples of BMI and body fat in a selection of athletes.

TABLE 3.5				
BMI and Body Fat Percentage in Selected Athletes				
	Males		**Females**	
Sport	BMI	% Fat	BMI	% Fat
Basketball	26.0	12.7	24.5	20.7
Wrestling	25.2	10.4		
Hockey	26.0	12.9		
Football	28.1	13.9		
Football lineman	36.0	27.7		
Rowing			24.2	26.4
Softball			25.7	26.0
Nonathletes	26.0	17.7	23.4	28.5

Modified from Neville A, Stewart A, Olds T, et al. Relationship between adiposity and body size reveals limitations of BMI. *Am J Phys Anthropol* 2006;129:151–56.

POSTURE AND MOVEMENT ASSESSMENTS

POSTURE

The production of movement depends on the structural integrity and alignment of the human movement system. This structural alignment is known as posture. Posture is the independent and interdependent alignment (static posture) and function (transitional and dynamic posture) of all

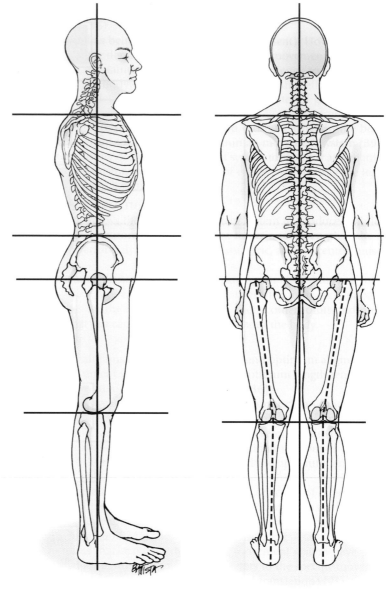

FIGURE 3.19 Postural alignment, lateral view.

FIGURE 3.20 Postural alignment, posterior view.

TRANSITIONAL AND DYNAMIC POSTURAL ASSESSMENT

Transitional and dynamic postural assessments (looking at movements) are a quick way to gain an impression of an athlete's overall functional status. Because posture is a dynamic quality, these observations show postural distortion and potential overactive and underactive muscles in its naturally dynamic setting.

Movement observations should relate to basic functions such as squatting, pushing, pulling, and balancing in addition to providing crucial information about muscle and joint interaction. The observation process should search for any movement impairments that may decrease an athlete's functional ability and potentially lead to injury (with indications both in and out of the athletic environment). The limited time that most Sports Performance Professionals have for observation requires a systematic sequence of assessments.

There are various movement assessment techniques that will be described. Each assessment described contains key human movement system checkpoints to observe. These checkpoints include:

- The feet
- Knees
- Lumbo-pelvic-hip complex
- Shoulders
- Head

TRANSITIONAL POSTURAL ASSESSMENTS

OVERHEAD SQUAT ASSESSMENT

Purpose: This is designed to assess dynamic flexibility, core strength, balance, and overall neuromuscular control. There is evidence to support the use of transitional movement assessments such as the overhead squat test (42). This assessment appears to be reliable and valid measures of lower extremity movement patterns when standard protocols are applied. The overhead squat test has been shown to reflect lower-extremity movement patterns during jump landing tasks (43). Knee valgus during the overhead squat test is influenced by decreased hip abductor and hip external rotation strength (10), increased hip adductor activity (44), and restricted ankle dorsiflexion (44,45). These results suggest that the movement impairments observed during this transitional movement assessment may be the result of alterations in available joint motion, muscle activation, and overall neuromuscular control that some feel point toward people with an elevated injury risk.

Procedure:

Position:

1. Athlete stands with the feet shoulder-width apart and pointed straight ahead. The foot and ankle complex should be in a neutral position. It is suggested that the assessment is performed with the shoes off to better view the foot and ankle complex.
2. Have athlete raise his/her arms overhead, with elbow fully extended. The upper arm should bisect the torso (Figs. 3.21 and 3.22).

FIGURE 3.21 Overhead squat assessment start, anterior view.

FIGURE 3.22 Overhead squat assessment start, lateral view.

FIGURE 3.24 Overhead squat assessment finish, lateral view.

FIGURE 3.23 Overhead squat assessment finish, anterior view.

Movement:

3. Instruct the athlete to squat to roughly the height of a chair seat and return to the starting position.
4. Repeat the movement 5 repetitions observing from each position (anterior and lateral).

Views:

5. View feet, ankles, and knees from the front (Fig. 3.23). The feet should remain straight with the knees tracking in line with the foot (second and third toe).
6. View the lumbo-pelvic-hip complex, shoulder, and cervical spine from the side (Fig. 3.24). The tibia should remain in line with the torso while the arms also stay in line with the torso.

Compensations: Anterior View

7. Feet: Do the feet flatten and/or turn out (Figs. 3.25 and 3.26)?
8. Knees: Do the knees move inward (adduct and internally rotate) (Fig. 3.27)?

FIGURE 3.25 Feet flatten.

FIGURE 3.26 Feet turn out.

FIGURE 3.27   Knees move inward.

FIGURE 3.28   Low back arches.

Compensations: Lateral View

    9. Lumbo-pelvic-hip complex:
        a. Does the low-back arch (Fig. 3.28)?
        b. Does the torso lean forward excessively (Fig. 3.29)?
    10. Shoulder: Do the arms fall forward (Fig. 3.30)?

FIGURE 3.29   Forward lean.

FIGURE 3.30   Arms fall forward.

View	Kinetic chain checkpoints	Movement observation	Yes
Anterior	Feet	• Flatten/Turn out	☐
	Knees	• Moves inward	☐
Lateral	Lumbo-pelvic-hip complex	• Excessive forward lean	☐
		• Low back arches	☐
	Shoulder complex	• Arm falls forward	☐

FIGURE 3.31 Checkpoints for the overhead squat.

When performing the assessment, record all of your findings (Fig. 3.31). You can then refer to Table 3.6 to determine potential overactive and underactive muscles that will need to be addressed through corrective flexibility and strengthening techniques to improve the athlete's quality of movement, decreasing the risk for injury and improving performance.

SINGLE-LEG SQUAT ASSESSMENT

Purpose: This transitional movement assessment also assesses dynamic flexibility, core strength, balance, and overall neuromuscular control. There is evidence to support the use of the single-leg squat as a transitional movement assessment (42). This assessment appears to be reliable and valid measures of lower-extremity movement patterns when standard application protocols are applied. Knee valgus has been shown to be influenced by decreased hip abductor and hip external rotation strength (10), increased hip adductor activity (44), and restricted ankle dorsiflexion (44,45). These results suggest that the movement impairments observed during the transitional movement assessments may be the result of alterations in available joint motion, muscle activation, and overall neuromuscular control.

Procedure:

Position:

1. Athlete should stand with hands on the hips and eyes focused on an object straight ahead.
2. Foot should be pointed straight ahead and the foot, ankle and knee and the lumbo-pelvic-hip complex should be in a neutral position.

TABLE 3.6

Checkpoints for the Overhead Squat

View	Checkpoint	Compensation	Probable Overactive Muscles	Probable Underactive Muscles
Lateral	LPHC	Excessive forward lean	Soleus Gastrocnemius Hip flexor complex Abdominal complex	Anterior tibialis Gluteus maximus Erector spinae
		Low back arches	Hip flexor complex Erector spinae Latissimus dorsi	Gluteus maximus Hamstrings Intrinsic core stabilizers (transverse abdominis, multifidus, transversospinalis, internal oblique pelvic floor muscles)
	Upper body	Arms fall forward	Latissimus dorsi Teres major Pectoralis major/minor	Mid/lower trapezius Rhomboids Rotator cuff
Anterior	Feet	Turn out	Soleus Lat. gastrocnemius Biceps femoris (short head)	Med. gastrocnemius Med. hamstring Gracilis Sartorius Popliteus
	Knees	Move inward	Adductor complex Biceps femoris (short head) TFL Vastus lateralis	Gluteus medius/maximus Vastus medialis oblique (VMO)

FIGURE 3.32 Single-leg squat.

FIGURE 3.33 Knee moves inward.

Movement:

3. Have the athlete squat to a comfortable level (Fig. 3.32) and return to the starting position.
4. Perform up to 5 repetitions before switching sides.

Views:

5. View the knee from the front. The knee should track in line with the foot (second and third toe).

Compensation:

6. Knee: Does the knee move inward (adduct and internally rotate) (Fig. 3.33)?

Like the overhead squat assessment, record your findings (Fig. 3.34). You can then refer to Table 3.7 to determine potential overactive and underactive muscles that will need to be addressed through corrective flexibility and strengthening techniques to improve the athlete's quality of movement, decreasing the risk for injury and improving performance.

View	Kinetic chain checkpoints	Movement observation	Right	Left
Anterior	Knees	• Moves inward	☐	☐

FIGURE 3.34 Checkpoints for the single-leg squat.

TABLE 3.7

Checkpoints for the Single-Leg Squat

Checkpoint	Compensation	Probable Overactive Muscles	Probable Underactive Muscles
Knee	Move inward	Adductor complex Biceps femoris (short head) TFL Vastus lateralis	Gluteus medius/maximus Vastus medialis oblique (VMO)

FIGURE 3.41 Pulling assessment position.

PULLING ASSESSMENT

Purpose: To assess movement efficiency and potential muscle imbalances during pulling movements.

Procedure:

Position:

1. Instruct athlete to stand with feet shoulder-width apart and toes pointing forward (Fig. 3.41).

Movement:

2. Viewing from the side, instruct athlete to pull handles toward their body and return to the starting position. Like the pushing assessment, the lumbar and cervical spines should remain neutral while the shoulders stay level (Fig. 3.42).
3. Perform 10 repetitions in a controlled fashion.

Compensations:

4. Low back: Does the low back arch (Fig. 3.43)?
5. Shoulders: Do the shoulders elevate (Fig. 3.44)?
6. Head: Does the head migrate forward (Fig. 3.45)?

Record your findings (Fig. 3.46). You can then refer to Table 3.9 to determine potential overactive and underactive muscles that will need to be addressed through corrective flexibility and strengthening techniques to improve the athlete's quality of movement, decreasing the risk for injury and improving performance.

 TIME OUT
Pulling Assessment Option

Like the pushing assessment, the pulling assessment can also be performed on a machine.

FIGURE 3.42 Pulling assessment movement.

FIGURE 3.43   Low back arch.

FIGURE 3.44   Shoulders elevate.

FIGURE 3.45   Head migrates forward.

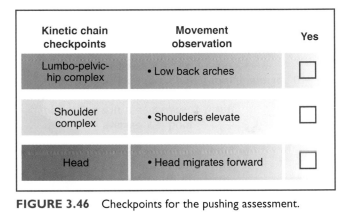

Kinetic chain checkpoints	Movement observation	Yes
Lumbo-pelvic-hip complex	• Low back arches	☐
Shoulder complex	• Shoulders elevate	☐
Head	• Head migrates forward	☐

FIGURE 3.46   Checkpoints for the pushing assessment.

TABLE 3.9

Checkpoints for Pulling Assessment

Checkpoint	Compensation	Probable Overactive Muscles	Probable Underactive Muscles
LPHC	Low back arches	Hip flexors, erector spinae	Intrinsic core stabilizers
Shoulder complex	Shoulder elevation	Upper trapezius, sternocleidomastoid, levator scapulae	Mid/lower trapezius
Head	Head protrudes forward	Upper trapezius, sternocleidomastoid, levator scapulae	Deep cervical flexors

CORE STABILITY ASSESSMENTS

DOUBLE-LEG LOWERING TEST

Purpose: The double-leg lowering test is one test with which the Sports Performance Professional can effectively assess neuromuscular control and strength of the core (17,36,46,47).

Procedure:

Position:

1. Individual is placed supine with a flat blood pressure cuff under the lumbar spine at approximately L4–L5 (Fig. 3.49).
2. The cuff pressure is raised to 40 mm Hg.
3. The individual's legs are maintained in full extension while flexing the hips to 90 degrees (or to the amount of hip flexion that does not cause a posterior pelvic tilt).
4. The individual is instructed to perform a drawing-in maneuver (pull bellybutton to spine) and maintain while keeping their lumbar spine in contact with the pressure cuff.

FIGURE 3.49 Double-leg lowering test position.

FIGURE 3.50 Double-leg lowering test movement.

Movement:

5. The individual is then instructed to lower their legs toward the table while maintaining the drawing-in maneuver.
6. The test is over when the pressure in the cuff decreases (back arches-synergistic dominance of psoas) or the pressure increases as the athlete allows the abdominal wall to protrude and synergistically compensate with the rectus abdominus and the external obliques (Fig. 3.50).
7. The hip angle is then measured with a goniometer to determine the angle (Fig. 3.51).
8. Core stability strength is determined by the below score (Fig. 3.52):
   a. 50% = Poor
   b. 60% = Fair
   c. 80% = Good
   d. 100% = Normal

FIGURE 3.51 Double-leg lowering test measure.

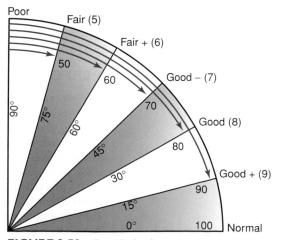

FIGURE 3.52 Double-leg lowering test scoring.

SORENSEN ERECTOR SPINAE TEST

Purpose: This assessment measures neuromuscular control and endurance of the spinal extensors.

Procedure:

Position:

1. The individual lies prone on a treatment table.
2. Align the adjustable arm of a goniometer with the lateral side of the torso while the stationary arm is aligned with the femur (Fig. 3.53).

Movement:

3. The individual is instructed to extend at the lumbar spine to 30 degrees and hold the position for as long as they can while the clinician times the test (Fig. 3.54).
4. A normal test is 30 seconds.

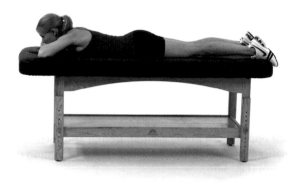

FIGURE 3.53   Sorensen Erector Spinae Test position.

FIGURE 3.54   Sorensen Erector Spinae Test movement.

SINGLE-LEG STAR BALANCE EXCURSION TEST

Purpose: This assessment measures dynamic balance and neuromuscular efficiency of the testing leg and also establishes objective range of motion measurements during closed chain functional movements.

Procedure:

Position:

1. The individual is instructed to stand on the testing leg.
2. They are instructed to squat down as far as they can control with the knee aligned in a neutral position (balance threshold) (Fig. 3.55).

FIGURE 3.55   Single-leg STAR Excursion Test position.

Movement:

2. Warm up with a light resistance that can be easily performed, 8 to 10 repetitions.
3. Rest for 1 minute.
4. Add 10 to 20 pounds (or 5 to 10% of initial load) and perform 3 to 5 repetitions.
5. Rest for 2 minutes.
6. Repeat steps 4 and 5 until the individual fails at 3 to 5 repetitions.
7. Use the 1-rep maximum estimation chart in the appendix to calculate estimated 1 repetition max.

185-POUND BENCH PRESS—BASKETBALL

Purpose: This is a test of maximum strength and repetition (strength) endurance. Each athlete is given one attempt at completing a maximum number of repetitions with 185 pounds.

Procedure:

1. Have the athlete perform 10 push-ups and then take a 60-second rest.
2. Next, have the athlete perform 5 repetitions at 135 pounds of the bench press.
3. Take a 90-second rest.
4. Finally, have the athlete perform the bench press using 185 pounds for the maximum number of repetitions.
5. Two spotters are used on each athlete. One spotter gives the athlete a lift off, counts the number of reps, and makes sure that each repetition is fully locked out at the top. The other spotter watches to make sure that the athlete's hips stay in contact with the bench (no arching).

LOWER-EXTREMITY STRENGTH ASSESSMENT: SQUAT

Purpose: This assessment is designed to estimate the 1-repetition squat maximum and overall lower body strength. This test can also be used to determine training intensities for the squat.

Procedure:

Position:

1. Feet should be shoulder-width apart, pointed straight ahead with knees in line with the toes. The low back should be in a neutral position (Fig. 3.61).

A   B

FIGURE 3.61 Squat assessment.

Movement:

2. Warm up with a light resistance that can be easily performed, 8 to 10 repetitions.
3. Rest for 1 minute.
4. Add 30 to 40 pounds (or 10 to 20% of initial load) and perform 3 to 5 repetitions.
5. Rest for 2 minutes.
6. Repeat steps 4 and 5 until the individual fails at 3 to 5 repetitions.
7. Use the 1-repetition maximum estimation chart in the appendix to calculate estimated 1-repetition maximum.

FIGURE 3.62 Pull-up test.

PULL-UPS

Purpose: This test measures muscular endurance of the upper body, primarily the pulling muscles.

Procedure:

Position:
1. Athlete grasps the bar with a pronated grip (Fig. 3.62).

Movement:
2. The athlete performs the pull-up to exhaustion.
3. Record the total number of repetitions without compensating with body swings, kicking, or creating momentum.
4. The athlete should be able to perform more pull-ups when reassessed.

PUSH-UPS

Purpose: This test measures muscular endurance of the upper body, primarily the pushing muscles.

Procedure:

Position:
1. In push-up position (ankles, knees, hips, shoulders, and head in a straight line), the athlete lowers body to touch partner's closed fist placed under chest, and repeats for 60 seconds or until exhaustion without compensating (low back arches, cervical spine extends; Fig. 3.63).
2. Record number of actual touches reported from partner.
3. The athlete should be able to perform more push-ups when reassessed.

FIGURE 3.63 Push-up test.

FIGURE 3.64 Rotation medicine ball throw.

POWER ASSESSMENTS

ROTATION MEDICINE BALL THROW

Purpose: This assessment measures total body transverse plane strength and power.

Procedure:

Position:

1. Athlete begins perpendicular to the throwing-zone holding the medicine ball with both hands (5 to 10% of body weight).

Movement:

2. The athlete rotates through the hips (similar to a batter's swing) and throws the medicine ball forward as far as possible (Fig. 3.64).
3. Compare right to left.

OVERHEAD MEDICINE BALL THROW

Purpose: This assessment measures total body strength and power.

Procedure:

Position:

1. Using a medicine ball that does not exceed 5% of the athlete's body weight, begin with medicine ball in hands with arms straight.

Movement:

2. Explosively throw the ball for maximal distance (Fig. 3.65).
3. Measure the relative distance from the starting line to the point of first contact of the medicine ball.

FIGURE 3.65 Overhead medicine ball throw.

FIGURE 3.66   Soccer throw.

STANDING SOCCER THROW

Purpose: This assessment measures total power of the core and upper extremities.

Procedure:

Position:

1. Keep feet in a staggered stance holding a medicine ball (5 to 10% of body weight).

Movement:

2. Using proper soccer throw-in technique, bring the arms over your head and throw the medicine ball forward as far as you can without moving your feet (Fig. 3.66).
3. Measure the distance thrown.

DOUBLE-LEG VERTICAL JUMP

Purpose: This assessment is designed to measure total body bilateral power.

Procedure:

Position:

1. Measure standing reach of the athlete with one arm fully extended upward.

Movement:

2. Have the athlete jump and touch the highest possible vane (Fig. 3.67).
3. Measure the high difference between the standing reach and jumping height.
4. Two attempts are provided. If on the second attempt, the athlete reaches a new height, a third attempt is awarded.
5. No shuffle step, no side step, no drop step, and no gather step was allowed (straight down and straight up)

FIGURE 3.67   Double-leg vertical jump.

FIGURE 3.68   Single-leg vertical hop.

SINGLE-LEG VERTICAL JUMP

Purpose: This assessment is designed to measure unilateral power and dynamic stabilization capabilities.

Procedure:

Position:

    1. Measure standing reach of the athlete with one arm fully extended upward.

Movement:

    2. Have the athlete balance on one leg.

    3. Using the balance leg, have the athlete jump and touch the highest possible vane (Fig. 3.68).

    4. Measure the height difference between the standing reach and jumping height.

    5. Two attempts are provided. If on the second attempt the athlete reaches a new height, a third attempt is awarded.

    6. No shuffle step, no side step, no drop step, and no gather step was allowed (straight down and straight up).

DOUBLE-LEG HORIZONTAL JUMP (LONG JUMP)

Purpose: This assessment is designed to measure total body bilateral power in a more dynamic fashion by jumping for distance rather than height. It can also be performed in the frontal and transverse planes.

Procedure:

Position:

    1. Extend a tape measure along a nonskid surface and make a start-line with athletic tape.

Movement:

    2. Athletes will jump forward as far as possible (Fig. 3.69).

FIGURE 3.69   Double-leg horizontal jump.

FIGURE 3.70   Single-leg horizontal hop.

3. Record relative distance from the edge of the starting line (edge closest to landing point) to the athlete's heel.
4. If they fall backward, record from the body part nearest the starting line.

SINGLE-LEG HORIZONTAL JUMP (LONG JUMP ON SINGLE LEG)

Purpose: This assessment is designed to measure unilateral power and dynamic stabilization capabilities in a more dynamic fashion by jumping for distance rather than height. It can also be performed in the frontal and transverse planes.

Procedure:

1. Extend a tape measure along a nonskid surface and make a start-line with athletic tape.
Movement:
2. Athletes will jump forward as far as possible with one leg and lands on that same leg (Fig. 3.70).
3. Record relative distance from the edge of the starting line (edge closest to landing point) to the athlete's heel.
4. If they fall backward, record from the body part nearest the starting line.

SHARK SKILL TEST

Purpose: This is designed to assess lower-extremity agility and neuromuscular control.

Procedure:

Position:
1. Position the athlete in the center box of a grid, with hands on hips and standing on one leg.
Movement:
2. Instruct the athlete to hop to each box in a designated pattern, always returning to the center box. Be consistent with the patterns (Fig. 3.71).
3. Perform one practice run through the boxes with each foot.
4. Perform the test twice with each foot (4 times total). Keep track of time.

FIGURE 3.71   Shark skill test.

b. Backpedal to Cone 1, touch cone
c. Side shuffle to Cone 2, touch cone
d. Side shuffle to Cone 1, touch cone
e. Carioca to Cone 2, touch cone
f. Carioca to Cone 1, touch cone
g. Forward sprint to Cone 2

2. The timer stands at Cone 2. Begin timing on first movement, and end when athlete crosses imaginary line between timer and Cone 2.

300-YARD SHUTTLE

Purpose: This test measures total anaerobic endurance.

Procedure:
1. Marker cones and lines are placed 25 yards apart to indicate the sprint distance.
2. Start with a foot on one line. When instructed by the timer, the player runs to the opposite 25-yard line, touches it with their foot, turns, and runs back to the start (Fig. 3.76).
3. This is repeated 6 times without stopping (covering 300 yards total). After a rest of 5 minutes, the test is repeated.

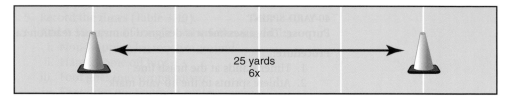

FIGURE 3.76 300-yard shuttle.

5-10-5 TEST

Purpose: This assessment is designed to measure lateral speed and agility.

Procedure:
1. Begin with three cones, placing two cones 10 m apart. Place the final cone at the midpoint.
2. The timer is facing the middle cone (Cone 1) with the athlete in a rested position facing the timer.
3. Start the timer on the athlete's first movement as they sprint to Cone 2, then to Cone 3, then to Cone 1 (Fig. 3.77).

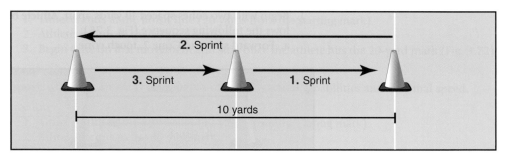

FIGURE 3.77 5-10-5 test.

5-0-5 TEST FOR HORIZONTAL AGILITY

Purpose: This assessment is designed to measure horizontal speed and agility.

Procedure:
1. Athletes begins to run as diagrammed at the start/finish point (Fig. 3.78).
2. Athletes sprint forward passing through the start-stop gate, starting the clock.
3. At the turning point, athletes perform a cutting maneuver off of the right or left leg (determined prior to repetition).
4. Athletes sprint back through the gates, stopping the clock.
5. Athletes should continue sprint through the start/finish point.

Note: Athletes should be instructed before testing regarding the following:
1. Which foot to cut off of prior to beginning each test trial.
2. To sprint maximally from the start through to the turning point.
3. Sprint all the way through the start/finish point.

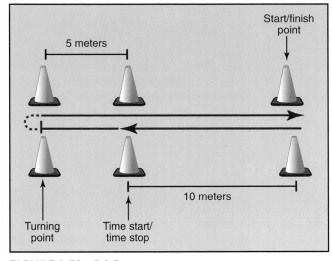

FIGURE 3.78 5-0-5 test.

7- × 30-M SPRINT TEST

Purpose: This test is designed to measure maximal anaerobic power and repeated sprint ability.

Procedure:

1. Athlete performs seven total sprints of 30 m.
2. As diagrammed (Fig. 3.79), athlete begins at the start point and follows the course to complete the sprint at the finish point, decelerating through the final set of markers at 40 m. Following each subsequent sprint, the athlete receives 25 seconds of active recovery in which they return to the start position to repeat the sprint task.
3. The following times are calculated, with the greatest interest being placed in the "fatigue time":
   a. Fastest Time: representative of the fastest sprint time.
   b. Total Time: representative of the athlete's total sprint duration.
   c. Mean Time: average sprint time over the seven trials.
   d. Fatigue Time: calculated as the percentage difference between the fastest time (usually the first or second sprint) and the slowest time (usually the sixth or seventh sprint).
4. A variation on this test is run along a straight course or a course with both a right and left turn where the athlete has to react to a signal during the run, dictating running direction.

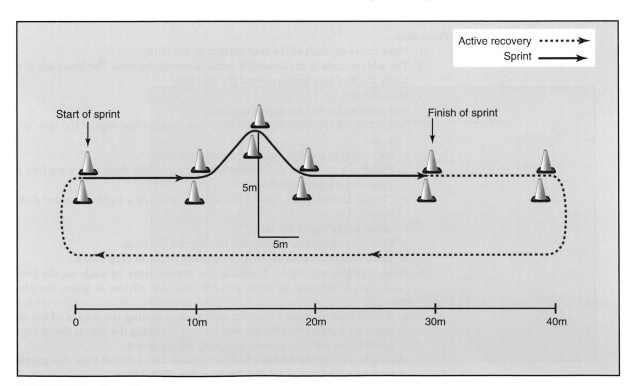

FIGURE 3.79 7- × 30-m sprint test.

CARDIORESPIRATORY ASSESSMENTS

HARVARD STEP TEST

Purpose: This test is a test of aerobic fitness. It is also used to estimate a cardiorespiratory starting point.

Procedure:

1. Determine the client's maximum heart rate by subtracting the client's age from the number 220 (220 − age). Then, take the maximum heart rate and multiply it by the following figures to determine the heart rate ranges for each zone (Table 3.11).

Zone One	Maximum Heart Rate × 0.65
	Maximum Heart Rate × 0.75
Zone Two	Maximum Heart Rate × 0.80
	Maximum Heart Rate × 0.85
Zone Three	Maximum Heart Rate × 0.86
	Maximum Heart Rate × 0.90

TABLE 3.11	
Heart Rate Training Zones	
Training Zone	**Purpose**
One	Builds aerobic base and aids in recovery
Two	Increases endurance and trains the anaerobic threshold
Three	Builds high-end work capacity

2. Begin the test. The athlete steps up and down on the platform (20 inches) at a rate of 30 steps per minute (every 2 seconds) for 5 minutes or until exhaustion (Fig. 3.83).
   a. Exhaustion is defined as when the athlete cannot maintain the stepping rate for 15 seconds.

A   B

FIGURE 3.83   Harvard Step Test.

FIGURE 3.84   Record heart rate.

3. The athlete immediately sits down on completion of the test, and the total number of heartbeats are counted between 1 and 1.5 minutes after finishing (Fig. 3.84).
   a. This is the only measure required if using the *short form* of the test. If the *long form* of the test is being conducted, there are additional heart rate measures at between 2 to 2.5 minutes, and between 3 to 3.5 minutes.
4. The Fitness Index score is determined by the following equations:
   a. **Fitness Index** (short form) = (100 × test duration in seconds) divided by (5.5 × pulse count between 1 and 1.5 minutes).
   b. **Fitness Index** (long form) = (100 × test duration in seconds) divided by (2 × sum of heartbeats in the recovery periods).
   c. Use Table 3.12 below to determine score:

TABLE 3.12	
Step Test Scoring	
Rating	**Fitness Index (long form)**
Excellent	>90
Good	80–89
High average	65–79
Low average	55–64
Poor	<55

5. Determine the appropriate starting cardiorespiratory program using the appropriate category:
   • Poor   Zone One
   • Low average   Zone One
   • High average   Zone Two
   • Good   Zone Two
   • Excellent   Zone Three

20-METER MULTISTAGE SHUTTLE TEST
Purpose: This test is a field test designed to estimate an aerobic power and predict $\dot{V}O_2$ max. It was originally designed for mass screening of aerobic power (49).

Procedure:
   1. Set up two rows of cones 20 meters apart (Fig. 3.85).
   2. Make sure athletes are sufficiently warmed-up. Start the audio CD and ensure that the athletes understand the directions. Begin the test at level one.
   3. The audio CD will sound a "beep" at designated time intervals. When the "beep" is heard, the athlete must be at the opposite end of the 20-meter run. Each time the recorded "beep" is heard, the athlete must have completed another 20-meter run.
   4. With every minute (60 seconds), the "beeps" will progressively get faster prompting the athlete to increase running speed (the "beeps" start out at a running speed of 8.5 kilometers per hour, or 5.3 miles per hour, and increase by 0.5 kph, or 0.3 mph, every minute thereafter).

REFERENCES

1. Thomas S, Reading J, Shephard R. Revision of the physical activity readiness questionnaire (PAR-Q). *Can J Sport Sci* 1992;17:338–45.
2. Bullock-Saxton JE. Local sensation changes and altered hip muscle function following severe ankle sprain. *Phys Ther* 1994;74:17–28; discussion 28–31.
3. Guskiewicz K, Perrin D. Effect of orthotics on postural sway following inversion ankle sprain. *J Orthop Sports Phys Ther* 1996;23:326–31.
4. Nitz A, Dobner J, Kersey D. Nerve injury and grades II and III ankle sprains. *Am J Sports Med* 1985;13:177–82.
5. Wilkerson G, Nitz A. Dynamic ankle stability: mechanical and neuromuscular interrelationships. *J Sport Rehab* 1994;3:43–57.
6. Barrack R, Lund P, Skinner H. Knee proprioception revisited. *J Sport Rehab* 1994;3:18–42.
7. Beard D, Kyberd P, O'Connor J et al. Reflex hamstring contraction latency in ACL deficiency. *J Orthop Res* 1994;12:219–28.
8. Fredericson M, Cookingham CL, Chaudhari AM et al. Hip abductor weakness in distance runners with iliotibial band syndrome. *Clin J Sport Med* 2000;10:169–75.
9. Hewett TE, Lindenfeld TN, Riccobene JV et al. The effect of neuromuscular training on the incidence of knee injury in female athletes. A prospective study. *Am J Sports Med* 1999;27:699–706.
10. Ireland ML, Willson JD, Ballantyne BT et al. Hip strength in females with and without patellofemoral pain. *J Orthop Sports Phys Ther* 2003;33:671–76.
11. Johansson H. Role of knee ligaments in proprioception and regulation of muscle stiffness. *J Electromyogr Kinesiol* 1991;1:158–79.
12. Johansson H, Sjolander P, Sojka P. A sensory role for the cruciate ligaments. *Clin Orthop Relat Res* 1991;268:161–78.
13. Nyland J, Smith S, Beickman K et al. Frontal plane knee angle affects dynamic postural control strategy during unilateral stance. *Med Sci Sports Exerc* 2002;34:1150–157.
14. Powers C. The influence of altered lower-extremity kinematics on patellofemoral joint dysfunction: a theoretical perspective. *J Orthop Sports Phys Ther* 2003;33:639–46.
15. Bullock-Saxton JE, Janda V et al. Reflex activation of gluteal muscles in walking. An approach to restoration of muscle function for patients with low-back pain. *Spine* 1993;18:704–708.
16. Hodges P, Richardson C, Jull G. Evaluation of the relationship between laboratory and clinical tests of transversus abdominis function. *Physiother Res Int* 1996;1:30–40.
17. Hodges PW, Richardson CA. Inefficient muscular stabilization of the lumbar spine associated with low back pain. A motor control evaluation of transversus abdominis. *Spine* 1996;21:2640–650.
18. Hodges PW, Richardson CA. Contraction of the abdominal muscles associated with movement of the lower limb. *Phys Ther* 1997;77:132–42; discussion 42–44.
19. Janda V. Muscles and Motor Control in Low Back Pain: Assessment and Management. In: Twomey L. Physical Therapy of the Low Back. New York, NY: Churchill Livingstone; 1987.
20. Lewit K. Muscular and articular factors in movement restriction. *Manual Med* 1985;1:83–85.
21. O'Sullivan P, Twomey L, Allison G et al. Altered patterns of abdominal muscle activation in patients with chronic low back pain. *Aust J Physiother* 1997;43:91–98.
22. Richardson C, Jull G, Toppenberg R et al. Techniques for active lumbar stabilization for spinal protection. *Aust J Physiother* 1992;38:105–12.
23. Glousman R, Jobe F, Tibone J et al. Dynamic electromyographic analysis of the throwing shoulder with glenohumeral instability. *J Bone Joint Surg Am* 1988;70A:220–26.
24. Howell S, Kraft T. The role of the supraspinatus and infraspinatus muscles in glenohumeral kinematics of anterior shoulder instability. *Clin Orthop Relat Res* 1991;263:128–34.
25. Kedgley A, Mackenzie G, Ferreira L et al. In vitro kinematics of the shoulder following rotator cuff injury. *Clin Biomech (Bristol, Avon)* 2007;22:1068–73.
26. Kronberg M, Broström L-Å, Nemeth G. Differences in shoulder muscle activity between patients with generalized joint laxity and normal controls. *Clin Orthop Relat Res* 1991;269:181–92.
27. Lambert E, Bohlmann I, Cowling K. Physical activity for health: understanding the epidemiological evidence for risk benefits. *Int J Sports Med* 2001;1:1–15.
28. Pate R, Pratt M, Blair S et al. Physical activity and public health: a recommendation from the Centers for Disease Control and Prevention and the American College of Sports Medicine. *JAMA* 1995;273:402–407.
29. Aasa U, Jaric S, Barnekow-Bergkvist M et al. Muscle strength assessment from functional performance tests: role of body size. *J Strength Cond Res* 2003;17:664–70.
30. Kuipers H, Keizer H. Overtraining in elite athletes. Review and directions for the future. *Sports Med* 1988;6:79–92.
31. Durnin J, Womersley J. Body fat assessed from total body density and its estimation from skinfold thickness measurements on 481 men and women aged 16–72 years. *Br J Nutr* 1974;32:77–97.
32. Nieman D. Fitness and Sports Medicine. Palo Alto, CA: Bull Publishing; 1995.
33. Neville AM, Stewart AD, Olds T, et al. Relationship between adiposity and body size reveals limitations of BMI. *Am J Phys Anthropol* 2006;129:151–56.
34. Hammer W. Functional Soft Tissue Examination and Treatment by Manual Methods. New York, NY: Aspen Publishers, Inc; 1999.
35. Sahrmann. Diagnosis and Treatment of Movement Impairment Syndromes. St. Louis: Mosby; 2002.
36. Sahrmann SA. Posture and Muscle Imbalance. Faulty lumbo-pelvic alignment and associated musculoskeletal pain syndromes. *Orthop Div Rev-Can Phys Ther* 1992;12:13–20.
37. Kendall. Muscle Testing and Function, 4th ed. Baltimore: Williams & Wilkins; 1993.

38. Norkin C, Levangie P. Joint Structure and Function, 2nd ed. Philadelphia, F.A. Davis Company; 1992.
39. Janda V. Muscle strength in relation to muscle length, pain, and muscle imbalance. In: Twomey L. International Perspectives in Physical Therapy. Edinburgh: Churchill Livingstone; 1993. p 83–91.
40. Powers CM, Ward SR, Fredericson M et al. Patellofemoral kinematics during weight-bearing and non-weight-bearing knee extension in persons with lateral subluxation of the patella: a preliminary study. *J Orthop Sports Phys Ther* 2003;33:677 85.
41. Newmann D. Kinesiology of the Musculoskeletal System: Foundations for Physical Rehabilitation. St. Louis: Mosby; 2002.
42. Zeller B, McCrory J, Kibler W et al. Differences in kinematics and electromyographic activity between men and women during the single-legged squat. *Am J Sports Med* 2003;31:449–56.
43. Buckley BD, Thigpen CA, Joyce CJ et al. Knee and hip kinematics during a double leg squat predict knee and hip kinematics at initial contact of a jump landing task. *J Athl Train* 2007;42:S–81.
44. Vesci BJ, Padua DA, Bell DR et al. Influence of hip muscle strength, flexibility of hip and ankle musculature, and hip muscle activation on dynamic knee valgus motion during a double-legged squat. *J Athl Train* 2007;42:S–83.
45. Bell DR, Padua DA. Influence of ankle dorsiflexion range of motion and lower leg muscle activation on knee valgus during a double-legged squat. *J Athl Train* 2007;42:S–84.
46. Ashmen K, Swanik C, Lephart S. Strength and flexibility characteristics of athletes with chronic low back pain. *J Sport Rehab* 1996;5:275–86.
47. O'Sullivan PB, Phyty GD, Twomey LT et al. Evaluation of specific stabilizing exercise in the treatment of chronic low back pain with radiologic diagnosis of spondylolysis or spondylolisthesis. *Spine* 1997;22:2959–967.
48. Goldbeck T, Davies GJ. Test-retest reliability of a closed kinetic chain upper extremity stability test: a clinical field test. *J Sport Rehab* 2000;9:35–45.
49. Leger L, Gadoury C. Validity of the 20 m shuttle run test with 1 minute stages to predict $\dot{V}O_2$ max in adults. *Can J Sport Sci* 1989;14:21–26.
50. Shvartz E, Reibold R. Aerobic fitness norms for males and females aged 6 to 75 years: a review. *Aviat Space Environ Med* 1990;62:3–11.

CHAPTER 4

Flexibility Training for Performance Enhancement

UPON COMPLETION OF THIS CHAPTER, YOU WILL BE ABLE TO:

Explain the effects of muscle imbalances on the human movement system.

Provide a scientific rationale for the use of an integrated flexibility training program.

Differentiate between the types of flexibility techniques.

Perform and instruct appropriate flexibility techniques for given situations.

Introduction

Integrated flexibility training (IFT) is a key component for all sports performance training programs. The general purposes of flexibility training are varied:

- Correct muscle imbalances
- Increase joint range of motion
- Decrease muscle hypertonicity
- Relieve joint stress
- Improve the extensibility of the musculotendinous junction
- Maintain the normal functional length of all muscles (1,2).

This chapter provides an overview of the most current rationale supporting flexibility training so that Sports Performance Professionals can not only understand the dynamic nature of IFT, but design IFT programs for their athletes for optimum performance and function.

Flexibility is the normal extensibility of all soft tissues that allows full range of motion of a joint and optimum neuromuscular efficiency throughout all functional movements. Although flexibility training is a key component for developing optimum neuromuscular efficiency, many Sports Performance Professionals lack an understanding of current concepts in flexibility training as human movement efficiency requires optimum levels of flexibility. Table 4.1 summarizes the significant benefits of integrated flexibility training without which optimum performance will not be possible.

Flexibility
The normal extensibility of all soft tissues that allows full range of motion of a joint and optimum neuromuscular efficiency throughout all functional movements.

Causes of Muscle Imbalances

Table 4.2 shows that muscle imbalances can be caused by problems ranging from postural stress to decreased recovery and delayed regeneration (18,19). These muscle imbalances result in altered reciprocal inhibition, synergistic dominance, arthrokinetic dysfunction, and decreased neuromuscular control.

Altered Reciprocal Inhibition

The concept of muscle inhibition caused by a tight agonist, decreasing the neural drive of its functional antagonist.

Synergistic Dominance

The neuromuscular phenomenon that occurs when synergists take over the function of a weak or inhibited prime mover.

Arthrokinetic Dysfunction

The biomechanical dysfunction in two articular partners that lead to abnormal joint movement (arthrokinematics) and proprioception.

TABLE 4.2	
Causes of Muscle Imbalances	
• Pattern overload	• Lack of core strength
• Poor technical skill	• Immobilization
• Aging	• Cumulative trauma
• Decreased recovery and regeneration following activity	• Lack of neuromuscular control
• Repetitive movement	• Postural stress

Altered reciprocal inhibition is the concept of muscle inhibition caused by a tight agonist, decreasing the neural drive of its functional antagonist (19–24). This results in altered force-couple relationships and synergistic dominance, which leads to the development of faulty movement patterns and poor neuromuscular control.

Synergistic dominance is the neuromuscular phenomenon that occurs when synergists take over the function of a weak or inhibited prime mover (24). This causes faulty movement patterns leading to tissue overload, decreased neuromuscular efficiency, and injury.

Arthrokinetic dysfunction is the biomechanical dysfunction in two articular partners that lead to abnormal joint movement (arthrokinematics) and proprioception (25). Altered reciprocal inhibition, synergistic dominance, and arthrokinetic dysfunction all lead to decreased neuromuscular control, tissue overload, and injury. This process initiates and continues to escalate the cumulative injury cycle (Fig. 4.2).

Muscle Tissue Structure and Function

To fully understand how a muscle lengthens, it is necessary to have a thorough understanding of muscle architecture. Anatomically, muscles share common characteristics at the cellular level, although they come in many sizes and perform various functions. Figure 4.5 illustrates the classical organization of skeletal muscle.

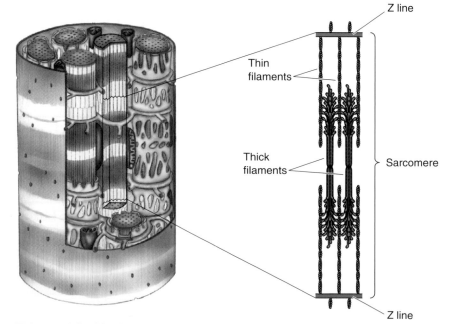

FIGURE 4.5   Muscle fiber structure.

The details on the subcellular structure of skeletal muscle and basic physiology of muscle contraction are beyond the scope of this chapter, but can be found in any introductory anatomy and physiology textbook. As seen in Figure 4.6, muscle is composed of strands of tissue called fascicles. Each individual fascicle is comprised of fasciculae, which are bundles of muscle fibers. Muscle fibers are composed of thousands of myofibrils, which contain the contractile components of the muscle tissue (Figure 4.5). The functional unit of muscle is the myofibrils called the sarcomere. Each sarcomere is made up of myofilaments, which include overlapping thick and thin contractile proteins, primarily actin and myosin and the regulatory proteins of troponin and tropomyosin (26).

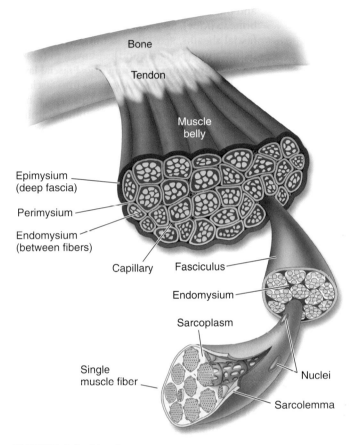

FIGURE 4.6   Muscle structure.

The process of muscular contraction occurs when a neural impulse (an action potential) from the brain to the alpha motor neuron crosses the neuromuscular junction. This impulse stimulates a similar action potential along the muscle fiber membrane, the sarcolemma, triggering an exchange of calcium and potassium to expose the active sites on the thin actin filament, and allows the myosin crossbridges to pull the actin filaments toward the center of the sarcomere and shortening the sarcomeres. This sliding of the actin filament past the myosin filament and resultant shortening of the sarcomere, which when multiplied over thousands of sarcomeres, lead to visible shortening of the muscle.

When a fiber is stimulated to contract, it contracts completely. This is known as the **All-Or-None Principle**. A muscle fiber is unable to vary the degree by which it contracts. If the action potential is strong enough to induce the molecular events of contraction, the fiber will contract completely. The amount of force generated by the whole muscle is dictated by a number of factors including the number of fibers recruited, the rate at which the central nervous system (CNS) stimulates the neuron, and the fibers the neuron controls.

All-Or-None Principle

When a muscle fiber is stimulated to contract, the entire fiber contracts completely.

CONNECTIVE TISSUE

Connective tissue has multiple functional categories:
- Enclose and separate tissues
- Connect dissimilar tissues

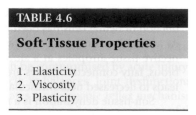

TABLE 4.6
Soft-Tissue Properties
1. Elasticity
2. Viscosity
3. Plasticity

Elasticity
The spring-like behavior of connective tissue that enables the tissue to return to its original shape or size when forces are removed.

forces are removed (1,29,30). The soft tissue of the human movement system demonstrates an elastic limit. The elastic limit is the smallest value of stress required to produce permanent strain in the tissue. Below this elastic limit, the soft tissue returns to its original length when the deforming forces are removed. However, the result of applying a force beyond the elastic limit is that the soft tissue does not return to its original length when the deforming forces are removed. The unrecoverable or permanent elongation in the soft tissue is called plasticity (1,29,30). When stress is applied beyond the elastic limit, deformation and force are no longer linearly proportional.

VISCOELASTICITY

Viscoelasticity
The fluid-like property of connective tissue that allows slow deformation with an imperfect recovery after the deforming forces are removed.

The fluid-like property of connective tissue that allows slow deformation with an imperfect recovery after the deforming forces are removed is **viscoelasticity** (1,29,30,59,60). Recovery is due to the elastic property of the connective tissue, but a lack of full recovery back to normal length is due to the viscous property of the connective tissue. The viscosity of the soft tissue is time-dependent (59,60). The faster one tries to move, the greater the resistance to elongation. Proper warm-up and flexibility training reduces tissue viscosity and consequently improves the extensibility of the soft tissue (61). When subjected to loads for prolonged periods of time, the soft tissue adapts with plastic deformation (22,27,28,49,62).

PLASTICITY

Plasticity
The residual or permanent change in connective tissue length due to tissue elongation.

When soft tissue permanently deforms in response to loading it is said to have undergone plastic deformation (27,29,30). Consequently, there is no tendency for elastic recoil or recovery. **Plasticity** is also referred to as the residual or permanent change in connective tissue length due to tissue elongation (as in flexibility training). Integrated flexibility training increases elongation of the interstitial collagenous interfiber matrix, allowing a plastic deformation of the connective tissue. There needs to be an increase of approximately 3 to 5% in tissue length to elicit a plastic deformation in the soft tissue (29,30). Tissue overload and microfailure occur at approximately 6 to 10% of tissue deformation (29,30). When forces exceed the tissue's adaptive potential, tissue microfailure occurs and this microfailure contributes to the development of the cumulative injury cycle (Fig. 4.2).

One aspect of the cumulative injury cycle (30) is the development of proinflammatory compounds, which stimulate nociceptors leading to pain and the development of protective muscle spasm. The chemical changes also lead to the development of fibrotic adhesions in the soft tissue within only 3 to 5 days following connective tissue insult. These fibrotic adhesions form a weak inelastic matrix in the connective tissue bundles, decreasing the normal tissue extensibility. This results in alterations of the normal-length tension relationships and the development of common muscle imbalances (19).

Davis's Law
Soft tissue models along the lines of stress.

Wolff's Law
Bone in a healthy person or animal will adapt to the loads it is placed under.

The nature of soft-tissue remodeling follows **Davis's Law** that states soft tissue models along the lines of stress; the soft-tissue equivalent of **Wolff's Law** for bone. If soft tissue has an inelastic collagen matrix that forms in a random fashion, then alterations in normal tissue extensibility can result (30). The Sports Performance Professional must follow the integrated flexibility continuum to restore the normal extensibility of the entire soft-tissue complex (29,30).

Neurophysiological Principles of Flexibility Training

Muscle stretching or elongation essentially begins with the sarcomere; the contractile element of muscle (1). During contraction, the thin actin myofilament is pulled over the thick myosin myofilament via the myosin crossbridges, pulling the Z lines toward the center of the sarcomere, effectively shortening the sarcomere. The initial length of the sarcomere largely dictates the tension produced. When the sarcomere is at less than its optimal length, the actin filaments can even overlap and produce less tension when stimulated because the sarcomere has less shortening capacity. With stretching, the overlap in the sarcomere decreases, which allows the muscle fiber to

Recruitment
An impulse transmitted simultaneously over an increasing number of nerve fibers, pulling in increasingly more muscle fibers for the task.

Rate Coding
The rate at which any individual nerve fiber transmits impulses per unit of time.

Muscle Spindles
The major sensory organs of the muscle that are sensitive to change in length and rate of length change.

become closer to its optimal length and makes peak tension production possible (1). Once the sarcomeres are fully stretched out, additional elongation comes from the surrounding connective tissue (fascia and muscle tendons). Because Davis's Law states that soft tissue models along the lines of stress (29,30), an increase in scar tissue develops following an injury secondary to the cumulative injury cycle. Scar tissue has many inelastic properties, but will realign its fibers into functional lines of stress with proper flexibility training (30,59,60).

Integrated flexibility training not only affects the muscular system, but it also affects the neural system through two basic forms of feedback: recruitment and rate coding (1). **Recruitment** is an impulse transmitted simultaneously over an increasing number of nerve fibers, pulling in increasingly more muscle fibers for the task. This is sensitive to the stretch intensity and the number of fibers recruited. For example, a moderate straight-leg hamstring stretch will only stimulate a few stretch receptors. But as the stretch intensity increases, a greater number of receptors are stimulated. **Rate coding** is a time sensitive feedback mechanism. This is the rate at which any individual nerve fiber transmits impulses per unit of time. As the stretch intensity increases, so does the frequency of impulses being sent to the spinal cord, which will usually result in some form of motor response (stretch reflex). Sensors within the musculotendinous unit provide the neural feedback. These sensors are collectively called mechanoreceptors (63). There are three basic types of mechanoreceptors: muscle spindles, Golgi tendon organs, and joint mechanoreceptors (1,63).

Muscle spindles (Fig. 4.10) are the major sensory organs of the muscle and are composed of microscopic intrafusal fibers that lie in parallel to the extrafusal muscle fibers. Muscle spindles are sensitive to change in length and rate of length change (63).

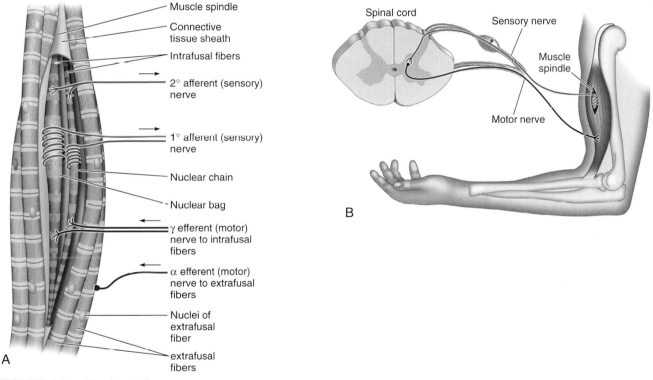

Muscle spindle
Connective tissue sheath
Intrafusal fibers
2° afferent (sensory) nerve
1° afferent (sensory) nerve
Nuclear chain
Nuclear bag
γ efferent (motor) nerve to intrafusal fibers
α efferent (motor) nerve to extrafusal fibers
Nuclei of extrafusal fiber
extrafusal fibers

Spinal cord
Sensory nerve
Muscle spindle
Motor nerve
B

A

FIGURE 4.10 Muscle spindle.

Golgi Tendon Organs
Mechanoreceptors located within the musculotendinous junction that are sensitive to tension and rate of tension change.

Joint Mechanoreceptors
Mechanoreceptors located in joints throughout the fibrous capsule and ligaments that respond to joint position, movement, and pressure changes.

Golgi tendon organs (Fig. 4.11) are located within the musculotendinous junction, and are sensitive to tension and rate of tension change (63–65). Prolonged Golgi tendon organ stimulation provides inhibitory action to muscle spindles located within the agonist muscle and is called autogenic inhibition (22). This occurs when the neural impulses sensing tension are greater than the impulses causing muscle contraction. The phenomenon is termed *autogenic*, because the contracting agonist is inhibited by its own receptors.

Joint mechanoreceptors are located in joints throughout the fibrous capsule and ligaments. These receptors signal joint position, movement, and pressure changes (1,63).

THE STRETCH REFLEX

The most basic reflex is a neuronal circuit consisting of a sensory neuron and a motor neuron with its effector muscle (1,63). When a stimulus of sufficient intensity is applied to the receptor ending, an impulse is created. This impulse travels to the spinal cord where a motor neuron is excited. The nerve impulse is conducted to the effector site on the muscle and a motor

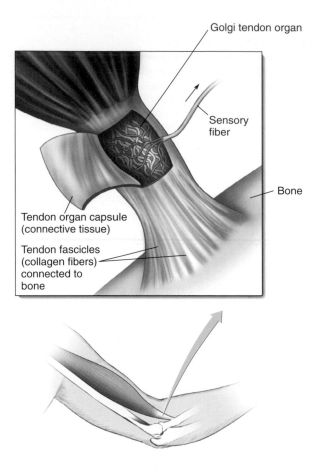

Golgi tendon organ

Sensory fiber

Bone

Tendon organ capsule (connective tissue)

Tendon fascicles (collagen fibers) connected to bone

FIGURE 4.11 Golgi tendon organ.

Myotatic Stretch Reflex

When a muscle is stretched very quickly, the muscle spindle contracts, which in turn stimulates the primary afferent fibers that causes the extrafusal fibers to fire, and tension increases in the muscle.

response is initiated. The reflex is a response to the stimulus (Fig. 4.12). As the stimulus intensity increases, the motor response (the reflex) is proportional. When extrafusal muscle fibers are stretched, the intrafusal (muscle spindles) fibers are also stretched. These relay information regarding changes in muscle length and rate of change of muscle length. This information is relayed to the spinal cord where a motor response (contraction), also called a **myotatic stretch reflex**, occurs (1,64,65). When a muscle is stretched very quickly, the muscle spindle contracts, which in turn stimulates the primary afferent fibers that causes the extrafusal fibers to fire, and tension increases in the muscle (myotatic stretch reflex). The rationale for holding a stretched position is to stimulate the Golgi tendon organ's inhibitory action to the muscle spindles, which will allow adaptive changes to muscle spindle sensitivity at the new range.

This myotatic stretch reflex has static (tonic) and dynamic (phasic) components (1,64,65). The tonic portion remains as long as the stretch is active. The phasic component is proportional to the velocity of the stretch. An understanding of these principles helps in the proper administration of a successful flexibility program (1).

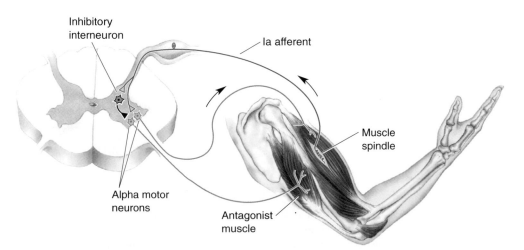

Inhibitory interneuron

Ia afferent

Muscle spindle

Alpha motor neurons

Antagonist muscle

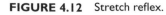

FIGURE 4.12 Stretch reflex.

Integrated Flexibility Continuum

 Corrective Flexibility
Stretching techniques designed to correct common postural dysfunctions, muscle imbalances, and joint dysfunctions.

 Active Flexibility
Stretching techniques designed to improve soft tissue extensibility in all planes of motion by employing the neurophysiological principle of reciprocal inhibition.

 Functional Flexibility
Stretching techniques designed to improve multiplanar soft tissue extensibility and provide optimum neuromuscular control throughout that full range of motion, while performing functional movements that utilize the body's muscles to control the speed, direction, and intensity of the stretch.

The Sports Performance Professional needs to understand the different types of flexibility training in order to prescribe the appropriate program based on needs and goals. Figure 4.13 illustrates the different types of flexibility on the integrated flexibility continuum. There are three categories of flexibility, including: corrective, active, and functional.

Corrective flexibility is designed to correct common postural dysfunctions, muscle imbalances, and joint dysfunctions. Corrective flexibility training incorporates self-myofascial release, static stretching, and neuromuscular stretching.

Active flexibility is designed to improve soft-tissue extensibility in all planes of motion by employing the neurophysiological principle of reciprocal inhibition (22,66–69). Active flexibility utilizes agonists and synergists to actively move a limb through a range of motion, while the functional antagonists are being stretched. Active flexibility incorporates self-myofascial release, neuromuscular stretching and active isolated stretching (68–70).

Functional flexibility is designed to improve multiplanar soft tissue extensibility and provide optimum neuromuscular control throughout that full range of motion, while performing functional movements that utilize the body's muscles to control the speed, direction, and intensity of the stretch. Lunges with rotation is a good example of a functional flexibility exercise. Remember that all functional movements occur in all three planes of motion, and injuries most often occur in the transverse plane. If the appropriate soft tissue is not extensible through the full range of movement, the risk of injury may increase because those with the least range of motion seem to have the most strain injuries (71). Exercises that increase multiplanar soft tissue extensibility and have high levels of neuromuscular demand are preferred.

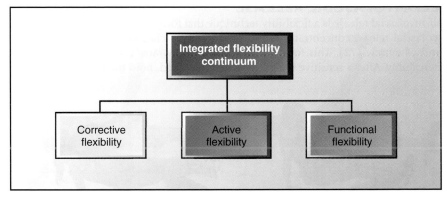

FIGURE 4.13   Integrated flexibility continuum.

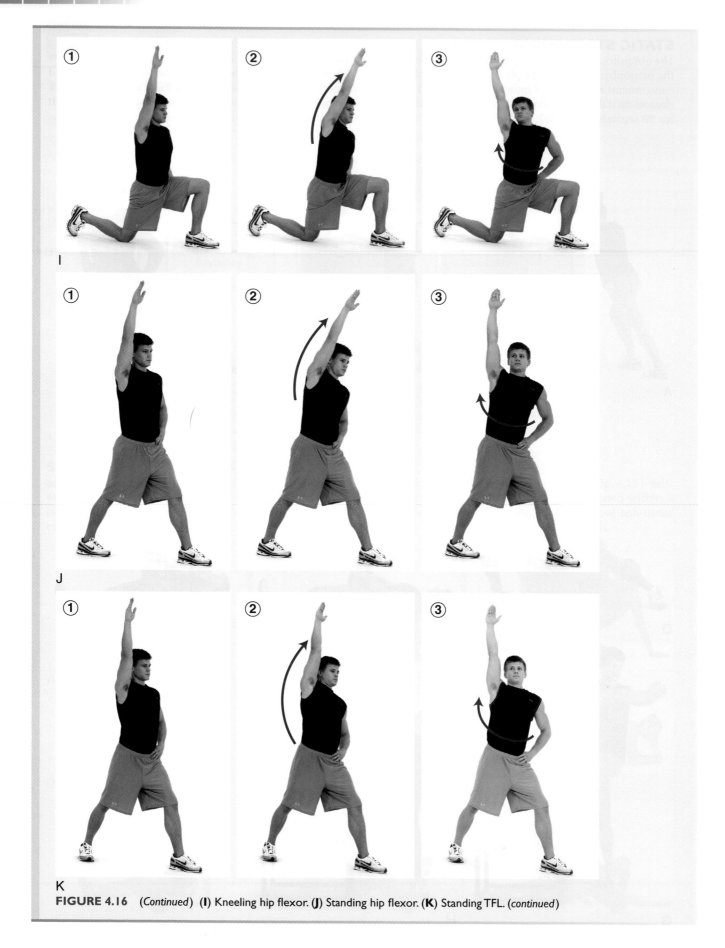

FIGURE 4.16 *(Continued)* **(I)** Kneeling hip flexor. **(J)** Standing hip flexor. **(K)** Standing TFL. *(continued)*

FIGURE 4.16 *(Continued)* **(L)** Supine piriformis. **(M)** Ball piriformis. **(N)** Erector spinae. **(O)** Ball lat. **(P)** Pectoral. **(Q)** Posterior shoulder. **(R)** Upper trapezius. **(S)** Levator scapulae. **(T)** Sternocleidomastoid.

FIGURE 4.19 *(Continued)* (**J**) Scorpion. (**K**) Iron cross. (**L**) Russian twist. (**M**) Single-leg squat touchdown. (**N**) Leg swings, front to back. (**O**) Leg swings, side to side.

The goal of any flexibility routine is to create multiplanar soft-tissue extensibility that is controlled by the CNS. Though there are many types of flexibility training, no single method can improve every flexibility deficit. The best flexibility program follows the integrated flexibility continuum.

EVIDENCE-BASED APPLICATION OF INTEGRATED FLEXIBILITY TRAINING

When it comes to discussing flexibility, opinions, theories, and applications vary from one professional to another. However, *flexibility* is a general term and one needs to be specific as to the type of flexibility being discussed.

To clarify current research, static stretching has been the subject of various studies that have helped to define the current thoughts behind the role of stretching in increasing range of motion, strength, and performance.

FLEXIBILITY TRAINING AND INCREASING JOINT RANGE OF MOTION

Flexibility has been the subject of debate for several decades and a lack of consensus allows researchers to continue to study the effects, duration, and methodologies behind stretching while practitioners struggle to recommend the ideal static flexibility program. To date, this subject might be one of the most profusely studied topics in fitness and sports medicine. Many believe static stretching provides the benefit of increased range of motion and decreased muscle stiffness. The debate seems to be centered on the basic prescription such as the type of stretch (e.g., static stretching or PNF/neuromuscular stretching), the duration of the stretch required to increase range of motion, and the mechanism of the adaptation to stretching (how stretching increases range of motion). Researchers continue to determine what form of stretching creates the greatest increase in range of motion around a joint, the mechanics of stretching, along with the duration of a stretch required to see a significant change in range of motion.

Evidence-Based Research on Flexibility Training's Effects on Range of Motion

According to several studies, both static stretching and PNF/NMS have shown positive effects on improving range of motion; however, PNF/NMS stretching created the largest gains in range of motion. Sady et al. (65) found PNF/NMS stretching superior to all types of flexibility when used to increase range of motion of the trunk, shoulder, and hamstring complex (65). Whether PNF/NMS was performed as either the contract-relax-contract technique or the hold-relax-contract technique, significant improvements in range of motion were seen over a 6-week span when compared to traditional static stretching (66). In fact, when tested head-to-head against a home program of static stretching, PNF/NMS stretching reigned supreme; a self-applied PNF stretching program using a contract-relax-contract method increased range of motion more than self-applied static stretching (67).

A full description of the mechanism of action about the adaptations to a stretching program will be unveiled in future research. Current theories equate increased range of motion to structural changes, changes in stretch sensation or both. Some theorize that structural changes, such as decreased stiffness of the muscle tendon unit and passive resistive force, take place when performing static stretching (61,68), whereas others hypothesize that the muscle structure does not actually change, but a change in the stretch sensation leads to increases in range of motion (69). The greater stretch tolerance might lead to increased range of motion around a joint (69).

While various stretching protocols exist, researchers have begun to understand the effect of stretching duration on increasing ranges of motion. In an important study by Bandy et al. (70), the duration of holding a stretch was measured against shorter or longer static stretching protocols for the hamstring complex. Thirty seconds of holding a single stretch, once a day, 5 days a week for 6 weeks resulted in increased range of motion at a joint (70). However, in contrast to Bandy's findings, Bazett-Jones et al. (71) found that a static stretching protocol (using 3 sets of 30-second holds) showed no effects on increasing range of motion of the hamstring complex and quadriceps as did the research of Youdas et al. (72), which showed no significant changes in range of motion in the gastrocnemius after implementing a 6-week stretching regimen (30-second duration stretches, performed once a day, 5 days a week) (81). Given the differences in research results, it is important to analyze a few different factors that may affect the relationship between static stretching and range of motion.

NASM's Position on the Use of Static Stretching to Enhance ROM

While more research must be done to understand some of the underlying factors on how stretching increases range of motion, there are a few determinants that NASM uses to understand the role of static stretching on increasing range of motion. First is the determination of muscle imbalances that may affect range of motion. When testing the range of motion of the hamstring complex, stretching the opposite muscles (the quadriceps) increases range of motion at the hips (73). When the quadriceps are tight, an anterior pelvic tilt of the hips is created, effectively increasing the length of the hamstring complex that decreases range of motion for hip flexion. Flexibility and range of motion require a thorough and integrated assessment process to evaluate all aspects or barriers to range of motion and not an isolated look at a singular muscle. A limited range of motion could be secondary to an issue at a neighboring joint. Second, the implementation of the method may be specific to certain muscles. When looking at the contrasting studies of Bandy et al. versus Youdas et al., Youdas et al. implemented an exact replica of the methodology of Bandy et al., but performed the stretches on the gastrocnemius muscle focusing on dorsiflexion range of motion. Although Youdas et al. found that the stretching regimen did not produce the at the performance effects of chronic static stretching (static stretching integrated into a 10-week program) versus the acute effects of static stretching (done immediately prior to performance assessment). The acute effects may not equate to decreases in muscle stiffness and therefore the results may not match those of Young and Elliot (80). Thus, the differences in the stretching protocols seem to play a factor in the results seen between each study.

The NASM Position on the Use of Flexibility Training and Performance Enhancement

Overall, research shows that performance is influenced by static stretching and may decrease jump height, balance, reaction times, and movement times. The acute effects of static stretching on performance have led NASM to determine pre-activity flexibility should be limited to active-isolated and dynamic stretches unless muscle imbalances are present that may impede proper movement and limit performance. If static stretching is used to address these imbalances, it should be followed with active-isolated and/or dynamic stretching to increase proper reciprocal inhibition, neuromuscular efficiency, and motor neuron excitability pre-activity.

Furthermore, while some evidence suggests that an acute bout of static stretching may inhibit muscular strength when performed in isolation (see the section on Flexibility and Strength), we are not ready to infer that specific static stretching performed to correct muscle imbalances and used in conjunction with active and dynamic stretching will equate to decreased performance. On the contrary, research currently underway at the University of North Carolina is beginning to show that a systematic approach that includes inhibition (foam roll), lengthening (static stretching), activation (active stretching), and integration (dynamic stretching) may improve human movement imbalances, decrease injury risk, and improve performance.

TIME OUT
Stretching Tips for Strength and Performance Enhancement

1. As a warm-up, static stretching prior to a strength training routine or competition should only be used on areas that are determined as tight/overactive from the assessment process.

2. Static stretching (if incorporated before a strength workout or as a warm-up prior to competition) should be followed by active-isolated and/or dynamic stretching to improve neuromuscular efficiency.

3. Static stretching should be used post-workout or event to return muscles to normal resting lengths and should be performed on the major muscles utilized during the workout or event.

4. Static stretching is contraindicated prior to activities requiring maximal effort *unless muscle imbalances are present.*

5. Active-isolated and/or dynamic stretching can be used:

    i. As a warm up by themselves if no muscle imbalances are present.

    ii. As a warm up after static stretching if muscle imbalances are present.

    iii. Prior to activities requiring maximal effort.

SUMMARY

There are many stretching exercises designed to improve flexibility. Regardless of the method chosen, individuals can achieve flexibility by manipulating the duration of the stretch, intensity of the stretch, velocity of the movement, and frequency of the movements performed. To achieve optimum soft-tissue extensibility with neuromuscular control, the individual should follow the integrated flexibility continuum (corrective, active, functional). The risk of injury is reduced when these stretching techniques are combined with an integrated training program that focuses on neuromuscular efficiency at all levels. Further research is needed to determine which flexibility technique is optimum for a given individual.

REFERENCES

1. Alter MJ. Science of Flexibility, 2nd ed. Champaign, IL: Human Kinetics; 1996.
2. Chaitow L. Muscle Energy Techniques. New York: Churchill Livingstone; 1991.
3. Bandy WD, Irion JM, Briggler M. The effect of time and frequency of static stretching on flexibility of the hamstring muscles. *Phys Ther* Oct 1997;77(10):1090–96.
4. Clanton TO, Coupe KJ. Hamstring strains in athletes: diagnosis and treatment. *J Am Acad Orthop Surg* Jul–Aug 1998;6(4):237–48.
5. Condon SA. Soleus muscle electromyographic activity and ankle dorsiflexion range of motion during four stretching procedures. *Phys Ther* 1987;67:24–30.
6. Janda V. Muscle spasm—a proposed procedure for differential diagnosis. *Man Med* 1991;199:6136–139.
7. Liebenson C. Rehabilitation of the Spine—A Practitioners Manual. Baltimore: Williams & Wilkins; 1995.
8. Poterfield J, DeRosa C. Mechanical Low Back Pain: Perspectives in Functional Anatomy. Philadelphia: WB Saunders; 1991.
9. Gossman MR, Sahrman SA, Rose SJ. Review of length-associated changes in muscle: experimental evidence and clinical implications. *Phys Ther* 1982;62:1799–808.
10. Halbertsma JPK, Van Bulhuis AI, Goeken LNH. Sports stretching: effect on passive muscle stiffness of short hamstrings. *Arch Phys Med Rehabil* 1996;77(7):688–92.
11. Holcomb WR. Improved stretching with proprioceptive neuromuscular facilitation. *J NSCA* 2000;22(1): 59–61.
12. Moore MA, Kukulka CG. Depression of Hoffmann reflexes following voluntary contraction and implications for proprioceptive neuromuscular facilitation therapy. *Phys Ther* Apr 1991;71(4):321–29.
13. Moore MA. Electromyographic investigation of muscle stretching techniques. *Med Sci Sports Exerc* 1980; 12:322–29.
14. Sady SP, Wortman M, Blanke D. Flexibility training: ballistic, static, or proprioceptive neuromuscular facilitation? *Arch Phys Med Rehabil* Jun 1982;63(6):261–63.
15. Sherrington C. The Integrative Action of the Nervous System. New Haven: Yale University Press; 1947.
16. Wang RY. Effect of proprioceptive neuromuscular facilitation on the gait of patients with hemiplegia of long and short duration. *Phys Ther* Dec 1994;74(12):1108–115.
17. Sapega A, Quedenfeld T, Moyer R. Biophysical factors in range of motion exercises. *Phys Sports Med* 1981;9:57.
18. Tardieu C. Adaptation of connective tissue length to immobilization in the lengthened and shortened position in the cat soleus muscle. *J Physiol* 1982;78:214.
19. Woo SLY, Buckwalter JA. Injury and Repair of the Musculoskeletal Soft Tissues. Rosemont, IL: American Academy of Orthopedic Surgeons; 1987.
20. Johns RJ, Wright V. The relative importance of various tissues in joint stiffness. *J App Physiol* 1962; 17(5):824–28.
21. Selye H. The Stress of Life. New York: McGraw-Hill; 1984.
22. Butler D, Magee DJ, Quillen WS. Nerve: Structure, Function, and Physiology. In Zachazewski JE, et al. Athletic Injuries and Rehabilitation. Philadelphia: WB Saunders; 1996. p 170–83.
23. Butler D. Mobilization of the Nervous System. Melbourne: Churchill Livingstone; 1991.
24. Hiromada J. On the nerve supply of connective tissue of some peripheral nervous system components. *Acta Anat* 1963;55:343.
25. Sunderland S. Nerves and Nerve Injuries, 2nd ed. Edinburgh: Churchill Livingstone; 1978.
26. Elvey RL. Brachial Plexus Tension Tests and the Pathoanatomical Origin of Arm Pain. In Glasgow EF, Twomey L. Aspects of Manipulative Therapy. Melbourne: Melbourne Lincoln Institute of Health Sciences; 1979. p 105–10.
27. Elvey RL. Abnormal Brachial Plexus Tension and Shoulder Joint Limitation. Proceedings I.F.O.M.T. Vancouver; 1984.
28. Frykholm R. Cervical nerve root compression resulting from disc degeneration and root sleeve fibrosis. A clinical investigation. *Acta Chirurgica Scandinavica* 1995;160:408–13.
29. Kuslich SD, Ulstrom RN, Michael CJ. The tissue origin of low back pain in sciatica. *Orth Clin North Amer* 1991;22(2):181–87.
30. Maitland GD. Vertebral Manipulation, 5th ed. London: Butterworths; 1986.
31. Smyth MJ, Wright V. Sciatica and the intervertebral disc. An experimental study. *J Bone Joint Surg* 1958; 40(A):1401–418.
32. Xaver Av, Chen L, Sharma P, et al. Does antidromic activation of nociceptors play a role in sciatic radicular pain? *Pain* 1990;40:77–79.
33. Lundborg G. Nerve Injury and Repair. Edinburgh: Churchill Livingstone; 1988.
34. Rydevik B, Lundborg G, Skalak R. Biomechanics of Peripheral Nerve. In Nordin M, Frankel VH. Basic Biomechanics of the Musculolskeletal System, 2nd ed. Philadelphia: Lea & Febiger; 1989.
35. Grieve GP. Sciatica and the straight leg raise test in manipulative treatment. *Physiotherapy* 1970;56: 337–46.
36. Brieg A, Troup JDG. Biomechanical considerations in the straight leg raising test. *Spine* 1974;4:243–50.
37. Gummerson T. Mobility Training for the Martial Arts. London: A & C Black; 1990.
38. Akeson WH, Woo SLY. The connective tissue response to immobility: biochemical changes in periarticular connective tissue of the immobilized rabbit knee. *Clin Orthop Related Res* 1973;93:356–62.
39. Akeson WH, et al. The connective tissue response to immobility: an accelerated aging response. *Exp Gerontol* 1968;3:289–301.
40. Baker JH, Matsumoto DE. Adaptation of skeletal muscle to immobilization in a shortened position. *Muscle Nerve* 1988;11:231–44.

41. Robinson GA, Enoka RM, Stuart DG. Immobilization induced changes in motor unit force and fatigability in the cat. *Muscle Nerve* 1991;14:563–73.

42. Tabary JC, Tabary C, Tardieu G et al. Physiological and structural changes in the cat's soleus muscle due to immobilization at different lengths by plaster casts. *J Physiol London* 1972;224:231–44.

43. Williams PR, Goldspink G. Changes in sarcomere length and physiological properties in immobilized muscle. *J Anat* 1978;127:459.

44. Williams PE. Effect of intermittent stretch on immobilized muscle. *Ann Rheum Dis* 1988;47:1014–016.

45. Williams PE, Catanese T, Lucey EG et al. The importance of stretch and contractile activity in the prevention of connective tissue accumulation in muscle. *J Anat* 1988;158:109–14.

46. Goldspink G. The Adaptation of Muscle to a New Functional Length. In Anderson DJ, Matthews B. Mastication. Bristol, England: Wright & Sons; 1976. p 90–99.

47. Goodfellow JW, Bullough PG. The pattern of aging of the articular cartilage of the elbow joint. *J Bone Joint Sur* 1967;49B(1):175–81.

48. Woo SLY, Matthews JV, Akeson WH et al. Connective tissue response to immobility. *Arthritis Rheum* 1975;18(3):257–64.

49. Arem M. Effect of stress on healing wounds: intermittent noncyclical tension. *J Surg Res* 1976;20:93–102.

50. Spencer AM. Practical Podiatric Orthopedic Procedures. Cleveland, OH: Ohio College of Podiatric Medicine; 1978.

51. Zairns B. Soft tissue injury and repair-biomechanical aspects. *Int Journal Sports Med* 1982;3:9–11.

52. Magnusson SP, Simonsen EB, Aagaard P et al. Viscoelastic response to repeated static stretching in the human hamstring muscle. *Scand J Med Sci Sports Dec* 1995;5(6):342–47.

53. Shilling BK, Stone MH. Stretching: acute effects on strength and power performance. *J NSCA* 2000;22(1):44–47.

54. Evjenth O, Hamburg J. Muscle Stretching in Manual Therapy—A Clinical Manual. Alfta, Sweden: Alfta Rehab; 1984.

55. Magnusson SP, Simonsen EB, Aagaard P et al. Biomechanical responses to repeated stretches in human hamstring muscle in vivo. *Am J Sports Med* 1996;24(5):622–28.

56. Grigg P. Peripheral neural mechanisms in proprioception. *J Sports Rehab* 1994;3:2–17.

57. Cornelius WL. Pain is not a part of effective stretching. *Biomech* 1999;2:39–44.

58. Basmajian JV. Therapeutic Exercise, 3rd ed. Baltimore: Williams & Wilkins; 1978.

59. Downey J, Darling R. Physiological Basis of Rehabilitation Medicine. Philadelphia: WB Saunders; 1971.

60. Beaulieu JA. Developing a stretching program. *Phys Sports Med* 1981;9:59.

61. Tannigawa M. Comparison of the hold-relax procedure and passive mobilization on increasing muscle length. *Phys Ther* 1972;52:725.

62. Voss DE, Ionla MK, Meyers BJ. Proprioceptive Neuromuscular Facilitation, 3rd ed. Philadelphia: Harper & Row; 1985.

63. Neumann DA. Kinesiology of the Musculoskeletal System: Foundations for Physical Rehabilitation. St. Louis: Mosby; 2002.

64. Etnyre BR, Abraham LD. Gains in range of ankle dorsiflexion using three popular stretching techniques. *Am J Phys Med* 1986;65:189.

65. Sady SP, Wortman M, Blanke D. Flexibility training: ballistic, static or proprioceptive neuromuscular facilitation? *Arch Phys Med Rehabil* 1982;63:261–63.

66. Decicco PV, Fisher MM. The effects of proprioceptive neuromuscular facilitation stretching on shoulder range of motion in overhand athletes. *J Sport Med Phys Fitness* 2005;45;183–87.

67. Schuback B, Hooper J, Salisbury L. A comparison of a self-stretch incorporating proprioceptive neuromuscular facilitation components and a therapist-applied PNF-techniques on hamstring flexibility. *Physiotherapy* 2004;90:151–57.

68. Reid DA, McNair PJ. Passive force, angle and stiffness changes after stretching of hamstring muscles. *Med Sci Sport Exerc* 2004;36(11):1944–948.

69. Bjorklund M, Hamburg J, Crenshaw AG. Sensory adaptation after a 2-week stretching regimen of the rectus femoris muscle. *Arch Physl Med Rehabil* 2001;82:1245–250.

70. Bandy WD, Irion JM. The effect of time on static stretch on the flexibility of the hamstring muscles. *Phys Ther* 1994;74(9):845–52.

71. Bazett-Jones DM, Winchester JB, McBride JM. Effect of potentiation and stretching on maximal force development, and range of motion. *J Strength Condition Res* 2005;19(2):421–26.

72. Youdas JW, Krause DA, Egen KS et al. The effect of static stretching on the calf muscle-tendon unit on active dorsiflexion range of motion. *J Orthop Sport Phys Ther* 2003;33(7):408–17.

73. Clark S, Christiansen A, Hellman DF et al. Effects of ipsilateral anterior thigh soft tissue stretching on passive unilateral straight-leg raise. *J Orthop Sport Phys Ther* 1999;29(1):4–12.

74. Bell DR, Padua DA, Clark MA. Muscle strength and flexibility characteristics of people displaying excessive medial knee displacement. *Arch Phys Med Rehabil.* 2008;89:1323–8.

75. Fowles JR, Sale DG, MacDougall JD. Reduced strength after passive stretch on the human plantar flexors. *J Appl Physiol* 2000;89:1179–188.

76. Marek SM, Cramer JT, Fincher AL et al. Acute effects of static and proprioceptive neuromuscular facilitation stretching on muscle strength and power output. *J Athl Train* 2005;40(2):94–103.

77. Kokkonen J, Nelson AG, Cornwell A. Acute muscle strength inhibits maximal strength performance. *Res Q Exerc Sport* 1998;69(4):411–15.

78. Knudson D, Noffal G. Time course of stretch-induced isometric strength deficits. *Eur J Appl Physiol* 2005;94:348–51.

79. Power K, Behm D, Cahill F et al. An acute bout of static stretching: effects on force and jumping performance. *Med Sci Sports Exerc* 2004;36(8):1389–396.
80. Behm DG, Bambury A, Cahill F et al. Effect of acute static stretching on force, balance, reaction time and movement time. *Med Sci Sports Exerc* 2004;36(8):1397–402.
81. Young W, Elliot S. Acute effects of static stretching, proprioceptive neurofacilitation stretching and maximum voluntary contractions on explosive force production and jumping performance. *RQES* 2001;72(3):273–79.
82. Hunter JP, Marshall RN. Effects of power and flexibility training on vertical jump technique. *Med Sci Sports Exerc* 2002;34(3):478–86.
83. Unick J, Kieffer HS, Cheesman W et al. The acute effects of static and ballistic stretching on vertical jump performance in trained women. *J Strength Cond Res* 2005;19(1):206–12.

CHAPTER 5

Cardiorespiratory Training for Performance Enhancement

UPON COMPLETION OF THIS CHAPTER, YOU WILL BE ABLE TO:

Describe how cardiorespiratory training is used within an integrated training program to improve performance.

Apply the guidelines for proper cardiorespiratory training.

Understand the importance of interval training and its effect on cardiorespiratory performance.

Design performance enhancing cardiorespiratory training programs through the use of Base and Interval training.

Introduction

Sports Performance Professionals must be creative in developing new cardiorespiratory training experiences. As such programs expand, becoming new and more diverse, athletes will want to know how to start and plan a safe program that will create success while minimizing the risk of injury and avoiding underperformance, staleness, overreaching, and overtraining.

The term *athlete*, as it is used throughout this text, encompasses people at all competitive levels including high school or college students, professional level athletes, as well as recreational athletes who compete in weekend races or local leagues. All athletes need goals and proper training guidelines to assure continued growth. Personalized cardiorespiratory training programs will go a long way toward achieving specific goals.

To have a complete cardiorespiratory training program, a Sports Performance Professional must first assess the athlete, then create a program with specific goals while applying a measurement tool (such as heart rate or watts) to measure the athlete's progress.

Basics of Cardiorespiratory Training

Of the various components that comprise an athlete's total physical fitness program, cardiorespiratory endurance is probably the most misunderstood and underrated. The athlete often fails to understand why building an aerobic base is such an important part of a complete

Anaerobic Threshold
The exercise intensity at which lactic acid starts to accumulate in the bloodstream. This happens when it is produced faster than it can be removed (metabolized).

to produce the ATP rapidly enough to meet these energy needs. The intensity level at which oxygen supply is unable to match the energy demands is referred to as the **anaerobic threshold**. It has also been termed *lactic threshold*. Even though these terms are often used interchangeably, true lactic threshold occurs before the anaerobic threshold. The academics of how this is actually determined and the difference between the two concepts is beyond the scope of this chapter.

In brief, the lactic threshold is determined by serial blood analysis at increasing intensities of exercise while the anaerobic threshold can be determined through submaximal VO_2 testing (such as the step test discussed in Chapter 3). Although the measurement of oxygen consumption requires some technical expertise and equipment, it is still more practical in the performance setting due to its ease of use versus the understandable reluctance of athletes to have repeated blood samples taken (1,2).

The primary fuel for anaerobic ATP production is glucose that is stored in muscles and the liver as glycogen, a large molecule made up of chains of glucose. This energy pathway is often referred to as the glycolytic (or lactic acid) system. During muscle contraction, stored glucose is broken down into lactic acid. During this breakdown of glucose, a small number of high-energy ATP molecules are produced. It is estimated that if glycolysis was the sole source of fuel for exercise, one could only continue for roughly one minute.

A second source of anaerobic ATP production is *creatine phosphate* (CP). The CP molecule is also a high energy compound. Once a ATP has been split and its energy released for mechanical work by the muscle, the energy in the CP molecule can be quickly transferred to the "used" adenosine diphosphate (ADP) and a free phosphate molecule is attached making a new ATP. This energy pathway is often referred to as the ATP-CP system. As with the muscle's store of ATP, there is an extremely limited supply of creatine phosphate. If this was the sole source of energy, exercise might be sustained for maybe 10–15 seconds.

At no time is only one system functioning. All three systems are supplying energy constantly. Which one is the prominent system depends on the duration and intensity of exercise, as seen in Table 5.1.

In skeletal muscle, this cycle goes on constantly at the myosin cross bridges and must be constantly resupplied by ATP from glycolytic and aerobic energy sources. The main advantage of the ATP-CP system is the speed at which energy can be supplied. The main drawback is that not as much ATP can be produced as with the aerobic system. If glycolysis is the prominent source of ATP, the result is an increasing level of lactic acid waste that can inhibit exercise. These anaerobic energy pathways are the main source of energy for high-intensity, short-duration activities (1,2).

Lactic acid is continuously being produced and removed, even when the body is at rest. When lactic is produced faster than it is removed, it spills out into the blood and symptoms of fatigue become evident. A major goal of training should be to minimize lactic acid production while enhancing lactic acid removal during exercise (2). One way to accomplish this is through a combination of high intensity interval training and prolonged submaximal training. Interval training helps maximize cardiorespiratory adaptations and increases VO_2 max (3). The more oxygen that is consumed, the less that will be reliant on the anaerobic (especially glycolytic) breakdown of carbohydrates. Prolonged submaximal training can help to induce an increase in mitochondrial structure and function. These adaptations will help reduce lactic acid formation by increasing the fractional utilization of fatty acids as a mitochondrial fuel source, while facilitating lactic acid removal (4,5).

Early work in exercise physiology was directed at determining the metabolic demands of different sports. The Sports Performance Professional who designs workouts for athletes can use

TABLE 5.1

Exercise Duration for Energy Systems and Supplies Used

Estimated Time	Energy System Used	Energy Supply Used
1–4 seconds	Anaerobic	ATP in muscle
4–20 seconds	Anaerobic	ATP + CP
20–45 seconds	Anaerobic	ATP + CP + muscle glycogen
45–120 seconds	Anaerobic and lactic	Muscle glycogen
120–240 seconds	Aerobic and anaerobic	Muscle glycogen + lactic acid
Over 240 seconds	Aerobic	Muscle glycogen + fatty acids

TABLE 5.2			
Percentage of Each Energy System Used During Sports Activities			
Sport	**ATP/CP**	**Glycolysis**	**Oxidative**
Basketball	60	20	20
Fencing	90	10	0
Field Events	90	10	0
Golf Swing	95	5	0
Gymnastics	80	15	5
Hockey	50	20	30
Running (distance)	10	20	70
Rowing	20	30	50
Skiing	33	33	33
Soccer	50	20	30
Sprints	90	10	0
Swimming (1,500 m)	10	20	70
Tennis	70	20	10
Volleyball	80	5	15

Table 5.2 to understand which system supplies the most energy as well as which system probably needs the most training emphasis for competition.

No sport is dependent on a single energy system, so each sport needs to focus on all energy systems during training. The relative training fraction devoted to each system can be estimated using data from these types of tables.

Consider an athlete starting to jog on a treadmill that is going 7 mph. After the first step, the muscles have to increase the rate of ATP to produce the required energy for the new physical demands of the 7 mph pace. In the transition from rest to light or moderate exercise, oxygen consumption (or VO_2) increases rapidly and reaches a steady state within 1 to 4 minutes depending on age and one's level of fitness. The fact that the VO_2 does not increase instantaneously to a steady state value means that an anaerobic energy source has to contribute to the overall production of ATP at the beginning of exercise. At 7 mph, the energy demand of the first steps (well before steady state is reached) is the same as the last steps (well after attaining steady state). The body has to get energy from somewhere while the aerobic system "catches up" with its production of energy. At the onset of exercise, the ATP-CP system is the first active bioenergetic pathway that gives way to glycolysis and then finally to aerobic energy production (4). After a steady state is reached, the body's ATP requirement is met via the balanced delivery and use of oxygen using aerobic metabolism. Energy needed for exercise and sports is not provided by any one bioenergetic pathway, but rather from a mixture of several metabolic systems that overlap based on the intensity and duration of work.

Understanding Heart Rate Formulas, Heart Rate Training Zones and Base Training

Heart rates and heart rate training zones are convenient tools for monitoring training intensity and are determined by mathematical formulas that are extremely useful when used to estimate the maximum heart rate or the appropriate training zones that an athlete could safely train at without risking harm.

HEART RATE FORMULAS: ESTIMATING HEART RATE MAXIMUM

Here are two common formulas for calculating heart rate maximum.

laboratory that use the RQ and oxygen consumption to determine the actual calories per minute and the proportion of calories that come from fat and carbohydrates.

An RQ of 0.80–0.90 is a great zone to work within (verified by the athlete using prescribed heart rate monitors provided by the consulting Sports Performance Professional). This RQ range can be used for a beginning or deconditioned athlete to improve the blood's capability of delivering oxygen and removing waste. With regular training, the heart increases its cardiac output, blood volume increases, and total peripheral resistance to blood flow decreases allowing blood a less restricted path to the cells. The result is a greater flow of oxygen to a greater number of cells throughout the body, which helps the muscle cells and the cardiorespiratory system work more efficiently.

RESPIRATORY QUOTIENT—ZONE 1

From this point on, this chapter will refer to an RQ of 0.80–0.90 (or, approximately 65–75% of maximum heart rate) as "Zone 1" although many people know this as the so-called "fat burning zone." Some may also refer to this as a "cardio base zone" or "recovery zone" (the intensity used between interval work bouts).

Athletes that train in this zone without variation will initially improve their oxygen consumption, but in the absence of further overload will quickly plateau in their training. When this occurs, weight loss is slowed (or sometimes ceases). If Zone 1 is maintained, the only solution to end the plateau is to keep increasing the training duration, frequency, or both. Increasing intensity will place a new stress to the cardiorespiratory system to adapt to (enhancement in cardiorespiratory efficiency, increases in caloric expenditure) without adding more time or frequency to the program.

RESPIRATORY QUOTIENT—ZONE 2

Exercise at an intensity that results in an RQ of 0.9–1.0 would be considered Zone 2, which corresponds to about 80–85% of maximum heart rate. Some athletes may mistakenly think that performing higher intensity (or, "cardio zone," not to be confused with the "cardio base zone" of Zone 1 above) workouts every time is preferred.

Zone 2 is close to the anaerobic threshold (which some say occurs when the RQ is around 1.0 during steady state exercise). In this zone, the body can no longer produce enough energy for the working muscles solely through aerobic metabolism, so the fraction of energy production from anaerobic metabolism increases. The higher the intensity the body can train at while remaining aerobic, the greater the number of calories burned from fat and the less lactic acid is produced. Thus, one of the outcomes of cardiorespiratory training is an increased anaerobic threshold and greater reliance on fat as a fuel at progressively higher percentages of the maximum.

For weight loss, the bottom line is to burn more calories than are consumed. By referring back to Table 5.3, it is easy to see that at higher intensities of exercise, such as at RQ values approaching 1.0, the body is using predominantly carbohydrates for fuel and the caloric expenditure per minute is high. Because total caloric expenditure is the most important issue, this approach is an effective one for weight loss if that is the athlete's goal.

As with Zone 1, staying in Zone 2 will also lead to a plateau for most athletes. Remember, to improve the athlete's fitness level, the body needs to be progressively overloaded.

RESPIRATORY QUOTIENT—ZONE 3

A true "high intensity" workout would be considered going to an RQ > 1.0 (approximately 90% of maximum heart rate), which could consist of several short 30–60 second sprints. This *overload* requires training close to, or at, peak exertion, which would be in Zone 3.

Most athletes may exercise in Zone 3 for 30–60 seconds (while some world class endurance athletes, such as rowers, triathletes, and cyclists, can maintain this intensity for 3–4 minutes). It would be advised to recover in Zone 1 after a high intensity bout of work in Zone 1 (for a prescribed amount of time depending on the goal). Then, return to Zone 3 for subsequent repetitions (interval training).

For most athletes, exercising in Zone 3 once a week is sufficient, but the highly competitive athlete may find it necessary for more frequent sessions depending on the seasonal cycle. Research has shown that regardless of whether an athlete performs interval training once a week or three times a week, both frequencies have the same cardiorespiratory benefits (3).

If weight loss is the goal, then an athlete would certainly burn more calories by training in Zone 3 more often. However, this may be more strenuous to an athlete and can lead to overtraining. Weight loss requires long-term commitment and solutions, which are challenging for an athlete to accomplish when time is taken off as a result of overtraining.

HEART RATE TRAINING ZONES

The information provided up to this point can be transferred into practical application by using the heart rate formulas mentioned earlier in this chapter to establish the athlete's training heart rate (THR). The THR will assist in determining the specific zones of training that an athlete can utilize to train safely and effectively in order to optimize aerobic capacity.

These Heart Rate Training Zones can be found by simply taking the appropriate percentage of the formula "220 – age" (or, any of the heart rate maximum formulas such as the Karronen formula) for each Heart Rate Training Zone (Table 5.4). The percentage that is appropriate will be determined by the goal or adaptation that the athlete is trying to achieve.

- **Zone 1** is 65–75% of HRmax (RQ of 0.80–0.90) and is used for recovery, or lower intensity.
- **Zone 2** is 80–85% of HRmax (RQ of 0.90–1.0) and is closer to the anaerobic threshold (AT), or higher intensity.
- **Zone 3** is 86–90% of HRmax (RQ > 1.0) and is considered closer to peak training, which is just below HRmax, but above anaerobic threshold.

For a 25-year-old athlete, the formula would work like this:

$$220 - 25 \ (the \ client's \ age) = 195$$

To find the Heart Rate Training Zone 1 for that athlete, the Sports Performance Professional would take 195 and multiply it by 0.65 and 0.75.

$$195 \times 0.65 = 127 \ bpm$$
$$195 \times 0.75 = 146 \ bpm$$

To find Heart Rate Training Zone 2 for that same athlete, the Sports Performance Professional would take 195 and multiply it by 0.80 and 0.85.

$$195 \times 0.80 = 156 \ bpm$$
$$195 \times 0.85 = 166 \ bpm$$

To find Heart Rate Training Zone 3 for that same athlete, the Sports Performance Professional would take 195 and multiply it by 0.86 and 0.90.

$$195 \times 0.86 = 168 \ bpm$$
$$195 \times 0.90 = 176 \ bpm$$

This method is simple to use. There is no equipment required to measure the appropriate Heart Rate Training Zones. Unfortunately, the simple way is not always the best way. As

---

TABLE 5.4

Heart Rate Training Zones

Training Zone	Heart Rate Formula	Purpose
Zone 1 65–75%	(220 – age) × 0.65 or 0.75	This zone builds an aerobic base that is critical for improving heart and lung capacity. This improved capacity affects the body's ability to store and transport oxygen and nutrients to produce energy. It is used for warm-up and recovery.
Zone 2 80–85%	(220 – age) × 0.80 or 0.85	This zone is used to increase anaerobic and aerobic capacity by straddling the energy systems. An athlete could work on both leg strength and cardiorespiratory capacity by sustaining this zone for long periods of time.
Zone 3 86–90%	(220 – age) × 0.86 or 0.90	Zone 3 is only used in interval training. It can increase speed, power, metabolism, and anaerobic capacity by repeatedly exposing active muscles to high intensity exercise, improving resistance to fatigue. An athlete will be able to sustain a given exercise intensity for a longer period of time, increasing endurance.

previously stated, heart rate formulas based solely on age are not always reliable. Because this formula is based on averages, almost every athlete's true max heart rate will be above or below the estimate given. In addition, putting the face and body in cold water (such as a swimmer) slows down the heart rate and the breeze on the face during cycling also can slow the heart rate based on certain inherent reflexes and a reduction in the thermal load. For these people, zones based on estimated heart rates can be excessive and hard for some to achieve.

The Sports Performance Professional can use estimations derived from formulas similar to estimating loads for a lifting session. Start with these formulas and adjust, based on the specific athlete's situation, needs, goals, and results. Remember that genetics can play a large part in establishing each person's heart rate zones. Thus, high or low heart rates are not necessarily an indicator of fitness. Rather, heart rate is simply a training tool.

The Benefits of Interval Training

As mentioned earlier, if the goal is to bring positive physical changes to an athlete's cardiorespiratory system, then overloading is necessary. The body must be presented with a workload that challenges its current fitness state. This increased workload will cause fatigue and, with the proper recovery, will eventually yield cardiorespiratory improvements.

If the workloads are of the right magnitude (i.e., slightly more than the body's current capabilities), then the body must adapt to be prepared for the next time such a demand is placed on the body. It is important to note that the overload stimulus happens during the *exercise*, while the adaptations occur during *recovery*. Recovery days, therefore, are a vital and underappreciated part of any athlete's program.

INTERVAL TRAINING

Interval training is widely practiced in one form or another at most all levels of training for competitive sports. While popularized for middle distance runners, variations on the technique have been incorporated into many sports. Consider the miler who could go out and train by running longer distances so that the actual race might seem short; however, this concept does not press training intensity. Fatigue during a mile race is largely due to lactic acid buildup and long distance running is limited by other factors. Thus, the long distance runner who wants to get faster will not have addressed glycolysis. Instead, the miler might do eight 200-meter runs at a much higher than race-paced intensity interspersed with recovery periods that are 2–3 times the duration of the running pace. Each 200-meter run would be at a much higher intensity that stresses both anaerobic systems, but also allows for some recovery to replenish phosphagens and eliminate some lactic acid. The fatigue from running, the time at high heart rates are both reduced, and the neuromuscular recruitment of muscle fibers to run at a high intensity is enhanced, which is, all in all, a better training stimulus.

Because recovery for the body is vital, the most effective workout is one that involves interval training, which is training at different intensities for certain periods of time in a given workout. A day of cardiorespiratory exercise utilizing interval training would start in Zone 1 (or, THR of 65–75%). The program would slowly work through Zone 2 (or, THR of 80–85%). Finally, it would reach Zone 3 (or, THR of 86–90%). This exercise session would typically yield a higher caloric expenditure than working in any one zone alone.

As an example, examine a 150-pound female athlete exercising on a stationary bike. She might burn approximately 82 calories during a 30-minute ride by staying in Zone 1 with about half of those calories coming from fat. As this athlete rides at a harder rate, she will raise her RQ over 0.90 (or, Zone 2) and burn up to 152 calories in that same 30 minutes. Although a smaller percentage of those calories will come from fat, the actual number of calories from fat will be higher.

There are three other, less-evident benefits of interval training. First, varying an athlete's programs will have a positive motivational impact by helping to avoid monotonous exercise intensities. Second, by overloading the heart and lungs, an athlete will increase cardiorespiratory efficiency. Finally, interval training will increase an athlete's metabolic rate during recovery (excess post-exercise oxygen consumption or EPOC).

TIME OUT
Excess Post-Exercise Oxygen Consumption

EPOC is the state where the body's metabolism is elevated following exercise. This means that the body is burning more calories following exercise than before the exercise was initiated. Think of EPOC as a caloric afterburner that is caused by exercise (much like a car engine stays warm for a period of time after it has been driven). Following exercise, the body must utilize increased amounts of oxygen to replenish energy supplies, lower tissue temperature, and return the body to a resting state, all of which requires calories to do.

In achieving weight loss, the amount of calories burned during the day is even more important than how many calories are burned during a workout. Studies have shown that interval training raises metabolism after a workout and keeps it higher for a longer period than any "steady state" workout (9–13).

The Phases of Cardiorespiratory Performance Training

When training for performance enhancement, there are typically five phases of cardiorespiratory training:
1. Base training
2. Interval training
3. Linear training
4. Multidirectional training
5. Sport specific training

The primary focus of this chapter will be the first 7 weeks of an athlete's cardiorespiratory training program, with the goals being to build a cardiorespiratory base and improve conditioning. This will be accomplished by reviewing the first two phases of training: base training and interval training. You can learn more about all five phases of the training program through further NASM continuing education courses.

In any sport, conditioning is obviously very important; however the Sports Performance Professional needs to take a close look at the energy systems for each event/sport and determine how to develop these systems for the long season. Conditioning is not just random sprints, but needs to be a well thought out progression through a series of systematic phases to create a cardiorespiratory base and then develop the work to rest needs specific to the sport. Throughout the training there should also be planned recovery periods and peaks—this holds true for the off-season as well as in-season.

PHASE 1: BASE TRAINING

The first phase of cardiorespiratory performance training is called base training. The main goal is to create a strong aerobic base, which will be the foundation for all the subsequent phases of training.

It is a little misleading calling it a "base," because many think this means staying at a low intensity for a long period of time. Although it is important to do some low intensity work, this phase will introduce intervals into the program.

Since this phase of training is primarily an off-season activity, it is wise to do this training on cardio equipment to reduce stress on the body. Most sports seasons are getting longer with more competitions crammed into an already dense competitive schedule, and athletes will be doing enough running during the pre-season and in-season. The off-season is to be used to build an aerobic base without overtraining or inducing injury. If weight loss is a goal, athletes will stay in this phase of training during the off-season for up to 7 weeks. For this athlete, it is even more important to stay on cardio equipment to reduce impact on their joints.

It is also prudent to use different pieces of cardio equipment as much as possible to enhance motivation and minimize boredom. Equipment can be changed within and between workouts.

During this phase of training, the athlete will have a low intensity day (Zone 1 or 65–75% of HRmax) and a higher intensity day in which the athlete will be slowly introduced to Zone 2 (80–85% of HRmax). This creates a 2-day rotation: Zone 1 on one day, while the second day will be used to do intervals in Zone 2, with the intensity of the recovery periods between intervals being in Zone 1 (Fig. 5.2).

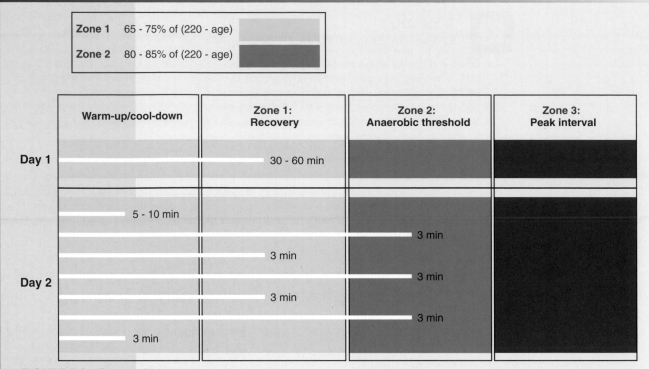

FIGURE 5.2 Example Phase 1 program: base training.

On the higher-intensity day, Zone 2 is introduced slowly, after a 5–10-minute warm-up in Zone 1. In this example, the athlete should do 3 minutes in Zone 2 followed by 3 minutes in Zone 1. Repeat the 3:3 rotation based on the time available for that day (each workout can be 20–60 minutes long). The length can be determined by the other activities they are doing in the training session, the program goal (e.g., weight loss), the demands of the sport, or all three.

After a couple of workouts using the 3:3 rotation, you can change the rotation to increase the time in Zone 2 while reducing the time in Zone 1. A common rotation is 5 minutes in Zone 2 with a 1 minute recovery in Zone 1. The 1 minute is a good time to switch equipment. For example, after a 5 minute warm-up, perform 5 minutes in Zone 2 on the bike, take 1 minute to switch to a treadmill, and repeat the 5 minutes in Zone 2.

Typically, this phase of training will last between 1–7 weeks, depending on the amount of aerobic work needed for the sport or the goal (e.g., weight loss).

PHASE 2: INTERVAL TRAINING

The second phase in cardiorespiratory performance training is interval training. The goal of this phase is to introduce the third training zone into the program as well as create the cardiorespiratory strength needed for the future phases. Most athletes will be in this phase for 1–2 weeks.

For most sports, the athlete will work 30–60 second sprints in this phase. Two minutes in Zone 3 (which is 85–90% of HRmax) is a good intensity to build cardiorespiratory strength for most sports. This will be the longest they will maintain in an anaerobic state (use of ATP-CP and muscle glycogen as an energy system). Endurance athletes (such as triathletes) may work at this intensity for as much as 3 to 4 minutes, but 2 minutes will probably be the maximum duration for most team sports (football, baseball, soccer, and basketball).

As in base training, it is also recommended to use equipment at the beginning of this phase to minimize stress on the joints. Many athletes might be doing some drills or pick-up games in the off-season, which will also prepare them for their sport. The goal of Phase 2 conditioning is to prepare the athlete for the season and it will be at a higher intensity than the sport specific drills. Using equipment will allow the Sports Performance Professional to concentrate on the cardiorespiratory conditioning without the stress that high-intensity running has on the legs and back. This phase will also be very important for the athletes still needing to lose weight.

Adding this workout creates a 3-day rotation, 1 day for each of the training zones (Fig. 5.3). Day 1 is still a low intensity day in Zone 1 that is a recovery day from the higher-intensity days. Athletes need to recover from high-intensity intervals, both within and between training days.

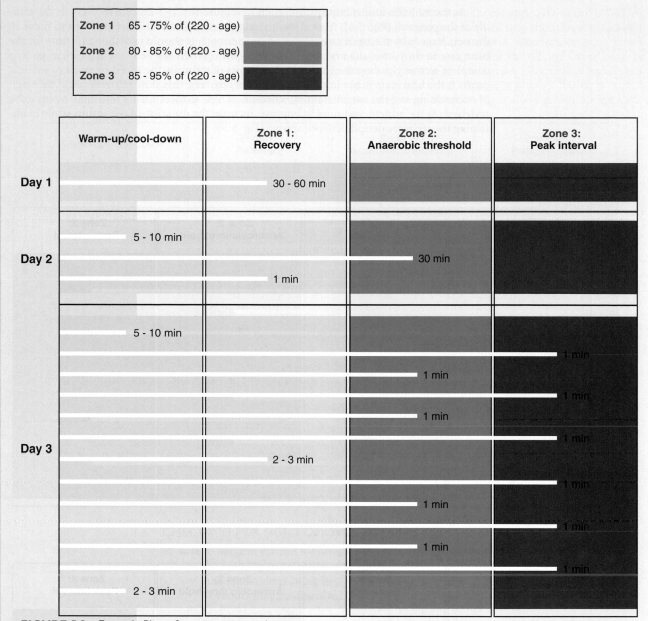

Zone 1	65 - 75% of (220 - age)	
Zone 2	80 - 85% of (220 - age)	
Zone 3	85 - 95% of (220 - age)	

	Warm-up/cool-down	Zone 1: Recovery	Zone 2: Anaerobic threshold	Zone 3: Peak interval
Day 1		30 - 60 min		
Day 2	5 - 10 min		30 min	
		1 min		
Day 3	5 - 10 min			1 min
			1 min	
				1 min
			1 min	
				1 min
		2 - 3 min		
				1 min
			1 min	
				1 min
			1 min	
				1 min
	2 - 3 min			

FIGURE 5.3 Example Phase 2 program: interval training

In day 2, the athlete spends the majority of the workout in Zone 2 (Fig. 5.3). The goal is to keep the heart rate up, but not to overload the athlete. For weight loss, this workout should be 30–60 minutes to burn extra calories. If weight gain is a goal, keep the workout to under 20 minutes.

Day 3 is the true interval day. For example, the athlete performs three 1-minute sprints in Zones 2 and 3 inside of a 5-minute interval followed by a true recovery in Zone 1 for the 2–3 recovery minutes (Fig. 5.3). The 1-minute recovery in Zone 2 is to give the body a short break while minimizing how much the heart rate can recover. An example on a treadmill could be doing the 1-minute sprints (Zone 3) at 8 mph and then break (Zone 2) at 6 mph for 1 minute. The true recovery (Zone 1) would be at 3 mph for a further 2–3 minutes for a total of 5 minutes at the lower intensity before repeating.

In the example provided, there are six sprints in the 30-minute workout. Make sure the first sprint and the last sprint are at the same workload; however, it would be optimal if the last sprint is harder than the first. This 30-minute workout would be followed by a 2–3-minute recovery period with the goal being to get to the low end of the athlete's Zone 1 by the end of the recovery period. Slow recovery can be a sign of poor fitness, but can also indicate dehydration or the onset of overtraining. In the presence of a slow recovery, the athlete should not attempt another series of sprints and instead should cool down and end the workout.

SUMMARY

The proper cardiorespiratory training program is very important for each athlete. Cardiorespiratory training is not a one-size-fits-all program. Personalized cardiorespiratory training programs can help any athlete reach any goal by maintaining program efficacy and client enthusiasm.

Using heart rate as the primary basis of measurement during training, the Sports Performance Professional must utilize appropriate equations to obtain an athlete's maximal heart rate and training heart rate. Developing a cardiorespiratory training program entails a comprehensive assessment process and designing a structured program to meet the athlete's goals and needs. It will also be important that the athlete develops a good cardiorespiratory base before engaging in higher-intensity training. This is accomplished through the use of base training.

Overloading is necessary to present the body with a workload that challenges its current state and bring about positive changes in the body. Likewise, rest and recovery are vital in allowing the body to recuperate from exercise and prepare for greater demands. The use of interval training allows an athlete to train at varying intensities to help avoid overtraining and better prepare for increased workloads. Interval training is also important for caloric expenditure, increasing metabolism, and avoiding boredom.

REFERENCES

1. Wilmore JH, Costill DL. Physiology of Sports and Exercise. Champaign, IL: Human Kinetics; 1994.
2. Brooks GA, Fahey TD, White TP. Exercise Physiology: Human Bioenergetics and its Application. Mountain View, CA: Mayfield Publishing Company; 1996.
3. Billat VL, Flechet B, Petit B et al. Interval training at VO₂ max: effects of aerobic performance and overtraining markers. *Med Sci Sport Exerc* 1999;31:156–63.
4. Brooks GA. The lactate shuttle during exercise and recovery. *Med Sci Sport Exerc* 1986;18:360–68.
5. Donovan CM, Brooks GA. Endurance training affects lactate clearance, not lactate production. *Am J Physiol* 1983;244:E83–E92.
6. Kolata G. 'Maximum' Heart Rate Theory Challenged. New York Times: New York, NY, 2001.
7. Visich PS. Graded Exercise Testing. In Ehrman JK, Gordon PM, Visich PS et al. Clinical Exercise Physiology. Champaign, IL: Human Kinetics; 2003. p 79–101.
8. Karvonen MJ, Kentala E, Mustala O. The effects of training on heart rate: a longitudinal study. *Ann Med Exp Biol Fenn* 1957;35:307–15.
9. Henritze J, Weltman A, Schurrer RL et al. Effects of training at and above the lactate threshold on the lactate threshold and maximal oxygen uptake. *Eur J Appl Physiol* 1985;54:84–88.
10. James DVB, Doust JH. Oxygen uptake during moderate intensity running: response following a single bout of interval training. *Eur J Appl Physiol* 1998;77:551–55.
11. Simoneau JA, Lortie G, Boulay MR et al. Human skeletal muscle fiber type alteration with high intensity intermittent training. *Eur J Appl Physiol* 1985;54:250–53.
12. Tabata I, Inrisawa K, Kousaki M et al. Metabolic profile of high intensity intermittent exercises. *Med Sci Sport Exerc* 1997;29:390–95.
13. Zavorsky GS, Montgomery DL, Pearsall DJ. Effect of intense interval workouts on running economy using three recovery durations. *Eur J Appl Physiol* 1998;77:224–30.

CHAPTER 6

Core Training Concepts for Performance Enhancement

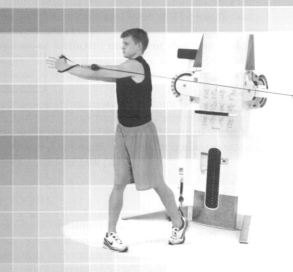

UPON COMPLETION OF THIS CHAPTER, YOU WILL BE ABLE TO:

Understand the importance of the core musculature and its relationship to performance enhancement.

Differentiate between the local stability, global stability, and movement systems of the core.

Rationalize the importance of core training for improving sports performance and injury prevention.

Design a systematic core training program for athletes at any level of training.

Introduction

In recent years, Sports Performance Professionals have increased the emphasis on core training in sports conditioning programs. Historically, physical therapists prescribed core exercises for individuals with low-back problems. Today, core training is a common practice for healthy athletes on sports teams and in sports conditioning centers.

Core Training Concepts

WHAT IS THE CORE?

Core
Defined by the structures that make up the lumbo-pelvic-hip complex (LPHC).

The neuromusculoskeletal **core** of the human movement system (HMS) is defined by the structures that make up the lumbo-pelvic-hip complex (LPHC) (1–3). An efficient core ensures optimal length-tension relationships of functional agonists and antagonists, which makes it possible for the HMS to maintain favorable force-couple relationships throughout the LPHC. Maintenance of optimum length-tension and force-couple relationships allows for optimum joint arthrokinematics in the LPHC during functional movements (4). This provides ideal neuromuscular efficiency throughout the entire HMS and allows for the best possible acceleration, deceleration, and dynamic stabilization during integrated, dynamic movements (Fig. 6.1).

compressive, shear, and rotational forces between spinal segments. These muscles also aid in proprioception and postural control because of their high density of muscle spindles (23). The primary muscles that make up the local stabilization system include the transverse abdominus, internal oblique, multifidus, pelvic floor musculature, and diaphragm. These muscles contribute to segmental spinal stability by increasing intra-abdominal pressure and generating tension in the thoracolumbar fascia, thus increasing spinal stiffness for improved intersegmental neuromuscular control (2,14,24–26).

GLOBAL STABILIZATION SYSTEM

Global Core Stabilizers

Muscles that attach from the pelvis to the spine.

The **global core stabilizers** are muscles that attach from the pelvis to the spine. These muscles act to transfer loads between the upper extremity and lower extremity and provide stability between the pelvis and spine (Table 6.1). These muscles provide stabilization and eccentric control of the core during functional movements. The primary muscles that make up the global stabilization system include the quadratus lumborum, psoas major, external oblique, portions of the internal oblique, rectus abdominus, gluteus medius, and adductor complex (2,27).

MOVEMENT SYSTEM

Movement System

Includes muscles that attach the spine and/or pelvis to the extremities.

The **movement system** includes muscles that attach the spine and/or pelvis to the extremities. These muscles are primarily responsible for concentric force production and eccentric deceleration during dynamic activities. The primary muscles that make up the movement system include the latissimus dorsi, hip flexors, hamstrings, and quadriceps (28).

All of these muscles provide dynamic stabilization and optimum neuromuscular control of the entire core (LPHC) and are reviewed in Chapter 2. These muscles not only produce force (concentric contractions), but also reduce force (eccentric contractions) and provide dynamic stabilization in all planes of movement during functional activities. In isolation, these muscles do not effectively achieve stabilization of the LPHC. It is their synergistic, interdependent functioning that enhances stability and neuromuscular control.

CORE STABILIZATION MECHANISMS

The core (LPHC) is stabilized during functional movement by two primary systems: the thoracolumbar stabilization mechanism and the intra-abdominal pressure stabilization mechanism (6,25,29–32).

The thoracolumbar fascia (TLF) stabilization mechanism is accomplished through a fascial network of noncontractile tissue that plays an essential role in the functional stability of the core and is divided into the posterior, anterior, and middle layers (Fig. 6.3).

Although the TLF is noncontractile, it can be engaged dynamically because of the contractile tissue that attaches to it. The muscles that attach to the TLF include: the deep erector spinae, multifidus, transverse abdominus, internal oblique, gluteus maximus, latissimus dorsi, and quadratus lumborum (28). The transverse abdominus and the internal oblique are particularly important for stabilization. They attach to the middle layer of the TLF via the lateral raphe and activation of both create a traction and tension force on the thoracolumbar fascia, which enhances the regional intersegmental stability in the core decreasing translational and rotational stress (25,31,32).

The second stabilization mechanism involves the intra-abdominal pressure mechanism (Fig. 6.4). Increased intra-abdominal pressure mechanism decreases compressive forces in the core. The abdominal muscles contract against the viscera, pushing the viscera superiorly into the diaphragm and inferiorly into the pelvic floor. This increase in the intra-abdominal pressure results in elevation of the diaphragm and contraction of pelvic floor musculature while also assisting in providing intersegmental stabilization to the core (LPHC) (25,29,30).

SCIENTIFIC RATIONALE FOR CORE TRAINING

When compared to other muscle groups, many athletes train their core muscles inadequately. Although adequate stability, strength, and power are important for sports performance, it is detrimental to perform exercises incorrectly or select exercises that are too advanced (33).

Several authors have found decreased firing of the transverse abdominus, internal oblique, and multifidus in individuals with chronic low-back pain (LBP) (31,32,34). Hungerford (35) found a delay in firing of the internal oblique, multifidus, and gluteus maximus in the stance leg of patients with sacroiliac joint pain. Laasonen (11) found 10–30% more paraspinal atrophy in patients with LBP on the affected side as compared to the unaffected side. It has been demonstrated that the multifidus atrophies on the affected side in patients with LBP that does not automatically regain its cross-sectional area or activation in the absence of LBP (9,36). Several studies have demonstrated that individuals with LBP have weaker back extensor muscles (37)

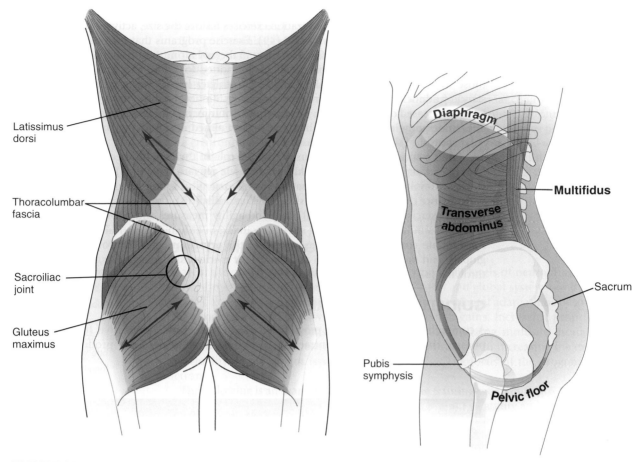

FIGURE 6.3 Thoracolumbar stabilization mechanism.

FIGURE 6.4 Intra-abdominal pressure mechanism.

and decreased muscle endurance (6,38). Trunk muscle weakness is a known risk factor for developing LBP (33).

There is also a close link between core stabilization with posture, balance, and proprioception of the LPHC. Individuals with LBP have altered postural control when compared to healthy controls. Single-leg stance balance in individuals with LBP is less efficient and effective than healthy controls (7). This can be seen in individuals with LBP who had failure rates more than four times that of controls in tasks that involved bilateral standing with the eyes closed (39). Individuals with LBP also do more poorly on unexpected balance challenges. With unexpected perturbations (balance challenges), the lumbar paraspinal muscles in individuals with LBP react significantly more slowly than healthy controls (40). It has also been demonstrated that individuals with LBP have altered spinal proprioception (26,31,41).

The hip is also a part of this integrated system. Bilateral hip extension strength deficits are a risk factor for developing LBP (42). Deficits of as much as a 26% reduction in hip abductor strength and a 36% deficit in hip external rotator strength is a factor in females with knee pain (43). Decreased hip adduction strength usually follows a simple ankle sprain (44). Further, weakness in hip abduction increases subtalar joint pronation (45) that can lead to increased internal rotation of the tibia and femur (46), further affecting neuromuscular control of the LPHC.

Fredericson (47) has reported that runners with iliotibial band syndrome had weaker hip abduction strength compared to healthy controls. It should be obvious, then, that in this highly interdependent system, an imbalance in one component of the system will lead to predictable patterns of compensation elsewhere.

This has important implications when designing a sports performance training program. Core training programs are an integral component of all sports performance programs with sound support in scientific research. It has been demonstrated that individuals/athletes who have suffered from ankle sprains, knee pain, muscle strains, and/or LBP have altered core neuromuscular control and decreased intersegmental stability and global stability.

Research has also demonstrated that proper application of a specific core training program can improve pain, function, and performance. Specific instructions on the neuromechanical activation of the local stabilization system (**drawing-in maneuver**) (1,48) and the global stabilization system (**bracing**) (23) have demonstrated preferential activation of these specific muscles during the core training continuum (Figure 6.2).

 Drawing-In Maneuver

A maneuver used to recruit the local core stabilizers by drawing the navel in towards your spine.

 Bracing

Occurs when you have contracted both the abdominal, lower back, and buttock muscles at the same time.

Example Core Exercises

CORE STABILIZATION EXERCISES

Core Stabilization Exercises

Involve little to no motion through the spine and pelvis.

To improve core stabilization, exercises involve little to no motion through the spine and pelvis (Figs. 6.6 through 6.11). These exercises are designed to improve neuromuscular efficiency and intervertebral stability by focusing on the local stabilization system (13,58). The athlete would traditionally spend 4 weeks at this level of core training (Figs 6.6 to 6.11).

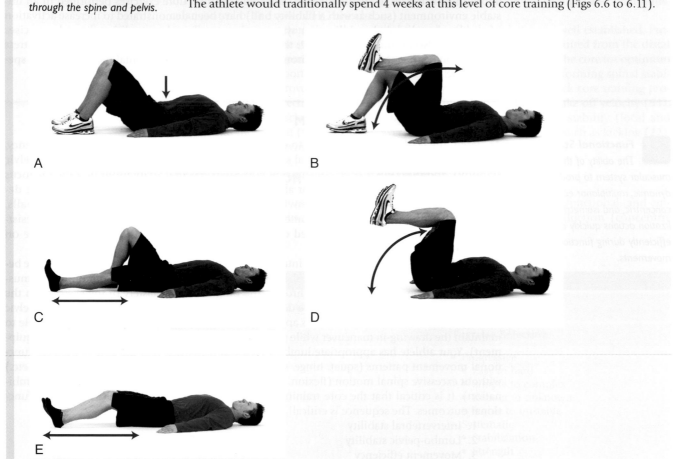

FIGURE 6.6 Drawing-in maneuver progression. (**A**) Supine. (**B**) Supine with march. (**C**) Supine with heel slide. (**D**) Supine with both knees to chest. (**E**) Supine with two-leg slide.

FIGURE 6.7 Iso-abdominal series. (**A**) Prone. (**B**) Prone with hip extension. (**C**) Side. (**D**) Side with hip abduction.

FIGURE 6.8 Prone progression. (**A**) Floor cobra. (**B**) Prone arm and opposite leg raise. (**C**) Superman. (**D**) Ball cobra.

FIGURE 6.9 Supine progression. (**A**) Two-leg floor bridge. (**B**) Ball bridge. (**C**) Bridge with feet on ball. (**D**) Floor bridge with march. (**E**) Floor bridge with knee extension.

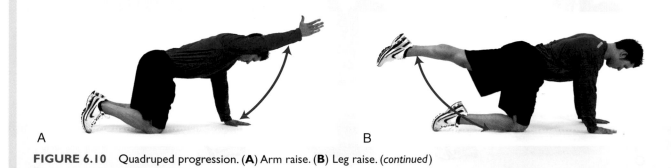

FIGURE 6.10 Quadruped progression. (**A**) Arm raise. (**B**) Leg raise. (*continued*)

FIGURE 6.12 (*Continued*) (**I**) Knee-ups with rotation. (**J**) Reverse hypers.

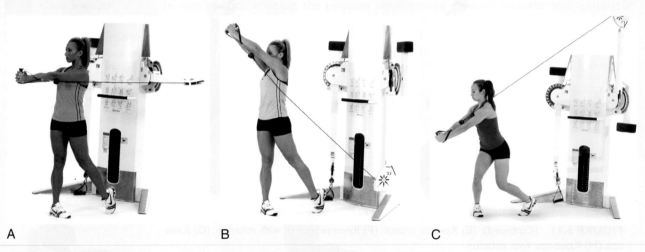

FIGURE 6.13 Cable progressions. (**A**) Rotation. (**B**) Lift. (**C**) Chop.

CORE POWER EXERCISES

Core Power Exercises

Designed to improve the rate of force production by the core musculature.

In core power training, exercises are designed to improve the rate of force production by the core musculature. These exercises prepare an athlete to stabilize and to generate force dynamically at more functionally applicable speeds. It is imperative that your athlete has the appropriate intervertebral stability and lumbo-pelvic stability prior to progressing to this phase of core training (Fig. 6.14).

FIGURE 6.14 Medicine ball exercises. (**A**) Pullover throw. (**B**) Rotation chest pass. (*continued*)

FIGURE 6.14   (*Continued*) (**C**) Front oblique throw. (**D**) Woodchop throw. (**E**) Overhead throw. (**F**) Overhead throw with rotation. (**G**) Side oblique throw. (**H**) Soccer throw.

44. Friel K, McLean N, Myers C et al. Ipsilateral hip abductor weakness after inversion ankle sprain. *J Athl Train* 2006;41:74–8.

45. Youdas, JW, Hollman J, Krause D. The effects of gender, age, and body mass index on standing lumbar curvature in persons without current low back pain. *Physiother Theory Pract* 2006;22:229–37.

46. Khamis S, Yizhar Z. Effect of feet hyperpronation on pelvic alignment in a standing position. *Gait Posture* 2007;25:127–34.

47. Fredericson M, Cookingham CL, Chaudhari AM et al. Hip abductor weakness in distance runners with iliotibial band syndrome. *Clin J Sport Med* 2000;10:169–75.

48. Karst GM, Willett GM. Effects of specific exercise instructions on abdominal muscle activity during trunk curl exercises. *J Orthop Sports Phys Ther* 2004;34:4–12.

49. Hides JA, Jull GA, Richardson CA. Long-term effects of specific stabilizing exercises for first-episode low back pain. *Spine* 2001;26:E243–8.

50. Yílmaz F, Yílmaz A, Merdol F et al. Efficacy of dynamic lumbar stabilization exercise in lumbar microdiscectomy. *J Rehabil Med* 2003;35:163–7.

51. Hölmich P UP, Ulnits L, Kanstrup IL et al. Effectiveness of active physical training as treatment for long-standing adductor-related groin pain in athletes: randomised trial. *Lancet* 1999;353:439–43.

52. Sherry MA, Best TM. A comparison of 2 rehabilitation programs in the treatment of acute hamstring strains. *J Orthop Sports Phys Ther* 2004;34:116–25.

53. Mills J, Taunton J. The effect of spinal stabilization training on spinal mobility, vertical jump, agility and balance. *Med Sci Sports Exerc* 2003;25:S323.

54. Butcher SJ CB, Chilibeck PD, Spink KS et al. The effect of trunk stability training on vertical takeoff velocity. *J Orthop Sports Phys Ther* 1996;37:223–31.

55. Kibler W, Chandler T, Livingston B et al. Shoulder range of motion in elite tennis players. Effect of age and years of tournament play. *Am J Sport Med* 1996;24:279–85.

56. Marshall R, Elliott B. Long-axis rotation: the missing link in proximal-to-distal segmental sequencing. *J Sports Sci* 2000;18:247–54.

57. Behm D, Leonard A, Young W et al. Trunk muscle electromyographic activity with unstable and unilateral exercises. *J Strength Cond Res* 2005;19:193–201.

58. Ng JK, Kippers V, Richardson CA et al. Range of motion and lordosis of the lumbar spine: reliability of measurement and normative values. *Spine* 2001;26:53–60.

CHAPTER 7

Balance Training Concepts for Performance Enhancement

UPON COMPLETION OF THIS CHAPTER, YOU WILL BE ABLE TO:

Describe balance and its purpose in performance enhancement and injury prevention.

Rationalize the importance of balance training.

Design a progressive balance training program for athletes at any level of training.

Introduction

Balance is the ability to maintain the body's center of gravity within its base of support. Balance is achieved through an interaction of active and passive restraints imposed by the muscular system, reflexive actions imposed by the peripheral nervous system, and anticipatory feed-forward control imposed by the central nervous system (CNS) (1). This entire process is referred to as sensorimotor control. Sensorimotor control, even for the easiest tasks, is a plastic process that undergoes constant review, feedback, and modification based on the integration of sensory information, motor commands, and resultant movements (2). Optimum sensorimotor control is designed to prepare, maintain, anticipate, and restore stability of the entire human movement system (postural stability) as well as each segment of the human movement system (joint stability) (3). Balance is a component of all movement no matter if strength, speed, skill, or flexibility dominates the movement in question. For example, a relatively simple activity such as sprinting is a highly complex movement pattern that requires losing, regaining, and maintaining balance on alternating legs all in less than one tenth of a second!

An understanding of the postural control system as well as the kinetic chain helps conceptualize the role of the chain in maintaining balance. Within the kinetic chain, each moving segment transmits forces to every other segment along the chain, and its motions are influenced by forces transmitted from other segments. The act of maintaining equilibrium or balance is associated with the closed kinetic chain, as the distal segment (foot) is fixed beneath the base of support. Changes along the distal kinetic chain can influence the efficiency of more core or central components, and position the center of gravity in either more or less optimal positions above the base of support. In other words, the coordination of automatic postural movements during the act of balancing is not determined solely by the muscles acting directly with one specific joint. Leg and trunk muscles exert indirect forces on neighboring joints through the inertial interaction forces among body segments. A combination of one or more strategies (ankle, knee, hip) are used to coordinate movement of the center of gravity back to a stable or balanced position when the length and its rate of length change in the muscle even after the muscle has been shortened. This improves the excitability and sensitivity of the CNS.

The GTO is a muscle mechanoreceptor located at the musculotendinous junction in series with the extrafusal muscle fibers (see Fig. 4.11) (4,9). The GTO is primarily sensitive to tension development and rate of tension development in skeletal muscle. The GTO has an inhibitory effect on the skeletal muscle. The more tension produced by the muscle, the greater the frequency of impulses from the GTO to the CNS leading to a reciprocal inhibition of the agonist and synergists, thereby limiting force production. Research postulates that the GTO functions as a protective mechanism to prevent overcontraction of the muscle (4,9,15).

JOINT MECHANORECEPTORS

Joint Mechanoreptors

Ruffini Afferents
Mechanically sensitive to tissue stresses that are activated during extremes of extension and rotation.

Paciniform Afferents
Mechanically sensitive to local compression and tensile loading, especially at extreme ranges of motion.

Golgi Afferents
Mechanically sensitive to tensile loads and are most sensitive at the end ranges of motion.

Nocioceptors
Sensitive to mechanical deformation and pain.

Joint rotation or deformation stretches the joint capsule on one side of the joint and may also compress it against the underlying bone on the other side of the joint. Ligamentous structures may also be loaded during joint rotation (4,9). There are several types of joint receptors. **Ruffini afferents** are large, encapsulated, multicellular structures located within the collagenous network of the joint's fibrous capsule (9,26). These receptors are slowly adapting sensory neurons that continue to discharge information as long as a mechanical stimulus is present. These receptors are mechanically sensitive to tissue stresses that are activated during extremes of extension and rotation. They are generally considered to be the limit detectors of motion (9,27). **Paciniform afferents** are large, cylindrical, thinly encapsulated, multicellular structures. These receptors are widely distributed around the joint capsule and surrounding periarticular tissue that are mechanically sensitive to local compression and tensile loading, especially at extreme ranges of motion. They exhibit a rapid burst of impulses following stimulation, after which there is a rapid decline in the impulse rate. These receptors are associated with the detection of acceleration, deceleration, or sudden changes in the deformation of the mechanoreceptors (9,26,28). **Golgi afferents** are high-threshold, slowly adapting sensory receptors located in ligaments and menisci. These receptors are mechanically sensitive to tensile loads and are most sensitive at the end ranges of motion (9,29). **Nocioceptors** are small diameter afferents located primarily in articular tissue and are sensitive to mechanical deformation and pain. The sensory receptors lack directional specificity, so optimum stimulation includes abnormal rotation, deformation, or chemical changes (30,31). The motto "No Pain, No Gain" has no place in a sports performance training program. Inflammation and abnormal sensory input to the CNS creates pain resulting in decreased neuromuscular efficiency and tissue overload.

LIGAMENTOUS MECHANORECEPTORS

Ligamentous mechanoreceptors are deformed during rotation and are mechanically sensitive to stretching. Movement of the joint in any limiting position results in sensory stimulation. Ligamentous receptors cause an increased level of response in the gamma efferent muscle spindle receptors. This is primarily responsible for the appropriate muscle firing patterns necessary to help protect the joint during stabilization (32–34). Joint and muscle receptors work interdependently to provide optimum proprioceptive input to the CNS. Joint receptors increase the response when muscle mechanoreceptors are losing their ability to signal changes about angular displacement. This results in maximal sensory input at the CNS level and optimum neuromuscular efficiency.

CENTRAL PROCESSING

Anticipatory postural adjustments play an important role in maintaining balance during the performance of any given task. It is known that postural adjustments of the legs and trunk may be initiated before the onset of voluntary movements of the trunk or upper limb (35,36). When the support is unstable, the activation of the stabilizing muscles preceded the force production of the prime movers (37). Slijper and Latash (38) reported an anticipatory increase in activity of the anterior tibialis, biceps femoris, erector spinae, and rectus abdominus during standing in an unstable environment. Furthermore, it has been demonstrated that the transverse abdominus become active prior to actual limb movement, and this preprogrammed (i.e., central processing) activation was used as an anticipatory, feed-forward postural mechanism in the core (lumbo-pelvic-hip complex) (39,40). It is speculated that these anticipatory postural adjustments serve the purpose to minimize subsequent postural destabilization (41).

When an athlete moves, we are usually unaware of the complex sensorimotor process that occurs to maintain balance by keeping the center of gravity over their base of support. The complex sensorimotor control process unites the proprioceptive feedback from the peripheral nervous system with the internal central processing within the brainstem and cerebellum. This meets the constant demands of changing postures, joint angles, and torques during activity to allow optimum balance and successful performance of complex motor skills.

SCIENTIFIC RATIONALE FOR BALANCE TRAINING

Inefficient neuromuscular stabilization leads to abnormal stress throughout the human movement system period. The HMS will not respond to the demands imposed during functional activities if the neuromuscular system is inappropriately trained. Just as a lack of joint stabilization predisposes an individual to functional instability, a lack of neuromuscular stabilization alters length-tension relationships, force-couple relationships, and joint kinematics, decreasing balance and performance leading to tissue overload and possible injury (16,22,23,27,42–54).

As the efficiency of the neuromuscular system decreases, the ability to maintain appropriate forces also decreases. This leads to compensations and substitute movement patterns, which then leads to excessive mechanical loading in both contractile and noncontractile tissues (18,35, 51,55–67).

The human movement system is only as strong as its weakest link. The CNS will allow recruitment of the prime movers only to the degree that the body maintains dynamic joint stabilization and postural equilibrium (Fig. 7.3) (10,68,69). The HMS will break down at the weak link or transfer forces elsewhere that can lead to tissue overload, compensation, adaptation, and further substitute patterns (51,57,63). Each tissue located in the HMS has a different breakdown threshold and rate. This is referred to as the tissue stress continuum (70). Microfailure occurs in collagen tissue when the tissue is deformed by as little as 6 to 8 percent (71). Therefore, with a lack of balance, the HMS compensates with an altered, less familiar motor pattern in order to maintain force production. When this compensation transfers forces to a weaker link in the HMS, alterations in stability and neuromuscular control occur. The CNS selects optimum movement strategies to maintain adequate force production. If a prime mover is weak or slow to activate, synergistic muscles are substituted to maintain force production (10). Synergistic muscles

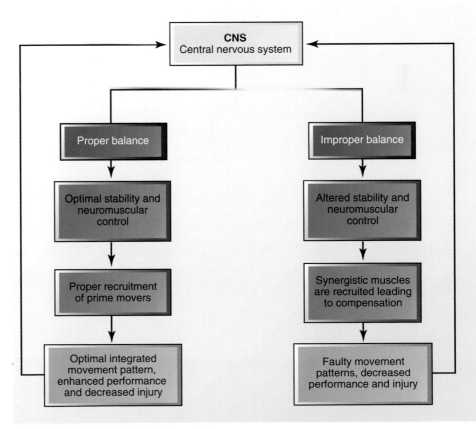

FIGURE 7.3 Proper and improper balance strategies.

fatigue more quickly and lack the precise neuromuscular control that the prime movers provide. This leads to faulty movement patterns, decreased performance, and injury.

Research has demonstrated that balance training restores dynamic stabilization mechanisms, improves neuromuscular efficiency, and stimulates joint and muscle receptors to encourage maximal sensory input to the CNS. Acting collectively, this improves proprioception, kinesthesia, and neuromuscular efficiency (central processing), which in turn can improve performance and decrease injury (16–18,20,22,23,25,43,49,52–54,72–75).

TIME OUT
Stability Terminology

Dynamic joint stabilization refers to the ability of the human movement system to stabilize a joint during movement.
EXAMPLE: The rotator cuff stabilizing the shoulder during all arm/shoulder motion.

Multisensory condition refers to a training environment that provides heightened stimulation to the proprioceptors and mechanoreceptors.
EXAMPLE: Standing on one foot on a 1/2-foam roll while throwing and catching a medicine ball.

Controlled instability refers to a training environment that is as unstable as can be SAFELY controlled for an athlete.
EXAMPLE: Standing on one foot for a 65-year-old athlete or standing on one foot on a 1/2-foam roll while squatting down and reaching across your body toward the floor for a 20-year-old athlete.

GUIDELINES FOR BALANCE TRAINING

As mentioned earlier, balance is a component of all movements, whether dominated by strength, speed, flexibility, or endurance. In sports, balance does not work in isolation; therefore, it should not be thought of as an isolated component of training. An integrated training program requires

TABLE 7.1

Balance Training Parameters

Exercise Selection	Variables

• Safe
• Progressive
  • Easy to hard
  • Simple to complex
  • Known to unknown
  • Stable to unstable
  • Static to dynamic
  • Slow to fast
  • Two-arms/legs to single-arm/leg
  • Stable to unstable
  • Eyes open to eyes closed
• Systematic
• Proprioceptively challenging
  1. Floor
  2. Balance beam
  3. Half foam roll
  4. Airex pad
  5. Dyna Disc
	• Plane of motion
	  • Sagittal
	  • Frontal
	  • Transverse
	• Range of motion
	  • Full
	  • Partial
	  • End-range
	• Multisensory
	  • Half foam roll
	  • Airex pad
	  • Dyna Disc
	• Type of resistance
	  • Body weight
	  • Dumbbells
	  • Tubing
	  • Cable
	• Body position
	  • Two-leg/Stable
	  • Single-leg/Stable
	  • Two-legs/Unstable
	  • Single-leg/Unstable
	• Speed of motion
	• Duration
	• Frequency
	• Amount of feedback

incorporating balance training into a comprehensive, multicomponent training program of flexibility, core, plyometrics, SAQ, resistance, and cardiorespiratory training (18,23,76).

The main objective of balance training is to continually increase your athlete's awareness of their balance threshold or limits of stability by creating controlled instability. Designing an integrated balance training progression requires creating a proprioceptively enriched environment and selecting the appropriate exercises. A balance program should be based on science and be systematic, progressive, and functional (Table 7.1).

Designing an integrated training program requires selecting the appropriate exercises. The exercises must be safe, challenging, stress multiple planes of motion, incorporate a multisensory approach, and be derived from fundamental movement skills that apply directly to an activity (Table 7.1).

When designing an integrated balance training program, the Sports Performance Professional should follow a continuum of function. The exercises should progress from slow to fast, simple to complex, known to unknown, low force to high force, static to dynamic, two arms to one arm, two legs to one leg, stable to unstable, eyes open to eyes closed, and most importantly quality before quantity (Table 7.1).

A balance training program can also be progressed by adding external resistance. External resistance comes from many forms including tubing, dumbbells, medicine balls, power balls, cobra belt, Bodyblade, and other forms of external resistance. Proprioception should be the key to progression and external resistance is added as each movement is mastered appropriately (Table 7.1).

BALANCE TRAINING PROGRAM

NASM has designed a systematic, progressive, and integrated balance training program utilizing the three levels of the Optimum Performance Training™ (OPT™) model (see Fig. 7.4).

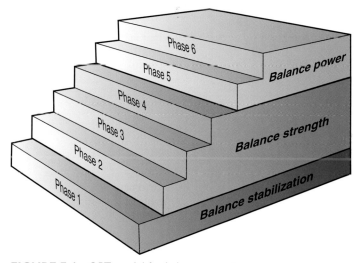

FIGURE 7.4 OPT model for balance exercises.

TIME OUT
Proprioceptive Progression Safety

The HMS is a neurological sponge that absorbs all sensory input, enabling it to learn how to adapt to the imposed demands. This demonstrates the importance of beginning an athlete with proprioceptively enriched environments, as seen in the Stabilization stage of the OPT™ model. By placing an athlete in environments that challenge stabilization requirements at the onset of their training program, you feed their nervous system appropriate stimuli to help ensure proper development and progression. However, it must be emphasized that the extent of the proprioceptive challenge to an athlete must be consistent with their ability level and progress systematically; otherwise, you perpetuate synergistic dominance and compensation that can lead to injury.

Example Balance Exercises

BALANCE STABILIZATION EXERCISES

Balance Stabilization Exercises

Balance exercises that involve little joint motion of the balance leg.

Little joint motion is involved in balance stabilization training. Exercises are designed to improve reflexive joint stabilization contractions to improve joint stability. Isometric contractions lead to static compression of the articular receptors, providing reflexive joint stabilization. Self-generated perturbations increase the interdependence between the receptors to create appropriate equilibrium reactions. This process assists in the sensitization of the muscle spindle, improving neuromuscular efficiency (Figs. 7.5 through 7.7).

FIGURE 7.5   Single-leg balance progression. (**A**) Floor. (**B**) Arm motion. (**C**) Leg motion. (**D**) Arm and leg motion. (*continued*)

E

F

FIGURE 7.7   (*Continued*) (**E**) Lift and chop. (**F**) Throw and catch.

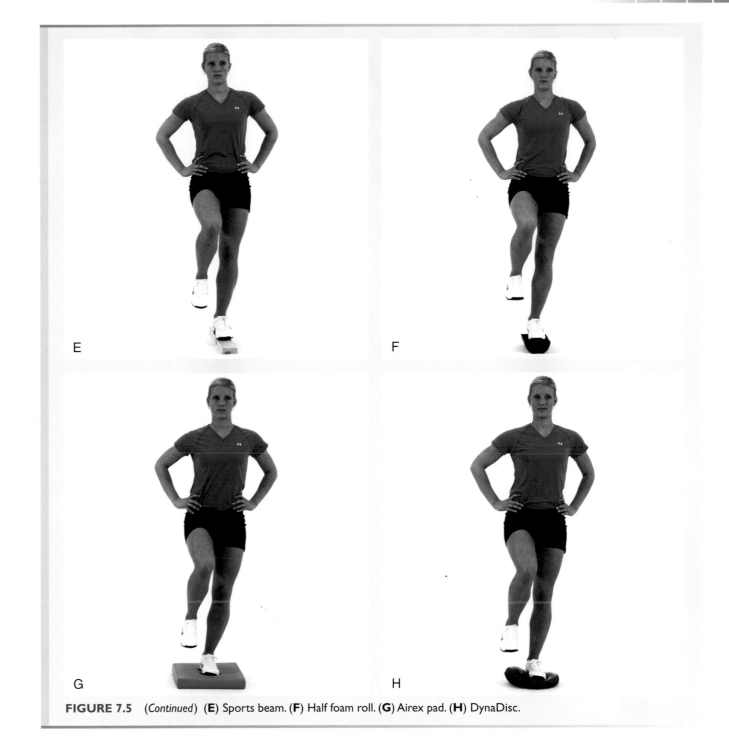

E

F

G

H

FIGURE 7.5   (*Continued*) (**E**) Sports beam. (**F**) Half foam roll. (**G**) Airex pad. (**H**) DynaDisc.

FIGURE 7.6 Single-leg balance reach progression. (**A**) Sagittal plane. (**B**) Frontal plane. (**C**) Transverse plane.

FIGURE 7.7 Single-leg balance with dynamic movement progression. (**A**) Pushing movement. (**B**) Pressing movement. (**C**) Pulling movement. (**D**) Rotation movement. (*continued*)

BALANCE STRENGTH EXERCISES

Balance Strength Exercises

Balance exercises involving eccentric and concentric movement of the balancing leg through a full range of motion.

In balance strength training, exercises become more dynamic, involving eccentric and concentric movement of the balancing leg through a full range of motion. These exercises are designed to improve the neuromuscular efficiency of the human movement system. Movements require dynamic control in the midrange of motion, with isometric stabilization at the end range of motion. The specificity, speed, and neural demand are progressed in at this level (Fig. 7.8).

FIGURE 7.8 Balance strength progression. (**A**) Single-leg squat. (**B**) Single-leg squat touchdown. (**C**) Single-leg squat touchdown with overhead press. (*continued*)

FIGURE 7.8 (*Continued*) (**D**) Single-leg Romanian deadlift. (**E**) Single-leg Romanian deadlift to overhead press. (**F**) Step-up to balance. (*continued*)

FIGURE 7.8   (*Continued*) (**G**) Step-up balance to overhead press. (**H**) Lunge to balance. (**I**) Lunge to balance to overhead press.

BALANCE POWER EXERCISES

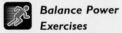 **Balance Power Exercises**

Balance exercises performed by hopping from one foot to another or performing hopping movements on the same foot.

In balance power training, exercises require high levels of eccentric strength, dynamic neuromuscular efficiency, and reactive joint stabilization. Exercises are performed by hopping from one foot to another or performing hopping movements on the same foot (Figs. 7.9 through 7.12) and holding the landing for 3–5 seconds.

FIGURE 7.9 Single-leg hop with stabilization progression. (**A**) Sagittal plane. (**B**) Frontal plane. (**C**) Transverse plane.

FIGURE 7.10 Single-leg box hop-up progression. (**A**) Sagittal plane. (**B**) Frontal plane. (**C**) Transverse plane.

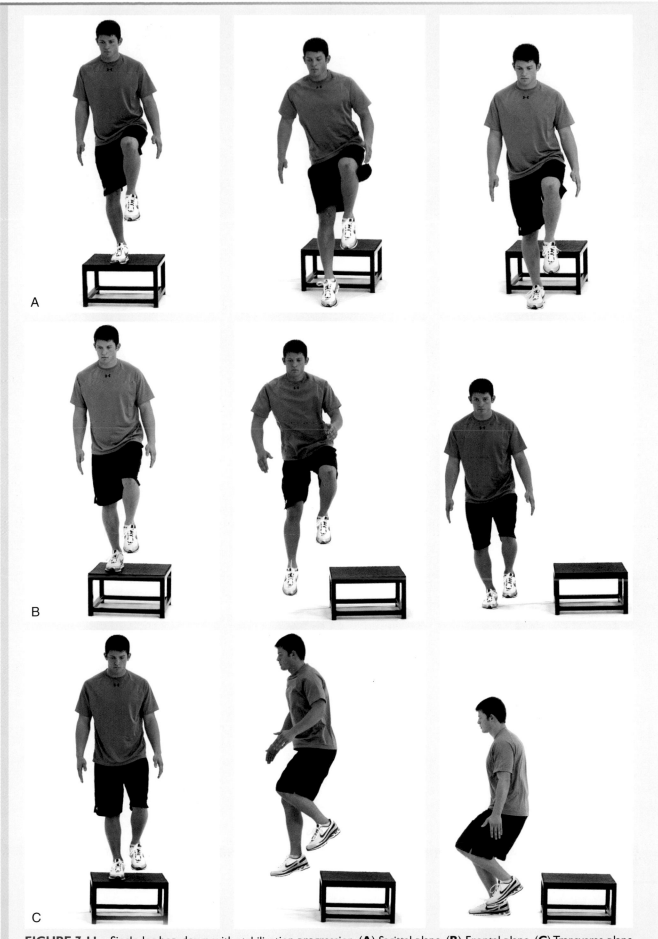

FIGURE 7.11   Single-leg hop-down with stabilization progression. (**A**) Sagittal plane. (**B**) Frontal plane. (**C**) Transverse plane.

FIGURE 7.12 Single-leg proprioceptive plyometric progression. (**A**) Front to back (sagittal). (**B**) Side to side (frontal). (**C**) Diagonal (transverse).

Balance Training Program Design Parameters

Implementing a balance training program requires that Sports Performance Professionals follow a systematic program strategy to ensure safety and effectiveness of the program. For example, if an athlete is in the stabilization level of training (Phase 1), select balance-stabilization exercises. For an athlete in the strength level of training (Phases 2, 3, or 4), select balance-strength exercises. For an athlete in the power level of training (Phase 5 or 6), select balance-power exercises (Table 7.2).

TABLE 7.2

Balance Program Design Parameters

OPT Level	Phase	Example Balance Exercises	Sets/Reps	Tempo	Rest
Stabilization	1	1–4 Balance-Stabilization Single-leg balance Single-leg balance reach Single-leg lift/chop	1–3 sets × 12–20 reps (or single-leg 6–10 ea.)	Slow (4/2/1)	0–90 s
Strength	2,3,4	*0–4 Balance-Strength Single-leg squats Single-leg Romanian deadlift Step-up to balance	2–3 sets × 8–12 reps	Medium (3/2/1–1/1/1)	0–60 s
Power	5,6	**0–2 Balance-Power Single-leg hops Single-leg box hop-ups Single-leg box hop-downs	2–3 sets × 8–12 reps	Controlled (Hold the landing position for 3–5 seconds)	0–60 s

*For some goals in this level of training (hypertrophy and maximal strength), balance exercises may not be required. Although recommended, balance training is optional in these phases of training.
**Because balance exercises are performed in the dynamic flexibility portion of this program and the goal of the program is power, balance training may not be necessary in this phase of training. Although recommended, balance training is optional.

SUMMARY

Balance training represents one of the most important components of an integrated training program. There is ample research demonstrating that poor posture, muscle imbalances, joint dysfunction, and injury decreases proprioception, kinesthesia, limits of stability, postural control, and balance poor which then cycle back to create poor posture, greater imbalances, joint dysfunction, and injury. Therefore, the Sports Performance Professional must understand the concepts of balance training before designing an integrated training program.

REFERENCES

1. Behm DG, Anderson KG. The role of instability with resistance training. *J Strength Cond Res* 2006; 20:716–22.
2. Hasler EM, Herzog W, Leonard TR et al. In vivo knee joint loading and kinematics before and after ACL transection in an animal model. *J Biomech* 1998;31:253–62.
3. Bergmark A. Stability of the lumbar spine. A study in mechanical engineering. *Acta Orthop Scand Suppl* 1989;230:1–54.
4. Lephart SM, Fu FHe. Proprioception and Neuromuscular Control in Joint Stability. Champaign, IL: Human Kinetics; 2000.
5. Guskiewicz K, Perrin D. Effect of orthotics on postural sway following inversion ankle sprain. *J Orthop Sports Phys Ther* 1996;23:326–31.
6. Horak FB, Nashner LM. Central programming of postural movements: adaptation to altered support-surface configurations. *J Neurophysiol* 1986;55:1369–381.
7. Kollmitzer J, Ebenbichler GR, Sabo A et al. Effects of back extensor strength training versus balance training on postural control. *Med Sci Sports Exerc* 2000;32:1770–776.
8. Nardone A, Tarantola J, Galante M et al. Time course of stabilometric changes after a strenuous treadmill exercise. *Arch Phys Med Rehabil* 1998;79:920–24.
9. Grigg P. Peripheral neural mechanisms in proprioception. *J Sport Rehab* 1994;3:2–17.
10. Edgerton VR, Wolf SL, Levendowski DJ et al. Theoretical basis for patterning EMG amplitudes to assess muscle dysfunction. *Med Sci Sports Exerc* 1996;28:744–51.
11. Newmann D. Kinesiology of the Musculoskeletal System: Foundations for Physical Rehabilitation. St. Louis: Mosby; 2002.
12. Sherrington CS. Flexion-reflex of the limb, crossed extension-reflex, and reflex stepping and standing. *J Physiol* 1910;40:28–121.
13. Schutte MJ, Dabezies EJ, Zimny ML et al. Neural anatomy of the human anterior cruciate ligament. *J Bone Joint Surg Am* 1987;69:243–47.
14. Edin BB. Quantitative analysis of static strain sensitivity in human mechanoreceptors from hairy skin. *J Neurophysiol* 1992;67:105–13.
15. Gandevia S, McCloskey D, Burke D. Kinaesthetic signals and muscle contraction. *Trends Neurosci* 1992;15:62–65.
16. Caraffa A, Cerulli G, Projett M et al. Prevention of anterior cruciate ligament injuries in soccer. A prospective controlled study of proprioceptive training. *Knee Surg Sports Traumatol Arthrosc* 1996;4:19–21.
17. Gioftsidou A, Malliou P, Pafis G et al. The effects of soccer training and timing of balance training on balance ability. *Eur J Appl Physiol* 2006;96:659–64.
18. Hewett TE, Myer GD, Ford KR. Reducing knee and anterior cruciate ligament injuries among female athletes: a systematic review of neuromuscular training interventions. *J Knee Surg* 2005;18:82–88.
19. Hewett TE, Zazulak BT, Myer GD et al. A review of electromyographic activation levels, timing differences, and increased anterior cruciate ligament injury incidence in female athletes. *Br J Sports Med* 2005;39:347–50.
20. Kovacs EJ, Birmingham TB, Forwell L et al. Effect of training on postural control in figure skaters: a randomized controlled trial of neuromuscular versus basic off-ice training programs. *Clin J Sport Med* 2004;14:215–24.
21. Mandelbaum BR, Silvers HJ, Wantanabe DS et al. Effectiveness of a neuromuscular and proprioception training program in preventing anterior cruciate ligament injuries in female athletes: a 2-year follow-up. *Am J Sports Med* 2005;33:1003–110.
22. Mykelbust G, Engebretsen L, Braekken IH et al. Prevention of anterior cruciate ligament injuries in female team handball players: a prospective study over three seasons. *Clin J Sport Med* 2003; 13:71–78.
23. Paterno MV, Myer GD, Ford KR et al. Neuromuscular training improves single-limb stability in young female athletes. *J Orthop Sports Phys Ther* 2004;34:305–16.
24. Rozzi SL, Lephart SM, Sterner R et al. Balance training for persons with functionally unstable ankles. *J Orthop Sports Phys Ther* 1999;29:478–86.
25. Sforza C, Grassi GP, Turci M et al. Influence of training on maintenance of equilibrium on a tilting platform. *Percept Mot Skills* 2003;96:127–36.
26. Rowinski MJ. Afferent Neurobiology of the Joint. In Gould JA. Orthopaedic and Sports Physical Therapy. St. Louis, MO: Mosby, 1990.
27. Lephart SM, Pincivero DM, Giraldo JL et al. The role of proprioception in the management and rehabilitation of athletic injuries. *Am J Sports Med* 1997;25:130–37.
28. Johnston RB 3rd, Howard ME, Cawley PW et al. Effect of lower extremity muscular fatigue on motor control performance. *Med Sci Sports Exerc* 1998;30:1703–707.
29. Wilkerson G, Nitz A. Dynamic ankle stability: mechanical and neuromuscular interrelationships. *J Sport Rehab* 1994;3:43–57.
30. Schaible H, Schmidt RF. Activation of groups III and IV sensory units in medial articular nerve by local mechanical stimulation of the knee joint. *J Neurophysiol* 1983;49:35–44.
31. Schaible HG, Schmidt RF. Responses of fine medial articular nerve afferents to passive movements of knee joint. *J Neurophysiol* 1983;49:1118–126.
32. Halata Z, Haus J. The ultrastructure of sensory nerve endings in human anterior cruciate ligament. *Anat Embryol (Berl)* 1989;179:415–21.
33. Johansson H. Role of knee ligaments in proprioception and regulation of muscle stiffness. *J Electromyogr Kinesiol* 1991;1:158–79.

34. Johansson H, Sjolander P, Sojka P. A sensory role for the cruciate ligaments. *Clin Orthop Relat Res* 1991;268:161–78.

35. Hodges PW, Richardson CA. Inefficient muscular stabilization of the lumbar spine associated with low back pain. A motor control evaluation of transversus abdominis. *Spine* 1996;21:2640–650.

36. Mizuno Y, Shindo M, Kuno S et al. Postural control responses sitting on unstable board during visual stimulation. *Acta Astronaut* 2001;49:131–36.

37. Kornecki, S, Kebel A, Siemieński A. Muscular co-operation during joint stabilisation, as reflected by EMG. *Eur J Appl Physiol* 2001;84:453–61.

38. Slijper H, Latash M. The effects of instability and additional hand support on anticipatory postural adjustments in leg, trunk, and arm muscles during standing. *Exp Brain Res* 2000;135:81–93.

39. Hodges PW, Richardson CA. Contraction of the abdominal muscles associated with movement of the lower limb. *Phys Ther* 1997;77:132–42; discussion 42-4.

40. Richardson CA, Jull GA, Hodges PW et al. Therapeutic exercise for spinal segment stabilization in low back pain: Scientific basis and clinical approach. London: Churchill Livingstone; 1999.

41. Andersen JC. Stretching before and after exercise: effect on muscle soreness and injury risk. *J Athl Train* 2005;40:218–20.

42. Bahr R, Bahr IA. Incidence of acute volleyball injuries: a prospective cohort study of injury mechanisms and risk factors. *Scand J Med Sci Sports* 1997;7:166–71.

43. Bahr R, Lian O, Bahr IA. A twofold reduction in the incidence of acute ankle sprains in volleyball after the introduction of an injury prevention program: a prospective cohort study. *Scand J Med Sci Sports* 1997;7:172–77.

44. Borsa PA, Lephart SM, Kocher MS et al. Functional assessment and rehabilitation of shoulder proprioception for glenohumeral instability. *J Sports Rehab* 1994;3:84–104.

45. Cholewicki J, Greene HS, Polzhofer GK et al. Neuromuscular function in athletes following recovery from a recent acute low back injury. *J Orthop Sports Phys Ther* 2002;32:568–75.

46. Cholewicki J, Silfies SP, Shah RA et al. Delayed trunk muscle reflex responses increase the risk of low back injuries. *Spine* 2005;30:2614–620.

47. Cholewicki J, VanVliet JJ. Relative contribution of trunk muscles to the stability of the lumbar spine during isometric exertions. *Clin Biomech Bristol* 2002;17:99–105.

48. Ebenbichler GR, Oddsson LI, Kollmitzer J et al. Sensory-motor control of the lower back: implications for rehabilitation. *Med Sci Sports Exerc* 2001;33:1889–898.

49. Hewett TE, Lindenfeld TN, Riccobene JV et al. The effect of neuromuscular training on the incidence of knee injury in female athletes. A prospective study. *Am J Sports Med* 1999;27:699–706.

50. Hodges P, Richardson C, Jull G. Evaluation of the relationship between laboratory and clinical tests of transversus abdominis function. *Physiother Res Int* 1996;1:30–40.

51. O'Sullivan P, Twomey L, Allison G et al. Altered patterns of abdominal muscle activation in patients with chronic low back pain. *Aust J Physiother* 1997;43:91–98.

52. Olsen OE, Mykelbust G, Engebretsen L et al. Exercises to prevent lower limb injuries in youth sports: cluster randomised controlled trial. *Br J Sports Med* 2005;330:449.

53. Padua DA, Marshall SW, Evidence supporting ACL-injury-prevention exercise programs: a review of the literature. *Athl Ther Today* 2006;11:11–23.

54. Verhagen AP, de Vet HC, de Bie RA et al. The Delphi list: a criteria list for quality assessment of randomized clinical trials for conducting systematic reviews developed by Delphi consensus. *J Clin Epidemiol* 1998;51:1235–241.

55. Chaudhari AM, Andriacchi TP. The mechanical consequences of dynamic frontal plane limb alignment for non-contact ACL injury. *J Biomech* 2006;39:330–38.

56. Denegar CR, Hertel J, Fonseca J. The effect of lateral ankle sprain on dorsiflexion range of motion, posterior talar glide, and joint laxity. *J Orthop Sports Phys Ther* 2002;32:166–73.

57. Fredericson M, Cookingham CL, Chaudhari AM et al. Hip abductor weakness in distance runners with iliotibial band syndrome. *Clin J Sport Med* 2000;10:169–75.

58. Friel K, McLean N, Myers C et al. Ipsilateral hip abductor weakness after inversion ankle sprain. *J Athl Train* 2006;41:74–78.

59. Hollman JH, Brey RH, Bang TJ et al. Does walking in a virtual environment induce unstable gait? An examination of vertical ground reaction forces. *Gait Posture* 2007;26:289–94.

60. Hossain M, Nokes LD. A model of dynamic sacro-iliac joint instability from malrecruitment of gluteus maximus and biceps femoris muscles resulting in low back pain. *Med Hypotheses* 2005;65:278–81.

61. Ireland ML, Willson JD, Ballantyne BT et al. Hip strength in females with and without patellofemoral pain. *J Orthop Sports Phys Ther* 2003;33:671–76.

62. Khamis S, Yizhar Z. Effect of feet hyperpronation on pelvic alignment in a standing position. *Gait Posture* 2007;25:127–34.

63. Leetun DT, Ireland ML, Willson JD et al. Core stability measures as risk factors for lower extremity injury in athletes. *Med Sci Sports Exerc* 2004;36:926–34.

64. O'Sullivan PB, Phyty GD, Twomey LT et al. Evaluation of specific stabilizing exercise in the treatment of chronic low back pain with radiologic diagnosis of spondylolysis or spondylolisthesis. *Spine* 1997;22:2959–967.

65. Stodden DF, Fleisig GS, McLean SP et al. Relationship of biomechanical factors to baseball pitching velocity: within pitcher variation. *J Appl Biomech* 2005;21:44–56.

66. Zazulak BT, Hewett TE, Reeves NP et al. Deficits in neuromuscular control of the trunk predict knee injury risk: a prospective biomechanical-epidemiologic study. *Am J Sports Med* 2007;35:1123–130.

67. Zazulak BT, Hewett TE, Reeves NP et al. The effects of core proprioception on knee injury: a prospective biomechanical-epidemiological study. *Am J Sports Med* 2007;35:368–73.

68. Falla DL, Hess S, Richardson C. Evaluation of shoulder internal rotator muscle strength in baseball players with physical signs of glenohumeral joint instability. *Br J Sports Med* 2003;37:430–32.

69. Hungerford BP, Gilleard WP, Hodges PP. Evidence of altered lumbopelvic muscle recruitment in the presence of sacroiliac joint pain. *Spine* 2003;28:593–600.

70. Arnheim DD, Prentice WE. Principles of athletic training, 10th ed. Boston, MA: McGraw-Hill; 2000.

71. Zachazewski JE, Magee DJ, Quillen WS. Athletic Injuries and Rehabilitation. Philadelphia: WB Saunders; 1996.

72. Emery CA, Cassidy JD, Klassen TP et al. Effectiveness of a home-based balance-training program in reducing sports-related injuries among healthy adolescents: a cluster randomized controlled trial. *CMAJ* 2005;172:749–54.

73. Junge A, Rosch D, Peterson L et al. Prevention of soccer injuries: a prospective intervention study in youth amateur players. *Am J Sports Med* 2002;30:652–59.

74. Soderman K, Werner S, Pietila T et al. Balance board training: prevention of traumatic injuries of the lower extremities in female soccer players? A prospective randomized intervention study. *Knee Surg Sports Traumatol Arthroscopy* 2000;8:356–63.

75. Wedderkopp N, Kaltoft M, Holm R et al. Comparison of two intervention programmes in young female players in European handball—with and without ankle disc. *Scand J Med Sci Sports* 2003;13:371–75.

76. Caraffa A, Cerulli G, Projetti M et al. Prevention of anterior cruciate ligament injuries in soccer. A prospective controlled study of proprioceptive training. *Knee Surg Sports Traumatol Arthrosc* 1996;4:19–21.

CHAPTER 8

Plyometric Training Concepts for Performance Enhancement

UPON COMPLETION OF THIS CHAPTER, YOU WILL BE ABLE TO:

Describe plyometric training and its purpose for performance enhancement and injury prevention.

Rationalize the importance of plyometric training.

Design a plyometric training program for athletes in any level of training.

Introduction

The ability of muscles to exert maximal force output in a minimal amount of time (also known as rate of force production) enhances performance during functional activities. All else being equal, success in most functional activities depends on the speed at which muscular force is generated. Power output and reactive neuromuscular control represents a component of function. Power and reactive neuromuscular control are perhaps the best measures of success in activities that require rapid force production. Plyometric training, also called reactive training, makes use of the stretch-shortening cycle to produce maximum force in the shortest amount of time and to enhance neuromuscular control efficiency, rate of force production, and reduce neuromuscular inhibition (1–20).

Plyometric Training Concepts

WHAT IS PLYOMETRIC TRAINING?

 Plyometric Training
Defined as a quick, powerful movement involving an eccentric contraction, followed immediately by an explosive concentric contraction.

Plyometric training is defined as a quick, powerful movement involving an eccentric contraction, followed immediately by an explosive concentric contraction (21–23). This is accomplished through the stretch-shortening cycle or an eccentric-concentric coupling phase. The eccentric-concentric coupling phase is also referred to as the integrated performance paradigm (Fig. 8.1), which states that in order to move with precision, forces must be loaded (eccentrically), stabilized (isometrically), and then unloaded/accelerated (concentrically). Plyometric exercise stimulates the body's proprioceptive and elastic properties to generate maximum force output in a minimum amount of time (24).

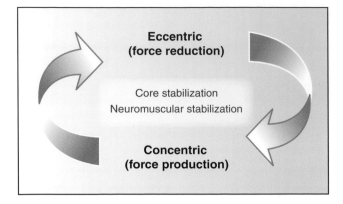

FIGURE 8.1 Integrated Performance Paradigm™.

Plyometric training is an effective mode of training as it enhances motor learning and neuromuscular efficiency by promoting the excitability, sensitivity, and reactivity of the neuromuscular system to increase the rate of force production (power), motor-unit recruitment, firing frequency (rate coding), and synchronization.

Muscles produce the necessary force to change the direction of an object's center of mass (24). All movement patterns that occur during functional activities involve a series of repetitive stretch-shortening cycles. The neuromuscular system must react quickly and efficiently following an eccentric muscle action to produce a concentric contraction and impart the necessary force (or acceleration) in the appropriate direction. Therefore, specific functional exercises that emphasize a rapid change in direction must be utilized to prepare each athlete for the functional demands of a specific activity.

Plyometric training provides the opportunity to train specific movement patterns in a biomechanically correct manner at a more functionally appropriate speed. This provides functional strengthening of the muscle, tendon, and ligaments specific to the demands of everyday activities and sports. The ultimate goal of plyometric training is to improve the reaction time of the muscle action spectrum (eccentric deceleration, isometric stabilization, and concentric acceleration).

The speed of muscular exertion is limited by neuromuscular coordination. This means that the body will move most effectively and efficiently within a range of speed that the nervous system has been programmed to allow. Plyometric training improves both neuromuscular efficiency and the range of speeds set by the central nervous system. Optimum reactive performance of any activity depends on the speed at which muscular forces can be generated (19).

TIME OUT
Evidence-Based Research to Support the Use of Reactive Training for Injury Prevention and Performance Enhancement

- In 2004, Chimera et al., in a pre-post test control group design with 20 healthy Division I female athletes, found that a 6-week plyometric training program improved hip abductor/adductor coactivation ratios to help control varus/valgus moments at the knee during landing (1).

- In 2004, Wilkerson et al., in a quasi-experimental design with 19 female basketball players, demonstrated that a 6-week plyometric training program improved hamstring-quadricep ratios, which has been shown to enhance dynamic knee stability during the eccentric deceleration phase of landing (2).

- In 2003, Luebbers et al., in a randomized controlled trial with 19 subjects demonstrated that a 4-week and 7-week plyometric training program enhanced anaerobic power and vertical jump height (3).

- In 1996, Hewett et al., in a prospective study, demonstrated decreased peak landing forces, enhanced muscle-balance ratio both with the quadriceps and hamstring complex, and decreased rate of ACL injuries in female soccer, basketball, and volleyball players that incorporated reactive neuromuscular training into their program (4).

1. Chimera NJ, Swanik CB, Straub SJ. Effects of plyometric training on muscle-activation strategies and performance in female athletes. *J Athl Train* 2004;39(1):24–31.
2. Wilkerson GB, Colston MA, Short Ni, Neal KL. Neuromuscular changes in female collegiate athletes resulting from a plyometric jump training program. *J Athl Train* 2004;39(1):17–23.
3. Luebbers PE, Potteiger JA, Hulver MW et al. Effects of plyometric training and recovery on vertical jump performance and anaerobic power. *J Strength Cond Res* 2003;17(4):704–09.
4. Hewett TE, Stroupe AL, Nance TA et al. Plyometric training in female athletes. Decreased impact forces and increased hamstring torques. *Am J Sports Med* 1996;24(6):765–73.

Eccentric Phase of Plyometrics

This phase increases muscle spindle activity by pre-stretching the muscle prior to activation.

Amortization Phase of Plyometrics

The time between the end of the eccentric contraction (the loading or deceleration phase) and the initiation of the concentric contraction (the unloading or force production phase).

Concentric Phase of Plyometrics

Occurs immediately after the amortization phase and involves a concentric contraction.

THREE PHASES OF PLYOMETRIC EXERCISE

There are three distinct phases involved in plyometric training including the eccentric, or loading, phase; the amortization, or transition, phase; and the concentric, or unloading, phase (25).

THE ECCENTRIC PHASE

The first stage of a plyometric movement can be classified as the eccentric phase, but it has also been called the deceleration, loading, yielding, countermovement, or cocking phase (26). This phase increases muscle spindle activity by pre-stretching the muscle prior to activation (27). Potential energy is stored in the elastic components of the muscle during this loading phase. A slower eccentric phase prevents taking optimum advantage of the myotatic stretch reflex (22,28).

THE AMORTIZATION PHASE

This phase involves dynamic stabilization and is the time between the end of the eccentric contraction (the loading or deceleration phase) and the initiation of the concentric contraction (the unloading or force production phase) (29). The amortization phase, sometimes referred to as the transition phase, is also referred to as the electromechanical delay between the eccentric and concentric contraction during which the muscle must switch from overcoming force to imparting force in the intended direction (30). A prolonged amortization phase results in less-than-optimum neuromuscular efficiency from a loss of elastic potential energy (31). A rapid switch from an eccentric contraction to a concentric contraction leads to a more powerful response (29,30).

THE CONCENTRIC PHASE

The concentric phase (or unloading phase) occurs immediately after the amortization phase and involves a concentric contraction (29,30,32), resulting in enhanced muscular performance following the eccentric phase of muscle contraction. This occurs secondary to enhanced summation and reutilization of elastic potential energy, muscle potentiation, and contribution of the myotatic stretch reflex (33–35).

PHYSIOLOGICAL PRINCIPLES OF PLYOMETRIC TRAINING

Plyometric training utilizes the elastic and proprioceptive properties of a muscle to generate maximum force production (29,30) by stimulating mechanoreceptors to facilitate an increase in muscle recruitment in a minimal amount of time. Muscle spindles and Golgi tendon organs (GTOs) provide the proprioceptive basis for plyometric training. The central nervous system then uses this sensory information to influence muscle tone, motor execution, and kinesthetic awareness (26). Stimulation of these receptors can cause facilitation, inhibition, and modulation of both agonist and antagonist muscle activity. This enhances neuromuscular efficiency and functional strength (Fig. 8.2) (36–40).

THE ELASTIC PROPERTIES OF MUSCLE

The concept of plyometrics is based on the three-component model of muscle (Fig. 8.3). Muscle is modeled with a contractile element and two elastic elements that are named according to their relationship to the contractile element—one in line with (the series elastic element) and one in parallel (the parallel elastic element). When a muscle contracts, tension is not directly transmitted to the ends of the tendon and the load is not overcome, leading to movement. This would only happen if the connection between the contractile element and its insertion were rigid and inelastic. In reality, the contractile element develops tension, stretching the series elastic element; the degree of stretch is dependent on the load to be moved. After sufficient tension has been generated, the tension at the ends of the muscle is sufficient to overcome the load and the load is moved. When a load is applied to a joint (eccentric phase), the elastic elements stretch and store potential energy (amortization phase) prior to the contractile element contracting (concentric phase).

An eccentric contraction immediately preceding a concentric contraction significantly increases the force generated concentrically as a result of the storage of elastic potential energy (21). During the loading of the muscle, the load is transferred to the series elastic components and stored as elastic potential energy. The elastic elements then contribute to the overall force production by converting the stored elastic potential energy to kinetic energy, which enhances the contraction (21,41). The muscle's ability to use the stored elastic potential energy is affected by the variables of time, magnitude of stretch, and velocity of stretch. Increased force generation during the concentric contraction is most effective when the preceding eccentric contraction is of short range and is performed without delay (31).

A simple example of the use of the energy stored in the elastic element is the basic vertical, or countermovement, jump. The initial squat (the countermovement) is the eccentric phase that stretches the elastic elements and stores elastic energy (amortization phase). When the jump is performed (the concentric phase), the stored energy is "added" to the tension produced leading to a higher jump. The amount of stored energy used is inversely proportional to the time spent

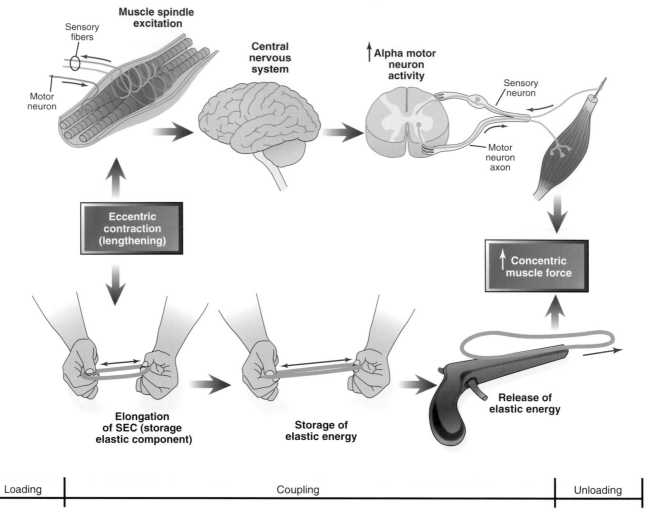

Muscle spindle excitation

Sensory fibers

Motor neuron

Central nervous system

↑ **Alpha motor neuron activity**

Sensory neuron

Motor neuron axon

↑ **Concentric muscle force**

Eccentric contraction (lengthening)

Elongation of SEC (storage elastic component)

Storage of elastic energy

Release of elastic energy

| Loading | Coupling | Unloading |

FIGURE 8.2   Physiological principles of plyometric training.

in the amortization phase. When doing a vertical jump, the longer one waits at the end of the countermovement before performing the jump, the lower the eventual jump height due to the inability to recover the stored elastic energy.

The improved muscular performance that occurs with the pre-stretch in a muscle is the result of the combined effects of both the storage of elastic potential energy and the proprioceptive properties of the muscle. The percentage that each component contributes is unknown at this time, but the degree of muscular performance, as stated earlier, is dependent upon the time in transition from the eccentric to the concentric contraction. Training that enhances neuromuscular efficiency decreases the time between the eccentric and concentric contraction, thereby, improving performance. This can be accomplished through integrated training.

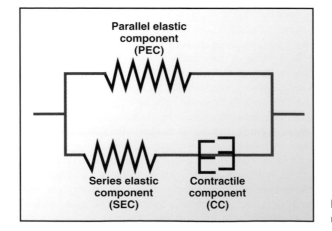

Parallel elastic component (PEC)

Series elastic component (SEC)

Contractile component (CC)

FIGURE 8.3   Elastic properties of muscle.

PROPOSED MECHANISM BY WHICH PLYOMETRIC TRAINING ENHANCES PERFORMANCE

There are three proposed mechanisms by which plyometric training improves performance: enhanced muscle spindle activity, desensitization of the GTO, and enhanced intramuscular and intermuscular neuromuscular efficiency.

ENHANCED MUSCLE SPINDLE ACTIVITY

The speed of a muscular contraction is regulated by the neuromuscular system. The human movement system will only move within a set speed range regardless of how strong a muscle is. The faster the eccentric loading, the greater the concentric force production (26,31). For example, the quadriceps are loaded more rapidly when dropping from a 1-m box versus a 0.25-m box.

DESENSITIZATION OF THE GOLGI TENDON ORGAN

Desensitizing the GTO increases the stimulation threshold for muscular inhibition. This promotes increased force production with a greater load applied to the musculoskeletal system (29,30).

ENHANCED NEUROMUSCULAR EFFICIENCY

Plyometric training may promote better neuromuscular control of the contracting agonists and synergists, thus enabling the central nervous system to become more reflexive. These neural adaptations lead to enhanced neuromuscular efficiency even in the absence of morphological adaptations, such as muscle hypertrophy. Exploiting the stretch reflex, inhibiting the GTO, and enhancing the ability of the nervous system to react with maximum speed to the lengthening muscle optimizes the force produced by the concentric contraction.

In the end, plyometric training has wide-ranging effects beyond power output. There is moderate evidence that when plyometric exercises are incorporated into an integrated training program, there are documented improvements in jumping ability, running economy, power output, and rate of force development, but not strength. When used in an isolated training program, there is moderate evidence that plyometrics have little positive benefits on performance. There is no evidence that youth athletes, when properly instructed and following directions, cannot use plyometrics in an integrated training program or that plyometrics should be reserved solely for athletes (8). A common fallacy when considering plyometric training is that plyometrics are only useful in training for jumping performance when there are randomized trials showing significant reductions in injury rates (2,42–44).

TIME OUT
Importance of Proper Stability with Plyometric Training

Ground reaction force places tremendous amounts of stress to one's structure. Not only do we have gravity pushing us downward, but we also have ground reaction force pushing from below back up through our body. This is like being placed in a trash compactor with forces coming from above and below. As the speed and amplitude of movement increases, so does the ground reaction force (1). While jumping, ground reaction force can be 4–11 times one's body weight (2–4). Inadequate stability under these types of forces places enormous amounts of stress to the athlete's structure, increasing the risk of injury. Having ample amounts of stability is crucial to the effectiveness and safety of plyometric training.

---

1. Voloshin A. The influence of walking speed on dynamic loading on the human musculoskeletal system. *Med Sci Sports Exerc* 2000;32:1156–159.
2. Witzke KA, Snow CM. Effects of plyometric jumping on bone mass in adolescent girls. *Med Sci Sports Exerc* 2000;32:1051–057.
3. Dufek JS, Bates BT. Dynamic performance assessment of selected sport, shoes on impact forces. *Med Sci Sports Exerc* 1991;23:1062–67.
4. McNitt-Gray JL. Kinematics and impulse characteristics of drop landings from three heights. *Int J Sports Biomech* 1991;7:201–24.

PLYOMETRIC TRAINING PROGRAM

A systematic and progressive plyometric training program is a vital component of any integrated training program. As plyometric training is one of the more advanced training tools, the athlete needs proper levels of flexibility, core strength, and balance before progressing into plyometric training. Sports Performance Professionals must follow very specific program guidelines, proper exercise selection criteria, and detailed program variables for the best outcome and lowest risk of injury (Table 8.1).

TABLE 8.1	
Plyometric Training Parameters	
Exercise Selection	**Variables**

• Safe
• Done with supportive shoes
• Performed on a proper training surface
  • Grass field
  • Basketball court
  • Tartan track surface
  • Rubber track surface
• Performed with proper supervision
• Progressive
  • Easy to hard
  • Simple to complex
  • Known to unknown
  • Stable to unstable
  • Body weight to loaded
• Activity-specific
	• Plane of motion
	  • Sagittal
	  • Frontal
	  • Transverse
	• Range of motion
	  • Full
	  • Partial
	• Type of resistance
	  • Medicine ball
	  • Power ball
	• Type of implements
	  • Tape
	  • Cones
	  • Boxes
	• Muscle action
	  • Eccentric
	  • Isometric
	  • Concentric
	• Speed of motion
	• Duration
	• Frequency
	• Amplitude of movement

As with all training programs, overload will need to be considered with plyometrics. Increasing the stretch load increases intensity. This can be accomplished by using body weight over a greater jump distance or drop height. Progressing from two-legged to one-legged jumps also increases intensity. As the athlete progresses, the duration of the amortization phase should be as brief as possible. The number of foot contacts monitors training volume; the more contacts, the greater the training volume. As always, training volume is inversely related to training intensity. Potach and Chu (45) offer the following suggestions for a single training session: low-intensity training = 400-foot contacts; moderate-intensity training = 350-foot contacts; high-intensity training = 300-foot contacts; very-high-intensity training = 200-foot contacts. Experience should also be considered when prescribing plyometrics. Athletes with minimal experience using plyometrics should keep the ground contacts to less than 100 maximal efforts per session, whereas those with considerable experience could have as many as 120–140 maximal effort ground contacts per session (45).

The Optimum Performance Training™ (OPT™) model provides a systematic, progressive, and integrated plyometric training program to safely and effectively progress an athlete through this portion of their program (see Fig. 8.4).

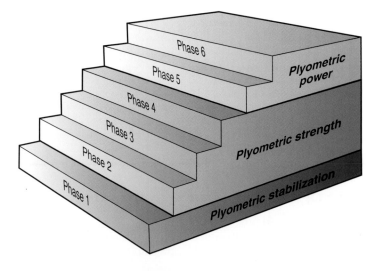

FIGURE 8.4 OPT™ model for plyometric exercises.

Example Plyometric Exercises

PLYOMETRIC STABILIZATION EXERCISES

Plyometric Stabilization Exercises

Plyometric exercises designed to establish optimum landing mechanics, postural alignment, and reactive neuromuscular efficiency.

Exercises in the stabilization level of plyometric training involve little joint motion. They are designed to establish optimum landing mechanics, postural alignment, and reactive neuromuscular efficiency. Upon landing, the athlete should hold the landing position (or stabilize) for 3–5 seconds before repeating (Figs. 8.5–8.7).

FIGURE 8.5   Box jump-up with stabilization progression. (**A**) Sagittal plane. (**B**) Frontal plane. (*continued*)

FIGURE 8.5 (*Continued*) (**C**) Transverse plane.

FIGURE 8.6 Box jump-down with stabilization progression. (**A**) Sagittal plane. (**B**) Frontal plane. (*continued*)

FIGURE 8.6 (*Continued*) (**C**) Transverse plane.

FIGURE 8.7 Squat jump with stabilization progression. (**A**) Squat jump with stabilization. (**B**) Sagittal plane jump with stabilization. (*continued*)

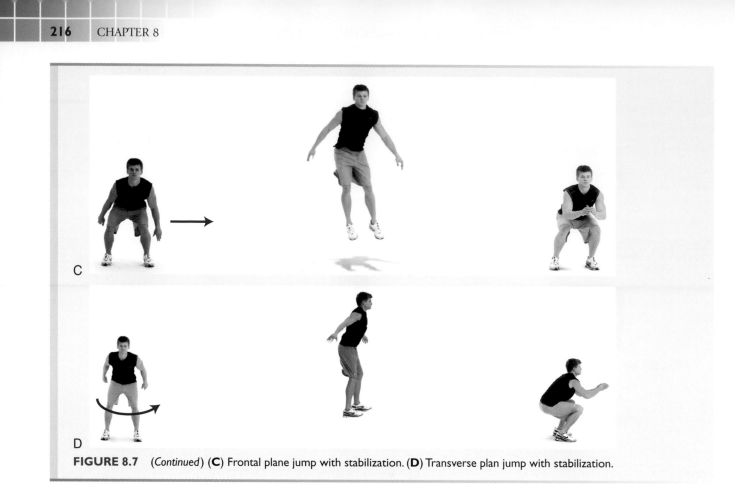

FIGURE 8.7 (*Continued*) (**C**) Frontal plane jump with stabilization. (**D**) Transverse plan jump with stabilization.

PLYOMETRIC-STRENGTH EXERCISES

Plyometric-Strength Exercises

Plyometric exercises designed to improve dynamic joint stabilization, eccentric strength, rate of force production, and neuromuscular efficiency of the entire human movement system. These exercises are performed in a more repetitive fashion by spending a shorter amount of time on the ground.

In the strength level of plyometric training, exercises are more dynamic, requiring eccentric and concentric movement throughout the full range of motion. The specificity, speed, and neural demand are also progressed within this level. Exercises in this level are designed to improve dynamic joint stabilization, eccentric strength, rate of force production, and neuromuscular efficiency of the entire human movement system. These exercises are performed in a more repetitive fashion by spending a shorter amount of time on the ground. Exercises in this level can also be performed in all three planes of motion (Fig. 8.8).

FIGURE 8.8   Plyometric-strength exercises. (**A**) Repeat squat jumps (**B**) Lunge jumps. (*continued*)

FIGURE 8.8   (*Continued*) (**C**) Power step-ups. (**D**) Butt kicks.

FIGURE 8.8   (*Continued*) (**E**) Tuck jumps. (**F**) Repeat box jumps.

These exercises can be varied and made more intense by adding any one of a variety of tools to increase external resistance such as a weight vest, tubing, medicine ball, or a Bodyblade.

PLYOMETRIC POWER EXERCISES

 Plyometric Power Exercises

Plyometric exercises are performed as fast and as explosively as possible.

In the power level of plyometric training, exercises involve the entire spectrum of muscle actions and contraction velocities important for integrated, functional movement. These exercises are designed to improve the rate of force production, eccentric strength, reactive strength, reactive joint stabilization, dynamic neuromuscular efficiency, and optimum force production. These exercises are performed as fast and as explosively as possible. Exercises in this level can also be performed in all three planes of motion (Figs. 8.9 through 8.11).

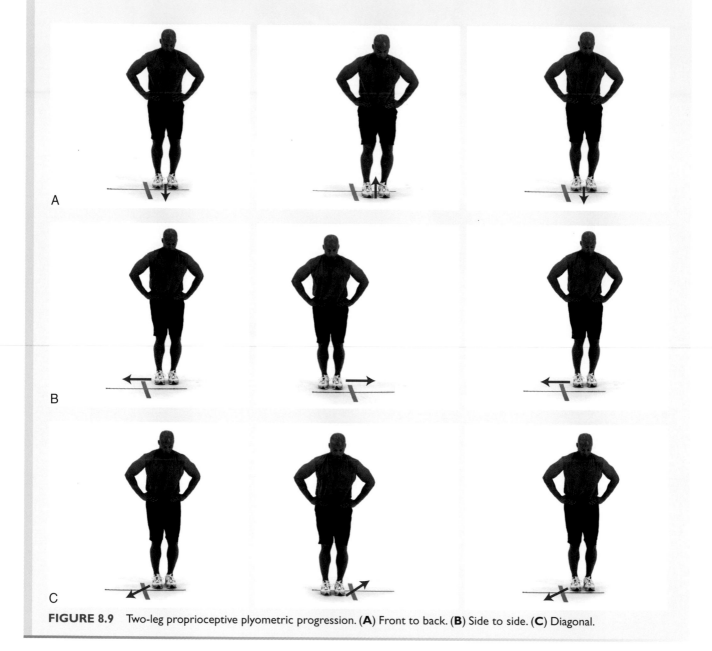

FIGURE 8.9   Two-leg proprioceptive plyometric progression. (**A**) Front to back. (**B**) Side to side. (**C**) Diagonal.

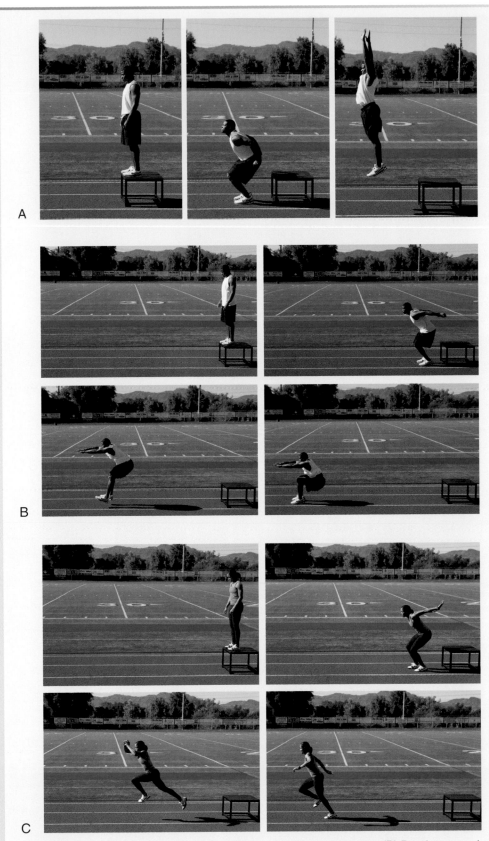

FIGURE 8.10 Depth jump progression. (**A**) Depth jump to squat jump. (**B**) Depth jump to long jump. (**C**) Depth jump to bounding. (*continued*)

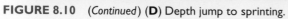

FIGURE 8.10 (*Continued*) (**D**) Depth jump to sprinting.

FIGURE 8.11 Obstacle jump progression. (**A**) Hurdle jump to squat jump. (**B**) Hurdle jump to long jump. (*continued*)

FIGURE 8.11 (*Continued*) (**C**) Hurdle jump to bounding. (**D**) Hurdle jump to sprinting.

Plyometric Training Program Design Parameters

Implementing a plyometric training program requires that Sports Performance Professionals follow a systematic program strategy to ensure safety and effectiveness of the program. For example, if an athlete is in the stabilization level of training (Phase 1), select plyometric-stabilization exercises. For an athlete in the strength level of training (Phase 2, 3, or 4), select plyometric-strength exercises. For an athlete in the power level of training (Phase 5 or 6), select plyometric-power exercises (Table 8.2).

TABLE 8.2

Plyometric Program Design Parameters

OPT Level	Phase	Example Plyometric Exercises	Sets/Reps	Tempo	Rest
Stabilization	1	*0–2 Plyometric Stabilization Squat jump with stab. Box jump-up with stab.	1–3 sets × 5–8 reps	Controlled (hold the landing position for 3–5 seconds)	0–90 s
Strength	2,3,4	**0–4 Plyometric-Strength Power step-ups Lunge jumps	2–3 sets × 8–10 reps	Repeating	0–60 s
Power	5,6	***0–2 Plyometric-Power Depth jump to bounding Hurdle jump to sprinting	2–3 sets × 8–12 reps	As fast as possible	0–60 s

*Plyometric exercises may not be appropriate for an athlete in this phase of training if they do not possess the appropriate amount of core strength and balance capabilities.

**Due to the goal of certain phases in this level (hypertrophy and maximal strength), plyometric training may not be necessary to do.

***Because one is performing plyometric exercises in the resistance training portion of this phase of training, separate plyometric exercises may not be necessary to perform.

SUMMARY

Plyometric training is an important component of all integrated performance training programs. All sporting activities require efficient use of the integrated performance paradigm. Therefore, all performance programs should include plyometric training to enhance neuromuscular efficiency and prevent injury. The human movement system responds to the imposed demands of training. Less than optimum results will occur if the training program does not systematically and progressively challenge the neuromuscular system. Following a progressive plyometric training program as demonstrated through the OPT™ model will ensure the athlete enhances their performance while decreasing their risk of injury.

REFERENCES

1. Chimera NJ, Swanik KA, Swanik CB et al. Effects of plyometric training on muscle-activation strategies and performance in female athletes. *J Athl Train* 2004;39:24–31.
2. Hewett TE, Lindenfeld TN, Riccobene JV et al. The effect of neuromuscular training on the incidence of knee injury in female athletes. A prospective study. *Am J Sports Med* 1999;27:699–706.

3. Hewett TE, Myer GD, Ford KR. Reducing knee and anterior cruciate ligament injuries among female athletes: a systematic review of neuromuscular training interventions. *J Knee Surg* 2005;18:82–88.
4. Hewett TE, Stroupe AL, Nance TA et al. Plyometric training in female athletes. Decreased impact forces and increased hamstring torques. *Am J Sports Med* 1996;24:765–73.
5. Hoffman JR, Ratamess NA, Cooper JJ et al. Comparison of loaded and unloaded jump squat training on strength/power performance in college football players. *J Strength Cond Res* 2005;19:810–15.
6. Junge A, Rosch D, Peterson L et al. Prevention of soccer injuries: a prospective intervention study in youth amateur players. *Am J Sports Med* 2002;30:652–59.
7. Luebbers PE, Potteiger JA, Hulver MW et al. Effects of plyometric training and recovery on vertical jump performance and anaerobic power. *J Strength Cond Res* 2003;17:704–09.
8. Markovic G. Does plyometric training improve vertical jump height? A meta-analytical review. *Br J Sports Med* 2007;41:349–55; discussion 55.
9. Markovic G, Jukic I, Milanovic D et al. Effects of sprint and plyometric training on muscle function and athletic performance. *J Strength Cond Res* 2007;21:543–49.
10. Matavulj D, Kukolj M, Ugarkovic D et al. Effects of plyometric training on jumping performance in junior basketball players. *J Sports Med Phys Fitness* 2001;41:159–64.
11. Myer GD, Ford KR, Palumbo JP et al. Neuromuscular training improves performance and lower-extremity biomechanics in female athletes. *J Strength Cond Res* 2005;19:51–60.
12. Newton RU, Kraemer WJ, Häkkinen K. Effects of ballistic training on preseason preparation of elite volleyball players. *Med Sci Sports Exerc* 1999;31:323–30.
13. Paterno MV, Myer GD, Ford KR et al. Neuromuscular training improves single-limb stability in young female athletes. *J Orthop Sports Phys Ther* 2004;34:305–16.
14. Petersen J, Holmich P. Evidence based prevention of hamstring injuries in sport. *Br J Sports Med* 2005;39:319–23.
15. Spurrs RW, Murphy AJ, Watsford ML. The effect of plyometric training on distance running performance. *Eur J Appl Physiol* 2003;89:1–7.
16. Stemm JD, Jacobson BH. Comparison of land- and aquatic-based plyometric training on vertical jump performance. *J Strength Cond Res* 2007;21:568–71.
17. Toumi H, Best TM, Martin A et al. Effects of eccentric phase velocity of plyometric training on the vertical jump. *Int J Sports Med* 2004;25:391–98.
18. Toumi H, Best TM, Martin A et al. Muscle plasticity after weight and combined (weight + jump) training. *Med Sci Sports Exerc* 2004;36:1580–588.
19. Wilkerson GB, Colston MA, Short NI et al. Neuromuscular changes in female collegiate athletes resulting from a plyometric jump-training program. *J Athl Train* 2004;39:17–23.
20. Wilson GJ, Newton RU, Murphy AJ et al. The optimal training load for the development of dynamic athletic performance. *Med Sci Sports Exerc* 1993;25(11):1279–286.
21. Bosco C, Viitasalo JT, Komi PV et al. Combined effect of elastic energy and myoelectrical potentiation during stretch-shortening cycle exercise. *Acta Physiol Scand* 1982;114:557–65.
22. Verhoshanski Y. Depth jumping in the training of jumpers. *Track Technique* 1983;51:1618–619.
23. Wilt F. Plyometrics, what it is and how it works. *Athl J* 1975;55:76–90.
24. Voight ML, Brady D. Plyometrics, 4th ed. Onalaska, WI: S&S Publishers; 1992.
25. Chmielewski TL, Myer GD, Kauffman D et al. Plyometric exercise in the rehabilitation of athletes: physiological responses and clinical application. *J Orthop Sports Phys Ther* 2006;36:308–19.
26. Lundin PE. A review of plyometric training. *Nat Strength Condition Assoc J* 1985;73:65–70.
27. Kubo K, Kanehisa H, Kawakami Y et al. Influence of static stretching on viscoelastic properties of human tendon structures in vivo. *J Appl Physiol* 2001;90:520–27.
28. Komi PV, Bosco C. Utilization of stored elastic energy in leg extensor muscles by men and women. *Med Sci Sports Exerc* 1978;10:261–5.
29. Wilk KE, Voight ML, Keirns MA et al. Stretch-shortening drills for the upper extremities: theory and clinical application. *J Orthop Sports Phys Ther* 1993;17:225–39.
30. Voight ML, Wieder DL. Comparative reflex response times of vastus medialis obliquus and vastus lateralis in normal subjects and subjects with extensor mechanism dysfunction. An electromyographic study. *Am J Sports Med* 1991;19:131–37.
31. Wilson GJ, Wood GA, Elliott BC. Optimal stiffness of series elastic component in a stretch-shorten cycle activity. *J Appl Physiol* 1991;70:825–33.
32. Ishikawa M, Niemelä E, Komi PV. Interaction between fascicle and tendinous tissues in short-contact stretch-shortening cycle exercise with varying eccentric intensities. *J Appl Physiol* 2005;99:217–23.
33. Fukunaga T, Kawakami Y, Kubo K et al. Muscle and tendon interaction during human movements. *Exerc Sport Sci Rev* 2002;30:106–10.
34. Gollhofer A, Strojnik V, Rapp W et al. Behaviour of triceps surae muscle-tendon complex in different jump conditions. *Eur J Appl Physiol* 1992;64:283–91.
35. Rassier DE, Herzog W. Force enhancement and relaxation rates after stretch of activated muscle fibres. *Proc Biol Sci* 2005;272:475–80.
36. Astrand P, Rodahl K, Dahl H et al. Textbook of Work Physiology, 4th ed. Champaign, IL: Human Kinetics; 2003.
37. Jacobson M. Developmental Neurobiology. New York: Rinehart & Winston, Inc; 1970.
38. O'Connell A, Gardner E. Understanding the scientific bases of human movement. Baltimore: Williams & Wilkins; 1972.
39. Schmidt RF. Motor Control and Learning. Champaign, IL: Human Kinetics; 1982.
40. Swash M, Fox K. Muscle spindle innervation in man. *J Anat* 1972;112:61–80.

41. Asmussen E, Bonde-Petersen F. Storage of elastic energy in skeletal muscles in man. *Acta Physiol Scand* 1974;91:385–92.

42. Heidt RS Jr, Sweeterman LM, Carlonas RL et al. Avoidance of soccer injuries with preseason conditioning. *Am J Sports Med* 2000;28:659–62.

43. Mandelbaum BR, Silvers HJ, Watanabe DS et al. Effectiveness of a neuromuscular and proprioceptive training program in preventing anterior cruciate ligament injuries in female athletes: 2-year follow-up. *Am J Sports Med* 2005;33:1003–10.

44. Myklebust G, Engebretsen L, Braekken IH et al. Prevention of anterior cruciate ligament injuries in female team handball players: a prospective intervention study over three seasons. *Clin J Sport Med* 2003;13:71–8.

45. Potach DH, Chu DA. Plyometric Training. In Baechle TR, Earle RW. Essentials of Strength Training and Conditioning, 2nd ed. Champaign, IL: Human Kinetics; 2000.

CHAPTER 9

Speed, Agility, and Quickness Training for Performance Enhancement

UPON COMPLETION OF THIS CHAPTER, YOU WILL BE ABLE TO:

Describe speed, agility, and quickness training and its purpose.

Rationalize the importance of speed, agility, and quickness training.

Design a speed, agility, and quickness training program for athletes at any level of training.

Perform, describe, and instruct various speed, agility, and quickness training exercises.

Introduction

Speed, agility, and quickness are some of the most significant, and visible, components of athletic success. An improvement in the ability to react quickly, apply significant force rapidly in the appropriate direction, and to redirect that force if needed is the ultimate goal of a program to improve speed, agility, and quickness. A carefully designed program that addresses these factors of athleticism significantly improves overall performance and reduces the risk of injury.

Speed, agility, and quickness all involve learned motor skills. Although the magnitude of proficiency will vary with each individual, learning the efficient and effective execution of these skills can improve overall athletic ability. This chapter aims to address the significant components of speed, agility/multidirectional speed (MDS), and quickness. Modalities and drills for improving these skills will also be introduced.

Training for Speed of Movement

Speed
The "rate of perform-ance" of an activity.

In the context of athletics, **speed** is best defined as the "rate of performance" of an activity. This can refer to any movement or action. In athletics, the velocity at which one executes a movement can be the difference between success and failure. Speed is a culmination of reactive ability, rapid force development, rapid force application, and effective movement technique. Generally, when the force demands of an activity increase, the velocity output of the movement decreases (1) as demonstrated by the force-velocity curve (Fig. 9.1). The goal of a speed-training program is to move this curve up and to the right, which would mean being able to create greater force at higher

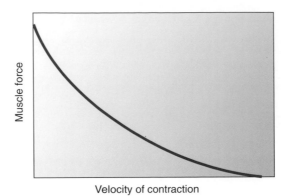

Velocity of contraction

FIGURE 9.1 Force-velocity curve.

velocities of movement. This, in combination with an ability to maintain biomechanically advantageous body and limb positioning, creates an increase in the velocity of movement.

Speed of movement greatly affects an athlete's abilities in regards to linear speed, agility/MDS, and quickness. The following are essential components of a well-designed program to improve speed of movement:

- Stability, strength, and power
- Muscle and joint elasticity
- Joint mobility and flexibility
- Movement technique
- Specialized drills

STABILITY, STRENGTH, AND POWER

Stability, strength, and power training help shift the force-velocity curve up and to the right (2). While stability training develops appropriate balance, strength training improves the body's ability to create force, and power training aids in decreasing the amount of time needed to create that force. These all have significant contributions in regards to improving speed. When performing stability, strength, and power drills specific for speed development, it is important to include exercises for contributing areas, such as the feet, anterior and posterior muscles of the shins, the core, and hip flexors/extensors as part of a whole-body program. In addition, movements that emphasize powerful plantar and dorsiflexion of the ankle, as well as extension and flexion of knee and hip are also important components. Please refer to Specialized Strength Exercises for Speed section in this chapter for these drills.

MUSCLE AND JOINT ELASTICITY

Ballistic movement, as found in speed, agility, and quickness training, is created by a forced and rapid lengthening of a muscle immediately followed by a shortening of the muscle, creating an elastic "rubber-band-like" effect of energy release. As mentioned in Chapter 8, this ability to store and release energy is referred to as the **stretch-shortening cycle** and is affected by the intrinsic qualities of the muscle and the involved musculotendinous junctions (2). This action is often reflexive, and referred to as the "stretch reflex." Training the muscle and tendon's ability to load eccentrically and rapidly release energy concentrically improves the magnitude and effectiveness of the stretch-shortening cycle (2). This is achieved through power training and plyometrics. Please refer to Chapter 8 in this text for more information on how to improve these components.

 Stretch-Shortening Cycle

An active stretch (eccentric contraction) of a muscle followed by an immediate shortening (concentric contraction) of that same muscle.

JOINT MOBILITY AND FLEXIBILITY

Joint mobility is the ability of a joint to move through its natural, effective range of motion and is further characterized as the balance of strength and flexibility regulating contrasting motions around a joint (i.e., flexion and extension). In addition, the integrity of the muscle tissue and its ability to relax and contract appropriately during movement is a limiting factor in producing effective joint mobility. For example, when a sprinter comes out of the blocks, proper range of motion during hip extension requires strength of the hip extenders, as well as the ability for the hip flexors to lengthen properly to allow for full hip extension (Fig. 9.2). If there is an imbalance of strength and flexibility about the hip, range of motion will be compromised, which will in turn affect force output and speed of movement. In addition, if the muscle tissue is not responding properly due to injury, adhesions, or other factors, performance will be diminished. This can be improved with flexibility training (Chapter 4).

FIGURE 9.2 Appropriate flexibility and range of motion.

MOVEMENT TECHNIQUE

Proper movement technique while executing speed, agility/MDS, and quickness drills allows the body and limbs to achieve biomechanically advantageous positions for optimal force production, thereby increasing speed of movement. Movement technique for speed, agility/MDS, and quickness skills will be discussed and demonstrated later in this chapter.

SPECIALIZED DRILLS

Most athletes wishing to improve speed of movement follow a very general program to develop strength, mobility, power, and general athletic ability. General movement patterns (e.g., running, jumping, throwing) are used to develop strength and power. These movement patterns also help develop the basic motor skills required to move efficiently in space and decrease an athlete's risk of injury. Although these programs function well for the beginner to intermediate athletes in a particular sport, more advanced methodologies are necessary for higher-level athletes. After sound mechanical proficiency is established, specialized drills are effective in facilitating the specific demands of an athlete's sport. These drills reinforce proper movement patterns in a sport-specific environment while adding heightened demands to the neuromuscular system. These drills often imitate sport scenarios while adding additional reactionary, force, or other neuromuscular demands. A common means of adding neuromuscular load to movement drills is by applying the concepts of resisted and assisted speed.

OVERSPEED OR ASSISTED DRILLS

Overspeed or "assisted" running drills involve apparatus or running surface grade changes that aid in accelerating an athlete's movement. Moderate grade (5–6%) downhill running, assisted bungee cord movement, and other "towing" mechanisms are used for this type of training (Fig. 9.3). The prevalent theory is that as the athlete is accelerated at a rate he or she is unaccustomed to, the adaptations involved will train the neuromuscular system to work at higher speeds. Assisted speed drills are effective for improving stride frequency, a key component to running speed (3,4). Because this type of training is done at speeds beyond the body's normal capabilities, it is important to have a sound mechanical foundation in order to attain maximal effectiveness and prevent injury. These drills are not recommended for beginners.

FIGURE 9.3   Assisted drills.   **FIGURE 9.4**   Resisted drills.

RESISTED SPEED DRILLS

Resisted speed drills involve the athlete moving against increased horizontal or vertical load (Fig. 9.4). This aids in improving force production during the drive phase of the running stride, aiding with improvements in stride length (3). As mentioned later in this chapter, this is significant in regards to increasing movement speed. Weight vests, sled pushes and pulls, uphill running, and partner-resisted drills are all types of resisted speed drills. Light loads (10% of body weight) are generally recommended for maximal skill carryover, because they allow for technique, joint velocities, and loads similar to that for competition (3,5). However, many coaches and trainers use loads much higher in order for further overload to develop leg strength specific to speed skills, such as acceleration. As with any load-intensive resistance program, it is important that proper progression is observed.

Developing Linear Speed, Agility/MDS, and Quickness

LINEAR SPEED

 Linear Speed
The ability to move the body in one intended direction as fast as possible.

 Stride Rate
The amount of time needed to complete a stride cycle and is limited by stride length.

 Stride Length
The distance covered with each stride and is improved by increasing the amount of force applied into the ground.

Although sports often have multidirectional movement demands, **linear speed** development establishes a basis for general, efficient movement technique. In addition, even during multidirectional movement after initial direction change, the body attempts to align itself as linearly as possible to maximize force production and running velocity. Linear speed in sports can be defined as the ability to move the body in one intended direction as fast as possible. Linear speed is a product of **stride rate** and **stride length** (3,6,7). Stride rate refers to the amount of time needed to complete a stride cycle and is limited by stride length. Stride length refers to the distance covered with each stride and is improved by increasing the amount of force applied into the ground (Fig. 9.5) (3). Research suggests that optimal stride length for maximal speed in sprinting is 2.3 to 2.5 times the athlete's leg length (8).

FIGURE 9.5   Stride length.

Improvements in stride length and frequency must happen by making adjustments in overall mechanics and force production (5). Attempting to "force" adaptations in either one of these factors is ineffective. For example, attempting to increase stride length by reaching for greater distance with each stride often results in "overstriding," where the foot contacts the ground well in front of the body's center of gravity, and is sometimes mentioned as a factor in hamstring strains (9). "Overstriding" creates a decelerative force and slows movement. Attempting to force faster foot contact to increase stride frequency results in a significantly shorter stride length. As you can see, achieving maximal running speed is a product of an optimal relationship between stride length and frequency (3,6,8). All training modalities in a linear speed program are focused on improving this relationship.

LINEAR SPEED TECHNIQUE

As previously mentioned, linear speed technique aids in establishing a foundation for effective movement. Although this section discusses movement technique in regards to a linear orientation of the body, nearly every one of these concepts is important to multidirectional movement as well. Posture, arm movement, and leg movement must all be executed correctly to achieve maximal performance during linear speed development. These can all have an effect on creating optimal frontside mechanics (dorsiflexion, knee and hip flexion) (Fig. 9.6), backside mechanics (plantarflexion, knee and hip extension), and ability to maintain a neutral pelvis (Fig. 9.6) (6). The three distinct phases during the stride cycle are the **drive phase**, when the foot is in contact with the ground; the **recovery phase**, when the leg swings from the hip while the foot clears the ground; and the **support phase**, where the runner's weight is carried by the entire foot (3). Posture, arm movement, and leg movement must all be executed correctly to optimize force production and velocity at each phase. The ideal technique for effective, efficient running speed depends on the specific needs of the desired task in the sport. For most sports, an ability to rapidly increase running or movement velocity is necessary; this is called acceleration. The maximal running speed one is able to attain is referred to as maximal speed. The mechanical differences between acceleration and maximal speed will be discussed later in this chapter. Athletic proficiency for many sports demands effective mechanical execution of both.

Please refer to Table 9.1 for proper movement mechanics for both maximal speed and acceleration.

Also listed in Table 9.1 are common errors observed, their common causes, and effective drills for correction. For illustration of these drills, please refer to "Drills for Speed, Agility/MDS, and Quickness" at the end of this chapter.

Proper execution of running technique is the foundation of improving running speed. Proficient movement mechanics during linear speed provides a foundation for other movement skills. Programs should aim to establish sound linear speed mechanics before progressing on to more advanced skills. For technique and specialized drills for linear speed, please refer to Technique and Specialized Drills for Linear Speed later in this chapter.

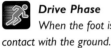

Drive Phase
When the foot is in contact with the ground.

Recovery Phase
When the leg swings from the hip while the foot clears the ground.

Support Phase
Where the runner's weight is carried by the entire foot.

FIGURE 9.6 Frontside and backside mechanics.

TABLE 9.1

Proper Linear Sprint Mechanics

Body Part	Motion Summary	Problem	Cause	Drills for Correction
Head	As an athlete initiates acceleration, the head must cast downward. This initiates forward movement by placing the weight of the head slightly in front of the body's center of gravity. As the athlete approaches maximal running speed, the head is raised to be in line with the vertical axis of the body.	Improper flexion or extension at the head	Fatigue or poor execution of proper mechanics	Coach to maintain proper eye focus ahead or slightly downcast, depending on the specific acceleration or maximal speed drills
Shoulders	Shoulders should create an exaggerated flexion and extension opposite lower-body movement (hip flexion/extension). During acceleration, shoulder extension (driving elbows backward) should cease when the hands are past the buttocks posteriorly (3). Shoulder flexion should cease as the hands rise above forehead level. Proper, aggressive shoulder extension during acceleration and maximal speed aids in proper contralateral movements, such as hip and shoulder flexion. Attempts should be made to minimize shoulder abduction and thoracic rotation, keeping the elbows close to the body (3). This results in the hands approaching, but not crossing, the body's vertical midline. As the athlete approaches maximal speed, shoulder flexion and extension maintains a high amount of force, but movement at the shoulder joint decreases in range of motion. The shoulder should flex to observe the hands even with the nose. Forcible shoulder extension is maintained to move the elbows "down and back". The role of arm action shifts from creating propulsive force during acceleration, to facilitating balance of the contralateral hip flexion during maximal speed (6). During acceleration and maximal speed, shoulders should stay relaxed and swing naturally.	Tight and elevated shoulders during running Movement of the hands across the midline during flexion and extension, causing excessive rotation of the upper body	Arm movement too forced and not natural Lack of coordination of contralateral hip and shoulder flexion/ extension; overcompensa-tion for poor hip flexion	Standing arm swings; relaxed shoulders while marching or skipping Standing arm swings; A-skips; cycling B-skips; weighted arm swings; proper technique focus during all drills
Elbows	Elbows should be bent at 90 degrees during shoulder flexion with fingers extended. During shoulder extension, the angle at the elbow may naturally open slightly, but must close to 90 degrees once again during shoulder flexion. Wrists should remain neutral with the fingers extended. This movement pattern is maintained as the athlete approaches maximal speed.	Excessive flexion or extension	Poor neural patterning	Standing arm swings; marches; A-skips; cycling B-skips; weighted arm swings; proper technique focus during all drills

(continued)

TABLE 9.1

Proper Linear Sprint Mechanics (*Continued*)

Body Part	Motion Summary	Problem	Cause	Drills for Correction
Hips	During acceleration, hip flexion, as a result of contralateral shoulder extension, should reach a point slightly below parallel to the ground. Hip extension should be explosive yet movement of the thigh posteriorly beyond the body's center of gravity should be minimized to less than 20 degrees (5). As the athlete approaches maximal running speed, hip flexion approaches 90 degrees. Hip extension should remain explosive, yet posterior movement past the body's center of gravity must still be minimized. The pelvis must stay neutral during acceleration and maximal speed.	Inadequate hip flexion	Poor neural patterning; weak hip flexors; tight hip extensors	Flexibility drills for piriformis, hamstrings, (refer to Chapter 4); resisted knee drives; marches; A-skips; 1/3/5 wall drill
		Inability to produce adequate force during hip extension (ground push-off)	Weak posterior chain; tight hip flexors; inadequate ankle mobility	Mobility and flexibility drills for ankle and hip flexors (see Chapter 4); strength, power, and plyometric drills focusing on triple extension of the ankle, knee, and hip (see Chapters 8 and 10); 1/3/5 wall drills; resisted speed drills
		Excessive lumbar extension throughout stride cycle	Weak core and glute muscles; tight hip flexors	Core strengthening drills (refer to Chapter 6); hip flexor flexibility drills (refer to Chapter 4); 1/3/5 wall drills; resisted sprints; superman planks
Knees	During the drive phase in acceleration, the knee is fully extended to allow for maximal hip extension with the foot slightly behind the center of mass. The knee then flexes as the hip flexes during the recovery, driving the heel directly up toward the buttocks and over the opposite knee (8). During maximal hip flexion, the knee is flexed, leaving the shin nearly parallel to the ground. As the hip begins to extend again, the knee is allowed to swing open to create an angle that is roughly 90 degrees with the shin before it is rapidly extended once again during foot contact. As the athlete approaches maximal speed, the more perpendicular body angle to the ground allows for greater hip flexion, and therefore higher knee and heel lift.	Knee height is too low during running stride, not allowing for adequate stride length	Inadequate hip flexion during the drive phase of the running stride	Resisted knee drives; marches; A-skips; resisted sprints
		Knee adduction during the stance phase of stride cycle	Poor ankle mobility; weak abductor/external rotators; tight adductors/internal rotators	Flexibility exercises for gastrocnemius/soleus/Achilles complex (see Chapter 4); tube walks; single-leg balance drills (see Chapter 7); single-leg strength drills (see Chapter 10)

(continued)

TABLE 9.1

Proper Linear Sprint Mechanics (*Continued*)

Body Part	Motion Summary	Problem	Cause	Drills for Correction
Ankle and heel	The ankle should remain dorsiflexed to allow for proper foot contact on the ball of the foot during the drive phase. At foot contact, the angle created between the shin and the foot should be close to 45 degrees, referred to as a "positive shin angle" (6). This allows for the appropriate amount of horizontal force to be applied in the posterior direction. As the foot comes off of the ground during recovery, the heel is raised toward the buttocks to "step" over the opposite knee. The height of the heel is related to the height of the knee during hip flexion, so the height of the heel begins rather low during acceleration and increases as maximal speed is approached. Due to overcoming initial inertia during acceleration, ground contact time of the foot is slightly greater than at maximal speed. As maximal speed is approached, foot contact is still on the ball of the foot, but is slightly higher toward the toes. The ankle remains dorsiflexed, but as the foot contact moves forward slightly to a point directly under or slightly in front of the body's center of gravity, the angle between the foot and shin becomes less acute. Ground contact time for the foot is decreased as maximal speed is achieved.	Inability to maintain dorsiflexion throughout stride cycle Foot contact time too long, resulting in decreased stride rate	Improper coaching ("run on the toes"); weak tibialis anterior, tight gastrocnemius/ soleus/Achilles complex Inability to maintain dorsiflexion; improper backside mechanics; foot contact too far in front of center of gravity	Mobility and flexibility exercises for gastrocnemius/ soleus/Achilles complex (see Chapter 4); reverse calf raises; A-skips; 1/3/5 wall drills Reverse calf raises; A-skips, cycling B-skips; assisted sprints
Body angle in relation to the ground	During initial acceleration, the body angle should be about 45 degrees to the ground. This allows for maximal force to be created posteriorly. A straight line should be observed from the top of the head, down the spine, through the extended rear leg. As the athlete approaches maximal speed, the body angle increases to near perpendicular to the ground. This allows the hips to continue to drive the body's center of gravity forward.	Improper body angle at phase of running (i.e., acceleration vs. maximal speed)	Improper coaching (bend forward, or "stay low" while sprinting); poor neural patterning	Core strengthening drills (see Chapter 6); superman planks; 1/3/5 wall drills; resisted and/or assisted speed drills

FIGURE 9.7 Agility and MDS.

 Agility
The ability to change direction or orientation of the body based on rapid processing of internal or external information quickly and accurately without significant loss of speed.

 Multidirectional Speed

Being able to create speed in any direction or body orientation (forward, backward, lateral, diagonal, etc.).

AGILITY AND MULTIDIRECTIONAL SPEED

Although running speed is generally correlated with athleticism, the ability to adapt and redirect speed appropriately to the needs of the game is an essential skill for athletic success, especially in team sports. The ability to change direction or orientation of the body based on rapid processing of internal or external information quickly and accurately without significant loss of speed is called **agility** (6,8). Being able to create speed in any direction or body orientation (forward, backward, lateral, diagonal, etc.) is referred to as **Multidirectional Speed (MDS)** (6). An athlete adept in these skills is effective at being able to create and control speed in any direction rapidly (Fig. 9.7). Castello and Kreis (10) observed a direct correlation between increased agility and development of athletic timing, rhythm, and movement. These are key coordinative components of athleticism.

Agility/MDS training often closely resembles the actual sporting activity and may, therefore, be the most effective way to address neuromuscular demands required to perform sport specific skills (11). The primary effect of agility/MDS training is improvement of overall body control and awareness (12). This aids in heightening overall athleticism, which improves proficiency at nearly every athletic activity.

General skills and concepts learned during linear speed training apply to agility/MDS, such as effective force production, posture, and proper lower- and upper-body orientation and movement. Agility/MDS has many specific skill demands, however, that must be addressed in creating a training program to improve these essential components of athleticism.

According to Gambetta (6) the key components of agility training are:

- Body control and awareness
- Recognition and reaction
- Starting and first step
- Acceleration
- Footwork
- Change of direction
- Stopping

These all involve development of motor skills and can therefore be trained.

Effective movement for agility/MDS is a culmination of these skills, in addition to others mentioned earlier in this chapter related to general speed of movement. Because these skills must be highly integrated during game performance, they are often trained simultaneously during agility/MDS drills. For beginners and other athletes wishing to work on specific aspects, agility drills can be broken down into individual components.

Much like movements in sports, agility/MDS drills can be planned or reactive based (6). In planned drills, athletes know ahead of time what is coming, so they know exactly how to react. Drills involving cones or other markers in which athletes knows ahead of time what action they are supposed to take when they reach the marker are planned drills. These are the most basic agility drills and can be used to teach proper movement patterns to beginners. Reactive drills incorporate an unpredictable environment that more closely mimic the athletic contest. The athletes may be required to react to a sound, an opponent or coach's movement, or other varying stimuli. They are unable to plan or predict when and what certain stimuli will be presented; thus, they must react once they see it. This requires a much higher level of neural processing as well as neuromuscular coordination. A large majority of agility/MDS drills for advanced athletes should be reactive in nature.

When you are selecting the appropriate drills for agility/MDS, keep in mind the demands of the sport and the level of the athlete. The development of agility/MDS skills should follow a progression, beginning by learning the appropriate movement skills for acceleration, deceleration, and change of direction. Introduction of these movements may be static, then as the athlete progresses, dynamic movements are utilized in planned drills, focusing on speed of movement. After proficiency is obtained, reactive drills are introduced. Figure 9.8 illustrates the progression model for agility/MDS skill acquisition and performance application. For techniques and specialized drills for agility/MDS, please refer to Technique and Specialized Drills for Agility and MDS in this chapter.

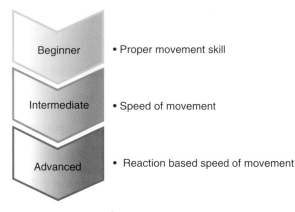

Beginner — • Proper movement skill

Intermediate — • Speed of movement

Advanced — • Reaction based speed of movement

FIGURE 9.8 Agility/MDS Progression Model.

QUICKNESS

Quickness

An athlete's ability to execute movement skill in a comparatively brief amount of time is part of the athleticism continuum.

Reaction Time

The time elapsed between the athlete's recognizing the need to act and initiating the appropriate action.

Total Response Time

The summation of the reaction time and the time it takes to execute the reactionary movement is of concern.

An athlete's ability to execute movement skill in a comparatively brief amount of time is part of the athleticism continuum referred to as **quickness**. Quickness addresses the quality and magnitude of the athlete's perceptive and reactive abilities and may be one of the most significant components contributing to athletic success (13). A "quick" athlete is able to assess a game situation and apply the necessary actions at a very high speed. Although many may possess a high level of performance for other variables such as speed, power, agility/MDS, and other game skills, the athlete who can apply these appropriate skills at the right time at the highest rate will be the most successful.

Quickness training involves developing biomotor skills related to decreasing **reaction time**. This is the time elapsed between the athlete's recognizing the need to act and initiating the appropriate action. In athletics, aside from the time it takes to initiate an appropriate reaction, the time it takes to execute the reactionary movement is of concern. The summation of these is referred to as total response time (13,14). The goal of quickness training is to address the mechanisms involved with **total response time** and improve the related motor and perceptual skills. Although elite athletes are often genetically predisposed to efficient, coordinated, high-level reactive motor skills, concepts of motor learning and control can aid in developing even faster reaction and total response times.

Training for quickness is a process of taking all of the skills required for effective speed and agility in addition to the specific skills needed in a sport, and applying them to the reactionary demands of that sport. This process begins with general coordination and teaching effective, sport-specific movement patterns. After proficiency is established, speed of movement is addressed. Efficient movement is then paired with specific reactionary demands the athlete will face while playing their sport. Finally, a large amount of competitive game experience will allow for accurate, game-specific application of these skills. Take a soccer athlete, for example. Soccer requires effective acceleration, top-end speed, deceleration, and direction change. In the initial phases of training, the focus of the program should be teaching the technique drills for the aforementioned skills. After these movements are mastered, an athlete can be practiced in game-like planned drills, such as the T and box drills described later. Execution of these drills can be timed to monitor speed and proficiency. After an established time criteria is met, the soccer ball can be added to make the drills game-specific. In addition, reactionary demands replace the practiced, predictable patterns of the above drills. Cones may be removed from the T drill and the athlete must then respond to a coach's whistle or visual cue. Finally, scrimmages and game scenarios are added to training, still keeping proper movement skills in mind, but adding the demands of the actual game. Continuous practice of the above process results in a quick, successful athlete.

Figures 9.9 through 9.45 are illustrated drills for improving the components of linear speed, MDS, and quickness. Refer to Table 9.2 in regards to which drills apply specifically to individual sports.

Example Drills for Speed, Agility/MDS, and Quickness

SPECIALIZED STRENGTH EXERCISES FOR SPEED

RESISTED KNEE DRIVES

FOCUS: Special strength for hip flexion
REPETITIONS: 10–20 each leg

FIGURE 9.9   Resisted knee drives.

SUPINE HEEL PUSHES

FOCUS: Special strength for hip extension
REPETITIONS: 10–20

FIGURE 9.10   Supine heel pushes.

TUBE WALKING

FOCUS: Special strength for hip ad/abduction
REPETITIONS: 10–20 each way

FIGURE 9.11   Tube walking.

A-SKIPS

FOCUS: General running technique
DISTANCE: 15–20 yards

FIGURE 9.17 A-skips.

CYCLING B-SKIPS

FOCUS: General running technique
DISTANCE: 15–20 yards

FIGURE 9.18 Cycling B-skips.

1/3/5 WALL DRILL

FOCUS: Linear acceleration technique
REPETITIONS: About 5

FIGURE 9.19 1/3/5 wall drill.

STANDING ARM SWINGS

FOCUS: General running technique
TIME: 5–10 seconds

FIGURE 9.20   Standing arm swings.

PUSH-UP SPRINTS

FOCUS: Specialized drill for acceleration
DISTANCE: 10–20 yards
DRILL PROGRESSION: Reaction can be introduced by having two athletes race, or by varying the start stimulus. Athlete can also begin supine, backward, etc.

FIGURE 9.21   Push-up sprints.

ALI SHUFFLE

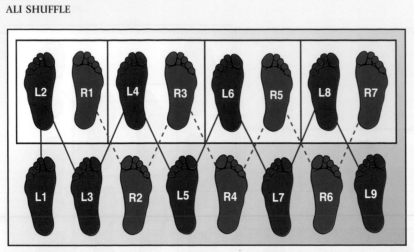

FIGURE 9.35   Ali shuffle.

ALI CROSSOVER

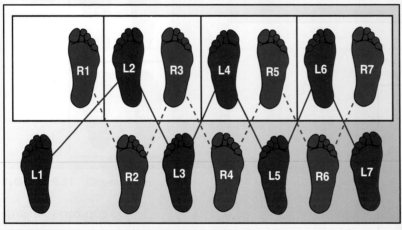

FIGURE 9.36   Ali crossover.

W-WEAVE

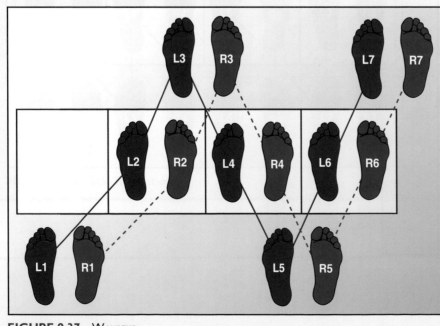

FIGURE 9.37   W-weave.

UPPER-BODY AGILITY DRILL

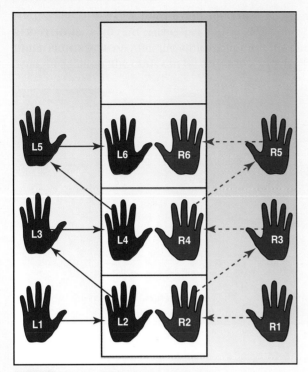

FIGURE 9.38   Upper-body agility drill.

CONE AGILITY DRILLS

FOCUS: Specialized drills for agility/MDS

5-10-5 DRILL

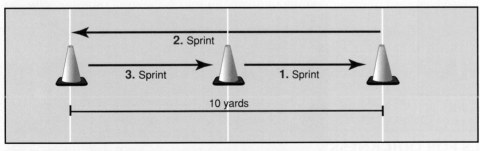

FIGURE 9.39   5-10-5 drill.

T-DRILL

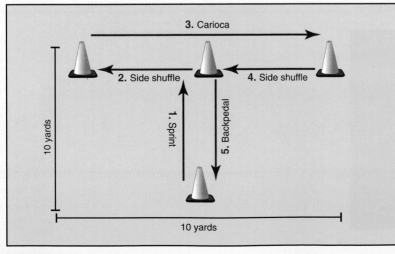

FIGURE 9.40   T-drill.

TABLE 9.2

Sport-Specific Drills

	Football	Basketball	Soccer	Baseball	Hockey	Volleyball
Resisted Knee Drives	x	x	x	x	x	x
Supine Heel Pushes	x		x	x	x	x
Lateral Cord Walks	x	x	x	x	x	x
Reverse Calf Raises	x	x	x	x		x
Superman Planks	x	x	x	x	x	x
Weighted Arm Swings	x		x	x		
Big Toe Cord Flexions	x	x	x	x		x
Barefoot Warm-Up	x	x	x	x		x
Tennis Ball Foot Roll	x	x	x	x	x	x
Marches	x		x	x		
A-Skips	x		x	x		
Cycling B-Skips	x		x	x		
1/3/5 Wall Drill	x	x	x	x		x
Standing Arm Swings	x		x	x		
Push-Up Sprints	x	x	x	x		x
Resisted Sprints	x	x	x	x	x	x
Assisted Sprints	x		x			
Lateral A-Skips	x	x	x	x	x	x
Lateral 1/3/5 Wall Drill	x	x	x	x	x	x
Line-Stop Deceleration Drill	x	x	x			x
Lateral Steps	x	x	x	x	x	x
Jumping Jacks	x	x	x	x	x	x
In and Out	x	x	x	x		x
LT Shuffle	x	x	x		x	x
Upper-Body Agility	x	x		x	x	x
5-10-5 Drill	x	x	x	x	x	x
T-Drill	x	x	x	x	x	x
Box Drill	x	x	x	x	x	x
Modified Box Drill	x	x	x	x	x	x
W-Drill	x	x	x		x	
Partner Mirror Drill	x	x	x		x	
Turn and Grab Card Drill	x	x		x		x
Agility Ball Drills	x	x	x	x		x

Program Design for Speed, Agility/MDS, and Quickness

Improvement in speed, agility/MDS, and quickness (SAQ) are the desired end result of a performance program. For nearly every athlete, the high demands placed on the central nervous system for coordination, reaction, and force production during these skills should be trained separately from other aspects of a program. Other aspects of a performance program, such as strength, power, and flexibility should be designed in a manner that complements SAQ. A program designed to accomplish this aids in creating high-force production at the correct time for effective, efficient movement. This improves speed of movement and overall athletic ability. For the purpose of this chapter, program design will be discussed and displayed in regards to implementing specific SAQ drills.

As previously mentioned, SAQ drills are best trained separately from other aspects of a training program. Because these skills are very closely related to skills demanded during game play, special attention is required. SAQ drills can be performed either before strength and power training or on different days to maximize effectiveness and decrease the negative effects of fatigue. When designing programs to improve SAQ, the needs of the athlete, the needs of the specific sport, and proper organization and integration should be addressed.

THE NEEDS OF THE ATHLETE

Every athlete has different strengths and weaknesses. These may be related to genetics, motivation, developmental level, or prior exposure to proper skill development. As a Sports Performance Professional, it is essential that the specific needs of the athlete are addressed. This is done by careful initial assessment (see Chapter 3) of the athlete. This may include assessments for the needs of the sport, their position, injury history, posture, criteria-based performance tests, or personality assessments. After this is accomplished, the program should be designed to facilitate the proper introduction and improvement of the skills related to performance for that particular athlete. Skill development should progress based on the proficiency demonstrated by that athlete and may happen on a daily, monthly, or yearly basis, depending on the athlete. A program that is effective for one may not be effective for another. A good Sports Performance Professional constantly monitors the effectiveness of their program by observing, assessing, and communicating with their athletes.

THE NEEDS OF THE SPORT

Different sports have different SAQ demands. The Sports Performance Professional must understand the specific metabolic, biomechanical, and neuromuscular demands for their athlete's sport. In this way, SAQ programs can be designed to accommodate the needs of that sport. For example, a study by McInnes (15) observed movements and exertion output by Australian League basketball players. The results showed that during a 48-minute game, side-to-side shuffling movements made up 31% of the game. Two-thirds of these movements were intense and lasted from 1–4 seconds. Sprints were found to last 1–5 seconds in duration. Average recovery between intensive bouts was found to be approximately 21 seconds. Other movements observed were jogging, running, and jumping. Gambetta says that the data of McInnes show jumping accounts for only about 41 seconds of the 48-minute game (6). Based on this data, a program for basketball players should observe a high amount of intensive shuffle and sprint movements lasting about 1–5 seconds. Recovery between repetitions should be about 20–21 seconds. In program design, this is referred to as the work-to-rest ratio. Each bout lasting 5 seconds with a rest time of 20 seconds would be a 1:4 work-to-rest ratio. The goal is for the athlete to "practice" these activities maximally in order to apply them maximally in competition. Although it is possible to modify the work-to-rest intervals during SAQ training in an attempt to achieve some metabolic overload, such training will fatigue the athlete and the quality of the activity will be significantly decreased; the fatigued player will train "slower" at a time when the goal is to get "faster." In true SAQ training, the overload will be the mechanical demands to be overcome, such as adding resistance or other criteria. This will improve the rate and quality of the desired movement.

In addition to the general movement and energy demands of the sport, different positions in each sport require different demands for movement. For example, a baseball infielder must react quickly in a relatively small area for movement to field ground balls. An outfielder often must run 20–30 yards or more to catch a ball. The more a program addresses these specific

REFERENCES

1. Komi PV. Neuromuscular performance: Factors influencing force and speed production. *Scand J Sports Sci.* 1979;1:2–15.
2. Komi PV. Stretch Shortening Cycle. In: Komi PV, ed. Strength and Power. Oxford, UK: Blackwell Scientific, 1992:181–93.
3. Dintiman GB, Ward RD, Tellez T. Sports Speed. Champaign, IL: Human Kinetics, 1997.
4. Ebben WP, Davies J, Clewien R. Effect of the Degree of Hill Slope on Acute Downhill Running Velocity and Acceleration. *J Strength Cond Res.* 2008;22:898–902.
5. Rogers J. USA Track and Field Coaching Manual. Champaign, IL: Human Kinetics, 2000.
6. Gambetta V. Athletic Development: The Art and Science of Functional Sports Conditioning. Champaign, IL: Human Kinetics, 2007.
7. Mero A, Komi PV, Gregor RJ. Biomechanics of sprint running. *Sports Med.* 1992;13:376–92.
8. Lentz D, Hardyk A. Speed Training. In: Brown LE, Ferrigno A, eds. Training for Speed, Agility and Quickness. Champaign, IL: Human Kinetics, 2005:17–70.
9. Thelen DG, Chumanov ES, Hoerth DM, et al. Hamstring muscle kinematics during treadmill sprinting. *Med Sci Sport Exer.* 2005;37:108–14.
10. Costello F, Kreis EJ. Sports Agility. Nashville, TN: Taylor Sports, 1993.
11. Cissik J, Barnes M. Sport Speed and Agility. Monterey, CA: Coaches Choice, 2004.
12. Graham J, Ferrigno V. Agility and balance training. In: Brown LE, Ferrigno A, eds. Training for Speed, Agility and Quickness, 2nd ed. Champaign, IL: Human Kinetics, 2005:71–136.
13. Vives D. Quickness and reaction time training. In: Brown L, Ferrigno A, eds. Training for Speed, Agility and Quickness, 2nd ed. Champaign, IL: Human Kinetics, 2005:137–222.
14. Schmidt R. Motor Learning Performance. Champaign, IL: Human Kinetics, 1991.
15. McInnes S, Carlson C, Jones J, McKenna M. The physiological load imposed on basketball players during competition. *J Sports Sci.* 1995;13:387–97.

CHAPTER 10

Integrated Resistance Training for Performance Enhancement

Introduction

The world of performance enhancement is changing drastically. Athletes demand to be bigger, faster, stronger, and leaner than ever before. To stay on the cutting edge, the Sports Performance Professional must follow a comprehensive, systematic approach to training. The broad scope of resistance training requires an understanding of the different programming schemes to meet the range of needs for different individuals. Given the wealth of information and research on this broad topic, this chapter will concentrate on providing an understanding of the progressive outcomes from resistance training and the systematic, progressive modeling that will allow the greatest performance benefit from resistance training.

Training Principles

Principle of Specificity OR Specific Adaptation to Imposed Demands (SAID Principle)
Principle that states the body will adapt to the specific demands placed on it.

There are several important resistance training principles that the Sports Performance Professional must understand. These principles include the following: the principle of specificity, overload, variation, individualization, and adaptation (1).

THE PRINCIPLE OF SPECIFICITY: THE SAID PRINCIPLE

The **principle of specificity** is often referred to as the *SAID principle*, which stands for **Specific Adaptation to Imposed Demands**. This means that the body will undergo specific adaptations to the specific type of demand placed upon it. For example, if an athlete trains by lifting heavy weights, the primary adaptations will support higher levels of maximal strength. If an athlete trains by lifting lighter weights for many repetitions, the primary adaptations will support higher levels of local muscle endurance.

This is a fairly simple concept to understand that implies, in essence, you get what you train for. However, the SAID principle is often used out of context and can be a misleading term when basic science is considered by the Sports Performance Professional. Remember, there are many different tissues in the body that each respond to a different stimulus to achieve specific goals. In order to make the SAID principle a safe and effective tool, it must be used appropriately within the context of the OPT™ model that progresses the program through a series of logical steps. Saying that the SAID principle is justification for jumping steps in the model simply because the planned performance occurs at some defined speed is not a proper application of the principle or the OPT™ model and can lead to injury.

The body must progress through progressive stages of adaptation to ensure that all of the necessary tissues are developed properly to meet the desired goal. Connective tissue adapts much more slowly than muscle, but also must be strong in order for muscles to generate high levels of tension. If emphasis is placed on training muscles to get big, strong, or both, an absence of prior training that allows connective tissue to increase in strength will increase the risk of injury.

Remember that type I muscle fibers, which are vitally important for postural stabilization, function differently than type II muscle fibers. In order to train with higher intensities, proper postural stabilization is a necessity. Therefore, both fiber types need to be trained specifically to prepare them to support higher levels of training. This is the primary purpose behind the three main outcomes of training within the OPT™ model.

The degree of adaptation that occurs during training is directly related to the mechanical, neuromuscular, and metabolic specificity of the training program (1,2). In other words, the more specifically a Sports Performance Professional manipulates the exercise routine to meet the actual goal, the greater the specific carryover the training program will have on that goal. It is important to remember that if a specific adaptation is required or desired, it must be trained for. The body can only adapt if it has a reason to adapt (3–7).

TIME OUT
Resistance Training in Proprioceptively Enriched Environments

Persons training with the same basic exercises and movement patterns (bench press, squats, leg press, pulldowns, etc.) will adapt by getting stronger, while using less motor units (1–4). This is partially the result of increased synchronization of motor unit activity (firing rates) (3,4). The body essentially becomes more efficient. While this adaptation is desirable for many sports, for an athlete who has the goals of getting stronger, bigger, and/or losing weight this is known as a plateau. By placing an athlete in a different environment (proprioceptively enriched), as seen in the Stabilization stage of the OPT™ model, you create a different stimulus to which the body must adapt (5). In turn, this forces increased motor unit recruitment as well as energy expenditure (6,7). If an athlete can recruit more motor units in synchrony, he or she can get stronger (1). The only way to increase the size of a muscle fiber is to be able to recruit it (8). Activating more motor units increases the number of muscle fibers that are utilized, creating greater potential for growth. The recruitment of more motor units increases the energy requirements of the human movement system chain, allowing for more energy expenditure and potential weight loss (9).

1. Sale DG. Neural adaptation to resistance training. *Med Sci Sports Exerc.* 1988;20(5):S135–45.
2. Enoka RM. Muscle strength and its development: new perspectives. *Sports Med* 1988;6:146–68.
3. Milner-Brown HS, Stein RB, Yemm R. Changes in firing rate of human motor units during linearly changing voluntary contractions. *J Physiol* 1973; 230:371–90.
4. Bernardi M, Solomonow M, Nguyen G. Motor unit recruitment strategies change with skill acquisition. *Eur J Appl Physiol* 1996;74:52–9.
5. Hakkinen K, Kallinen M, Komi PV, et al. Neuromuscular adaptations during short-term "normal" and reduced training periods in strength athletes. *Electromyogr Clin Neurophysiol* 1991;31:35–42.
6. Enoka RM. Neuromechanical basis of kinesiology. 2nd edition. Champaign, IL: Human Kinetics; 1994.
7. Ogita F, Stam RP, Tazawa HO, et al. Oxygen uptake in one-legged and two-legged exercise. *Med Sci Sports Exerc* 2000;32(10):1737–42.
8. Kraemer WJ, Ratamess NA. Physiology of resistance training. *Ortho Phys Ther Clin North Am* 2000;9(4): 467–513.
9. Brooks GA, Fahey TD, White TP. Exercise Physiology: Human Bioenergetics and Its Application. 2nd edition. Mountain View, CA: Mayfield Publishing Company; 1996.

Mechanical Specificity

Refers to the weight and movements required of the body.

 Neuromuscular Specificity

Refers to the speed of contraction and exercise selection.

Mechanical specificity refers to the weight and movements required of the body (3,5). To develop endurance in the legs, light weights must be used over many repetitions of leg exercises. To develop maximal strength in the chest, heavy weights must be used during chest-related exercises.

Neuromuscular specificity refers to the speed of contraction and exercise selection (4,8). To develop higher levels of power in the legs, low weight at high velocity of contraction must be performed in a plyometric manner (such as those seen in the Plyometric Training, Chapter 8) (Fig. 10.1). To develop higher levels of stability while pushing, chest exercises will need to be performed using controlled, unstable exercises at slower speeds (3,9). An example would be a dumbbell chest press performed on a stability ball (Fig. 10.2).

FIGURE 10.1   Training for power.

FIGURE 10.2   Training for stability.

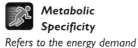 *Metabolic Specificity*

Refers to the energy demand required for a specific activity.

Metabolic specificity refers to the metabolic route needed to supply energy quickly for a specific exercise. To develop endurance, training will require prolonged bouts of exercise with minimal rest periods between sets that produce energy through the aerobic pathways. To develop maximal strength or power, training will require longer rest periods, so the intensity of each bout of exercise remains high. Energy will be supplied via the anaerobic pathways (10,11).

TIME OUT

Intramuscular Coordination versus Intermuscular Coordination

Intramuscular coordination is the ability of the neuromuscular system to allow optimum levels of motor unit recruitment and motor unit synchronization within a single muscle using single joint exercises (e.g., leg extensions, leg curls).

Intermuscular coordination is the ability of the neuromuscular system to allow *all* muscles to work together using multiple joint exercises (e.g., squats, lunges).

THE PRINCIPLE OF OVERLOAD

The principle of overload involves providing the appropriate training stimulus to elicit optimum physical, physiological, and performance adaptations. A tissue will adapt when it is asked, on a regular basis, to do more; the tissue needs the overload or it will not adapt. A well-designed, resistance training program imposes demands that force progressive adaptations (12). The human movement system responds to the imposed demands incurred during training (the SAID principle) with specific adaptations. The overload can occur through appropriate variable manipulation of volume (repetitions, sets), intensity, contraction velocity, muscle action, rest interval, training frequency, plane of motion, exercise selection, sensorimotor challenge, and exercise order (1,13–19).

THE PRINCIPLE OF VARIATION

Planned variations in a resistance training program are essential to enable continuous adaptations over a training period while preventing injury. Periodized resistance training programs lead to superior physical, physiological, and performance improvements when compared to a nonperiodized training program (20). Specific combinations of volume and intensity produce specific training adaptations (high volume = cellular/hypertrophic changes; high intensity = neural adaptations). A planned training program with progressive and systematic variation produces long-term, consistent adaptations and prevents overtraining and injury (1,2,20–31).

THE PRINCIPLE OF INDIVIDUALIZATION

Although it may sound obvious, when designing a resistance training program, the Sports Performance Professional must consider the athlete. Specifically, consider the athlete's age, general medical history, injury history, training background, work capacity, recoverability, structural integrity, training needs/goals, and sport. Each athlete will respond to a program that is designed specifically to address the individual's specific needs/goals (1,13,15).

PRINCIPLE OF ADAPTATION

One of the many unique qualities of the human body is its ability to adapt or adjust its functional capacity to meet the desired needs. Humans are the most adaptable of all. This is perhaps the root of all training and conditioning; the desire to seek an adaptation is the driving force behind most athletes and training programs (Table 10.1) (2,32).

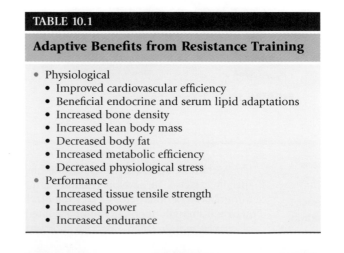

TABLE 10.1

Adaptive Benefits from Resistance Training

- Physiological
  - Improved cardiovascular efficiency
  - Beneficial endocrine and serum lipid adaptations
  - Increased bone density
  - Increased lean body mass
  - Decreased body fat
  - Increased metabolic efficiency
  - Decreased physiological stress
- Performance
  - Increased tissue tensile strength
  - Increased power
  - Increased endurance

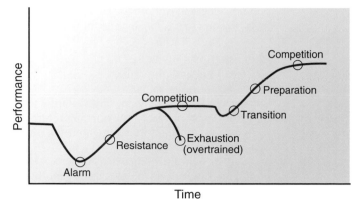

FIGURE 10.3   General adaptation syndrome.

General Adaptation Syndrome

The human movement system's ability to adapt to stresses placed on it.

GENERAL ADAPTATION SYNDROME

The human movement system seeks to maintain a state of physiological balance (or homeostasis) (33). To do this, the body must be able to adapt to stresses placed on it. Adaptation to stress follows a predictable pattern commonly called the **general adaptation syndrome**. This general pattern of adaptation was proposed by Hans Selye who showed that we all respond and adapt in a predictable manner to the stresses placed on us. In order to respond, however, the body must be confronted with a stressor or some form of stress that creates the need for a response (Fig. 10.3) (34). Selye outlined three stages of response to stress:

- Alarm reaction
- Resistance development
- Exhaustion

ALARM REACTION

This is the initial reaction to a stressor (Fig. 10.3). It allows for the activation of protective processes within the body. For example, an athlete who decides to begin resistance training places his/her body under the stress of increased amounts of force on the bones, joints, muscles, connective tissues, and nervous system. This creates a need for increased oxygen and blood supply to the right areas in his/her body, as well as increased neural recruitment to the muscles. Initially, the athlete's body is very inefficient at responding to the demands placed on it. Thus, the body must increase its ability to meet these new demands (34).

Consider the typical response to either unaccustomed exercise or a sudden increase in a training program. The new work is performed and over the next 2–3 days, the muscles may exhibit classic delayed onset muscle soreness or DOMS. During this period of DOMS, any attempt at replicating or advancing the soreness will be limited by the factors contributing to the soreness. This could be considered an "alarm reaction."

RESISTANCE DEVELOPMENT

During the resistance development stage, the body increases its functional capacity as it adapts to the stressor (Fig. 10.3). After repeated training sessions, the human movement system will increase its capability to efficiently recruit muscle fibers and distribute oxygen and blood to the proper areas in the body. After adaptation occurs, the body will require further stress to produce a new response and a higher level of performance (34).

Sports Performance Professionals often understand this adaptation response, but use it improperly by only manipulating the amount of weight the athlete uses when, in fact, this is but one of many ways to increase stress on the body. Chapter 12 will discuss the importance of manipulating the many acute variables for optimal adaptation while avoiding breakdown or exhaustion.

In the example of unaccustomed exercise, after the DOMS subsides, further work will be met with less and less soreness so that performance may gradually advance. This would be "resistance development." Performance will continue to improve until some new performance plateau is reached and will be maintained if training is maintained.

EXHAUSTION

Prolonged stress or stress that is intolerable to an athlete will produce exhaustion or distress (Fig. 10.3). When the stressor is too much for the system to handle, performance declines because of injury, staleness, or both (34). The athlete who is in this exhaustion stage can suffer from a variety of issues that can reduce performance, such as:

- Stress fractures
- Muscle strains
- Joint and muscle pain
- Emotional fatigue

Resistance training (and any other forms of training) must be cycled through different stages that increase stress placed on the human movement system and also allow for sufficient rest and recuperation. More information about the **periodization** of training (OPT™ model) will be detailed in Chapter 12.

There may be a point where further advancement in a training program fails to lead to any improvement in performance and actual performance may decline. This would be the exhaustion stage.

A continual increase in resistance with the intent of stressing the muscles of the body to produce a size and/or strength change can lead to injury of the muscle, joint, or connective tissue. Remember that connective tissues (such as ligaments, and tendons) do not adapt as quickly as muscles, due to their individual nature and the lack of blood supply (35,36).

The different tissues in the body (muscle, connective, epithelial, and nervous) each have a different potential to adapt to stress. This means that training programs should provide a variety of intensities and stresses to optimize the adaptation of each tissue for the best possible results. Adaptations result from the specific application of stresses to specific aspects of the human movement system using different training techniques. This is evident by the SAID principle.

Periodization
Division of a training program into smaller, progressive stages.

Progressive Outcomes of Resistance Training

The concept of adaptation makes it clear that some specific type of change will occur based on the specific stresses placed upon the body. Resistance training programs are designed to produce changes to factors across the entire power output continuum. Whether the goal is to increase muscle mass, develop better athletic performance, or reduce body fat, the use of resistance training is an important component of any program. This will help ensure optimum athletic performance. The healthier athletes remain and the longer they can train, the greater amount of adaptation they will realize without developing tissue breakdown, injury, or entering the exhaustion stage of the general adaptation syndrome. The main adaptations that occur from resistance training include stabilization, muscular endurance, hypertrophy, strength, and power.

STABILIZATION

Stabilization is the human movement system's ability to provide optimal dynamic joint support and maintain correct posture during all movements. This requires high levels of muscular endurance for optimal recruitment of prime movers to increase concentric force production and reduce eccentric force. Recent research has demonstrated repeatedly that training with controlled, unstable exercises increases the body's ability to stabilize and balance itself (37–39). Conversely, if training is not performed with controlled, unstable exercises, athletes will not gain the same level of stability and may even become worse. (39–41). This is an important consideration during rehabilitation after injury (41).

Stabilization
The human movement system's ability to provide optimal dynamic joint support and maintain correct posture during all movements.

MUSCULAR ENDURANCE

Muscular endurance is the ability to produce and maintain force production over prolonged periods of time. Training for muscular endurance is not the sole domain of the endurance athlete; muscular endurance is an integral component of all sports performance programs. Creating muscular endurance will help the athlete increase core and joint stabilization–the foundation for which hypertrophy, strength, and power are built. Training for muscular endurance of the core focuses on the recruitment of muscles responsible for postural stability, namely, type I muscle fibers.

Research has shown that resistance training protocols with higher repetitions are most effective at improving local muscular endurance (14,20,29). Current research also shows that a periodized, structured resistance training program can enhance local muscular endurance (12,20,42). Research also shows that after the initial training effect in previously untrained individuals, multiple sets of periodized training may reign superior to single-set training in increasing local muscle endurance (20). Campos (14) found that higher repetitions (2 sets/20–28 repetitions with 1-minute rest periods beginning at 2 days per week) increased local muscle endurance and hypertrophy in untrained males following an 8-week training program. Marx (20) found that after the initial 12 weeks of training, multiple sets of up to 15 repetitions, 4 times a week for 6 months resulted in a threefold decrease in body fat and an increase in local muscle

Muscular Endurance
The ability to produce and maintain force production over prolonged periods of time.

endurance as well as a significant increase in lean body mass. In addition, Marx's data showed that after the initial 12 weeks of training, multiple set training was superior to low-volume single-set training for maximal strength, endurance, and power.

HYPERTROPHY

Hypertrophy
Enlargement of skeletal muscle fibers in response to overcoming force from high-tension requirements.

Hypertrophy is the enlargement of skeletal muscle fibers in response to being recruited to develop increased levels of tension. Early work suggested that the initial improvement in strength was due mostly to recruitment and further increases in strength followed by hypertrophy (43). The general nature of hypertrophy is an increase in cross-sectional area of individual muscle fibers due to an increase in myofibril protein synthesis. Although hypertrophy is not externally visible for many weeks (4–8 weeks) in a beginner, research on the nature of the hypertrophic response has demonstrated that protein synthesis begins in the early stages of training, regardless of the intensity (44–46).

Resistance training protocols that use low- to intermediate-repetition ranges with progressive overload lead to hypertrophy. And this is not limited to young adult males. Structured, progressive resistance training programs using multiple sets will help to increase hypertrophy in older ages as well as both males and females alike (12,14,47–50). In a project directed at women, Kraemer et al. demonstrated that 24 weeks of training 3 days per week with 3 sets of 8–12 repetitions per exercise improved muscle hypertrophy and body composition (32). Thus, progressive resistance training programs using moderate to low-repetition protocols with progressively higher loads will result in increased hypertrophy in older adults, and men, and women.

STRENGTH

Strength
The ability of the neuromuscular system to produce internal tension in order to overcome an external force.

Strength is the ability of the neuromuscular system to produce internal tension to overcome an external load. Regardless of whether the external load demands that the neuromuscular system produce stability, endurance, maximal strength, or power, internal tension is still required. As external loads increase, there is a demand for greater internal tension which, when applied in a systematic manner, leads to *strength adaptations*. Although the muscle fibers only produce tension, the specific form of strength performance that is visible from training is the "sum" total of a number of mechanical and physiological factors (e.g., recruitment, hypertrophy, summation, length-tension, force-velocity, rate coding) based on the style of training used (SAID principle).

Traditionally, resistance training programs have focused on developing maximal strength in individual muscles, emphasizing single planes of motion. Because all muscles function eccentrically, isometrically, and concentrically in all three planes of motion at different speeds of movement, a training program should use a progressive approach that emphasizes the appropriate exercise selection, all muscle actions, and repetition tempos. This is discussed in greater detail in Chapter 12.

Because muscles operates under the control of the central nervous system, strength needs to be thought of not as a function of muscle, but as a result of activating the neuromuscular system. Strength gains can occur rapidly in beginning athletes and can increase with a structured, progressive resistance training program. One factor in increased strength is an increase in the number of motor units recruited, especially early in a training program (43,51). Using heavier loads increases the neural demand and recruitment of more muscle fibers until a recruitment plateau is reached, after which further increases in strength are a result of fiber hypertrophy (9,52). But remember, research shows that improper stabilization can negatively affect a muscle's force production (53), so stabilization training precedes strength training according to the OPT™ model.

Strength cannot be thought of in isolation. Strength is built on the foundation of stabilization requiring muscle, tendon, and ligaments to be prepared for the load that will be required to increase strength beyond the initial stages of training. Where stabilization training is designed with the characteristics of type I muscle fibers in mind (slow contracting, low-tension output, and resistance to fatigue), strength training is designed to match the characteristics of type II muscle fibers (quick contracting, high-tension output, prone to fatigue). Due to their characteristics of each fiber type, the acute variables are manipulated to take advantage of the specific characteristics of each fiber type. The majority of strength increases will occur during the first 12 weeks of resistance training from increased recruitment and hypertrophy (20,26,42,47,54). Beyond the initial gains, novice exercisers will continue to benefit by recruitment and hypertrophy when using multiple sets, and training a minimum of two times per week at 80% of 1 repetition maximum (55,56). Experienced lifters will find it necessary to carry out a more demanding program in terms of training volume and intensity following a sound periodized schedule (see Chapter 12 for more details).

POWER

Power
The ability to generate the greatest possible force in the shortest amount of time.

Power is the ability to generate the greatest possible force in the shortest amount of time. Power is also defined by the neuromuscular system's ability to increase the rate of force production through increased motor unit activation, synchronization, and rate coding (the speed at which the motor units are activated) (57).

Power is built on the foundation of stabilization and strength because power requires both neuromuscular efficiency (from stabilization training) and increased motor unit activation (from strength training). The adaptation to power training uses stabilization and strength adaptations that are applied at more realistic speeds and forces. As power is the product of force × velocity, power can be enhanced through an increase in either force or velocity. The force-velocity curve dictates that the higher the load, the slower the speed of movement and conversely, the lower the load, the faster the speed of movement. To maximize training, both heavy and light loads must be moved as fast as possible to create the adaptation of power. Hence, using both training methods in superset fashion may create the necessary adaptations to enhance the body's ability to recruit a large number of motor units and increase the rate (speed) of activation (21,58,59). Early isokinetic work underscored the importance of speed of exercise showing that training performed at high speeds led to better performance at the training speed and all movement speeds below the training speed.

Resistance Training Systems

Power lifters, Olympic lifters, and bodybuilders were the original architects of most resistance training programs. These training programs are popular because of marketing or "gym science," not necessarily because they have been scientifically proven to be superior over other programs increasing strength, hypertrophy, and performance. Research has shown that following a systematic, integrated training program and manipulating key training variables achieves optimum gains in strength, neuromuscular efficiency, hypertrophy, and performance (12,29,32).

There are many training systems currently being followed. Several of the most common training systems that are currently used in the sports performance industry will be reviewed prior to discussing the OPT™ model in Chapter 12. For the most complete and eloquent description of the systems described subsequently, the reader is referred to the text by Steven Fleck and William Kraemer (15).

RESISTANCE TRAINING SYSTEMS EXPLAINED

THE SINGLE-SET SYSTEM

As the name suggests, the single-set system uses 1 set of each exercise. Each set usually consists of 8–12 repetitions of each exercise at a controlled tempo. It is usually recommended that this system be performed two times per week in order to promote sufficient development and maintenance of muscle mass.

THE MULTIPLE-SET SYSTEM

The multiple-set system, on the other hand, consists of performing multiple sets for each exercise. The resistance, sets, and repetitions that are performed can be selected according to the goals and needs of the athlete. Multiple-set training can be appropriate for both novice and advanced athletes.

THE PYRAMID SYSTEM

The pyramid system involves a progressive or regressive step approach that either increases weight with each set, or decreases weight with each set (Fig. 10.4).

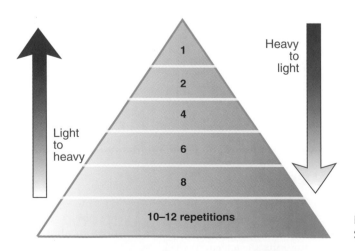

FIGURE 10.4 Pyramid System.

In the *light-to-heavy system*, the athlete performs 10–12 repetitions with a light load and increases the resistance for each set that follows until the athlete can perform 1–2 repetitions, usually in 4–6 sets. This system can easily be used for workouts that involve only 2–4 sets or higher repetition schemes (12–20 repetitions).

The *heavy-to-light system* works in the opposite direction. Following a warm-up, the athlete begins with a heavy load for 1–2 repetitions then decreases the load and increases the repetitions for 4–6 sets. This system leads to early muscle fatigue of a large fraction of fibers. Thus, to continue through the workout, more motor units need to be recruited to successfully perform subsequent sets. When heavy resistance fatigues a large number of motor units, more fibers will be activated overall throughout the workout than might occur with the *light-to-heavy system.*

THE SUPERSET SYSTEM

The superset system utilizes two exercises performed in rapid succession. This system features the use of independent subsystems with similar principles (namely, compound-set and tri-set systems).

Compound sets involve the performance of two exercises for antagonistic muscles. For example, an athlete may perform a set of bench presses followed by cable rows (chest/back). Working opposing musculature allows for better recovery before the start of another set.

Tri-sets use three exercises in rapid succession for the same muscle group or body part. For example, a chest tri-set might be an incline dumbbell press, cable chest press, and ball push-ups all in succession.

Typically, supersetting involves sets of 8–12 repetitions with no rest between sets or exercises. However, any number of repetitions can be employed. The superset system is popular among bodybuilders and may be beneficial for muscular hypertrophy and muscular endurance.

THE CIRCUIT TRAINING SYSTEM

The circuit training system consists of a series of exercises that an athlete performs one after the other with minimal rest (Table 10.2). The typical acute variables for a circuit training program include 1–3 sets of 8–15 repetitions with 15–60 seconds of rest between exercises. However, these variables can be manipulated to enhance the desired effect (60).

TABLE 10.2
Example Stabilization Circuit
1. Ball Two-Arm Dumbbell Chest Press
2. Single-Leg Cable Row
3. Single-Leg Dumbbell Shoulder Press
4. Single-Leg Dumbbell Curl
5. Supine Ball Dumbbell Triceps Extension
6. Step-Up to Balance
7. Rest

THE PERIPHERAL HEART ACTION SYSTEM

The Peripheral Heart Action System (PHA)
A variation of circuit training that alternates upper- and lower-body exercises throughout the circuit.

The peripheral heart action (PHA) system is another variation of circuit training that alternates upper- and lower-body exercises throughout the circuit. The number of exercises per sequence varies with the program's goal. The athlete performs 8-20 repetitions per exercise, depending on the desired adaptation and phase of training he or she is using in the OPT™ model. This system is very beneficial for incorporating an integrated, multidimensional program and for altering body composition (15,43). Examples for each of the three main adaptations are shown in Table 10.3.

THE SPLIT-ROUTINE SYSTEM

A split-routine system involves breaking the body up into parts to be trained on separate days. Many bodybuilders, as well as mass dominant and strength athletes (football, shot put, etc.), use the split-routine system. Bodybuilders typically perform many exercises for the same body part to bring about optimal muscular hypertrophy. By breaking up the body into parts that can be trained on different days, more work can be performed for the allotted time per workout. Split-routines come in all sizes and shapes. A few typical split-routines are shown in Table 10.4.

Any derivative of these outlined routines can be used. The important issue with some of these routines is recovery time. When training each body part more than once a week, volume and intensity should be taken into account.

FIGURE 10.5 (*Continued*) (**B**) Step-up balance to overhead press: sagittal plane. (**C**) Step-up balance to overhead press: frontal plane. (**D**) Step-up balance to overhead press: transverse plane. (*continued*)

FIGURE 10.5   (*Continued*) (**E**) Lunge to balance to overhead press: sagittal plane. (**F**) Lunge to balance to overhead press: frontal plane. (**G**) Lunge to balance to overhead press: transverse plane. (*continued*)

FIGURE 10.6 (*Continued*) (**D**) Push-up progression: floor. (**E**) Push-up progression: feet on ball. (**F**) Push-up progression: hands on ball. (**G**) Push-up progression: with roll. (**H**) Push-up progression: with oblique roll. (**I**) Cable chest press progression: two legs and two arms. (*continued*)

FIGURE 10.6 (*Continued*) (**J**) Cable chest press progression: two legs and alternate arm. (**K**) Cable chest press progression: two legs and single arm. (**L**) Cable chest press progressions: single leg and two arms. (**M**) Cable chest press progressions: single leg and alternate arm. (**N**) Cable chest press progressions: single leg and single arm.

FIGURE 10.7 (*Continued*) (**M**) Standing lat pulldown. (**N**) Single-leg lat pulldown. (**O**) Single-leg straight-arm pulldown.

FIGURE 10.8 SHOULDERS STABILIZATION EXERCISES. (**A**) Single-leg scaption. (**B**) Single-leg overhead press progression: two arms. (*continued*)

FIGURE 10.8 (*Continued*) (**C**) Single-leg overhead press progression: alternate arm. (**D**) Single-leg overhead press progression: single arm. (**E**) Single-leg PNF. (*continued*)

FIGURE 10.8 *(Continued)* **(F)** Prone ball scaption. **(G)** Prone ball horizontal abduction. **(H)** Prone ball military press progression: two arms. **(I)** Prone ball military press progression: alternate arm. **(J)** Prone ball military press progression: single arm. *(continued)*

FIGURE 10.8 (*Continued*) (**K**) Ball lift and chop with side lunge. (**L**) Ball combo I. (**M**) Ball combo II.

FIGURE 10.9   BICEPS STABILIZATION EXERCISES. (**A**) Single-leg dumbbell curl progression: two arms. (**B**) Single-leg dumbbell curl progression: alternate arm. (**C**) Single-leg dumbbell curl progression: single arm. (*continued*)

FIGURE 10.9 (*Continued*) (**D**) Single-leg barbell curl. (**E**) Single-leg cable curl. (*continued*)

FIGURE 10.9 (*Continued*) (**F**) Single-leg hammer curl progression: two arms. (**G**) Single-leg hammer curl progression: alternate arm. (**H**) Single-leg hammer curl progression: single arm.

FIGURE 10.10 TRICEPS STABILIZATION EXERCISES. (**A**) Supine ball dumbbell extension progression: two arms. (**B**) Supine ball dumbbell extension progression: alternate arm. (**C**) Supine ball dumbbell extension progression: single arm. (**D**) Prone ball dumbbell extension progression: two arms. (*continued*)

FIGURE 10.10 *(Continued)* **(E)** Prone ball dumbbell extension progression: alternate arm. **(F)** Prone ball dumbbell extension progression: single arm. **(G)** Single-leg cable press-down.

FIGURE 10.11 LEG STABILIZATION EXERCISES. (**A**) Ball squat. (**B**) Step-up to balance: sagittal plane. (**C**) Step-up to balance: frontal plane. (**D**) Step-up to balance: transverse plane. (**E**) Lunge to balance: sagittal plane. (**F**) Lunge to balance: frontal plane. (*continued*)

FIGURE 10.11 *(Continued)* (**G**) Lunge to balance: transverse plane. (**H**) Single-leg squat. (**I**) Single-leg squat touchdown. (**J**) Single-leg Romanian deadlift.

STRENGTH EXERCISES

GOAL: These exercises are designed to enhance prime mover strength by performing them in more stable environments (Figs. 10.12 to 10.18). This places more emphasis on the prime movers and allows the athlete to handle heavier loads.

A

B

FIGURE 10.12 TOTAL BODY STRENGTH EXERCISES. (**A**) Squat, curl to overhead press. (**B**) Step-up to overhead press: sagittal plane. (*continued*)

FIGURE 10.12   (*Continued*) (**C**) Step-up to overhead press: frontal plane. (**D**) Step-up to overhead press: transverse plane. (*continued*)

E

F

FIGURE 10.12 (*Continued*) (**E**) Lunge to overhead press: sagittal plane. (**F**) Lunge to overhead press: frontal plane. (*continued*)

FIGURE 10.12 (*Continued*) (**G**) Lunge to overhead press: transverse plane. (**H**) Romanian deadlift shrug to calf raise. (*continued*)

I

FIGURE 10.12 (*Continued*) (**I**) Deadlift shrug to calf raise.

A

B

FIGURE 10.13 CHEST STRENGTH EXERCISES. (**A**) Dumbbell bench press. (**B**) Incline dumbbell bench press. (*continued*)

C

D

E

FIGURE 10.13   (*Continued*)   (**C**) Barbell bench press. (**D**) Incline barbell bench press. (**E**) Chest press machine.

FIGURE 10.14 BACK STRENGTH EXERCISES. (**A**) Seated cable row. (**B**) Seated lat pulldown. (*continued*)

FIGURE 10.14   (*Continued*) (**C**) Straight-arm pulldown. (**D**) Pull-up. (*continued*)

E

F

FIGURE 10.14 (*Continued*) (**E**) Supported dumbbell row. (**F**) Bent-over barbell row.

FIGURE 10.15   SHOULDER STRENGTH EXERCISES. (A) Seated overhead dumbbell press. **(B)** Seated dumbbell lateral raise. (*continued*)

C

D

E

FIGURE 10.15   (*Continued*) (**C**) Shoulder press machine. (**D**) Overhead barbell press. (**E**) Seated dumbbell scaption.

FIGURE 10.16 BICEPS STRENGTH EXERCISES. (**A**) Seated dumbbell curl. (**B**) Seated hammer curl. (**C**) Standing barbell curl. (*continued*)

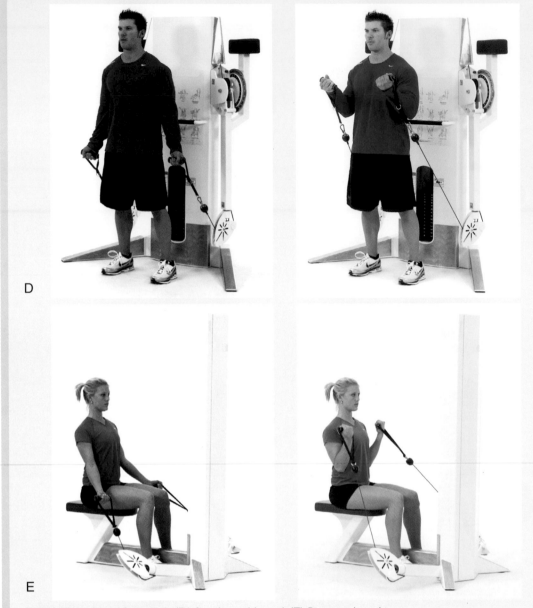

D

E

FIGURE 10.16 (*Continued*) (**D**) Standing cable curl. (**E**) Bicep curl machine.

A

FIGURE 10.17 TRICEPS STRENGTH EXERCISES. (**A**) Supine dumbbell extension. (*continued*)

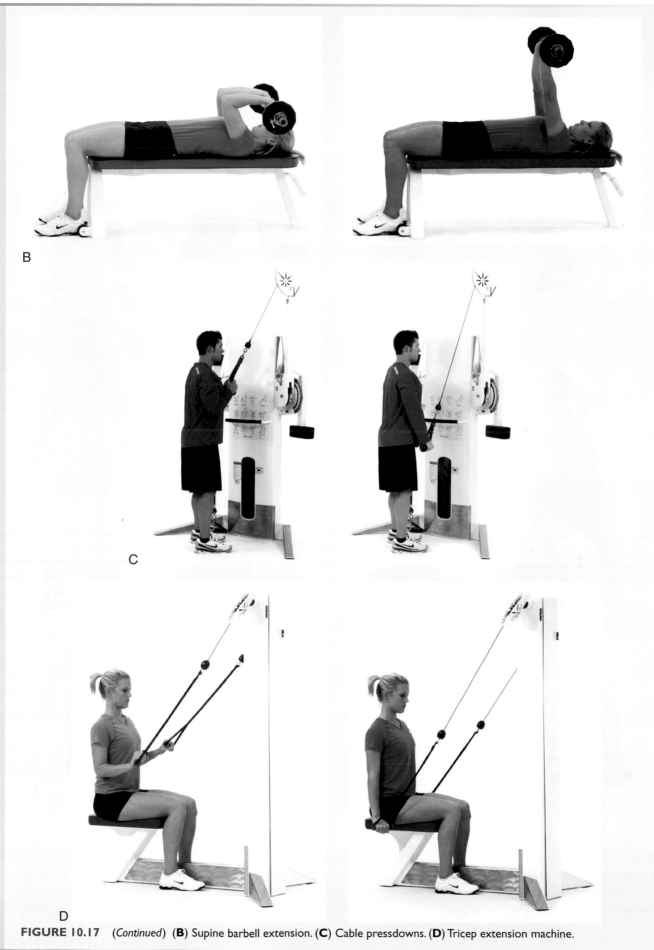

FIGURE 10.17   (*Continued*) (**B**) Supine barbell extension. (**C**) Cable pressdowns. (**D**) Tricep extension machine.

FIGURE 10.18 LEG STRENGTH EXERCISES. (**A**) Barbell squat. (**B**) Dumbbell squat. (**C**) Step-up: sagittal plane. (**D**) Step-up: frontal plane. (**E**) Step-up: transverse plane. (**F**) Lunge: sagittal plane. (*continued*)

FIGURE 10.18   (*Continued*) (**G**) Lunge: frontal plane. (**H**) Lunge: transverse plane. (**I**) Deadlift. (**J**) Romanian deadlift. (**K**) Leg press.

POWER EXERCISES

GOAL: These exercises are designed to improve rate of force productions and overall muscular power by performing them as fast and explosively as can be controlled (Figs. 10.19 to 10.23). Ideally, the athlete must have ample amounts of stability and strength to ensure the safety and effectiveness of these exercises.

FIGURE 10.19 TOTAL BODY POWER EXERCISES. (**A**) Dumbbell snatch. (**B**) Barbell clean. (*continued*)

C

FIGURE 10.19 *(Continued)* (**C**) Push-press.

A

FIGURE 10.20 CHEST POWER EXERCISES. (**A**) Medicine ball chest press. *(continued)*

B

FIGURE 10.20 (*Continued*) (**B**) Rotational chest pass.

A

FIGURE 10.21 BACK POWER EXERCISES. (**A**) Ball/medicine ball pullover throw. (*continued*)

FIGURE 10.21   (*Continued*) (**B**) Woodchop throw. (**C**) Soccer throw.

FIGURE 10.22 SHOULDERS POWER EXERCISES. (**A**) Overhead medicine ball throw. (**B**) Oblique throw.

FIGURE 10.23   LEG POWER EXERCISES. (**A**) Squat jump. (**B**) Tuck jump. (**C**) Butt kick. (**D**) Ice skaters. (*continued*)

FIGURE 10.23 (*Continued*) (**E**) Lunge jump. (**F**) Box jump. (**G**) Power step-up.

SUMMARY

A well-designed, integrated training program produces optimum levels of strength, neuro-muscular control, power, flexibility, endurance, and alterations in body composition. To achieve this, the body is required to adapt specifically to impose demands. Adaptation is, therefore, one of the most important concepts to understand. It is important also to understand how adaptation relates to the design of a program and a client's goals. It is also important to realize that there are different types of strength and different systems of resistance training that the Sports Performance Professional can use to create a far more individualized and systematic program.

REFERENCES

1. Tan B. Manipulating resistance training program variables to optimize maximum strength in men: a review. *J Strength Cond Res* 1999;13:289–304.
2. Kraemer WJ, Ratamess NA. Physiology of resistance training. *Orthop Clin J N Am* 2000;9:467–513.
3. Behm DB. Neuromuscular implications and applications of resistance training. *J Strength Cond Res* 1995;9:264–74.
4. Hakkinen K. Neuromuscular adaptation during strength training, aging, detraining and immobilization. *Crit Rev Phys Med* 1994;6:161–98.
5. Rutherford OM, Greig CA, Sargent AJ et al. Strength training and power output: transference effects in the human quadriceps muscle. *J Sports Sci* 1986;4:101–07.
6. Rutherford OM, Jones DA. The role of learning and coordination in strength training. *Eur J Appl Physiol* 1987;55:100–05.
7. Sale DG. Influence of exercise and training on motor unit activation. *Exerc Sport Sci Rev* 1987;15:95–151.
8. McEvoy KP, Newton RU. Baseball throwing speed and base running speed: the effects of ballistic resistance training. *J Strength Cond Res* 1991;12:216–21.
9. Sale DG. Neural adaptation to resistance training. *Med Sci Sports Exerc* 1988;20:S135–45.
10. Viru A, Viru M. Nature of the Training Response. In Garrett Jr WE, Kirkendall DT. Exercise and Sport Science. Philadelphia: Lippincott, Williams & Wilkins; 2000. p 67–95.
11. Parra J, Cadefau JA, Rodas G et al. The distribution of rest periods affects performance and adaptations of energy metabolism induced by high-intensity training in human muscle. *Acta Physiol Scand* 2000;169:157–65.
12. Kraemer WJ, Ratamess NA. Fundamentals of resistance training: progression and exercise prescription. *Med Sci Sports Exerc* 2004;36:674–88.
13. Bompa TO. Theory and Methodology of Training. Dubuque, IA: Kendall/Hunt; 1983.
14. Campos GE, Luecke TJ, Wendeln HK et al. Muscular adaptations in response to three different resistance-training regimens: specificity of repetition maximum training zones. *Eur J Appl Physiol* 2002;88:50–60.
15. Fleck SJ, Kraemer WJ. Designing Resistance Training Programs, 2nd ed. Champaign, IL: Human Kinetics; 1997.
16. Graves JE, Pollock ML, Jones AE et al. Specificity of limited range of motion variable resistance training. *Med Sci Sport Exerc* 1989;21:84–89.
17. Hass CJ, Feigenbaum MS, Franklin BA. Prescription of resistance training for healthy populations. *Sports Med* 2001;31:953–64.
18. McCall GE, Byrnes WC, Fleck SJ et al. Acute and chronic hormonal responses to resistance training designed to promote muscle hypertrophy. *Can J Appl Physiol* 1999;24:96–107.
19. Morrissey MC, Harman EA, Johnson MJ. Resistance training modes; Specificity and effectiveness. *Med Sci Sport Exerc* 1986;18:612–24.
20. Marx JO, Ratamess NA, Nindl BC et al. Low-volume circuit versus high-volume periodized resistance training in women. *Med Sci Sports Exerc* 2001;33:635–43.
21. Baker D, Wilson G, Carlyon R. Periodization: the effects on strength of manipulating volume and intensity. *J Strength Cond Res* 1994;8:235–42.
22. Blazevich AJ, Gill ND, Bronks R et al. Training-specific muscle architecture adaptation after 5-wk training in athletes. *Med Sci Sports Exerc* 2003;35:2013–22.
23. Hakkinen A, Sokka T, Kotaniemi A et al. A randomized two-year study of the effects of dynamic strength training on muscle strength, disease activity, functional capacity, and bone mineral density in early rheumatoid arthritis. *Arthritis Rheum* 2001;44:515–22.
24. Hakkinen K, Pakarinen A, Hannonen P et al. Effects of strength training on muscle strength, cross-sectional area, maximal electromyographic activity, and serum hormones in premenopausal women with fibromyalgia. *J Rheumatol* 2002;29:1287–295.
25. Izquierdo M, Hakkinen K, Ibanez J et al. Effects of strength training on muscle power and serum hormones in middle-aged and older men. *J Appl Physiol* 2001;90:1497–507.
26. Kraemer WJ, Mazzetti SA, Nindl BC. Effect of resistance training on women's strength/power and occupational performances. *Med Sci Sports Exerc* 2001;33:1011–25.
27. Mazzetti SA, Kraemer WJ, Volek JS et al. The influence of direct supervision of resistance training on strength performance. *Med Sci Sports Exerc* 2000;32:1175–184.
28. Rhea MR, Alvar BA, Ball SD et al. Three sets of weight training superior to 1 set with equal intensity for eliciting strength. *J Strength Condition Res* 2002;16:525–29.

29. Rhea MR, Alvar BA, Burkett LN et al. A meta-analysis to determine the dose response for strength development. *Med Sci Sports Exerc* 2003;35:456–64.

30. Rhea MR, Ball SD, Phillips WT et al. A comparison of linear and daily undulating periodized programs with equated volume and intensity for strength. *J Strength Condition Res* 2002;16:250–55.

31. Willoughby DS. The effects of mesocycle length weight training programs involving periodization and partially equated volumes on upper and lower body strength. *J Strength Cond Res* 1993;7:2–8.

32. Kraemer WJ, Nindl BC, Ratamess NA et al. Changes in muscle hypertrophy in women with periodized resistance training. *Med Sci Sports Exerc* 2004;36:697–708.

33. Brooks GA, Fahey TD, White TP. Exercise Physiology: Human Bioenergetics and its Application. Mountain View, CA: Mayfield Publishing Company; 1996.

34. Selye H. The Stress of Life. New York: McGraw-Hill; 1976.

35. Nordin M, Lorenz T, Campello M. Biomechanics of Tendons and Ligaments. In Nordin M, Frankel VH. Basic Biomechanics of the Musculoskeletal System. Philadelphia: Lippincott Williams & Wilkins; 2001. p 102–125.

36. Kannus P. Structure of the tendon connective tissue. *Scan J Med Sci Sports* 2000;10:312–20.

37. Behm DG, Anderson K, Curnew RS. Muscle force and activation under stable and unstable conditions. *J Strength Cond Res* 2002;16:416–22.

38. Cosio-Lima LM, Reynolds KL, Winter C et al. Effects of physioball and conventional floor exercises on early phase adaptations in back and abdominal core stability and balance in women. *J Strength Cond Res* 2003;17:721–25.

39. Heitkamp HC, Horstmann T, Mayer F et al. Gain in strength and muscular balance after balance training. *Int J Sports Med* 2001;22:285–90.

40. Bellew JW, Yates JW, Gater DR. The initial effects of low-volume strength training on balance in untrained older men and women. *J Strength Cond Res* 2003;17:121–28.

41. Cressey EM, West CA, Tiberio DP et al. The effects of ten weeks of lower-body unstable surface training on markers of athletic performance. *J Strength Cond Res* 2007;21:561–67.

42. Hass CJ, Garzarella L, de Hoyos D et al. Single versus multiple sets in long-term recreational weightlifters. *Med Sci Sports Exerc* 2000;32:235–42.

43. Moritani T, deVries HA. Neural factors versus hypertrophy in the time course of muscle strength gain. *Am J Phys Med* 1979;58:115–30.

44. Kraemer WJ, Fleck SJ, Evans WJ. Strength and Power Training: Physiological Mechanisms of Adaptation. In Holloszy JO. Exercise and Sport Science Reviews. Baltimore: Williams & Wilkins; 1998. p 363–97.

45. Mayhew TP, Rothstein JM, Finucane SD et al. Muscular adaptation to concentric and eccentric exercise at equal power levels. *Med Sci Sport Exerc* 1995;27:868–73.

46. Staron RS, Karapondo DL, Kraemer WJ et al. Skeletal muscle adaptations during early phase of heavy-resistance training in men and women. *J Appl Physiol* 1994;76:1247–255.

47. Brandenburg JP, Docherty D. The effects of accentuated eccentric loading on strength, muscle hypertrophy, and neural adaptations in trained individuals. *J Strength Condition Res* 2002;16:25–32.

48. Hakkinen K, Alen M, Kraemer WJ et al. Neuromuscular adaptations during concurrent strength and endurance training versus strength training. *Eur J Appl Physiol* 2003;89:42–52.

49. Hakkinen K, Kraemer WJ, Newton RU et al. Changes in electromyographic activity, muscle fibre and force production characteristics during heavy resistance/power strength training in middle-aged and older men and women. *Acta Physiologica Scandinavica* 2001;171:51–62.

50. McCall GE, Byrnes WC, Fleck SJ. Acute and chronic hormonal responses to resistance training designed to promote muscle hypertrophy. *Can J Appl Physiol* 2003;89:42–52.

51. Gabriel DA, Kamen G, Frost G. Neural adaptations to resistive exercise: mechanisms and recommendations for training practices. *Sports Med* 2006;36:133–49.

52. Sale DG. Neural Adaptation in Strength and Power Training. In Jones NL, McCartney N, McComas AJ. Human Muscle Power. Champaign, IL: Human Kinetics; 1986. p 289–307.

53. Edgerton VR, Wolf SL, Levendowski DJ et al. Theoretical basis for patterning EMG amplitudes to assess muscle dysfunction. *Med Sci Sports Exerc* 1996;28:744–51.

54. Chilibeck PD, Calder AW, Sale DG et al. A comparison of strength and muscle mass increases during resistance training in young women. *Eur J Appl Physiol Occup Physiol* 1998;77:170–75.

55. Peterson MD, Rhea MR, Alvar BA. Maximizing strength development in athletes: a meta-analysis to determine the dose-response relationship. *J Strength Cond Res* 2004;18:377–82.

56. Rhea MR, Alderman BL. A meta-analysis of periodized versus nonperiodized strength and power training programs. *Res Q Exerc Sport* 2004;75:413–22.

57. Enoka RM. Neuromechanics of Human Movement, 3rd ed. Champaign, IL: Human Kinetics; 2002.

58. Baker D. Selecting the appropriate exercises and loads for speed-strength development. *Strength Cond Coach* 1995;3:8–16.

59. Ebben WP, Watts PB. A review of combined weight training and plyometric training modes: complex training. *Strength Cond* 1998;20:18–27.

60. Haltom RW, Kraemer RR, Sloan RA et al. Circuit weight training and its effects on excess postexercise oxygen consumption. *Med Sci Sport Exerc* 1999;31:1613–618.

CHAPTER 11

Olympic Lifting for Performance Enhancement

UPON COMPLETION OF THIS CHAPTER, YOU WILL BE ABLE TO:

Describe the rationale for the utilization of Olympic lifts for improving performance.

Qualify an athlete to perform Olympic lifts.

Coach proper lifting techniques and be able to identify improper techniques.

Understand where the OPT™ model Olympic lifting would be most appropriately used to ensure safety and effectiveness of the program.

Introduction

The scientific rationale for incorporating Olympic lifts, and their derivatives into an athlete's program, to enhance sports performance is evident both practically and scientifically. The utilization of the Olympic lifts has long been in practice. As performance specialists become more knowledgeable in the process of program design, more information on Olympic lifting is necessary to make the most effective exercise prescriptions. The purpose of this chapter is to shed light on the proven effectiveness of the Olympic lifts as well as to describe and illustrate the established techniques to properly execute the lifts.

Olympic weightlifting is a sport in and of itself. The competition lifts are the snatch and the clean and jerk. Although these lifts can improve explosiveness, even more popular among athletes and coaches are the derivatives of the Olympic lifts, such as the power snatch, power clean, and clean pulls, as well as squatting and deadlifting. One reason the derivative lifts are more widely accepted is that many athletes cannot realize the deep positions necessary in the snatch and clean and jerk. This chapter will assist the Sports Performance Professional to understand how flexibility, mobility, stability, posture, and neuromuscular control affect the athlete's ability to execute the Olympic lifts and their derivatives. Also, the Olympic lifts are oftentimes performed improperly. This will reduce the effectiveness of the lifts and can lead to compensations or injury. The common compensations observed, in training with the lifts, will also be addressed.

The Scientific Rationale for Olympic Lifting

PRINCIPLE OF SPECIFICITY OF TRAINING

When considering a program designed for enhancing sports performance, one of the variables is exercise selection (1). As mentioned in the previous chapter, the exercises chosen to improve performance in a particular sport should follow the specific adaptation to imposed demand (SAID) principle. The concept of specificity was first put forth in DeLorme's classic 1945 paper on progressive resistance training, but became a popular research topic in the middle 1970s when the concept was expanded far beyond resistance exercise. Bompa explains this principle stating that an exercise modality specific to the skill set of a particular sport will elicit a more rapid performance enhancement (2). Siff (3) points out that there are at least 10 variables when considering the idea of specificity, such as the velocity of movement, force of contraction, muscle fiber recruitment, movement pattern, muscle contraction type, region of movement, metabolism, biomechanical adaptation, flexibility, and fatigue.

TIME OUT
High-Load and Low-Load Speed Strength

Work output has a speed component based on the characteristics of the hyperbolic force-velocity curve. According to the force-velocity curve, the highest forces are generated at slow contraction velocities. When converted to power, these motions are at lower power output due to the longer duration of time necessary to execute the movement. Low loads can be moved at high-contraction velocities (i.e., quickly). When converted to power, these motions are at higher-power output due to the short duration to execute the movement.

Maximum Strength
Strength is usually defined as the ability to exert a force against a resistance. Maximum strength would be the greatest amount of force generated, typically measured during a 1-RM.

Reactive Strength
Reactive strength is a ready response to a stimulus that would be the necessary strength required in response to some sort of stimulus, be it physical, visual, or auditory.

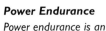

Power Endurance
Power endurance is an athlete's ability to sustain high-power output for an extended period of time. Athletes with exceptional power endurance might be 400-m sprinters, 400-m hurdlers, individual medley swimmers, or wrestlers, for example.

A myriad of sports require explosive power to be successful and Olympic lifts are a valuable set of exercises for a program designed to enhance explosive power. In applying the SAID principle, it has been suggested that "7 independent qualities contribute to an athlete's power capacity: **maximum strength,** high-load speed strength, low-load speed strength, rate of force production, **reactive strength,** skill performance, and **power endurance**" (4); the Olympic lifts have been shown to improve many of these qualities (5). Siff goes on to explain how the principle of specificity can be misconstrued with simulation training by stating that the SAID principle looks to enhance the variables specific to the demands of the athlete's sport. Simulation training is mimicking the specific sport skill that may be resisted lightly with bands, tubes, or weights so as not to interrupt the neurological movement pattern (3). Although the Olympic lifts do not mimic many sport skills, they do develop the specific variables necessary to enhance performance in sports requiring explosive power. In fact, the second pull phase of the snatch and power snatch exhibit the highest power outputs of any resistance training exercise (6). These two exercises alone will increase velocity of movement, high-load speed strength, and rate of force development while maximum strength can be enhanced by squats, clean deadlifts, and snatch deadlifts. In this respect, the Olympic lifts adhere to the SAID principle and can be a potent exercise selection within a program design.

TIME OUT
Rate of Force Development

Force is not produced in a "square wave" response, meaning strength does not go from nothing immediately, without delay, to maximal force. The mechanical, electrical, and elastic properties of the neuromuscular system respond in an orderly manner that takes time (in milliseconds). The rate of force development is the time, from the stimulus, to reach the required force. The muscle physiologist measures this during a muscle twitch as time to peak tension in an isolated muscle preparation. In humans, it is measured during an isometric contraction, either voluntary or in response to an electrical stimulus.

MOVEMENT PATTERNS AND REGION OF MOVEMENT

The SAID principle, in part, recognizes that in order for an exercise to improve performance, it must display similar movement patterns and regions of movement of the targeted sport skills. The Olympic lifts fulfill these criteria through the universal athletic position (UAP). The UAP is the most common position in all of sports. It is easily recognized as the static starting position, such as a linebacker's ready position or the defensive position in baseball (Figs. 11.1 and 11.2). It is also seen dynamically (7) as in the countermovement jump or the second pull phase in the snatch or the clean (Figs. 11.3 and 11.4). This position is described as being in a standing ¼ squat with feet flat, weight on the balls of the feet, hands in front, hips back, knees over the toes, shoulders over the knees, and a **neutral spine.** Because "posture modulates the ability to generate strength" (8), the UAP ensures a posture where maximum force

Neutral Spine
A posture where there is no exaggeration of any of the normal curvatures of the spine.

FIGURE 11.1 Ready football position.

FIGURE 11.2 Defensive position in baseball.

FIGURE 11.3 Countermovement jump.

FIGURE 11.4 Pull phase in the snatch or clean.

can be generated from the hips. To exhibit explosive power, the athlete must avoid exaggerated movement of the spine; the spine must be in neutral and stable to generate maximum power through the hips, knees, and ankles. The Olympic lifts, when performed correctly, move through the UAP between the first and second pull phases allowing the powerful hip muscles to explode the bar vertically. Empirically, the Olympic lifts augment explosive power from the UAP and, therefore, increase sports performance.

TIME OUT
Skill Performance

The Merriam Webster Collegiate Dictionary defines skill as *the dexterity or coordination in the execution of learned physical tasks.* The learning of a new skill follows a predictable course whereby unnecessary motor units are eliminated and the skill progressively becomes relegated to almost a subconscious level, executed almost in a reactive state. Skills are learned through a process called deliberate practice; practice that is not inherently "fun."

THE HIP HINGE

 Hip Hinge
The concept of the hip hinge can be described as the spine remaining stiff and neutral while movement occurs about the hip joint.

As previously mentioned, the spine must remain stable and neutral in order to create powerful lower body movements. The athlete must also learn to disassociate hip movement from spinal movement (Fig. 11.5). The concept of **hip hinge** is best described as the spine remaining stiff and neutral while movement occurs about the hip joint (8). This movement pattern is learned cognitively, beginning with only the body weight as resistance before progressing to the Olympic lifts that reinforce the hip hinge with the use of a load. This will be more evident later when the proper techniques of the Olympic lifts are described.

FIGURE 11.5 Hip hinge.

Olympic Lifts and the Vertical Jump: Their Relationship to Sports Performance

The vertical jump test is the most widely accepted test for assessing explosive lower body power. In the 2004 and 2005 NFL combine, drafted skill players (e.g., receivers, defensive backs, running backs) jumped, on average, 4 cm higher than nondrafted skill players and drafted big skill players (e.g., linebackers, tight ends, fullbacks, defensive ends) as well as linemen also jumped higher than their nondrafted counterparts (9). In football, there is a strong relationship between playing ability and vertical jump, even stronger than the 40-yard dash (10). Female Division 1 volleyball players jumped, on average, 4.6 inches higher than Division II players and 6.2 inches higher than Division III players (11). Vertical jump performance seems to be correlated with success in sports where explosive power is necessary.

Two articles highlighting the importance of weightlifting point to similar studies in support of Olympic lifts to improve vertical jump performance and thus athletic performance (4,5). Studies in the performance literature include:

- Canavan et al. who showed that the kinematics and kinetics of the Olympic lifts were notably similar to the vertical jump (12).
- Carlock et al. concluded that vertical jump peak power was strongly associated with weightlifting ability (13).
- Garhammer and Gregor showed that ground reaction forces were comparable between countermovement vertical jump and the snatch (14).
- Burkhardt and Garhammer found kinematic similarities between the hang clean and the vertical jump that may account for the training transfer between these two activities (15).
- Stone et al. stated that the Olympic lifts improved vertical jump performance (16).
- Hori et al. compared hang power clean performance to performance in sprinting, jumping, and change of direction and reported that high performance in the hang power clean was significantly related to jumping and sprinting (17).

There is ample scientific rationale to incorporate Olympic lifts into a performance enhancement program. Although no study can be considered as definitive, the literature consistently provides evidence that the Olympic lifts improve rate of force development, high-load speed strength, maximum strength, explosive power, and vertical jump performance using movement patterns similar to many sports skills. The combination of all these factors will undoubtedly improve sports performance.

Olympic Lifting Prerequisites and How they Affect Lifting Techniques

FLEXIBILITY AND MOBILITY

To perform the full Olympic lifts (snatch, clean and jerk), an athlete must be able to perform the deep catch positions. This requires maximum flexibility of the plantar flexors, knee extensors, hip extensors, elbow extensors, and wrist flexors. Not only does the involved musculature need to be flexible, but the involved joints need to display full mobility.

For example, maximum ankle dorsiflexion is 20 degrees, knee flexion is 135 degrees, and hip flexion is 120 degrees (18). If any of these joint ranges cannot be achieved, then the full depth cannot be achieved and compensations can occur (Fig. 11.6). When considering the snatch and the clean exercises, the athlete must achieve the full deep catch position. With normal ankle dorsiflexion being 20 degrees, it becomes difficult to sit in the full clean and snatch positions without shifting the center of gravity too far posteriorly. In order to achieve the full deep catch position, a specialized weightlifting shoe with a heel lift is sometimes used. If the weightlifting shoe is not going to be used and dorsiflexion is limited, the athlete should focus on the power clean and power snatch as opposed to the full lifts. These lifts use a higher catch position, making full ankle dorsiflexion, knee flexion, and hip flexion unnecessary. Flexibility techniques to improve calf extensibility and ankle dorsiflexion should be practiced in order to perform the full Olympic lifts with less compensation.

FIGURE 11.6 Full depth.

A second example involves the snatch and jerk. In the catch phase of both the snatch and of the jerk, the bar is held directly overhead, which requires full shoulder flexion. A limited range of shoulder flexion due to tightness in the latissimus dorsi can lead to compensations in the low back region (excessive lumbar extension) (Fig. 11.7). This is due to the latissimus dorsi's attachment to this region via the thoracolumbar fascia (TLF). This can increase stress to the lumbar spine and lead to potential injury. In this case, the athlete may have to compromise by using the snatch pull variations and avoiding the jerk (no overhead motion) while incorporating flexibility techniques in their program to enhance latissimus dorsi extensibility and thus shoulder range of motion.

FIGURE 11.7 Lumbar extension.

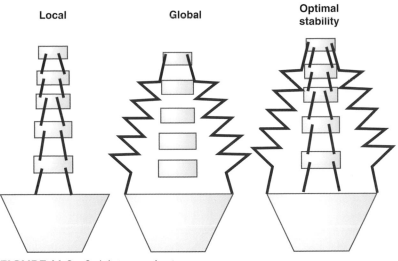

FIGURE 11.8   Stabilizing mechanisms.

STABILITY

Siff has described all dynamic movement as being "triphasic" in nature (3). He describes movement as beginning with a stabilizing contraction followed by a concentric contraction then an eccentric contraction. All human movement is preceded by a stabilizing contraction. As stated in Chapter 6, the human movement system is comprised of local stabilizers, global stabilizers, and global movers. In functional movements, like lifting free weights, the local and global stabilizers must be recruited prior to the movement in order to safely perform the movement (19). As also mentioned in Chapter 6, Hodges and Richardson (20) have suggested the need for a "drawing-in" maneuver to activate the local stabilizers (Fig. 11.8), whereas McGill offers the abdominal brace as a method to provide trunk stability (activation of the global stabilizers) (Fig. 11.8) (8). Several recent studies have found that an antagonistic torso co-contraction increases spinal stability during lifting tasks (21,22) and one of these studies (21) suggested that another benefit to the torso co-contraction (Fig. 11.8) may be to increase control of the path of the object being lifted. These stability cues (drawing-in and bracing) are a must before performing any Olympic lifting movement, whether starting from the floor, off a box, or from the hang position due to the importance of a stiff stable spine during lifting tasks. The athlete must develop this neuromuscular control before engaging in any Olympic lifts to ensure the safety and effectiveness of the lifts. This is one of the reasons why stabilization training (phase 1) should precede strength and power training. After neuromuscular control is established, Olympic lifts are an excellent progression to incorporate the stability cues into a dynamic movement that the lifter must cognitively create. This will be reinforced over time through high repetition to create neural pathways that will occur with less conscious thought and become more automatic. As the athlete learns how to stabilize the trunk and can perform the lifting techniques properly, load can then be increased allowing for greater strength gains of both the local and global systems of the core.

One other stability cue that is important prior to lifting the bar from any starting position is scapular retraction (1). Although the torso antagonistic co-contractions help to stabilize the spine, scapular retraction enhances global stabilization of the spine and a local stabilization of the glenohumeral joint. On top of this, Olympic lifting coaches recommend contracting the latissimus dorsi in order to control the path of the bar to keep the bar close to the body.

POSTURE

Proper posture makes lifting tasks easier due to the decreased load and sheer on the spine and thus increases the biomechanical advantage. The neutral tri-curve spine posture provides for the highest levels of spinal stability, biomechanical advantage, and efficient muscle activation during lifting. A 2007 study showed that when the global spinal extensor muscles take on curved paths, muscle forces and spinal compression significantly decreases, but shear forces increase at L5-S1 (23), suggesting that a slight flattening of the lumbar spine reduces load and shear at the level of L5-S1. This suggests that there is not one perfect neutral posture for all human movement and tasks, and that this neutrality changes slightly with various tasks. The proper lifting posture must be trained with high repetitions and low load until the neuromuscular system can accurately and efficiently reproduce the proper positions. Failure to achieve the proper posture can produce low performance and injury. The athlete who is unable to achieve the posture necessary to lift a weight from the floor should have their starting position changed (8) with the use of blocks combined with flexibility and stability exercises to improve postural control. When performing the Olympic lifts or any explosive movement, poor posture should be corrected first by stopping the exercise and resetting the three torso stability cues (drawing-in, bracing, and scapular retraction). After neutral posture is achieved and stabilized, then the exercise can be continued. Lacking postural control may also be an indicator that the athlete does not have proper amounts of flexibility, stability or both and may need to eliminate these lifts from their program until these components are improved.

NEUROMUSCULAR CONTROL

Perturbation

A disturbance in motion. When applied to human movement, this would entail any disruption in the normal pattern of movement; a disturbance in the relationship of the center of mass to the base of support. An example might be balancing on a wobble board or the use of a Swedish ball as part of the base of support.

The Olympic lifts and their derivatives are functional closed chain exercises whose main actions occur in the frontal and sagittal planes, although stability is occurring in all three planes. Complete neuromuscular control is necessary to perform the Olympic lifts as any **perturbation** in the desired movement patterns increase the chance of a breakdown in the human movement system (24–26). Adding an external load to this inefficient system can only worsen the problem and lead to injury.

The thoracolumbar fascia (TLF) transfers loads between the upper and lower body while at the same time stabilizing the lower lumbar spine and sacroiliac joints (27). Vleeming goes on to say that the latissimus dorsi may be functionally coupled to the gluteus maximus via the TLF (Fig. 11.9). In the Olympic lifts, as well as in the vertical jump, the proper proximal to distal neuromuscular firing sequence should be core and trunk stability, hip extension, knee extension, and finally plantar flexion. This sequential firing pattern combines both the proper timing and intensity of muscular contractions. The highest intensity of muscle activation occurs in the hip extensors and decreases as it moves down the chain through knee extension and plantar flexion. If core stability is poor or nonexistent, then the gluteus maximus may not fire with the proper timing and intensity as the primary hip extensor (altering the desired force-couple relationship), meaning the hamstrings and the lumbar extensors take over as the primary hip extensors in a compensatory reaction (synergistic dominance) (28).

The Olympic lifts are complex, loaded exercises that require normal function of the neuromuscular system. For proper and efficient movement, poor movement patterns need to be

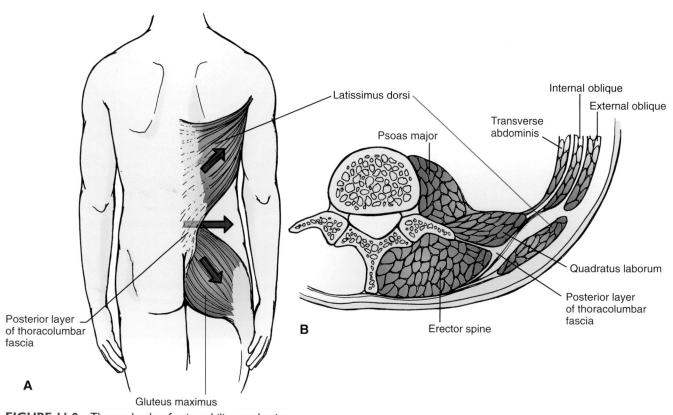

FIGURE 11.9 Thoracolumbar fascia stability mechanism.

resolved prior to performing the Olympic lifts. Perturbed movement patterns need to be addressed and improved in phase 1 (Stabilization Endurance Training) of the OPT™ model. Once corrected, Olympic lifts can then be incorporated in phases 4 and 5 of the model where maximal strength and power is the goal.

Many of the issues surrounding an athlete's functional qualifications for the use of Olympic lifts can be determined easily by performing the overhead and single-leg squat assessments discussed in Chapter 3. If compensations are present when performing the assessments, Olympic lifting may not be a viable option until movement deficiencies are corrected. Once corrected, the athlete will have an enhanced ability to generate force more effectively (through optimal length-tension and force-couple relationships) and decrease the risk of injury.

Example Olympic Lifts

SNATCH

This is the first of the two Olympic lifts and is sometimes described as a single movement as the weight is pulled from the floor with two hands and explosively lifted to arm's length over the head with no pause in the movement.

EXECUTION: GETTING SET

The lifter approaches the barbell perpendicular to the long axis and places the feet at approximately hip-width with the metatarsal-phalangeal joint directly beneath the bar. The feet should point straight ahead. The lifter then overgrips the bar with both hands at a distance approximately equal to the distance from the left middle finger tip to the right elbow when both arms are out to the sides of the body perpendicular to the sagittal plane (Fig. 11.10). Athletes whose grip lengths extend beyond the collars of the bar should use the snatch pull as an alternative to the snatch. Use of the snatch pull eliminates the need to raise the bar overhead. Most lifters use a technique known as "hooking", where the index and middle finger squeeze down on the thumb. While maintaining a neutral spine, the lifter then lowers the hips by squatting so that the shins touch the bar. The shoulders should be slightly ahead of the vertical plane of the bar and the cervical spine should be in its neutral position. Incorporate the stability cues by drawing-in, bracing, and retracting the scapulae (Fig. 11.11).

FIGURE 11.10   Start position for the snatch.   **FIGURE 11.11**   Getting set for the snatch.

EXECUTION: THE FIRST PULL PHASE

The first phase occurs when the knees extend and the barbell is lifted from the floor to knee height. The angle of the torso in relationship to the floor should not change. The shoulders should be kept slightly ahead of the path of the bar through contraction of the latissimus dorsi (Fig. 11.12).

FIGURE 11.12 First pull phase of the snatch.

EXECUTION: THE SHIFT OR SCOOP

In this transitional phase, the barbell is elevated from the knees to an area between the mid-thigh and the pubic bone depending upon the relative limb and torso segment lengths. The greater the ratio between arm length and torso length, the lower the bar will be when this re-flexing occurs. During this phase, there is a slight rebending of the knees as the main balance point shifts from the front of the heel to the ball of the foot. The shoulders will remain slightly in front of, or directly in line with, the bar pathway and the arms remain straight. This task is similar to the countermovement in jumping, taking advantage of the stretch-shortening cycle (Fig. 11.13).

FIGURE 11.13 Shift or scoop phase of the snatch.

EXECUTION: THE TOP PULL

This phase begins with a violent extension of the hips, knees, and ankles (hence the triple extension) that help drive the bar upward and slightly forward off the upper thigh or pubic area. A rapid contraction of the trapezius and lateral raising of the humerus by the deltoids follow this immediately (Fig. 11.14).

FIGURE 11.14   Top pull phase of the snatch.

EXECUTION: THE AMORTIZATION AND CATCH

As soon as the previous pull is completed, the lifter drops rapidly into a squat position, moving the feet quickly sideways and extending the arms overhead to catch the bar and stop its descent (Fig. 11.15). Foot movement needs to be quick to enable a quick drop under the bar. Alternatively, some lifters use the split, dropping quickly into a deep lunge position to catch the bar. Officially, the lift is completed when the lifter stands erect with the barbell overhead and under control (Fig. 11.16).

FIGURE 11.15   Amortization and catch.

FIGURE 11.16   Standing up with snatch completed.

CLEAN AND JERK

The second of the two Olympic lifts is considered a double movement. The "clean" involves lifting the barbell from the floor to the shoulders and the "jerk" is the explosive lifting of the barbell from shoulders overhead. It is this lift by which humans achieve the heaviest weights overhead.

EXECUTION: GETTING SET

Like the snatch, the lifter approaches the barbell perpendicular to the long axis and places the feet at a distance slightly wider than hip width with the metatarsal-phalangeal joint directly under the bar. The feet should point straight ahead. The lifter then takes an overgrip (again, "hooking" is an option) with the distance between the two hands being slightly wider than shoulder width. The shoulders should be slightly ahead of the vertical plane of the barbell. The hips are lowered with the spine in a neutral position until the shins touch the bar. The angle between the torso and the floor may be slightly greater than that used at the beginning of the snatch. Create the three stability cues (Fig. 11.17).

FIGURE 11.17   Start position for the clean and jerk.

EXECUTION: THE FIRST PULL

The barbell is lifted from the floor to knee height through an extension of the knees and the hips. The angle of the back relative to the floor should be maintained and the hips and barbell should rise at the same speed. The tendency of the barbell to move forward and away from the body should be counteracted by the isometric contraction of the latissimus dorsi (Fig. 11.18).

FIGURE 11.18   First pull phase for the clean and jerk.

EXECUTION: THE SHIFT OR SCOOP

The barbell is lifted from the top of the knees to the upper thigh to the pubic area (the bar may hit lower on the thigh in athletes with longer arms). The hips move forward and the knee rebends slightly so that the main balance point shifts from the front of the heel to the ball of the foot. Again, the barbell should contact the body, but at a lower point than it does in the snatch due to the closer grip width. The shoulders should remain slightly in front of or directly in line with the vertical path of the bar. Again, the rebending of the knee creates an eccentric load taking advantage of the stretch-shortening cycle (Fig. 11.19).

FIGURE 11.19   Shift or scoop phase of the clean and jerk.

EXECUTION: THE TOP PULL

A powerful extension of the hips and knees followed by plantar flexion violently and forcibly ejects the bar off the upper thigh/pubic area into a rapid ascent. Very shortly thereafter, the trapezius contracts forcefully to add speed to the bar (Fig. 11.20).

FIGURE 11.20   Top pull phase of the clean and jerk.

EXECUTION: THE CATCH, AMORTIZATION, AND POSSIBLE REBOUND

As soon as the body is fully extended and the trapezius contraction has taken place, the lifter drops rapidly into the full squat position. The elbows revolve rapidly forward as the grip is relaxed and the bar is caught on the shoulders that have moved forward. A skillfully performed catch will allow the lifter to employ the elastic component of the barbell to gain some momentum in recovery from the deep squat. (Figs. 11.21 and 11.22).

FIGURE 11.21   Catch of the clean and jerk.   **FIGURE 11.22**   Amortization and possible rebound of the clean and jerk.

EXECUTION: THE GET SET, DIP, AND DRIVE OF THE JERK

It is common for the hands to move closer together when transitioning from the top pull to the catch, so upon recovering from the squat, many lifters find it advantageous to heave the barbell up off the shoulders and reset the grip width. The narrower grip width is not conducive to proper extension of the arms during the jerk and supporting the jerk directly overhead. After the appropriate grip is established, the lifter should take a fresh breadth and reengage the core musculature prior to dipping (Fig. 11.23).

The dip can commence after the stance is at a width slightly wider than the hips and the toes pointing forward (Fig. 11.24). The main pressure point should be on the heels and the upper arms should be approximately 45 degrees in relation to the vertical axis of the torso. This may not always be possible with lifters who have an exceptionally large ratio of humerus length to radius length. The hands should be relaxed. The dip should commence with the torso vertical. The knees and hips bend until the knees reach the same angle as in the UAP. Without pausing, the knees and hips extend violently followed shortly thereafter by contraction of the trapezius to drive the barbell rapidly straight up. Experienced lifters elevating heavy weights can take advantage of the elastic component of the bar, but the timing is slightly different from brand to brand of bar. This task also utilizes an eccentric loading pattern.

FIGURE 11.23   Standing position after the clean, getting ready for the Jerk.

FIGURE 11.24   Dip and drive of the jerk.

EXECUTION: THE CATCH AND RECOVERY

After the drive is generated, most lifters drop into a split (in this case, a shallow lunge) (Fig. 11.25). Because the bar is in front of the neck to begin with, but should end up directly over the head, the back foot should make contact first. This will drive the lifter slightly forward so that the vertical axis of the torso is in line with the bar pathway. Thus, the rear foot should skim while the front foot takes a more prancing movement. To recover from the split, the lifter leans backward and the posterior momentum will enable the front foot to slide back to the starting position, and then the rear foot can recover forward ensuring that the bar moves only in a vertical pathway completing the lift (Fig. 11.26).

Some lifters are strong enough in the jerk drive that they can power jerk or catch the jerk in a quarter- to half-squat position. This is allowable. A few lifters will drop into a full squat, but this style is not advisable to most people.

The grip width can be varied from the drive to the catch, and some lifters employ this tactic to lessen the distance the bar must travel before the elbows lock, but it does require some practice.

FIGURE 11.25 Catch of the jerk.

FIGURE 11.26 Recovery of the jerk.

POWER CLEAN

The power clean is a popular variation of the classic clean and jerk. It does not require the same degree of leg strength, and it is generally more conducive to speed development, but it does have to be used in conjunction with other strength-building movements for optimum results and continued progress. This exercise is a good alternative to the clean and jerk when the full squat position cannot be achieved.

EXECUTION: THE SETUP, FIRST PULL, SHIFT, AND TOP PULL

These phases are identical to those for the clean and jerk.

EXECUTION: THE CATCH

Immediately after the top pull is performed, the lifter should drop into a quarter-to half-squat by moving the feet sideways a few centimeters each, and rapidly moving the elbows and shoulders forward so that the bar will be supported across the front of the deltoids with the arms serving as brackets that prevent the bar from falling off the shoulders (Fig. 11.27). The core musculature should be contracted and the racking motion of the arms should cease at the same time that the knees stop bending. The recovery from the catch should be deliberate.

FIGURE 11.27   Catch of the power clean.

VARIATION: THE HANG CLEAN

This variation can be performed to below the knee or to above the knee. The hang below the knees is more taxing on the spinal erectors and latissimus dorsi muscles and should be performed with the shoulders slightly in front of the bar's vertical pathway. Power cleaning from the knee can be used to strengthen the back musculature or to improve the shift phase of the movement. The latter variant, above the knees, focuses more on the development of explosive force and requires that the lifter bend forward to the UAP before commencing the movement proper. There is an obvious elastic component in this variation. The grip will be developed with both variants, although not to the extent as with hang snatches.

VARIATION: CLEAN FROM HIGH BLOCKS

High blocks will place the bar at the mid to upper thigh so the body is ready to begin from the UAP. This variant will develop explosive power from this position specifically and is noteworthy in that it does not tax the grip musculature as severely as performing repetitions from the hang (Fig. 11.28).

FIGURE 11.28   Power clean from blocks.

SNATCH DEADLIFT

This movement is best used to develop stability of the supportive musculature, thus the techniques are similar to the first pull and shift phases of the snatch. Straps to aid in securing the grip are frequently used. The movement can be performed either to the knees, through the shift or with halts (about 3 seconds), and/or even ultra slow descents (about 10 seconds). Several different modes may be employed in a single set.

EXECUTION: GETTING SET, THE FIRST PULL, THE SHIFT

These phases correspond to the same phases as in the snatch proper. Most of the value of the movement is completed at the end of the shift phase when the barbell reaches the upper thigh region (Figs. 11.29 through 11.31).

FIGURE 11.29 Getting set for the snatch deadlift.

FIGURE 11.30 First pull of the snatch deadlift.   **FIGURE 11.31** Shift of the snatch deadlift.

VARIATION: ON BLOCKS

This challenging variation is performed while standing on a block and with the barbell resting on the floor. This is an especially good exercise for working the thighs, hips, and the latissimus dorsi.

BACK SQUAT

The back squat is an exceptional exercise for increasing leg, back and core strength, and affecting anabolic metabolism. Many see the obvious leg strengthening features, but overlook the amount of back development necessary to support the requisite weight for developing stronger legs.

EXECUTION: UNRACKING AND GETTING READY

The squat rack needs to be adjusted so that the top of the front lip is lower than the lowest point of the bar resting on the shoulders of the lifter. The lifter needs to face the rack and take a symmetrical grip on the bar; the width is a matter of personal comfort. The lifter should then bend forward, step forward under the bar, and position the bar against the trapezius and shoulders (Fig. 11.32). Inexperienced lifters often place the bar against the top two thoracic vertebrae and experience a great deal of discomfort. The lifter can now stand erect and the bar should clear the squat rack. The lifter can now take the minimum number of skating steps back to begin the squatting movement (Fig. 11.33). Athletes new to lifting need to minimize the amount of energy spent on nonproduct movements surrounding an exercise. Minimizing the energy spent on the setup is just one example. The knees should be straight, but not locked.

FIGURE 11.32   Unracking for the back squat.

FIGURE 11.33   Getting ready for the back squat.

EXECUTION: THE DESCENT

The lifter then begins the descent in a controlled manner, keeping the core musculature engaged. The resistive forces are primarily generated by the gluteals. (Fig. 11.34).

FIGURE 11.34 Descent and bottom position of the back squat.

EXECUTION: THE ASCENT

The lifter, using momentum generated by the elastic component, pushes the resistance upward as it goes through the mechanically most disadvantageous point in the pathway. This is generally at a point at or near where the thigh is parallel to the floor (Fig. 11.35). The lifter should then complete the movement rising to an unlocked knee position, which minimizes stress on the back. The lifter is now ready to begin a second repetition or to rerack the bar.

FIGURE 11.35 Ascent of the back squat.

EXECUTION: THE RERACK

After the requisite number of reps has been completed, the lifter is now ready to rerack the bar. If the prescribed minimum number of steps were taken to assume the get-set position, the walk back into the rack should be short and accurate. When the bar makes contact with the taller rear lip, the lifter knows that the bar is directly over the supporting portion of the rack and merely has to bend the knees to lower the barbell safely into the rack (Fig. 11.36).

FIGURE 11.36   Reraking

SPOTTING

Spotting is the process of assisting a lifter during the course of a set of an exercise either as a safety measure or to slightly lessen the resistance so the lifter can perform the requisite number of repetitions. Spotting can be performed by a single person in many cases, but must be performed by two or more persons in other circumstances. When two or more persons are spotting, there must be cooperative teamwork taking place in order to avoid asymmetrical assistance or possible injury.

A one-person spot of a squat involves the spotter standing directly behind the lifter. The spotter can provide assistance through the "sticking point" (the range of greatest mechanical disadvantage), by either squeezing against the hips with both hands from the sides and pushing upwards or by providing some upward force against the barbell with both hands, placing each hand lateral to the lifter's shoulders (Fig. 11.37). The disadvantage of a single-person spot is that a single individual cannot lift the weight from a failed squat off of the lifter.

FIGURE 11.37   One-person spot.

One-person spots can be used on flat bench presses, incline bench presses, lat pull-downs, chin-ups, and curls.

A two-person spot can often be used to help a lifter lower a jerk when jerking blocks are not available. Some of today's lifters raise such heavy weights that the barbells cannot be lowered safely without some assistance. This is the only instance in which spotting is employed in training the Olympic lifts.

Two-person spots are even more common in the assistance of lifters performing squats in case the lifter cannot attain the prescribed number of squats (Fig. 11.38). The problem with a two-person spot is that the two spotters must be of comparable experience in order to safely and accurately perform the spot. Familiarity with the trainee's squatting rhythm allows both spotters to know exactly when to offer support and to what degree. An inexperienced spotter can provide too much upward force too soon and cause an injury or an accident that leads to an injury. In extreme cases, a five-person spot can be used on a squat with two on each side and one in the center in the back.

FIGURE 11.38 Two-person spot.

Compensations: Possible Causes and How to Correct Them

TRUNK FLEXION IN THE POWER CLEAN

In the power clean, the bar is racked on the shoulders and clavicles. A common problem found in this position is the poor posture of trunk flexion (Fig. 11.39). This may be due to inner unit instability or weak core extensors. The remedy for trunk flexion during these actions is to actively engage the local and global stabilizers (the stability cues of the drawing-in and the abdominal brace) and retract the scapula prior to initiating the movements. If this does not remedy the problem, the weight may simply be too heavy. In this case, simply decrease the weight, cue the stabilizers, and repeat the movement. The thought process should be "big chest, elbows high." If a movement cannot be performed technically correct, stop the movement, reset, and try again. Do not repeat poor movement patterns. Poor posture reduces performance and increases the risk of injury. It has been stated that a neutral spine posture is the best position from which to perform any exercise.

EXCESSIVE LUMBAR EXTENSION AND ANTERIOR PELVIC TILT IN THE OVERHEAD POSITIONS

Excessive lumbar extension in any movement pattern normally causes low-back pain. For example, when performing a clean and jerk, it is common to see excessive lumbar extension while standing with the bar overhead. (Fig. 11.40). This may be due to weak core stabilizers combined with tight hip flexors and latissimus dorsi. This posture would also put disproportionate stress on the hamstrings as hip extensors as well as the lumbor spine.

FIGURE 11.39 Trunk flexion during a power clean.

FIGURE 11.40 Lumbar extension during overhead positions.

Again, postures away from neutral spine position reduce performance and increase the risk for injury. The first four stages of the OPT™ model should address weak core stabilizers and tight hip flexors and latissimus dorsi. The other way to maintain neutral spinal position and avoid lumbar extension is to use the stability cues. Always cue up the drawing-in maneuver, bracing, and then scapula retraction prior to lifting.

IMPROPER KNEE TRACKING DURING SQUATTING MOVEMENTS

When performing traditional squats or movements off the floor, the knee should track appropriately in line with the toes (Figs. 11.41 and 11.42). Excessive knee valgus can increase shear forces to the ACL ligament, increasing the risk of injury. Excessive knee valgus can also decrease force production by altering length-tension relationships and force-couple relationships, leading to further compensation and injury.

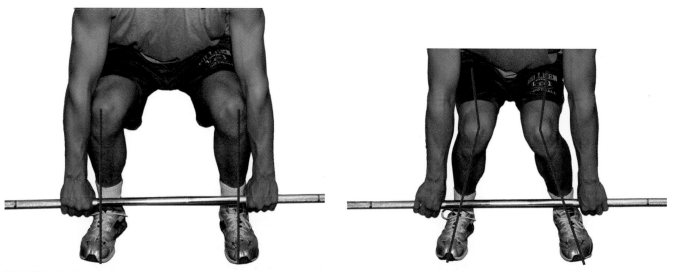

FIGURE 11.41 Proper foot and knee alignment.

FIGURE 11.42 Improper foot and knee alignment.

The Appropriate Phases for Olympic Lifting in the OPT™ Model

PERIODIZATION WITHIN THE OPT™ MODEL

> **Work Capacity**
> *Work is defined as the force expressed through a distance (W = F × D) with no consideration of time. Capacity then is the maximum amount that can be accommodated. Thus, work capacity is the maximum amount of work that a person can handle and will vary based on the intensity-duration relationship of the task. The international unit of work is the joule.*

At its most basic level, the typical athletic cycle consists of four periods: preparatory, first transition, competition, and second transition (29). The preparatory period addresses endurance, **work capacity**, strength, and then power. The first transition phase shifts to a short unloading period, whereas the goal of the competition phase is to maintain all of these qualities. The second transition is a period of active rest. This is known as periodization of training and is systematically applied using the OPT™ model (Chapter 12). As mentioned in previous chapters, the early phases of the OPT™ model are designed to train the stability system and restore flexibility, mobility, and neuromuscular control. After proper function is restored (force-tension relationships, sequential firing patterns, etc.) strength and power can be addressed.

The Olympic lifts primarily develop strength and power; qualities desired in the latter stages of this periodized training program that also require ample flexibility, stability, and neuromuscular control. Within the OPT™ model, the Olympic lifts are most appropriate in phases 4 and 5. (Fig. 11.43), maximal strength training and power training.

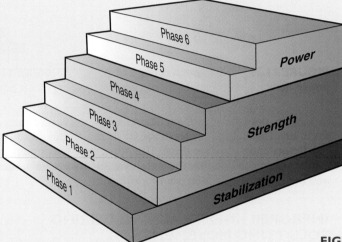

FIGURE 11.43 OPT™ model.

PHASE 4 OF THE OPT™ MODEL: MAXIMUM STRENGTH

Lifts to be used in this phase of training would be back squats, front squats, snatch deadlifts, and bench presses. While building strength with these auxiliary exercises, the technical aspects of the classic lifts, such as the snatch and clean and jerk, can begin to be taught. The Sports Performance Professional may want to start training sessions with snatch and clean technique work and then move on to strength work so the athlete will not be exhausted while trying to learn the more technical tasks. Volume and intensity of training should be modified according to the experience and talent level of the athlete. Beginning athletes start with higher volumes and lower intensities. As the athlete gains technical mastery and conditioning, the volume decreases while the intensity increases. As the athlete becomes a veteran at these lifts, squats and deadlifts become the most important exercises in this phase for maximal strength, and as such, should be performed first in the daily plan. The snatch and clean and jerk are executed at the end of the program.

PHASE 5 OF THE OPT™ MODEL: POWER TRAINING

The primary resistance training exercises designed to enhance power are the snatch and the clean and jerk or their derivatives, such as the power clean. Phase 5 is the phase where these lifts can become an integral part of the training program. Speed and quality are the important coaching components; do not sacrifice these for increased load. In any daily training plan, the most important exercises are scheduled first. Thus, when training for power, the Olympic lifts are performed before the strength derivatives, such as squats and deadlifts.

SUMMARY

Olympic lifts and their derivatives have long been a popular form of training to enhance athletic performance. The goal of this form of training is to improve maximal strength and explosive power that would transfer to the demands of the sport. Before engaging in an Olympic lifting program, it is important that the athlete possess the proper prerequisites to perform Olympic lifts safely and effectively. Flexibility, stability, and neuromuscular control must be established first before engaging into an Olympic lifting program. Proper coaching on technique and stability cues should also be provided prior to increasing training intensity of these lifts. Finally, due to the adaptation goals, these lifts are useful for developing maximal strength and power, or in phases 4 and 5 of the OPT™ model.

REFERENCES

1. Baechle TR, Earle RW. Essentials of Strength and Conditioning, 2nd ed. Champaign, IL: Human Kinetics; 2000.
2. DeLorme TL. Resportation of muscle power by heavy resistance exercises. *J Bone Joint Surg* 1945; 27:645–67.
3. Siff MC. Supertraining. Denver, CO: Supertraining Institute; 2003.
4. Hori N, Newton RU, Nosaka K. Weightlifting exercises enhance athletic performance that requires high-load speed strength. *Strength Cond J* 2005;27:50–55.
5. Waller M, Townsend R, Gattone M. Application of the power snatch for athletic conditioning. *Strength Cond J* 2007;29:11–20.
6. Garhammer J. Power production by Olympic weightlifters. *Med Sci Sport Exerc* 1980;12:54–60.
7. Plisk S. Functional Training. CITY: NSCA; 2006. http://www.nsca-lift.org/HotTopic/download/Functional%20Training%20modified[1].pdf, Jan 11, 2006. p 8.
8. McGill S. Ultimate Back Fitness and Performance. Waterloo, Ontario: BackFitPro, Inc; 2006.
9. Sierer SP, Battaglini CL, Mihalik JP. The National Football League combine: performance differences between drafted and nondrafted players entering the 2004 and 2005 drafts. *J Strength Cond Res* 2008;22:6–12.
10. Sawyer DT, Ostarello JZ, Suess EA. Relationship between football playing ability and selected performance measures. *J Strength Cond Res* 2002;16:611–16.
11. Barnes jL, Schilling BK, Falvo MJ. Relationship of jumping and agility performance in female volleyball athletes. *J Strength Cond Res* 2007;21:1192–196.
12. Canavan PK, Garrett GE, Armstrong LE. Kinematic and kinetic relationships between an Olympic-style lift and the vertical jump. *J Strength Cond Res* 1996;10:127–30.
13. Carlock JM, Smith SL, Hartman MJ et al. The relationship between vertical jump power estimates and weightlifting ability: a field-test approach. *J Strength Cond Res* 2004;18:534–39.
14. Garhammer J, Gregor RJ. Propulsion forces as a function of intensity for weightlifting and vertical jumping. *J Appl Sport Sci Res* 1992;6:129–34.
15. Burkhardt E, Garhammer J. Biomechanical comparison of hang cleans and vertical jumps. *J Appl Sport Sci Res* 1988;2:57.
16. Stone MH, Cyrd R, Twe J. Relationship between anaerobic power and Olympic weightlifting performance. *J Sports Med Phys Fitness* 1980;20:99–102.
17. Hori N, Newton RU, Andrews AW. Does performance of hang power clean differentiate performance of jumping, sprinting, and changing of direction? *J Strength Cond Res* 2008;22:412–18.
18. Reese NB, Bandy WD. Joint Range of Motion and Muscle Length Testing. Philadelphia, PA: Elsevier Health Sciences; 2001.
19. Faries MD, Greenwood M. Core training: stabilizing the confusion. *Strength Cond J* 2007;29:11–25.
20. Hodges PW, Richardson CA. Inefficient muscular stabilization of the lumbar spine associated with low back pain. A motor control evaluation of transversus abdominis. *Spine* 1996;21:2640–650.
21. van Dieen JH, Kingma I, van der Bug P. Evidence for a role of antagonistic cocontraction in controlling trunk stiffness during lifting. *Clin Biomech* 2006;21:668–75.
22. Vera-Garcia FJ, Brown SH, Gray JR. Effects of different levels of torso coactivation on trunk muscular and kinematic responses to posteriorly applied sudden load. *J Biomech* 2003;36:1829–836.
23. Arjmand N, Shirazi-Adl A, Bazrgari B. Wrapping of trunk thoracic extensor muscles influences muscle forces and spinal loads in lifting tasks. *Eur Spine J* 2007;16:668–75.
24. Bell DR, Padua DA. Influence of ankle dorsiflexion range of motion and lower leg muscle activation on knee valgus during a double-legged squat. *J Athl Train* 2007;42:S–84.
25. Buckley BD, Thigpen CA, Joyce CJ, Bohres SM et al. Knee and hip kinematics during a double leg squat predict knee and hip kinematics at initial contact of a jump landing task. *J Athl Train* 2007;42:S–81.
26. Vesci BJ, Padua DA, Bell DR et al. Influence of hip muscle strength, flexibility of hip and ankle musculature, and hip muscle activation on dynamic knee valgus motion during a double-legged squat. *J Athl Train* 2007;42:S–83.
27. Vleeming A, Pool-Goudzwaard AL, Stoeckart R. The posterior layer of the thoracolumbar fascia. Its function in load transfer from spine to legs. *Spine* 2001;26:E114–21.
28. Boyle M. Functional Training for Sports. Champaign, IL: Human Kinetics; 2004.
29. Wathen D, Baechle TR, Earle RW. Training Variation: Periodization. In Baechle TR, Earle RW. Essentials of Strength Training and Conditioning, 2nd ed. Champaign, IL: Human Kinetics; 2000. p 513–27.

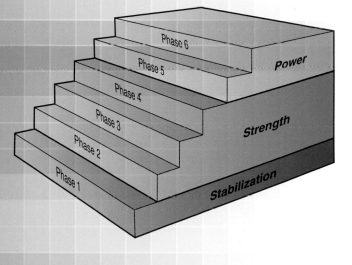

Phase 6
Phase 5
Phase 4
Phase 3
Phase 2
Phase 1

Power
Strength
Stabilization

SECTION 4

Program Design Principles and Application

CHAPTER 12

The Science of Periodization and The Optimum Performance Training (OPT™) Model

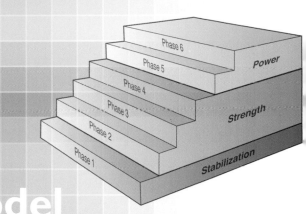

UPON COMPLETION OF THIS CHAPTER, YOU WILL BE ABLE TO:

Define and describe the acute training variables within the Optimum Performance Training (OPT™) model.

Describe the phases within the OPT™ model.

Design sports performance programs for each phase of training of the OPT™ model.

Introduction

To achieve consistent success with athletes, the Sports Performance Professional must be able to design an integrated training program that addresses all the needs of the athlete. A well-designed program must be systematically organized to provide a planned progression over a period of time. The training program should be a methodical approach to improve physical, physiological, psychological, and performance adaptations. The best way to achieve consistent, superior results is to follow a periodized training program (1–12). Evidence also exists showing that a multi-component program that includes, but is not limited to, flexibility, core, balance, plyometrics, speed/agility/quickness, resistance, and cardiorespiratory training can decrease injury and improve performance (13–30).

What is Program Design?

Program Design
A purposeful system or plan put together to help an individual achieve a specific goal.

Program design involves making use of a purposeful system or plan to achieve a specific goal. The key words here are *purposeful system* that provides a path for athletes to achieve individual goals. Providing a path requires a comprehensive understanding of a few key concepts.

ACUTE VARIABLES

- What are they?
- How do they affect the desired adaptation?
- How do they affect the overall training program?

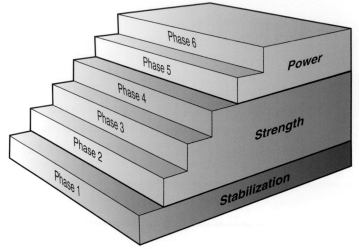

FIGURE 12.1   OPT™ model.

THE OPT™ MODEL: PLANNED SPORTS PERFORMANCE TRAINING PERIODIZATION

- How and why must the physiological, physical, and performance adaptations of stabilization, strength and power take place in a planned, progressive manner to establish the proper foundation for each subsequent adaptation?

THE PHASES OF TRAINING IN THE OPT™ MODEL

- How do these phases promote specific adaptations?
- What are the acute variables for each of the phases?

APPLICATION

- Selecting the right exercises.
- Selecting the right acute variables.
- Applying both in a systematic manner to different athletes with different goals.

TAKING THE GUESSWORK OUT

A proven system can be followed when the needed information is inserted, removing the worry of using the correct formula for success. This is exactly what the OPT™ model provides (Fig. 12.1).

NASM designed the OPT™ model as a planned, systematic, periodized training program for concurrent improvement of all functional abilities, such as flexibility, core stabilization, balance, power, strength, and cardiorespiratory endurance. The OPT™ program has been extremely successful in helping professional athletes (e.g., NFL, NBA, MLB, NHL, MLS, and Olympic), as well as college, high school, and recreational athletes to consistently achieve optimum results.

The remainder of this chapter will detail acute variables of planned sports performance training (or periodization) as it relates to the OPT™ model, the phases of the OPT™ model, and how to apply the OPT™ program design model with athletes.

Acute Variables of Training

Acute Variables
Important components that specify how each exercise is to be performed.

Acute variables are the most fundamental components of designing a training program. They determine the amount of stress placed on the body and, ultimately, what adaptation the body will incur.

The body will specifically adapt to the demands placed on it (Principle of Specificity). The acute variables dictate these demands.

TABLE 12.1				
Program Design Continuum				
Adaptation	**Reps**	**Sets**	**Intensity**	**Rest Period**
Power	1–10	3–6	30–45% of rep max or ≤10% of body weight	3–5 min.
Strength	1–12	2–6	70–100%	45 sec.–5 min.
Stabilization	12–20	1–3	50–70%	0 sec.–1.5 min.

The OPT™ model takes the guesswork out of program design and allows for a planned, systematic progression by pre-assigning specific acute variables for each of the phases of training to elicit the desired adaptation (2–5,7,9–12,31–41). Collectively, the acute variables are the foundation of program design and fall within the Program Design Continuum seen in Table 12.1.

To ensure proper development and progression of an integrated training program, the Sports Performance Professional must understand the acute training variables shown in Table 12.2. Each of the acute variables will be explained in this chapter, as they relate to the OPT™ model.

TABLE 12.2		
Acute Variables of Training		
Repetitions	Repetition Tempo	Training Frequency
Sets	Training Volume	Training Duration
Training Intensity	Rest Interval	Exercise Selection

REPETITIONS

Repetition (or "Rep")

One complete movement of a single exercise.

A **repetition** is one complete movement of a particular exercise. Most repetitions will involve the three muscle actions: concentric, isometric, and eccentric (not necessarily in that order) (42–44).

These muscle actions can be seen in the example of a biceps curl. A single repetition includes raising the dumbbell up against the direction of resistance (a concentric contraction), pausing for any specified amount of time (an isometric contraction), and then lowering the dumbbell with the direction of resistance back to its starting position (an eccentric contraction).

Another example of this can be seen when performing a squat. Starting from a standing position, one repetition includes lowering the body (with the direction of resistance) toward the ground (eccentric), pausing for any specified amount of time (isometric), and then raising back up (against the direction of resistance) to the starting position (concentric).

Repetitions are simply a means to count the number of movements performed in a given amount of time. They can, therefore, be a means to count the time the muscles are under tension.

Each phase of training in the OPT™ model has specific goals that requires a specific number of repetitions to achieve these goals. The number of repetitions performed in a given set depends on the athlete's work capacity, intensity of the exercise, and the specific phase of training.

Keep in mind that all acute variables are interdependent. This means that the specific use of one will affect the others. For example, the more intense the exercise or heavier the load, the fewer the number of repetitions that the individual can perform (40,45).

Research demonstrates that training in a specific range of repetitions yields very specific adaptations. The specific goals of the athlete and the phase of training dictate the precise repetition range (Table 12.3) (7,32,40,45).

- Endurance is best achieved by performing 12–20 repetitions at 50–70% of the 1 RM.
- Hypertrophy is best achieved utilizing 6–12 repetitions at 75–85% of the 1 RM.
- If maximal strength adaptations are desired, the repetition range is 1–5 at 85–100% of the 1 RM.
- Power adaptations require 1–10 repetitions at 30–45% of the 1-repetition maximum (1 RM) or approximately 10% of body weight.

TABLE 12.3
Repetition Continuum
Stabilization/Endurance: 12–20 Hypertrophy: 6–12 Maximal Strength: 1–5 Power : 1–10

The OPT™ model utilizes the specified repetition continuum to provide the stimulus for the desired adaptations in a systematic manner. The beginning phases consist of higher-repetition schemes that help build stability, endurance, and connective tissue strength. This is especially important for the beginning athlete. A common mistake of many advanced athletes, however, is failing to follow a planned training program that provides periods of low-repetition training alternated with periods of high-repetition training. Higher intensities of training (with fewer repetitions) can only be sustained for a short period of time without running the risk of overtraining (46,47). The OPT™ model guides the Sports Performance Professional and the athlete through a systematic training approach that minimizes the risk of overtraining and maximizes specific results using planned intervals of training.

SETS

Set
A group of consecutive repetitions.

A **set** is a group of consecutive repetitions (42–44). As all the acute variables are interrelated, the quantities of the other acute variables (i.e., repetitions, training intensity, number of exercises, training level and recoverability) determine the number of sets an individual performs (42,48).

There is an inverse relationship between sets, repetitions (the product of which is daily training volume) and intensity. The athlete usually performs fewer sets when performing higher repetitions at a lower intensity (endurance and hypertrophy adaptations) and more sets when performing lower repetitions at a higher intensity (43,44) (strength and power adaptations), as shown in Table 12.4 (7,32,40).

- Endurance is best developed with 1–3 sets of 12–20 repetitions at 50–70% 1 RM intensity.
- Hypertrophy adaptations require 3–5 sets of 6–12 repetitions at 75–85% 1 RM intensity.
- Maximal strength adaptations are best developed with 4–6 sets of 1–5 repetitions at 85–100% 1 RM intensity.
- Power adaptations are best developed with 3–6 sets of 1–10 repetitions at 85–100% 1 RM intensity or approximately 10% of body weight.

TABLE 12.4
Set Continuum
Stabilization/Endurance: 1–3 Hypertrophy: 3–5 Maximal Strength: 4–6 Power: 3–6

TRAINING INTENSITY

Training Intensity
An individual's level of effort, compared to their maximal effort, which is usually expressed as a percentage.

Training intensity is one of the most important acute variables in an integrated training program. Training intensity is defined as an athlete's level of effort compared to their maximum effort (7,40,43,44,49).

The specific training phase and an athlete's training goal will determine the number of sets and repetitions for an exercise. Intensity is then determined by the number of sets and repetitions to be performed, which is based on the athlete's specific training goals (Table 12.5).

- Endurance is best developed with a training intensity of 50–70% of 1 RM.
- Hypertrophy is best achieved by training with 75–85% of 1 RM.
- Maximal strength adaptations require training with 85–100% of 1 RM.
- Power (high velocity) adaptations are best attained with 30–45% of 1 RM when using conventional weight training or approximately 10% of body weight, when using medicine balls.

Training in an unstable environment, as seen in the stabilization phases of the OPT™ model, increases the training intensity because it requires more motor unit recruitment (50–53) and more energy expenditure per exercise (54–56), leading to optimal development of neuromuscular efficiency. Changing other acute training variables such as rest periods and tempo also changes the training intensity. Thus, intensity is a function of more than just external resistance. An integrated training program will focus on a holistic approach that leads to continued adaptations.

TABLE 12.5
Intensity Continuum
Stabilization/Endurance: 50–70% Hypertrophy: 75–85% Maximal Strength: 85–100% Power: 30–45% or ≤10% of body weight

REPETITION TEMPO

Repetition Tempo
The speed with which each repetition is performed.

Repetition tempo refers to the speed with which each repetition is performed. This is an important variable for achieving specific training objectives such as endurance, hypertrophy, strength, and power (40,42–44). Movement occurs at different velocities in order to get the appropriate results from training (e.g., slower tempo for endurance and faster tempo for power) based on the Repetition Tempo Spectrum (Table 12.6).

TABLE 12.6
Tempo Continuum (Eccentric/Isometric/Concentric)
Stabilization/Strength Endurance: Slow (4/2/1) Hypertrophy: Moderate (2/0/2) Maximal Strength: Moderate/Fast Power: Fast/Explosive

REST INTERVAL

Rest Interval
The time taken to recuperate between sets.

The **rest interval** is the time taken to recuperate between sets, exercises, or both and can have a dramatic effect on the outcome of the training program (40,42–44). Each exercise requires energy and the primary type of energy used during training depends on the training phase, exercise intensity, and goal (Table 12.7).

Power and maximal strength adaptations may require up to 5 minutes of rest between sets and exercises, depending on the athlete's level of fitness. Hypertrophic adaptations are maximized when the rest intervals are decreased to 45–90 seconds between sets and exercises, but are, of course, dependent on the load being used. Stability and endurance adaptations are best achieved with 30–60 seconds of rest (57).

TABLE 12.7
Rest Interval Continuum
Stabilization/Strength Endurance: 30–60 seconds Hypertrophy: 45–90 seconds Maximal Strength: 3–5 minutes Power: 3–5 minutes

Dynamic resistance training, as well as isometric training, can significantly reduce ATP and creatine phosphate (CP) supplies (58–60). The ability to replenish these supplies rapidly is crucial for optimal performance and the desired adaptation. By adjusting the rest interval, energy supplies can be regained according to the goal of the training program. Phosphagen recovery has a half-time of approximately 20–30 seconds (61), thus rest intervals of:

- 20–30 seconds will allow approximately 50% recovery of ATP/CP
- 40 seconds will allow approximately 75% recovery of ATP/CP
- 60 seconds will allow approximately 85–90% recovery of ATP/CP
- Three minutes will allow approximately 100% recovery of ATP/CP

The rest interval between sets determines to what extent the energy resources are replenished prior to the next set (40,62). The shorter the rest interval, the less ATP-CP will be replenished and consequently less energy will be available for the next set and the more energy must be drawn from other sources (57). This can result in fatigue which can lead to decreased neuromuscular control, force production, and stabilization by decreasing motor unit recruitment (63).

Therefore, inadequate rest intervals decreases performance and can lead to excessive compensation and even injury. As the athlete advances, this can be used as a means to increase the intensity of the workout and promote better adaptations, especially for stability, endurance, and hypertrophy.

Conversely, if rest periods are too long between sets or exercises, the potential effects include a reduced adaptation to training and decreased neuromuscular activity. After a prolonged recovery period, if the beginner athlete is asked to perform an intense bout of exercise, this could entail a potential increased risk of injury. For the advanced athlete, extended recovery periods may be necessary if heavy weight is being used repetitively. The goal of the training program should establish the appropriate rest periods (7,40,57). There are several factors to consider when prescribing appropriate rest intervals (Table 12.8).

TABLE 12.12

Exercise Selection—Examples

Level	Total Body	Multi-Joint	Single-Joint
Stabilization	Step-Up, Balance to Overhead Press	Ball Dumbbell Chest Press Ball Dumbbell Row Ball Military Press	Single-Leg Dumbbell Curl
Strength	Squat, Curl to Overhead Press	Bench Press Seated Row Machine Shoulder Press Machine	Standing Barbell Curl
Power	Squat Jump	Two-arm Medicine Ball Chest Pass Medicine Ball Pullover Throw Medicine Ball Oblique Throw	N/A

In the OPT™ model, exercises from all components (flexibility, core, balance, plyometrics, speed/agility/quickness, and resistance training) are categorized by the adaptation for which they are primarily used. For example, exercises that are used in Phase 1 of the OPT™ model (stabilization endurance) are termed *stabilization level* exercises because they are used and progressed for the stabilization adaptation. Similarly, the exercises used in Phases 2–4 are termed *strength level* exercises and exercises used in Phase 5 and 6 are termed *power level* exercises (Table 12.11).

Exercises can be broken down simplistically into three different types based upon the number of joints used, movements performed, and adaptation desired (Table 12.12) (72).

1. Single-joint: These exercises focus on isolating one major muscle group or joint.
2. Multi-joint: These exercises require the involvement of two or three joints.
3. Total-body: These exercises include multiple joint movements such as a squat, clean, and a lunge with biceps curl to a shoulder press (lunge, curl, and press).

The OPT™ model enables the Sports Performance Professional to effectively select the appropriate exercise for each athlete. Completing a sports performance assessment and reviewing the specific training goals will lead to inclusion of appropriate exercises into a properly planned integrated training program.

For example, to develop optimum stability, traditional stable exercises can be *progressed* to a more unstable environment, such as standing up (two-leg, staggered-stance, single-leg) or by using unstable modalities (Airex pad, stability ball, bosu ball, etc.). Research has shown that exercises performed in unstable environments produce superior results for the goal of stabilization and training the core stabilizing muscles (16,76,77). Stabilization exercise examples include:

- Chest press on a stability ball
- Single-leg cable rows
- Single-leg dumbbell shoulder press on a 1/2-foam roll
- Single-leg squat

To develop optimum strength, the use of more stable total-body and multi-joint exercises has been shown most beneficial (78). Strength exercise examples include:

- Bench press (barbell or dumbbell)
- Rows (machine, seated cable, barbell)
- Shoulder press (seated barbell, seated dumbbell, machine)
- Leg press

To develop optimum power, plyometrics and explosive medicine ball exercises can be performed during functional movement patterns (79–91). Power exercise examples include:

- Overhead medicine ball throw
- Medicine ball chest pass
- Medicine ball soccer throw
- Squat jump
- Tuck jump
- Box jump

All exercises, once selected, can be progressed or regressed in a systematic fashion, by following the Exercise Progression Continuum (Table 12.13).

TABLE 12.13

Exercise Progression Continuums

Stabilization Continuum	Lower Body	Upper Body
Floor ↓	Two-leg stable ↓	Two-arm ↓
Sport beam ↓	Staggered-stance stable ↓	Alternating arms ↓
Half foam roll ↓	Single-leg stable ↓	Single-arm ↓
Airex pad ↓	Two-leg unstable ↓	Single-arm with trunk rotation
Dyna disc	Staggered-stance unstable ↓	
	Single-leg unstable	

TIME OUT
Neural Demand Continuum

Neural demand refers to the challenge that an exercise places on the balance and stabilization systems of the human movement system. Integrated training progressively and systematically alters the base of support, center of gravity, and neural demand to improve neuromuscular efficiency, dynamic joint stabilization, and functional strength. The most important aspect to remember when altering the neural demand is safety. Progression should proceed from stable to unstable if the goal is to enhance stability.

Periodization and the OPT™ Model: Implementing the Planned Sports Performance Training Program

Understanding the need for program design and the purpose of acute variable manipulation is important fundamental information that can ultimately determine the success of a Sports Performance Professional. A system is required to properly organize this base level of information.

The science behind the OPT™ model is based on the concept of periodization. Periodization is a systematic approach to program design that uses the general adaptation syndrome and principle of specificity to vary the amount and type of stress placed on the body to produce adaptation and prevent injury. Periodization (or planned sports performance training) varies the focus of a training program at regularly planned periods of time (weeks, months, etc.) to produce optimal adaptation. It involves two primary objectives:

1. Dividing the training program into distinct periods (or phases) of training
2. Training for different adaptations in each period (or phase) to control the volume of training and to prevent injury (40,72,92).

THE TRAINING PLAN

To accomplish these objectives, an athlete's training program should be organized into a training plan that involves both short- and long-term planning. A **training plan** is a specific plan designed to meet the athlete's training and performance goals. This plan will determine the forms of training to be used, how long the plan will take, how often the plan will change, and what specific exercises will be performed. The long-term aspect of the training plan in the OPT™ model is known as an *annual plan*, whereas the short-term aspects are termed *monthly* and *weekly plans*. When the plan is viewed from the weekly to the annual, the athlete will be able to see the future advancement toward individual goals in a timely, organized fashion.

An **annual plan** organizes the training program over a 1-year period (Fig. 12.2) that provides the athlete with a blueprint (or map) of how the OPT™ training program will progress over the long term, month by month, to meet the desired goal. This gives the athlete a clear representation of how the Sports Performance Professional plans to get the athlete to his/her goal and how long it will take to get there.

Training Plan
The specific outline, created by a Sports Performance Professional to meet an athlete's goals, that details the form of training, length of time, future changes, and specific exercises.

Annual Plan
Generalized training plan that spans 1 year to show when the athlete will progress between phases.

The OPT™ Model

The different periods (or phases) of training seen in a traditional periodization model include a preparatory period (termed anatomical adaptation), a hypertrophy period, a maximum strength period, and a power period.

In the OPT™ model, these are simplified into stabilization (anatomical adaptation), strength (strength endurance, hypertrophy, and maximum strength), and power. The OPT™ model seen in a phase-specific model of training includes six different phases of training. These phases systematically progress all athletes through the three main adaptations of stabilization, strength, and power (see Fig. 12.1).

Think of the OPT™ model as a staircase, guiding an athlete to different adaptations. This journey will involve going up and down the stairs, stopping at different steps and moving to various heights, depending on the athlete's goals, needs, and abilities. This section will detail the various phases of training in the OPT™ model.

CORRECTIVE EXERCISE

Corrective Exercise Training

A form of training designed to correct muscle imbalances, joint dysfunctions, neuromuscular deficits, and postural distortion patterns that the athlete may have developed during the season. This may be a form of training an athlete may have to start in before starting Phase 1 of the OPT™ Model.

Before discussing the different levels of the OPT™ model, it will be important to briefly discuss **corrective exercise training**. At the end of a season, an athlete may be required to spend some time performing this form of training prior to starting the phases of the OPT™ model. Corrective exercise training is designed to correct muscle imbalances, joint dysfunctions, neuromuscular deficits, and postural distortion patterns the athlete may have developed during the season. It is also designed to recondition each athlete and improve total kinetic chain structural integrity. Corrective exercise will help prepare the athlete for the higher-intensity training that will come in the phases of the OPT™ model. To learn more about corrective exercise training, see Chapter 13 of this textbook or refer to NASM's Corrective Exercise Specialist course.

STABILIZATION LEVEL

The first level of training in the OPT™ model focuses on the main adaptation of stabilization (or anatomical adaptation) and is designed to prepare the body for the demands of higher levels of training to follow. This period is as crucial for the beginner as it is for the experienced athlete coming back from a detrained state. It is also necessary to cycle back through this phase after periods of strength and power training in order to maintain a high degree of core and joint stability. In addition, it allows the body to rest from more intense bouts of training. Stabilization training:

- Improves muscle imbalances
- Improves stabilization of the core musculature
- Prevents tissue overload by preparing muscles, tendons, ligaments, and joints for the upcoming imposed demands of training
- Improves overall cardiorespiratory and neuromuscular condition
- Establishes proper movement patterns and exercise technique

The above goals are accomplished through low-intensity, high-repetition training programs that emphasize core and joint stabilization (as opposed to increasing the strength of the arms and legs). This phase incorporates exercises that progressively challenge the body's stability requirements (or proprioception), as opposed to how much weight is being used.

Therefore, the primary means of advancing throughout this phase is to increase the intensity of training by increasing the proprioceptive demands of the exercises. This form of training has been shown to be extremely effective for increasing neuromuscular efficiency (76,77).

The stabilization period of training in the OPT™ model consists of a single phase of training: stabilization endurance (see Fig. 12.1).

STABILIZATION ENDURANCE TRAINING (PHASE 1)

Stabilization endurance training is designed to create optimum levels of stabilization strength and postural control (Table 12.14). Although this phase is the first phase of training in the OPT™ model, as previously stated, it will also be important to cycle back through this phase of training between periods of higher-intensity training seen in Phases 2 through 6. This will allow for proper recovery and maintenance of high levels of stability that will ensure optimal adaptations for strength, power, or both. The primary focus when progressing in this phase is on increasing the proprioception (controlled instability) of the exercises, rather than just the load. This phase of training focuses on:

- Increasing stability
- Muscular endurance

TABLE 12.14

Phase 1: Stabilization Endurance Training

	Reps	Sets	Tempo	% Intensity	Rest Interval	Frequency	Duration	Exercise Selection
Flexibility	1	1–3	30–sec hold	n/a	n/a	3–7x/week	4–6 weeks	SMR and static
Core	12–20	1–4	Slow 4/2/1	n/a	0–90 sec	2–4x/week	4–6 weeks	1–4 core-stabilization
Balance	12–20 6–10 (SL)	1–3	Slow 4/2/1	n/a	0–90 sec	2–4x/week	4–6 weeks	1–4 balance-stabilization
*Plyometric	5–8	1–3	3–5 sec hold on landing	n/a	0–90 sec	2–4x/week	4–6 weeks	0–2 plyometric-stabilization
SAQ	15–20 yd	3–4 2–4	Controlled	n/a •	**1:3 **1:5	2–4x/week	4–6 weeks	3–4 technique drills 3–5 speed of movement drills (linear/MDS)
Resistance Training	12–20	1–3	Slow 4/2/1	50–70%	0–90 sec	2–4x/week	4–6 weeks	1–2 stabilization progression

SL = single-leg (6–10) on each leg; SMR = self-myofascial release; n/a = not applicable.
*If an athlete does not have ample amounts of core stability and balance, plyometric exercises may not be included in this phase of training until these components are developed.
**1:3 = 3 minutes of rest for 1 minute of work, 1:5 = 5 minutes of rest for 1 minute of work.

- Increasing neuromuscular efficiency of the core musculature
- Improving intermuscular and intramuscular coordination.

Acute variables can be progressed if the athlete is starting in the stabilization endurance phase, with minimal to no training background and is also fairly conditioned, with no major muscle imbalances (Table 12.15). The Sports Performance Professional will design the program to increase repetitions and challenge proprioception in order to establish the necessary core muscle endurance. The intensity of the weight will remain low to allow the athlete to focus on proprioceptive control and neuromuscular efficiency. A well-designed program will have an athlete in this phase of training for about 4 weeks in preparation for the demands of the strength endurance phase (Phase 2).

Acute variables can also be progressed if the athlete is fairly conditioned and has a good level of training background (Table 12.16). The program designed should progress the athlete by slowly increasing intensity and decreasing the repetitions, to establish the necessary levels of endurance and strength in the stabilizing muscles.

TABLE 12.15

Stabilization Endurance Progressions for Beginning Athletes

		Weekly Progression			
		Week 1	Week 2	Week 3	Week 4
Core	Sets	1	2	2	3
	Reps	12	15	20	20
Balance	Sets	1	2	2	3
	Reps	12	15	20	20
Plyometric	Sets	1	2	2	2
	Reps	5	5	6	8
SAQ	Sets	*3/2	3/3	4/3	4/4
	Reps	15 yd	15 yd	20 yd	20 yd
Resistance Training	Sets	1	2	2	3
	Reps	12	15	20	20
	Intensity	60%	60%	60%	60%

*3/2 = 3 sets of technique drills, 2 sets of speed of movement drills, etc.

TABLE 12.16

Stabilization Endurance Progressions for Athletes that are Fairly Conditioned with Good Training Background

		Weekly Progression			
		Week 1	Week 2	Week 3	Week 4
Core	Sets	1	2	3	3
	Reps	20	20	15	15
Balance	Sets	1	2	3	3
	Reps	20	20	15	15
Plyometric	Sets	1	2	3	3
	Reps	6	6	6	8
SAQ	Sets	3/3	3/3	4/3	4/4
	Reps	15 yd	20 yd	20 yd	20 yd
Resistance Training	Sets	1–2	2	3	3
	Reps	20	15	15	12
	Intensity	60%	65%	65%	70%

EXAMPLE PHASE 1: STABILIZATION ENDURANCE TRAINING PROGRAM

WARM-UP		Sets	Reps		Time
Foam Roll					
Calves		1			30 sec
IT-Band		1			30 sec
Lats		1			30 sec
Static Stretch					
Gastrocnemius Stretch		1			30 sec
Kneeling Hip Flexor		1			30 sec
Ball Lat Stretch		1			30 sec

CORE & BALANCE		Sets	Reps	Tempo	Rest
Prone Iso-Ab		1	15	Slow	0
Floor Bridge		1	15	Slow	0
Single-leg Balance Reach		1	15	Slow	60 sec

PLYOMETRICS		Sets	Reps	Tempo	Rest
Squat Jump with Stabilization		1	6	Hold Landing for 3–5 sec.	60 sec

SPEED/AGILITY/QUICKNESS		Sets	Reps	Distance	Rest
Speed Ladder: 6-Exercises		2			60 sec

RESISTANCE		Sets	Reps	Tempo	Intensity	Rest
Total Body	Optional					
Chest	Standing Cable Chest Press	1	20	4/2/1	60%	0 sec
Back	Stability Ball Cobra	1	20	4/2/1	60%	0 sec
Shoulders	Single-Leg Dumbbell Scaption	1	20	4/2/1	60%	0 sec
Biceps	Single-Leg DB Bicep Curl	1	20	4/2/1	60%	0 sec
Triceps	Supine Ball Dumbbell Extensions	1	20	4/2/1	60%	0 sec

(*continued*)

(continued)						
RESISTANCE		**Sets**	**Reps**	**Tempo**	**Intensity**	**Rest**
Legs	Single-leg Squat	1	20	4/2/1	60%	90 sec
COOL DOWN						
Repeat Foam Roll and/or Static Stretching Exercises from WARM-UP						

STRENGTH LEVEL

The second level of training in the OPT™ model focuses on the main adaptation of strength, which includes strength endurance, hypertrophy, and maximal strength. It is designed to enhance stability while increasing the amount of stress placed upon the body to increase muscle size and strength. This period of training is a necessary progression to develop muscle size, muscle strength, and improve overall performance. The focus of the strength level of training includes:

- Increasing the ability of the core musculature to stabilize the pelvis and spine under heavier loads through more complete ranges of motion
- Increasing the load bearing capabilities of muscles, tendons, ligaments, and joints
- Increasing the volume of training with more reps, sets, and intensity
- Increasing the metabolic demand by taxing the ATP/CP and glycolytic energy systems to induce cellular changes in muscle (weight loss, hypertrophy, or both)
- Increasing motor unit recruitment, frequency of motor unit recruitment, and motor unit synchronization (maximal strength)

The strength level of training in the OPT™ model consists of three phases: Phase 2: Strength Endurance Training, Phase 3: Hypertrophy Training, and Phase 4: Maximal Strength Training (Fig. 12.1).

STRENGTH ENDURANCE TRAINING (PHASE 2)

Strength endurance training is a hybrid form of training that promotes increased stabilization endurance, hypertrophy, and strength. This form of training entails the use of *superset* techniques where a more stable exercise (such as a bench press) is immediately followed with a stabilization exercise with similar biomechanical motions (such as a stability ball push-up). Thus, for every set of an exercise/body part performed according to the acute variables, there are actually two exercises or 2 sets being performed. High amounts of volume can be generated in this phase of training (Table 12.17).

TABLE 12.17

Strength Endurance Acute Variables

Phase 2: Strength Endurance Training

	Reps	Sets	Tempo	% Intensity	Rest Interval	Frequency	Duration	Exercise Selection
Flexibility	5–10	1–2	1–2 sec. hold	n/a	n/a	3–7x/week	4 weeks	SMR and *active
Core	8–12	2–3	Medium	n/a	0–60 sec	2–4x/week	4 weeks	1–3 core-strength
Balance	8–12	2–3	Medium	n/a	0–60 sec	2–4x/week	4 weeks	1–3 balance-strength
Plyometric	8–10	2–3	Repeating	n/a	0–60 sec	2–4x/week	4 weeks	1–3 plyometric-strength
SAQ	15–20 yd	3–4	Controlled	n/a	1:3	2–4x/week	4 weeks	2–3 technique drills
		2–4			1:5			5–7 speed of movement drills (linear/MDS)
Resistance Training	8–12	2–4	(Str) 2/0/2 (Stab) 4/2/1	70–80%	0–60 sec	2–4x/week	4 weeks	1 strength superset w/1 stabilization
Comments	Each resistance training exercise is a superset of a strength level exercise immediately followed by a stabilization level exercise (e.g., bench press followed by a ball push-up)							

*Depending on the athlete, static stretching may still need to be used in this phase of training.

Acute variables can be progressed if an athlete with the goal of increasing lean body mass and general performance has properly progressed through Phase 1 of the OPT™ model (Table 12.18). Because the goal of this phase of training is strength and hypertrophy, the Sports Performance Professional will want to increase intensity and decrease the repetitions to establish the necessary levels of strength. An athlete in this category will generally stay in this phase of training for a 4-week duration.

TABLE 12.18

Strength Endurance Progressions for Athlete with Goals of Increased Lean Body Mass and/or General Performance

		Weekly Progression			
		Week 1	Week 2	Week 3	Week 4
Core	Sets	2	2	3	3
	Reps	12	12	10	8
Balance	Sets	2	2	3	3
	Reps	12	12	10	8
Plyometric	Sets	2	3	3	3
	Reps	8	8	10	10
SAQ	Sets	3/3	3/3	4/3	4/4
	Reps	15 yd	20 yd	20 yd	20 yd
Resistance Training	Sets	2	3	3	4
	Reps	12 strength	10 strength	8 strength	8 strength
		12 stabilization	10 stabilization	8 stabilization	8 stabilization
	Intensity	70%	75%	80%	80%

EXAMPLE PHASE 2: STRENGTH ENDURANCE TRAINING PROGRAM

WARM-UP	Sets	Reps	Time
Foam Roll			
IT Band	1		60 sec
Lats	1		60 sec
Calf	1		60 sec
Active Stretch			
Gastrocnemius (supination/pronation)	1	5–10	
Hip Flexors	1	5–10	
Lats	1	5–10	

CORE & BALANCE	Sets	Reps	Tempo	Rest
Ball Crunch	2	12	Medium	0 sec
Bench Back Extension with Rotation	2	12	Medium	0 sec
Single-leg Squat Touchdown	2	12	Medium	60 sec

PLYOMETRICS	Sets	Reps	Tempo	Rest
Power Step-Ups	2	8	Repeating	60 sec

SPEED/AGILITY/QUICKNESS	Sets	Reps	Distance	Rest
Speed Ladder: 6-Exercises	2			60 sec
Lateral A-Skips	2		15–20 yds	30 sec
Line-Stop Deceleration Drill	2		15–20 yds	60 sec

(continued)

(continued)

RESISTANCE		Sets	Reps	Tempo	Intensity	Rest
Total Body	Optional					
Chest	1. Incline DB Bench Press 2. Ball Push Up	2	12 12	2/0/2 4/2/1	70%	0 sec
Back	1. Lat Pulldown 2. Ball DB Row	2	12 12	2/0/2 4/2/1	70%	0 sec
Shoulders	1. Seated Shoulder Press 2. Single-leg Lateral Raise	2	12 12	2/0/2 4/2/1	70%	0 sec
Biceps	Optional					
Triceps	Optional					
Legs	1. Leg Press 2. Single-leg Squat	2	12 12	2/0/2 4/2/1	70%	90 sec
COOL DOWN						
Foam Roll and/or Static Stretching						

HYPERTROPHY TRAINING (PHASE 3)

Hypertrophy training is specific for the adaptation of maximal muscle growth, focusing on high levels of volume with minimal rest periods to force cellular changes that result in an overall increase in muscle size (Table 12.19).

TABLE 12.19

Hypertrophy Acute Variables

Phase 3: Hypertrophy Training

	Reps	Sets	Tempo	% Intensity	Rest Interval	Frequency	Duration	Exercise Selection
Flexibility	5–10	1–2	1–2 sec hold	n/a	n/a	3–7x/week	4 weeks	SMR and active
*Core	8–12	2–3	Medium	n/a	0–60 sec	3–6x/week	4 weeks	0–4 core-strength
*Balance	8–12	2–3	Medium	n/a	0–60 sec	3–6x/week	4 weeks	0–4 balance-strength
*Plyometric	8–10	2–3	Repeating	n/a	0–60 sec	3–6x/week	4 weeks	0–4 plyometric-strength
*SAQ	15–20 yd	3–4	Controlled	n/a	1:3	2–4x/week	4 weeks	2–3 technique drills
		2–4			1:5			5–7 speed of movement drills (linear/MDS)
Resistance Training	6–10	3–5	2/0/2	75–85%	0–60 sec	3–6x/week	4 weeks	2–4 strength level exercises/body part
Comments	Total of 24–36 sets per workout Light day = 20–24 total sets Moderate day = 24–30 total sets Heavy day = 30–36 total sets							

*Because of the goal, core, balance, plyometric, and SAQ training may be optional in this phase of training (although recommended). They can also be trained on non-resistance training days.

TABLE 12.20

Hypertrophy Progressions for Athletes with Goals of Increased Lean Body Mass and/or General Performance

		Weekly Progression			
		Week 1	Week 2	Week 3	Week 4
Core	Sets	2	2	3	3
	Reps	12	12	10	8
Balance	Sets	2	2	3	3
	Reps	12	12	10	8
Plyometric	Sets	2	3	3	3
	Reps	8	8	10	10
SAQ	Sets	3/3	3/3	4/3	4/4
	Reps	15 yd	20 yd	20 yd	20 yd
Resistance Training	Sets	3	3	4	5
	Reps	12	10	8	6
	Intensity	75%	80%	80%	85%

Acute variables can be progressed if an athlete has properly progressed through Phases 1 and 2 of the OPT™ model (Table 12.20). Because the goal of this phase of training is primarily hypertrophy, the Sports Performance Professional will want to increase intensity and volume.

An athlete in this category will generally stay in this phase of training for 4 weeks before cycling back through Phases 1 or 2 or progressing on to Phases 4, 5, or 6.

EXAMPLE PHASE 3: HYPERTROPHY TRAINING (Chest, Shoulders, Triceps) PROGRAM

WARM-UP		Sets	Reps	Time
Foam Roll				
IT Band		1		30 sec
Calves		1		30 sec
Lats		1		30 sec
Active Stretch				
Gastrocnemius (supination/pronation)		1	5–10	
Hip Flexors		1	5–10	
Lats		1	5–10	
CORE & BALANCE	Sets	Reps	Tempo	Rest
Ball Crunch with Rotation	2	12	Medium	0 sec
Back Extension w/Cobra	2	12	Medium	0 sec
Single-leg Squat	2	12	Medium	60 sec
PLYOMETRICS	Sets	Reps	Tempo	Rest
Tuck Jump	2	10	Fast	60 sec
SPEED/AGILITY/QUICKNESS	Sets	Reps	Distance	Rest
No SAQ on this day/Optional				

(continued)

(continued)

RESISTANCE		Sets	Reps	Tempo	Intensity	Rest
Total Body	**Optional**					
Chest	DB Bench Press	4	8	2/0/2	80%	60 sec
Chest	Chest Press Machine	4	8	2/0/2	80%	60 sec
Shoulders	Seated DB Shoulder Press	4	8	2/0/2	80%	60 sec
Shoulders	Standing Lateral Raise	4	8	2/0/2	80%	60 sec
Triceps	Cable Pressdowns	4	8	2/0/2	80%	60 sec
Triceps	Triceps Extension Machine	4	8	2/0/2	80%	60 sec
COOL DOWN						
Foam Roll and/or Static Stretching						

EXAMPLE PHASE 3: HYPERTROPHY TRAINING (Back, Biceps, Legs) PROGRAM

WARM-UP		Sets	Reps	Time
Foam Roll				
IT Band			1	30 sec
Calves			1	30 sec
Lats			1	30 sec
Active Stretch				
Gastrocnemius (supination/pronation)			1	5–10
Hip Flexors			1	5–10
Lats			1	5–10

CORE & BALANCE	Sets	Reps	Tempo	Rest
Reverse Crunch	2	12	Medium	0 sec
Cable Rotations	2	12	Medium	0 sec
Lunge to Balance	2	12	Medium	60 sec

PLYOMETRICS	Sets	Reps	Tempo	Rest
Butt Kicks	2	10	Fast	60 sec

SPEED/AGILITY/QUICKNESS	Sets	Reps	Distance	Rest
No SAQ on this day/Optional				

RESISTANCE		Sets	Reps	Tempo	Intensity	Rest
Total Body	**Optional**					
Back	Pull Ups	4	8	2/0/2	80%	60 sec
Back	Seated Row Machine	4	8	2/0/2	80%	60 sec
Biceps	Barbell Curls	4	8	2/0/2	80%	60 sec
Biceps	Bicep Curl Machine	4	8	2/0/2	80%	60 sec
Legs	Barbell Squat	4	8	2/0/2	80%	60 sec
Legs	Leg Press	4	8	2/0/2	80%	60 sec
COOL DOWN						
Foam Roll and/or Static Stretching						

MAXIMAL STRENGTH TRAINING (PHASE 4)

The Maximal Strength Training Phase focuses on increasing the load placed upon the tissues of the body. Maximal strength training improves:

- Recruitment of more motor units
- Rate of force production
- Motor unit synchronization

Maximal strength training has also been shown to help increase the benefits of power training used in Phases 5 and 6 (Table 12.21).

TABLE 12.21

Maximal Strength Acute Variables

Phase 4: Maximal Strength Training

	Reps	Sets	Tempo	% Intensity	Rest Interval	Frequency	Duration	Exercise Selection
Flexibility	5–10	1–2	1–2 sec hold	n/a	n/a	3–7x/week	4 weeks	SMR and active
Core	8–12	2–3	Medium 1/1/1	n/a	0–60 sec	2–4x/week	4 weeks	0–3 core-strength
Balance	8–12	2–3	Medium 1-1-1	n/a	0–60 sec	2–4x/week	4 weeks	0–3 balance-strength
Plyometric	8–10	2–3	Repeating	n/a	0–60 sec	2–4x/week	4 weeks	0–3 plyometric-strength
SAQ	15–20 yd	3–4 2–4	Fast	n/a	1:3 1:5	2–4x/week	4 weeks	2–3 technique drills 5–7 speed of movement drills (linear/MDS)
Resistance Training	1–5	4–6	As fast as can be controlled	85–100%	3–5 min	2–4x/week	4 weeks	1–3 strength

Acute variables can be progressed if an athlete has properly progressed through Phases 1 and 2 (and possibly Phase 3) (Table 12.22). Because the goal of this phase of training is primarily maximal strength, the focus will be on the increase in intensity.

An athlete in this category will generally stay in this phase of training for a 4-week duration before cycling back through Phases 1 or 2 or progressing on to Phase 5.

TABLE 12.22

Maximal Strength Training Progressions for Athletes with Goals of Increased Strength and/or General Performance

		Weekly Progression			
		Week 1	Week 2	Week 3	Week 4
Core	Sets	2	2	3	3
	Reps	12	12	10	8
Balance	Sets	2	2	3	3
	Reps	12	12	10	8
Plyometric	Sets	2	3	3	3
	Reps	8	8	10	10
SAQ	Sets	3/3	3/3	4/3	4/4
	Reps	15 yd	20 yd	20 yd	20 yd
Resistance Training	Sets	4	5	5	6
	Reps	5	5	4	3
	Intensity	85%	85%	90%	95%

EXAMPLE PHASE 4: MAXIMAL STRENGTH TRAINING PROGRAM

WARM-UP		Sets	Reps	Time
Foam Roll				
IT Band		1		30 sec
Lats		1		30 sec
Calf		1		30 sec
Active Stretch				
Gastrocnemius (supination/pronation)		1	5–10	
Hip Flexor Stretch		1	5–10	
Lat Stretch		1	5–10	

CORE & BALANCE	Sets	Reps	Tempo	Rest
Cable Rotations	2	12	Medium	0 sec
Cable Lift	2	12	Medium	0 sec
Lunge to Balance: Frontal Plane	2	12	Medium	90 sec

PLYOMETRICS	Sets	Reps	Tempo	Rest
No Plyometrics on this day				

SPEED/AGILITY/QUICKNESS	Sets	Reps	Distance	Rest
No SAQ on this day				

RESISTANCE		Sets	Reps	Tempo	Intensity	Rest
Total Body	**Optional**					
Chest	Bench Press	4	5	Controlled	85%	3 min
Back	Lat Pulldown	4	5	Controlled	85%	3 min
Shoulders	Seated Barbell Shoulder Press	4	5	Controlled	85%	3 min
Biceps	Optional					
Triceps	Optional					
Legs	Barbell Squats	4	5	Controlled	85%	3 min

COOL DOWN
Foam Roll and/or Static Stretching

POWER

The third level of training is power training and is designed to increase the rate of force production (or, speed of muscle contraction). This form of training uses both the strength and stabilization adaptations acquired in the previous phases of training and then applies them with more realistic speeds and forces that the body will encounter in sport.

Power is simply defined as force multiplied by velocity ($P = F \times V$). Therefore, any increase in either force and/or velocity will produce an increase in power. This is accomplished by either increasing the load (or force) at any velocity as might be seen in progressive strength training or increasing the speed (or velocity) with which a load is moved. The combined effect is a better rate of force production during athletic activities.

To develop optimum levels of power, individuals must train both with heavy loads (85–100%) at low speeds and light loads (30–45%) at high speeds. The focus of power training is to increase the rate of force production by increasing the number of motor units activated, the synchrony between them, and the speed at which they are excited (29,94–96).

The power level of training in the OPT™ model consists of two phases of training: Phase 5: Power Training and Phase 6: Maximal Power Training.

POWER TRAINING (PHASE 5)

The Power Training Phase focuses on both high force and velocity to increase power (Table 12.23). This is accomplished by using a form of complex training, supersetting a strength exercise with a power exercise for each body part (such as performing a barbell bench press superset with a medicine ball chest pass).

The 85–100% refers to the intensity for traditional strength training exercises. It increases power by increasing the *force* side of the power equation.

The 30–45% intensity, on the other hand, is used for "speed" exercises such as speed squats where the squats are performed as fast as possible with a low load. Approximately 10% of body weight intensity is used for medicine ball training that will require the release of a medicine ball. These last two forms of training affect the *velocity* side of the power equation. By using heavy weight with explosive movement and low resistance with a high velocity, you can produce high power outputs (90,94–97).

TABLE 12.23

Power Acute Variables

Phase 5: Power Training

	Reps	Sets	Tempo	% Intensity	Rest Int.	Frequency	Duration	Exercise Selection
Flexibility	10–15	1–2	Controlled	n/a	n/a	3–7x/week	4 weeks	SMR and dynamic 3–10 exercises
*Core	8–12	2–3	As fast as can be controlled	n/a	0–60 sec	2–4x/week	4 weeks	0–2 core-power
*Balance	8–12	2–3	Controlled	n/a	0–60 sec	2–4x/week	4 weeks	0–2 balance-power
*Plyometric	8–12	2–3	As fast as possible	n/a	0–60 sec	2–4x/week	4 weeks	0–2 plyometric-power
**SAQ	15–20 yd	3–4 / 2–4	Fast	n/a	1:3 / 1:5	2–4x/week	4 weeks	1–2 technique drills / 7–10 speed of movement drills (linear/MDS)
Resistance Training	1–5 (S) 8–10 (P)	3–5	(S) Controlled (P) As fast as can be controlled	(S) 85–100% (P) up to 10% BW or 30–45% 1 RM	1–2 min b/w pairs 3–5 min b/w circuits	2–4x/week	4 weeks	1 strength superset w 1 power
Comments	BW = body weight 1 RM = 1 repetition maximum							

*Because of the use of core-power, balance-power, and plyometric-power exercises in the resistance training portion of this program, it may not be necessary to perform these exercises prior to the resistance training portion of the program. They can be performed as part of a dynamic flexibility warm-up or performed on non-resistance training days.
**SAQ drills may be performed on non-resistance training days.

Acute variables can be progressed if the athlete has properly progressed through the rest of the OPT™ model (Table 12.24). Because the goal of this phase of training is primarily power, the program design will focus on progressing intensity and velocity.

An athlete in this category will generally stay in this phase of training for a 4-week duration, before cycling back through Phases 1 or 2 or progressing to Phase 6 (maximal power training).

TABLE 12.24

Power Progressions for Athletes with Goals of Increased Power and Performance

		Weekly Progression			
		Week 1	Week 2	Week 3	Week 4
Core	Sets	2	2	3	3
	Reps	12	12	10	8
Balance	Sets	2	2	3	3
	Reps	12	12	10	8
Plyometric	Sets	2	3	3	3
	Reps	8	8	10	10
SAQ	3/3	3/3	4/3	4/4	3/3
	15 yd	20 yd	20 yd	20 yd	15 yd
Resistance Training	Sets	3	4	4	5
	Reps	5 strength	4 strength	4 strength	2–3 strength
		10 power	10 power	8 power	8 power
	Intensity	Strength 85%	Strength 90%	Strength 90%	Strength 95%
		Power 5% BW	Power 5% BW	Power 8% BW	Power 10% BW

EXAMPLE PHASE 5: POWER TRAINING PROGRAM

WARM-UP	Sets	Reps	Time
Foam Roll			
Calf	1		30 sec
IT-Band	1		30 sec
Lats	1		30 sec
Dynamic Warm-Up			
Lateral Tube Walking	1	10	0 sec
Prisoner Squats	1	10	0 sec
Walking Lunge with Rotation	1	10	0 sec
Leg Swings: Front to Back	1	10	0 sec
Push-Up with Rotation	1	10	0 sec
Medicine Ball Rotations	1	10	0 sec
Scorpion	1	10	60 sec

CORE, BALANCE AND PLYOMETRICS	Sets	Reps	Tempo	Rest
No CORE, BALANCE and PLYOMETICS (Incorporated into Dynamic Warm-Up and Resistance Training Program)				

SPEED/AGILITY/QUICKNESS	Sets	Reps	Distance	Rest
Speed Ladder: 8 Exercises	1			60 sec
T-Drill	4			30 sec
Box Drill	4			30 sec

(continued)

(continued)						
RESISTANCE		**Sets**	**Reps**	**Tempo**	**Intensity**	**Rest**
Total Body	Power Cleans	3	5	Fast	85%	2 Min
Chest	1. Barbell Bench Press	3	5	Controlled	85%	2 min
	2. Rotational Chest Press		10	Fast	2% of BW	
Back	1. Lat Pulldown	3	5	Controlled	85%	2 min
	2. Soccer Throw		10	Fast	2% of BW	
Shoulders	1. Seated Shoulder Press	3	5	Controlled	85%	2 min
	2. Overhead Medicine Ball Throw		10	Fast	2% of BW	
Legs	1. Barbell Squat	3	5	Controlled	85%	2 min
	2. Power Step-Ups		10	Fast	2% of BW	
COOL DOWN						
Foam Roll and/or Static Stretching						

MAXIMAL POWER TRAINING (PHASE 6)

The maximal power training phase focuses on high-velocity training for further increases in power (Table 12.25). This is accomplished by training with 30–45% of an athlete's maximum strength and by accelerating through the entire range of motion. This is a specialized form of training and should be implemented only for those athletes who require maximum power and who have already developed optimum levels of stabilization strength and eccentric strength.

TABLE 12.25

Maximal Power Training Acute Variables

Phase 6: Maximal Power Training

	Reps	Sets	Tempo	% Intensity	Rest Int.	Frequency	Duration	Exercise Selection
Flexibility	10–15	1–2	Controlled	n/a	n/a	3–7x/week	2 weeks	SMR and dynamic 3–10 exercises
Core	N/A	N/A	N/A	N/A	N/A	N/A	N/A	N/A
Balance	N/A	N/A	N/A	N/A	N/A	N/A	N/A	N/A
Plyometric	N/A	N/A	N/A	N/A	N/A	N/A	N/A	N/A
***SAQ**	15–20 yd	3–4	Fast	n/a	1:3	2–4x/week	2 weeks	1–2 technique drills
		2–4			1:5			7–10 speed of movement drills (linear/MDS)
Resistance Training	10	4–6	As fast as can be controlled	30–45% 1RM or 10% BW	3–5 min	1–2x/week	2 weeks	Power level
Comments	4–6 total exercises							

N/A = Because of the use of core-power, balance-power, and plyometric-power exercises in the resistance training portion of this program, it is not necessary to perform these exercises prior to the resistance training portion of the program. These components can be included in the dynamic flexibility warm-up portion of this program.

*SAQ drills should be done on separate days.

Traditional training techniques do not allow maximal acceleration throughout the entire range of motion. Research demonstrates that approximately 25–40% of a traditional "explosive power" lift requires deceleration (72). Therefore, the athlete who follows traditional training techniques is unable to express their speed strength throughout the entire range of motion. This prevents optimum performance improvements.

Because the exercises performed in this phase of training are strictly power exercises being performed at very high intensities, performing core-power, balance-power, and plyometric-power exercises would not be necessary to ensure that the athlete does not overtrain. These components will be trained during the dynamic warm-up of this program. Additionally, SAQ drills should be done on separate days to further ensure the athlete does not become overly fatigued prior to the power exercises.

Acute variables can be progressed if the athlete has properly progressed through the rest of the OPT™ model (Table 12.26). Because the goal of this phase of training is primarily power, the program design will focus on increasing velocity. An athlete in this category will generally stay in this phase of training for a 2-week duration, before cycling back through Phases 1 or 2.

TABLE 12.26

Progressions for Athletes with Goals of Increased Power and Performance

		Weekly Progression			
		Week 1	Week 2	Week 3	Week 4
Core	Sets	N/A	N/A	N/A	N/A
	Reps	N/A	N/A	N/A	N/A
Balance	Sets	N/A	N/A	N/A	N/A
	Reps	N/A	N/A	N/A	N/A
Plyometric	Sets	N/A	N/A	N/A	N/A
	Reps	N/A	N/A	N/A	N/A
SAQ	Sets	3/3	3/3	4/3	4/4
	Reps	15 yd	20 yd	20 yd	20 yd
Resistance Training	Sets	3	4	4	5
	Reps	10 power	10 power	8 power	8 power
	Intensity	Power 5% BW	Power 5% BW	Power 8% BW	Power 10% BW
Comments					

EXAMPLE PHASE 6: MAXIMAL POWER TRAINING PROGRAM

WARM-UP	Sets	Reps	Time
Foam Roll			
Calf	1		30 sec
IT-Band	1		30 sec
Lats	1		30 sec
Dynamic Warm-Up			
Lateral Tube Walking	1	10	0 sec
Prisoner Squats	1	10	0 sec
Walking Lunge with Rotation	1	10	0 sec
Leg Swings: Front to Back	1	10	0 sec
Push-Up with Rotation	1	10	0 sec
Medicine Ball Rotations	1	10	0 sec
Scorpion	1	10	60 sec

(continued)

(continued)					
CORE, BALANCE, AND PLYOMETRICS		**Sets**	**Reps**	**Tempo**	**Rest**
No CORE, BALANCE, and PLYOMETRICS (Incorporated into Dynamic Warm-Up and Resistance Program)					
SPEED/AGILITY/QUICKNESS		**Sets**	**Reps**	**Distance**	**Rest**
Performed on different day					
RESISTANCE		**Sets**	**Reps**	**Tempo**	**Intensity**	**Rest**
Total Body				Fast		
Chest	Rotational Chest Pass	3	10	Fast	10% of BW	3 min
Back	Ball Medicine Ball Pullover Throw	3	10	Fast	10% of BW	3 min
Shoulders	Overhead Medicine Ball Throw	3	10	Fast	10% of BW	3 min
Legs	Squat Jumps	3	10	Fast	10% of BW	3 min
COOL DOWN						
Foam Roll and/or Static Stretching						

Applying the OPT™ Model

The concepts of program design, periodization and the OPT™ model have all been described. Program design was defined as creating a purposeful system or plan to achieve a goal. Periodization is the scientific basis that allows the Sports Performance Professional to strategically plan, design programs, and achieve goals while minimizing the risk of placing improper stresses on the body that can lead to overuse or acute injuries when there is too rapid a progression in the training stimulus.

The OPT™ model is a proven, easy to use system of periodization that can be used to create programs for athletes to meet their various goals. Although the understanding of these concepts is paramount, what matters the most is the ability to apply the information in multiple situations to a variety of athletes. See Appendix A in the textbook for comprehensive assessment strategies, OPT™ periodization strategies, and sample programs for baseball, basketball, football, hockey, golf, and soccer.

SUMMARY

Program design is creating a purposeful system or plan to achieve a specific goal. To do so, the Sports Performance Professional must understand acute variables, the OPT™ model and its phases, as well as how to apply it all. The OPT™ model provides the Sports Performance Professional with all the necessary tools to properly utilize acute variables (repetitions, sets, etc.), scientific concepts, and exercises to design programs.

The different levels of training seen in a traditional periodization model include anatomical adaptation, hypertrophy, maximal strength, and power. In the OPT™ model, these are simplified into stabilization, strength, and power. These are further broken down into six different phases of training—stabilization endurance training, strength endurance training, hypertrophy training, maximal strength training, power training, and maximal power training. Sports Performance Professionals must be able to apply the information in multiple situations, to a variety of athletes.

REFERENCES

1. Hakkinen K, Kraemer WJ, Newton RU et al. Changes in electromyographic activity, muscle fibre and force production characteristics during heavy resistance/power strength training in middle-aged and older men and women. *Acta Physiologica Scandinavica* 2001;171:51–62.

2. Hakkinen K, Pakarinen A, Hannonen P et al. Effects of strength training on muscle strength, cross-sectional area, maximal electromyographic activity, and serum hormones in premenopausal women with fibromyalgia. *J Rheum* 2002;29:1287–95.

3. Hass CJ, Garzarella L, de Hoyos D et al. Single versus multiple sets in long-term recreational weightlifters. *Med Sci Sports Exerc* 2000;32:235–42.

4. Izquierdo M, Hakkinen K, Ibanez J et al. Effects of strength training on muscle power and serum hormones in middle-aged and older men. *J Appl Physiol* 2001;90:1497–507.

5. Kraemer WJ, Hakkinen K, Triplett-Mcbride NT et al. Physiological changes with periodized resistance training in women tennis players. *Med Sci Sports Exerc* 2003;35:157–68.

6. Kraemer WJ, Mazzetti SA, Nindl BC. Effect of resistance training on women's strength/power and occupational performances. *Med Sci Sports Exerc* 2001;33:1011–025.

7. Kraemer WJ, Ratamess N, Fry AC et al. Influence of resistance training volume and periodization on physiological and performance adaptations in collegiate women tennis players. *Am J Sports Med* 2000;28:626–33.

8. Kraemer WJ, Ratamess NA. Fundamentals of resistance training: progression and exercise prescription. *Med Sci Sports Exerc* 2004;36:674–88.

9. Mazzetti SA, Kraemer WJ, Volek JS et al. The influence of direct supervision of resistance training on strength performance. *Med Sci Sports Exerc* 2000;32:1175–84.

10. Rhea MR, Alvar BA, Ball SD et al. Three sets of weight training superior to 1 set with equal intensity for eliciting strength. *J Strength Cond Res* 2002;16:525–9.

11. Rhea MR, Ball SD, Phillips WT et al. A comparison of linear and daily undulating periodized programs with equated volume and intensity for strength. *J Strength Cond Res* 2002;16:250–55.

12. Rhea MR, Phillips WT, Burkett LN et al. A comparison of linear and daily undulating periodized programs with equated volume and intensity for local muscular endurance. *J Strength Cond Res* 2003 Feb;17:82–87.

13. Baker D. Improving vertical jump performance through general, special and specific strength training: a brief review. *J Strength Cond Res* 1996;10:131–36.

14. Bruhn S, Kullmann N, Gollhofer A. The effects of a sensorimotor training and a strength training on postural stabilisation, maximum isometric contraction and jump performance. *Int J Sports Med* 2004;25:56–60.

15. Caraffa A, Cerulli G, Projetti M et al. Prevention of anterior cruciate ligament injuries in soccer. A prospective controlled study of proprioceptive training. *Knee Surg Sports Traumatol Arthrosc* 1996;4:19–21.

16. Cosio-Lima LM, Reynolds KL, Winter C et al. Effects of physioball and conventional floor exercises on early phase adaptations in back and abdominal core stability and balance in women. *J Strength Cond Res* 2003;17:721–25.

17. Hanten WP, Olson SL, Butts NL et al. Effectiveness of a home program of ischemic pressure followed by sustained stretch for treatment of myofascial trigger points. *Phys Ther* 2000;80:997–1003.

18. Hewett TE, Lindenfeld TN, Riccobene JV et al. The effect of neuromuscular training on the incidence of knee injury in female athletes. A prospective study. *Am J Sports Med* 1999;27:699–706.

19. Junge A, Rosch D, Peterson L et al. Prevention of soccer injuries: a prospective intervention study in youth amateur players. *Am J Sports Med* 2002;30:652–59.

20. Kokkonen J, Nelson AG, Eldredge C et al. Chronic static stretching improves exercise performance. *Med Sci Sports Exerc* 2007;39:1825–31.

21. Luebbers PE, Potteiger JA, Hulver MW et al. Effects of plyometric training and recovery on vertical jump performance and anaerobic power. *J Strength Cond Res* 2003;17:704–709.

22. Mandelbaum BR, Silvers HJ, Wantanabe DS et al. Effectiveness of a neuromuscular and proprioception training program in preventing anterior cruciate ligament injuries in female athletes: a 2-year follow-up. *Am J Sports Med* 2005;33:1003–110.

23. Myer GD, Ford KR, Brent JL et al. The effects of plyometric vs. dynamic stabilization and balance training on power, balance, and landing force in female athletes. *J Strength Cond Res* 2006;20:345–53.

24. Paterno MV, Myer GD, Ford KR et al. Neuromuscular training improves single-limb stability in young female athletes. *J Orthop Sports Phys Ther* 2004;34:305–16.

25. Rimmer E, Sleivert G. Effects of a plyometrics intervention program on sprint performance. *J Strength Cond Res* 2000;14(3):295–301.

26. Thompson CJ, Cobb KM, Blackwell J. Functional training improves club head speed and functional fitness in older golfers. *J Strength Cond Res* 2007;21:131–37.

27. Vera-Garcia FJ, Grenier SG, McGill SM. Abdominal muscle response during curl-ups on both stable and labile surfaces. *Phys Ther* 2000;80:564–69.

28. Willson JD, Ireland ML, Davis I. Core strength and lower extremity alignment during single leg squats. *Med Sci Sports Exerc* 2006;38:945–52.

29. Wilson GD, Murphy AJ, Giorgi A. Weight and plyometric training: Effects on eccentric and concentric force production. *Can J Appl Physiol* 1996;21(4):301–15.

30. Witvrouw E, Danneels L, Asselman P et al. Muscle flexibility as a risk factor for developing muscle injuries in male professional soccer players. A prospective study. *Am J Sports Med* 2003;31:41–46.

31. Blazevich AJ, Gill ND, Bronks R et al. Training-specific muscle architecture adaptation after 5-wk training in athletes. *Med Sci Sports Exerc* 2003;35:2013–22.

32. Campos GE, Luecke TJ, Wendeln HK et al. Muscular adaptations in response to three different resistance-training regimens: specificity of repetition maximum training zones. *Eur J Appl Physiol* 2002;88:50–60.

33. Hakkinen A, Sokka T, Kotaniemi A et al. A randomized two-year study of the effects of dynamic strength training on muscle strength, disease activity, functional capacity, and bone mineral density in early rheumatoid arthritis. *Arthritis Rheum* 2001;44:515–22.

34. Hakkinen K, Alen M, Kraemer WJ et al. Neuromuscular adaptations during concurrent strength and endurance training versus strength training. *Eur J Appl Phys* 2003;89:42–52.

35. Harber MP, Fry AC, Rubin MR et al. Skeletal muscle and hormonal adaptations to circuit weight training in untrained men. *Scand J Med Sci Sports* 2004;14:176–85.

36. Kraemer WJ, Mazzetti SA, Nindl BC et al. Effect of resistance training on women's strength/power and occupational performances. *Med Sci Sports Exerc* 2001;33:1011–25.

37. Kraemer WJ, Nindl BC, Ratamess NA et al. Changes in muscle hypertrophy in women with periodized resistance training. *Med Sci Sports Exerc* 2004;36:697–708.

38. Marx JO, Ratamess NA, Nindl BC et al. Low-volume circuit versus high-volume periodized resistance training in women. *Med Sci Sports Exerc* 2001;33:635–43.

39. McCall GE, Byrnes WC, Fleck SJ et al. Acute and chronic hormonal responses to resistance training designed to promote muscle hypertrophy. *Can J Appl Physiol* 1999;24:96–107.

40. Tan B. Manipulating resistance training program variables to optimize maximum strength in men: a review. *J Strength Cond Res* 1999;13:289–304.

41. Willardson JM. A brief review: factors affecting the length of the rest interval between resistance exercise sets. *J Strength Cond Res* 2006;20:978–84.

42. Fleck SJ, Kraemer WJ. Designing Resistance Training Programs, 2nd ed. Champaign, IL: Human Kinetics; 1997.

43. Kraemer WJ, Adams K, Cafarelli E et al. American College of Sports Medicine position stand. Progression models in resistance training for healthy adults. *Med Sci Sports Exerc* 2002;34:364–80.

44. Spiering BA, Kraemer WJ. Resistance Exercise Prescription. In Chandler TJ, Brown LE. Conditioning for Strength and Human Performance. Baltimore: Wolters Kluwer, Lippincott Williams & Wilkins; 2008. pp. 273–291.

45. Baker D, Wilson G, Carlyon R. Periodization: the effects on strength of manipulating volume and intensity. *J Strength Cond Res* 1994;8:235–42.

46. Hakkinen K, Pakarinen A, Alen M. Neuromuscular and hormonal responses in elite athletes to two successive strength training sessions in one day. *Eur J Appl Physiol* 1988;57:133–39.

47. Peterson MD, Rhea MR, Alvar BA. Maximizing strength development in athletes: a meta-analysis to determine the dose-response relationship. *J Strength Cond Res* 2004;18:377–82.

48. Bompa TO. Variations of periodization of strength. *Strength Cond J* 1996;18:58–61.

49. Rhea MR, Alvar BA, Burkett LN et al. A meta-analysis to determine the dose response for strength development. *Med Sci Sports Exerc* 2003;35:456–64.

50. Anderson K, Behm DG. The impact of instability resistance training on balance and stability. *Sports Med* 2005;35:43–53.

51. Behm DB. Neuromuscular implications and applications of resistance training. *J Strength Cond Res* 1995;9:264–74.

52. Behm DG, Anderson KG. The role of instability with resistance training. *J Strength Cond Res* 2006;20:716–22.

53. Kornecki S, Kebel A, Siemieński A. Muscular co-operation during joint stabilisation, as reflected by EMG. *Eur J Appl Physiol* 2001;84:453–61.

54. Ogita F, Stam RP, Tazawa HO et al. Oxygen uptake in one-legged and two-legged exercise. *Med Sci Sport Exerc* 2000;32:1737–42.

55. Williford HN, Olson MS, Gauger S et al. Cardiovascular and metabolic costs of forward, backward, and lateral motion. *Med Sci Sport Exerc* 1998;30:1419–23.

56. Cressey EM, West CA, Tiberio DP et al. The effects of ten weeks of lower-body unstable surface training on markers of athletic performance. *J Strength Cond Res* 2007;21:561–67.

57. Willardson JM, Burkett LN. The effect of rest interval length on the sustainability of squat and bench press repetitions. *J Strength Cond Res* 2006;20:400–403.

58. Baker JS, Graham MR, Davies B. Metabolic consequences of resistive force selection during cycle ergometry exercise. *Res Sports Med* 2007;15:1–11.

59. Chandler TJ, Arnold CE. Bioenergetics. In Chandler TJ, Brown LE. Conditioning for Strength and Human Performance. Baltimore: Wolters Kluwer, Lippincott Williams & Wilkins; 2008. pp. 3–19.

60. Tesch PA, Karlsson J. Lactate in fast and slow twitch skeletal muscle fibres of man during isometric contraction. *Acta Physiol Scand* 1977;99:230–36.

61. Harris RC, Edwards RH, Hultman E et al. The time course of phosphorylcreatine resynthesis during recovery of the quadriceps muscle in man. *Pflugers Archiv* 1976;367:137–42.

62. Brooks GA, Fahey TD, White TP. Exercise Physiology: Human Bioenergetics and its Application. Mountain View, CA: Mayfield Publishing Company; 1996.

63. Fitts RH. Cellular mechanisms of muscle fatigue. *Physiol Rev* 1994;74:49–94.

64. Hakkinen K. Neuromuscular adaptation during strength training, aging, detraining and immobilization. *Crit Rev Phys Med* 1994;6:161–98.

65. Kaneko M, Ito A, Fuchimoto T et al. Effects of running speed on the mechanical power and efficiency of sprint- and distance-runners. *Nippon Seirigaku Zasshi* 1983;45:711–13.

66. Hickson RC, Rosenkoetter MA. Reduced training frequencies and maintenance of increased aerobic power. *Med Sci Sport Exerc* 1981;13:13–16.

67. Mujika I, Padilla S. Detraining: loss of training-induced physiological and performance adaptations. Part I: short term insufficient training stimulus. *Sports Med* 2000;30:79–87.

68. Mujika I, Padilla S. Detraining: loss of training-induced physiological and performance adaptations. Part II: long term insufficient training stimulus. *Sports Med* 2000;30:145–54.

69. Kraemer WJ, Fleck SJ, Callister R et al. Training responses of plasma beat-endorphin, adrenocorti-cotrophin, and cortisol. *Med Sci Sport Exerc* 1989;21:146–53.
70. Kraemer WJ, Marchitelli L, Gordon SE et al. Hormonal growth factor responses to heavy resistance pro-tocols. *J Appl Physiol* 1990;69:1442–50.
71. Kraemer WJ, Patton JF, Gordon SE et al. Compatibility of high-intensity strength and endurance training on hormonal and skeletal muscle adaptations. *J Appl Physiol* 1995;78:976 89.
72. Kraemer WJ, Ratamess NA. Physiology of resistance training. *Orthop Clin J N Am* 2000;9:467–513.
73. Bompa TO. Periodization of Strength: The New Wave in Strength Training. Toronto, ON: Verita Publish-ing, Inc; 1993.
74. Enoka RM. Muscle strength and its development: new perspectives. *Sports Med* 1988;6:146–68.
75. Sale DG. Neural adaptation to resistance training. *Med Sci Sports Exerc* 1988;20:S135–45.
76. Behm DG, Anderson K, Curnew RS. Muscle force and activation under stable and unstable conditions. *J Strength Cond Res* 2002;16:416–22.
77. Heitkamp HC, Horstmann T, Mayer F et al. Gain in strength and muscular balance after balance training. *Int J Sports Med* 2001;22:285–90.
78. Azegami M, Ohira M, Miyoshi K et al. Effect of single and multi-joint lower extremity muscle strength on the functional capacity and ADL/IADL status in Japanese community-dwelling older adults. *Nurs Health Sci* 2007;9:168–76.
79. Carter AB, Kaminski TW, Douex AT Jr et al. Effects of high volume upper extremity plyometric training on throwing velocity and functional strength ratios of the shoulder rotators in collegiate baseball play-ers. *J Strength Cond Res* 2007;21:208–15.
80. Chimera NJ, Swanik KA, Swanik CB et al. Effects of plyometric training on muscle-activation strategies and performance in female athletes. *J Athl Train* 2004;39:24–31.
81. Hoffman JR, Ratamess NA, Cooper JJ et al. Comparison of loaded and unloaded jump squat training on strength/power performance in college football players. *J Strength Cond Res* 2005;19:810–15.
82. Markovic G. Does plyometric training improve vertical jump height? A meta-analytical review. *Br J Sports Med* 2007;41:349–55; discussion 355.
83. Markovic G, Jukic I, Milanovic D et al. Effects of sprint and plyometric training on muscle function and athletic performance. *J Strength Cond Res* 2007;21:543–49.
84. Matavulj D, Kukolj M, Ugarkovic D et al. Effects of plyometric training on jumping performance in jun-ior basketball players. *J Sports Med Phys Fitness* 2001;41:159–64.
85. Newton RU, Kraemer WJ, Häkkinen K. Effects of ballistic training on preseason preparation of elite vol-leyball players. *Med Sci Sports Exerc* 1999;31:323–30.
86. Saunders PU, Telford RD, Pyne DB et al. Short-term plyometric training improves running economy in highly trained middle and long distance runners. *J Strength Cond Res* 2006;20:947–54.
87. Spurrs RW, Murphy AJ, Watsford ML. The effect of plyometric training on distance running performance. *Eur J Appl Physiol* 2003;89:1–7.
88. Stemm JD, Jacobson BH. Comparison of land- and aquatic-based plyometric training on vertical jump performance. *J Strength Cond Res* 2007;21:568–71.
89. Toumi H, Best TM, Martin A et al. Effects of eccentric phase velocity of plyometric training on the verti-cal jump. *Int J Sports Med* 2004;25:391–98.
90. Wilson GJ, Newton RU, Murphy AJ et al. The optimal training load for the development of dynamic ath-letic performance. *Med Sci Sports Exerc* 1993;25(11):1279–86.
91. Young WB, Wilson GJ, Byrne C. A comparison of drop jump training methods: effects on leg extensor strength qualities and jumping performance. *Int J Sports Med* 1999;20:295–303.
92. Plisk SS, Stone MH. Periodization strategies. *Strength Cond J* 2003;25:19–37.
93. Graham J. Periodization research and an example application. *Strength Cond J* 2002;24:62–70.
94. Ebben WP, Blackard DO. Complex training with combined explosive weight and plyometric exercises. *Olympic Coach* 1997;7:11–12.
95. Newton RU, Hakkinen K, Hakkinen A et al. Mixed-methods resistance training increases power and strength of young and older men. *Med Sci Sports Exerc* 2002;34:1367–75.
96. Schmidtbleicher D. Training for Power Events. In Chem PV. Strength and Power in Sports. Boston: Blackwell Scientific; 1992. p 381–96.
97. Crewther B, Cronin J, Keogh J. Possible stimuli for strength and power adaptation: acute mechanical responses. *Sports Med* 2005;35:967–89.

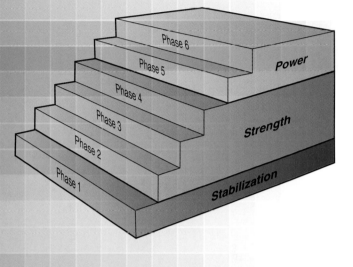

SECTION 5

Injury Prevention and Reconditioning

CHAPTER 13

Current Concepts in Injury Prevention

UPON COMPLETION OF THIS CHAPTER, YOU WILL BE ABLE TO:

Understand the frequency of injuries for the foot and ankle, knee, low back, and shoulder.

Understand the mechanisms for injury in each segment.

Determine common risk factors that can lead to an injury of each segment.

Incorporate exercises into the athlete's program to help decrease the risk of injury and enhance reconditioning.

Introduction

Very specific injuries, such as ankle sprains, anterior cruciate ligament (ACL) injuries, low-back pain, and shoulder pain, create an enormous challenge to athletes and training professionals alike. Athletes in sports that require cutting and jumping are particularly affected by injuries due to over-training, poor neuromuscular control, arthrokinetic dysfunction, or improper biomechanics. The number of injuries to areas, such as the foot and ankle, knees, hips, low back, and shoulders, are staggering and necessitate a comprehensive programming strategy to help prevent injury or help to recondition athletes once an injury has occurred. This chapter will review common injuries that occur in athletics and provide general guidelines for prevention and reconditioning.

Epidemiology of Common Foot Injuries

There are numerous foot injuries that can be a result of either traumatic injury or due to overuse. For the purpose of this text, the focus will be on three common injuries encountered in a physically active population: Achilles tendonitis, plantar fasciitis, and metatarsal stress fractures. In a study of Marine Corps recruits, Achilles tendonitis was reported in 2.8% of all cases in men, whereas women reported plantar fasciitis in 3.7% of all cases (1). In the general population, plantar fasciitis accounted for over 1 million ambulatory care (doctor) visits per year (2). In a study of over 300 athletes with stress fractures, almost 9% were to the metatarsals (3). In one study on 131 military conscripts with x-rays negative for stress fracture, magnetic resonance imaging (MRI) indicated fracture, and 35.7% of those injuries occurred to the metatarsals (4). In a group of female military recruits with suspected stress fractures, metatarsal fractures accounted for 16.2% of all injuries (5). Certain populations have been reported to be more at risk for these injuries, including overground runners (6), females (7), and individuals with a high body mass index (8).

Common Foot Injuries in Physical Activities

ACHILLES TENDONITIS

The calf complex, which consists of the gastrocnemius and soleus muscles, shares the Achilles tendon to insert on the base of the calcaneus (Fig. 13.1). Tendonitis, or inflammation of this tendon or its sheath, is a common sports-related injury. Mechanisms of injury include overuse, poorly fitted shoes, and eccentric loading. Jumping and running with poor form (overpronation) are common causes of Achilles tendonitis (9). Signs and symptoms include pain during physical activities or at rest, inflammation, swelling, and thickening of the tendon. The incidence of Achilles tendonitis is reported to be approximately 6.8% of physically active individuals and risk factors include cold weather and previous injury (10). Some drugs have also been reported to increase risk of Achilles injury, specifically quinolone antimicrobials such as ciprofloxacin (11). The risk of injury may also increase with age and male gender (1).

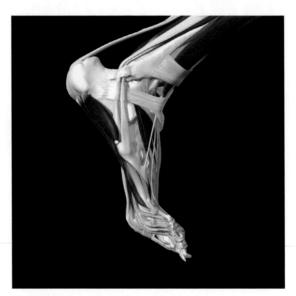

FIGURE 13.1   Achilles tendon.

PLANTAR FASCIITIS

The plantar fascia is a thick, fibrous band of tissue that runs from the calcaneus and fans out to insert on the metatarsal heads to support the longitudinal arch of the foot. An inflamed and irritated plantar fascia can be very painful. Plantar fasciitis is a common cause of heel pain and most patients report pain in the heel region, particularly after getting out of bed in the morning or after sitting for extended periods. The typical mechanism of injury is overuse, often involving sudden increases in running, walking, or standing (9). Plantar fasciitis may be aggravated by training on a certain surface or wearing certain shoes. Acute irritation of the fascia can occur, but plantar fasciitis is primarily an overuse syndrome (9). Risk factors for plantar fasciitis include having less than 0 degrees ankle dorsiflexion (23 times greater risk), a body mass index (BMI) greater than 30 (5 times greater risk), and working on one's feet (3 times greater risk) (8). Increased foot pronation (feet flatten) has also been identified as a risk factor for plantar fasciitis (12).

METATARSAL STRESS FRACTURES

Stress fractures can occur to the metatarsals, or the long bones of the foot between the phalanges (the toes) and the tarsals (Fig. 13.2). Any metatarsal may experience a stress fracture; however, stress fractures occur most commonly to the second and fifth metatarsals (4,13). The mechanism of injury is overuse through repeated loading of the foot, often through increases in running and walking (9). Injuries may develop from any combination of the following factors: sudden increases in intensity or duration of activity, decreases in the amount of rest and recovery, changes in training surface, changes in footwear, and inadequate nutrition (9). Risk factors for metatarsal stress fractures include Achilles tendon contracture, low bone mass, and length differences between the first and second metatarsals (13).

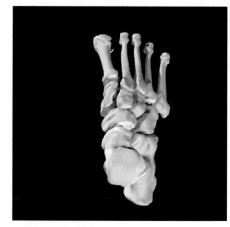

FIGURE 13.2 Metatarsals.

TIME OUT
Shoes and Preventing Foot Injury

Wearing the right type of shoe can be extremely important in preventing foot injury. Athletes should wear a shoe designed for the type of activity in which they participate. The shoe should be fitted for the athlete's specific foot type and size, preferably by a trained professional. Shoes should be replaced on a regular basis as they wear. Off-the-shelf or custom-made orthotics inserts for the shoes may also help prevent injury and increase comfort.

Foot Injury Prevention Strategies

Some common foot injury prevention and rehabilitation programs may help avoid the foot injuries discussed. Ensuring proper range of motion through stretching is paramount (9). The Achilles tendon can be stretched as pictured and should be stretched with the knee both bent (Fig. 13.3) and straight (Fig. 13.4); this ensures the gastrocnemius and soleus contributions to the tendon are stretched. The plantar fascia can be stretched by pulling back on the toes. Stretching should be relatively pain-free, performed several times a day, and may be most effective after a whole-body warm-up.

Other exercises can be incorporated to strengthen the musculotendinous structures of the foot and improve proprioception. Calf strengthening can be done through heel raises on both legs or one, and can be paired with resisted dorsiflexion to strengthen the anterior tibialis (Fig. 13.5). Strengthen the toe flexors and the intrinsic muscles of the foot by performing towel crunches (Fig. 13.6) or marble pick-ups, which may improve arch strength and function.

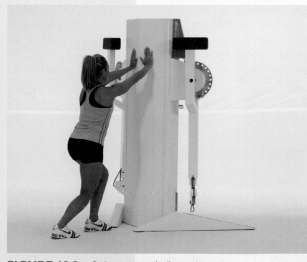

FIGURE 13.3 Soleus stretch (knee bent).

FIGURE 13.4 Gastrocnemius stretch (knee straight).

(*continued*)

(continued)

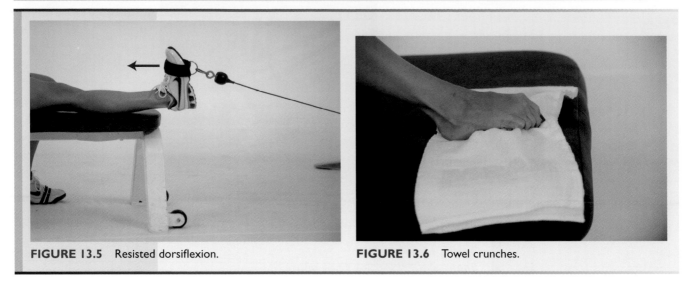

FIGURE 13.5 Resisted dorsiflexion.

FIGURE 13.6 Towel crunches.

Epidemiology of Ankle Sprains

Ankle sprains are reported to be the most common sports-related injury (14), and the number one injury for time lost (15). The ankle is the most commonly injured body site in most sports, and sprains are the most common ankle injury in those sports (16). The game injury rate has been reported to be 3.85/1,000 exposures in recreational basketball (17), whereas the rate in selected high school sports was roughly one ankle injury for every 17 participants per season (18). It is estimated that collegiate athletes suffer over 11,000 ankle sprains per year (19).

A lateral ankle sprain is the most common type of sprain (14); however, medial ankle and syndesmosis (high ankle) sprains do occur, but at a far lower rate (20). There is also a lack of data on the estimated annual health-care costs attributable to ankle spcains; medical charges ranged from $100 to $6,414, but the majority of patient expenses were between $250 and $749 (21) with patients requiring surgery being encumbered with significantly greater expenses (21). Besides the pain, swelling, and loss of function associated with ankle sprains, there are also long-term consequences. It is estimated that approximately 47–73% of individuals who suffer an initial ankle sprain will resprain their ankle again (22,23). Ankle trauma and history of ankle sprains is also associated with developing osteoarthritis (OA) with approximately 70% of ankle arthritis being attributable to trauma (24,25). Of those with ankle arthritis (approximately 13% developed OA following ligamentous injury), sports participation was responsible for half of those sprains. Of those individuals, 82% reported that osteoarthritis forced them to decrease their activity level (25). The average time from injury to development of post-traumatic osteoarthritis at the ankle was 34.3 years and it is often presented in younger patients compared to those who develop degenerative or systemic ankle arthritis (25). There is some evidence that women and girls are more at risk for ankle sprain than men and boys (26,27). As a common injury with high potential for re-injury and long-term consequences, prevention of ankle sprains is important (Table 13.1).

Ankle Injuries

LATERAL ANKLE SPRAINS

During a lateral ankle sprain, any of the lateral ligaments including the anterior talofibular ligament (ATFL), calcaneofibular ligament (CFL), and posterior talofibular ligament (PTFL) may be injured (Fig. 13.7). The ATFL is the most commonly injured of the lateral ligaments (28), followed by the CFL and PTFL (29). Additionally, there is risk of an avulsion fracture to the base of the fifth metatarsal if the forces at the ankle are great enough (30).

TABLE 13.1

Common Ligament Injuries

Ligament	Function	Injuries
Anterior Talofibular	Prevents anterior translation of the talus on the fibula and ankle mortise. Taut when foot is in plantarflexion.	Most commonly injured ligament. Injured with plantarflexion and inversion.
Calcaneofibular	Prevents supination of talocrural and subtalar joints; limits rearfoot inversion and internal rotation. Taut in dorsiflexion.	Second most commonly injured ligament. Injured with plantarflexion and inversion.
Posterior Talofibular	Limits inversion and internal rotation. Taut in extreme dorsiflexion.	Third most commonly injured ligament. Injured with dorsiflexion and internal rotation.
Deltoid	Limits eversion. Taut in eversion.	Not often injured. Injured with eversion.
Anterior and posterior inferior tibiofibular	Stabilizes the ankle mortise.	Involved with high ankle sprains. Injured with eversion and extreme dorsiflexion.

TIME OUT
Ankle Joint Neutral Position

The ankle joint's neutral or "close pack position" is most stable when the joint surfaces meet and match to each other. In this situation, or in dorsiflexion, the tibia and fibula articulate with a larger portion of the talus, because of the talus' wedge-shaped anterior surface (27a).

1. Spaulding SJ, Livingston LA, Hartsell HD. The influence of external orthotic support on the adaptive gait characteristics of individuals with chronically unstable ankles. *Gait Posture.* 2003;17(2):152–8.

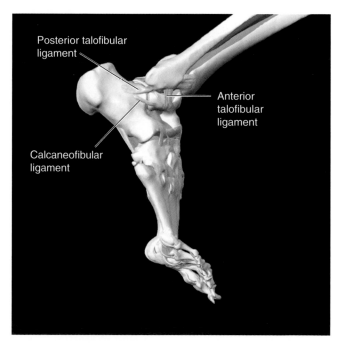

FIGURE 13.7   Lateral ankle ligaments.

MECHANISM OF INJURY FOR LATERAL ANKLE SPRAINS

The typical mechanism of injury for a lateral ankle sprain is forced plantar flexion and inversion of the ankle during landing on an unstable or uneven surface. Bony congruency establishes joint stability during weight bearing (31,32), whereas the body relies on ligamentous and musculotendinous stability during weight acceptance. The latter two contribute less stability to the joint than bony congruency (31). An inversion moment may cause an ankle sprain if the ankle is too inverted, plantarflexed, or both, and bony stability is lost or decreased, or if the subtalar joint is too inverted (33). The avulsion fracture of the base of the fifth metatarsal occurs when the insertion of the peroneus brevis muscle on the lateral side of the leg pulls a small piece of bone off the metatarsal's base (30). This may occur with a forceful peroneal contraction with the inverted foot, during tripping, or other spraining mechanisms (30).

RISK FACTORS FOR LATERAL ANKLE SPRAINS

The most common risk factor for lateral ankle sprains is a history of a prior sprain (34,35). Athletes with a previous sprain were almost five times more likely to suffer an ankle injury (17). Other risk factors included shoes with air cells in the heels and not stretching before the game (34). High school basketball players with greater postural sway (poorer balance) experienced almost seven times as many ankle sprains as those with low sway (better balance) (36). It is unclear if female athletes are more at risk for ankle sprains. Some report an increased risk for females (26,27), whereas others do not (37). A recent literature review indicated that there is insufficient evidence to determine if height, weight, limb dominance, anatomic foot type, ankle joint laxity, and ankle range of motion are risk factors for sprain (35). It is also unclear if muscle strength and reaction time are risk factors. Few studies have noted differences in ankle strength between injured and uninjured groups (15), and the mechanism of injury may be too fast for everting muscles to react and prevent injury (31).

MEDIAL ANKLE SPRAINS

ANATOMICAL STRUCTURES INVOLVED

Medial ankle sprains involve the deltoid ligament of the ankle and may include avulsion fractures of the tibia or other bone of the foot (Fig. 13.8 and Table 13.1).

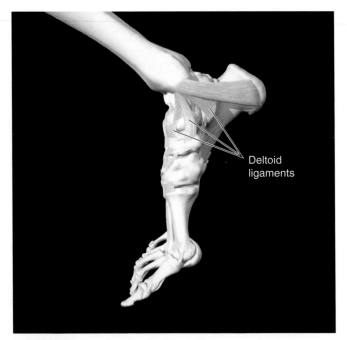

Deltoid
ligaments

FIGURE 13.8 Medial ankle ligaments.

MECHANISM OF INJURY AND RISK FACTORS FOR MEDIAL ANKLE SPRAINS

The mechanism of injury for a medial ankle sprain involves forceful and rapid eversion of the foot (38). This may be combined with external rotation and plantar flexion. There is little literature regarding medial ankle sprains, because they are not as common as lateral ankle sprains. Because the deltoid ligament is so strong, injury to this area may be more severe and involve fractures to bony structures. Risk factors for medial ankle sprains have not been established.

HIGH ANKLE SPRAINS

ANATOMICAL STRUCTURES INVOLVED

A syndesmotic sprain involves the distal tibiofibular joint just proximal to the ankle. The anterior inferior tibiofibular ligament, the posterior inferior tibiofibular ligament, and the interosseous ligament are all involved in syndesmotic sprains (Fig. 13.9) (20,39).

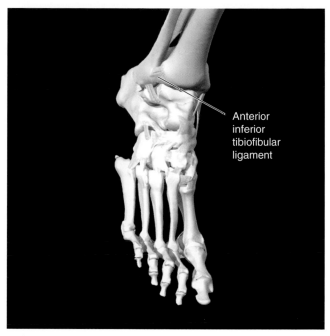

Anterior
inferior
tibiofibular
ligament

FIGURE 13.9   High ankle sprain.

MECHANISM OF INJURY FOR HIGH ANKLE SPRAINS

The proposed mechanism of injury for high ankle sprains includes external foot rotation, talar eversion in the ankle mortise, and excessive dorsiflexion (20,39). The mechanism typically involves widening of the mortise, often from the talus being driven into the articulation, whether by eversion, external rotation, or dorsiflexion (20). When the mortise is widened, the distal fibula is pushed laterally, prying bones out of parallel and expanding the space in the syndesmosis (20).

TIME OUT
Relevant Research

Using the Star Excursion Balance Test, and factoring in for other variables, high school girl basketball players with anterior right and left reach distance differences of ≥4 cm and decreased normalized anterior, posteromedial, posterolateral, and composite reach distances bilaterally had significant association with increased lower-extremity injury risk. Only anterior right and left reach distance differences of ≥4 cm were significantly associated with lower-extremity injury risk in boys (1).

1. Plisky PJ, Rauh MJ, Kaminski TW et al. Star Excursion Balance Test as a predictor of lower extremity injury in high school basketball players. 2006;36(12):911–19.

RISK FACTORS FOR HIGH ANKLE SPRAINS

There are limited prospective studies for risk factors in high ankle sprains (20). This injury is associated most often with sports involving planting and cutting or with rigid boots. Thus, skiing, ice hockey, football, soccer, rugby, wrestling, and lacrosse are the sports with the highest risk of high ankle sprain (20,39). Theoretically, athletes with flat feet, or pes planus, may be more likely to be in a position of external ankle rotation when their foot is planted, thus increasing the risk of high ankle sprain (39).

Lateral Ankle Sprain Injury Prevention

PREVENTION AND REHABILITATION PROGRAMS

Ankle sprain prevention and rehabilitation programs have proved effective at decreasing the incidence of ankle sprain in physically active individuals and improving ankle function (40). Most programs incorporated proprioceptive or balance training with or without sport specific movements on a daily or multiple times per week schedule. Several studies utilized single-leg stance exercises on a wobble board (Fig. 13.10), in either a home exercise program with sport

FIGURE 13.10 Wobble board.

specific balance training (41,42) or with eyes open or closed on different surfaces (43). Similarly, foam pads have been used to provide unstable surfaces to improve balance (44). Other general ankle injury prevention and rehabilitation programs include restoring range of motion at the ankle, particularly in closed kinetic chain dorsiflexion utilizing gastrocnemius and soleus muscle stretching (see Figs. 13.3 and 13.4). Strengthening of the ankle musculature is incorporated, either using resistance bands, weights, or body weight, as are functional activities like hopping, lateral movements, and cutting maneuvers (40). Programs typically progress in number of repetitions, speed, and direction over the course of several weeks (40). There is limited evidence for the effectiveness of rehabilitation programs on medial or syndesmotic ankle sprains. Prevention programs appear to be most effective for individuals with a history of ankle sprain (45). See Chapters 7, 8, and 9 for exercises that could be utilized in a progressive ankle injury prevention program.

Knee Injury Epidemiology

Lower-extremity injuries account for over 50% of injuries in college (46) and high school athletes (47). Among lower-extremity injuries, the knee is one of the most commonly injured regions of the body. Two of the more common diagnoses resulting from physical activity are patellofemoral pain (PFP) and ACL sprains/tears. PFP is defined as "pain in the knee region that is provoked or accentuated by actions that involve motion at the patellofemoral joint and/or increase pressure of patella against the femoral condyles" (48). The ACL is one of the primary stabilizing ligaments of the knee with a primary function of preventing anterior displacement of the tibia relative to the femur that can result in either a partial or complete tearing of the ligament substance (Fig. 13.11). It is also possible for secondary injuries to the medial collateral ligament, medial meniscus, and/or lateral meniscus to occur simultaneously with an ACL injury.

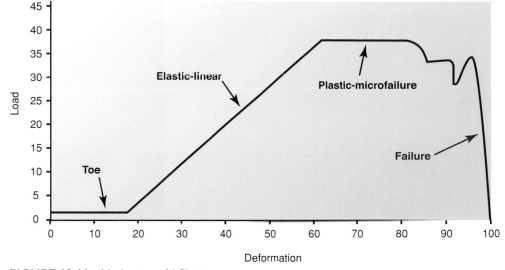

FIGURE 13.11 Mechanism of ACL injury.

Both PFP and ACL injuries are public health concerns because of the frequency of injury, cost burden on the health-care system, and potential for future debilitating injuries. Across multiple sports, the overall incidence of ACL injuries is pretty stable between genders (49). However, in sports where both men and women compete (e.g., soccer, basketball), the injury rate is higher in women (50). Researchers have estimated health-care costs to be approximately $2.5 billion annually for ACL injuries (51); however, similar data on the annual costs for treatment of PFP are unavailable. Those individuals who suffer an ACL injury and undergo surgical intervention face a lengthy rehabilitation process ranging from 6–36 months and only 75% of these individuals are able to return to their previous activity levels (52). Furthermore, individuals suffering acute knee injury, such as an ACL injury, are seven times more likely to develop knee osteoarthritis approximately 25 years following the initial injury as compared to those individuals with no history of acute knee injury (53). The development of PFP can also be devastating due to the recurrence of symptoms. Surgical treatment is an option for PFP; however, no studies have provided evidence favoring surgical intervention over conservative management (54). In a retrospective investigation, 91% of patients diagnosed with PFP reported continued knee pain for 4–18 years after initial presentation and, in 36% of these patients, PFP restricted their physical activity (55). Additionally, PFP has been associated with the development of patellofemoral osteoarthritis and is, therefore, a major concern for long-term disability.

To prevent these injuries from occurring and allow individuals to maintain healthy and physically active lifestyles, it is important to understand the anatomy, causes, and most appropriate exercise strategies for prevention and management. This is especially important in young females who are at greater risk for suffering both PFP and ACL injuries (56,57). Although there are a multitude of knee injuries that can occur from physical activity, an understanding of the mechanisms, risk factors, and prevention strategies for these two common problems will aid the Sports Performance Professional in identifying individuals at risk and develop effective prevention strategies for these and other knee injuries.

Causes of PFP Syndrome and ACL Injury

PATELLOFEMORAL SYNDROME

One of the most commonly accepted causes of PFP syndrome is abnormal tracking of the patella within the femoral trochlea (Fig. 13.12). When the patella is not properly aligned within the femoral trochlea, the stress per unit area on the patellar cartilage increases due to a smaller contact area between the patella and the trochlea (58). Abnormal tracking of the patella may be due to static or dynamic lower-extremity malalignment, altered muscle activation of surrounding knee musculature, decreased strength of the hip musculature, or various combinations (59–61).

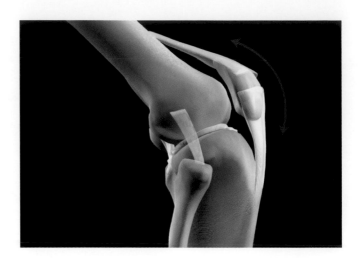

FIGURE 13.12 Patellar tracking.

Malalignment of the patella within the femoral trochlea is commonly associated with an excessive Q-angle. The Q-angle is formed by a line drawn from the anterior superior iliac spine to the central patella and a second line drawn from central patella through the tibial tubercle (Fig. 13.13). Holmes and Clancy (62) describe the Q-angle as "an attempt to measure the vector forces applied to the patella" and is responsible for guiding the patella within the femoral trochlea during knee flexion and extension. A large Q-angle is believed to facilitate excessive lateral tracking of the patella, which may lead to the development of PFP (63). The underlying causes of an excessive Q-angle include femoral anteversion, external tibial torsion, genu valgum, and foot hyperpronation (64). Muscle activation of the quadriceps, which attaches to the patella, may also influence patellar alignment and subsequent PFP. Researchers have suggested that the oblique fibers of the vastus medialis must activate earlier or at the same time as the vastus lateralis because a delay in vastus medialis oblique activation may lateralize the patella, leading to suboptimal tracking, increased stress on the patellar surface, cartilage damage, and pain (65).

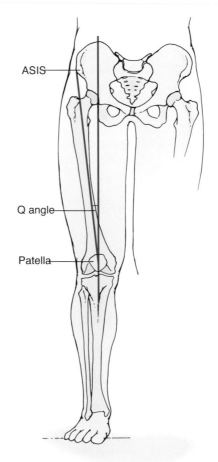

FIGURE 13.13 Q-angle.

Abnormal transverse and frontal plane motions of the femur can also alter patellofemoral mechanics and be a causative factor in PFP (64). Lee et al. (66) reported that 30 degrees of femoral internal rotation caused a significant increase in patellofemoral joint stress. Also, femoral adduction has been proposed to cause an increase in the knee valgus angle and, in turn, lateral tracking of the patella (Fig. 13.14) (59,64). Weakness of the hip external rotators and abductors may allow the femur to move into excessive hip adduction and internal rotation, further increasing the lateral contact pressure of the patella on the femur (63). Also, femoral adduction has been proposed to cause an increase in the knee valgus angle and, in turn, lateral tracking of the patella (59,64).

FIGURE 13.14 Excessive knee valgus.

The few prospective cohort investigations that have been performed report that people with PFP have decreased quadriceps flexibility, shortened reflex time of the vastus medialis oblique, reduction in vertical jump performance, increased medial patellar mobility, increased distance between the medial tibial condyles of the right and left legs (tibial bowing), and increased quadriceps strength as factors associated with the incidence of PFP (67,68). The modifiable findings (i.e., quadriceps flexibility) from the two prospective risk factor investigations support that both static alignment and strength of the lower-extremity musculature may play a role in the development of PFP (67,68). As a result, the risk factors for PFP are thought to include increased femoral rotation, adduction, and knee valgus during functional tasks, decreased strength of the surrounding hip and knee musculature, and increased Q-angle and foot pronation (64). When implementing prevention programs for PFP, these proposed risk factors should be targeted through the use of exercises.

ACL INJURIES

ACL injuries are overwhelmingly (70–75%) non-contact in nature and almost always occur as the body undergoes rapid deceleration (52,69–73). The three major non-contact events described as being responsible for ACL injury are: (1) planting and cutting (29%); (2) straight knee landing (28%); and (3) one-step landing with a hyperextended knee (26%) (74). Large shear forces are placed across the knee when performing these types of maneuvers and may result in a high degree of ACL strain (Fig. 13.15).

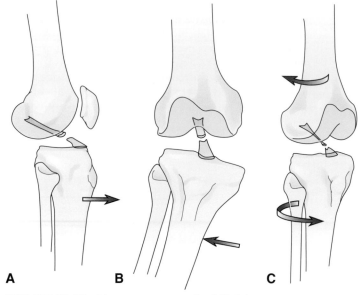

A   B   C

FIGURE 13.15   Noncontact events for ACL injury.

Specific movement patterns commonly occurring during ACL and lower-extremity injuries include knee valgus (knock knee), excessive leg rotation, and decreased knee flexion (71,75). Knee flexion angle influences ACL stress, as vigorous quadriceps contractions at low-knee flexion angles (0–30 degrees) may generate enough anterior tibial shear force to rupture the ACL (76,77). Large amounts of ACL loading occur during the combined loading state of tibial rotation and knee valgus (Fig. 13.16) (78,79). Although the knee may appear to be in valgus, a true opening of the medial joint space is not thought to occur. This visible valgus largely comes from internal rotation of the femur at the hip (79). As such, lower-extremity rotation (tibial and femoral) and knee valgus occurring during cutting and landing maneuvers are viewed to be of sufficient magnitude to generate extreme loading across the ACL, causing spontaneous rupture of the ligament (80–83). It is during this combined loading state of excessive tibial rotation and knee valgus that researchers have described the ACL to be at greatest risk of injury (78,79).

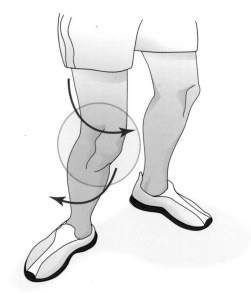

FIGURE 13.16   Combination of tibial rotation and knee valgus.

Movement patterns are important and modifiable factors that may influence the risk of ACL injury (75,84). Lower-extremity movement patterns play a critical role in injury mechanisms, as they are known to influence the load and deformational forces on ligaments, meniscus, cartilage, and bone (71,78,79,85,86). Although other factors such as sex hormones and bony alignment may also influence the risk of PFP, ACL, and other knee injuries (87–89), these factors are not modifiable through exercise-based interventions.

Movement patterns may influence the muscle's stabilizing capacity by impacting the length-tension relationship of muscle (90). As mentioned earlier, specific movement patterns commonly occurring during ACL and lower-extremity injury include knee valgus (knock knee), excessive rotation, and decreased knee flexion (71,75). Thus, exercise-based injury prevention programs that successfully alter movement patterns to decrease this visible knee valgus, minimize tibial rotation, and increase knee flexion angle may have great promise for reducing the incidence of knee injury during sport and recreational activities (91,92).

PFP and ACL Injury Prevention

A variety of exercise programs have been described in the literature to rehabilitate and prevent both PFP and ACL injuries. PFP-related exercises commonly focus on strengthening of the hip and surrounding knee musculature. Strengthening of the hip muscles is thought to assist in decreasing hip internal rotation, adduction, and knee valgus during functional activities (Fig. 13.17) (93). The use of exercises to strengthen the quadriceps is also regularly performed because many individuals with PFP are reported to have quadriceps weakness (94–96).

FIGURE 13.17 Example hip strengthening exercise: tube walking.

Most individuals with patellofemoral syndrome respond favorably to conservative intervention (59,97,98) with the most common treatment being quadriceps and hip musculature strengthening using nonweight-bearing and weight-bearing exercises (93,99,100). Weight-bearing exercises are more functional than nonweight-bearing exercises because the multijoint movement requirement facilitates a more functional pattern of muscle recruitment and stimulating proprioceptors (Fig. 13.18) (101). Because of these advantages, clinicians often recommend weight-bearing exercises in the rehabilitation of individuals with PFP (102,103).

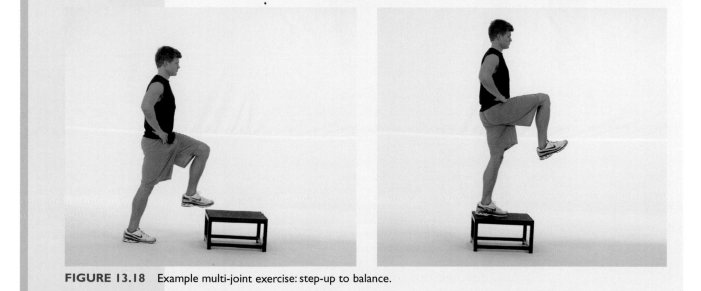

FIGURE 13.18 Example multi-joint exercise: step-up to balance.

(*continued*)

(continued)

Two main types of preventive training programs have been published for ACL injury: proprioception-balance training (Fig. 13.19) (104–108) and plyometric-agility training (Fig. 13.20) (91,92,109,110). Proprioception-balance training is designed to improve coordination and balance by performing exercises that include, but are not limited to, balancing on a single leg, balancing on an unstable platform, and single-leg balancing while performing various tasks involving the upper extremity. Plyometric agility training is designed to improve an individual's agility, dynamic stability, and technique during dynamic tasks. Typically, plyometric agility exercises involve performing various jumping, landing, and cutting maneuvers in different directions of motion at varying intensity levels. Other common training techniques incorporated in an ACL injury prevention exercise program are movement-technique awareness training (105,106,109,110), strength training (91,92,106,108–110), and flexibility training (91,92,109).

FIGURE 13.19 Example balance exercise: single-leg balance reach.

FIGURE 13.20 Example plyometric exercise: hop to stabilization.

There may be a considerable amount of confusion when attempting to determine the most appropriate exercises to incorporate into a PFP and ACL injury prevention program. Therefore, a systematic exercise selection process based on the individual's movement patterns observed during the overhead and single-leg squat (Chapter 3) may provide the most effective option. Because altered movement patterns are believed to be one of the primary causes for PFP and ACL injury, selecting exercises to correct faulty movement patterns would seem a logical approach to preventing these injuries from occurring. See Chapters 7, 8, and 9 for exercises that could be utilized in a progressive knee injury prevention program.

Low Back Injury Epidemiology

Back injuries can be costly to both the individual and to health-care systems. It has been estimated that the annual costs attributable to low back pain in the United States are greater than $26 billion (111). In addition, 6–15% of athletes experience low-back pain in a given year (112,113). Although it is apparent that athletes are not immune to a variety of back problems, for them the greater concern is the associated decrease in training level, conditioning, and performance as a result of such injuries. The symptoms associated with generalized low back pain take 4–6 weeks to resolve (114) and depending on the particular sport, this length of time can account for a significant portion of a competitive season. The time lost to a back injury may not be limited to an isolated injury over the course of an athlete's career. It is important to remember that athletes who suffer one low-back injury are significantly more likely to suffer additional low-back injuries, further increasing their time lost to training and competition (115). Repeated injuries to the back may predispose the athlete to future osteoarthritis and long-term disability. Ultimately, this course of events may limit an athlete's career and definitive level of performance. Due to the high incidence of recurrent back injury, prevention of the first injury is the most effective means to promote the health and performance of athletes.

Low Back Injuries and Etiology

DISC INJURY

Vertebral disc injuries occur when the outer fibrous structure of the disc (annulus fibrosus) fails, allowing the internal contents of the disc (nucleus pulposus) to be extruded and irritate the nerves that exit the spinal cord at the intervertebral foramen (Fig. 13.21). The exact mechanism underlying injury to the intervertebral disc is unclear, but it is generally thought to be due to a combination of motion with compressive loading. Increases in disc pressures and stresses are influenced by the kinematics of the lumbar spine (116–121). Disc pressure increases with lumbar flexion (e.g., excessive forward trunk lean) (118,120,121) and decreases in lordosis (e.g., low back rounding) (117,121). In addition, a combination of flexion (excessive forward trunk lean) and lateral bending has been demonstrated to increase the strain placed on the discs (120,121).

Proper activation of the local muscles and maintenance of a proper lordotic posture may contribute to a reduction in the compression and torques generated about the discs and may minimize their risk of injury. Notably, transverse abdominus and multifidus activation is diminished in patients with low back pain (122,123). Although it is not possible to determine which came first, the deficit in activation or low back pain, it may be used as evidence of the relationship between proper muscle activation as a means to avoid injury.

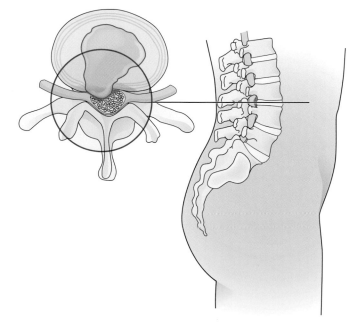

FIGURE 13.21   Disc injury.

MUSCLE STRAIN/LIGAMENT SPRAIN

As previously described, the loads, forces, and movements that occur about the lumbar spine are controlled by a considerable number of ligaments and muscles. The ligaments that surround the spine limit intersegmental motion maintaining the integrity of the lumbar spine. These ligaments may fail when proper motion cannot be created, proper posture cannot be maintained, or excessive motion cannot be resisted by the surrounding musculature (117,118,124,125). Therefore, decreasing the ability of local and global stabilizing muscles to produce adequate force can lead to ligamentous injury (Fig. 13.22).

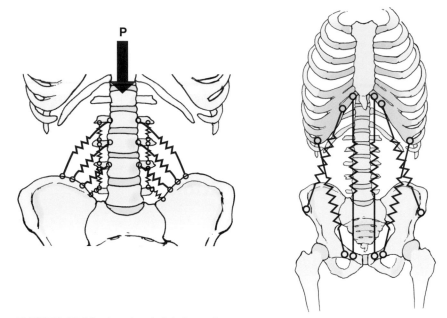

FIGURE 13.22 Local and global muscles.

The performance of these muscles is determined by the posture of the lumbar spine during functional activities (117,118,124,125). If the neutral lordotic curvature of the lumbar spine is not maintained (e.g., low back arching, excessive forward lean, or low-back rounding), the activation (117) and relative moment arm of the muscle fibers is decreased (124,125), disrupting normal muscle force production. This forces the muscles to generate greater forces than would be necessary had a neutral lordotic posture were maintained (see Chapter 3). When this occurs, muscles can become overloaded, which can lead to injury. In fact, maintenance of a proper lordotic posture is associated with increased muscle activation in the lumbar spine (124).

SACROILIAC JOINT DYSFUNCTION

The sacroiliac joint (SIJ) is subjected to considerable forces as loads are transferred between the trunk and legs. The flat surfaces of the sacrum and ilium make the joint susceptible to shearing forces (Fig. 13.23) (126). If SIJ stability is not maintained, loads cannot be transferred efficiently between the trunk and legs, which may result in abnormal loading of the tissues at the joint and the development of pain (126). Compressive forces across the SIJ contribute to its stability, and are provided in part by muscles that cross the joint interfaces (126). In particular, the transverse abdominis and internal oblique play a significant role in resisting shear loads across the SIJ and maintaining stability (126–129). Contraction of the transverse abdominis is more effective at

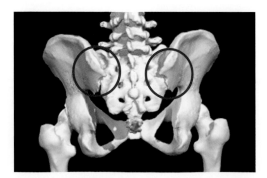

FIGURE 13.23 SI joint.

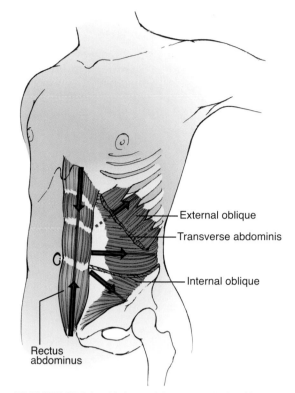

FIGURE 13.24 Abdominal force-couple for SI joint stability.

increasing SIJ stability than the larger abdominal muscles like the rectus abdominus and external oblique (128,129). Therefore, proper execution of an abdominal drawing-in maneuver during performance should enhance the stability of the SIJ and allow for the most efficient transfer of forces between the trunk and legs (Fig. 13.24).

Low Back Injury Prevention Strategies

Exercise is clearly an important component to treating nonspecific low back pain (128–132). Exercise is also believed to be a vital component in preventing the occurrence of low back pain and injury. What is unclear, however, is the type of exercises that should be performed as part of a low back pain prevention and rehabilitation program. Liddle et al. (132) concluded that strengthening exercises targeting the lumbar spine, lower limbs, and abdominal muscles were the predominant exercises performed in successful exercise programs that decreased pain and improved function. The systematic review by Hayden et al. (131) concluded that programs including strengthening or trunk-stabilizing exercises were most effective. A separate meta-analysis (130) indicated that the most effective programs consist of a supervised, individually designed set of stretching and strengthening exercises.

In agreement with the observations and recommendations from the scientific literature, a low-back injury prevention program that includes a variety of exercises aimed at improving flexibility of tight and overactive muscles, strengthening weak and inhibited muscles, and improving neuromuscular control is recommended. In addition, low back injury prevention program design should be based on a systematic assessment of the athlete and the exercises prescribed should be specific to the athlete's needs.

There can be a considerable amount of confusion when attempting to determine the most appropriate exercises for preventing low back pain. Therefore, the most effective option may be a systematic selection process based on the specific movement patterns observed during the movement assessment (see Chapter 3). Because altered movement patterns are believed to be one of the primary causes for low back pain, a logical approach to preventing these injuries would be to select exercises that correct these faulty movement patterns. Thus, prevention exercises will focus on a systematic progression to correct these undesirable movement patterns. Because core stability is also a critical component to maintaining neutral spine alignment, exercises to promote core stability will also be important to include in the prevention program. See Chapters 4 and 6 for exercises that could be utilized in a progressive low back injury prevention program.

Epidemiology of Shoulder Pain

Shoulder pain is reported to occur in up to 21% of the general population (133,134) with 40% persisting for at least 1 year (135) at an estimated annual cost of $39 billion (136). Shoulder impingement is the most prevalent diagnosis accounting for 40–65% of reported shoulder pain (137), whereas traumatic shoulder dislocations account for an additional 15–25% of shoulder pain (138–140). The persistent nature of shoulder pain may be the result of degenerative changes to the shoulder's capsuloligamentous structures, articular cartilage, and tendons as the result of altered shoulder mechanics. As many as 70% of individuals suffering shoulder dislocations experience recurrent instability within 2 years (141) and are at risk to develop glenohumeral osteoarthritis secondary to the increased motion at the glenohumeral joint (142,143). Degenerative changes may also affect the rotator cuff by weakening the tendons over time through intrinsic and extrinsic risk factors (137,144–148), such as repetitive overhead use ($>60°$ of shoulder elevation), increased loads raised above shoulder height (149), forward head and rounded shoulder posture (150), as well as altered scapular kinematics and muscle activity (151–154). Those factors are theorized to overload the shoulder muscles, especially the rotator cuff, which can lead to shoulder pain and dysfunction. Given the cost, rate of occurrence and difficult resolution of shoulder pain, preventive exercise solutions that address these factors are essential in preventing shoulder injuries.

Common Shoulder Injuries

Shoulder injuries can be broadly categorized into those that affect the rotator cuff muscles (Fig. 13.25) or those that affect the capsuloligamentous structures of the shoulder. Rotator cuff conditions such as strains, ruptures, and tendonopathies account for approximately 75–80% of shoulder injuries. Rotator cuff strains occur when a muscle group is overexerted, causing microdamage within the muscle belly and tendon resulting in immediate inflammation and decreased muscle function. In contrast, injuries to the capsuloligamentous structures lead to deficits in the passive stabilizing structures of the shoulder such as the anterior, posterior, or inferior glenohumeral ligaments, and the glenoid labrum. Rotator cuff and capsuloligamentous injuries are devastating to the ability of the shoulder to facilitate function of the upper extremity in reaching forward or overhead tasks.

FIGURE 13.25 Rotator cuff.

SHOULDER IMPINGEMENT

Subacromial impingement syndrome (SAIS) is a common diagnosis broadly defined as compression of the structures that run beneath the coracoacromial arch, most often from a decrease in the subacromial space (Fig. 13.26). The impinged structures include the supraspinatus and infraspinatus tendons, the subacromial bursa, and the long head of the biceps tendon (Fig. 13.27). Repetitive compression of these structures with the overhead motions required of many sports can lead to irritation and inflammation (155). In turn, prolonged inflammation can cause muscular inefficiency, specifically affecting the rotator cuff muscles. SAIS may be the result of bony deformity of the acromion, underlying rotator cuff weakness, shoulder instability, or scapular dyskinesis (156).

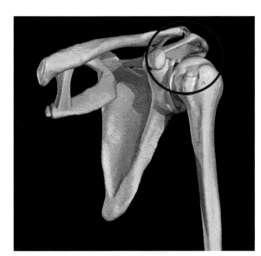

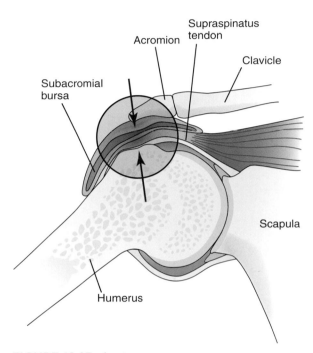

FIGURE 13.26   Coracoacromial arch.

FIGURE 13.27   Impingement.

SHOULDER INSTABILITY

Shoulder instability results from many different mechanisms, but regardless of the mechanism, instability most often manifests itself as anterior or multidirectional. These forms of instability differ greatly in terms of the involved structures and injury mechanisms. Even though the exact injury mechanism may differ, all forms of shoulder instability may occur via atraumatic injury mechanisms associated with improper mechanics and poor conditioning (157).

The most common is traumatic anterior instability as the result of an abducted and externally rotated arm that might occur during a fall on an outstretched arm or reaching behind and to the side to tackle someone (138,139,158). This results in damage to the anterior/inferior glenohumeral ligament and often the glenoid labrum. The resulting instability usually leads to significant disability with overhead activities that in most cases requires surgical repair (159,160).

Shoulder Injury Prevention Strategies

Soft-tissue mobilization and self-myofascial release techniques should be used to increase extensibility of the overactive muscles such as the pectorals and/or latissimus dorsi (see Chapter 4). Static or neuromuscular stretching exercises should then be performed for 30–45 seconds on these muscles (see Chapter 4). Isolated strengthening exercises should be used to facilitate the underactive muscles of the scapulae. Auditory and tactile feedback while performing these exercises can also help develop endurance with proper kinetic chain positioning and control. For example, the Prone Ball Combo I exercise (Fig. 13.28) emphasizes scapular stability on the thorax as the athlete externally rotates then retracts

(continued)

(continued)

and depresses the scapulae, these by restoring the functional balance between the under-active rhomboids and lower trapezius with the overactive latissimus and pectoralis minor. Exercises can be progressed by incorporating activities that integrate the entire kinetic chain. This can be accomplished by performing squat concurrent with a row (Fig. 13.29). Athletes should be instructed to maintain scapular retraction, and depression during the row while limiting winging by keeping the scapula on the costal surface.

FIGURE 13.28   Ball Combo I.

FIGURE 13.29   Squat to row.

SUMMARY

Sports-related injuries are considered commonplace in athletics, whether caused by contact or the result of faulty mechanics or neuromuscular inefficiency. Ranging from the foot and ankle to the shoulder, common injuries require knowledge of the epidemiology of the injury and an understanding of prevention strategies to prepare athletes for the demands of sport.

Prevention strategies are key to an athlete's health and career longevity. In most cases, the influence of poor biomechanics, neuromuscular efficiencies, overtraining, and decreased flexibility contribute to injury. This has lead researchers and clinicians to strategies that include various preventative methods such as implementing integrated flexibility, proprioceptive training, proper biomechanics during cutting and jumping as well as implementing progressive plyometric and strength intervention strategies. To learn more about human movement deficiencies and corrective strategies for injury prevention, see NASM's Corrective Exercise Specialist course.

REFERENCES

1. Almeida SA, Trone DW, Leone DM et al. Gender differences in musculoskeletal injury rates: a function of symptom reporting? *Med Sci Sports Exerc* 1999;31:1807–12.
2. Riddle DL, Schappert SM. Volume of ambulatory care visits and patterns of care for patients diagnosed with plantar fasciitis: a national study of medical doctors. *Foot Ankle Int* 2004;25:303–10.
3. Matheson GO, Clement DB, McKenzie DC et al. Stress fractures in athletes. A study of 320 cases. *Am J Sports Med* 1987;15:46–58.
4. Niva MH, Sormaala MJ, Kiuru MJ et al. Bone stress injuries of the ankle and foot: an 86-month magnetic resonance imaging-based study of physically active young adults. *Am J Sports Med* 2007;35:643–49.
5. Hod N, Ashkenazi I, Levi Y et al. Characteristics of skeletal stress fractures in female military recruits of the Israel defense forces on bone scintigraphy. *Clin Nucl Med* 2006;31:742–9.
6. Milgrom C, Finestone A, Segev S et al. Are overground or treadmill runners more likely to sustain tibial stress fracture? *Br J Sports Med* 2003;37:160–3.
7. Bennell KL, Malcolm SA, Thomas SA et al. Risk factors for stress fractures in track and field athletes. A twelve-month prospective study. *Am J Sports Med* 1996;24:810–8.
8. Riddle DL, Pulisic M, Pidcoe P et al. Risk factors for Plantar fasciitis: a matched case-control study. *J Bone Joint Surg Am* 2003;85-A:872–7.
9. Krivickas LS. Anatomical factors associated with overuse sports injuries. *Sports Med* 1997;24:132–46.
10. Milgrom C, Finestone A, Zin D et al. Cold weather training: a risk factor for Achilles paratendinitis among recruits. *Foot Ankle Int* 2003;24:398–401.
11. Shortt P, Wilson R, Erskine I. Tendinitis: the Achilles heel of quinolones! *Emerg Med J* 2006;23:e63.
12. Irving DB, Cook JL, Young MA et al. Obesity and pronated foot type may increase the risk of chronic plantar heel pain: a matched case-control study. *BMC Musculoskelet Disord* 2007;8:41.
13. Chuckpaiwong B, Cook C, Pietrobon R et al. Second metatarsal stress fracture in sport: comparative risk factors between proximal and non-proximal locations. *Br J Sports Med* 2007;41:510–4.
14. Hertel J. Functional anatomy, pathomechanics, and pathophysiology of lateral ankle instability. *J Athl Train* 2002;37:364–75.
15. Kaminski TW, Hartsell HD. Factors contributing to chronic ankle instability: a strength perspective. *J Athl Train* 2002;37:394–405.
16. Fong DT, Hong Y, Chan LK et al. A systematic review on ankle injury and ankle sprain in sports. *Sports Med* 2007;37:73–94.
17. McKay GD, Goldie PA, Payne WR et al. Ankle injuries in basketball: Injury rate and risk factors. *Br J Sports Med* 2001;35:103–08.
18. Garrick JG. The frequency of injury, mechanism of injury, and epidemiology of ankle sprains. *Am J Sports Med* 1977;5:241–42.
19. Hootman JM, Dick R, Agel J. Epidemiology of collegiate injuries for 15 sports: summary and recommendations for injury prevention initiatives. *J Athl Train* 2007;42:311–9.
20. Lin CF, Gross ML, Weinhold P. Ankle syndesmosis injuries: anatomy, biomechanics, mechanism of injury, and clinical guidelines for diagnosis and intervention. *J Orthop Sports Phys Ther* 2006;36:372–84.
21. Grimm DJ, Fallat L. Injuries of the foot and ankle in occupational medicine: a 1-year study. *J Foot Ankle Surg* 1999;38:102–8.
22. Yeung MS, Chan KM, So CH et al. An epidemiological survey on ankle sprain. *Br J Sports Med* 1994;28:112–16.
23. Ekstrand J, Gillquist J. Soccer injuries and their mechanisms: a prospective study. *Med Sci Sports Exerc* 1983;15:267–70.
24. Saltzman CL, Salamon ML, Blanchard GM et al. Epidemiology of ankle arthritis: report of a consecutive series of 639 patients from a tertiary orthopaedic center. *Iowa Orthop J* 2005;25:44–6.
25. Valderrabano V, Hintermann B, Horisberger M et al. Ligamentous posttraumatic ankle osteoarthritis. *Am J Sports Med* 2006;34:612–20.
26. Hosea TM, Carrey CC, Harrer MF. The gender issue: epidemiology of knee and ankle injuries in high school and college players. *Clin Orthoped* 2000;372:45–9.
27. Leininger RE, Knox CL, Comstock RD. Epidemiology of 1.6 million pediatric soccer-related injuries presenting to US emergency departments from 1990 to 2003. *Am J Sports Med* 2007;35:288–93.
28. Safran MR, Benedetti RS, Bartolozzi AR et al. Lateral ankle sprains: a comprehensive review. Part I: etiology, pathoanatomy, histopathogenesis, and diagnosis. *Med Sci Sports Exerc* 1999;31:S429–37.
29. Peters JW, Trevino SG, Renstrom PA. Chronic lateral ankle instability. *Foot Ankle* 1991;12:182–91.
30. Stevens MA, El-Khoury GY, Kathol MH et al. Imaging features of avulsion injuries. *Radiographics* 1999;19:655–72.
31. Konradsen L, Voigt M, Hojsgaard C. Ankle inversion injuries: the role of the dynamic defense mechanism. *Am J Sports Med* 1997;25:54–8.
32. Stormont DM, Morrey BF, An K et al. Stability of the loaded ankle. *Am J Sports Med* 1985;13:295–300.
33. Konradsen L. Sensori-motor control of the uninjured and injured human ankle. *J Electromyogr Kinesiol* 2002;12:199–203.
34. McKay GD, Goldie PA, Payne WR et al. Ankle injuries in basketball: injury rate and risk factors. *Br J Sports Med* 2001;35:103–08.
35. Beynnon BD, Murphy DF, Alosa DM. Predictive factors for lateral ankle sprains: a literature review. *J Athl Train* 2002;37:376–80.
36. McGuine TA, Greene JJ, Best T et al. Balance as a predictor of ankle injuries in high school basketball players. *Clin J Sport Med* 2000;10:239–44.

37. Beynnon BD, Renstrom PA, Alosa DM et al. Ankle ligament injury risk factors: a prospective study of college athletes. *J Orthop Res* 2001;19:213–20.

38. Hoppenfeld S. Physical Examination of the Spine and the Extremities, 1st ed. London: Prentice Hall; 1976.

39. Williams GN, Jones MH, Amendola A. Syndesmotic ankle sprains in athletes. *Am J Sports Med* 2007; 35:1197–207.

40. Hale SA, Hertel J, Olmsted-Kramer LC. The effect of a 4-week comprehensive rehabilitation program on postural control and lower extremity function in individuals with chronic ankle instability. *J Orthop Sports Phys Ther* 2007;37:303–11.

41. Emery CA, Rose MS, McAllister JR et al. A prevention strategy to reduce the incidence of injury in high school basketball: a cluster randomized controlled trial. *Clin J Sport Med* 2007;17:17–24.

42. McGuine TA, Keene JS. The effect of a balance training program on the risk of ankle sprains in high school athletes. *Am J Sports Med* 2006;34:1103–11.

43. Mohammadi F. Comparison of 3 preventive methods to reduce the recurrence of ankle inversion sprains in male soccer players. *Am J Sports Med* 2007;35:922–6.

44. McHugh MP, Tyler TF, Mirabella MR et al. The effectiveness of a balance training intervention in reducing the incidence of noncontact ankle sprains in high school football players. *Am J Sports Med*. 2007; 35:1289–94.

45. Luime JJ, Koes BW, Hendriksen IJ et al. Prevalence and incidence of shoulder pain in the general population: a systematic review. *Scand J Rheumatol* 2004;33:73–81.

46. Hootman JM, Dick R, Agel J. Epidemiology of collegiate injuries for 15 sports: summary and recommendations for injury prevention initiatives. 2007;42:311–9.

47. Fernandez WG, Yard EE, Comstock RD. Epidemiology of lower extremity injuries among U.S. high school athletes. *Acad Emerg Med*. 2007;14:641–45.

48. Arnoldi C. The patellar pain syndrome. *Acta Orthopedica Scandinavica* 1991;244:62.

49. Mountcastle SB, Posner M, Kragh Jr JF et al. Gender differences in anterior cruciate ligament injury vary with activity: epidemiology of anterior cruciate ligament injuries in a young, athletic population. *Am J Sports Med* 2007;35:1635–42.

50. Agel J, Arendt E, Bershadsky B. Anterior cruciate ligament injury in national collegiate athletic association basketball and soccer: a 13-year review. *Am J Sports Med* 2005;33:524–30.

51. Garrick JG, Requa RK. Chapter 1: ACL Injuries in Men and Women—How Common are They? In Griffin LY. Prevention of Noncontact ACL Injuries. Rosemont, IL: American Academy of Orthopaedic Surgeons; 2001.

52. Noyes FR, Mooar PA, Matthews DS et al. The symptomatic anterior cruciate-deficient knee. Part I: the long-term functional disability in athletically active individuals. *J Bone Joint Surg AM*. 1983;65:154–62.

53. Wilder FV, Hall BJ, Barrett JPJ et al. History of acute knee injury and osteoarthritis of the knee: a prospective epidemiological assessment. The Clearwater Osteoarthritis Study. *Osteoarthritis Cartilage* 2002;10:611–6.

54. Sandow MJ, Goodfellow JW. The natural history of anterior knee pain in adolescents. *J Bone Joint Surg* 1985;67B:36–8.

55. Stathopulu E, Baildam E. Anterior knee pain: a long term follow-up. *Rheumatology*. 2003;42:380–2.

56. DeHaven KE, Lintner DM. Athletic injuries: comparison by age, sport, and gender. *Am J Sports Med* 1986;14:218–24.

57. Prodromos CC, Han Y, Rogowski J et al. A meta-analysis of the incidence of anterior cruciate ligament tears as a function of gender, sport, and a knee injury-reduction regimen. *Arthroscopy* 2007;23:1320–5.

58. Greslamer RP, Klein JR. The biomechanics of the patellofemoral joint. *J Orthop Sports Phys Ther* 1998;28:286–98.

59. Fulkerson JP. Diagnosis and treatment of patients with patellofemoral pain. *Am J Sports Med* 2002;30:447–56.

60. Ireland ML, Willson JD, Ballantyne BT et al. Hip strength in females with and without patellofemoral pain. *J Orthop Sports Phys Ther* 2003;33:671–6.

61. Thomee R, Augustsson J, Karlsson J. Patellofemoral pain syndrome: a review of current issues. *Sports Med* 1999;28:245–62.

62. Holmes SW, Clancy WG. Clinical classification of patellofemoral pain and dysfunction. *J Orthop Sports Phys Ther* 1998;28:299–306.

63. Huberti HH, Hayes WC. Patellofemoral contact pressures. The influence of Q angle and tendofemoral contact. *J Bone Joint Surg* 1984;66A:715–24.

64. Powers CM. The influence of altered lower-extremity kinematics on patellofemoral joint dysfunction: a theoretical perspective. *J Orthop Sports Phys Ther* 2003;33:639–46.

65. Voight ML, Wieder DL. Comparative reflex response times of the vastus medialis obliquus and vastus lateralis in normal subjects and subjects with extensor mechanism. *Am J Sports Med* 1991;19:131–7.

66. Lee TQ, Anzel SH, Bennett KA et al. The influence of fixed rotational deformities of the femur on the patellofemoral contact pressures in human cadaver knees. *Clin Orthop* 1994;302:69–74.

67. Milgrom C, Kerem E, Finestone A et al. Patellofemoral pain caused by overactivity. A prospective study of risk factors in infantry recruits. *J Bone Joint Surg* 1991;73A:1041–43.

68. Witvrouw E, Lysens R, Bellemans J et al. Intrinsic risk factors for the development of anterior knee pain in an athletic population: A two-year prospective study. *Am J Sports Med* 2000;28:480–9.

69. Arendt E, Dick R. Knee injury patterns among men and women in collegiate basketball and soccer. NCAA data and review of literature. *Am J Sport Med* 1995;23:694–701.

70. Arendt EA, Agel J, Dick R. Anterior cruciate ligament injury patterns among collegiate men and women. *J Ath Train* 1999;34:86–92.

71. Boden BP, Dean GS, Feagin JA et al. Mechanisms of anterior cruciate ligament injury. *Orthoped* 2000; 23:573–78.
72. Engstrom B, Johansson C, Tornkvist H. Soccer injuries among elite female players. *Am J Sport Med* 1991;19:372–75.
73. Ireland ML, Wall C. Epidemiology and comparison of knee injuries in elite male and female United States basketball athletes. *Med Sci Sports Exerc* 1990;22:S82.
74. Arendt E. Anterior cruciate ligament injuries in women. *Sport Med Arthroscop Rev* 1997;5:149–55.
75. Ireland ML. Anterior cruciate ligament injury in female athletes: epidemiology. *J Ath Train* 1999;34: 150–54.
76. Beynnon BD, Fleming BC, Johnson RJ et al. Anterior cruciate ligament strain behavior during rehabilitation exercises in vivo. *Am J Sports Med* 1995;23:24–34.
77. Markolf KL, Gorek JF, Kabo M et al. Direct measurement of resultant forces in the anterior cruciate ligament. *J Bone Joint Surg* 1990;72-A:557–67.
78. Markolf K, Burchfield D, Shapiro M et al. Combined knee loading states that generate high anterior cruciate ligament forces. *J Orthop Res* 1995;13:930–35.
79. Arms S, Pope M, Johnson R et al. The biomechanics of anterior cruciate ligament rehabilitation and reconstruction. *Am J Sports Med* 1984;12:8–18.
80. Zarins B, Rowe C, Harris B et al. Rotational motion of the knee. *Am J Sports Med.* 1983;11:152–6.
81. Zarins B, Nemeth V. Acute knee injuries in athletes. *Orthop Clin J North Am* 1985;16:285–302.
82. Wang J, Rubin R, Marshall J. A mechanism of isolated anterior cruciate ligament rupture. *J Bone Joint Surg* 1975;57A:411–13.
83. Andrews J, McLeod W, Ward T et al. The cutting mechanism. *Am J Sports Med* 1979;5:111–21.
84. Hewett TE, Myer GD, Ford KR. Decrease in neuromuscular control about the knee with maturation in female athletes. *J Bone Joint Surg* 2004;86-A:1601–8.
85. Shelbourne K, Davis T, Klootwyk T. The relationship between intercondylar notch width of the femur and the incidence of anterior cruciate ligament tears: a prospective study. *Am J Sports Med* 1998; 26:402–08.
86. Devita P, Skelly WA. Effect of landing stiffness on joint kinetics and energetics in the lower extremity. *Med Sci Sport Exer* 1992;24:108–15.
87. Lee CY, Liu X, Smith CL et al. The combined regulation of estrogen and cyclic tension on fibroblast biosynthesis derived from anterior cruciate ligament. *Matrix Biol* 2004;23:323–9.
88. Uhorchak JM, Scoville CR, Williams GN et al. Risk factors associated with noncontact injury of the anterior cruciate ligament: a prospective four-year evaluation of 859 West Point cadets. *Am J Sport Med* 2003;31:831–42.
89. Zazulak BT, Paterno MV, Myer GD et al. The effects of menstrual cycle on anterior knee laxity: a systematic review. *Sports Med* 2006;36:847–62.
90. Diveta JM, Walker ML, Skibinski B. Relationship between performance of selected scapula muscles and scapula abduction in standing subjects. *Phys Ther* 1990;70:470–9.
91. Junge A, Rosch D, Peterson L et al. Prevention of soccer injuries: a prospective intervention study in youth amateur players. *Am J Sport Med* 2002;30:652–9.
92. Mandelbaum BR, Silvers HJ, Wantanabe DS et al. Effectiveness of a neuromuscular and proprioception training program in preventing anterior cruciate ligament injuries in female athletes: a 2-year follow-up. *Am J Sports Med* 2005;33:1003–110.
93. Mascal CL, Landel R, Powers C. Management of patellofemoral pain targeting hip, pelvis, and trunk muscle function: 2 case reports. *J Orthop Sports Phys Ther* 2003;33:647–60.
94. Callaghan MJ, Oldham JA. Quadriceps atrophy: to what extent does it exist in patellofemoral pain syndrome? *Br J Sports Med* 2004;38:295–9.
95. Dvir Z, Shklar A, Halperin N et al. Concentric and eccentric torque variations of the quadriceps femoris in patellofemoral pain syndrome. *Clin Biomech* 1990;5:68–72.
96. Thomee R, Renstrom P, Karlsson J et al. Patellofemoral pain syndrome in young women: a clinical analysis of alignment, pain parameters, common symptoms, functional activity level. *Scand J Med Sci Sports* 1995;5:237–44.
97. Bizzini M, Childs JD, Piva SR et al. Systematic review of the quality of randomized controlled trials for patellofemoral pain syndrome. *J Orthop Sports Phys Ther.* 2003;33:4–20.
98. Crossley K, Bennell K, Green S et al. A systematic review of physical interventions for patellofemoral pain syndrome. *Clin J Sport Med.* 2001;11:103–10.
99. Boling MC, Bolgla LA, Mattacola CG et al. Outcomes of a weight-bearing rehabilitation program for patients diagnosed with patellofemoral pain syndrome. *Arch Phys Med Rehab* 2006;87:1435.
100. Tyler TF, Nicholas SJ, Mullaney MJ et al. The role of hip muscle function in the treatment of patellofemoral pain syndrome. *Am J Sports Med* 2006;34:630–6.
101. Selseth A, Dayton M, Cordova M et al. Quadriceps concentric EMG activity is greater than eccentric EMG activity during the lateral step-up exercise. *J Sport Rehab* 2000;9:124–34.
102. Powers CM. Rehabilitation of patellofemoral joint disorders: a critical review. *J Orthop Sports Phys Ther* 1998;28:345–54.
103. Prentice W, Voight M. Techniques in Musculoskeletal Rehabilitation. New York: McGraw-Hill; 2001.
104. Caraffa A, Cerulli G, Projett M et al. Prevention of anterior cruciate ligament injuries in soccer. A prospective controlled study of proprioceptive training. *Knee Surg Sports Traumatol Arthrosc* 1996; 4:19–21.
105. Mykelbust G, Engebretsen L, Braekken IH et al. Prevention of anterior cruciate ligament injuries in female team handball players: a prospective study over three seasons. *Clin J Sport Med* 2003;13:71–8.

106. Olsen OE, Mykelbust G, Engebretsen L et al. Exercises to prevent lower limb injuries in youth sports: cluster randomised controlled trial. *Br J Sports Med* 2005;330:449.

107. Soderman K, Werner S, Pietila T et al. Balance board training: prevention of traumatic injuries of the lower extremities in female soccer players? A prospective randomized intervention study. *Knee Surg Sports Traumatol Arthroscopy* 2000;8:356–63.

108. Wedderkopp N, Kaltoft M, Lundgaard B et al. Prevention of injuries in young female European team handball. A prospective intervention study. *Scand J Med Sci Sports* 1999;9:41–7.

109. Heidt RS Jr, Sweeterman LM, Carlonas RL et al. Avoidance of soccer injuries with preseason conditioning. *Am J Sports Med* 2000;28:659–62.

110. Hewett TE, Lindenfeld TN, Riccobene JV et al. The effect of neuromuscular training on the incidence of knee injury in female athletes. A prospective study. *Am J Sports Med* 1999;27:699–706.

111. Luo X, Pietrobon R, Sun SX et al. Estimates and patterns of direct health care expenditures among individuals with back pain in the United States. *Spine* 2004;29:79–86.

112. Nadler SF, Malanga GA, DePrince M et al. The relationship between lower extremity injury, low back pain, and hip muscle strength in male and female collegiate athletes. *Clin J Sport Med* 2000;10:89–97.

113. Nadler SF, Malanga GA, Feinberg JH et al. Functional performance deficits in athletes with previous lower extremity injury. *Clin J Sport Med* 2002;12:73–8.

114. Trainor TJ, Wiesel SW. Epidemiology of back pain in the athlete. *Clin Sports Med* 2002;21:93–103.

115. Greene HS, Cholewicki J, Galloway MT et al. A history of low back injury is a risk factor for recurrent back injuries in varsity athletes. *Am J Sports Med* 2001;29:795–800.

116. Drake JD, Aultman CD, McGill SM et al. The influence of static axial torque in combined loading on intervertebral joint failure mechanics using a porcine model. *Clin Biomech (Bristol)* 2005;20:1038–45.

117. Holmes JA, Damaser MS, Lehman SL. Erector spinae activation and movement dynamics about the lumbar spine in lordotic and kyphotic squat-lifting. *Spine* 1992;17:327–34.

118. Kong WZ, Goel VK, Gilbertson LG et al. Effects of muscle dysfunction on lumbar spine mechanics. A finite element study based on a two motion segments model. *Spine* 1996;21:2197–206.

119. Lu YM, Hutton WC, Gharpuray VM. Do bending, twisting, and diurnal fluid changes in the disc affect the propensity to prolapse? A viscoelastic finite element model. *Spine* 1996;21:2570–79.

120. Schmidt H, Kettler A, Heuer F et al. Intradiscal pressure, shear strain, and fiber strain in the intervertebral disc under combined loading. *Spine* 2007;32:748–55.

121. Shirazi-Adl A. Biomechanics of the lumbar spine in sagittal/lateral moments. *Spine* 1994;19:2407–14.

122. Ferreira PH, Ferreira ML, Hodges PW. Changes in recruitment of the abdominal muscles in people with low back pain: ultrasound measurement of muscle activity. *Spine* 2004;29:2560–66.

123. Hodges PW, Richardson CA. Inefficient muscular stabilization of the lumbar spine associated with low back pain. A motor control evaluation of transversus abdominis. *Spine* 1996;21:2640–50.

124. Arjmand N, Shirazi-Adl A. Biomechanics of changes in lumbar posture in static lifting. *Spine* 2005; 30:2637–48.

125. McGill SM, Hughson RL, Parks K. Changes in lumbar lordosis modify the role of the extensor muscles. *Clin Biomech (Bristol)* 2000;15:777–80.

126. Snijders CJ, Ribbers MT, de Bakker HV et al. EMG recordings of abdominal and back muscles in various standing postures: validation of a biomechanical model on sacroiliac joint stability. *J Electromyogr Kinesiol* 1998;8:205–14.

127. Hungerford B, Gilleard W, Hodges P. Evidence of altered lumbopelvic muscle recruitment in the presence of sacroiliac joint pain. *Spine* 2003;28:1593–600.

128. Pel JJ, Spoor CW, Pool-Goudzwaard AL et al. Biomechanical analysis of reducing sacroiliac joint shear load by optimization of pelvic muscle and ligament forces. *Ann Biomed Eng* 2008;36:415–24.

129. Richardson CA, Snijders CJ, Hides JA et al. The relation between the transversus abdominis muscles, sacroiliac joint mechanics, and low back pain. *Spine* 2002;27:399–405.

130. Hayden JA, van Tulder MW, Malmivaara A et al. Exercise therapy for treatment of non-specific low back pain. *Cochrane Database Syst Rev* 2005:CD000335.

131. Hayden JA, van Tulder MW, Tomlinson G. Systematic review: strategies for using exercise therapy to improve outcomes in chronic low back pain. *Ann Intern Med* 2005;142:776–85.

132. Liddle SD, Baxter GD, Gracey JH. Exercise and chronic low back pain: what works? *Pain* 2004;107: 176–90.

133. Bongers PM. The cost of shoulder pain at work. *Br Med J* 2001;322:64–65.

134. Urwin M, Symmons D, Allison T et al. Estimating the burden of musculoskeletal disorders in the community: the comparative prevalence of symptoms at different anatomical sites, and the relation to social deprivation. *Ann Rheum Dis* 1998;57:649–55.

135. Van der Heijden G. Shoulder disorders: a state of the art review. *Baillieres Best Pract Res Clin Rheumatol* 1999;13:287–309.

136. Johnson M, Crosley K, O'Neil M et al. Estimates of direct health care expenditures among individuals with shoulder dysfunction in the United States. *J Orthop Sports Phys Ther* 2005;35:A4–PL8.

137. van der Windt DA, Koes BW, Boeke AJ et al. Shoulder disorders in general practice: prognostic indicators of outcome. *Br J Gen Pract* 1996;46:519–23.

138. Hovelius L. Shoulder dislocation in Swedish ice hockey players. *Am J Sports Med* 1978;6:373.

139. Hovelius L. Incidence of shoulder dislocation in Sweden. *Clin Orthop Related Res* 1982;166:127–31.

140. Simonet WT, Melton III J, Cofield RH et al. Incidence of anterior shoulder dislocation in Olmsted County, Minnesota. *Clin Orthop Related Res* 1983;186:186–91.

141. Simonet WT, Cofield RH. Prognosis in anterior shoulder dislocation. *Am J Sports Med* 1984;12:19–24.

142. Buscayret F, Edwards TB, Szabo I et al. Glenohumeral arthrosis in anterior instability before and after surgical intervention. *Am J Sports Med* 2004;32:1165–72.

143. Cameron ML, Kocher MS, Briggs KK et al. The prevalence of glenohumeral osteoarthrosis in unstable shoulders. *Am J Sports Med* 2003;31:53–55.

144. Bigliani LU, Levine WN. Subacromial impingement syndrome. *J Bone Joint Surg Am* 1997;79:1854–68.

145. Carpenter JE, Flanagan CL, Thomopoulos S et al. The effects of overuse combined with intrinsic or extrinsic alterations in an animal model of rotator cuff tendinosis. *Am J Sports Med* 1998;26:801–07.

146. Soslowsky LJ, Carpenter JE, Bucchieri JS et al. Biomechanics of the rotator cuff. *Orthop Clin N Am* 1997;28:17–30.

147. Yamaguchi K, Ditsios K, Middleton WD et al. The demographic and morphological features of rotator cuff disease. A comparison of asymptomatic and symptomatic shoulders. *J Bone Joint Surg Am* 2006; 88:1699–704.

148. Yamaguchi K, Sher JS, Andersen WK et al. Glenohumeral motion in patients with rotator cuff tears: a comparison of asymptomatic and symptomatic shoulders. *J Shoulder Elbow Surg* 2000;9:6–11.

149. Bernard BP. Musculoskeletal Disorders (MSD's) and Workplace Factors: A Critical Review of Epidemiologic Evidence for Work-Related Musculoskeletal Disorders of the Neck, Upper Extremity, and Low Back. In Cincinnati, OH: Centers for Disease Control and Prevention; 1997.

150. Szeto GPY, Straker L, Raine S. A field comparison of neck and shoulder postures in symptomatic and asymptomatic office workers. *Appl Ergonomics.* 2002;33:75–84.

151. Lukasiewicz AC, McClure P, Michener L et al. Comparison of 3-dimensional scapular position and orientation between subjects with and without shoulder impingement. *J Orthop Sports Phys Ther* 1999; 29:574–83; discussion 84–86.

152. Ludewig PM, Cook TM. Alterations in shoulder kinematics and associated muscle activity in people with symptoms of shoulder impingement. *Phys Ther* 2000;80:276–91.

153. Thigpen CA, Padua DA, Karas SG. Comparison of scapular kinematics between individuals with and without multidirectional shoulder instability. *J Athl Train* 2005;34(4):644–52.

154. Thigpen CA, Padua DA, Xu N et al. Comparison of scapular muscle activity between individuals with and without multidirectional shoulder instability. *J Orthop Sports Phys Ther* 2005;35:A4–PL18.

155. Arnheim DD, Prentice WE. Principles of Athletic Training, 10th ed. Boston, MA: McGraw-Hill; 2000.

156. Schmitt L, Snyder-Mackler L. Role of scapular stabilizers in etiology and treatment of impingement syndrome. *J Orthop Sports Phys Ther* 1999;29:31–8.

157. Mesiter K. Injuries to the shoulder in the throwing athlete. Part 1: Biomechanics/pathophysiology/classification of injury. *Am J Sport Med* 2000;28:265–75.

158. Rowe MCR, Harilaos T, Sakellarides M. Factors related to recurrences of anterior dislocations of the shoulder. *Clin Orthop* 1961;20:40–7.

159. Buss DD, Lynch GP, Meyer CP et al. Nonoperative management for in-season athletes with anterior shoulder instability. *Am J Sports Med* 2004;32:1430–33.

160. Warner JJ, Micheli LJ, Arslanian LE et al. Patterns of flexibility, laxity, and strength in normal shoulders and shoulders with instability and impingement. *Am J Sports Med* 1990;18:366–75.

CHAPTER 14

Performance Nutrition

UPON COMPLETION OF THIS CHAPTER, YOU WILL BE ABLE TO:

Understand the scope of practice of Sports Performance Professionals to provide nutritional advice.

Describe the macronutrients and their functions as it relates to performance.

Understand the role of micronutrients and their role in performance enhancement.

Suggest pre-exercise and post-exercise nutrition strategies.

Provide hydration recommendations and identify signs of dehydration.

Provide basic nutritional recommendations for optimizing health, performance, and weight control.

Introduction

Performance Nutrition

A combination of strategies to enhance physical and athletic performance through specific food and nutrient choices, timing, and quantities.

Performance nutrition is described as a combination of strategies to enhance physical and athletic performance through specific food and nutrient choices, timing, and quantities. Decades of research have shown us an exciting field of practice where one can improve strength, power, and endurance when these strategies are employed. More specifically, performance nutrition can delay fatigue, enhance the anabolic effect of strength training, promote the regeneration of energy stores, stabilize the immune function while training, and improve cognitive performance factors such as hand-eye coordination, concentration, and focus. Perhaps one of the most important benefits of executing performance nutrition strategies is injury prevention. Fatigue is a significant variable for athletes who are training and competing. As an athlete fatigues, the risk of injury increases. Therefore, if one can prevent or delay the onset of fatigue, the risk of injury can be reduced. Performance nutrition is an athlete's last legal edge in training and competition.

TABLE 14.1

Educational and Professional Requirements for the RD

Bachelor's Degree	RDs receive their degrees at an accredited college or university with course work approved by the Commission on Accreditation for Dietetics Education (CADE).
Supervised Practice Program	RDs then complete a CADE accredited program, typically 6–12 months in length, with focused practice and study in clinical and community nutrition, and food service management. Graduate study is often combined.
National Exam	After completing the supervised practice program, candidates must pass the national exam to receive their RD credential.
Continuing Education	One must complete continuing education requirements in order to maintain an active RD credential.

Overview of the Field

Sports Performance Professionals should be familiar with the concepts of performance nutrition. Integrating nutritional strategies with training designs will help athletes achieve their desired outcomes. It is important, however, to recognize and respect the scope of practice of each professional field. The professional legally qualified to practice in the field of nutrition is a registered dietitian (RD), who can be recognized by the use of the "RD" credential. The RD is a specialized food and nutrition expert with extensive training who meets specified criteria. Table 14.1 describes the RD's educational and professional requirements.

The practice of nutrition, more formally called dietetics, is governed by national credentialing programs and state licensing laws. The practice of dietetics is regulated in most states. A person practicing dietetics without a license would be breaking the law. In these states, the scope of practice is well defined, legally enforced with licensure laws being subject to misdemeanor or felony penalties. The following Web site can help the Sports Performance Professional identify the laws by state of residence:

www.eatright.org/ada/files/STATE_LICENSURE_SUMMARY_7_07_PDF.pdf.

A general understanding of basic nutrition and weight management should exist in order to educate athletes and provide general guidance in this area. It is likely that a Sports Performance Professional will be the first person approached with nutrition questions, so being confident about the nature of the relationship between nutrition and performance is essential. However, providing individual nutrition assessments, dietary advice, meal plans, or recommendations for nutrient intakes are best left to an RD. The skills and abilities required to calculate, counsel, or prescribe an individualized nutrition or weight management plan exceeds the training and expertise of the Sports Performance Professional (1). This means a qualified RD should be a valued partner to professionally and legally work with the athlete. This becomes especially important if the athlete has health and medical concerns such as obesity, diabetes, heart disease, allergies, or hypertension. Table 14.2 offers examples of nutrition topics that the Sports Performance Professional should be prepared to discuss with athletes.

TABLE 14.2

Examples of Nutrition Topics of Discussion for the Sports Performance Professional

Food preparation methods	Food guidance systems (i.e., Food Guide Pyramid)
Healthy snacks	Carbohydrate, protein, and fat basics
Statistical information on the relationship between chronic disease and the excesses or deficiencies of specific nutrients	Nutrients contained in foods or supplements
Vitamins and minerals as essential nutrients	Importance of water and hydration status

Training Diet Components

MACRONUTRIENTS

CARBOHYDRATE

The fuel burned during exercise depends on the intensity and duration of the activity being performed. As intensity increases so does the contribution of carbohydrate as an energy source. If blood glucose cannot be stabilized, performance intensity must decrease. Because carbohydrate availability is a limiting factor in selected activities, it should be clear that it is a primary fuel source during physical activity and is critical for optimal performance. Athletes typically train and compete at 65% or more of $\dot{V}O_2$max. At this level, carbohydrates are the predominant fuel. Muscle glycogen, a stored carbohydrate, is the major source of carbohydrates in the body followed by liver glycogen and blood glucose. Muscle glycogen can be depleted within 2 hours of exercise and liver glycogen stores can be depleted by a 15-hour fast. With such limited stores of carbohydrates, it makes sense that the greater the pre-exercise glycogen content, the longer an athlete can exercise (2). So, by consuming adequate carbohydrate and energy, the training athlete can delay the onset of fatigue caused by glycogen depletion.

Carbohydrate recommendations for athletes range from 6–10 g/kg/day, whereas the typical American diet provides 4–5 g/kg/day. Recommended intakes for endurance training are slightly higher than general training needs. Ultra-endurance athletes (e.g., those involved in exercise lasting longer than 4 hours), require the highest intakes at 11 g/kg/day or more (2). Table 14.3 outlines daily carbohydrate recommendations.

TIME OUT
Carbohydrate Depletion and Exercise

An athlete who exercises in a carbohydrate-depleted state experiences larger increases in stress hormones and greater disturbances of many immune function indicators. By consuming carbohydrates during exercise, one can limit exercise-induced immunosuppression (3).

Carbohydrate-containing foods can be categorized by the type or form of carbohydrate or its glycemic index (GI). A food can be said to have a low, moderate, or high GI. The GI indicates the effect of the food or fluid on circulating blood glucose and insulin levels; high-GI foods cause a rapid rise in blood glucose (and subsequent release of insulin), whereas low-GI foods cause a slower, more gradual rise in blood glucose (and a blunted insulin response). For example, sports drinks and potatoes have a high GI, whereas milk and apples have a low GI. The GI can be a useful tool when the rate of digestion and absorption is important. For example, in the post-exercise period, an athlete wants to ingest foods and fluids that are digested and absorbed quickly to help enhance muscle recovery and glycogen repletion. Foods with a higher GI are digested and thus absorbed more quickly than lower-GI foods, hence the more rapid rise in blood glucose.

Perhaps the most famous performance enhancing strategy related to carbohydrate intake is glycogen supercompensation (i.e., carbohydrate loading). Carbohydrate loading can almost double muscle glycogen concentrations, which can ultimately impact endurance potential and is most effective for athletes performing intense, continuous endurance activities lasting longer than 90 minutes (2). To achieve glycogen supercompensation, one must allow 2–6 days for increases to take place. Athletes consume a typical mixed diet on the first 3 days then progress to a

TABLE 14.3	
Daily Carbohydrate Intakes and Recommendations for Athletes	
Typical U.S. intake	4–5 g/kg/day
General Training Needs	5–7 g/kg/day
Endurance Training Needs	7–10 g/kg/day
Ultra-endurance Training Needs	11 g/kg/day or more

Source: Adapted from (2).

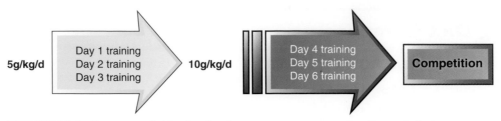

FIGURE 14.1   Recommended intakes for glycogen supercompensation (i.e., carbohydrate loading).

high-carbohydrate diet for 3 days before competition. Figure 14.1 illustrates carbohydrate loading recommendations. When working with athletes, be sure they understand the important food sources of carbohydrates. For example, foods from the cereals and grains, fruits and vegetable food groups, as well as milk, yogurt, beans, legumes from the dairy and protein groups can all contribute to one's daily carbohydrate intake.

PROTEIN

The protein needs of athletes receive considerable interest and attention. Protein requirements as well as supplementation of individual amino acids and specific protein types have been the primary areas of focus. Given the important functions of protein, it is easy to see why athletes are so concerned. A few key roles of proteins include:

- Supporting growth and maintenance of body tissues
- Synthesizing enzymes, hormones, and other peptides
- Building antibodies
- Maintaining fluid and electrolyte balance
- Repairing exercise-associated muscle damage
- Providing energy and glucose (4).

Protein contributes to energy both at rest and during exercise, but in fed individuals, protein likely provides less than 5% of expended energy (5). However, as exercise duration increases and glycogen levels fall, protein may help sustain blood glucose levels via liver **gluconeogenesis**.

Dietary protein requirements reflect the need to balance daily turnover and losses. Proteins are continually being synthesized and degraded; therefore, assessing and meeting needs is an important component of an athlete's diet. The type, intensity, and duration of activity are important variables that can induce significant changes in protein turnover. Another important factor is energy balance. Negative energy balance (where calories expended exceed calories ingested) increases protein requirement to prevent protein from being used as an energy source. The need to repair exercise-related muscle damage, support lean mass gains, and replace proteins used as energy are a few reasons athletes have increased requirements. Resistance exercise protein needs are greater than those of endurance exercise. Strength and power athletes should consume 1.6–1.8 g/kg of body mass per day. Eating more protein beyond this recommended level has not been proven to be any more effective at increasing lean mass.

The protein tissue accrual rate is limited. Endurance athletes are generally recommended to ingest 1.2–1.4 g/kg/day, whereas the current dietary reference intake (DRI) for protein is 0.8 g/kg/day. Sports Performance Professionals should also be aware that the need for protein may be higher during the first 3–6 months of training when muscle hypertrophy rates are accelerated (2). Despite the increased need for protein, the typical diets of most athletes provide sufficient intake. Too much protein could displace dietary carbohydrates below recommended levels, which would impact performance.

Dietary protein can be found in many different foods. Meats, poultry, fish, eggs, beans, nuts, nut butters, milk, vegetables, such as broccoli, and carbohydrates, such as bread, all contribute high-quality protein to the training diet. There is no evidence that protein supplements are necessary or more effective in meeting an athlete's protein requirements than consuming protein from these standard food sources. However, protein supplements can be helpful under certain circumstances and be useful in many situations. Common forms of supplemental protein are whey and casein and can be found in either isolated powder form or as a component of other products. **Whey proteins** are often considered "fast" proteins due to the quick rise of plasma amino acids after consumption. On the other hand, **casein** is often considered a "slow" protein because of its moderate, prolonged amino acid increase. This is helpful to know when considering the timing of protein ingestion. For example, the periods before and after a bout of resistance exercise are crucial for promoting muscle protein synthesis (6). Whey protein may be a wise choice during these periods, given its quick absorption. The faster the amino acids can get into the body, the faster the body can reduce degradation and facilitate synthesis.

Gluconeogenesis
A metabolic pathway that results in the generation of glucose from non-carbohydrate carbon substrates such as pyruvate, lactate, glycerol, and glucogenic amino acids.

Whey Protein
The collection of globular proteins that can be isolated from whey, a by-product of cheese manufactured from cow's milk. Whey has the highest biological value of any known protein.

Casein
The predominant phosphoprotein that accounts for nearly 80% of proteins in milk and cheese.

TIME OUT
Protein Sources

Beef, pork, and salmon are all great sources of protein and also contain approximately 1.0 g of naturally occurring creatine per 8-oz serving!

FATS

Fat has several essential functions, one of which includes serving as an energy source through a wide range of exercise intensities. After 15–20 minutes of endurance exercise, the oxidation of fats is stimulated. As exercise intensity increases, the contribution of fat begins to decrease due to carbohydrate's increasing role. In addition to energy, fat helps athletes meet daily calorie needs, maintain body temperature, protect organs, deliver and absorb fat-soluble vitamins and carotenoids, enhance taste and texture of foods, and improve the satiety of meals and snacks.

Fatty acids are simple, single chain lipids. They serve as regulators of fat production, inflammation, insulin action, and neurological function (2). Fatty acids are classified based on the chain length and presence of double bonds (no double bond compared to more than one double bond). Saturated fat, which can be synthesized in the body, is found primarily in land animal fats such as whole milk, cream, whole milk cheese, lard, butterfat, or so-called tropical oils like palm or coconut oils. Olive oil, canola oil, almonds, and avocados all contain monounsaturated fatty acids (MUFAs), whereas vegetable and fish oils predominantly contain polyunsaturated fatty acids (PUFAs). Polyunsaturated fatty acids play a major role in **eicosanoid** synthesis that has hormonal functions, which regulate many functions, such as smooth muscle contraction and inflammatory functions. Therefore, the types of fats consumed in the diet can become active participants in health and performance.

The recommended daily allowance for total fat has not been established. However, an acceptable macronutrient distribution range for all adults has been established as 20–35% of daily energy intake as total fat. National surveys have reported that total fat consumption for both men and women average 32.8% of total calorie intake. Athlete intake patterns vary depending on the sport, training, and performance. For example, rowers have been reported consuming diets containing 30–40% fat, whereas gymnasts report intake ranges from 15–31% fat (2). Very-low-fat diets (<15% of total calories as fat) compared to moderate-fat diets (20–25% of total calories as fat) have shown no performance benefit and athletes should not restrict dietary fat intake to such low levels. Very-low-fat diets can disrupt menstrual function in female athletes and contribute to low serum testosterone levels in male athletes (2). The Dietary Guidelines for Americans have recommended that 25–30% of energy intake come from fat with 10% coming from saturated fatty acids, 10% from PUFAs, and 10% from MUFAs. Athletes should follow these general guidelines and recommendations to prevent fat intake from becoming too low (5).

Interestingly, gender-based research has shown that dietary recommendations may be specific for exercising women. Several reports describe subtle differences in the sources of energy used. For example, women may utilize more fat and less carbohydrates than men. It has been shown that women have higher intramuscular muscle triglyceride stores and may have greater breakdown during submaximal exercise (8). Thus, the female endurance athlete in energy balance needs at least 30% of calories from fat to replace muscle triglyceride used during training. If fat intake is too low, depletion would continue, which may ultimately limit performance capacity in succeeding workouts (8).

Meats, poultry, and fish are major sources of total fat in the national food supply, contributing 30% of total energy intakes. Grain products contribute to 25% of our total intake, whereas milk and milk products supply 18%. Fats and oils, such as table spreads and salad dressings, represent 11%, vegetables 9%, and other foods contribute 7% (2).

MICRONUTRIENTS

VITAMINS AND MINERALS

Micronutrients play key roles in energy metabolism, bone health, hemoglobin production, immune function, and protection from oxidative damage. All of these functions are important to an athlete's health and performance. Exercising on a regular basis may result in increased micronutrient losses or an increased rate of turnover. During strenuous physical activity, the rate of energy turnover in skeletal muscle may be increased up to 20–100 times the resting rate (5, 9). A higher turnover increases the need for greater total food intake to balance the increase in energy expenditure. The higher energy intakes of physically active people and competitive

Eicosanoid
Signaling molecules made by oxygenation of 20-carbon essential fatty acids (EFAs). They exert complex control over many bodily systems, mainly in inflammation or immunity, and as messengers in the central nervous system.

TABLE 14.4

Terms Related to Daily Recommended Nutrient Intakes

DRI	**Dietary Reference Intakes**: a family of four nutrient reference values including RDA, AI, EAR, and TUL. The primary goals of the DRI values are to prevent nutrient deficiencies and reduce the risk of chronic diseases such as osteoporosis, cancer, and cardiovascular disease.
RDA	**Recommended Daily Allowance**: the average daily dietary intake level that adequately meets the nutrient requirements of nearly all healthy individuals in a particular life stage and gender group.
AI	**Adequate Intake**: used when an RDA cannot be determined. The AI is a recommended intake value based on observed or experimentally determined nutrient intake estimates of a group of healthy people.
EAR	**Estimated Average Requirement**: used to assess dietary adequacy and is the basis for the RDA. An EAR is a daily nutrient intake value estimated to meet half of the healthy individual's requirement.
TUL	**Tolerable Upper Level**: the highest level of daily nutrient intake not likely to pose a risk of adverse health effects for almost all individuals in the general population. Potential risk of adverse effects increase as intake increases above the TUL.

athletes will ensure adequate ingestion of most essential dietary components (9). A diet with plenty of variety should supply adequate protein, vitamins, minerals, and other nutrient requirements. If energy needs are being met, there is no evidence to suggest that specific supplementation is necessary or that it will improve performance (5). Those athletes at greatest risk for micronutrient deficiencies or poor status are those who restrict calorie intake, who eliminate one or more food groups from their daily diet, or those who consume high-calorie, low-nutrient dense diets. These behaviors may prompt the suggestion of a multivitamin and mineral supplement to improve overall status. Table 14.4 lists terms related to the current reference intakes of vitamins and minerals. However, there is data available that suggest exercise may slightly increase the need for these vitamins to approximately twice the recommended amount. See Chapter 15 for more information on micronutrient requirements for the athlete and their effects on performance.

ANTIOXIDANTS

The antioxidant nutrients (e.g., vitamins A, E, and C; beta-carotene; and selenium) play important roles in balancing the oxidative stress produced by free radicals. As exercise can increase oxygen consumption by 10–15 times more than a resting metabolism, exercise itself may induce oxidative stress. In response, well-trained athletes may compensate by developing a more powerful endogenous antioxidant system than a sedentary person (2). There have been questions about whether athletes really need more antioxidants in the form of supplements, especially vitamins C and E. We know that free radicals act as secondary messengers that control a variety of physiological responses and many of these responses may be important to training adaptation, so disturbing the natural processes may limit significant performance or training benefits (10).

The concept of "too much of a good thing" may be true with regard to antioxidants. At very high doses, vitamins and minerals can be as toxic as any other known, harmful ingredient. For example, high doses of vitamin E can interfere with platelet function via vitamin K disruption, and high doses of vitamin C can act as a pro-oxidant. This is a major reason why current data do not support the use of excessive antioxidant doses. However, athletes following a low-fat diet, those who restrict energy intakes, or have limited fruit and vegetable intakes may want to pay special attention to their food choices and antioxidant status. Under the direction of a health-care provider, supplemental antioxidants may be suggested.

When considering dietary strategies to help reduce free radical damage, one should consider ways to reduce foods and dietary components that promote oxidative stress (for example, saturated fats), as well as efforts to include nutrients that have high-antioxidant properties. A diet high in fruits and vegetables reduces the risk of oxidative stress by increasing plasma antioxidant vitamins (10). Specifically, consuming adequate vitamin C may help reduce muscle soreness and damage induced by exercise-associated oxidative stress. In addition, although supplemental vitamin C will not prevent colds, it does seem to help reduce upper respiratory tract infection duration (2). Alternatively, studies on vitamin E's impact on exercise-related muscle injury are equivocal (10).

The consensus on the need for antioxidant supplementation continues to evolve. This makes applying practical recommendations challenging for athletes and Sports Performance Professionals. In general, we can say that supplementation does not appear to improve performance, but may be helpful in reducing exercise-induced muscle damage. Research interest in antioxidant supplementation will continue, but until further conclusions become clear, it is important to determine antioxidant intakes and supplement needs on an individual basis.

Performance Nutrition Concepts

ENERGY BALANCE

DAILY ENERGY BALANCE

The concepts of performance nutrition mean little in the absence of a state of energy balance. An individual is in energy balance when sufficient calories are consumed in order to match daily energy expenditure. Exercise increases the rate of energy utilization and water loss through higher energy metabolism and heat production. Compensating for these increases should be the first nutrition priority for athletes. Failure to meet energy needs leads to decreases in performance and an overall reduction in weight, lean body mass, or both. Energy balance is also essential for the maintenance of immune and reproductive function (5). Despite what may seem like an obvious foundation to performance nutrition, surveys routinely report that athletes do not eat or drink enough (11). For example, a 2004 study reported that 62% of female athletes wanted to lose weight, which was associated with inadequate energy intake. Only 15% of the athletes studied were consuming adequate carbohydrate intake (12). Limited energy intakes set the body up to use of fat and lean tissue for fuel. Loss of muscle ultimately results in decreased strength and endurance. Low-energy intakes are also associated with poor nutrient intakes, especially of the micronutrients. In such a situation, the use of a multivitamin supplement would be warranted. A stable weight and lean mass is the best indicator of adequate energy balance. Typical energy intakes for endurance athletes can range from 3,000–5,000+ kcal/day. Many strength athletes need to ingest approximately 44–50 kcal/kg body mass per day and some may need more. Low-energy intakes of 1,800–2,000 kcal/day or less in female athletes often are associated with weight loss and disruption of reproductive function (5).

INTERDAY ENERGY BALANCE

In addition to daily energy balance, the concept of interday energy balance can also be of importance. Body composition and performance can be impacted by meal and snack frequency. For example, Deutz et al. found that those who deviated most widely from energy balance *during the day* had the highest body fat levels (13). One of the most interesting findings was that this held true regardless of whether the person was in positive or negative energy balance (13). Knowing that blood glucose levels fluctuate approximately every 3 hours helps to explain why higher body fat levels occur. If eating is delayed, blood glucose levels will drop, forcing amino acids to be recruited from muscle tissue in order to be converted by the liver to glucose. The result is blood glucose stabilization at the cost of muscle mass.

A typical meal pattern for athletes and many individuals consists of infrequent meals and a large meal at the end of the day. This pattern creates large energy deficits during the day. Therefore, the athlete who reports weight stability but is having difficulty reaching desired body composition goals may be in energy balance at the end of the day, but the within-day energy intakes may need examining and/or adjusting. Because the amount of an individual's lean body mass influences metabolism and ultimately the amount of calories expended, it makes sense to preserve and optimize lean mass in order to achieve desired body composition ranges and performance levels. An ideal way to lower muscle mass and increase fat mass is to eat infrequent meals and a large meal at the end of the day. So, practically speaking, this concept supports the recommendation of 4–6 smaller, frequent meals and snacks per day. Incorporating midmorning snacks, as well as midafternoon or pre-training snacks and fluid intake is a good way to prevent hunger and avoid marked energy deviations during the day.

TIME OUT
Energy Consumption and Performance

Performance nutrition concepts mean little in the face of negative energy balance. Adequate or positive energy balance is crucial to optimal health and performance outcomes unless the goal is weight loss.

NUTRIENT TIMING

FUELING BEFORE AND AFTER EXERCISE

Nutrient timing is an important performance concept for pre- and post-fueling strategies, muscle and energy recovery, and muscle building plans. Foods and fluids before and after workouts will need to be individually planned according to physiological characteristics (e.g., gastrointestinal sensitivity, workout intensity, and personal preferences). However, there are several concepts and strategies that form the base for improved performance. First, eating before exercise has been shown to improve performance versus exercising in the fasted state. The goal is to arrive at training or competition in a fed state (i.e., not hungry) and prevent having undigested food in the stomach. Consuming a pre-event or exercise meal that follows these general guidelines should help individuals achieve this goal:

- Sufficient fluids to maintain hydration
- Low in fat and fiber to encourage gastric emptying and minimize gastrointestinal distress
- High in carbohydrates to optimize glycogen stores
- Moderate in protein
- Contain familiar foods.

If time permits, larger meals can be consumed 3–4 hours before exercise and contain approximately 200–300 g of carbohydrates. Meals closer to training or competition should be smaller (5). Carbohydrates and hydration are two of the most important factors affecting performance. Both have a defined storage capacity and are continually being utilized. It has been stated that there may be an upper limit of carbohydrate intake. Consumption greater than approximately 500–600 g/day may offer no further contribution to glycogen storage capacity or athletic performance (14). Sports drinks containing 4–8% carbohydrates improve performance, even in events lasting 1 hour or less. It is good practice to consume sports drinks, especially during morning workouts, because liver glycogen levels may be low from the overnight fast and blood glucose levels may not be adequate if the athlete has difficulty consuming an early morning pre-exercise meal or snack. Athletes can extend endurance performance when participating in longer events by consuming approximately 30–60 g of carbohydrates per hour (5) that appears to be independent of the ingested form (e.g., fluids, gels, or solid foods). Post-exercise meals and snacks will depend on the length and intensity of exercise and when the next workout will be. For example, a post-morning workout snack or meal will be crucial if an afternoon training session is planned.

MUSCLE AND ENERGY RECOVERY

Muscle recovery and energy repletion are critical objectives for athletes training on a regular basis. The choices an individual makes regarding foods, fluids, and timing in the immediate post-workout period make a significant impact. Although long-term muscle adaptations are the result of the cumulative effects of repeated exercise, the initial responses that lead to these changes occur during and after each and every training session. Therefore, the recovery periods are key opportunities to influence training outcomes. For example, during the first few hours of recovery, many exercise-related genes are activated, which may be linked to the repletion of muscle energy stores (i.e., glycogen) (14). If carbohydrate needs are ignored after training, one potentially diminishes training gains. Similarly, it has been reported that ingesting protein with carbohydrates immediately after endurance exercise reduces muscle soreness (14). The ability to sustain high-level performance day after day is limited by how well glycogen stores are recovered and muscle tissues are repaired.

The key to maximizing recovery is to consume high-glycemic carbohydrates and proteins in a 4:1 ratio within 30–45 minutes immediately after exercise (15). The timing is essential in part because there is a narrow window of time where muscle cells are insulin receptive after exercise. Insulin is responsible for transporting glucose and amino acids into cells and initiating glycogen and protein synthesis. Insulin also reduces muscle protein breakdown (16). Individuals should aim for approximately 1.5 g carbohydrates/kg post exercise and at 2-hour intervals thereafter. Adding protein beyond the 4:1 ratio does not improve glycogen repletion, but can provide amino acids for protein repair and an enhanced anabolic environment (5).

MUSCLE BUILDING STRATEGIES

Muscle tissue is sensitive to muscular activity itself, carbohydrates, proteins, and fat intake, and hormonal fluctuations. The interaction of these variables determines the balance of muscle synthesis and breakdown. Increased muscle protein results from a positive net protein balance (i.e., synthesis is greater than breakdown). Positive balance is achieved through use of the following strategies:

- Consume a mixture of carbohydrates and amino acids before and immediately after strength workouts
- Adequately replenish glycogen stores immediately after workouts
- Meet daily carbohydrate needs
- Avoid high-protein diets.

TIME OUT
Gender Differences and Muscle Gain

Some attention has been given to gender-based response differences. It has been suggested that women use less glycogen during resistance exercise than men and may need to consume more protein afterward in order to achieve the same anabolic environment (8).

Greater improvements in 1-repetition maximum strength and body composition have been reported with pre-training and post training carbohydrate and protein supplementation (17). Consuming such a mixture counteracts the post-exercise catabolic state by making more amino acids available for transport into the muscle, thereby allowing protein synthesis to occur. These strategies activate synthesis due in part to an improved anabolic hormone environment. Carbohydrates are central to this process, given their ability to elevate insulin levels. The amount of protein necessary to elicit a positive effect appears to be only about 6 g. Further, recent data suggest that high-protein diets may actually inhibit muscle protein synthesis (14). Additional evidence advises against low-carbohydrate diets because such diets may actually result in reduced hypertrophy (18). This confirms the recommendation that athletes consume a high-carbohydrate, moderate-protein diet, especially those strength athletes looking to increase muscle mass.

HYDRATION AND FLUID STATUS

PERFORMANCE EFFECTS

Fluid intake and hydration status may be one of the most widely studied, but overlooked performance factors in athletic training and competition. A great deal of research demonstrates the proven effects of dehydration on endurance performance, but hydration status may also affect strength, power, and high-intensity endurance (19). Measurements of core temperature, heart rate, and perceived exertion demonstrate the physiologic strain of dehydration. In a dehydrated state, the same exercise task is perceived as requiring more effort than if it was performed in a well-hydrated state. Dehydration of more than 2% of body mass can decrease aerobic exercise performance, particularly in warm and hot weather. Various cognitive tasks including visuomotor tracking, short-term memory, response time, coordination, attention, and mental focus are all consequences that can be attributed to dehydration (20). It is important to note that an individual's tolerance to dehydration is very individual, so it can be difficult to quantify specific performance decrements for all types of activities, sports, or individual performances (21). However, there is recent evidence that basketball players attempt and make fewer absolute shots when dehydrated (20). This would put a player and the team at a distinct disadvantage when playing against a hydrated team. Additionally, dehydration consistently decreased strength by approximately 2%, power by approximately 3%, and high-intensity endurance by approximately 10% (19). The relative importance of the strength and power reductions is assumed to have little effect on the casual resistance exerciser. However, these small performance decrements can significantly affect outcomes of competitions and races because extremely small differences define winning versus losing.

TIME OUT
The Difference between First and Second Place

The difference between the first and eighth place finisher in the 100-m dash at the 1996, 2000, and 2004 Olympic Games was on average just a 3% margin (19). Slight performance edges can significantly affect the outcomes of competition.

FLUID RECOMMENDATIONS

A well-executed hydration plan allows an individual to show up to practices and workouts already hydrated, ready to keep pace with fluid and sweat losses during exercise, and adequately replace fluid losses in order to return to a hydrated state. The 2004 DRIs recommend an adequate intake for water to be 130 oz/day for males (16 cups) and 95 oz/day (12 cups/day) for females. Fluids from all foods and beverages count toward this total. In general, approximately

TABLE 14.5	
American Dietetic Association, Dietitians of Canada, and the American College of Sports Medicine's Fluid Replacement Guidelines	
Before Exercise	14–22 oz of fluid 2 hours before exercise
During Exercise	6–12 oz of water or sports drink every 15–20 minutes of exercise
After Exercise	16–24 oz of water or sports drink for every pound of body mass lost during exercise

20% of daily water comes from foods, leaving the remaining 80% to come from ingested fluids (2). For athletes, fluid needs increase due to increased heat production and water loss from exercise. Fluid guidelines for before, during, and after exercise have been prepared to help athletes and active individuals to properly hydrate themselves. Table 14.5 outlines the American Dietetic Association, Dietitians of Canada, and the American College of Sports Medicine's fluid recommendations.

Athletes should prehydrate several hours before exercise to allow for fluid absorption and urine output. The goal of drinking during exercise is to keep fluid losses to 2% or less as dehydration levels in excess of this can lead to significant performance decrements. Fluids should be cool, not cold, to promote consumption and optimize gastric emptying. Rehydration practices should aim to fully replace fluid and electrolyte losses. Those beverages containing sodium will help the body stimulate thirst and retain ingested fluids. For those individuals needing to achieve rapid and complete recovery from dehydration, approximately 1.5 L of fluid should be consumed for each kilogram of body mass lost after exercise. The Institute of Medicine (IOM) has recommended that replacement beverages contain -20–30 $mEq \cdot L^{-1}$ sodium, -2–5 $mEq \cdot L^{-1}$ potassium, and 5–10% carbohydrates for prolonged activity in hot weather (21).

Eating food also promotes fluid intake and retention; therefore, adequate meals and snacks throughout the day are critical to daily hydration practices. Evidence suggests that caffeine consumed in foods and beverages at levels less than 180 $mg \cdot d^{-1}$ will likely not increase urine outputs or cause dehydration. Food and beverage manufacturers are not required to list caffeine amounts; however, as a reference, an average cup of home-brewed coffee contains approximately 100 mg caffeine/8 oz and a 16-oz commercial, gourmet black coffee can range between 200 and 350 mg, whereas a 12-oz can of caffeinated soda contains approximately 22–55 mg. On the other hand, alcohol can delay full rehydration because it can act as a diuretic and increase urine output. Therefore, alcohol consumption should be limited, especially in the several days prior to competition or intense training and the post-exercise period (21).

HYDRATION ASSESSMENT

Individuals can monitor their own hydration status through a number of ways. Body mass changes, urine color, and thirst can all indicate the need for additional fluids. Measuring body mass before and after exercise and calculating the difference will give an athlete an indication of his or her sweat rate. Having an idea of what one's sweat rate is can then help determine fluid needs to be replaced after exercise. Monitoring urine color upon waking and throughout the day is another way to tell if an individual is hydrated. A urine color that is pale yellow or like light-colored lemonade is desirable and likely indicates a well-hydrated state. Darker colors, like apple juice, would indicate that the athlete should drink additional fluids. In addition to these self-monitoring techniques, precise readings of urine-specific gravity can be measured with a refractometer and can be used as another general indicator of hydration status. Well-hydrated states are reflected by readings of less than 1.01, whereas readings of more than 1.02 indicate dehydration (22).

DEHYDRATION SIGNS AND SYMPTOMS

Active individuals should be familiar with dehydration warning signs and be able to recognize these symptoms before heat illness progresses. Early signs and symptoms include thirst, discomfort, and complaints. These are generally followed by flushed skin, muscle cramps, and apathy. As water loss continues, dizziness, headache, vomiting, nausea, chills, and shortness of breath may be observed. Identifying these signs and symptoms can help prevent exertional heat illnesses and potentially life-threatening conditions (22).

EXERTIONAL HYPONATREMIA

Hyponatremia
An electrolyte disturbance (disturbance of the salts in the blood) in which the sodium concentration in the plasma is too low (below 135 mmol/L). Hyponatremia is most often a complication of other medical illnesses in which fluids rich in sodium are lost or excess water accumulates in the body at a higher rate than it can be excreted.

Along with heat illness, another dangerous condition related to fluid and hydration is **hyponatremia** or water intoxication. Overdrinking hypotonic fluids combined with excessive losses of sodium leads to hyponatremia. Consumption of (typically) water in excess of sweat rates results in dangerously low or falling serum sodium levels. Both women and children have lower sweating rates than adult males and, therefore, can be at increased risk. Endurance athletes, such as distance runners, cyclists, triathletes, and those with small body mass and large sodium losses, are also at risk for hyponatremia. Older adults have slower kidney responses to water and can, therefore, also be at higher risk (22).

The body cannot excrete the consumed fluid fast enough to prevent intracellular swelling. Symptoms can include headache, vomiting, swollen hands and feet, restlessness, fatigue, confusion and disorientation, and wheezing. Seizure, coma, respiratory arrest, and death are severe consequences of hyponatremia. Many of these symptoms can easily be mistaken for dehydration, so it is important that individuals experiencing symptoms be evaluated by a qualified health-care professional to determine the correct diagnosis and treatment. Risks can be minimized and most likely avoided if sodium is consumed with beverages during and after exercise. Fluid intake and replacement should not exceed sweat loss replacement recommendations (22).

Weight and Body Composition

GOALS AND STANDARDS

Weight and body composition are topics of great interest to athletes, coaches, and health-care professionals working with athletes. There are a variety of factors that can affect performance, but these two alone cannot solely predict one's optimal performance range. Competitive body weight and relative body fatness is best determined during a healthy, peak performance period. A weight that can be realistically maintained allows for performance improvements, minimizes injury and illness risk, and reduces chronic disease risk factors. Similarly, minimal levels of body fat, estimated at approximately 5% for males and approximately 12% for females, are associated with health. Many studies have published data on sport-specific body composition and Table 14.6 shows examples body fat ranges for various sports. Targets should be determined on an individual basis because optimal body fat ranges may be much higher than estimated minimums or different than the published reference ranges. Due to various sources of measurement error of the different assessment methods, body composition target *ranges* should be recommended rather than a *specific* body fat percentage goal.

TABLE 14.6

Typical Body Composition Ranges by Sport

Male Athletes	
<6% Body Fat (BF)	Middle- and Long-Distance Runners, Bodybuilders
6–15% BF	Basketball Players, Cyclists, Gymnasts, Sprinters, Jumpers, Triathletes, Wrestlers
6–19% BF	Football, Rugby, Ice Hockey, and Field Hockey Players
Female Athletes	
6–15% BF	Bodybuilders, Cyclists, Triathletes, Runners
10–20% BF	Racquetball Players, Skiers, Soccer Players, Swimmers, Tennis and Volleyball Players

Source: Data from reference (5).

ASSESSMENT METHODS

An athlete's speed, endurance, and power can be affected by body *mass*, whereas strength, agility, and appearance are influenced by body *composition*. Depending on which area of training and performance needs improvement, the most appropriate strategy designed to affect the most

TIME OUT
Nutrition and Chronic Training Adaptations

Pathways important to chronic training adaptations are activated during the first few hours of recovery (16). This fact highlights the role nutrition choices can have in promoting optimal outcomes.

relevant variable can be addressed. Body mass is assessed by scale weight as well as body mass index (BMI). BMI is a ratio of body mass to height (BMI = mass [kg]/height^2 [meters]). In large heterogeneous samples, BMI is fairly well correlated with fat mass and percent body fat (23). However, it does not account for varying degrees of fat mass, fat-free mass, and fat distribution, which can be a particular problem in its application to athletes. Therefore, it is suggested that BMI be used in conjunction with other assessments to help set weight loss or weight gain goals (2). Body composition can be measured using several different techniques. Common field methods include skinfold calipers, bioelectrical impedance (BIA), and near-infrared interactance. Skinfold thickness measured by an experienced technician and careful BIA measures can estimate body fat percentage with a 3–4% error range (5). Other techniques, such as plethysmography (e.g., the BOD POD), hydrostatic weighing that uses an underwater weigh tank, or dual-energy x-ray absorptiometry, which uses low-level x-rays, yield a more accurate result, but are not as practical or cost-effective for regular use. Further details on body composition assessment are found in Chapter 3.

STRATEGIES FOR ALTERING BODY MASS AND COMPOSITION

One can reduce body fat or increase total lean body mass in order to proportionally reduce body fat and increase metabolism. After a realistic weight and body composition goal is set, flexible and achievable dietary goals are outlined. Sports Performance Professionals should help athletes plan strategies for dealing with identified barriers and pitfalls to success.

It is important to recognize that low calorie diets will not sustain training or performance. What is preferred is creating a 10–20% deficit of normal intake to help initiate weight loss without feelings of hunger or deprivation. Athletes can substitute lower-fat foods into their diets, reduce energy-dense snacks, and become aware of times where he or she may be eating when not hungry. Dietary fat should not be eliminated or restricted beyond those recommended levels because it is essential for health and ultimately performance. However, those consuming higher fat diets (e.g., >35% fat) should reduce their fat intake to the recommended 20–35% range. Athletes should begin to increase intakes of whole grains and cereals, beans, and legumes and increase fruit and vegetable servings to five or more. It is also important to maintain adequate protein and calcium intakes as well as meeting daily fluid requirements including before, during, and after exercise. Behavioral strategies include not skipping meals, eating 4–6 smaller meals throughout the day to prevent hunger, keeping nutritious foods and snacks available, and not depriving oneself of favorite foods by labeling foods "good" or "bad" (5).

Strategies for increasing lean body mass mimic fat-loss recommendations but do so in a state of positive energy balance (i.e., consuming more calories than needed to maintain current body mass). If the goal is to increase total lean body mass, these strategies also include specific nutrient timing concepts described earlier in this chapter, such as post workout carbohydrate and protein consumption. Meal and snack timing will help put the body in an optimal anabolic state and maintain existing lean body mass. The combination of adequate and appropriate food choices and nutrient timing coupled with expertly designed fitness and exercise programs will provide athletes with optimal results.

SUMMARY

After physical training, nutrition probably has the greatest impact on physical performance. The athlete wanting to optimize exercise and sport performance needs to understand and follow sound nutrition and hydration practices. Sports Performance Professionals working with athletes should be knowledgeable of performance nutrition strategies and be able to educate appropriately on these topics. They should also be aware of national and state regulations and laws governing scope of practice. Ultimately, the synergistic effect of both diet and exercise will best help individuals reach their training potential and desired outcomes.

Carbohydrates are the primary energy source for athletes. Proteins serve as the building blocks of all body tissues, especially lean body mass. Fats are an important dietary component as well, because they help athletes reach their overall energy needs and can be an important fuel source for some forms of exercise. Micronutrient supplementation is generally recommended; however some nutrients need special dietary attention. Vitamins C and D and the minerals iron and calcium can be of particular relevance to the athletic population. Conclusions on antioxidants remain unclear; therefore, one's status and needs should be evaluated on an individual basis.

Athletes who put the latest performance nutrition concepts into practice will have a distinct advantage over their peers and competitors who do not. Both daily energy balance and interday energy balance are important in maintaining desired weight and body composition. Nutrient timing can ensure that proper fuel is available when athletes begin exercise and allow them to work through and finish training sessions intensely. Special attention to post-workout meal and snack timing can facilitate muscle recovery and energy repletion through enhanced nutrient delivery to muscles and the promotion of an anabolic environment. The coupling of adequate carbohydrates and moderate protein intakes with nutrient timing can help stimulate and maximize muscle synthesis. Hydration is an important performance component and sound practices should not be ignored. Athletes should hydrate on a schedule based on recommended guidelines and self-monitor their hydration status. Active individuals as well as Sports Performance Professionals should be aware of the signs and symptoms of dehydration as well as the risk of exertional hyponatremia. Overdrinking water or other hypotonic fluids is the primary cause of exertional hyponatremia and should be avoided.

Body mass and composition are two of many important factors in an athlete's performance. Realistic goals should be set using appropriate standards after conducting accurate and reliable assessments. Changes in body composition can occur safely by using strategies and behaviors that decrease body fat and increase lean body mass.

The quality and overall performance of regular workouts, practices, and competitions greatly depends on how well many of the fueling strategies presented in this chapter are executed. Peak mental and physical performance can be achieved when training adaptations are maximized and the body is fueled and functioning optimally.

REFERENCES

1. Sass C, Eickhoff-Shemek JM, Manore MM et al. Crossing the line: understanding the scope of practice between registered dieticians and health/fitness professionals. *ACSM Health Fitness J* 2007;11(3):12–19.
2. Dunford M. Sports Nutrition: A Practice Manual for Professionals, 4th ed. SCAN dietetic practice group, American Dietetic Association, 2006.
3. Gleeson M, Lancaster GI, Bishop NC. Nutritional strategies to minimize exercise-induced immunosuppression in athletes. *Can J Appl Physiol* 2001;26 (Suppl):s23–35.
4. Wein D. Protein update: how much protein is enough? *NSCA Performance Training J* 2007;6(6):14–6.
5. Position of the American Dietetic Association, Dietitians of Canada, and the American College of Sports Medicine: Nutrition and athletic performance. *J AM Diet Assoc* 2000;100(12):1543–6.
6. Campbell B, Kreider R, Ziegenfuss T et al. International Society of Sports Nutrition position stand: protein and exercise. *J Int Soc Sports Nutr* Sep 2007;4:8.
7. Tipton KD, Elliott TA, Cree MG et al. Stimulation of net muscle protein synthesis by whey protein ingestion before and after exercise. *Am J Physiol Endocrinol Metab* 2007;292:E71–76.
8. Volek JS, Forsythe CE, Kraemer WJ. Nutritional aspects of women strength athletes. *Br J Sports Med* 2006;40:742–8.
9. Maughan RJ. Role of micronutrients in sport and physical activity. *Br Med Bull* 1999;55(3):683–90.
10. Atalay M, Lappalainen J, Sen CK. Dietary antioxidants for the athlete. *Curr Sports Med Rep* 2006;5:182–6.
11. Benardot D. Never Get Hungry, Never Get Thirsty: A Drug-Free Nutritional Strategy for Optimizing Athletic Performance. *Olympic Coach.* 2004;16(4):4–7.
12. Hinton PS, Sanford TC, Davidson MM et al. Nutrient intakes and dietary behaviors of male and female collegiate athletes. *Int J Sport Nutr Exerc Metab* 2004;14:389–405.
13. Deutz RC, Benardot D, Martin DE et al. Relationship between energy deficits and body composition in elite female gymnasts and runners. *Med Sci Sports Exerc* 2000;32(3):659–68.
14. Hawley JA, Tipton KD, Millard-Stafford ML. Promoting training adaptations through nutritional interventions. *J Sports Sci* 2006;24(7):709–21.
15. Ivy J, Portman R. Nutrient Timing. New York: Basic Health; 2004.

16. Houston ME. Gaining weight: the scientific basis of increasing skeletal muscle mass. *Can J Appl Physiol* 1999;24(4):305–16.

17. Cribb PJ, Hayes A. Effects of supplement timing and resistance exercise on skeletal muscle hypertrophy. *Med Sci Sports Exerc* 2006;38(11):1918–25.

18. Churchley EG, Coffey VG, Pedersen DJ et al. Influence of preexercise muscle glycogen content on transcriptional activity of metabolic and myogenic genes in well-trained humans. *J Appl Physiol* 2007;102: 1604–611.

19. Judelson DA, Maresh CM, Anderson JM et al. Hydration and muscular performance. Does fluid balance affect strength, power and high-intensity endurance? *Sports Med* 2007;37(10):907–21.

20. Baker LB, Dougherty KA, Chow M et al. Progressive dehydration causes a progressive decline in basketball skill performance. *Med Sci Sports Exerc* 2007;39(7):1114–23.

21. American College of Sports Medicine, Sawka MN, Burke LM et al. American College of Sports Medicine position stand. Exercise and fluid replacement. *Med Sci Sports Exerc* 2007;39(2):377–90.

22. Casa DJ, Armstrong LE, Hillman SK et al. National Athletic Trainers' Association position statement: fluid replacement for athletes. *J Athl Train* 2000;35(2):212–24.

23. Malina RM. Body composition in athletes: assessment and estimated fatness. *Clin Sports Med* 2007;26: 37–68.

CHAPTER 15

Ergogenic Aids

UPON COMPLETION OF THIS CHAPTER, YOU WILL BE ABLE TO:

Define the term *ergogenic* and common substances used to enhance performance.

Understand basic recommendations for optimizing performance.

Answer questions, handle issues, and dispel myths regarding the relationship of ergogenic aids and successful performance enhancement.

Introduction

Ergogenic Aid
Something that aids (enhances) athletic performance.

The term *ergogenic* literally means work generating. In popular use, the term **ergogenic aid** is something that aids (enhances) athletic performance. There are many ways that athletes attempt to boost their performance and training capacity. Some purported ergogenic aids make sense, and some do not. It can be challenging for athletes, trainers, and coaches to sort out which aids are potentially safe and effective and which are primarily unreasonable marketing hype based on questionable science or pseudoscience. Dr. Ron Maughan, the prolific sport supplements researcher from the United Kingdom, states a reasonable axiom when considering ergogenic aids to improve performance: "If it works, it's probably banned. If it's not banned, it probably doesn't work."

This chapter provides an overview of substances marketed primarily as dietary supplements that are promoted as potential ergogenic aids. The components of these supplements include nutrients, herbs, and various non-nutrient compounds that are involved in metabolism, affect biochemical functions in the body in a potentially beneficial fashion, or both. For in-depth reviews of nutritional, pharmacological, and physiological ergogenic aids, see references 1–6. Also, for a brief assessment of a variety of purported ergogenic aids and related substances, see Appendix D.

An effective physiological, pharmacological, or nutritional ergogenic aid generally enhances the body's ability to perform specific types of biochemical or physiological functions that are highly involved in supporting specific types of sports performance, training adaptations required for the sport, or both. Because ergogenic aids might enhance performance in a wide variety of ways, the assessment of the ergogenic aid's effectiveness and its evaluation of potential risks can be rather complex.

Generalized Concepts Related to Ergogenic Aids

ACUTE EFFECTS ON EXERCISE PERFORMANCE

Some ergogenic aids, like caffeine, can affect mental and physiological functions shortly after ingestion. Similarly, within a few minutes, ingestion of water, carbohydrate, and salt can significantly affect blood levels and muscle function.

CHRONIC EFFECTS ON TRAINING ADAPTATIONS

When taken over a period of weeks in conjunction with training, ergogenic aids like creatine can enhance strength and muscle mass adaptations to certain types of strength training. However, a single, acute ingestion of creatine is unlikely to have any significant effects on exercise performance.

CONDITIONAL ERGOGENIC EFFECTS

The conditions under which an ergogenic aid produces a predictable, beneficial response can be very specific. For example, an ergogenic aid that enhances performance in hot weather may not enhance performance at lower temperatures and vice versa.

CONDITIONAL ERGOLYTIC EFFECTS

Certain ergogenic aids can be beneficial for some, potentially ergolytic (impair performance), or even harmful to health for others. For example, iron supplementation can have ergogenic effects in someone with poor iron status, but could seriously impair performance and health in someone with the genetic condition of hemochromatosis (iron overload predisposition) if their iron stores are already high. Also, the specific type of activity can determine ergogenicity. Carbohydrate loading is proven to enhance endurance performance, but could be ergolytic for short-term, high-intensity sprint performance due to the water weight gain associated with glycogen storage.

SPECIFICITY OF ACTION

Most ergogenic aids enhance only specific types of performance. For example, an ergogenic aid that enhances strength performance may not benefit endurance performance and vice versa.

NUTRITIONAL STATUS DEPENDENT EFFECTS

Nutritional status can be thought of as a specific type of condition that will determine nutrient-related conditional effects. For example, nutrient supplementation generally will enhance performance only in individuals that are deficient in the specific nutrient. Virtually any essential nutrient can be an effective ergogenic aid for someone who is deficient enough in the nutrient to impair biochemical reactions that depend on that nutrient. However, after a deficiency is corrected, consuming more than an adequate intake of that essential nutrient is unlikely to further enhance performance. In fact, intake of a nutrient at an excessively high dosage could become ergolytic and some can even seriously harm health.

The specific amounts of nutrient intake that are considered to be inadequate, adequate, optimal, and excessive are very difficult to define. The physical performance differences between athletes with a nutrient deficiency and those with nutrient adequacy can be very pronounced. However, the performance differences between adequate and optimal intake are likely minor, subtle, or nonexistent for most nutrients. Yet, the difference between winning and losing can be small, so the potential of even a minor benefit to performance is a tempting option for many athletes. Because "optimal" intake is unknown, it is also difficult to determine the point at which a theoretically optimal intake becomes excessive and potentially ergolytic.

NUTRITIONAL STRATEGIES AS ERGOGENIC AIDS

Nutritional planning that matches the demands of a particular sport may be the best ergogenic aid available to athletes. See Chapter 14 for nutritional concepts that help athletes plan proper food and nutrient intake for enhanced performance. Adequate and properly timed intake of water, carbohydrate, protein, and fat is the foundation for meeting the physiological demands of a particular sport.

PROTEIN AND AMINO ACID SUPPLEMENTATION

As mentioned in Chapter 14, adequate consumption of dietary protein is required for many of the training adaptations that take place in the body. Although excessively high-protein intake may be detrimental to training adaptations, athletes involved in heavy training need significantly more protein than the average moderately active individual (7–9). As summarized in Table 15.1, some athletes may need twice as much daily protein as the average individual. Protein recommendations are typically increased by 10% for those consuming vegetarian diets to allow for the lower quality of plant proteins.

TABLE 15.1

Estimated Protein Needs for Various Types of Athletes

Type of Activity and Diet	Daily Protein Intake (g/kg body weight)	Reference
Moderately Active Adults	0.8	(14)
Strength Athletes	1.6–1.7	(15)
Strength Athletes (vegetarian)	1.7–1.8	(15)
Endurance Athletes	1.2–1.4	(15)
Endurance Athletes (vegetarian)	1.3–1.5	(15)
All Exercising Individuals	1.4–2.0	(16)

Specific amino acids and amino acid mixtures are available in various types of sports products (Table 15.2). Athletes have used these products in attempts to boost various types of exercise performance and build body muscle mass; however, research support for ergogenic effects is mixed and rather limited. Besides contributing to protein synthesis, many amino acids have other specific functions in the body.

TABLE 15.2

Essential and Nonessential Amino Acids

Essential Amino Acids	Nonessential Amino Acids
Leucine	Alanine
Isoleucine	Arginine*
Valine	Asparagine
Lysine	Aspartic Acid
Tryptophan	Cysteine*
Threonine	Glutamic Acid
Methionine	Glutamine*
Phenylalanine	Glycine*
Histidine	Proline*
	Serine
	Tyrosine*

*Conditionally indispensable amino acids that are normally synthesized from other amino acids in the body in adequate amounts but can be required in the diet under certain physiological conditions or pathological states.

Arginine supplementation has beneficial clinical applications for individuals compromised by various disease conditions. Arginine is known to enhance the synthesis of growth hormone and insulin, benefit immune regulation, and stimulate dilation of blood vessels via nitric oxide synthesis. Consequently, studies have explored arginine as a potential ergogenic aid for sports. However, the limited research conducted to date does not support effects of arginine supplementation on performance (9). Additional research is warranted and needed to explore the effects of arginine supplementation on specific types of exercise.

Aspartate (aspartic acid) is an amino acid that can contribute to metabolic pathways for energy production (Krebs cycle). It has been tested as an ergogenic aid mainly in the form of potassium magnesium aspartate. Most of the research has been inconclusive, but there may be some benefit for performance of sports that involve high-intensity running or repetitive high-intensity efforts (10).

The branched chain amino acids (BCAAs) of leucine, isoleucine, and valine have the theoretical potential to enhance muscle protein synthesis, support immune function by promoting glutamine production by muscles, and reduce the perception of fatigue (11). Consequently, BCAA supplements have been used widely in sport products. Leucine, in particular, appears to play a role in stimulating muscle protein synthesis and may help to protect muscle protein from catabolism during and after exercise (12). This potential benefit of leucine supplementation may be dependent on an athlete's total protein intake, because their diets already may contain liberal amounts of leucine and the other BCAAs.

BCAA supplementation has been proposed as a potential means to prevent "central fatigue" (the mental sensation of fatigue). The "Central Fatigue Hypothesis" proposes that increased brain levels of the neurotransmitter **serotonin** may cause the sensation of tiredness and fatigue. Serotonin is synthesized in the brain from the essential amino acid tryptophan, so serotonin levels are affected by the amount of tryptophan available in the brain. Tryptophan enters the brain via a transport mechanism that also transports BCAAs. Consequently, BCAA supplementation should increase blood levels of BCAAs, making greater amounts of BCAAs available to bind competitively with the transporter, reducing the capacity for tryptophan transport into the brain, preventing the elevation of serotonin (13).

Serotonin

A neurotransmitter in the modulation of anger, aggression, body temperature, mood, sleep, sexuality, appetite, and metabolism.

Glutamine is another amino acid widely studied for its potential ergogenic effects. Glutamine is not an essential amino acid (not required in the diet) since it can be synthesized from other amino acids in the body. Skeletal muscle and the liver use amino acids from protein catabolism to synthesize glutamine and release it for use elsewhere in the body. Under conditions of infection, stress, and trauma, glutamine can be termed a *conditionally essential amino acid* that can support recovery when consumed in supplemental form (14).

As the major energy source for cells of the immune and gastrointestinal systems, glutamine is used clinically to enhance recovery from conditions that overly challenge these systems. Since rigorous training and competition can stress these same systems, glutamine supplementation of athletes has been studied as a means to help athletes recover from major efforts and to reduce the risk of contracting cold and flu virus infections. In addition to potential immune-enhancing effects, glutamine supplementation theoretically can help prevent muscle protein breakdown. Despite these potential benefits of glutamine supplementation, the current state of research is not conclusively supportive of its use. Simply consuming an adequate amount of dietary protein may be capable of maintaining optimal glutamine levels in the athlete (14). Consequently, athletes with low-protein intakes may be more likely to benefit from glutamine supplementation.

Lysine is the amino acid most likely to be limited in diets that are low in total energy and total protein. The lysine recommended dietary allowance (RDA) for a 70-kg (154-pound) person is 2.7 g/day (7). To obtain this amount of lysine from foods requires eating 150 to 200 kcals of beef, chicken, or fish (about 5 oz). About 400 kcals of milk (about 3.5 cups), yogurt (about 2.5 cups), or tofu (about 2 cups) contain a comparable amount of lysine. However, to obtain the lysine RDA from almonds or most grains would require over 2,000 kcal (about 15 oz of almonds or 35 slices of bread). Vegan vegetarian diets that do not include copious amounts of legumes (beans, peas, lentils, tofu) are likely to contain inadequate lysine. Lysine supplementation that results in total lysine intake above the RDA is unlikely to benefit sports performance. However, chronic lysine deficiency would inhibit normal protein synthesis and certainly impair normal adaptive responses to strength and endurance training and compromise normal function of the immune system (15).

Amino acid mixtures have been used as sports supplements with some benefit demonstrated in very specific conditions. In particular, balanced essential amino acid mixtures consumed after heavy exercise can significantly enhance muscle protein synthesis (16,17). Under some conditions, an essential amino acid mixture may stimulate post-exercise muscle protein synthesis to a greater extent than a comparable amount of a high-quality protein (18).

VITAMINS

Supplementation with most any vitamin is likely to be ergogenic if an individual has inadequate intake of the vitamin. However, studies evaluating ergogenic aspects of supplementation with very high intakes of specific vitamins have yielded conflicting results. What seems to be clear is that those with low-energy intake (for weight loss, low physical activity, or both) are most likely to benefit from vitamin supplementation. It is difficult to meet nutrient needs when limited amounts of foods are consumed. Similarly, extreme dietary patterns can create the need for dietary supplements or fortified foods. For example, a strict vegetarian diet must be supplemented with vitamin B_{12}. Physically active people generally eat greater amounts of food than average to balance greater than average energy expenditure. In the process of eating more food from a varied and balanced diet, they obtain greater amounts of vitamins.

Traditionally, dieticians prefer that vitamins be obtained from a varied and adequate diet because the foods that provide vitamins often contain other beneficial compounds that may not be absolutely essential, but still contribute to health. A Harvard Medical School team writing in the *Journal of the American Medical Association,* however, proposed that there is adequate evidence to conclude that it is prudent for all adults to take vitamin supplements (19).

Although excessive intake of some vitamins can seriously damage health, moderate supplementation is likely safe. A possible exception to this statement is vitamin A. Recent research indicates that excessive intake of vitamin A can lead to reduced bone mineral density and increased fracture risk (20,21). This concern does not apply to the beta-carotene precursor form of vitamin A, but is specifically related to the retinol form commonly used in dietary supplements and fortified foods. The retinol form is usually listed in food or supplement ingredients as retinyl palmitate (vitamin A palmitate) or retinyl acetate (vitamin A acetate).

A dietary supplement that provides 100% of the daily value (DV) for vitamin A (from a retinol form) supplies 5,000 IU of the vitamin. Long-term intakes of 4,500 IU of retinol per day or greater increase the risk of bone loss and eventual bone fractures, thus the vitamin A DV of 5,000 IU or more (as stated on food and supplement labels) is set too high. Currently, the adult RDA for vitamin A is 2,333 IU (700 μg) per day for a woman and 3,000 IU (900 μg) per day for a man. This appears to be the optimal level of vitamin A intake for bone health (20).

Those taking a supplement with 100% of the DV for vitamin A (5,000 IU) may want to reconsider their use of that supplement. This level of supplementation combined with eating foods fortified with vitamin A can place vitamin A intake into a range that could be damaging to bones over time. The safest way to meet vitamin A needs is by eating fruits and vegetables. Since there are studies that did not find this correlation between vitamin A and fracture risk, this relationship remains controversial, but certainly worthy of attention. At this time, moderation in vitamin A intake seems prudent, because there is no theoretical rationale for high dose vitamin A to be ergogenic and bone loss can certainly be ergolytic. Too little vitamin A in the diet also is associated with bone loss.

Vitamin D is another vitamin of current interest in nutrition research. Studies in the elderly are finding poor vitamin D status and supplementation often leads to improved neuromuscular function and a reduced incidence of falling (22,23). Vitamin D status of athletes is not well studied; however, a Finnish study found that military recruits with low vitamin D status were much more likely to suffer from stress fractures during training (24). Studies in the United States are finding low vitamin D status to be rather common among the otherwise healthy population (25). Recently, an international group of top vitamin D researchers expressed the urgent need to adjust vitamin D recommendations to reflect more recent research (26) stating that "Randomized trials using the currently recommended intakes of 400 IU of vitamin D per day have shown no appreciable reduction in fracture risk. In contrast, trials using 700–800 IU of vitamin D per day found less fracture incidence, with and without supplemental calcium." Their editorial continues to point out that to normalize vitamin D status in someone who is clinically deficient in the nutrient requires an intake more like 1,700 IU vitamin D/day (26). The editorial also stresses that the current tolerable upper intake level of 2,000 IU/day is set too low. Risk assessment of vitamin D using current studies suggests that the upper level for vitamin D consumption by adults should be 10,000 IU/day, five times the current upper limit (27).

A relatively inexpensive blood test for serum 25-hydroxyvitamin D levels can identify individuals that may benefit from vitamin D supplementation. Expect to see more research on the potential ergogenic effects of normalizing vitamin D status in athletes. Athletes with darker skin and limited sun exposure are at greatest risk for low vitamin D status.

MINERAL ELEMENTS

Like vitamins, all of the essential mineral elements are needed in reasonable amounts and proportions to support optimal function of the body. Also like vitamins, mineral supplements are not known to be ergogenic unless an individual has a predisposing deficiency of that mineral. Consequently, determining if increased intake of a mineral may be ergogenic for an individual athlete requires proper assessment and identification of the deficient state.

Iron is one of the minerals most likely to be deficient in athletes, especially females. It has long been known that iron deficiency anemia reduces the capacity for physical exertion. There is growing recognition amongst iron researchers that nonanemic iron deficiency also causes reduced performance capacity (28–30) and miscellaneous health problems (31).

Nonanemic iron deficiency (also called functional iron deficiency) represents a state in which iron reserves have been depleted and the body is drawing on limited tissue sources of iron to maintain red blood cell production (32,33). Iron is required as an enzyme cofactor in at least 50 different chemical reactions in the body and it is logical that chronic marginal iron status has the potential to drain iron from selected tissues to maintain more critical red blood cell production. Nonanemic iron deficiency can and does adversely affect many body functions that are not directly related to red blood cell adequacy. Often, these functions are affected before iron deficiency anemia is diagnosed from low hemoglobin and hematocrit measurements (31–33).

Common symptoms related to iron deficiency (with and without anemia) include fatigue, impaired cognitive function, depression, reduced immune function, and poor body temperature regulation (32). Other potential consequences include restless legs syndrome, thinning of hair, deformed nails (spooned or ridged), difficulty swallowing (Plummer-Vinson syndrome), dizziness, cardiac arrhythmia, distorted olfactory sense, disturbed thyroid function, increased insulin sensitivity, arthritis-type symptoms, and more. Even altered drug metabolism can occur. This mainly affects drugs metabolized by the liver cytochrome P450 system. Apparently, the iron-containing cytochrome levels can be compromised (31).

Individuals who are at increased risk for iron deficiency include: women of childbearing age (especially those who donate blood); women during and after pregnancy; women and men consuming vegetarian or near-vegetarian diets; men who donate blood frequently; adolescents and young adults who are still growing; those who exercise heavily; those with internal blood loss related to drug-induced gastritis, ulcer, *Helicobacter pylori* infection, and those with bariatric surgery; and those with colon cancer (28,34,35–37). Iron deficiency can be especially common in female athletes. A Swedish study of 28 elite female soccer players found that 57% had iron deficiency and 29% had iron deficiency anemia (38).

Iron deficiency can creep up on an athlete and even evade detection by standard medical practice that assumes no iron problem exists if blood levels of hemoglobin and hematocrit (measures of red blood cell adequacy) are normal. To detect nonanemic iron deficiency requires measurement of serum iron, transferrin saturation, total iron binding capacity, and serum ferritin.

Sports Performance Professionals are hesitant to recommend iron supplements without adequate assessment of iron status since some people are genetically predisposed to an iron overload condition called hemochromatosis. Also contributing to this reluctance is the theory that iron accumulation in the body is associated with increased risk of chronic diseases. Whether this theory proves correct or not, it should also be recognized that low iron status may contribute to early development of degenerative diseases associated with aging (39). Also, it should be appreciated that individuals carrying the hemochromatosis gene can suffer from iron deficiency if their dietary intake of iron is inadequate.

Zinc, like iron, is an important nutrient that can be inadequate in the diets of those who are attempting to "eat healthy" by consuming a primarily vegetarian diet that is not carefully designed. Zinc is a component of over 100 enzymes in the body and is involved in immune function, protein synthesis, and blood cell production (40–42). Consequently, low zinc intake can have an adverse effect on many body functions. The demands of strenuous exercise training increase zinc loss from the body (43). A 2-hour cycling session resulted in a loss of zinc in sweat in some athletes that was equivalent to almost 10% of the RDA for zinc (about 1 mg). As approximately 40% of the zinc in the typical diet can be absorbed, a 1-mg loss increases zinc needs by about 2 mg. Athletes meeting their calorie needs with a balanced typical diet easily obtain these additional zinc needs. This may not be the case for some types of vegetarian diets (44).

Sodium needs can be substantial for athletes who experience typical sweat losses during training and competition. It is common for athletes to lose 1,500 to 2,000 mg of sodium in sweat during an hour of exercise (9). Currently, the upper limit for sodium established by the Institute of Medicine for the average person is 2,300 mg/day (45). Physically active people can lose this much sodium in sweat in less than two hours of exercise, so this is one recommendation that does not apply to highly active individuals. If an athlete becomes sodium depleted, salt can become an ergogenic aid for that individual until sodium status is normalized.

A deficiency of any essential mineral can impair health and athletic performance. In general, athletes meeting energy needs with a varied and balanced diet will obtain plenty of these minerals. However, those limiting calorie intake or restricting specific food groups are likely to need and benefit from a dietary supplement that provides a balance of essential mineral elements.

Athletes recognize calcium's important role in muscle contraction, nerve impulse conduction, regulation of blood pressure and water balance, immune function, energy and fat metabolism, and nutrient transport. Although calcium serves many functions, one of the most important roles for calcium is bone health. It is noteworthy that calcium deficiencies often parallel low-protein and vitamin D intakes, which also affect bone health. Exercise and physical activity does not increase the requirement for dietary calcium, but electrolyte losses from high sweat rates, exercising in hot conditions, and poor intakes may require special attention on improving food choices and possibly supplementation (46).

When considering bone health and calcium intakes, the female athlete triad is a major concern for active girls and women. This syndrome is the interaction of disordered eating, amenorrhea, and osteoporosis. During training, female athletes who do not meet energy and calcium needs by either intentionally restricting intakes or simply failing to consume enough calories in relation to daily energy outputs, can result in a disruption of normal menstrual cycling and ultimately bone loss. **Amenorrheic athletes** should automatically increase calcium intakes to a minimum of 1,500 mg/day, compared to the standard 1,200 mg/day for adolescents. For most people, 70% of calcium in the diet comes from milk and dairy products (46); however, other options include dark leafy greens, broccoli, soybeans, enriched breads and grains, and calcium-fortified orange juice. Calcium supplementation may be warranted if the athlete's diet excludes these good food sources for the mineral.

Amenorrheic Athletes

Female athletes with the absence of a menstrual period during reproductive ages.

Non-nutrient Ergogenic Aids

There is a multitude of non-nutrient compounds that have been promoted as potential ergogenic aids. Some of these substances are hormone precursors such as DHEA, androstenedione, and 5-hydroxytryptophan. Others are compounds that the human body can produce, such as carnitine, creatine, lipoic acid, and taurine. Similarly, various metabolic intermediates such as aspartate, alpha-ketoglutarate, and pyruvate have been studied. Other substances that affect basic physiology, such as bicarbonates, citrates, phosphates, and glycerol, have interested athletes and researchers. Many herbal sources of pharmacological compounds have been promoted, such as ephedra (source of ephedrine), herbal sources of caffeine, ginseng, and a wide variety of other herbs and their extracts. The numbers of these substances exceed the capacity of this chapter and many of them are summarized briefly in Appendix D. Again, for in-depth reviews of these substances, see references 1–6. Historically, athletes have attempted to enhance performance with a wide variety of legal and illegal means. Some of the most common practices include the use of stimulants, anabolic and anticatabolic agents, and blood doping.

STIMULANTS

Athletes have tried a wide variety of legal and illegal stimulants to obtain potential ergogenic benefits. These have ranged from herbal and synthetic sources of caffeine and ephedrine to controlled drugs such as amphetamines and cocaine. Some of these substances have been used legally by athletes, whereas others are prohibited substances. Because stimulants can affect both physical function and mental state, athletes involved in many different types of sports have attempted to get ergogenic benefits from the use of stimulants.

CAFFEINE

Many consider caffeine to be the most widely used drug in the world. Many athletes consume caffeine daily in coffee, tea, cocoa, and other beverages with added caffeine. Foods such as chocolate and a wide variety of herbal supplements also provide caffeine. Caffeine acts as a stimulant that primarily affects the central nervous system, heart, and skeletal muscles.

Most carefully controlled studies have demonstrated ergogenic effects from caffeine, especially when tested on well-trained athletes performing endurance exercise (over an hour) or high-intensity short-duration exercise lasting approximately 5 minutes. However, there does not appear to be an ergogenic effect on performance of sprint type efforts with durations up to 90 seconds (47).

The most effective ergogenic response has been observed when the dosage of caffeine is approximately 3–6 mg/kg body weight and it is ingested approximately 1 hour before exercise. For a 70-kg person (154 pounds), this dose is equivalent to 210–420 mg of caffeine. To put that into a coffee perspective, as mentioned in Chapter 14, 16 oz of black coffee likely ranges from about 200–350 mg of caffeine. The caffeine content of coffee can vary tremendously depending on the type of coffee, the amount used, and the brewing process. Caffeine doses greater than 6 mg/kg body weight generally show less performance benefit and have more risk of adverse effects (47).

Legal limits for urinary caffeine have been established by the International Olympic Committee (12 mcg caffeine per milliliter) and by the National Collegiate Athletic Association (15 mcg caffeine per milliliter). A 70-kg athlete would likely need to consume more than 9 mg of caffeine per kg body weight an hour prior to exercise to exceed these levels at the time of testing after a 1- to 2-hour event. However, there are no guarantees, because kidney clearance rates vary greatly from one person to another. Also, studies usually have used pure caffeine and it is not known if the body will handle caffeine from natural sources in exactly the same way.

Caffeine sources often hide in the ingredients of herbal products. For example, guarana, maté, and cola nut are all sources of caffeine that can be listed as ingredients using a variety of names.

Potential negative effects of caffeine can vary greatly from one person to another. Possible adverse effects range from the well known insomnia and nervousness to lesser known effects like nausea, rapid heart and breathing rates, convulsions, and diuresis (increased urine production). Other symptoms that have been reported include headaches, anxiety, chest pain, and irregular heart rhythm (48).

TIME OUT
Alternative Names for Some Caffeine-Containing Herbs

Cocoa: cacao, chocola, theobroma, cocoa bean, seed, etc. (Not to be confused with coca, the source of cocaine.)
Cola nut: cola, cola seed, kola nut, guru nut, bissy nut
Guarana: Brazilian cocoa, guarana bread, guarana gum, guarana seed paste, paullina, zoom
Maté: hervea, ilex, Jesuit's Brazil tea, Jesuit's tea, maté folium, Paraguay tea, St. Bartholomew's tea, yerba maté.

Source: Natural Medicines Comprehensive Database.

BANNED STIMULANTS

The World Anti-Doping Agency lists over 50 different stimulants that are prohibited in sports competition. The list includes amphetamines, cocaine, ephedrine, along with less commonly known drugs and substances with similar chemical structures or biological effects (49). Historically, athletes have been known to abuse these illegal stimulants and there is some evidence for possible ergogenic effects. However, many adverse side effects are common, including altered behavior (especially increased aggression), headache, disrupted heart function, and overheating. Several athletes have died while competing in the heat under the influence of amphetamines. One of the earliest amphetamine-related fatalities was Tom Simpson, who died during the 1967 Tour de France. Chronic use of these illegal stimulants can lead to addiction and the problems associated with withdrawal (50).

ANABOLIC AND ANTICATABOLIC SUBSTANCES

For many sports, building muscle mass and strength are major goals. A wide variety of natural and synthetic substances have been tried (both legally and illegally) by athletes to assist the body's natural responses to strength training. Ergogenic aids that encourage strength development usually promote increased muscle mass and sometimes are referred to as hypertrophic compounds. Some of the mechanisms are very direct such as with creatine supplementation that provides muscles with additional high-energy phosphate to promote increased capacity for maximal intensity efforts. Other mechanisms are less direct, primarily focusing on techniques to manipulate anabolic hormone levels in order to speed protein synthesis.

CREATINE SUPPLEMENTATION

Creatine is synthesized naturally in the human body from the amino acids methionine, glycine, and arginine. In resting skeletal muscle, about two thirds of the creatine exists in a phosphorylated form that can rapidly regenerate ATP from ADP to maintain high-intensity muscular efforts for up to about 10 seconds. Supplementation with creatine can increase muscle creatine levels and may enhance certain types of brief high-intensity efforts. When creatine supplementation is combined with a strength training program, it has been shown to increase muscle mass and strength when compared to a placebo treatment in most individuals (51). In this sense, creatine can have an anabolic effect on the body. The typical dosing scheme begins with 5–7 days of supplementation at 20 g/day to rapidly increase muscle creatine. This is then followed by a maintenance phase of 2–5 g/day to sustain maximal muscle creatine levels. Creatine supplementation as part of a strength training program typically causes an initial weight gain of 4–5 pounds that may be due to the osmotic effect of creatine drawing water into muscles along with increased muscle protein synthesis (52).

The maintenance dose of creatine (2–5 g/day) is apparently safe for normal healthy individuals for up to 5 years. However, possible effects of longer chronic use remain unknown. People with kidney problems should use creatine supplements only with medical guidance (48). Consuming creatine supplements in combination with carbohydrates can enhance muscle uptake of creatine and potentially increase muscle levels above that achieved without concurrent carbohydrate consumption (53). Creatine supplementation is under study for several therapeutic uses in various neuromuscular and neurodegenerative diseases and it is now known that creatine plays an essential role in normal brain function (52).

Creatine supplementation is not banned by major sports governing bodies; however, the NCAA rules prohibit institutions from supplying creatine supplements to athletes. Creatine use is widespread in sports and reasonable testing procedures for abnormal levels of this natural compound would be difficult to establish. It has been argued that creatine loading should be considered no different than carbohydrate loading, because creatine is a substance found naturally in animal foods like red meat (54).

ANTICATABOLIC SUBSTANCES

Anticatabolic substances are those thought to reduce muscle protein catabolism (breakdown) by protecting muscle protein and promoting building and maintaining muscle mass. Most of the substances tested for this purpose are amino acids or specific types of proteins. The amino acid glutamine (discussed under Protein and Amino Acids) has been reported to have anticatabolic effects in a variety of medical applications and a limited number of studies on athletes also support the anticatabolic effect of glutamine (55). Further study is required to identify the specific conditions and sports under which glutamine may be beneficial. Doses of glutamine from 5 to 40 g/day appear to be safe for normal healthy individuals, but may not be advisable for those with impaired kidney function (48).

Branched chain amino acids, and leucine in particular, have been shown to have anticatabolic effects that may benefit recovery from exercise and promote muscle mass and strength gains. However, additional research is needed to ascertain if the benefits exceed those obtained with high-quality protein alone (12).

A compound called β-hydroxy-β-methylbutyrate (HMB) has been studied for its anticatabolic effects. It is formed naturally in the body from the metabolism of the amino acid leucine. Supplementation with HMB appears to be safe and can enhance adaptations to strength training programs. In addition, it has been found to contribute to lowering blood pressure and cholesterol (56).

Various protein supplements such as milk protein isolates (whey protein and casein) and soy protein have been studied for anticatabolic effects in athletes. There is growing interest in ways to combine these proteins to optimize their effects. It has been suggested that the more slowly absorbed casein be consumed at night and before training and the rapidly absorbed whey protein be consumed at other times, such as following exercise (55). To date, a protein version of the glycemic index has not been established.

PROHORMONES

A variety of dietary supplements with hormone precursors have been used to promote building of strength and muscle mass. In general, research on these substances has demonstrated a lack of benefit and significant risk potential in young to middle-aged athletes. Dehydroepiandrosterone (DHEA) is produced naturally in the body and can serve as a precursor for androstenedione that, in turn, can be converted into testosterone or estrogens. There is some evidence that older individuals who have low levels of naturally produced DHEA can benefit from DHEA supplementation (57). However, high-serum DHEA levels are associated with various health risks such as cancer (58). Consequently, it is recommended that supplementation with DHEA be conducted under medical supervision. Older athletes are the most likely to benefit from medical use of DHEA supplementation.

Androstenedione, a compound that the body can convert to testosterone or estrogens, has been used widely in an attempt to boost testosterone levels in men. Because androstenedione supplementation in men has been shown to boost estrogen levels more than testosterone levels (59), studies have been conducted with concurrent supplementation with natural compounds thought to inhibit the formation of estrogen from androstenedione to theoretically favor testosterone production. However, a combination of these inhibitors (Tribulis terrestris, chrysin, indole-3-carbinol, and saw palmetto) has failed to enhance testosterone production from androstenedione (60). Due to the apparent lack of potential benefit of these hormone precursors and blockers and the risks inherent in affecting natural hormone production, athletes should avoid the use of these products without careful medical supervision. Also, most of these substances are on the prohibited list of the World Anti-Doping Code (49). Despite all the hype, androstenedione is unlikely to be ergogenic for any athlete in normal health and is clearly not worth its potential downsides.

ANDROGENIC ANABOLIC STEROIDS AND OTHER HORMONES

Androgenic anabolic steroids are drugs designed to mimic the effects of testosterone. These drugs have a long history of abuse by athletes and their use is banned by all major athletic organizations. There is evidence that these drugs can promote the building of muscle mass and strength and loss of body fat. However, these beneficial changes are accomplished at the risk of serious adverse health effects (61,62). Some of these undesirable health effects can persist even after drug withdrawal. Of particular concern, is that the use of androgenic anabolic steroids by adolescents can cause early closure of the growth plates in bones and stunt the development of normal height. For a summary of potential adverse effects of anabolic androgenic steroid use, see Table 15.3.

TABLE 15.3	
Partial Listing of Potential Adverse Effects of Androgenic-Anabolic Steroid Use*	
Men	**Women****
Acne	General development of masculine traits
Increased body hair	Increased facial and body hair
Loss of head hair	Deepening of voice (more like a male's voice)
Gynecomastia (female-like breast/nipple enlargement)	Increased aggressiveness
Irritability	Increased appetite
Aggressive behavior	Acne
Increased or decreased sexual drive	Altered libido
Mood extremes (from well-being to depression)	Loss of head hair
Increased appetite	Alteration in pubic hair growth
Sleeplessness	Fluid retention
Fluid retention	Menstrual irregularities
Testicular shrinkage	Reduction of breast size
Decreased sperm production and infertility	Clitoris enlargement
Prostate gland enlargement	
Increased blood pressure	
Decreased HDL-cholesterol	
Increased LDL-cholesterol	
Stroke	
Impaired glucose tolerance	

*Adverse effects may vary due to individual differences and variation in the doses and types of steroids used.
**Availability of data on females is limited.

BLOOD DOPING

Blood doping (also called blood boosting, blood packing, or induced erythrocythemia) is a practice that can increase maximal oxygen uptake ($\dot{V}O_2$max) and enhance endurance performance. The practice is considered to be unethical and is banned by all major athletic organizations. Blood doping involves removing blood from an athlete and storing the red blood cells in a frozen form until red blood cells (in a saline solution) are infused back into the athlete at a later date. The time span between removal and infusion of the red blood cells allows the athlete to resynthesize their red blood cells back to a normal level so that the infusion results in supraphysiological levels of these oxygen-carrying cells. Because blood removal can temporarily compromise training, athletes also have used transfusions of blood from others such as family members (which carries additional risks) (63).

It also is possible to increase red blood cell numbers by taking the drug erythropoietin (EPO) to stimulate red blood cell production in the body. The resulting increase in red blood cells with this technique is also a form of blood doping, having the same ultimate effect of increasing the total amount of red blood cells (64) and is also banned by all major sporting associations.

There are risks inherent in receiving blood transfusions that include contracting blood-borne diseases and bacterial infections. Risks also are associated with maintaining an artificially high mass of red blood cells (high hematocrit). Blood with a high hematocrit is more viscous, creating greater resistance to blood flow (sluggish blood). This blood flow resistance can increase the risk of a stroke or heart attack (64).

Ethical and Legal Issues with Ergogenic Aids

When deciding to explore the use of a potential ergogenic aid, the athlete is presented with challenging decisions. The first question of most athletes is, "Does it work?" The answer to that question is not always simple and is generally heavily dependent on the type of physical activity that the athlete seeks to enhance and the population the research is based upon. In reality, the first question should be "Is it safe?" The answer to this question is not always simple or obvious and must take into account many individual variables that may determine safety for a given individual. Not of least importance is the question, "Is it legal or ethical?" Again, the answer is not always simple. Even seemingly common herbal products can contain pharmaceutically active compounds that are banned and can result in a positive blood test for the banned substance. An international study that analyzed over 600 nonhormonal nutritional supplements found that approximately 15% of the supplements contained undeclared anabolic androgenic steroids that could trigger a positive doping test. In some countries, 20–25% of the supplements were contaminated (65). Consequently, elite athletes who might qualify for a drug test must be especially careful in their choice of supplements; however, all athletes need to be on notice, as drug testing is moving beyond international and professional competitions and into scholastic arenas. The temptation to use illegal performance enhancing substances is great for many competitive athletes. The governing bodies of various sports are ethically bound to enforce controls on the use of banned substances. Unfortunately, the reputations of many great athletes have been sullied by illegal use of banned substances. For individual sports to maintain their reputations, their governing bodies carry the obligation to establish regulations for banned substance use and to enforce those regulations.

TIME OUT
International Regulations on Banned Substances

World Anti-Doping Agency
www.wada-ama.org
International Association of Athletic Federations
www.iaaf.org/antidopin

SUMMARY

Maximizing one's potential during high-level competition involves exploiting all available resources within known, healthful guidelines. There is no substitute for an appropriate training regime and attitude, nor is there a magic pill that creates a world-class athlete out of anyone. However, when an athlete has obtained all he or she can from food intake, talent, and motivation, specific compounds used in proper dosages, forms, and schedules offer a safe and viable means of maximizing their potential and enhancing results during training and competition. Keep in mind that individual results from the ingestion of similar specific compounds may vary because those results can be related to the physiological and psychological state of the competitive athletes who use them. See Appendix D of this textbook for a summary of common ergogenic aids and an evaluation of their effectiveness.

REFERENCES

1. Williams MH. Nutritional Aspects of Human Physical and Athletic Performance, 2nd ed. Springfield, IL: Thomas; 1985.
2. Bucci L. Nutrients as Ergogenic Aids for Sports and Exercise. Boca Raton: CRC Press; 1993.
3. Spruce N, Titchenal A. An Evaluation of Popular Fitness-Enhancing Supplements, A Fitness Professional's Desk Reference. Strongsville, Ohio: Evergreen Communications; 2001.
4. Antonio J, Stout J. Sports Supplements. Philadelphia: Lippincott Williams & Wilkins; 2001.
5. Wolinsky I, Driskell JA. Nutritional Ergogenic Aids. Boca Raton: CRC Press; 2004.
6. Driskell JA. Sports Nutrition: Fats and Proteins. Boca Raton: CRC Press; 2007.
7. Food and Nutrition Board, Institute of Medicine. Dietary Reference Intakes for Energy, Carbohydrate, Fiber, Fat, Fatty Acids, Cholesterol, Protein, and Amino Acids. Washington, DC: National Academy Press; 2005.
8. Campbell B, Kreider RB, Ziegenfuss T et al. International Society of Sports Nutrition position stand: protein and exercise. J Int Soc Sports Nutr 2007;26:4–8.
9. Guest JE, Lewis NM, Guest JR. Arginine. In Wolinsky I, Driskell JA. Nutritional Ergogenic Aids. Boca Raton: CRC Press; 2004. p 21–35.
10. Kalman DS. Aspartate. In Wolinsky I, Driskell JA. Nutritional Ergogenic Aids. Boca Raton: CRC Press; 2004. p 37–45.
11. Wildman REC. Branched-Chain Amino Acids. In Wolinsky I, Driskell JA. Nutritional Ergogenic Aids. Boca Raton: CRC Press; 2004. p 47–59.
12. Gleeson, M. Branched-Chain Amino Acids. In Driskell JA. Sports Nutrition: Fats and Proteins. Boca Raton: CRC Press; 2007. p 243–59.
13. Newsholme EA, Blomstrand E. Branched-chain amino acids and central fatigue. J Nutr 2006;136:274S–6S.
14. Jonnalagadda SS. Glutamine. In Driskell JA ed. Sports Nutrition: Fats and Proteins. Boca Raton: CRC Press; 2007. p 261–77.
15. Spruce N, Titchenal CA. Lysine. In Wolinsky I, Driskell JA. Nutritional Ergogenic Aids. Boca Raton: CRC Press; 2004. p 171–96.
16. Volpi E, Kobayashi H, Sheffield-Moore M et al. Essential amino acids are primarily responsible for the amino acid stimulation of muscle protein anabolism in healthy elderly adults. Am J Clin Nutr 2003;78:250–8.
17. Spruce N, Titchenal CA. Other Individual Amino Acids. In Driskell JA. Sports Nutrition: Fats and Proteins. Boca Raton: CRC Press; 2007. p 261–77.
18. Borsheim E, Tipton KD, Wolf SE et al. Essential amino acids and muscle protein recovery from resistance exercise. Am J Physiol Endocrinol Metab 2002;283:E648–57.
19. Fletcher RH, Fairfield KM. Vitamins for chronic disease prevention in adults: clinical applications. J Am Med Assoc 2002;287:3127–9.
20. Anderson JJ. Oversupplementation of vitamin A and osteoporotic fractures in the elderly: to supplement or not to supplement with vitamin A. J Bone Miner Res 2002;17:1359–62.
21. Promislow JH, Goodman-Gruen D, Slymen DJ et al. Retinol intake and bone mineral density in the elderly: the Rancho Bernardo Study. J Bone Miner Res 2002;17:1349–58.
22. Dhesi JK, Jackson SH, Bearne LM et al. Vitamin D supplementation improves neuromuscular function in older people who fall. Age Ageing 2004;33:589–95.
23. Pérez-López FR. Vitamin D and its implications for musculoskeletal health in women: an update. Maturitas 2007;58:117–37.
24. Ruohola JP, Laaksi I, Ylikomi T et al. Association between serum 25(OH)D concentrations and bone stress fractures in Finnish young men. J Bone Miner Res 2006;21:1483–8.
25. Binkley N, Novotny R, Krueger D et al. Low vitamin D status despite abundant sun exposure. J Clin Endocrinol Metab 2007;92:2130–5.
26. Vieth R, Bischoff-Ferrari H, Boucher BJ et al. The urgent need to recommend an intake of vitamin D that is effective. Am J Clin Nutr 2007;85:649–50.

27. Hathcock JN, Shao A, Vieth R et al. Risk assessment for vitamin D. *Am J Clin Nutr* 2007;85:6–18.
28. Haas JD. The Effects of Iron Deficiency on Physical Performance. In National Academic Press: Mineral Requirements for Military Personnel: Levels Needed for Cognitive and Physical Performance During Garrison Training. Washington, DC: Committee on Mineral Requirements for Cognitive and Physical Performance of Military Personnel, Committee on Military Nutrition Research; 2006. p 451–70.
29. Hinton PS, Sinclair LM. Iron supplementation maintains ventilatory threshold and improves energetic efficiency in iron-deficient nonanemic athletes. *Eur J Clin Nutr* 2007;61:30–9.
30. Hinton PS, Giordano C, Brownlie T et al. Iron supplementation improves endurance after training in iron-depleted, nonanemic women *J Appl Physiol* 2000;88:1103–11.
31. Kanjaksha G. Nonhaematological effects of iron deficiency—a perspective. *Indian J Med Sci* 2006; 60:30–7.
32. Beard JL, Green W, Miller L et al. Effect of iron-deficiency anemia on hormone levels and thermoregulation during cold exposure. *Am J Physiol Regul Integrative Comp Physiol* 1984;247:R114–9.
33. Hallberg L. Perspectives on nutritional iron deficiency. *Ann Rev Nutr* 2001;21:1–21.
34. Anderson WA, Foresta L. Nutritional Consequences Following Bariatric Surgery. In Farraye FA, Forse RA. Bariatric Surgery. A primer for Your Medical Practice. New Jersey: Slack Incorporated; 2006.
35. Centers for Disease Control. Iron deficiency—United States 1999–2000. *MMWR* 2002;51(40):897–900.
36. Craig WJ. Iron status of vegetarians. *Am J Clin Nutr* 1994;59:1233–7.
37. Marx JJ. Iron deficiency in developed countries: prevalence, influence of lifestyle factors and hazards of prevention. *Eur J Clin Nutr* Aug 1997;51(8):491–4.
38. Landahl G, Adolfsson P, Börjesson M et al. Iron deficiency and anemia: a common problem in female elite soccer players. *Int J Sport Nutr Exerc Metab* 2005;15:689–94.
39. Ames BN. Low micronutrient intake may accelerate the degenerative diseases of aging through allocation of scarce micronutrients by triage. *Proceed Nat Acad Sci* 2006;103:17589–94.
40. Messina M, Messina V. Vegetarian Diets for Athletes. In Messina M, Messina V. The Dietitian's Guide to Vegetarian Diets: Issues and Applications. Gaithersburg, MD: Aspen Publishers; 1996. p 124–35, 354–67.
41. Berning J. The Vegetarian Athlete. In Maughan RJ. Nutrition in Sport. Oxford: Blackwell Science; 2000. p 442–56.
42. Hunt JR. Bioavailability of iron, zinc, and other trace minerals from vegetarian diets. *Am J Clin Nutr* 2003;78:633S–9S.
43. DeRuisseau KC, Cheuvront SN, Haymes EM et al. Sweat iron and zinc losses during prolonged exercise. *Int J Sport Nutr Exerc Metab* 2002;12:428–37.
44. Food and Nutrition Board, Institute of Medicine. Dietary Reference Intakes for Vitamin A, Vitamin K, Arsenic, Boron, Chromium, Copper, Iodine, Iron, Manganese, Molybdenum, Nickel, Silicon, Vanadium, and Zinc. Washington, DC: National Academy Press; 2001.
45. Food and Nutrition Board, Institute of Medicine. Dietary Reference Intakes for Water, Potassium, Sodium, Chloride, and Sulfate. Washington, DC: National Academy Press; 2005.
46. Kunstel K. Calcium requirements for the athlete. *Curr Sports Med Rep* 2005;4:203–6.
47. Spriet LL. Caffeine and performance. *Int J Sport Nutr* 1995;5:S84–S99.
48. Jellin JM, Gregory PJ, Batz F et al. Pharmacist's Letter/Prescriber's Letter Natural Medicines Comprehensive Database, 5ᵗʰ ed. Stockton: Therapeutic Research Faculty; 2003.
49. World Anti-Doping Agency. The World Anti-Doping Code: The 2008 Prohibited List. Available at: http://www.wada-ama.org/rtecontent/document/2008_List_En.pdf (accessed March 20, 2008).
50. Nuzzo NA, Waller DP. Drug Abuse in Athletes. In Thomas JA. Drugs, Athletes, and Physical Performance. New York: Plenum Publishing Corporation; 1988. p 141–67.
51. Branch JD. Effect of creatine supplementation on body composition and performance: a meta-analysis. *Int J Sport Nutr Exerc Metab* 2003;13:198–226.
52. Brosnan JT, Brosnan ME. Creatine: endogenous metabolite, dietary, and therapeutic supplement. *Ann Rev Nutr* 2007;27:241–61.
53. Green AL, Simpson EJ, Littlewood JJ et al. Carbohydrate ingestion augments creatine retention during creatine feeding in humans. *Acta Physiologica Scandinavica* 1996;158:195–202.
54. Kreider RB. Creatine. In Driskell JA. Sports Nutrition: Fats and Proteins. Boca Raton: CRC Press; 2007. p 165–86.
55. Incledon T, Antonio J. The Anticatabolics. In Antonio J, Stout JR. Sports Supplements. Philadelphia: Lippincott Williams & Wilkins; 2001. p 111–36.
56. Nissen SL. β-Hydroxy-β-Methylbutyrate. In Driskell JA. Sports Nutrition: Fats and Proteins. Boca Raton: CRC Press; 2007. p 221–41.
57. Villareal DT, Holloszy JO. DHEA enhances effects of weight training on muscle mass and strength in elderly women and men. *Am J Physiol Endocrinol Metab* 2006;291:E1003–E1008.
58. Johnson MD, Bebb RA, Sirrs SM. Uses of DHEA in aging and other disease states. *Ageing Res Rev* 2002;1:29–41.
59. King DS, Sharp RL, Vukovich MD et al. Effect of oral androstenedione on serum testosterone and adaptations to resistance training in young men: a randomized controlled trial. *J Am Med Assoc* 1999; 281:2020–8.
60. Brown GA, Vukovich M, King DS. Testosterone prohormone supplements. *Med Sci Sports Exerc* 2006;38:1451–61.
61. Bahrke MS, Yesalis CE. Abuse of anabolic androgenic steroids and related substances in sport and exercise. *Curr Opin Pharmacol* 2004;4:614–20.
62. Hartgens F, Kuipers H. Effects of androgenic-anabolic steroids in athletes. *Sports Med* 2004;34:513–54.

63. Spriet LL. Blood Doping and Oxygen Transport. In: Lamb DR, Williams MH. Perspectives in Exercise Science and Sports Medicine, Volume 4: Ergogenics—Enhancement of Performance in Exercise and Sport. Dubuque: Wm. C. Brown Publishers; 1991. p 213–48.

64. Sawka MN, Joyner MJ, Miles DS et al. American College of Sports Medicine position stand. The use of blood doping as an ergogenic aid. *Med Sci Sports Exerc* 1996;28:i–viii.

65. Geyer H, Parr MK, Mareck U et al. Analysis of non-hormonal nutritional supplements for anabolic-androgenic steroids–results of an international study. *Int J Sports Med* 2004;25:124–9.

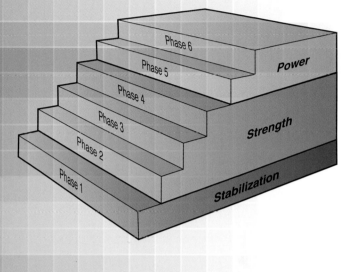

SECTION 7

Sports Psychology

CHAPTER 16

Performance Psychology: Integrating Physical and Mental Training

UPON COMPLETION OF THIS CHAPTER, YOU WILL BE ABLE TO:

Understand the principles and concepts of performance psychology and their importance in achieving athletic excellence.

Understand mental skill strategies and how to apply them into an integrated training program for the athlete.

Introduction

"You cannot know if you will be successful or not. You can only prepare for battle, and it must be done with all of your heart and with all of your consciousness. In that manner, you will have an edge."

— Sun Tzu, The Art of War (translated by Kaufman)

An inner quest of the warrior is to touch excellence, to experience oneself at the highest level. Likewise, athletes can have a similar mission, to achieve the objective, the task at hand, with the highest level of performance excellence. According to Eastern traditions and Zen masters, one of the highest forms of experience is the state "no-mind" (1). In sports, it is often referred to as the Zone. Both refer to the seemingly elusive experience in which all things "click" and the person is free to respond at the highest level. It is that state of effortless action that people report to be the best moments in their lives (2). One of the most challenging aspects of this experience is that it cannot be willed into existence. In fact, the entrance into the "no mind" performance state is often a result of letting go of what has been trained.

Performance Psychology

This chapter will explore mental skill strategies that appropriately trained Sports Performance Professionals can use to integrate mental training within the framework of physical development. These strategies have been linked to increasing the likelihood of performers to experience the state of "no mind." One of the objectives of this chapter is to assist you, the Sports Performance

Professional, in your quest to increase your athlete's performance objectives, especially during the most critical moments in sport and in life.

When the training environment is blended with the consistent will of the athlete to get the most out of oneself and with a Sports Performance Professional that is proficient in the assistance and guidance of the ideal mindset, a synergistic alliance is produced in which the performance sum is far greater than its parts. The questions then are: How can you assist in this process? How can you, while asking the athlete to engage the core or find proprioceptive balance during an exercise, assist the athlete in finding that ideal mindset? What can you possibly say to help the athlete find the strength and balance amid instability, to help the athlete to discover the transference of mental and physical training proficiency into the intensity of competition? How can this aim be achieved in the training environment, which can be riddled with monotony, and can lack the inherent intensity that often comes with competition, opponents, spectators, outcomes, and judges?

To answer such questions, you must first discover how this is achieved in your own life. This begins with a series of probing questions:

- Do I ask the most out of myself on a consistent basis?
- What is my vision, mission, or purpose in my chosen craft?
- Do I understand how to live aligned with my highest self, independent of my surroundings?
- If so, what do I do that allows me to be calm, intense, confident, focused, and fluid in any given moment?
- How can I assist others in training, competing, and living in a way that is aligned with their highest form of themselves?

Prior to reading this chapter you probably already have a working understanding of some of the basic tenets of psychology (the study of the mind and behavior), such as motivation, determination, mood, optimism, and confidence. Through the craft of dynamic physical training, you are in a unique position to apply the science of performance psychology. With proper training in both the theory and application of mental skills training, you would have the opportunity to integrate both physical and mental skill development, and subsequently aid others in their search for athletic excellence.

It is well understood that dynamic physical training that engages the core leads to the development of efficient functional movement (as discussed in Chapter 6) through dynamic exercises that integrate proper physical positioning and proprioceptive balance. Just as we have a physical core that relates to balance and strength, we also have reciprocal balance and strength in the emotional and psychological planes, which is referred to here as the "ideal mindset." During training, you can remind the athlete to engage the core, but how can you also ask the athlete to engage his "psychological core"? Is there a process or protocol that you can incorporate in the training program or a mental skill that can be integrated to assist the athlete in the quest for emotional and psychological balance? As a Sports Performance Professional, you are in a unique position to either teach or support the understanding and practice of psychological balance as well as physical balance. I firmly believe that integrated mental skills and physical core training offers athletes the optimal opportunity to explore, discover, and replicate that ideal performance state. Therefore, it follows that you can deliver a mental training curriculum to increase athletes' ability to achieve such an aim.

USING WHAT'S ALREADY THERE

"The quality of a person's life is in direct proportion to their commitment to excellence, regardless of their chosen field."

—Vince Lombardi

Let's assume that the athlete you are training has achieved a certain level of performance success. We might also assume that your athlete has also, at least once, experienced the "no-mind" state of performance. And by definition, without assumption, each athlete has achieved a personal best (not to be confused with "potential best"). If those assumptions are correct, it then follows that the athlete already possesses the knowledge of how that state-of-being was achieved. This knowledge might not be consciously available (after all, it is invisible) or easily articulated, but with a bit of exploration by the athlete, the process to engage in the ideal mindset can become more familiar. Familiarity with this process could certainly enhance the likelihood of increasing the time spent with one's ideal mindset.

If this line of thought is correct, then the prompting of appropriate questions to reveal how the athlete reached that state-of-being could be one of the most important challenges for the athlete on a given day. Simple, yet challenging questions can be framed as:

- Can you tell me a time when you were on the field (or court, etc.) and you were performing at your highest level?

- Can you think of a time when it all came together for you?
- What do you remember?
- What were your thoughts?
- What were you doing?
- What were you aware of that allowed you to perform at that level?
- What did you do to perform at your highest level?

This inner-work might allow the athlete to better understand that ideal mindset. The recollection of, and subsequent activities that promote this state-of-being (i.e., ideal mindset), are part of an athlete's inner-work that directly relates to the understanding of this ideal mindset. You, as the Sports Performance Professional, can recognize this inner-work as some of the athlete's most challenging work of the day.

Consistent inner-work can assist athletes with developing their own roadmap of successful performance. If you follow this approach, you might be the first person that helps that athlete unlock the hidden potential that lies within the subconscious. Therefore, the answers that are revealed by the athlete might seem simple or obvious. Keep three things in mind:

1. This process allows your athlete to be the expert on his or her own ideal way. This tends to fare well during decisive moments when the athlete is required to rely on personal inner strength and wisdom.
2. This process also allows the athlete to understand the roadmap that works best.
3. The importance of bringing this roadmap to life can increase the chances of the athlete finding and training their own ideal mindset.

Well-designed mental and physical training can develop optimal habits of neuromuscular and motor control. The often-sought goal is to establish highly skilled and proficient patterns of thinking and movement, so that the athlete can have a default pattern (of excellence) during the demands of performance, especially during critical moments. The questions that reveal an athlete's most proficient mental state are similar in structure to physical core stabilization and balance. You can, from time to time, re-engage the athlete's ideal mindset by asking questions that direct focus to the present moment. A present focus on the task at hand has been referred to as a key ingredient in optimal performance (2–4). Questions that guide the athlete toward the present moment, toward activities that the athlete is in control of, and toward harnessing the key ingredients of the optimal mindset can assist in eliminating or reducing mental obstacles, emotional obstacles, or both.

"What can you do right now to be in it?"
"What can you do to increase your physical intensity?"
"What can you do to increase your mental intensity?"
"Can you find a sense of calmness in that intensity?"
"What can you say to yourself right now to generate confidence?"
"What can you focus on to bring out your personal best?"

These questions help to turn the seemingly invisible to be more visible. Such questions that focus on the here and now can also help to reinforce the importance of attending to the process (versus the outcome) of excellence. The shift away from outcome-focused thinking has been linked to peak performance states in sport (5), which is often connected to a sense of being able to perform under pressure (3). Focusing on process-related strengths helps athletes to be relaxed, confident, and empowered (4). Accordingly, this ideal state is a complex recipe of cognitions, emotions, and associated physiological parameters that leads to optimal performance (4). You will be challenged continually to better understand and to create the habit of the ideal mindset or the ideal way of being. These patterns can allow your athletes to function in their most optimal way.

NO MIND AND FLOW

The precise mixture of thoughts, emotions, and behaviors have an individualistic quality to each athlete; however, research has revealed common elements that accompany the ideal performance state, which includes self-efficacy, arousal regulation, positive mood, self-determination, clear goals, internal locus of control, and present-time awareness (2,4,5). In conjunction, identified mental skills that assist in the ideal performance state include process-oriented goal setting, relaxation strategies, imagery, self-talk, mental preparation strategies, present-focus awareness, pre-performance and performance routines, the automation of routines, and simulation training (5).

Csikszentmihalyi (2), a leading expert in **flow** (also known as "the zone"), explains flow as "a state of consciousness where one becomes totally absorbed in what one is doing to the exclusion of all other thoughts and emotions. Flow is about focus. It's a harmonious experience where mind and body are working together effortlessly, leaving the person feeling that something special has just occurred. Flow lifts experience from the ordinary to the optimal, and it is in those moments that we feel truly alive and in tune with what we are doing" (3).

Flow
A state of consciousness where one becomes totally absorbed in what one is doing to the exclusion of all other thoughts and emotions.

Flow is more likely to occur in moments when the demands of the situation are challenging and the athlete perceives his or her skills to be sufficient to meet those demands. Csikszentmihalyi noted that it "tends to occur when a person's skills are fully involved in overcoming a challenge that is just about manageable. Optimal experiences usually involve a fine balance between one's ability to act and the available opportunities for action. If challenges are too high, one gets frustrated, then worried, and eventually anxious" (2). Conversely, if challenges are perceived to be too low, boredom is the likely result. It is when high challenges and high skills are matched that athletes are able to experience flow, the zone, or the no-mind state.

The skill of focus also is integral in the process of the zone. Athletes who are completely absorbed and focused on the task at hand are able to receive unambiguous feedback given by their own body (i.e., when internal physiological feedback is conscious to the athlete as described in the motor learning section of Chapter 2). This absorption in the present moment, with unambiguous feedback, allows for appropriate and skilled adjustment (a relative term) to the demands of the task(s). Csikszentmihalyi explained that there is "no space in consciousness for distracting thoughts, irrelevant feelings. Self-consciousness disappears, yet one feels stronger than usual" (2).

Zen master Takuan Soho explained that the ultimate place for the mind is for it to be clear and flexible like water. The concept of no-mind, which is a trainable skill, allows the person to become absorbed in the demands of the environment. Soho noted, "When no-mind has been well developed, the mind does not stop with one thing nor does it lack any one thing. It is like water overflowing and exists within itself. It appears appropriately when facing a time of need" (1). According to Soho, the state of no-mind is trained through meditation.

Integrated Physical and Mental Training

"You have to train your mind like you train your body."

—Bruce Jenner

The following sections in this chapter will outline mental skills that can assist athletes in performance enhancement. In particular, they include Settling-In, Here; The Winds of Progress; and Fine-Tuning Intensity.

SETTLING-IN, HERE

The mindset of being present (i.e., the letting go of both past and future awareness) is the foundation from which you can help athletes achieve performance excellence. Many have developed the fundamental physical and technical skills needed to perform at the highest level (albeit, a relative term); however, those skills are best revealed when the mind is absorbed in the here and now. The good news is that "settling-in" and becoming more present is a trainable skill. The skill development requires great awareness of the activity of the mind combined with the disciplined skill of directing the mind to the most relevant factors in the here-and-now. Just as Chapter 6 describes how the physical core requires proper functioning to harness the power, speed, and balance of the body, the proper functioning of the mind is a complete absorption in present moment, allowing the athlete the best chance to respond and adjust to the immediate demands of the environment (2). Therefore, the quest for optimal performance is a matter of training the human performance system to adjust, in the most skillful manner, to the immediate demands of the task at hand. With that in mind, the intensity of the technically proficient physical and mental training environment that you choreograph can provide an optimal atmosphere for the athlete (or nonathlete) to discover and train an ideal mindset in the quest of performance excellence.

Attention is fundamental to the execution of skilled motor performance (6). Experts in sport psychology have reported that the ability to focus on task-relevant cues is a necessary ingredient for performance success (3,7,8). According to Nideffer, Farrell, and O'Hara (7), successful performance relies on an individual's ability to adjust attention in response to dynamic environmental demands of the performance situation (7,9). In layman's terms, this skill is often referred to as "being present" or being "focused." You can design training protocols that force the athlete to appropriately shift attention between external (those things in the environment), internal (thoughts, feelings, or internal images), narrow (attending to details), and/or, broad (attending to the big picture) (Fig. 16.1). In regards to sport performance, the more one focuses on the environment, the more slowly time seems to pass. The more one focuses internally, the more quickly time seems to pass (10). You can assist in slowing down the game by training athletes to focus their attention externally during critical and decisive moments in training.

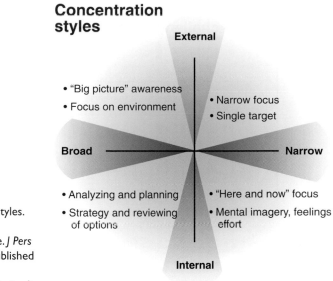

FIGURE 16.1 Concentration styles. (From RM Nideffer et al. Test of attentional and interpersonal style. *J Pers Social Psychol* 1976;34:394–404. Published by the American Psychological Association. Reprinted with permission.)

"Fight or Flight"
A physiological response stating that animals/humans react to threats with a general discharge of the sympathetic nervous system, priming the animal/human for fighting or fleeing.

It is a commonly held belief that increased anxiety leads to attentional narrowing (often referred to as tunnel vision). In other words, the breadth of attention is reduced and distractibility is increased (11), often resulting in an increase in visual search rate (12,13) that may lead to less proficient performance (14–16). As the perception of pressure increases (to the point when the athlete perceives to lack the necessary skills to perform), a cascade of physical and mental occurrences takes place. In short order, the autonomic nervous system activates the sympathetic division, which is responsible for arousal with the release of epinephrine, acetylcholine, norepinephrine, and steroid stress hormones into the body (17). Under this condition, often referred to as **"fight or flight,"** key physiological reactions that take place include muscle tension (bracing), increased respiration rate, and increased heart rate. Muscle tension (or more than normal tension) can affect performance by creating unfamiliar physical movements that may affect timing, rhythm, quickness/power, and pace. Changes in respiration and heart rate can also affect timing in performance as well as increase the rate of energy expenditure (think of an anxious person who finds it hard to catch his breath) (10). Additionally, key concentration reactions take place during the sympathetic activation to include reactions that may be deleterious to performance, such as a narrowed focus of concentration and internally focused attention (toward inner dialog). The narrowing of attention during this state reduces the availability of attending to possibly important peripheral awareness cues. Figure 16.2 explains the physiological and psychological variables that occur during the perception of fear and/or pressure. As the athlete perceives importance in a situation, a cascade of physical, mental, and emotional responses follow. The intended purpose of these responses is to prepare us to respond to the perceived challenge (18). When appraisals of the environmental demands are greater than perceived internal skills, it is reasonable to acknowledge that an emotional response will ensue. The perception of the inability to cope may lead to a less-optimal emotional state and subsequent performance decrements.

Accordingly, the assessment of a situation is then paramount during such situations. The athlete who perceives competence in the ability to perform (e.g., confident) will likely be able to maintain control over physical arousal and mental focus (18). It is also imperative to teach athletes how to manage the effects of anxiety once pressure has been perceived. Later in this chapter is a brief discussion on strategies to manage the "fight-or-flight" condition (e.g., breathing and self-talk).

At this point, however, questions of attention may arise, "How do I know what to focus on?" or "How do I know what to tell my athletes to focus on?" The answer is somewhat simple, yet it can be difficult to put into action. The answers to the above questions are revealed when the performer lets go, and quiets the mind. It is this form of trust that allows the mind and body to integrate into one action. It is this settling-in to the here and now when the automatic habits (the athlete's physiological and psychological default patterns) are revealed in their full potential. True potential is revealed upon the art of effortless concentration. The so-to-speak portal for this form of concentration (i.e., no-mind) occurs through the learning to "see" nonjudgmentally. That is, observe what is happening rather judging the standards of the performance (19). Teaching this concept can be challenging. It first requires that you be able to "see" yourself nonjudgmentally. This can take awhile, but the journey is often fruitful. See Gallwey's "The Inner Game of Tennis," and Lynch's "The Way of the Champion" (19,20) for further reading on this topic.

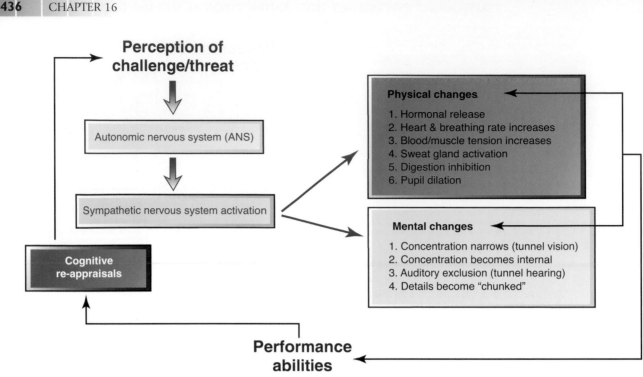

FIGURE 16.2 Response activity from perceived pressure.

THE WINDS OF PROGRESS

"You must have dreams and goals if you are ever going to achieve anything in this world."
—Lou Holtz

Creating a vision is no more than having a clear picture of what one is working toward. Likewise, goal setting is the task of identifying how to achieve the identified vision. In the most basic form, developing a vision uses the art of goal setting and mental imagery. At the most basic level, the goal-setting process helps to clarify both direction and purpose.

The true power of goal setting for athletes is clarifying and anchoring their vision. Stephen Covey (author of *The 7 Habits of Highly Successful People*) used the idea of "start with the end in mind" (21). When taking this approach, athletes can clarify what they are working toward. In my practice, we ask all athletes to think about how they are at their highest self. We ask them to finish this statement in three sentences or less: "In my life, I am on a mission to _____." In an effort to assist in the development of your athlete's vision, this exercise might prove useful.

Effective goal setting has been linked to performance enhancement (22). Operationally defined, a goal "is that which an individual is trying to accomplish; it is the object or aim of an action" (23). Leading researchers have included effective goal setting as a key component of their programs (24). A leading expert in exercise motivation, Annesi, cited behavioral contracts and goal setting as effective strategies to increase exercise retention (Fig. 16.3). He also mentions that within the first 6 months of beginning an exercise program, nearly 50% of all exercisers drop out of participation (25). Other researchers have also cited behavioral contracting as a way to change (or shape) behavior by specifying expectations, responsibilities, and contingencies for behavior. Such contracts should include realistic goals and consequences for not meeting those goals (26). Anshel (26) asserted that such contracting is among the most sophisticated forms of behavior management to promote accountability for a person's actions. Others have noted, "The key to developing personal competence is to be able to identify, set, and attain goals. When individuals can set and attain goals, they are able to gain control over their lives because they feel able to direct their future" (27). Furthermore, the skill of goal setting can provide objective feedback related to performance and skill development (28).

Goal setting can be a tricky strategy to navigate. Let's face it, the goal-setting process can be a bit tedious. It can also be really hard to keep athletes connected to their goal plan. Additionally, popular culture would have you believe that all successful performers set goals, and that if you do not set goals somehow you are "blowin' it." Truth is, the data are mixed on the efficacy of goal setting (5), but consensus holds that goals that are within the performer's control are most useful. When helping athletes set goals, keep the following themes in mind:

1. Write goals down; pick a realistic target date for completion. This helps anchor the process.
2. The goals should identify specific targets and strategies. In other words, what specifically do you want and how do you plan on attaining it?

3. Focus on goals in which performers have 100% control over. That is, focus on process-oriented goals. It is fine to have outcome goals (like winning or making the all-star team), but research suggests that outcome-focused goals may increase anxiety and tension (5).

4. Identify goals that have meaning. Athletes are likely to stay committed to the goals that have personal meaning. During a recent training camp, an NFL Pro-Bowler and soon to be member of the NFL Hall of Fame told me that each year his goal-setting process began with the following phrase at the top of the page: "REFUSE TO BE AVERAGE." He explained to me that this motto was his vision and his personal mission in life.

5. Keep in mind that the process of life is dynamic. If we are to connect with the order of "the way" of the world, then we need to be flexible and dynamic with our goal planning.

6. Use the goal-setting process to identify those things that really get you going. What is it that challenges you? Strive for those accomplishments.

Behavioral contract

My goal is (be specific, realistic, and challenging):

_____

_____

My target time frame for this goal is:

_____

My goal is (be specific, realistic, and challenging):

1. _____

2. _____

3. _____

When I accomplish (smaller goal): _____ I will reward myself with: _____

Activities that support my goal is/are:

1. _____

2. _____

3. _____

This is a challenging goal. Skills that will help me reach this goal (list your inner skills) are:

1. _____

2. _____

3. _____

A few barriers and success-strategies to reaching my goal are:

1. _____

2. _____

3. _____

This contract will be evaluated every: _____

Date: _____

Signed: _____

Signed: _____

FIGURE 16.3   Sample behavior contract.

FINE TUNING INTENSITY

Intensity is one of the most critical factors in the competitive arena. Independent of the technical skill proficiency or confidence, if the athlete is unable to harness the body's intensity, substandard performance is likely to follow. Due to the integrated nature that intensity has on all physiological and psychological systems within the body, the management of such becomes of paramount importance in an effort to reach optimal performance.

You can play a significant role in providing athletes with opportunities to explore how to manage differing levels of physiological intensity. This process is likely to take shape in three phases:

1. help the athlete understand how intensity affects performance;
2. help the athlete identify his/her ideal performance intensity; and
3. assist athletes to understand the unique tools that best harness the intensity of competition.

It might be important to note my use of the phrase "intensity," whereas other authors and researchers might use phrases such as arousal, nervousness, or anxiety. The term *intensity* has a favorable connotation and allows judgment to be removed from the experience. Intensity has three distinct components:

1. physiological activation that includes heart rate, as well as glandular and cortical activity;
2. behavioral responses that include motor activity, coordination, and pace; and
3. cognitive and emotional responses that are exhibited in terms of thought patterns and emotional reactions to environmental evaluations (29). Athletes experience the spectrum of levels of intensity ranging from deep sleep and boredom to extreme fear. The seasoned athlete is aware of being able to find a personal, optimal intensity level. In an effort to raise this awareness, you are encouraged to create training situations in which hyper-intensity might be expected (either by creating intensity through exertion or through the creation of situations that induce hormonal responses to perceived fear or threat).

The relationship between intensity and performance is based on the inverted-U hypothesis (Fig. 16.4) (30). This hypothesis suggests that moderate levels of intensity are best served for motor skills. Different sports require varying degrees of gross and fine motor movement. Those sports that require greater gross motor skills can withstand higher levels of performance intensity. For example, a football lineman would benefit from greater intensity than the rather moderate intensity best served with golfers. Although the intuitive appeal for this construct makes sense for most, recent investigations have failed to support clinical evidence (31). Therefore, the inverted-U model seems to pass the experiential test with most athletes. That is, most athletes understand that they have a unique level of optimal intensity, and that it is their responsibility to manage the intensity prior to and during competition. One of the desired goals of a well-designed and integrated physical and psychological training program is to shift this curve to the right and up so that the athlete can perform at a higher level at increasingly higher intensities.

There are many reasons for athletes to enter the competition with over-intensity. The primary culprit of this experience is often found associated with low self-confidence. Factors that negatively impact confidence include negative self-talk, focusing on the outcome of the performance, misunderstanding the natural body sensations that occur with intensity (i.e., butterflies, sweaty palms, increased heart rate, cotton-mouth), a narrowing of attention on performance mistakes,

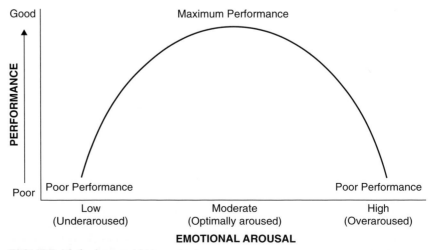

FIGURE 16.4 Inverted-U hypothesis.

fixation with the skill level of the opponent, and/or coaches or parents' perceptions of performance. Although under-intensity is also a concern for both you and the athlete, it is my experience that under-intensity is quite rare in the competitive sports arena and is often a function of boredom, staleness, burnout, or overconfidence.

There are many tools to manage over-intensity, including self-talk, familiarization with the competitive arena, having contingency plans, controlling the controllable, breathing, centering, muscle relaxation, imagery, cue words, pre-performance routines, smiling, laughter, and music (5,29,31). Although each of the above tools has been explored in more extensive presentations, this chapter is best served by examining self-talk, breathing, and imagery.

SELF-TALK

Self-Talk
The inner and outer dialog that forms our thoughts and shared ideas.

Self-talk occurs whenever a person thinks. It is the inner and outer dialog that forms our thoughts and shared ideas. Awareness of self-statements is important in guiding attention into a positive frame of mind. Self-talk can be positive, negative, or neutral that can also be focused on relevant techniques, tasks, or both. One of the best-served utilities of self-talk is to direct the focus of the mind, when in a critical or negative state, toward technical, positive, or neutral thoughts. Part of the zone, or flow, or no-mind experience occurs when the mind is completely absorbed in the present moment and focus. A number of sport psychologists have reported that the ability to focus on task-relevant cues is a necessary ingredient for performance success (3,18). Hence, negative thought, critical thoughts, or both are detractors from the state of flow, and subsequent guidance of self-talk toward the affirming or neutral patterns is well served. Self-talk can also be useful when learning new skills, when focusing attention to the here and now, to enhance self-confidence, and to modify intensity levels toward the optimal.

BREATHING

Possibly one of the simplest, yet most powerful tools that can be used to adjust intensity is breathing (32,33). Breathing is a tool that allows for moderation of heart rate in which a sense of relaxation and calm often follows. In fact, many anxious people demonstrate shallow breathing due to tight chest muscles, whereas deep breathing can provide instant and noticeable calming results (32). Deep rhythmic breathing can replenish the limited oxygen supply, which is often associated with muscular tension and anxiety. Deep breathing can also reduce an athlete's tendency to focus on excessive internal or nonrelevant cues, such as butterflies, negative self-talk, or uncontrollable factors, such as the expectations of others, the opponent, and so on. Ultimately, deep breathing (and other relaxation techniques) can be integrated into athlete's training sessions as a way to find their optimal level of intensity and thereby enhance performance.

IMAGERY

Creating mental images is not a special technique created by sport psychologists. The creation of mental images is an activity that humans do for a multitude of psychological processes. When used properly, however, it can be a very powerful process to enhance athletic performance. Imagery has been found to enhance motivation, confidence, attention and focus, the acquisition of new skills, as a method to reduce competitive anxiety, to psych up for training or competition, and to build competitive plans and strategies (34). Imagery can be external (like watching oneself from a fan's perspective) or internal (as if the person were seeing that activity through his/her own eyes). Additionally, imagery can be visual, auditory, or kinesthetic with kinesthetic imagery being most effective (35). Last, images that involve all five senses are vivid and controllable and are key elements toward effective performance imagery.

Murphy (34) noted two fascinating findings on imagery, emphasizing why this cognitive activity has such an impact on performance. He noted that positron emission tomography scanning and functional magnetic resonance imaging allow researchers to look into the function of the conscious brain. These methods have revealed that when people simply "see" activities taking place in their "mind's eye," the parts of the brain that are responsible for the actual physical movement "light up" (i.e., shows increased activity). When a person imagines a complex movement, the areas that are responsible for motor activity, sensory perception, proprioceptive feedback, and motor control (the cerebral cortex and cerebellum) both activate. The second finding revealed that while athletes at rest were doing imagery of an activity, electrodes placed on various muscles found activation in those muscles. That is, the activity of imagery also activated muscular contraction (just beneath conscious or noticeable thresholds). This finding supports the understanding that when skills are performed, the physical and cognitive pathways become stronger (34). Mental imagery promotes performance enhancement through neurological, cognitive, and muscular activation; all without breaking a sweat.

In a survey of athletes at the Olympic Training Center in Colorado Springs, 90% of athletes and 94% of coaches used imagery in their sport. Imagery was used by 80% of athletes to prepare for an event, by 48% of athletes to deal with correcting technical errors, by 44% of athletes during the skill acquisition phase, and by 20% of athletes every day (36). In addition, 97% of athletes and 100% of coaches believed that imagery enhances performance. With that understanding, it makes sense that your properly designed "performance enhancement" training session would include mental imagery.

SUMMARY

As a Sports Performance Professional, you are in a unique position to facilitate the integration of dynamic physical and mental training. You can assist athletes in understanding their ideal performance state, which can then bring to life the athlete's roadmap or recipe for performance excellence. You have the opportunity to create a training environment that supports the continual search for the optimal mental and physical performance state. The often-sought experience, otherwise known as flow, the zone, or no-mind, might occur more frequently when both you and the athlete consistently train the engagement of mental strategies such as being present, setting and monitoring effective goals, fine tuning intensity, self-talk, breathing, imagery, and self-confidence.

REFERENCES

1. Soho T. The Unfettered Mind: Writings from a Zen Master to a Master Swordsman. Tokyo: Kodansha America, Inc; 2002.
2. Csikszentmihalyi M. The Psychology Engagement with Everyday Life. New York, NY: Basic Books; 1997.
3. Jackson S, Csikszentmihalyi M. Flow in Sports: The Keys to Optimal Experiences and Performances. Champaign, IL: Human Kinetics; 1999.
4. Lynch J. Creative Coaching. Champaign, IL: Human Kinetics; 2001.
5. Hardy L, Jones G, Gould D. Understanding Psychological Preparation for Sport: Theory and Practice of Elite Performers. New York, NY: Wiley and Sons; 1996.
6. Abernethy B. Attention. In Singer RN, Hausenblas HA, Janelle CM. Handbook of Sports Psychology. New York, NY: Wiley & Sons; 2001. p 53–86.
7. Nideffer RM, Farrell J, O'hara J. Leadership in the 21st Century—A Handbook for Closures Managers. New Market, Ontario: Intier Automotive, Inc; 2002.
8. Orlick T. In Pursuit of Excellence: How to Win in Sport and Life Through Mental Training, 2nd ed. Champaign, IL: Leisure Press; 1990.
9. Nideffer RM, Farrell J, O'Hara J. Test of attentional and interpersonal style. *J Pers Social Psychol* 1976;34:394–404.
10. Nideffer RM, Sagal M. Assessment in Sport Psychology. Mogantown, WV: Fitness Information Technologies; 2001.
11. Easterbrook JA. The effect of emotion on cue utilization and the organization of behavior. *Psychol Rev* 1959;86:183–201.
12. Janelle CM, Singer RN, Williams AM. External distraction and attentional narrowing: Visual search evidence. *J Sport Exerc Psychol* 1999;21:70–91.
13. Murray NP, Janelle CM. Anxiety and performance: a visual search examination of the processing efficiency theory. *J Sport Exerc Psychol* 2003;25:171–87.
14. Eysenck M, Calvo M. Anxiety and performance: the processing efficiency theory. *Cogn Emotion* 1992;6:409–34.
15. Janelle CM. Anxiety, arousal and visual attention: a mechanistic account of performance variability. *J Sports Sci* 2002;20:237–51.
16. Taylor JG, Fragopanagos NF. The interaction of attention and emotion. *Neural Networds* 2005;18:353–69.
17. Carlson N. Physiology of Behavior: Structure of the Nervous System, 7th ed. Boston, MA: Allyn and Bacon; 2001.
18. Nideffer RM. Athlete's Guide to Mental Training, 2nd ed. Champaign, IL: Leisure Press; 1985.
19. Gallwey T. The Inner Game of Tennis. New York, NY: Random House, Inc; 1974.
20. Lynch J. The Way of the Champion. North Clarendon, VT: Tuttle Publishing; 2006.
21. Covey SR. The 7 Habits of Highly Effective People. New York, NY: Simon & Schuster; 1989.
22. Gould D. Goal Setting for Peak Performance. In Williams J. Applied Sport Psychology: Personal Growth to Peak Performance. Mountain View, CA: Mayfield; 1998.
23. Weinberg R. Goal Setting in Sport and Exercise: Research into Practice. In VR JL , Brewer B. Exploring Sport and Exercise Psychology, 2nd ed. Washington, DC: American Psychological Association; 2002.
24. Danish S, Nellen V. New roles for sports psychologists: teaching life skills through sport to at-risk youth. *Quest* 1997;49:100–13.
25. Annesi J. Enhancing Motivation: A Guide to Increasing Fitness Center Member Retention. Los Angeles, CA: Fitness Management; 1996.
26. Anshel M. Drug Abuse in Sport: Causes and Cures. In Williams J. Applied Sport Psychology: Personal Growth to Peak Performance, 4th ed. Mountain View, CA: Mayfield; 2001.
27. Danish SJ, Petitpas AJ, Hale BD. A developmental-educational intervention model of sport psychology. *Sport Psychol* 1992;6:403–15.

28. Martin G. Sport Psychology Consulting: Practical Guideline from Behavior Analysis. Winnipeg, Canada: Sport Science Press; 1997.

29. Taylor JG, Wilson GS. Intensity Regulation and Sport Performance. In Van Raalte JL, Brewer BW. Exploring Sport and Exercise Psychology, 2nd ed. Washington, DC: American Psychological Association; 2002.

30. Yerkes RM, Dodson JD. The relation of strength of stimulus to rapidity of habit formation. *J Comp Neurol Psychol* 1908;18:459–82.

31. Le Unes A, Nation J. Sport Psychology, 2nd ed. Chicago, IL: Nelson Hall, Inc; 1996.

32. Balague G. Anxiety: From Pumped to Panicked. In Murphy SM. The Sport Psych Handbook. Champaign, IL: Human Kinetics; 2005. pp. 73–92.

33. Williams JM, Harris DV. Relaxation and Energizing Techniques of Regulation of Arousal. In Williams JM. Applied Sport Psychology: Personal Growth to Peak Performance. Mountain View, CA: Mayfield; 1998.

34. Murphy SM. The Sport Psych Handbook. Champaign, IL: Human Kinetics; 2005.

35. Hardy L. Three myths about applied consultancy work. *J Appl Sport Psychol* 1997;9:277–94.

36. Jowdy DP, Murphy SM, Durtschi S. An Assessment of the Use of Imagery by Elite Athletes: Athlete, Coach, and Psychological Perspectives. Colorado Springs, CO: 1989.

APPENDIX A

Sport-Specific Assessment and Program Strategies

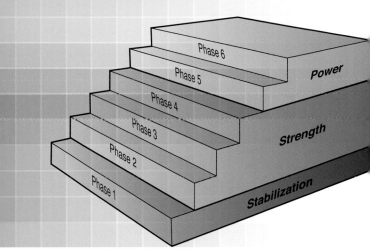

Baseball

Note: For the purposes of this book, the baseball programming will be a methodology shared across pitchers and position players. Although a case can be made for different programming strategies between pitchers and position players, clinical implementation has proven that the same OPT™ program can have tremendous impacts on injury prevention and performance enhancement for both pitchers and position players due to the overall demands of the sport.

DEMANDS OF THE SPORT (1)

GENERAL INFORMATION

- 4.3–4.4 seconds: Sprint time from home plate to first base
- 3.6 seconds or less: Sprint time to steal from first base to second base
- 9 minutes: Average time spent on defense for a half inning

PITCHERS

- Starting Pitcher: 6 1/3 innings pitched per game
- Nine-inning game: A pitcher will go nine innings 15% of all starts
- Average number of pitches per inning: 15
- Average fastball velocity (first inning): 87 mph

CATCHERS

- Total throws: 221
- Throws from standing position: 89
- Throws from knees: 76
- Total sprints: 15 @ 30 yards/2 @ 5 yards
- Total squat movements: 238
- Time on defense: 1 hour 40 minutes 50 seconds per game

SUGGESTED ASSESSMENTS FOR BASEBALL

TRANSITIONAL POSTURAL ASSESSMENTS

- Overhead Squat Test
- Single-leg Squat Test

CARDIORESPIRATORY ASSESSMENT

- Harvard Step Test

POWER ASSESSMENTS

- Double-leg Vertical Jump
- Rotation Medicine Ball Throw (left and right)

SPEED ASSESSMENTS

- Timed: Home-to-First Base
- Timed: Home-to-Second Base
- Timed: Home-to-Third Base
- Timed: Second Base-to-Home
- Timed: First Base-to-Home

AGILITY ASSESSMENT

- LEFT (Lower-Extremity Functional) Test

SPEED ENDURANCE ASSESSMENTS

- 300-yard Shuttle Test
- Timed 1-mile run

STABILIZATION ENDURANCE ASSESSMENT

- Davies Test (15 seconds)

STRENGTH ASSESSMENTS

- Squat (5 Repetition Max)
- Pull-ups

OFF-SEASON GOALS AND CONSIDERATIONS FOR BASEBALL

- Physical and mental reconditioning.
- Correcting impaired movement patterns based on results of transitional postural assessments.
- Improving range of motion, joint stability, and muscle strength and endurance.
- Improving cardiorespiratory endurance (anaerobic/aerobic).
- Improving total body stabilization.
- Improving total body strength.
- Improving total body power.
- Increasing arm and shoulder strength and stability.
- Increase speed, agility, and quickness (position players).
- Determine through assessment, demand of sport analysis, and athlete goals the plan and program that should be created to achieve each.
- Developing a systematic off-season plan that incorporates integrated training, including core training, balance training, plyometric training, speed, agility, and quickness training, integrated resistance training, and cardiorespiratory training combined with a proper nutrition plan to maximize training and recovery.
- Appropriate rest should be given between workouts.
- Developing an off-season training schedule that works backwards from commencement of spring training/season to allow for maximum injury prevention and performance gains without the athlete overtraining.
- Athlete will continue to increase baseball skill activities as the off-season progresses. Therefore, the performance program should be modified appropriately from a volume and exercise standpoint to accommodate these baseball-specific activities to avoid overtraining and maximize results.

SAMPLE OFF-SEASON OPT™ BASEBALL PLAN (OCTOBER–FEBRUARY)

Level	Phase	JAN OFF-Season (4)	FEB OFF-Season (5)	MAR PRE-Season	APR IN-Season	MAY IN-Season	JUN IN-Season	JUL IN-Season	AUG IN-Season	SEP IN-Season	OCT OFF-Season (1)	NOV OFF-Season (2)	DEC OFF-Season (3)
Corrective											X		
Stabilization	1		X									X	
Strength	2		X										X
	3												
	4												
Power	5	X	X										
	6												

SAMPLE OFF-SEASON WEEKLY OPT™ BASEBALL SCHEDULE

Month 1: 3 days/week

	Monday	Tuesday	Wednesday	Thursday	Friday	Saturday	Sunday
OPT™ Phase	Corrective	OFF	Corrective	OFF	Corrective	OFF	OFF

Month 2: 3 days/week

	Monday	Tuesday	Wednesday	Thursday	Friday	Saturday	Sunday
OPT™ Phase	Stabilization Endurance	OFF	Stabilization Endurance	OFF	Stabilization Endurance	OFF	OFF

Month 3: 4 days/week

	Monday	Tuesday	Wednesday	Thursday	Friday	Saturday	Sunday
OPT™ Phase	Strength Endurance		Strength Endurance	OFF	Strength Endurance	OFF	OFF
Other	Conditioning	Conditioning			Conditioning		

Month 4: 5 days/week

	Monday	Tuesday	Wednesday	Thursday	Friday	Saturday	Sunday
OPT™ Phase	Power	OFF	Power	OFF	Power	OFF	OFF
Other		Conditioning		Conditioning			

Month 5: 5 days/week

	Monday	Tuesday	Wednesday	Thursday	Friday	Saturday	Sunday
OPT™ Phase	Strength Endurance		Stabilization Endurance		Power	OFF	OFF
Other		Conditioning		Conditioning			

Conditioning = cardio training and/or sport-specific drills.

SAMPLE OFF-SEASON OPT™ BASEBALL PROGRAMS

CORRECTIVE EXERCISE TRAINING

INHIBIT			Sets	Reps	Time
Foam Roll: Tensor Fascia Latae				1	30 sec
Foam Roll: IT Band				1	30 sec
Foam Roll: Thoracic Spine				1	30 sec
Foam Roll: Lats				1	30 sec
LENGTHEN			**Sets**	**Reps**	**Time**
Gastrocnemius Stretch				1	30 sec
Supine Piriformis Stretch				1	30 sec
Posterior Shoulder Stretch				1	30 sec
Ball Lat Stretch				1	30 sec

ACTIVATE		Sets	Reps	Tempo	Intensity	Rest
Side-lying Hip Abduction		2	10	4/2/1		0 sec
Floor Bridge		2	10	4/2/1		0 sec
Standing Shoulder External Rotation		2	10	4/2/1		0 sec
Ball DB Cobra		2	10	4/2/1		90 sec
INTEGRATE		**Sets**	**Reps**	**Tempo**	**Intensity**	**Rest**
Back	Single-leg Cable Row	2	10	4/2/1	60%	0 sec
Shoulders	Single-leg Shoulder Scaption	2	10	4/2/1	60%	90 sec

PHASE I: STABILIZATION ENDURANCE TRAINING

WARM-UP	Sets	Reps	Time
Foam Roll			
Tensor Fascia Latae		1	30 sec
Piriformis		1	30 sec
Lats		1	30 sec
Static Stretch			
Gastrocnemius Stretch		1	30 sec
Kneeling Hip Flexor Stretch		1	30 sec
Posterior Shoulder Stretch		1	30 sec

CORE & BALANCE	Sets	Reps	Tempo	Rest
Quadruped Arm Opposite Leg Raise on Ball	2	15	4/2/1	0
Floor Bridge	2	15	4/2/1	0
Single-leg Med Ball Lift and Chop	2	15	4/2/1	60 sec
PLYOMETRICS	**Sets**	**Reps**	**Tempo**	**Rest**
Box Jump-up with Stabilization	2	10	Hold Landing	60 sec
SPEED/AGILITY/QUICKNESS	**Sets**	**Reps**	**Distance**	**Rest**
Speed Ladder: Four Exercises	2			60 sec

(continued)						
RESISTANCE		**Sets**	**Reps**	**Tempo**	**Intensity**	**Rest**
Total Body	Step-up, Balance to Overhead Press	2	15	4/2/1	65%	0 sec
Chest	Ball DB Chest Press	2	15	4/2/1	65%	0 sec
Back	Single-leg Cable Row	2	15	4/2/1	65%	0 sec
Shoulders	Single-leg Scaption	2	15	4/2/1	65%	0 sec
Biceps	Optional					
Triceps	Optional					
Legs	Single-leg Romanian Deadlift	2	15	4/2/1	65%	90 sec
COOL DOWN						
Repeat Foam Roll and Static Stretching Exercises from WARM-UP						

PHASE 2: STRENGTH ENDURANCE

WARM-UP		**Sets**	**Reps**	**Time**
Foam Roll				
IT Band			1	30 sec
Thoracic Spine			1	30 sec
Lats			1	30 sec
Static Stretch				
Standing Adductor Stretch			1	30 sec
Standing Psoas Stretch			1	30 sec
Ball Lat Stretch			1	30 sec
CORE & BALANCE		**Sets**	**Reps**	**Tempo**	**Rest**
Cable Rotation		2	10	1/1/1	0 sec
Cable Chop		2	10	1/1/1	0 sec
Single-leg Squat Touchdown		2	10	1/1/1	60 sec
PLYOMETRICS		**Sets**	**Reps**	**Tempo**	**Rest**
Cone Jumps: Site to Site		3	10	Repeating	0 sec
Power Step-ups		3	10	Repeating	60 sec
SPEED/AGILITY/QUICKNESS		**Sets**	**Reps**	**Distance**	**Rest**
Speed Ladder: Six Exercises		2			60 sec
T-Drill		4		10 yd	60 sec
RESISTANCE		**Sets**	**Reps**	**Tempo**	**Intensity**	**Rest**
Total Body	Optional					
Chest	1. Incline DB Press 2. Cable Chest Press	3	8 8	2/0/2 4/2/1	80%	0 sec
Back	1. Seated Lat Pulldown 2. Single-leg Cable Row	3	8 8	2/0/2 4/2/1	80%	0 sec
Shoulders	1. Seated Overhead DB Press 2. Ball Combo II	3	8 8	2/0/2 4/2/1	80%	0 sec
Biceps	Optional					

(continued)

(continued)						
RESISTANCE		**Sets**	**Reps**	**Tempo**	**Intensity**	**Rest**
Triceps	Optional					
Legs	1. Barbell Squats 2. Side Lunge to Balance	3	8 8	2/0/2 4/2/1	80%	60 sec
COOL DOWN						
Foam Roll and Static Stretching						

PHASE 5: POWER TRAINING

WARM-UP	**Sets**	**Reps**	**Time**
Foam Roll			
Tensor Fascia Latae	1		30 sec
Piriformis	1		30 sec
Lats	1		30 sec
Dynamic Warm-up (Some athletes may still require static stretching prior to the Dynamic Warm-up)			
Lateral Tube Walking	1	10	0 sec
Lunge w/ Rotation	1	10	0 sec
Push-up with Rotation	1	10	0 sec
Iron Cross	1	10	0 sec
Russian Twist	1	10	60 sec

CORE, BALANCE, & PLYOMETRICS	**Sets**	**Reps**	**Tempo**	**Rest**
No CORE, BALANCE, & PLYOMETRICS (Incorporated into Dynamic Warm-up and Resistance Training)				

SPEED/AGILITY/QUICKNESS	**Sets**	**Reps**	**Distance**	**Rest**
Speed Ladder: Six Exercises	3			60 sec
300-yd Shuttle	2			2 min

RESISTANCE		**Sets**	**Reps**	**Tempo**	**Intensity**	**Rest**
Total Body	Optional					
Chest	1. Incline DB Press 2. Rotational Chest Pass	3	5 10	Controlled Explosive	85% 2% of BW	2 min
Back	1. Seated Cable Row 2. Soccer Throw	3	5 10	Controlled Explosive	85% 2% of BW	2 min
Shoulders	1. Shoulder Press Machine 2. Overhead Medicine Ball Throw	3	5 10	Controlled Explosive	85% 2% of BW	2 min
Legs	1. Barbell Squat 2. Ice Skater	3	5 10	Controlled Explosive	85% BW	2 min
COOL DOWN						
Foam Roll and Static Stretching						

PRESEASON GOALS AND CONSIDERATIONS FOR BASEBALL

- Correcting impaired movement patterns based on results of preseason assessments.
- Maintain physical health, decrease chance of injury for participation in practice and games, and optimal performance within such activities.
- Maintain range of motion, joint stability, and muscle strength and endurance.
- Maintain cardiorespiratory endurance (anaerobic/aerobic).

- Maintain total body stabilization, strength, and power.
- Maintenance of speed, agility, and quickness (position players).
- Developing a systematic preseason plan that transitions the athlete from performance enhancement to injury prevention and maintenance of off-season gains. This transition should be implemented with the consideration that the athlete's sport participation level is increasing dramatically from what they have become used to in the off-season.
- The proper recovery and reconditioning should be applied during this time of increased activity.
- Consider the exercise volume of injury prevention and performance training based on the athlete's increased activity level.
- Establish with the athlete an in-season strategy and plan that works based on what the athlete needs, wants, and will have the capability to do.

SAMPLE PRESEASON OPT™ BASEBALL PLAN (MARCH)

Level	Phase	JAN OFF-Season	FEB OFF-Season	MAR PRE-Season (1)	APR IN-Season	MAY IN-Season	JUN IN-Season	JUL IN-Season	AUG IN-Season	SEP IN-Season	OCT OFF-Season	NOV OFF-Season	DEC OFF-Season
Corrective				X									
Stabilization	1			X									
Strength	2			X									
	3												
	4												
Power	5												
	6												

SAMPLE PRESEASON WEEKLY OPT™ BASEBALL SCHEDULE

Month 1

	Monday	Tuesday	Wednesday	Thursday	Friday	Saturday	Sunday
OPT™ Phase	Strength Endurance	Corrective	OFF	Stabilization Endurance	Corrective	OFF	OFF
Other	Game	Game	Game		Game	Game	

SAMPLE PRESEASON OPT™ BASEBALL PROGRAMS

CORRECTIVE EXERCISE TRAINING

INHIBIT			Sets	Reps	Time
Foam Roll: Tensor Fascia Latae			1		30 sec
Foam Roll: Piriformis			1		30 sec
Foam Roll: Lat			1		30 sec
LENGTHEN			**Sets**	**Reps**	**Time**
Gastrocnemius Stretch			1		30 sec
Supine Biceps Femoris Stretch			1		30 sec
Standing Pec Stretch			1		30 sec
Ball Lat Stretch			1		30 sec
ACTIVATE	**Sets**	**Reps**	**Tempo**	**Intensity**	**Rest**
Single-leg Calf Raise	2	10	4/2/1		0 sec
Standing Shoulder External Rotation	2	10	4/2/1		0 sec
Ball Combo I	2	10	4/2/1		90 sec

(continued)

(continued)						
INTEGRATE		**Sets**	**Reps**	**Tempo**	**Intensity**	**Rest**
Back	Single-leg, Single-arm Cable Pulldown	2	12	4/2/1	60%	0 sec
Shoulders	Single-leg, Single-arm Scaption	2	12	4/2/1	60%	90 sec

PHASE 1: STABILIZATION ENDURANCE TRAINING

WARM-UP		**Sets**	**Reps**	**Time**
Foam Roll				
Tensor Fascia Latae			1	30 sec
Piriformis			1	30 sec
Lats			1	30 sec
Static Stretch				
Gastrocnemius Stretch			1	30 sec
Supine Biceps Femoris Stretch			1	30 sec
Posterior Shoulder Stretch			1	30 sec

CORE & BALANCE	**Sets**	**Reps**	**Tempo**	**Rest**
Side Iso-Abs with Hip Abduction	2	15	4/2/1	0
Ball Cobra	2	15	4/2/1	0
Single-leg Balance Reach	2	15	4/2/1	60 sec

PLYOMETRICS	**Sets**	**Reps**	**Tempo**	**Rest**
No PLYOMETRICS because of increased activity				

SPEED/AGILITY/QUICKNESS	**Sets**	**Reps**	**Distance**	**Rest**
No SAQ because of on-field drills and conditioning				

RESISTANCE		**Sets**	**Reps**	**Tempo**	**Intensity**	**Rest**
Total Body	Optional					
Chest	Ball Push Up: Hands on Ball	2	15	4/2/1	65%	0 sec
Back	Ball DB Row	2	15	4/2/1	65%	0 sec
Shoulders	Single-leg Scaption	2	15	4/2/1	65%	0 sec
Biceps	Optional					
Triceps	Optional					
Legs	Step-up to Balance: Transverse Plane	2	15	4/2/1	65%	90 sec

COOL DOWN
Repeat Foam Roll and Static Stretching Exercises from WARM-UP

PHASE 2: STRENGTH ENDURANCE

WARM-UP	**Sets**	**Reps**	**Time**
Foam Roll			
Piriformis		1	30 sec
Adductor		1	30 sec
Thoracic Spine		1	30 sec

(continued)

WARM-UP		Sets	Reps	Time
Static Stretch				
Gastrocnemius Stretch		1		30 sec
Standing Adductor Stretch		1		30 sec
Standing Pec Stretch		1		30 sec

CORE & BALANCE		Sets	Reps	Tempo	Rest
Ball Crunch		2	10	1/1/1	0 sec
Back Extension		2	10	1/1/1	0 sec
Step-up to Balance: Transverse plane		2	10	1/1/1	60 sec

PLYOMETRICS		Sets	Reps	Tempo	Rest
No PLYOMETRICS because of increased activity					

SPEED/AGILITY/QUICKNESS		Sets	Reps	Distance	Rest
No SAQ because of on-field drills and conditioning					

RESISTANCE		Sets	Reps	Tempo	Intensity	Rest
Total Body	Optional					
Chest	1. Machine Chest Press 2. Ball Push-up: Hands on Ball	2	12 12	2/0/2 4/2/1	70%	0 sec
Back	1. Seated Cable Row 2. Ball DB Cobra	2	12 12	2/0/2 4/2/1	70%	0 sec
Shoulders	1. Seated DB Scaption 2. Prone Ball Scaption	2	12 12	2/0/2 4/2/1	70%	0 sec
Biceps	Optional					
Triceps	Optional					
Legs	1. Lunge: Sagittal Plane 2. Single-leg Squat	2	12 12	2/0/2 4/2/1	70%	60 sec

COOL DOWN
Foam Roll and Static Stretching

IN-SEASON GOALS AND CONSIDERATIONS FOR BASEBALL

- Perform assessments and testing to ensure program considerations are being made to prevent overuse injuries and maintain performance levels.
- Continued attention to impaired movement patterns with corrective exercise strategies being implemented.
- Maintain range of motion, joint stability, and muscle strength and endurance.
- Maintain cardiorespiratory endurance (anaerobic/aerobic).
- Maintain total body stabilization, strength, and power.
- Maintenance of speed, agility, and quickness (position players).
- Maintain arm and shoulder strength.
- Developing a systematic in-season maintenance plan that allows the athlete to minimize decreases in performance and chance of injury over a long season with repetitive sport movement patters (hitting and throwing).
- Consider the exercise volume of injury prevention and performance training based on the athlete's increased travel and activity level.

• Establish with the athlete a communication process for monitoring in-season maintenance and a plan that works based on what the athlete needs, wants, and will have the capability to do while playing baseball.

IN-SEASON OPT™ BASEBALL PLAN (APRIL–SEPTEMBER)

Level	Phase	JAN OFF-Season	FEB OFF-Season	MAR PRE-Season	APR IN-Season (1)	MAY IN-Season (2)	JUN IN-Season (3)	JUL IN-Season (4)	AUG IN-Season (5)	SEP IN-Season (6)	OCT OFF-Season	NOV OFF-Season	DEC OFF-Season
Corrective					X	X	X	X	X	X			
Stabilization	1				X	X	X	X	X	X			
Strength	2				X	X	X	X	X	X			
	3												
	4												
Power	5												
	6												

SAMPLE IN-SEASON WEEKLY OPT™ BASEBALL SCHEDULE

Any Month

	Monday	Tuesday	Wednesday	Thursday	Friday	Saturday	Sunday
OPT™ Level	Strength Endurance	OFF	Corrective	OFF	Stabilization Endurance	Corrective	OFF
Other	Game	Game	Game		Game	Game	Game

SAMPLE IN-SEASON OPT™ BASEBALL PROGRAMS

CORRECTIVE EXERCISE TRAINING

INHIBIT		Sets	Reps	Time
Foam Roll: Tensor Fascia Latae		1		30 sec
Foam Roll: Piriformis		1		30 sec
Foam Roll: Lats		1		30 sec

LENGTHEN		Sets	Reps	Time
Gastrocnemius Stretch		1		30 sec
Supine Biceps Femoris Stretch		1		30 sec
Standing Pec Stretch		1		30 sec
Ball Lat Stretch		1		30 sec

ACTIVATE	Sets	Reps	Tempo	Intensity	Rest
Single-leg Hip Extension	1	15	4/2/1		0 sec
Ball Bridge	1	15	4/2/1		0 sec
Ball DB Cobra	1	15	4/2/1		90 sec

INTEGRATE		Sets	Reps	Tempo	Intensity	Rest
Total Body	Cable Squat to Row	3	10	4/2/1	60%	0 sec
Total Body	Side Lunge, Curl to Overhead Press: Single-arm	3	10	4/2/1	60%	90 sec

PHASE I: STABILIZATION ENDURANCE TRAINING

WARM-UP			Sets	Reps	Time
Foam Roll					
Tensor Fascia Latae				1	30 sec
Piriformis				1	30 sec
Lats				1	30 sec
Static Stretch					
Gastrocnemius Stretch				1	30 sec
Standing Adductor Stretch				1	30 sec
Standing Pec Stretch				1	30 sec

CORE & BALANCE		Sets	Reps	Tempo	Rest
Side Iso-Ab		2	15	4/2/1	0
Floor Bridge: Single-leg		2	15	4/2/1	0
Single-leg Balance Reach		2	15	4/2/1	60 sec

PLYOMETRICS		Sets	Reps	Tempo	Rest
Multiplanar Hop with Stabilization Box Jump-down		2	10	Hold Landing	60 sec

RESISTANCE		Sets	Reps	Tempo	Intensity	Rest
Total Body	Cable Squat to Row	2	15	4/2/1	65%	0 sec
Chest	Ball Push-up: Hands on Ball	2	15	4/2/1	65%	0 sec
Back	Ball DB Cobra	2	15	4/2/1	65%	0 sec
Shoulders	Single-leg Cable Lift	2	15	4/2/1	65%	0 sec
Biceps	Optional					
Triceps	Optional					
Legs	Step-up to Balance: Frontal Plane	2	15	4/2/1	65%	90 sec

COOL DOWN
Foam Roll and Static Stretching

PHASE 2: STRENGTH ENDURANCE TRAINING

WARM-UP	Sets	Reps	Time
Foam Roll			
Tensor Fascia Latae	1		30 sec
IT Band	1		30 sec
Lats	1		30 sec
Static Stretch			
Gastrocnemius Stretch	1		30 sec
Standing Adductor Stretch	1		30 sec
Standing Pec Stretch	1		30 sec

(continued)

(continued)					
CORE & BALANCE		**Sets**	**Reps**	**Tempo**	**Rest**
Reverse Crunch		3	10	1/1/1	0 sec
Back Extension		3	10	1/1/1	0 sec
Turning Step-up to Balance		3	10	1/1/1	60 sec
PLYOMETRICS		**Sets**	**Reps**	**Tempo**	**Rest**
Front Power Step-up		3	10	Repeating	60 sec
SPEED/AGILITY/QUICKNESS		**Sets**	**Reps**	**Distance**	**Rest**
Speed Ladder: Six Exercises		2			60 sec

RESISTANCE		**Sets**	**Reps**	**Tempo**	**Intensity**	**Rest**
Total Body	Optional					
Chest	1. Incline DB Press 2. Cable Chest Press	2	10 10	2/0/2 4/2/1	75%	0 sec
Back	1. Seated Cable Row 2. Single-leg Straight Arm Pulldown	2	10 10	2/0/2 4/2/1	75%	0 sec
Shoulders	1. Seated DB Scaption 2. Single-leg Cable Lift	2	10 10	2/0/2 4/2/1	75%	0 sec
Biceps	Optional					
Triceps	Optional					
Legs	1. Lunge: Frontal Plane 2. Single-leg Squat Touchdown	2	10 10	2/0/2 4/2/1	75%	60 sec

COOL DOWN
Foam Roll and Static Stretching

Basketball

Note: For the purposes of this book, the basketball programming will be a methodology shared across "bigs" (centers and forwards) and "smalls" (guards). Through years of clinical application of the OPT™ model with basketball players, from youth leagues through the professional association, there has not been a need to treat the athletes differently from a strength and conditioning aspect. At a fundamental level, all positions on the court experience the same movement patterns and energy expenditure demands; therefore, we will focus on how the OPT™ model can be used for all basketball positions alike. If there is an individual need to modify the model based on the athlete's needs, then it is very appropriate to do so based on the assessment process and the goals set for the athlete.

DEMANDS OF THE SPORT

GENERAL INFORMATION (2,3)

- Jumps Classification:
  - Low: A shot or unchallenged rebound.
  - Medium: Most rebounds, defending jump shots, and a jump shot.
  - High: Maximal or near maximal as would occur with a dunk, blocked shot, or a challenged jump shot.
- Jumps in a Game:
  - Low: 30%
  - Medium: 45%
  - High: 25%

- Average number of jumps per game: 70
  - Guards: 55
  - Centers: 83
  - Forward: 72
- Ground reaction forces:
  - Running:
    - Vertical: $3 \times$ Body Weight (BW)
    - Anterior/Posterior: $0.5 \times$ BW
    - Mediolateral: $0.25 \times$ BW
  - Vertical Forces:
    - Starting: $0.8 \times$ BW
    - Lay-up Landing: $8.9 \times$ BW
    - Stopping: $2.7 \times$ BW
    - Cutting: $3.0 \times$ BW
  - Anterior/Posterior Forces:
    - Stopping: $1.3 \times$ BW
  - Mediolateral Direction:
    - Shuffling: $1.4 \times$ BW

ACTIVITY INFORMATION (1)

- Total Game Time (Professional): 48 minutes
  - $4 \times$ 12-minute quarters
  - 15 minute halftime
  - 2 minutes between quarters
- Activity Type
  - Walking or Standing: 4 minutes
  - Jogging: 4 minutes
  - Running: 4 minutes
  - Sprinting: 3 minutes
  - Shuffling (low to medium intensity): 9 minutes
  - Shuffling (high intensity): 2 minutes
  - Jumping: 41 seconds
- Movement
  - While ball is in play, a change in movement category happens every 2 seconds.
  - There were 1,000 different movements during a game.
  - 28% of all court time was spent in strenuous exertion.
  - Intense activity happened for 13–14 seconds at a time.
  - 105 intense activities per game, every 21 seconds
  - 31% of the game is devoted to side-to-side movements (66% of these movements are intense efforts).
  - Individual shuffle movements are 1–4 seconds in duration.
  - Sprints are 1–5 seconds in duration.

SUGGESTED ASSESSMENTS FOR BASKETBALL

TRANSITIONAL POSTURAL ASSESSMENTS

- Overhead Squat Test
- Single-leg Squat Test

CARDIORESPIRARORY ASSESSMENTS

- Harvard Step Test

POWER ASSESSMENTS

- Double-leg Vertical Jump
- Single-leg Vertical Jump
- Vertical Jump (15 foot approach, single-leg or two-legs)
- Shark Skill Test

SPEED ASSESSMENTS

- $^{3}/_{4}$ Court Sprint (Baseline to farthest free throw line)

AGILITY ASSESSMENTS

- LEFT (Lower-Extremity Functional) Test
- Pro-Lane Agility Drill

CORE STABILITY ASSESSMENTS

- Davies Test (15 seconds)

STRENGTH ASSESSMENTS

- 185 lb. Bench Press

OFF-SEASON GOALS AND CONSIDERATIONS FOR BASKETBALL

- Physical and mental reconditioning.
- Correcting impaired movement patterns and muscle imbalances based on results of transitional postural assessments.
- Improving range of motion, joint stability, and muscle strength and endurance.
  - Typical areas of focus for enhanced flexibility or range of motion include: ankle dorsiflexion, hip internal rotation, rectus femoris, and lats.
  - Typical areas of focus for enhanced strengthening include: gluteus medius, pectineus, gluteus maximus, posterior tibialis, medial gastrocnemius, and core musculature.
- Improving cardiorespiratory endurance (anaerobic/aerobic).
- Improving total body stabilization.
- Improving total body strength.
- Improving total body power.
- Increase reaction time, speed, agility, and quickness
- Determine through assessment, demand of sport analysis, and athlete goal the plan and program that should be created to achieve each.
- Developing a systematic off-season plan that incorporates integrated training including core training, balance training, power training, speed, agility, and quickness training, integrated resistance training, and cardiorespiratory training combined with a proper nutrition plan to maximize training and recovery.
- Appropriate rest should be given between workouts.
- Developing an off-season training schedule that works backward from commencement of the preseason to allow for maximum injury prevention and performance gains without the athlete overtraining.
- Consider that conditioning for basketball should be as similar to the game as possible.
- Consider that although the sport of basketball is a very dynamic activity, many basketball players enter the off-season having diminished stabilization mechanisms that must be trained and reconditioned.
- Athletes will continue to increase basketball skill activities as the off-season progresses. Therefore, an athlete's performance program should be modified appropriately from a volume and exercise standpoint to accommodate these specific activities to avoid overtraining and maximize results.

SAMPLE OFF-SEASON OPT™ BASKETBALL PLAN (MAY–SEPTEMBER)

Level	Phase	JAN IN-Season	FEB IN-Season	MAR IN-Season	APR IN-Season	MAY OFF-Season (1)	JUN OFF-Season (2)	JUL OFF-Season (3)	AUG OFF-Season (4)	SEP OFF-Season (5)	OCT PRE-Season	NOV IN-Season	DEC IN-Season
Corrective						X							
Stabilization	1						X			X			
Strength	2							X		X			
	3												
	4												
Power	5								X	X			
	6												

SAMPLE OFF-SEASON WEEKLY OPT™ BASKETBALL SCHEDULE

Month 1: 3 days/week

	Monday	Tuesday	Wednesday	Thursday	Friday	Saturday	Sunday
OPT™ Phase	Corrective	OFF	Corrective	OFF	Corrective	OFF	OFF

Month 2: 3 days/week

	Monday	Tuesday	Wednesday	Thursday	Friday	Saturday	Sunday
OPT™ Phase	Stabilization Endurance	OFF	Stabilization Endurance	OFF	Stabilization Endurance	OFF	OFF
Other	On-court Conditioning				On-court Conditioning		

Month 3: 5 days/week

	Monday	Tuesday	Wednesday	Thursday	Friday	Saturday	Sunday
OPT™ Phase	Strength Endurance TOTAL BODY	OFF	Strength Endurance UPPER BODY	OFF	Strength Endurance LOWER BODY	OFF	OFF
Other		On-court Conditioning		On-court Conditioning			

Month 4: 5 days/week

	Monday	Tuesday	Wednesday	Thursday	Friday	Saturday	Sunday
OPT™ Phase	Power	OFF	Power	OFF	Power	OFF	OFF
Other	On-court Conditioning	On-court Conditioning		On-court Conditioning			

Month 5: 5 days/week

	Monday	Tuesday	Wednesday	Thursday	Friday	Saturday	Sunday
OPT™ Phase	Strength Endurance		Stabilization Endurance		Power	OFF	OFF
Other		On-court Conditioning		On-court Conditioning			

SAMPLE OFF-SEASON OPT™ BASKETBALL PROGRAMS

CORRECTIVE EXERCISE TRAINING

INHIBIT		Sets	Reps	Time
Foam Roll: Calves		1		30 sec
Foam Roll: IT Band		1		30 sec
Foam Roll: Tensor Fascia Latae		1		30 sec
LENGTHEN		**Sets**	**Reps**	**Time**
Gastrocnemius Stretch		1		30 sec
Soleus Stretch		1		30 sec
Supine Biceps Femoris Stretch		1		30 sec

ACTIVATE	Sets	Reps	Tempo	Intensity	Rest
Posterior Tibialis Strengthening	2	12	4/2/1		0 sec
Single-leg Calf Raise	2	12	4/2/1		0 sec
Single-leg Hip Adduction: Pectineus	2	12	4/2/1		0 sec
Single-leg Hip Abduction: Gluteus Medius	2	12	4/2/1		90 sec
INTEGRATE	**Sets**	**Reps**	**Tempo**	**Intensity**	**Rest**
Total Body — Step-up, Balance to Overhead Press	2	12	4/2/1	60%	90 sec

PHASE 1: STABILIZATION ENDURANCE TRAINING

WARM-UP		Sets	Reps	Time
Foam Roll				
Tensor Fascia Latae		1		30 sec
Piriformis		1		30 sec
Static Stretch				
Gastrocnemius Stretch		1		30 sec
Kneeling Hip Flexor Stretch		1		30 sec
Standing Biceps Femoris Stretch		1		30 sec

CORE & BALANCE	Sets	Reps	Tempo	Rest
Side Iso-Ab	2	15	4/2/1	0
Floor Bridge	2	15	4/2/1	0
Single-leg Balance Reach	2	15	4/2/1	60 sec
PLYOMETRICS	**Sets**	**Reps**	**Tempo**	**Rest**
Box Jump-down with Stabilization	2	8	Hold Landing	60 sec
SPEED/AGILITY/QUICKNESS	**Sets**	**Reps**	**Distance**	**Rest**
Speed Ladder: Six Exercises	2			60 sec

(continued)						
RESISTANCE		**Sets**	**Reps**	**Tempo**	**Intensity**	**Rest**
Total Body	Step-up, Balance to Overhead Press: Sagittal Plane	2	15	4/2/1	65%	0 sec
Chest	Cable Chest Press	2	15	4/2/1	65%	0 sec
Back	Single-leg Cable Row	2	15	4/2/1	65%	0 sec
Shoulders	Single-leg Lateral Raise	2	15	4/2/1	65%	0 sec
Biceps	Optional					
Triceps	Optional					
Legs	Single-leg Romanian Deadlift	2	15	4/2/1	65%	90 sec
COOL DOWN						
Repeat Foam Roll and Static Stretching Exercises from WARM-UP						

PHASE 2: STRENGTH ENDURANCE TRAINING

WARM-UP	**Sets**	**Reps**	**Time**
Foam Roll			
IT Band		1	30 sec
Piriformis		1	30 sec
Calf		1	30 sec
Static Stretch			
Standing Adductor Stretch		1	30 sec
Standing Hip Flexor Stretch		1	30 sec
Ball Lat Stretch		1	30 sec

CORE & BALANCE	**Sets**	**Reps**	**Tempo**	**Rest**
Knee-ups	2	12	1/1/1	0 sec
Back Extension	2	12	1/1/1	0 sec
Single-leg Squat Touchdown	2	12	1/1/1	60 sec

PLYOMETRICS	**Sets**	**Reps**	**Tempo**	**Rest**
Power Step-ups	2	8	Repeating	0 sec
Butt Kicks	2	8	Repeating	60 sec

SPEED/AGILITY/QUICKNESS	**Sets**	**Reps**	**Distance**	**Rest**
Speed Ladder: Six Exercises	2			60 sec
Box Drill	6			30 sec
LEFT Test	2			60 sec

(continued)

(continued)						
RESISTANCE		**Sets**	**Reps**	**Tempo**	**Intensity**	**Rest**
Total Body	Optional					
Chest	1. Bench Press 2. Cable Chest Press	2	10 10	2/0/2 4/2/1	75%	0 sec
Back	1. Seated Lat Pulldown 2. Standing Cable Row: Alternate-arm	2	10 10	2/0/2 4/2/1	75%	0 sec
Shoulders	1. Standing Lateral Raise 2. Single-leg DB Press	2	10 10	2/0/2 4/2/1	75%	0 sec
Biceps	Optional					
Triceps	Optional					
Legs	1. Lunge: Frontal Plane 2. Step-up to Balance	2	10 10	2/0/2 4/2/1	75%	60 sec
COOL DOWN						
Foam Roll and Static Stretching						

PHASE 5: POWER TRAINING

WARM-UP	**Sets**	**Reps**	**Time**
Foam Roll			
Calf	1		30 sec
Tensor Fasciae Latae	1		30 sec
Piriformis	1		30 sec
Dynamic Warm-up (Some athletes may still require static stretching prior to the Dynamic Warm-up)			
Lateral Tube Walking	1	10	0 sec
Prisoner Squats	1	10	0 sec
Multiplanar Lunge	1	10	0 sec
Leg Swings: Front to Back	1	10	0 sec
Leg Swings: Side to Side	1	10	0 sec
Medicine Ball Rotations	1	10	0 sec
Russian Twist	1	10	0 sec
Multiplanar Hop to Stabilization	1	10	60 sec
CORE, BALANCE, & PLYOMETRICS	**Sets**	**Reps**	**Tempo**	**Rest**
No CORE, BALANCE, & PLYOMETRICS (Incorporated into Dynamic Warm-up)				
SPEED/AGILITY/QUICKNESS	**Sets**	**Reps**	**Distance**	**Rest**
Speed Ladder: Eight Exercises	1			60 sec
Box Drill	4			15 sec
T-Drill	4			25 sec
Shuttle: Six lengths of basketball court	2			60 sec

(continued)						
RESISTANCE		**Sets**	**Reps**	**Tempo**	**Intensity**	**Rest**
Total Body	1. DB Squat, Curl, to Overhead Press 2. DB Snatch	3	5 10	Controlled Explosive	85% 45%	2 min
Chest	1. DB Chest Press 2. Medicine Ball Chest Pass	3	5 10	Controlled Explosive	85% 2% of BW	2 min
Back	1. Seated Cable Row 2. Soccer Throw	3	5 10	Controlled Explosive	85% 2% of BW	2 min
Shoulders	Incorporated in Total Body Exercises					
Legs	1. Barbell Squat 2. Squat Jump	3	5 10	Controlled Explosive	85% of BW	2 min
COOL DOWN						
Foam Roll and Static Stretching						

PRESEASON GOALS AND CONSIDERATIONS FOR BASKETBALL

- Correcting impaired movement patterns based on results of preseason assessments.
- Maintain physical health, and decrease the chance of injury for participation in practice and games and optimal performance within such activities.
- Maintain range of motion, joint stability, and muscle strength and endurance.
- Maintain cardiorespiratory endurance (anaerobic/aerobic).
- Maintain total body stabilization, strength, and power.
- Maintenance of speed, agility, and quickness.
- Developing a systematic preseason plan that transitions the athlete from performance enhancement to injury prevention and maintenance of off-season gains. This transition should be implemented with the consideration that the athlete's sport participation level is increasing dramatically from what they have become used to in the off-season.
- The proper recovery and reconditioning should be applied during this time of increased activity.
- Consider the exercise volume of injury prevention and performance training based on the athlete's increased activity level.
- Establish with the athlete an in-season strategy and plan that works based on what the athlete needs, wants, and will have the capability to do.

PRESEASON OPT™ BASKETBALL PLAN (OCTOBER)

Level	Phase	JAN IN-Season	FEB IN-Season	MAR IN-Season	APR IN-Season	MAY OFF-Season	JUN OFF-Season	JUL OFF-Season	AUG OFF-Season	SEP OFF-Season	OCT PRE-Season (1)	NOV IN-Season	DEC IN-Season
Corrective											X		
Stabilization	1										X		
Strength	2										X		
	3												
	4												
Power	5												
	6												

IN-SEASON GOALS AND CONSIDERATIONS FOR BASKETBALL

- Perform assessments and testing to ensure program considerations are being made to prevent overuse injuries and maintain performance levels.
- Continued attention to impaired movement patterns with corrective strategies being implemented.
- Maintain range of motion, joint stability, and muscle strength and endurance.
- Maintain cardiorespiratory endurance (anaerobic/aerobic).
- Maintain total body stabilization, strength, and power.
- Maintenance of speed, agility, and quickness.
- Consider additional conditioning for athletes who may not get the same type of on the court minutes during games than others.
- For athletes who may get limited to no playing time during games, consider progressing athletes to the strength and power phases of the OPT™ model to offset the lack of on-court power/explosive movements that they are missing due to lack of playing time.
- Develope a systematic in-season maintenance plan that allows the athlete to minimize decreases in performance and chance of injury over a long season with repetitive sport movement patterns.
- It is important to assess coaching styles and their practice routines and adjust your workouts accordingly in-season. Making adjustments to avoid over- and undertraining is important.
- Consider the exercise volume of injury prevention and performance training based on the athlete's increased travel and activity level.
- Establish with the athlete a communication process for monitoring in-season maintenance and a plan that works based on what the athlete needs, wants, and will have the capability to do, while focusing on playing basketball.

IN-SEASON OPT™ BASKETBALL PLAN (NOVEMBER–APRIL)

Level	Phase	JAN IN-Season (3)	FEB IN-Season (4)	MAR IN-Season (5)	APR IN-Season (6)	MAY OFF-Season	JUN OFF-Season	JUL OFF-Season	AUG OFF-Season	SEP OFF-Season	OCT PRE-Season	NOV IN-Season (1)	DEC IN-Season (2)
Corrective		X	X	X	X							X	X
Stabilization	1	X	X	X	X							X	X
Strength	2	X	X	X	X							X	X
	3												
	4												
Power	5												
	6												

SAMPLE IN-SEASON WEEKLY OPT™ BASKETBALL SCHEDULE

Any Month

	Monday	Tuesday	Wednesday	Thursday	Friday	Saturday	Sunday
OPT™ Level	Strength Endurance UPPER BODY	OFF	Corrective	Corrective	Stabilization Endurance	OFF	Corrective
Other	Game			Game		Game	

SAMPLE IN-SEASON OPT™ BASKETBALL PROGRAMS

CORRECTIVE EXERCISE TRAINING

INHIBIT		Sets	Reps	Time
Foam Roll: Tensor Fascia Latae		1		30 sec
Foam Roll: Piriformis		1		30 sec
Foam Roll: Lats		1		30 sec
LENGTHEN		**Sets**	**Reps**	**Time**
Gastrocnemius Stretch		1		30 sec
Standing Biceps Femoris Stretch		1		30 sec
Kneeling Hip Flexor Stretch		1		30 sec
Ball Lat Stretch		1		30 sec

ACTIVATE	Sets	Reps	Tempo	Intensity	Rest
Single-leg Calf Raise	1	15	4/2/1		0 sec
Single-leg Hip Extension	1	15	4/2/1		0 sec
Ball Bridge	1	15	4/2/1		90 sec
INTEGRATE	**Sets**	**Reps**	**Tempo**	**Intensity**	**Rest**
Total Body Cable Squat to Row	3	10	4/2/1	60%	90 sec

PHASE 1: STABILIZATION ENDURANCE TRAINING

WARM-UP		Sets	Reps	Time
Foam Roll				
Tensor Fascia Latae		1		30 sec
Piriformis		1		30 sec
IT Band		1		30 sec
Static Stretch				
Gastrocnemius Stretch		1		30 sec
Standing Biceps Femoris Stretch		1		30 sec
Kneeling Hip Flexor Stretch		1		30 sec
Supine Piriformis Stretch		1		30 sec

CORE & BALANCE	Sets	Reps	Tempo	Rest
Side Iso-Abs	3	12	4/2/1	0
Floor Cobra	3	12	4/2/1	0
Single-leg Lift and Chop	3	12	4/2/1	60 sec
PLYOMETRICS	**Sets**	**Reps**	**Tempo**	**Rest**
No PLYOMETRICS because of increased activity				

SPEED/AGILITY/QUICKNESS	Sets	Reps	Distance	Rest
No SAQ because of on-court drills and conditioning				

(continued)

(continued)						
RESISTANCE		**Sets**	**Reps**	**Tempo**	**Intensity**	**Rest**
Total Body	Cable Squat to Row	3	12	4/2/1	70%	0 sec
Chest	Ball DB Chest Press: Alternate-arm	3	12	4/2/1	70%	0 sec
Back	Incorporated in Total Body Exercise					
Shoulders	Single-leg Overhead DB Press	3	12	4/2/1	70%	0 sec
Biceps	Optional					
Triceps	Optional					
Legs	Lunge to Balance: Frontal Plane	3	12	4/2/1	70%	60 sec
COOL DOWN						
Repeat Foam Roll and Static Stretching Exercises from WARM-UP						

PHASE 2: STRENGTH ENDURANCE TRAINING (UPPER BODY)

WARM-UP		**Sets**	**Reps**	**Time**
Foam Roll				
Piriformis			1	30 sec
Adductor			1	30 sec
Thoracic Spine			1	30 sec
Static Stretch				
Gastrocnemius Stretch			1	30 sec
Standing Adductor Stretch			1	30 sec
Standing Pec Stretch			1	30 sec

CORE & BALANCE		**Sets**	**Reps**	**Tempo**	**Rest**
Cable Chop		3	10	1/1/1	0 sec
Single-leg Squat		3	10	1/1/1	60 sec

PLYOMETRICS		**Sets**	**Reps**	**Tempo**	**Rest**
No PLYOMETRICS because of increased activity					

SPEED/AGILITY/QUICKNESS		**Sets**	**Reps**	**Distance**	**Rest**
No SAQ because of on-court drills and conditioning					

RESISTANCE		**Sets**	**Reps**	**Tempo**	**Intensity**	**Rest**
Chest	1. Bench Press	3	8	2/0/2	80%	0 sec
	2. Push-up		8	4/2/1		
Back	1. Seated Lat Pulldown	3	8	2/0/2	80%	0 sec
	2. Ball DB Cobra		8	4/2/1		
Shoulders	1. Shoulder Press Machine	3	8	2/0/2	80%	60 sec
	2. Prone Ball Scaption		8	4/2/1		
COOL DOWN						
Foam Roll and Static Stretching						

Football

Note: The Sports Performance Professional will focus on the design and assessment of a program for football players that considers the demands of the sport, the movement patterns, and the physical conditioning required for the sport. In the case of a performance program for football players, both skill position players and linemen can be treated separately with individual programs for each; however, in this section, we will explore football as a sport without a tremendous amount of specificity to the multiple positions and the various types of training that can be implemented with each.

NASM has implemented the OPT™ model with multiple ability levels (high school, college, combine prep, and NFL) and a variety of positions within football and had success to correct movement imbalances, prevent injury, and improve performance (speed, agility, quickness, strength, power). A football player of any skill and ability will receive tremendous benefits by following the application guidelines and techniques presented.

Consider that within football and the training progression that takes place, each position can be treated similarly in the early phases and then the program becomes more specific to the individual, their position, conditioning, and the demands and skills necessary to be able to excel at that position. The progression does not happen quickly, but it does occur over the course of an off-season or structured strength and conditioning program.

DEMANDS OF THE SPORT

GENERAL INFORMATION

- Activity characterized by high-intensity, intermittent movement with physical contact
- High-intensity movement followed by active rest periods after each play
- For the most part, all movement occurs from a completely stationary start position.
- Aerobic and anaerobic energy systems important to cardiorespiratory conditioning
- Change of direction includes stopping, backwards running, lateral movement, and engaging in physical activity while in a stationary position.
- Players wear equipment that adds 15–20 pounds of additional load they are carrying throughout the game.
- Frequent body contact (player to player) that adds additional stress to body

SPECIFIC INFORMATION (1)

- Duration of Game: 60 minutes (4 × 15 minute quarters)
- Team A Offense
    - Plays per game: 74.7 (Plays per quarter: 18.7)
    - Drives per game: 13.3 (Drives per quarter: 3.3)
    - Yards per drive: 24
    - Plays per drive: 5.6 (Each play averages: 5.0 seconds of work; 26.8 seconds of relief)
    - Runs per drive: 2.3–41.5% (Each run averages: 4.3 seconds of work; 27.9 seconds of relief)
    - Passes per drive: 3.3–58.5% (Each play averages: 5.5 seconds of work; 26.0 seconds of relief)
- Team B Offense
    - Plays per game: 64.7 (Plays per quarter: 16.2)
    - Drives per game: 12.3 (Drives per quarter: 3.1)
    - Yards per drive: 29
    - Plays per drive: 5.3 (Each play averages: 5.0 seconds of work; 36.4 seconds of relief)
    - Runs per drive: 3.0 − 57.2% (Each run averages: 4.4 seconds of work; 36.1 seconds of relief)
    - Passes per drive: 2.3 − 42.8% (Each play averages: 5.8 seconds of work; 36.8 seconds of relief)
- Position Specific Metrics

	Total Yards	Total Time (Min)	Avg. Yd/Play	Avg. Sec/Play
OL	484	3.54	6.05	2.67
RB	732	3.30	9.15	2.48
WR	1224	4.03	15.3	3.0

SUGGESTED ASSESSMENTS FOR FOOTBALL

TRANSITIONAL POSTURAL ASSESSMENTS

- Overhead Squat Assessment
- Single-leg Squat Assessment

CARDIORESPIRATORY ASSESSMENTS

- Harvard Step Test

POWER ASSESSMENTS

- Double-leg Vertical Jump
- Overhead Medicine Ball Throw (ball not to exceed 5% of athlete's body weight)
- Shark Skill Test

SPEED ASSESSMENT

- 40-yard Sprint

AGILITY ASSESSMENTS

- LEFT (Lower-Extremity Functional) Test
- 5-10-5 (Pro Agility Shuttle) Test

SPEED ENDURANCE ASSESSMENT

- 300-yard Shuttle

STRENGTH ASSESSMENTS

- Bench Press (5 RM)
- Squat (5 RM)
- Power Clean (5 RM)

OFF-SEASON GOALS AND CONSIDERATIONS FOR FOOTBALL

- Physical and mental reconditioning.
- Reconditioning from the physical contact and additional stress placed on the body.
- Correcting impaired movement patterns and muscle imbalances based on results of movement assessments.
- Improving range of motion, joint stability, and muscle strength and endurance.
- Improving cardiorespiratory endurance (anaerobic/aerobic).
- Improving total body stabilization.
- Improving total body strength.
- Improving total body power.
- Increasing lean body mass and size.
- Improving speed, agility, and quickness.
- Determine through assessment, demand of sport analysis, and athlete goal the plan and program that should be created to achieve both the needs and the goals.
- Developing a systematic off-season plan that incorporates integrated training, including core training, balance training, power training, speed, agility, and quickness training, integrated resistance training, and cardiorespiratory training combined with a proper nutrition plan to maximize training and recovery.
- Appropriate rest should be given between workouts.
- Developing an off-season training schedule that works backwards from commencement of the preseason to allow for maximum injury prevention and performance gains without athlete overtraining.
- Consider that conditioning for football should be as similar to the game demands as possible. Circuit-based training, and conditioning utilizing cardio machines and exercises incorporating ground reaction forces should be considered when designing a conditioning program.

OFF-SEASON OPT™ FOOTBALL PLAN (JANUARY–JUNE)

Level	Phase	JAN OFF-Season (1)	FEB OFF-Season (2)	MAR OFF-Season (3)	APR OFF-Season (4)	MAY OFF-Season (5)	JUN OFF-Season (6)	JUL PRE-Season	AUG PRE-Season	SEP IN-Season	OCT IN-Season	NOV IN-Season	DEC IN-Season
Corrective		X											
Stabilization	1	X											
Strength	2		X				X						
	3			X									
	4				X		X						
Power	5					X	X						
	6												

SAMPLE OFF-SEASON WEEKLY OPT™ FOOTBALL SCHEDULE

Month 1: 3 days/week

	Monday	Tuesday	Wednesday	Thursday	Friday	Saturday	Sunday
OPT™ Phase	Corrective	OFF	Stabilization Endurance	OFF	Corrective	OFF	OFF

Month 2: 3 days/week

	Monday	Tuesday	Wednesday	Thursday	Friday	Saturday	Sunday
OPT™ Phase	Strength Endurance BACK, BICEPS, LEGS	OFF	Strength Endurance CHEST, SHOULDERS, TRICEPS	OFF	Strength Endurance TOTAL BODY	OFF	OFF

Month 3: 4 days/week

	Monday	Tuesday	Wednesday	Thursday	Friday	Saturday	Sunday
OPT™ Phase	Hypertrophy CHEST, SHOULDERS, TRICEPS	Hypertrophy BACK, BICEPS, LEGS	OFF	Hypertrophy CHEST, SHOULDERS, TRICEPS	Hypertrophy BACK, BICEPS, LEGS	OFF	OFF
Other	Conditioning				Conditioning		

Month 4: 5 days/week

	Monday	Tuesday	Wednesday	Thursday	Friday	Saturday	Sunday
OPT™ Phase	Maximal Strength CHEST	Maximal Strength LEGS	Maximal Strength BACK	Maximal Strength SHOULDERS	Maximal Strength TOTAL BODY, ARMS	OFF	OFF
Other	Conditioning		Conditioning		Conditioning		

Month 5: 4 days/week

	Monday	Tuesday	Wednesday	Thursday	Friday	Saturday	Sunday
OPT™ Phase	Power	Power	OFF	Power	Power	OFF	OFF
Other	Conditioning	Conditioning		Conditioning	Conditioning		

(*continued*)

(continued)

Month 6: 5 days/week

	Monday	Tuesday	Wednesday	Thursday	Friday	Saturday	Sunday
OPT™ Phase	Maximal Strength	OFF	Strength Endurance	OFF	Power	OFF	OFF
Other		Conditioning		Conditioning			

SAMPLE OFF-SEASON OPT™ FOOTBALL PROGRAMS

CORRECTIVE EXERCISE TRAINING

INHIBIT		Sets	Reps	Time
Foam Roll: IT Band		1		30 sec
Foam Roll: Adductor		1		30 sec
Foam Roll: Tensor Fascia Latae		1		30 sec
LENGTHEN		**Sets**	**Reps**	**Time**
Gastrocnemius Stretch		1		30 sec
Supine Biceps Femoris Stretch		1		30 sec
Kneeling Hip Flexor Stretch		1		30 sec
Ball Lat Stretch		1		30 sec

ACTIVATE	Sets	Reps	Tempo	Intensity	Rest
Single-leg Calf Raise	3	10	4/2/1		0 sec
Side-lying Hip Abduction	3	10	4/2/1		0 sec
Ball Cobra	3	10	4/2/1		60 sec
INTEGRATE	**Sets**	**Reps**	**Tempo**	**Intensity**	**Rest**
Total Body Cable Squat to Row	3	10	4-2-1	60%	60 sec

PHASE 1: STABILIZATION ENDURANCE TRAINING

WARM-UP		Sets	Reps	Time
Foam Roll				
Tensor Fasciae Latae		1		30 sec
IT Band		1		30 sec
Piriformis		1		30 sec
Static Stretch				
Gastrocnemius Stretch		1		30 sec
Kneeling Hip Flexor Stretch		1		30 sec
Standing Adductor Stretch		1		30 sec
Ball Lat Stretch		1		30 sec

CORE & BALANCE	Sets	Reps	Tempo	Rest
Side Iso-Ab	3	12	4/2/1	0 sec
Ball Bridge	3	12	4/2/1	0 sec
Single-leg Balance Reach	3	12	4/2/1	60 sec

(continued)					
PLYOMETRICS		**Sets**	**Reps**	**Tempo**	**Rest**
Box Jump with Stabilization		3	10	Hold Landing	60 sec
SPEED/AGILITY/QUICKNESS		**Sets**	**Reps**	**Distance**	**Rest**
Speed Ladder: Six Exercises		2			60 sec

RESISTANCE		**Sets**	**Reps**	**Tempo**	**Intensity**	**Rest**
Total Body	Single-leg Squat Touchdown to Overhead Press	3	15	4/2/1	65%	0 sec
Chest	Ball DB Chest Press	3	15	4/2/1	65%	0 sec
Back	Ball DB Row: Alternate-arm	3	15	4/2/1	65%	0 sec
Shoulders	Single-leg PNF	3	15	4/2/1	65%	0 sec
Biceps	Optional					
Triceps	Optional					
Legs	Lunge to Balance: Frontal Plane	3	12	4/2/1	65%	90 sec
COOL DOWN						
Foam Roll and Static Stretching Exercises from WARM-UP						

PHASE 2: STRENGTH ENDURANCE TRAINING (BACK, BICEPS, LEGS)

WARM-UP	**Sets**	**Reps**	**Time**
Foam Roll			
IT Band	1		30 sec
Piriformis	1		30 sec
Lats	1		30 sec
Static Stretch			
Standing Adductor Stretch	1		30 sec
Standing Hip Flexor Stretch	1		30 sec
Standing Biceps Femoris Stretch	1		30 sec

CORE & BALANCE	**Sets**	**Reps**	**Tempo**	**Rest**
Reverse Crunches	2	10	1/1/1	0 sec
Back Extension	2	10	1/1/1	0 sec
Single-leg Romanian Deadlift	2	10	1/1/1	60 sec
PLYOMETRICS	**Sets**	**Reps**	**Tempo**	**Rest**
Repeat Box Jump-up	2	10	Repeating	0 sec
Tuck Jumps	2	10	Repeating	60 sec
SPEED/AGILITY/QUICKNESS	**Sets**	**Reps**	**Distance**	**Rest**
Speed Ladder: Six Exercises	3			60 sec

(continued)

(continued)

RESISTANCE		Sets	Reps	Tempo	Intensity	Rest
Back	1. Pull-ups 2. Ball DB Cobra	3	8 8	2/0/2 4/2/1	80%	0 sec
Biceps	1. Barbell Curls 2. Single-leg DB Curl: Alt.-arm	3	8 8	2/0/2 4/2/1	80%	0 sec
Legs	1. Lunge: Sagittal Plane 2. Single-leg Squat Touchdown	3	8 8	2/0/2 4/2/1	80%	60 sec
COOL DOWN						
Foam Roll and Static Stretching						

PHASE 2: STRENGTH ENDURANCE TRAINING (CHEST, SHOULDERS, TRICEPS)

WARM-UP			Sets	Reps	Time
Foam Roll					
IT Band				1	30 sec
Piriformis				1	30 sec
Lats				1	30 sec
Static Stretch					
Standing Adductor Stretch				1	30 sec
Standing Psoas Stretch				1	30 sec
Standing Biceps Femoris Stretch				1	30 sec

CORE & BALANCE	Sets	Reps	Tempo	Rest
Knee-ups	2	10	1/1/1	0 sec
Cable Lifts	2	10	1/1/1	0 sec
Step-up to Balance: Frontal Plane	2	10	1/1/1	60 sec
PLYOMETRICS	**Sets**	**Reps**	**Tempo**	**Rest**
Butt Kickers	2	10	Repeating	0 sec
Tuck Jumps	2	10	Repeating	60 sec
SPEED/AGILITY/QUICKNESS	**Sets**	**Reps**	**Distance**	**Rest**
Speed Ladder: Six Exercises	3			60 sec

RESISTANCE		Sets	Reps	Tempo	Intensity	Rest
Chest	1. Barbell Bench Press 2. Ball Push-up: Feet on Ball	3	8 8	2/0/2 4/2/1	80%	0 sec
Shoulders	1. Seated Overhead DB Press 2. Prone Ball Scaption	3	8 8	2/0/2 4/2/1	80%	0 sec
Triceps	1. Triceps Pressdowns 2. Supine Ball DB Extensions	3	8 8	2/0/2 4/2/1	80%	60 sec
COOL DOWN						
Foam Roll and Static Stretching						

PHASE 3: HYPERTROPHY TRAINING (CHEST, SHOULDERS, TRICEPS)

WARM-UP				Sets	Reps	Time
Foam Roll						
IT Band					1	30 sec
Piriformis					1	30 sec
Adductors					1	30 sec
Static Stretch						
Gastrocnemius Stretch					1	30 sec
Kneeling Hip Flexor Stretch					1	30 sec
Standing Adductor Stretch					1	30 sec
Standing Pec Stretch					1	30 sec

CORE & BALANCE			Sets	Reps	Tempo	Rest
Ball Crunch with Rotation			2	12	1/1/1	0 sec
Russian Twists			2	12	1/1/1	0 sec
Lunge to Balance: Sagittal Plane			2	12	1/1/1	60 sec

PLYTOMETRICS			Sets	Reps	Tempo	Rest
Power Step-ups			2	10	Repeating	0 sec
Tuck Jump			2	10	Repeating	60 sec

SPEED/AGILITY/QUICKNESS			Sets	Reps	Distance	Rest
No SAQ on this day						

RESISTANCE		Sets	Reps	Tempo	Intensity	Rest
Chest	DB Bench Press	3	8	2/0/2	80%	1 min
Chest	Incline Bench Press	3	8	2/0/2	80%	1 min
Shoulders	Seated Overhead Barbell Press	3	8	2/0/2	80%	1 min
Shoulders	Seated Lateral Raise	3	8	2/0/2	80%	1 min
Triceps	Triceps Pressdown	3	8	2/0/2	80%	1 min
Triceps	Triceps Extension Machine	3	8	2/0/2	80%	1 min

COOL DOWN
Foam Roll and Static Stretching

PHASE 3: HYPERTROPHY TRAINING (BACK, BICEPS, LEGS)

WARM-UP	Sets	Reps	Time
Foam Roll			
IT Band		1	30 sec
Piriformis		1	30 sec
Adductors		1	30 sec
Static Stretch			
Gastrocnemius Stretch		1	30 sec

(continued)

(continued)				
WARM-UP		**Sets**	**Reps**	**Time**
Kneeling Hip Flexor Stretch		1		30 sec
Standing Adductor Stretch		1		30 sec
Standing Pec Stretch		1		30 sec

CORE & BALANCE		**Sets**	**Reps**	**Tempo**	**Rest**
Cable Chop		2	12	1/1/1	0 sec
Knee-ups w/ Rotation		2	12	1/1/1	0 sec
Lunge to Balance: Frontal Plane		2	12	1/1/1	60 sec

PLYOMETRICS		**Sets**	**Reps**	**Tempo**	**Rest**
Lunge Jumps		2	10	Repeating	0 sec
Power Step-ups		2	10	Repeating	60 sec

SPEED/AGILITY/QUICKNESS		**Sets**	**Reps**	**Distance**	**Rest**
No SAQ on this day					

RESISTANCE		**Sets**	**Reps**	**Tempo**	**Intensity**	**Rest**
Back	Seated Lat Pulldown	3	8	2/0/2	80%	1 min
Back	Seated Cable Row	3	8	2/0/2	80%	1 min
Biceps	Barbell Curl	3	8	2/0/2	80%	1 min
Biceps	Seated DB Curl	3	8	2/0/2	80%	1 min
Legs	Leg Press	3	8	2/0/2	80%	1 min
Legs	Barbell Romanian Deadlift	3	8	2/0/2	80%	1 min

COOL DOWN
Foam Roll and Static Stretching

PHASE 4: MAXIMAL STRENGTH TRAINING (TOTAL BODY)

WARM-UP	**Sets**	**Reps**	**Time**
Foam Roll			
IT Band	1		30 sec
Piriformis	1		30 sec
Calf	1		30 sec
Active Stretch (Some athletes may still require static stretching)			
Standing Adductor Stretch	1	5–10	
Standing Hip Flexor Stretch	1	5–10	
Ball Lat Stretch	1	5–10	
Standing Pec Stretch	1	5–10	

CORE & BALANCE		**Sets**	**Reps**	**Tempo**	**Rest**
Cable Rotations		2	12	1/1/1	0 sec
Cable Lift and Chop		2	12	1/1/1	0 sec
Lunge to Balance: Transverse Plane		2	12	1/1/1	60 sec

PLYOMETRICS		**Sets**	**Reps**	**Tempo**	**Rest**
No PLYOMETRICS on this day					

(continued)						
SPEED/AGILITY/QUICKNESS			**Sets**	**Reps**	**Distance**	**Rest**
No SAQ on this day						
RESISTANCE		**Sets**	**Reps**	**Tempo**	**Intensity**	**Rest**
Chest	Bench Press	4	5	Controlled	85%	3 min
Back	Seated Lat Pulldown	4	5	Controlled	85%	3 min
Shoulders	Seated Overhead DB Press	4	5	Controlled	85%	3 min
Biceps	Optional					
Triceps	Optional					
Legs	Barbell Squats	4	5	Controlled	85%	3 min
COOL DOWN						
Foam Roll and Static Stretching						

PHASE 5: POWER TRAINING

WARM-UP		**Sets**	**Reps**	**Time**
Foam Roll				
Tensor Fascia Latae		1		30 sec
Piriformis		1		30 sec
Thoracic Spine		1		30 sec
Dynamic Warm-up (Some athletes may still require static stretching prior to the Dynamic Warm-up)				
Prisoner Squats		1	10	0 sec
Multiplanar Lunges		1	10	0 sec
Single-leg Squat Touchdown		1	10	0 sec
Push-up with Rotation		1	10	0 sec
Leg Swings: Front-Back		1	10	0 sec
Medicine Ball Lift Chop		1	10	0 sec
Medicine Ball Rotations		1	10	60 sec
CORE, BALANCE, & PLYOMETRICS		**Sets**	**Reps**	**Tempo**	**Rest**
No CORE , BALANCE, & PLYOMETRICS (Incorporated into Dynamic Warm-up)					
SPEED/AGILITY/QUICKNESS		**Sets**	**Reps**	**Distance**	**Rest**
Speed Ladder: Six Exercises		2			60 sec
Box Drill		4			30 sec
T-Drill		4			30 sec
RESISTANCE		**Sets**	**Reps**	**Tempo**	**Intensity**	**Rest**
Total Body	1. Deadlift Shrug to Calf Raise 2. DB Snatch	4	5 8	Controlled Explosive	85% 4% of BW	2 min
Chest	1. Bench Press 2. Rotational Chest Pass	4	5 8	Controlled Explosive	85% 4% of BW	2 min

(*continued*)

(continued)						
RESISTANCE		**Sets**	**Reps**	**Tempo**	**Intensity**	**Rest**
Shoulders	Incorporated in Total Body Exercises					
Legs	1. Barbell Squats 2. Squat Jumps	4	5 8	Controlled Explosive	85% BW	2 min
COOL DOWN						
Foam Roll and Static Stretching						

PRESEASON GOALS AND CONSIDERATIONS FOR FOOTBALL

- Correcting impaired movement patterns based on results of preseason assessments.
- Maintain physical health, and decrease chance of injury for participation in practice and games and optimal performance within such activities.
- Maintain range of motion, joint stability, and muscle strength and endurance.
- Maintain cardiorespiratory endurance (anaerobic/aerobic).
- Maintain total body stabilization, strength, and power.
- Developing a systematic preseason plan that transitions the athlete from performance enhancement to injury prevention and maintenance of off-season gains. This transition should be implemented with the consideration that the athlete's sport participation level is increasing dramatically from what the athlete has become used to in the off-season.
- The proper recovery and reconditioning should be applied during this time of increased activity.
- Consider the exercise volume of injury prevention and performance training based on the athlete's increased activity level.
- Establish with the athlete a preseason strategy and plan that works based on what the athlete needs, wants, and will have the capability to do.

PRESEASON OPT™ FOOTBALL PLAN (JULY–AUGUST)

Level	Phase	JAN OFF-Season	FEB OFF-Season	MAR OFF-Season	APR OFF-Season	MAY OFF-Season	JUN OFF-Season	JUL PRE-Season (1)	AUG PRE-Season (2)	SEP IN-Season	OCT IN-Season	NOV IN-Season	DEC IN-Season
Corrective								X	X				
Stabilization	1							X	X				
Strength	2							X	X				
	3							X	X				
	4												
Power	5												
	6												

SAMPLE PRESEASON WEEKLY OPT™ FOOTBALL SCHEDULE

Month 1 & 2

	Monday	Tuesday	Wednesday	Thursday	Friday	Saturday	Sunday
OPT™ Phase	Corrective	Strength Endurance SHOULDERS, LEGS	Hypertrophy CHEST, BACK	Corrective		Hypertrophy SHOULDERS, LEGS	Strength Endurance CHEST, BACK
Other					Game		

SAMPLE PRESEASON OPT™ FOOTBALL PROGRAMS

CORRECTIVE EXERCISE TRAINING

INHIBIT		Sets	Reps	Time
Foam Roll: Piriformis			1	30 sec
Foam Roll: Tensor Fascia Latae			1	30 sec
Foam Roll: Lat			1	30 sec
LENGTHEN		**Sets**	**Reps**	**Time**
Gastrocnemius Stretch			1	30 sec
Ball Lat Stretch			1	30 sec
Standing Psoas Stretch			1	30 sec
Erector Spinae Stretch			1	30 sec

ACTIVATE		Sets	Reps	Tempo	Intensity	Rest
Prone Iso-Ab		2	12	4/2/1		0 sec
Ball Bridge		2	12	4/2/1		60 sec
INTEGRATE		**Sets**	**Reps**	**Tempo**	**Intensity**	**Rest**
Total Body	Cable Squat to Row	2	12	4/2/1	60%	60 sec

PHASE I: STABILIZATION ENDURANCE TRAINING

WARM-UP		Sets	Reps	Time
Foam Roll				
Tensor Fascia Latae			1	30 sec
IT Band			1	30 sec
Piriformis			1	30 sec
Static Stretch				
Gastrocnemius Stretch			1	30 sec
Kneeling Hip Flexor Stretch			1	30 sec
Standing Adductor Stretch			1	30 sec
Ball Lat Stretch			1	30 sec

CORE & BALANCE		Sets	Reps	Tempo	Rest
Side Iso-Ab w/ Hip Abduction		2	12	4/2/1	0
Ball DB Cobra		2	12	4/2/1	0
Single-leg Lift and Chop		2	12	4/2/1	60 sec
PLYOMETRICS		**Sets**	**Reps**	**Tempo**	**Rest**
No PLYOMETRICS due to increased on-field activity					
SPEED/AGILITY/QUICKNESS		**Sets**	**Reps**	**Distance**	**Rest**
No SAQ, included in on-field conditioning					

RESISTANCE		Sets	Reps	Tempo	Intensity	Rest
Total Body	Optional					
Chest	Ball Push-up: Feet on Ball	2	15	4/2/1	65%	0 sec

(continued)

(continued)

RESISTANCE		Sets	Reps	Tempo	Intensity	Rest
Back	Single-leg Lat Pulldown	2	15	4/2/1	65%	0 sec
Shoulders	Single-leg Overhead DB Press	2	15	4/2/1	65%	0 sec
Biceps	Optional					
Triceps	Optional					
Legs	Lunge to Balance: Transverse Plane	2	12	4/2/1	65%	90 sec

COOL DOWN
Foam Roll and Static Stretching

PHASE 2: STRENGTH ENDURANCE TRAINING (CHEST, BACK)

WARM-UP	Sets	Reps	Time
Foam Roll			
IT Band		1	30 sec
Tensor Fasciae Latae		1	30 sec
Piriformis		1	30 sec
Static Stretch			
Gastrocnemius Stretch		1	30 sec
Kneeling Hip Flexor Stretch		1	30 sec
Standing Biceps Femoris Stretch		1	30 sec
Standing Pec Stretch		1	30 sec

CORE & BALANCE	Sets	Reps	Tempo	Rest
Cable Rotations	2	10	1/1/1	0 sec
Cable Lift	2	10	1/1/1	0 sec
Step-up to Balance: Frontal Plane	2	10	1/1/1	60 sec

PLYOMETRICS	Sets	Reps	Tempo	Rest
No PLYOMETRICS due to increased on-field activity				

SPEED/AGILITY/QUICKNESS	Sets	Reps	Distance	Rest
No SAQ, included in on-field conditioning				

RESISTANCE		Sets	Reps	Tempo	Intensity	Rest
Chest	1. Bench Press 2. Ball Push-up: Feet on Ball	2	12 12	2/0/2 4/2/1	70%	0 sec
Back	1. Seated Cable Row 2. Ball DB Cobra: Alt.-arm	2	12 12	2/0/2 4/2/1	70%	0 sec
Chest	1. Incline Bench Press 2. Ball DB Chest Press: Single-arm	2	12 12	2/0/2 4/2/1	70%	0 sec
Back	1. Seated Lat Pulldown 2. Single-leg Cable Row	2	12 12	2/0/2 4/2/1	70%	60 sec

COOL DOWN
Foam Roll and Static Stretching

PHASE 2: STRENGTH ENDURANCE TRAINING (SHOULDERS, LEGS)

WARM-UP			Sets	Reps	Time
Foam Roll					
IT Band				1	30 sec
Tensor Fasciae Latae				1	30 sec
Piriformis				1	30 sec
Static Stretch					
Gastrocnemius Stretch				1	30 sec
Kneeling Hip Flexor Stretch				1	30 sec
Standing Biceps Femoris Stretch				1	30 sec
Standing Pec Stretch				1	30 sec

CORE & BALANCE			Sets	Reps	Tempo	Rest
Knee-ups			2	10	1/1/1	0 sec
Back Extension with Rotation			2	10	1/1/1	0 sec
Single-leg Romanian Deadlift			2	10	1/1/1	60 sec

PLYOMETRICS			Sets	Reps	Tempo	Rest
No PLYOMETRICS due to increased on-field activity						

SPEED/AGILITY/QUICKNESS			Sets	Reps	Distance	Rest
No SAQ, included in on-field conditioning						

RESISTANCE			Sets	Reps	Tempo	Intensity	Rest
Shoulders	1.	Shoulder Press Machine	2	12	2/0/2	70%	0 sec
	2.	Prone Ball Military Press		12	4/2/1		
Legs	1.	Lunge: Frontal Plane	2	12	2/0/2	70%	0 sec
	2.	Single-leg Squat		12	4/2/1		
Shoulders	1.	Seated Lateral Raises	2	12	2/0/2	70%	0 sec
	2.	Prone Ball Scaption		12	4/2/1		
Legs	1.	Barbell Squats	2	12	2/0/2	70%	60 sec
	2.	Step-up to Balance: Transverse Plane		12	4/2/1		

COOL DOWN
Foam Roll and Static Stretching

PHASE 3: HYPERTROPHY TRAINING (CHEST, BACK)

WARM-UP	Sets	Reps	Time
Foam Roll			
IT Band		1	30 sec
Tensor Fascia Latae		1	30 sec
Thoracic Spine		1	30 sec
Static Stretch			
Gastrocnemius Stretch		1	30 sec
Kneeling Hip Flexor Stretch		1	30 sec

(*continued*)

(continued)

WARM-UP		Sets	Reps	Time
Standing Biceps Femoris Stretch		1		30 sec
Standing Pec Stretch		1		30 sec

CORE & BALANCE		Sets	Reps	Tempo	Rest
Knee-ups		2	12	1/1/1	0 sec
Reverse Hypers		2	12	1/1/1	0 sec
Single-leg Squat		2	12	1/1/1	60 sec

PLYOMETRICS		Sets	Reps	Tempo	Rest
No PLYOMETRICS on this day					

SPEED/AGILITY/QUICKNESS		Sets	Reps	Distance	Rest
No SAQ on this day					

RESISTANCE		Sets	Reps	Tempo	Intensity	Rest
Chest	Chest Press Machine	2	10	2/0/2	75%	0 min
Back	Lat Pull-down	2	10	2/0/2	75%	1 min
Chest	Incline DB Chest Press	2	10	2/0/2	75%	0 min
Back	Seated Cable Row	2	10	2/0/2	75%	1 min
Chest	DB Bench Press	2	10	2/0/2	75%	0 min
Back	Pull-up	2	10	2/0/2	75%	1 min

COOL DOWN
Foam Roll and Static Stretching

PHASE 3: HYPERTROPHY TRAINING (SHOULDERS, LEGS)

WARM-UP	Sets	Reps	Time
Foam Roll			
IT Band	1		30 sec
Tensor Fascia Latae	1		30 sec
Thoracic Spine	1		30 sec
Static Stretch			
Gastrocnemius Stretch	1		30 sec
Kneeling Hip Flexor Stretch	1		30 sec
Standing Biceps Femoris Stretch	1		30 sec
Standing Pec Stretch	1		30 sec

CORE & BALANCE	Sets	Reps	Tempo	Rest
Back Extension	2	12	1/1/1	0 sec
Reverse Crunch	2	12	1/1/1	0 sec
Single-leg Squat Touchdown	2	12	1/1/1	90 sec

PLYOMETRICS	Sets	Reps	Tempo	Rest
No PLYOMETRICS on this day				

(continued)					
SPEED/AGILITY/QUICKNESS	**Sets**	**Reps**	**Distance**	**Rest**
No SAQ on this day				

RESISTANCE		**Sets**	**Reps**	**Tempo**	**Intensity**	**Rest**
Shoulders	Shoulder Press Machine	2	10	2/0/2	75%	0 min
Legs	Lunge: Frontal Plane	2	10	2/0/2	75%	1 min
Shoulders	Seated Lateral Raise	2	10	2/0/2	75%	0 min
Legs	Barbell Squat	2	10	2/0/2	75%	1 min
Shoulders	Seated Overhead Barbell Press	2	10	2/0/2	75%	0 min
Legs	Barbell Romanian Deadlift	2	10	2/0/2	75%	1 min

COOL DOWN
Foam Roll and Static Stretching

IN-SEASON GOALS AND CONSIDERATIONS FOR FOOTBALL

- Perform assessments and testing to ensure program considerations are being made to prevent overuse injuries and maintain performance levels.
- Continued attention to impaired movement patterns with corrective strategies being implemented.
- Maintain range of motion, joint stability, and muscle strength and endurance.
- Maintain cardiorespiratory endurance (anaerobic/aerobic).
- Maintain total body stabilization, strength, and power.
- Consider additional conditioning for athletes who may not get the same type of on-field practice or game minutes.
- Developing a systematic in-season maintenance plan that allows the athlete to minimize decreases in performance and chance of injury over a long season with repetitive sport movement patterns and physical contact.
- Consider the exercise volume of injury prevention and performance training based on the athlete's increased travel and activity level.
- Establish with the athlete a communication process for monitoring in-season maintenance and plan that works for them based on what they need, want, and will have the capability to do focusing on their job of playing football.

IN-SEASON OPT™ FOOTBALL PLAN (SEPTEMBER–DECEMBER)

Level	Phase	JAN OFF-Season	FEB OFF-Season	MAR OFF-Season	APR OFF-Season	MAY OFF-Season	JUN OFF-Season	JUL PRE-Season	AUG PRE-Season	SEP IN-Season (1)	OCT IN-Season (2)	NOV IN-Season (3)	DEC IN-Season (4)
Corrective										X	X	X	X
Stabilization	1									X	X	X	X
Strength	2									X	X	X	X
	3												
	4												
Power	5												
	6												

SAMPLE IN-SEASON WEEKLY OPT™ FOOTBALL SCHEDULE

Any Month

	Monday	Tuesday	Wednesday	Thursday	Friday	Saturday	Sunday
OPT™ Phase	Stabilization Endurance	Corrective	Strength Endurance	Corrective	Stabilization Endurance	Corrective	
Other							Game

SAMPLE IN-SEASON OPT™ FOOTBALL PROGRAMS

CORRECTIVE EXERCISE TRAINING

INHIBIT		Sets	Reps	Time
Foam Roll: Calves		1		30 sec
Foam Roll: IT Band		1		30 sec
Foam Roll: TFL		1		30 sec
LENGTHEN		**Sets**	**Reps**	**Time**
Gastrocnemius Stretch		1		30 sec
Soleus Stretch		1		30 sec
Supine Biceps Femoris Stretch		1		30 sec

ACTIVATE		Sets	Reps	Tempo	Intensity	Rest
Floor Bridge		2	12	4/2/1		0 sec
Single-leg Calf Raise		2	12	4/2/1		0 sec
INTEGRATE		**Sets**	**Reps**	**Tempo**	**Intensity**	**Rest**
Total Body	Step-up, Balance, to Overhead Press	2	12	4/2/1	60%	60 sec

PHASE I: STABILIZATION ENDURANCE TRAINING

WARM-UP	Sets	Reps	Time
Foam Roll			
Tensor Fascia Latae	1		30 sec
IT Band	1		30 sec
Piriformis	1		30 sec
Static Stretch			
Gastrocnemius Stretch	1		30 sec
Kneeling Hip Flexor Stretch	1		30 sec
Standing Adductor Stretch	1		30 sec
Ball Lat Stretch	1		30 sec

CORE & BALANCE	Sets	Reps	Tempo	Rest
Side Iso-Ab w/ Hip Abduction	2	12	4/2/1	0
Ball Cobra	2	12	4/2/1	0
Single-leg Lift and Chop	2	12	4/2/1	60 sec
PLYOMETRICS	**Sets**	**Reps**	**Tempo**	**Rest**
No PLYOMETRICS due to increased on-field activity				

(continued)

SPEED/AGILITY/QUICKNESS		Sets	Reps	Distance	Rest
No SAQ due to increased on-field activity					

RESISTANCE		Sets	Reps	Tempo	Intensity	Rest
Total Body	Optional					
Chest	Standing Cable Chest Press	2	15	4/2/1	65%	0 sec
Back	Single-leg Straight-Arm Pulldown	2	15	4/2/1	65%	0 sec
Shoulders	Prone Ball Scaption	2	15	4/2/1	65%	0 sec
Biceps	Optional					
Triceps	Optional					
Legs	Lunge to Balance: Sagittal Plane	2	15	4/2/1	65%	90 sec

COOL DOWN
Repeat Foam Roll and Static Stretching Exercises from WARM-UP

PHASE 2: STRENGTH ENDURANCE TRAINING

WARM-UP	Sets	Reps	Time
Foam Roll			
IT Band		1	30 sec
Tensor Fascia Latae		1	30 sec
Piriformis		1	30 sec
Static Stretch			
Gastrocnemius Stretch		1	30 sec
Kneeling Hip Flexor Stretch		1	30 sec
Standing Biceps Femoris Stretch		1	30 sec
Standing Pec Stretch		1	30 sec

CORE & BALANCE	Sets	Reps	Tempo	Rest
Long Lever Ball Crunch	2	10	1/1/1	0 sec
Cable Lift	2	10	1/1/1	0 sec
Step-up to Balance: Frontal Plane	2	10	1/1/1	60 sec

PLYOMETRICS	Sets	Reps	Tempo	Rest
No PLYOMETRICS due to increased on-field activity				

SPEED/AGILITY/QUICKNESS	Sets	Reps	Distance	Rest
No SAQ, included in on-field conditioning				

RESISTANCE		Sets	Reps	Tempo	Intensity	Rest
Total Body	Optional					
Chest	1. DB Bench Press 2. Push-up	2	12 12	2/0/2 4/2/1	70%	0 sec

(continued)

(continued)						
RESISTANCE		**Sets**	**Reps**	**Tempo**	**Intensity**	**Rest**
Back	1. Straight Arm Pulldown 2. Ball DB Row: Alt.-arm	2	12 12	2/0/2 4/2/1	70%	0 sec
Shoulders	1. Shoulder Press Machine 2. Single-leg Overhead DB Press: Single-arm	2	12 12	2/0/2 4/2/1	70%	0 sec
Biceps	Optional					
Triceps	Optional					
Legs	1. Leg Press 2. Lunge to Balance: Sagittal Plane	2	12 12	2/0/2 4/2/1	70%	60 sec
COOL DOWN						
Foam Roll and Static Stretching						

Golf

Note: Research has shown that golf-specific exercise programs improve strength, flexibility, and balance in golfers. Improvements in these areas result in increased upper torso axial rotational velocity, which results in increased club head speed, ball velocity, and driving distance (4).

Better golfers possess unique physical characteristics that are important for greater proficiency. These characteristics have also been demonstrated to be modifiable through golf-specific training programs (5).

Implementing a progressive functional training program including flexibility core, balance, and integrated resistance exercises has been shown to provide significant improvements in club head speed and several components of functional fitness (6).

Golf may not look as physically demanding as other sports; however, the entire movement system must be functioning and trained in order to perform at the highest levels. Correcting muscle imbalances, increasing flexibility, and improving functional performance has been shown to improve a golfer's on-course results. The Sports Performance Professional should consider a progressive and systematic program for a golfer looking to prevent overuse injury and improve play.

All programs should be designed from an assessment that identifies the needs of the athlete and then strategically apply the assessment results into the training plan. The nature of golf, probably more than any other sport, is defined by one repetitive movement (i.e., the golf swing) and requires a blend of mobility and stability in order to properly execute the skill of the golf swing.

In many places, golf is a year-round activity and is not defined by a season (in-season/off-season). Considering that many play or practice year-round and that there is not a truly defined season for most, the golf programming strategies will be an undulating programming model. Because golf requires a unique blend of stabilization, strength, and power, an undulating model can address these needs within a shortened period of time.

It is important to remember that as a Sports Performance Professional, one must understand the functional movement of the golf swing; however, any golf-specific instruction should be left to a trained golf teaching professional.

DEMANDS OF THE SPORT

GENERAL INFORMATION

- Sport played by a wide range of age groups
- Physical demands, regardless of age, are typically the same for each individual.
- Sport consists of repetitive movement patterns in the transverse plane.
- Golf can cause chronic musculoskeletal problems from repetitive movement patterns (7).
- Cardiorespiratory conditioning may not seem as important as in other sports; however, the average golfer walks between 4 and 5 miles per round and endurance can become a factor in a golfer's performance.

- A proper golf-specific warm-up prior to play and practice has shown a significant increase in golfers' performances compared with not performing a warm-up (8). The Sports Performance Professional should consider designing a proper warm-up for a golfer beyond their strength and conditioning program. A warm-up has also been shown to reduce golf injuries (9).
- Golf requires a unique combination of stabilization, strength, and power throughout the entire human movement system and specifically in the spine, hips, and shoulders.
- Muscular imbalances throughout the human movement system, described as overactive muscles (tightness) and underactive muscles (weakness), can cause faulty movement patterns and can limit the golfer's ability to swing effectively.
- Flexibility has been shown to be the most important variable regarding performance and injury through clinical trials.

SUGGESTED ASSESSMENTS FOR GOLF

TRANSITIONAL POSTURAL ASSESSMENT

- Overhead Squat Assessment
- Single-leg Squat Assessment
- Trunk Rotation Assessment

CARDIORESPIRATORY ASSESSMENT

- Harvard Step Test

POWER ASSESSMENTS

- Rotation Medicine Ball Throw (left and right)

STABILIZATION ENDURANCE ASSESSMENTS

- Single-leg Balance Excursion Test
- Davies Test

CORRECTIVE EXERCISE GOALS AND CONSIDERATIONS

- Correcting impaired movement patterns and muscle imbalances based on results of movement assessments
- Ability to look at the results of the assessment and at the physical demand of the golf swing and understand what muscles must have the proper amount of range of motion throughout the swing
- Improving range of motion, joint stability, and muscle strength and endurance
- Improving total body stabilization
- Creating the proper warm-up while considering and incorporating the corrective exercise program
- Because of the repetitive nature of the golf swing, the corrective program should be consistently implemented and performed.
- Balance training to improve sensorimotor and proprioceptive skills

STRENGTH AND CONDITIONING GOALS AND CONSIDERATIONS

- Continued correction and maintenance of impaired movement patterns based on results of assessment
- Maintain physical health and decrease the chance of injury for participation in practice and games and optimal performance within such activities.
- Maintain range of motion, joint stability, and muscle strength and endurance.
- Maintain cardiorespiratory endurance (aerobic).
- Maintain total body stabilization, strength, and power.
- Developing a systematic plan that implements an undulating programming model integrating corrective exercise, stabilization, strength, and power
- The golf swing is a perfect example of the three phases of the OPT™ model being incorporated at one time, as the body must maintain posture and balance (stabilization), enhance joint stabilization and increase prime mover strength (strength), and increase rate of force production and velocity (power).
- It is necessary to incorporate the power phase into the program to improve velocity and rate of force production.
- Consider the exercise volume of injury prevention and performance training based on the athlete's activity level.

PRE-PRACTICE/PLAY WARM-UP GOALS AND CONSIDERATIONS

- Integrated corrective exercise programming and dynamic warm-up activities for a proper warm-up.
- Warm-up should be multiplanar and increase tissue temperature, elasticity, and activation of muscles specific to the golf swing.
- Warm-up should transition from exercises directly into hitting golf balls. Should be implemented as part of the pre-practice or pre-play routine for each session.

ANNUAL OPT™ GOLF PLAN (JANUARY–DECEMBER)

Level	Phase	JAN	FEB	MAR	APR	MAY	JUN	JUL	AUG	SEP	OCT	NOV	DEC
Corrective		X	X	X	X	X	X	X	X	X	X	X	X
Stabilization	1	X	X	X	X	X	X	X	X	X	X	X	X
Strength	2	X	X	X	X	X	X	X	X	X	X	X	X
	3												
	4												
Power	5	X	X	X	X	X	X	X	X	X	X	X	X
	6												

SAMPLE MONTHLY OPT™ GOLF SCHEDULE

Month 1

Week 1: 2 days/week

	Monday	Tuesday	Wednesday	Thursday	Friday	Saturday	Sunday
OPT™ Phase	Corrective	OFF	OFF	Stabilization Endurance	OFF	Warm-Up	OFF
Other						Play	

Week 2: 3 days/week

	Monday	Tuesday	Wednesday	Thursday	Friday	Saturday	Sunday
OPT™ Phase	Strength Endurance	OFF	Corrective	Stabilization Endurance	OFF	Warm-Up	OFF
		Practice				Play	

Week 3: 2 days/week

	Monday	Tuesday	Wednesday	Thursday	Friday	Saturday	Sunday
OPT™ Phase	OFF	Corrective	OFF	Power	OFF	Warm-Up	Warm-Up
Other						Play	Play

Week 4: 3 days/week

	Monday	Tuesday	Wednesday	Thursday	Friday	Saturday	Sunday
OPT™ Phase	Strength Endurance	OFF	Stabilization	OFF	Warm-Up	OFF	Corrective
Other					Play		

SAMPLE OPT™ GOLF PROGRAMS

CORRECTIVE EXERCISE TRAINING

INHIBIT	Sets	Reps	Time
Foam Roll: Tensor Fascia Latae	1		30 sec
Foam Roll: Piriformis	1		30 sec
Foam Roll: Lat	1		30 sec
Foam Roll: Thoracic Spine	1		30 sec

LENGTHEN	Sets	Reps	Time
Gastrocnemius Stretch	1		30 sec
Standing Biceps Femoris Stretch	1		30 sec
Supine Piriformis Stretch	1		30 sec
Ball Lat Stretch	1		30 sec

ACTIVATE	Sets	Reps	Tempo	Intensity	Rest
Side-lying Hip Abduction	2	12	4/2/1		0 sec
Standing Hip Adduction	2	12	4/2/1		0 sec
Quadruped Arm Opposite Leg Raise	2	12	4/2/1		90 sec

INTEGRATE		Sets	Reps	Tempo	Intensity	Rest
Total Body	Cable Squat to Row: Single-arm	2	12	4/2/1	60%	90 sec

PHASE 1: STABILIZATION ENDURANCE TRAINING

WARM-UP	Sets	Reps	Time
Foam Roll			
Tensor Fascia Latae	1		30 sec
Piriformis	1		30 sec
Thoracic Spine	1		30 sec
Static Stretch			
Gastrocnemius Stretch	1		30 sec
Supine Piriformis	1		30 sec
Ball Lat Stretch	1		30 sec
Erector Spinae Stretch	1		30 sec

CORE & BALANCE	Sets	Reps	Tempo	Rest
Side Iso-Ab	2	12	4/2/1	0 sec
Ball Bridge	2	12	4/2/1	0 sec
Single-leg Balance Reach	2	12	4/2/1	60 sec

PLYOMETRICS	Sets	Reps	Tempo	Rest
Box Jump-up with Stabilization	2	6	Hold Landing	60 sec

(continued)

(continued)						
RESISTANCE		**Sets**	**Reps**	**Tempo**	**Intensity**	**Rest**
Total Body	Optional					
Chest	Ball Push-up: Hands on Ball	2	15	4/2/1	60%	0 sec
Back	Ball DB Cobra	2	15	4/2/1	60%	0 sec
Shoulders	Single-leg Cable Lift: Single-arm	2	15	4/2/1	60%	0 sec
Biceps	Optional					
Triceps	Optional					
Legs	Lunge to Balance: Frontal Plane	2	15	4/2/1	60%	90 sec
COOL DOWN						
Repeat Foam Roll and Static Stretching Exercises from WARM-UP						

PHASE 2: STRENGTH ENDURANCE TRAINING

WARM-UP	**Sets**	**Reps**	**Time**
Foam Roll			
IT Band		1	30 sec
Piriformis		1	30 sec
Lats		1	30 sec
Static Stretch			
Standing Adductor Stretch		1	30 sec
Supine Biceps Femoris Stretch		1	30 sec
Kneeling Hip Flexor Stretch		1	30 sec
Standing Pec Stretch		1	30 sec

CORE & BALANCE	**Sets**	**Reps**	**Tempo**	**Rest**
Ball Crunch with Rotation	2	12	1/1/1	0 sec
Cable Lift	2	12	1/1/1	0 sec
Step-up to Balance: Transverse Plane	2	12	1/1/1	60 sec

PLYOMETRICS	**Sets**	**Reps**	**Tempo**	**Rest**
Power Step-up	2	8	Repeating	60 sec

RESISTANCE		**Sets**	**Reps**	**Tempo**	**Intensity**	**Rest**
Total Body	Optional					
Chest	1. Incline DB Chest Press 2. Ball Push-up: Hands on Ball	2	12 12	2/0/2 4/2/1	70%	0 sec
Back	1. Seated Cable Row 2. Single-leg Cable Row: Alternate-arm	2	12 12	2/0/2 4/2/1	70%	0 sec
Shoulders	1. Seated Overhead DB Press 2. Single-leg Shoulder PNF	2	12 12	2/0/2 4/2/1	70%	0 sec
Biceps	Optional					
Triceps	Optional					

(continued)						
RESISTANCE		**Sets**	**Reps**	**Tempo**	**Intensity**	**Rest**
Legs	1. DB Squat 2. Lunge to Balance: Frontal Plane	2	12 12	2/0/2 4/2/1	70%	60 sec
COOL DOWN						
Foam Roll and Static Stretching						

PHASE 5: POWER TRAINING

WARM-UP	**Sets**	**Reps**	**Time**
Foam Roll			
Tensor Fascia Latae	1		30 sec
Piriformis	1		30 sec
Lats	1		30 sec
Dynamic Warm-up (Some golfers may still require static stretching prior to the Dynamic Warm-up)			
Lateral Tube Walking	1	10	0 sec
Lunge with Rotation	1	10	0 sec
Russian Twist	1	10	60 sec

CORE & BALANCE	**Sets**	**Reps**	**Tempo**	**Rest**
Cable Rotation	2	12	Fast	0 sec
Cable Lift	2	12	Fast	0 sec
Mulitplanar Hop w/ Stabilization	2	12	Controlled	60 sec

RESISTANCE		**Sets**	**Reps**	**Tempo**	**Intensity**	**Rest**
Total Body	Optional					
Chest	1. Incline DB Press 2. Rotational Chest Pass	3	5 10	Controlled Explosive	85% 2% of BW	2 min
Back	1. Seated Cable Row 2. Woodchop Throw	3	5 10	Controlled Explosive	85% 2% of BW	2 min
Shoulders	1. Seated Overhead DB Press 2. Oblique Throw	3	5 10	Controlled Explosive	85% 2% of BW	2 min
Biceps	Optional					
Triceps	Optional					
Legs	1. DB Squat 2. Squat Jump	3	5 10	Controlled Explosive	85% BW	2 min
COOL DOWN						
Foam Roll and Static Stretching						

WARM-UP AT COURSE (PRE-PRACTICE/PRE-PLAY)

STATIC STRETCH	Sets	Reps	Time
Gastrocnemius Stretch	1		30 sec
Ball Lat Stretch	1		30 sec
Standing Biceps Femoris Stretch	1		30 sec
Standing Pec Stretch	1		30 sec
Standing Hip Flexor Stretch	1		30 sec
Erector Spinae Stretch	1		30 sec
DYNAMIC WARM-UP	**Sets**	**Reps**	**Time**
Medicine Ball Rotations (Use golf club instead of MB)	1	12	0 sec
Lunge with Rotations	1	12	0 sec
Medicine Ball Flexion/Extension (Use golf club instead of MB)	1	12	0 sec
Single-leg Romanian Deadlift	1	12	60 sec

Hockey

Note: The Sports Performance Professional will focus on position players within the sport of hockey and not specifically on the goal-tending position. In the case of a performance program with hockey players, both position players and goalies will receive tremendous benefits by following the application guidelines and techniques presented subsequently. The goal-tending position is a unique position within the sports; however, the same basic fundamentals should be considered when analyzing movement patterns, demand of the sport/position, and enhancing performance. If there is an individual need to modify the model based on the athlete's needs, then it is very appropriate to do so based on the assessment process, the position's needs, and the goals set for the athlete. The Sports Performance Professional will focus on "off-ice" performance training for the purposes of decreased injury and increased "on-ice" performance.

DEMANDS OF THE SPORT

GENERAL INFORMATION

- Activity characterized by high-intensity intermittent skating, rapid changes in velocity and duration.
- Aerobic and anaerobic energy systems important to cardiorespiratory conditioning.
- Movement is primarily skating forward without the puck; however, movement is rarely linear for more than a couple of strides. This should not be confused with lateral motion; turns can range from gradual to sharp and therefore loading of the legs is rarely equal.
- Change of direction includes stopping, backwards skating, and some lateral movement.

SPECIFIC INFORMATION (10)

- Duration of game: 60 minutes (3 × 20-minute periods)
- Player on ice (shift): 15–20 minutes, defensemen typically play more minutes than forwards
- Duration of each shift: 30–80 seconds
- Average shift length: 39 seconds
- Recovery between shifts: 3–4 minutes
- Work to rest ratio of 1:2–1:3
- Brief periods of accelerated sprints while on the ice: 4–7 seconds
- Frequent body contact (player to player, player to boards), which adds additional stress to body

SUGGESTED ASSESSMENTS FOR HOCKEY

TRANSITIONAL POSTURAL ASSESSMENTS

- Overhead Squat Test
- Single-leg Squat Test

CARDIORESPIRATORY ASSESSMENTS

- Harvard Step Test or
- Multistage Shuttle Test

POWER ASSESSMENTS

- Double-leg Vertical Jump
- Shark Skill Test

AGILITY ASSESSMENTS

- 5–10–15 (Pro Agility Shuttle) Test
- T-Test

SPEED ENDURANCE ASSESSMENT

- 300-yard Shuttle

STRENGTH ASSESSMENTS

- Bench Press (5 RM)
- Squat Test (5 RM)

OFF-SEASON GOALS AND CONSIDERATIONS FOR HOCKEY

- Physical and mental reconditioning.
- Correcting impaired movement patterns and muscle imbalances based on results of movement assessments.
- Improving range of motion, joint stability, and muscle strength and endurance.
- Improving cardiorespiratory endurance (aerobic/anaerobic).
- Improving total body stabilization.
- Improving total body strength.
- Improving total body power.
- Determine through assessment, demand of sport analysis, and athlete goals which plan and program should be created to achieve both the needs and the goals.
- Developing a systematic off-season plan that incorporates integrated training, including core training, balance training, power training, speed, agility, and quickness training, integrated resistance training, and cardiorespiratory training combined with a proper nutrition plan to maximize training and recovery.
- Appropriate rest should be given between workouts.
- Developing an off-season training schedule that works backwards from commencement of the preseason to allow for maximum injury prevention and performance gains without athlete overtraining.
- Consider that conditioning for hockey should be as similar to the game demands as possible. Off-ice conditioning utilizing cardio machines and exercises incorporating ground reaction forces should be considered when designing a conditioning program.

Note: Annual programming and periodization is based on elite level hockey schedules. Lower-level and younger athletes may play shortened seasons and, therefore, will have a longer off-season. Off-season programming should be adjusted in this case to progress the athlete at the proper pace to reach preseason in optimal condition

OFF-SEASON OPT™ HOCKEY PLAN (MAY–AUGUST)

Level	Phase	JAN IN-Season	FEB IN-Season	MAR IN-Season	APR IN-Season	MAY OFF-Season (1)	JUN OFF-Season (2)	JUL OFF-Season (3)	AUG OFF-Season (4)	SEP PRE-Season	OCT IN-Season	NOV IN-Season	DEC IN-Season
Corrective						X							
Stabilization	1					X			X				
Strength	2						X	X	X				
	3												
	4								X				
Power	5							X	X				
	6												

SAMPLE OFF-SEASON WEEKLY OPT™ HOCKEY SCHEDULE

Month 1: 3 days/week

	Monday	Tuesday	Wednesday	Thursday	Friday	Saturday	Sunday
OPT™ Phase	Stabilization Endurance	OFF	Corrective	OFF	Stabilization Endurance	OFF	OFF

Month 2: 4 days/week

	Monday	Tuesday	Wednesday	Thursday	Friday	Saturday	Sunday
OPT™ Phase	Strength Endurance UPPER BODY	Corrective	Maximal Strength TOTAL BODY	OFF	Strength Endurance LOWER BODY	OFF	OFF

Month 3: 5 days/week

	Monday	Tuesday	Wednesday	Thursday	Friday	Saturday	Sunday
OPT™ Phase	Power	Conditioning	Strength Endurance	Conditioning	Power	OFF	OFF

Month 4: 5 days/week

	Monday	Tuesday	Wednesday	Thursday	Friday	Saturday	Sunday
OPT™ Phase	Strength Endurance	OFF	Stabilization Endurance	OFF	Power	OFF	OFF
Other		Conditioning	Conditioning	Conditioning			

SAMPLE OFF-SEASON OPT™ HOCKEY PROGRAMS
CORRECTIVE EXERCISE TRAINING

INHIBIT	Sets	Reps	Time
Foam Roll: IT Band	1		30 sec
Foam Roll: Adductor	1		30 sec
Foam Roll: Tensor Fascia Latae	1		30 sec
LENGTHEN	**Sets**	**Reps**	**Time**
Gastrocnemius Stretch	1		30 sec
Supine Biceps Femoris Stretch	1		30 sec
Standing Adductor Stretch	1		30 sec
Standing Psoas Stretch	1		30 sec

(continued)					
ACTIVATE	Sets	Reps	Tempo	Intensity	Rest
Single-leg Hip Abduction: Gluteus Medius	3	10	4/2/1		0 sec
Single-leg Hip Adduction: Pectineus	3	10	4/2/1		0 sec
Ball Cobra	3	10	4/2/1		60 sec
INTEGRATE	Sets	Reps	Tempo	Intensity	Rest
Total Body Turning Step-up, Balance, to Overhead Press: Single-arm	3	10	4/2/1	60%	60 sec

PHASE 1: STABILIZATION ENDURANCE TRAINING

WARM-UP		Sets	Reps	Time	
Foam Roll					
Tensor Fascia Latae		1		30 sec	
Adductors		1		30 sec	
Static Stretch					
Gastrocnemius Stretch		1		30 sec	
Kneeling Hip Flexor Stretch		1		30 sec	
Standing Biceps Femoris Stretch		1		30 sec	

CORE & BALANCE	Sets	Reps	Tempo	Rest
Quadruped Arm Opposite Leg Raise	3	12	4/2/1	0
Floor Cobra	3	12	4/2/1	0
Single-leg Lift and Chop	3	12	4/2/1	60 sec

PLYOMETRICS	Sets	Reps	Tempo	Rest
Box Jump-downs with Stabilization	3	8	Hold Landing	60 sec

SPEED/AGILITY/QUICKNESS	Sets	Reps	Distance	Rest
Speed Ladder: Six Exercises	2			60 sec

RESISTANCE		Sets	Reps	Tempo	Intensity	Rest
Total Body	Optional					
Chest	Cable Chest Press: Alternate-Arm	3	12	4/2/1	70%	0 sec
Back	Ball DB Row	3	12	4/2/1	70%	0 sec
Shoulders	Single-leg Overhead DB Press: Single-arm	3	12	4/2/1	70%	0 sec
Biceps	Optional					
Triceps	Optional					
Legs	Single-leg Squat	3	12	4/2/1	70%	90 sec

COOL DOWN
Repeat Foam Roll and Static Stretching Exercises from WARM-UP

(continued)			
WARM-UP	**Sets**	**Reps**	**Time**
Lunge with Rotation	1	10	0 sec
Leg Swings: Side to Side	1	10	0 sec
Medicine Ball Lift and Chop	1	10	0 sec
Medicine Ball Rotations	1	10	0 sec
Push-up with Rotation	1	10	60 sec

CORE, BALANCE, & PLYOMETRICS	**Sets**	**Reps**	**Tempo**	**Rest**
No CORE, BALANCE, & PLYOMETRICS (Incorporated into Dynamic Warm-up)				

SPEED/AGILITY/QUICKNESS	**Sets**	**Reps**	**Distance**	**Rest**
Speed Ladder: Six Exercises	2			60 sec
T-Drill	4			60 sec

RESISTANCE		**Sets**	**Reps**	**Tempo**	**Intensity**	**Rest**
Total Body	1. Deadlift, Shrug to Calf Raise 2. Push Press	4	4 8	Controlled Explosive	90% 4% of BW	2 min
Chest	1. Bench Press 2. Rotational Chest Pass	4	4 8	Controlled Explosive	90% 4% of BW	2 min
Back	1. Seated Cable Row 2. Ball Medicine Ball Pullover Throw	4	4 8	Controlled Explosive	90% 4% of BW	2 min
Shoulders	Done in Total Body exercise					
Legs	1. Barbell Squat 2. Power Step-up	4	4 8	Controlled Explosive	90% 4% of BW	2 min

COOL DOWN
Foam Roll and Static Stretching

PRESEASON GOALS AND CONSIDERATIONS FOR HOCKEY

- Correcting impaired movement patterns based on results of preseason assessments.
- Maintain physical health and decrease the chance of injury for participation in practice and games and optimal performance within such activities.
- Maintain range of motion, joint stability, and muscle strength and endurance.
- Maintain cardiorespiratory endurance (anaerobic/aerobic).
- Maintain total body stabilization, strength, and power.
- Developing a systematic preseason plan that transitions the athlete from performance enhancement to injury prevention and maintenance of off-season gains. This transition should be implemented with the consideration that the athlete's sport participation level is increasing dramatically from what they have become used to in the off-season.
- The proper recovery and reconditioning should be applied during this time of increased activity.
- Consider the exercise volume of injury prevention and performance training based on the athlete's increased activity level.
- Establish with the athlete an in-season strategy and plan that works based on what the athlete needs, wants, and will have the capability to do.

PRESEASON OPT™ HOCKEY PLAN (SEPTEMBER)

Level	Phase	JAN IN-Season	FEB IN-Season	MAR IN-Season	APR IN-Season	MAY OFF-Season	JUN OFF-Season	JUL OFF-Season	AUG OFF-Season	SEP PRE-Season (1)	OCT IN-Season	NOV IN-Season	DEC IN-Season
Corrective											X		
Stabilization	1										X		
Strength	2										X		
	3												
	4												
Power	5												
	6												

SAMPLE PRESEASON WEEKLY OPT™ HOCKEY SCHEDULE

Month 1

	Monday	Tuesday	Wednesday	Thursday	Friday	Saturday	Sunday
OPT™ Phase	Strength Endurance	OFF	Corrective Exercise	OFF	Stabilization Endurance	OFF	Corrective
Other				Game		Game	

SAMPLE PRESEASON OPT™ HOCKEY PROGRAMS

CORRECTIVE EXERCISE TRAINING

INHIBIT		Sets	Reps	Time
Foam Roll: Tensor Fascia Latae		1		30 sec
Foam Roll: IT Band		1		30 sec
Foam Roll: Adductors		1		30 sec

LENGTHEN		Sets	Reps	Time
Supine Biceps Femoris Stretch		1		30 sec
Kneeling Hip Flexor Stretch		1		30 sec
Standing Adductor Stretch		1		30 sec
Ball Lat Stretch		1		30 sec

ACTIVATE	Sets	Reps	Tempo	Intensity	Rest
Side-lying Hip Adduction	1	15	4/2/1		0 sec
Ball Bridge	1	15	4/2/1		90 sec

INTEGRATE		Sets	Reps	Tempo	Intensity	Rest
Total Body	Squat, Curl to Overhead Press	1	15	4/2/1	60%	90 sec

PHASE 1: STABILIZATION ENDURANCE TRAINING

WARM-UP		Sets	Reps	Time
Foam Roll				
Tensor Fasciae Latae		1		30 sec
Piriformis		1		30 sec
Static Stretch				
Standing Adductor Stretch		1		30 sec
Kneeling Hip Flexor Stretch		1		30 sec
Posterior Shoulder Stretch		1		30 sec

CORE & BALANCE	Sets	Reps	Tempo	Rest
Side Iso-ab with Hip Abduction	2	15	4/2/1	0
Floor Bridge: Single-leg	2	15	4/2/1	0
Single-leg Throw and Catch	2	15	4/2/1	60 sec

PLYOMETRICS	Sets	Reps	Tempo	Rest
No PLYOMETRICS due to increased activity				

SPEED/AGILITY/QUICKNESS	Sets	Reps	Distance	Rest
No SAQ due to increased on-ice conditioning				

RESISTANCE		Sets	Reps	Tempo	Intensity	Rest
Total Body	Cable Squat to Row	2	15	4/2/1	65%	0 sec
Chest	Ball DB Chest Press	2	15	4/2/1	65%	0 sec
Back	Done in Total Body exercise					
Shoulders	Single-leg Scaption	2	15	4/2/1	65%	0 sec
Biceps	Optional					
Triceps	Optional					
Legs	Single-leg Romanian Deadlift	2	15	4/2/1	65%	90 sec

COOL DOWN
Repeat Foam Roll and Static Stretching Exercises from WARM-UP

PHASE 2: STRENGTH ENDURANCE TRAINING

WARM-UP		Sets	Reps	Time
Foam Roll				
Tensor Fascia Latae		1		30 sec
Adductors		1		30 sec
Static Stretch				
Standing Adductor Stretch		1		30 sec
Kneeling Hip Flexor Stretch		1		30 sec
Supine Biceps Femoris Stretch		1		30 sec

(continued)

CORE & BALANCE		Sets	Reps	Tempo	Rest
Ball Crunch with Rotation		2	12	1/1/1	0 sec
Back Extension		2	12	1/1/1	0 sec
Single-leg Squat Touchdown		2	12	1/1/1	60 sec

PLYOMETRICS		Sets	Reps	Tempo	Rest
No PLYOMETRICS due to increased activity					

SPEED/AGILITY/QUICKNESS		Sets	Reps	Distance	Rest
No SAQ due to increased on-ice conditioning					

RESISTANCE		Sets	Reps	Tempo	Intensity	Rest
Total Body	Optional					
Chest	1. DB Bench Press 2. Ball Push-up: Hands on Ball	2	12 12	2/0/2 4/2/1	70%	0 sec
Back	1. Bent Over Row 2. Single-leg Cable Pulldown	2	12 12	2/0/2 4/2/1	70%	0 sec
Shoulders	1. Seated Overhead DB Press 2. Single-leg Lateral Raise	2	12 12	2/0/2 4/2/1	70%	0 sec
Biceps	Optional					
Triceps	Optional					
Legs	1. Step-up: Frontal Place 2. Single-leg Romanian Deadlift	2	12 12	2/0/2 4/2/1	70%	60 sec

COOL DOWN
Foam Roll and Static Stretching

IN-SEASON GOALS AND CONSIDERATIONS FOR HOCKEY

- Perform assessments and testing to ensure program considerations are being made to prevent overuse injuries and maintain performance levels.
- Continued attention to impaired movement patterns with corrective strategies being implemented.
- Maintain range of motion, joint stability, and muscle strength and endurance.
- Maintain cardiorespiratory endurance (anaerobic/aerobic).
- Maintain total body stabilization, strength, and power.
- Consider additional conditioning for athletes that may not get the same type of on-ice minutes during games than others.
- Developing a systematic in-season maintenance plan that allows the athlete to minimize decreases in performance and chance of injury over a long season with repetitive sport movement patterns and physical contact.
- Consider the exercise volume of injury prevention and performance training based on the athlete's increased travel and activity level.
- Establish with the athlete a communication process for monitoring in-season maintenance and plan that works based on what the athlete needs, wants, and will have the capability to do.

IN-SEASON OPT™ HOCKEY PLAN (OCTOBER–APRIL)

Level	Phase	JAN IN- Season (4)	FEB IN- Season (5)	MAR IN- Season (6)	APR IN- Season (7)	MAY OFF- Season	JUN OFF- Season	JUL OFF- Season	AUG OFF- Season	SEP PRE- Season	OCT IN- Season (1)	NOV IN- Season (2)	DEC IN- Season (3)
Corrective		X	X	X	X						X	X	X
Stabilization	1	X	X	X	X						X	X	X
Strength	2		X		X						X		X
	3												
	4	X		X								X	
Power	5												
	6												

SAMPLE IN-SEASON WEEKLY OPT™ HOCKEY SCHEDULE

Any Month

	Monday	Tuesday	Wednesday	Thursday	Friday	Saturday	Sunday
OPT™ Phase	Maximal Strength	OFF	Corrective	OFF	Stabilization Endurance	OFF	Corrective
Other	Game			Game		Game	

CORRECTIVE EXERCISE TRAINING

INHIBIT			Sets	Reps	Time
Foam Roll: Tensor Fascia Latae			1		30 sec
Foam Roll: Adductors			1		30 sec
Foam Roll: Thoracic Spine			1		30 sec
LENGTHEN			**Sets**	**Reps**	**Time**
Supine Biceps Femoris Stretch			1		30 sec
Kneeling Hip Flexor Stretch			1		30 sec
Standing Adductor Stretch			1		30 sec
Standing Pec Stretch			1		30 sec

ACTIVATE		Sets	Reps	Tempo	Intensity	Rest
Side-lying Hip Adduction		1	15	4/2/1		0 sec
Ball Bridge		1	15	4/2/1		0 sec
Single-leg Hip Extension		1	15	4/2/1		90 sec
INTEGRATE		**Sets**	**Reps**	**Tempo**	**Intensity**	**Rest**
Total Body	Side Lunge to Overhead Press	1	15	4/2/1	60%	90 sec

PHASE 1: STABILIZATION ENDURANCE TRAINING

WARM-UP		Sets	Reps		Time
Foam Roll					
Tensor Fascia Latae			1		30 sec
Piriformis			1		30 sec
Static Stretch					
Standing Adductor Stretch			1		30 sec
Kneeling Hip Flexor Stretch			1		30 sec
Posterior Shoulder Stretch			1		30 sec
CORE & BALANCE		Sets	Reps	Tempo	Rest
Prone Iso Ab		2	15	4/2/1	0 sec
Ball Cobra		2	15	4/2/1	0 sec
Single-leg Balance Reach		2	15	4/2/1	60 sec
PLYOMETRICS		Sets	Reps	Tempo	Rest
No PLYOMETRICS due to increased activity					
SPEED/AGILITY/QUICKNESS		Sets	Reps	Distance	Rest
No SAQ due to increased on-ice conditioning					
RESISTANCE		Sets	Reps	Tempo	Intensity	Rest
Total Body	Lunge, Balance to Overhead Press	2	15	4/2/1	65%	0 sec
Chest	Ball DB Chest Press: Alternate-arm	2	15	4/2/1	65%	0 sec
Back	Single-leg Cable Row	2	15	4/2/1	65%	0 sec
Shoulders	Done in Total Body exercise					
Biceps	Optional					
Triceps	Optional					
Legs	Step-up to Balance: Transverse Plane	2	15	4/2/1	65%	90 sec
COOL DOWN						
Foam Roll and Static Stretching						

PHASE 2: STRENGTH ENDURANCE TRAINING

WARM-UP	Sets	Reps	Time
Foam Roll			
Tensor Fascia Latae	1		30 sec
Thoracic Spine	1		30 sec
Static Stretch			
Standing Adductor Stretch	1		30 sec
Standing Hip Flexor Stretch	1		30 sec
Ball Lat Stretch	1		30 sec

(*continued*)

(continued)					
CORE & BALANCE		**Sets**	**Reps**	**Tempo**	**Rest**
Cable Rotation		2	12	1/1/1	0 sec
Ball Crunch		2	12	1/1/1	0 sec
Single-leg Romanian Deadlift		2	12	1/1/1	60 sec
PLYOMETRICS		**Sets**	**Reps**	**Tempo**	**Rest**
No PLYOMETRICS due to increased activity					
SPEED/AGILITY/QUICKNESS		**Sets**	**Reps**	**Distance**	**Rest**
No SAQ due to increased on-ice conditioning					

RESISTANCE		**Sets**	**Reps**	**Tempo**	**Intensity**	**Rest**
Total Body	1. Cable Squat to Row 2. Step-up, Balance to Overhead Press	2	12 12	2/0/2 4/2/1	70%	0 sec
Chest	1. Incline Bench Press 2. Push-up	2	12 12	2/0/2 4/2/1	70%	0 sec
Back	Done in Total Body exercise					
Shoulders	Done in Total Body exercise					
Biceps	1. Standing DB Curl	2	12	2/0/2	70%	0 sec
Triceps	2. Supine Ball Triceps Extensions	2	12	4/2/1	70%	0 sec
Legs	1. Barbell Squat 2. Lunge to Balance: Frontal Plane	2	12 12	2/0/2 4/2/1	70%	60 sec

COOL DOWN
Foam Roll and Static Stretching

PHASE 4: MAXIMAL STRENGTH TRAINING

WARM-UP	**Sets**	**Reps**	**Time**
Foam Roll			
IT Band		1	30 sec
Adductors		1	30 sec
TFL		1	30 sec
Dynamic Warm-up (Some athletes may still require static stretching prior to the Dynamic Warm-up)			
Prisoner Squats		1	10	0 sec
Multiplanar Lunges		1	10	0 sec
Push-up with Rotation		1	10	0 sec
Medicine Ball Rotations		1	10	60 sec

CORE & BALANCE	**Sets**	**Reps**	**Tempo**	**Rest**
Knee-ups	2	12	1/1/1	0 sec
Back Extension	2	12	1/1/1	0 sec
Step-up to Balance	2	12	1/1/1	90 sec

(continued)						
PLYOMETRICS		**Sets**	**Reps**	**Tempo**		**Rest**
No PLYOMETRICS on this day						
SPEED/AGILITY/QUICKNESS		**Sets**	**Reps**	**Distance**		**Rest**
No SAQ on this day						
RESISTANCE		**Sets**	**Reps**	**Tempo**	**Intensity**	**Rest**
Total Body	Deadlift Shrug to Calf Raise	4	5	Explosive	85%	3 min
Chest	Bench Press	4	5	Controlled	85%	3 min
Back	Seated Cable Row	4	5	Controlled	85%	3 min
Shoulders	Seated Overhead Barbell Press	4	5	Controlled	85%	3 min
Biceps	Optional					
Triceps	Optional					
Legs	Barbell Squat	4	5	Controlled	85%	3 min
COOL DOWN						
Foam Roll and Static Stretching						

Soccer

DEMANDS OF THE SPORT

GENERAL INFORMATION

- Less than 2% of total distance covered during a game is with the ball.
- The aerobic energy system predominates, responsible for as much as 98% of the energy utilized (11).
- Matches are typically decided at the highest speeds with the ATP-PCr and glycolytic systems dominant.

ACTIVITY INFORMATION

- Distance covered by a player in a match ranges from 10–13 km (12).
- 1,000–1,200 changes in locomotion pattern occur during the course of a match. There is approximately one change every 4.5 seconds of play (13).
- Activity pattern defined by running intensity/speed:
  - Standing: 17.1% of total activity
  - Walking: 40.4% of total activity
  - Low-intensity Running: 35.1% of total activity
  - High-intensity Running: 8.1% of total activity
  - Sprinting: 0.7% of total activity
- Average sprint: 15 meters
- Average one sprint every 90 seconds
- Variations in all are position specific and vary between matches.
- Higher-level players will cover more ground and spend more time at higher intensities than lower-level players (14).
- Distance covered in the second half of play is typically less than that covered in the first half of play (14).

SUGGESTED ASSESSMENTS FOR SOCCER

TRANSITIONAL POSTURAL ASSESSMENTS

- Overhead Squat Assessment
- Single-leg Squat Assessment

CARDIORESPIRATORY ASSESSMENTS

- Harvard Step Test or
- 20-meter Multistage Shuttle Test

POWER ASSESSMENTS

- Standing Soccer Throw
- Double-leg Vertical Jump
- Overhead Medicine Ball Throw
- Shark Skill Test

SPEED ASSESSMENT

- 30-yard Sprint, measured 0–10 yards (acceleration speed), 10–30 yards (maximal speed)

AGILITY ASSESSMENTS

- LEFT (Lower-Extremity Functional) Test
- T-Test
- 5-0-5 Test for horizontal agility (15)

SPEED ENDURANCE ASSESSMENT

- 7- $\times$ 30-m sprint test (16)

STABILIZATION ENDURANCE ASSESSMENT

- Single-leg Balance Excursion Test

STRENGTH ASSESSMENTS

- Squat (5 RM)
- Push-up for Test for Endurance
- Pull-up Test

OFF-SEASON GOALS AND CONSIDERATIONS FOR SOCCER

- Physical and mental reconditioning.
- Correcting impaired movement patterns and muscle imbalances based on results of movement assessments.
- Improving range of motion, joint stability, and muscle strength and endurance.
- Improving cardiorespiratory endurance (anaerobic/aerobic).
- Improving total body stabilization.
- Improving total body strength.
- Improving total body power.
- Increase reaction time, speed, agility, and quickness.
- Determine through assessments, demand of sport analysis, and athlete goals which plan and program should be created to achieve each goal.
- Developing a systematic off-season plan that incorporates integrated training, including core training, balance training, power training, speed, agility, and quickness training, integrated resistance training and cardiorespiratory training combined with a proper nutrition plan to maximize training and recovery.
- Appropriate rest should be given between workouts.
- Developing an off-season training schedule that works backwards from commencement of the preseason to allow for maximum injury prevention and performance gains without the athlete overtraining.
- Consider that conditioning for soccer should be as similar to the game as possible. Ground reaction forces, starting and stopping, and change of direction must also be considered when designing a conditioning program.
- Consider that although the sport of soccer is a very dynamic activity, many soccer players enter the off-season having diminished stabilization mechanisms that must be trained and reconditioned.

- Athlete will continue to increase soccer skill activities as the off-season progresses. Therefore, their performance program should be modified appropriately from a volume and exercise standpoint to accommodate these specific activities to avoid overtraining and maximize results.

Note: The annual training plan and the seasonal periodization models are based on a collegiate competition calendar.

OFF-SEASON OPT™ SOCCER PLAN (JANUARY–JULY)

Level	Phase	JAN OFF-Season (1)	FEB OFF-Season (2)	MAR OFF-Season (3)	APR OFF-Season (4)	MAY OFF-Season (5)	JUN OFF-Season (6)	JUL OFF-Season (7)	AUG PRE-Season	SEP IN-Season	OCT IN-Season	NOV IN-Season	DEC IN-Season
Corrective		X											
Stabilization	1		X			X		X					
Strength	2			X			X	X					
	3												
	4												
Power	5				X			X					
	6												

SAMPLE OFF-SEASON WEEKLY OPT™ SOCCER SCHEDULE

Month 1: 2 days/week

	Monday	Tuesday	Wednesday	Thursday	Friday	Saturday	Sunday
OPT™ Phase	Corrective	OFF	OFF	Corrective	OFF	OFF	OFF

Month 2: 2 days/week

	Monday	Tuesday	Wednesday	Thursday	Friday	Saturday	Sunday
OPT™ Phase	Stabilization Endurance	OFF	OFF	Stabilization Endurance	OFF	OFF	OFF

Month 3: 4 days/week

	Monday	Tuesday	Wednesday	Thursday	Friday	Saturday	Sunday
OPT™ Phase	Strength Endurance		OFF	Strength Endurance		OFF	OFF
Other		Conditioning			Conditioning		

Month 4: 4 days/week

	Monday	Tuesday	Wednesday	Thursday	Friday	Saturday	Sunday
OPT™ Phase	Power		OFF	Power		OFF	OFF
Other		Conditioning			Conditioning		

Month 5: 5 days/week

	Monday	Tuesday	Wednesday	Thursday	Friday	Saturday	Sunday
OPT™ Phase	Stabilization Endurance		Stabilization Endurance		Stabilization Endurance	OFF	OFF
Other		Conditioning		Conditioning			

(*continued*)

(continued)

Month 6: 5 days/week

	Monday	Tuesday	Wednesday	Thursday	Friday	Saturday	Sunday
OPT™ Phase	Strength Endurance		Strength Endurance		Strength Endurance	OFF	OFF
Other		Conditioning		Conditioning			

Month 7: 5 days/week

	Monday	Tuesday	Wednesday	Thursday	Friday	Saturday	Sunday
OPT™ Phase	Strength Endurance		Stabilization Endurance		Power	OFF	OFF
Other	Conditioning	Conditioning		Conditioning			

SAMPLE OFF-SEASON OPT™ SOCCER PROGRAMS

CORRECTIVE EXERCISE TRAINING

INHIBIT			Sets	Reps	Time
Foam Roll: Calf			1		30 sec
Foam Roll: Tensor Fascia Latae			1		30 sec
Foam Roll: IT Band			1		30 sec
Foam Roll Adductor			1		30 sec
LENGTHEN			**Sets**	**Reps**	**Time**
Gastrocnemius Stretch			1		30 sec
Soleus Stretch			1		30 sec
Supine Biceps Femoris Stretch			1		30 sec
Kneeling Hip Flexor Stretch			1		30 sec
Standing Adductor Stretch			1		30 sec

ACTIVATE	Sets	Reps	Tempo	Intensity	Rest
Single-leg Calf Raise	2	12	4/2/1		0 sec
Single-leg Hip Adduction: Pectineus	2	12	4/2/1		0 sec
Single-leg Hip Abduction: Gluteus Medius	2	12	4/2/1		0 sec
Floor Bridge	2	12	4/2/1		90 sec
INTEGRATE	**Sets**	**Reps**	**Tempo**	**Intensity**	**Rest**
Total Body Cable Squat to Row	2	12	4/2/1	60%	0 sec

PHASE 1: STABILIZATION ENDURANCE TRAINING

WARM-UP	Sets	Reps	Time
Foam Roll			
Tensor Fascia Latae	1		30 sec
Piriformis	1		30 sec
Static Stretch			
Gastrocnemius Stretch	1		30 sec
Kneeling Hip Flexor Stretch	1		30 sec
Standing Biceps Femoris Stretch	1		30 sec

(continued)					
CORE & BALANCE		**Sets**	**Reps**	**Tempo**	**Rest**
Side Iso-Ab		1	15	4/2/1	0
Floor Bridge: Single-leg		1	15	4/2/1	0
Single-leg Balance Reach		1	15	4/2/1	60 sec
PLYOMETRICS		**Sets**	**Reps**	**Tempo**	**Rest**
Squat Jump with Stabilization		1	6	Hold Landing	60 sec
SPEED/AGILITY/QUICKNESS		**Sets**	**Reps**	**Distance**	**Rest**
Speed Ladder: Six Exercises		2			60 sec

RESISTANCE		**Sets**	**Reps**	**Tempo**	**Intensity**	**Rest**
Total Body	Lunge, Balance to Overhead Press: Single-arm	1	20	4/2/1	60%	0 sec
Chest	Cable Chest Press: Alternate-arm	1	20	4/2/1	60%	0 sec
Back	Ball DB Cobra	1	20	4/2/1	60%	0 sec
Shoulders	Done in Total Body exercise					
Biceps	Single-leg DB Curl: Alternate-arm	1	20	4/2/1	60%	0 sec
Triceps	Supine Ball Triceps Extensions	1	20	4/2/1	60%	0 sec
Legs	Single-leg Squat	1	20	4/2/1	60%	90 sec

COOL DOWN
Repeat Foam Roll and Static Stretching Exercises from WARM-UP

PHASE 2: STRENGTH ENDURANCE TRAINING

WARM-UP	**Sets**	**Reps**	**Time**
Foam Roll			
IT Band		1	30 sec
Piriformis		1	30 sec
Calf		1	30 sec
Static Stretch			
Standing Adductor Stretch		1	30 sec
Standing Hip Flexor Stretch		1	30 sec
Standing Pec Stretch		1	30 sec
CORE & BALANCE	**Sets**	**Reps**	**Tempo**	**Rest**
Knee-ups	2	12	1/1/1	0 sec
Back Extension with Rotation	2	12	1/1/1	0 sec
Single-leg Squat Touchdown	2	12	1/1/1	60 sec
PLYOMETRICS	**Sets**	**Reps**	**Tempo**	**Rest**
Butt Kicks	2	8	Repeating	0 sec
Cone Hops: Side-Side	2	8	Repeating	60 sec

(continued)

(continued)					
SPEED/AGILITY/QUICKNESS		**Sets**	**Reps**	**Distance**	**Rest**
Speed Ladder: Six Exercises		2			60 sec
LEFT test		2			60 sec
RESISTANCE		**Sets**	**Reps**	**Tempo**	**Intensity**	**Rest**

RESISTANCE		**Sets**	**Reps**	**Tempo**	**Intensity**	**Rest**
Total Body	Optional					
Chest	1. Incline DB Press 2. Cable Chest Press: Single-arm	2	12 12	2/0/2 4/2/1	70%	0 sec
Back	1. Seated Lat Pulldown 2. Ball DB Row: Alternate-arm	2	12 12	2/0/2 4/2/1	70%	0 sec
Shoulders	1. Seated Overhead DB Press 2. Single-leg Lateral Raise	2	12 12	2/0/2 4/2/1	70%	0 sec
Biceps	Optional					
Triceps	Optional					
Legs	1. Lunge: Frontal Plane 2. Single-leg Squat	2	12 12	2/0/2 4/2/1	70%	60 sec
COOL DOWN						
Foam Roll and Static Stretching Exercises						

PHASE 5: POWER TRAINING

WARM-UP	**Sets**	**Reps**	**Time**
Foam Roll			
Calf		1	30 sec
Tensor Fascia Latae		1	30 sec
Adductor		1	30 sec
Dynamic Warm-up (Some athletes may still require static stretching prior to the Dynamic Warm-up)			
Lateral Tube Walking		1	10	0 sec
Prisoner Squats		1	10	0 sec
Lunge with Rotation		1	10	0 sec
Leg Swings: Front to Back		1	10	0 sec
Push-up with Rotation		1	10	0 sec
Scorpion		1	10	0 sec
Multiplanar Hop to Stabilization		1	10	60 sec
CORE, BALANCE, & PLYOMETRICS	**Sets**	**Reps**	**Tempo**	**Rest**
No CORE, BALANCE, & PLYOMETRICS (Incorporated into Dynamic Warm-up and the Resistance Workout)				
SPEED/AGILITY/QUICKNESS	**Sets**	**Reps**	**Distance**	**Rest**
Speed Ladder: Eight Exercises	1			60 sec
Box Drill	4			30 sec

(continued)						
RESISTANCE		**Sets**	**Reps**	**Tempo**	**Intensity**	**Rest**
Total Body	1. Lunge, Curl to Overhead Press	3	5	Controlled	85%	2 min
	2. Overhead Medicine Ball Throw		10	Explosive	2% of BW	
Chest	1. DB Chest Press	3	5	Controlled	85%	2 min
	2. Rotational Chest Pass		10	Explosive	2% of BW	
Back	1. Seated Lat Pulldown	3	5	Controlled	85%	2 min
	2. Soccer Throw		10	Explosive	2% of BW	
Shoulders	Done in Total Body Exercise					
Legs	1. Barbell Squat	3	5	Controlled	85%	2 min
	2. Power Step-ups		10	Explosive	2% of BW	
COOL DOWN						
Foam Roll and Static Stretching						

PRESEASON GOALS AND CONSIDERATIONS FOR SOCCER

- Correcting impaired movement patterns based on results of preseason assessments.
- Maintain physical health and decrease the chance of injury for participation in practice and games and optimal performance within such activities.
- Maintain range of motion, joint stability, and muscle strength and endurance.
- Maintain cardiorespiratory endurance (anaerobic/aerobic).
- Maintain total body stabilization, strength, and power.
- Maintenance of speed, agility, and quickness.
- Developing a systematic preseason plan that transitions the athlete from performance enhancement to injury prevention and maintenance of off-season gains. This transition should be implemented with the consideration that the athlete's sport participation level is increasing dramatically from what they have become used to in the off-season.
- The proper recovery and reconditioning should be applied during this time of increased activity.
- Consider the exercise volume of injury prevention and performance training based on the athlete's increased activity level.
- Establish with the athlete an in-season strategy and plan that works based on what the athlete needs, wants, and will have the capability to do.

PRESEASON OPT™ SOCCER PLAN (AUGUST)

Level	Phase	JAN	FEB	MAR	APR	MAY	JUN	JUL	AUG	SEP	OCT	NOV	DEC
		OFF-Season	OFF-Season	OFF-Season	OFF-Season	OFF-Season	OFF-Season	OFF-Season	PRE-Season (1)	IN-Season	IN-Season	IN-Season	IN-Season
Corrective													
Stabilization	1								X				
Strength	2								X				
	3												
	4												
Power	5												
	6												

IN-SEASON OPT™ SOCCER PLAN (SEPTEMBER–DECEMBER)

Level	Phase	JAN OFF-Season	FEB OFF-Season	MAR OFF-Season	APR OFF-Season	MAY OFF-Season	JUN OFF-Season	JUL OFF-Season	AUG PRE-Season	SEP IN-Season (1)	OCT IN-Season (2)	NOV IN-Season (3)	DEC IN-Season (4)
Corrective										X	X	X	X
Stabilization	1									X	X	X	X
Strength	2									X	X	X	X
	3												
	4												
Power	5												
	6												

SAMPLE IN-SEASON WEEKLY OPT™ SOCCER SCHEDULE

Any Month

	Monday	Tuesday	Wednesday	Thursday	Friday	Saturday	Sunday
OPT™ Phase	Corrective	Strength Endurance	OFF	Corrective	Corrective	OFF	
Other					Game		Game

SAMPLE IN-SEASON OPT™ SOCCER PROGRAMS

CORRECTIVE EXERCISE TRAINING

INHIBIT			Sets	Reps	Time
Foam Roll: Quads			1		30 sec
Foam Roll: Tensor Fascia Latae			1		30 sec
Foam Roll: IT Band			1		30 sec
Foam Roll: Adductor			1		30 sec
LENGTHEN			Sets	Reps	Time
Gastrocnemius Stretch			1		30 sec
Supine Piriformis Stretch			1		30 sec
Supine Biceps Femoris Stretch			1		30 sec
Kneeling Hip Flexor Stretch			1		30 sec
Standing Adductor Stretch			1		30 sec

ACTIVATE	Sets	Reps	Tempo	Intensity	Rest
Single-leg Hip Adduction: Pectineus	2	12	4/2/1		0 sec
Single-leg Calf Raise	2	12	4/2/1		60 sec

INTEGRATE		Sets	Reps	Tempo	Intensity	Rest
Total Body	Side Step-up, Balance to Overhead Press	2	12	4/2/1	60%	60 sec

PHASE 1: STABILIZATION ENDURANCE TRAINING

WARM-UP		Sets	Reps	Time
Foam Roll				
Tensor Fascia Latae			1	30 sec
IT Band			1	30 sec
Piriformis			1	30 sec
Static Stretch				
Gastrocnemius Stretch			1	30 sec
Kneeling Hip Flexor Stretch			1	30 sec
Supine Biceps Femoris Stretch			1	30 sec

CORE & BALANCE		Sets	Reps	Tempo	Rest
Prone Iso-Ab		2	15	4/2/1	0
Standing Cable Iso-Rotation		2	15	4/2/1	0
Single-leg Rotation		2	15	4/2/1	60 sec

PLYOMETRICS		Sets	Reps	Tempo	Rest
Box Jump-up with Stabilization		2	6	Controlled	60 sec

SPEED/AGILITY/QUICKNESS		Sets	Reps	Distance	Rest
No SAQ due to increased activity					

RESISTANCE		Sets	Reps	Tempo	Intensity	Rest
Total Body	Optional					
Chest	Ball DB Chest Press: Alternate-arm	2	15	4/2/1	65%	0 sec
Back	Single-leg Cable Row: Single-arm	2	15	4/2/1	65%	0 sec
Shoulders	Prone Ball Military Press	2	15	4/2/1	65%	0 sec
Biceps	Optional					
Triceps	Optional					
Legs	Ball Squat	2	15	4/2/1	65%	90 sec

COOL DOWN
Repeat Foam Roll and Static Stretching Exercises from WARM-UP

PHASE 2: STRENGTH ENDURANCE TRAINING

WARM-UP	Sets	Reps	Time
Foam Roll			
IT Band	1		30 sec
Piriformis	1		30 sec
Thoracic Spine	1		30 sec
Static Stretch			

(*continued*)

(continued)				
WARM-UP		**Sets**	**Reps**	**Time**
Gastrocnemius Stretch		1		30 Sec
Standing Hip Flexor Stretch		1		30 Sec
Erector Spinae Stretch		1		30 Sec

CORE & BALANCE		**Sets**	**Reps**	**Tempo**	**Rest**
Ball Crunch with Rotation		2	12	1-1-1	0 sec
Cable Rotations		2	12	1-1-1	0 sec
Side Step-up to Balance		2	12	1-1-1	60 sec

PLYOMETRICS		**Sets**	**Reps**	**Tempo**	**Rest**
No PLYOMETRICS due to increased activity					

SPEED/AGILITY/QUICKNESS		**Sets**	**Reps**	**Distance**	**Rest**
No SAQ due to increased activity					

RESISTANCE		**Sets**	**Reps**	**Tempo**	**Intensity**	**Rest**
Total Body	Optional					
Chest	1. DB Bench Press 2. Ball Push-up: Hands on Ball	3	10 10	2/0/2 4/2/1	75%	0 sec
Back	1. Seated Cable Row 2. Ball DB Cobra	3	10 10	2/0/2 4/2/1	75%	0 sec
Shoulders	1. Seated Overhead DB Press 2. Single-leg Scaption	3	10 10	2/0/2 4/2/1	75%	0 sec
Biceps	Optional					
Triceps	Optional					
Legs	1. DB Squat 2. Single-leg Romanian Deadlift	3	10 10	2/0/2 4/2/1	75%	60 sec

COOL DOWN
Repeat Foam Roll and Static Stretching Exercises from WARM-UP

REFERENCES

1. Gambetta V. Building the Complete Athlete, 5th Edition. Sarasota, FL: Gambetta Sports Training Systems, 1999.
2. McClay IS, Robinson JR, Andriacchi TP, Fredrick EC, Gross T, Martin P, Valiant G, Williams KR, Cavanagh PR. A kinematic profile of skills in professional basketball players. *J Applied Biomech*. 1994;10(3): 205–221.
3. McClay IS, Robinson JR, Andriacchi TP, Fredrick EC, Gross T, Martin P, Valiant G, Williams KR, Cavanagh PR. A profile of ground reaction forces in professional basketball. *J Applied Biomech*. 1994;10(3): 221–236.
4. Lephart SM, Smoliga JM, Myers JB, Sell TC, Tsai YS. An eight-week golf-specific exercise program improves physical characteristics, swing mechanics, and golf performance in recreational golfers. *J Strength Cond Res*. 2007;21(3):860–9.
5. Sell TC, Tsai YS, Smoliga JM, Myers JB, Lephart SM. Strength, flexibility, and balance characteristics of highly proficient golfers. *J Strength Cond Res*. 2007;21(4):1166–71.
6. Thompson CJ, Cobb KM, Blackwell J. Functional training improves club head speed and functional fitness in older golfers. *J Strength Cond Res*. 2007;21(1):131–7.
7. Gosheger G, Liem D, Ludwig K, Greshake O, Winkelmann W. Injuries and overuse syndromes in golf. *Am J Sports Med*. 2003;31(3):438–43.
8. Fradkin AJ, Sherman CA, Finch CF. Is there an association between self-reported warm-up behavior and golf related injury in female golfers? *J Sports Med*. 2004;38(6):762–5.

9. Montgomery DL. Physiology of Ice Hockey. *Sports Med.* 1988;5(2): 99–126. Review.

10. Bangsbo J. The physiology of soccer—with special reference to intense intermittent exercise. *Acta Physiol Scand Suppl.* 1994b;619:1–155.

11. Bangsbo J, Mohr M, Krustrup P. Physical and metabolic demands of training and match-play in the elite football player. *J Sports Sci.* 2006;24(7):665–674.

12. Bangsbo J, Norregaard L, Thorso F. Activity profile of competition soccer. *Can J Sport Sci.* 1991;16(2): 110–116.

13. Mohr M, Krustrup P, Bangsbo J. Match performance of high-standard soccer players with special reference to development of fatigue. *J Sports Sci.* 2003;21(7):519–528.

14. Bangsbo J. Fitness Training in Football: A Scientific Approach. Vol. 1994. Bagsvaerd, Denmark: HO Storm; pp. 58–62.

15. Gore CJ. Physiological tests for elite athletes. Champaign, IL: Human Kinetics, 2000.

APPENDIX B

Percent of One Rep Maximum (I-RM) Conversion

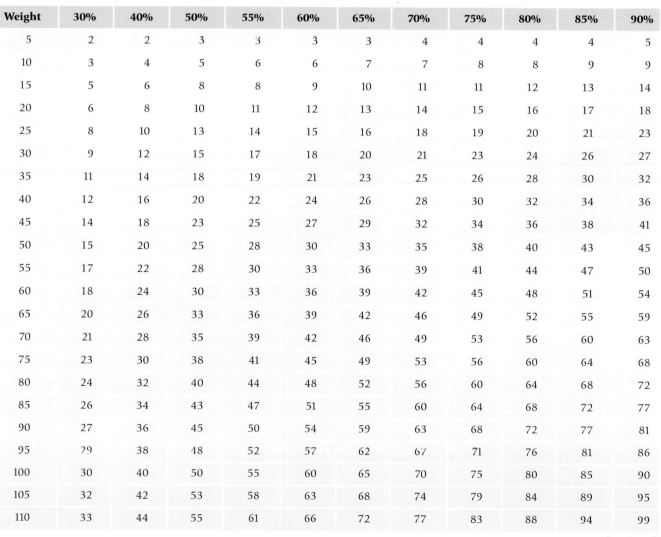

Weight	30%	40%	50%	55%	60%	65%	70%	75%	80%	85%	90%
5	2	2	3	3	3	3	4	4	4	4	5
10	3	4	5	6	6	7	7	8	8	9	9
15	5	6	8	8	9	10	11	11	12	13	14
20	6	8	10	11	12	13	14	15	16	17	18
25	8	10	13	14	15	16	18	19	20	21	23
30	9	12	15	17	18	20	21	23	24	26	27
35	11	14	18	19	21	23	25	26	28	30	32
40	12	16	20	22	24	26	28	30	32	34	36
45	14	18	23	25	27	29	32	34	36	38	41
50	15	20	25	28	30	33	35	38	40	43	45
55	17	22	28	30	33	36	39	41	44	47	50
60	18	24	30	33	36	39	42	45	48	51	54
65	20	26	33	36	39	42	46	49	52	55	59
70	21	28	35	39	42	46	49	53	56	60	63
75	23	30	38	41	45	49	53	56	60	64	68
80	24	32	40	44	48	52	56	60	64	68	72
85	26	34	43	47	51	55	60	64	68	72	77
90	27	36	45	50	54	59	63	68	72	77	81
95	29	38	48	52	57	62	67	71	76	81	86
100	30	40	50	55	60	65	70	75	80	85	90
105	32	42	53	58	63	68	74	79	84	89	95
110	33	44	55	61	66	72	77	83	88	94	99

(continued)

(continued)

Weight	30%	40%	50%	55%	60%	65%	70%	75%	80%	85%	90%
115	35	46	58	63	69	75	81	86	92	98	104
120	36	48	60	66	72	78	84	90	96	102	108
125	38	50	63	69	75	81	88	94	100	106	113
130	39	52	65	72	78	85	91	98	104	111	117
135	41	54	68	74	81	88	95	101	108	115	122
140	42	56	70	77	84	91	98	105	112	119	126
145	44	58	73	80	87	94	102	109	116	123	131
150	45	60	75	83	90	98	105	113	120	128	135
155	47	62	78	85	93	101	109	116	124	132	140
160	48	64	80	88	96	104	112	120	128	136	144
165	50	66	83	91	99	107	116	124	132	140	149
170	51	68	85	94	102	111	119	128	136	145	153
175	53	70	88	96	105	114	123	131	140	149	158
180	54	72	90	99	108	117	126	135	144	153	162
185	56	74	93	102	111	120	130	139	148	157	167
190	57	76	95	105	114	124	133	143	152	162	171
195	59	78	98	107	117	127	137	146	156	166	176
200	60	80	100	110	120	130	140	150	160	170	180
205	62	82	103	113	123	133	144	154	164	174	185
210	63	84	105	116	126	137	147	158	168	179	189
215	65	86	108	118	129	140	151	161	172	183	194
220	66	88	110	121	132	143	154	165	176	187	198
225	68	90	113	124	135	146	158	169	180	191	203
230	69	92	115	127	138	150	161	173	184	196	207
235	71	94	118	129	141	153	165	176	188	200	212
240	72	96	120	132	144	156	168	180	192	204	216
245	74	98	123	135	147	159	172	184	196	208	221
250	75	100	125	138	150	163	175	188	200	213	225
255	77	102	128	140	153	166	179	191	204	217	230
260	78	104	130	143	156	169	182	195	208	221	234
265	80	106	133	146	159	172	186	199	212	225	239
270	81	108	135	149	162	176	189	203	216	230	243
275	83	110	138	151	165	179	193	206	220	234	248
280	84	112	140	154	168	182	196	210	224	238	252
285	86	114	143	157	171	185	200	214	228	242	257
290	87	116	145	160	174	189	203	218	232	247	261
295	89	118	148	162	177	192	207	221	236	251	266
300	90	120	150	165	180	195	210	225	240	255	270
305	92	122	153	168	183	198	214	229	244	259	275

Weight	30%	40%	50%	55%	60%	65%	70%	75%	80%	85%	90%
310	93	124	155	171	186	202	217	233	248	264	279
315	95	126	158	173	189	205	221	236	252	268	284
320	96	128	160	176	192	208	224	240	256	272	288
325	98	130	163	179	195	211	228	244	260	276	293
330	99	132	165	182	198	215	231	248	264	281	297
335	101	134	168	184	201	218	235	251	268	285	302
340	102	136	170	187	204	221	238	255	272	289	306
345	104	138	173	190	207	224	242	259	276	293	311
350	105	140	175	193	210	228	245	263	280	298	315
355	107	**142**	178	195	213	231	249	266	284	302	320
360	108	**144**	180	198	216	234	252	270	288	306	324
365	110	**146**	183	201	219	237	256	274	292	310	329
370	111	**148**	185	204	222	241	259	278	296	315	333
375	113	**150**	188	206	225	244	263	281	300	319	338
380	114	**152**	190	209	228	247	266	285	304	323	342
385	116	**154**	193	212	231	250	270	289	308	327	347
390	117	**156**	195	215	234	254	273	293	312	332	351
395	119	**158**	198	217	237	257	277	296	316	336	356
400	120	**160**	200	220	240	260	280	300	320	340	360
405	122	**162**	203	223	243	263	284	304	324	344	365
410	123	**164**	205	226	246	267	287	308	328	349	369
415	125	**166**	208	228	249	270	291	311	332	353	374
420	126	**168**	210	231	252	273	294	315	336	357	378
425	128	**170**	213	234	255	276	298	319	340	361	383
430	129	**172**	215	237	258	280	301	323	344	366	387
435	131	**174**	218	239	261	283	305	326	348	370	392
440	**132**	**176**	220	242	264	286	308	330	352	374	396
445	**134**	**178**	223	245	267	289	312	334	356	378	401
450	**135**	**180**	225	248	270	293	315	338	360	383	405
455	137	182	228	250	273	296	319	341	364	387	410
460	138	184	230	253	276	299	322	345	368	391	414
465	140	186	233	256	279	302	326	349	372	395	419
470	141	188	235	259	282	306	329	353	376	400	423
475	143	190	238	261	285	309	333	356	380	404	428
480	144	192	240	264	288	312	336	360	384	408	432
485	146	194	243	267	291	315	340	364	388	412	437
490	147	196	245	270	294	319	343	368	392	417	441
495	149	198	248	272	297	322	347	371	396	421	446

(continued)

(continued)

Weight	30%	40%	50%	55%	60%	65%	70%	75%	80%	85%	90%
500	150	200	250	275	300	325	350	375	400	425	450
505	152	202	253	278	303	328	354	379	404	429	455
510	153	204	255	281	306	332	357	383	408	434	459
515	155	206	258	283	309	335	361	386	412	438	464
520	156	208	260	286	312	338	364	390	416	442	468
525	158	210	263	289	315	341	368	394	420	446	473
530	159	212	265	292	318	345	371	398	424	451	477
535	161	214	268	294	321	348	375	401	428	455	482
540	162	216	270	297	324	351	378	405	432	459	486
545	164	218	273	300	327	354	382	409	436	463	491
550	165	220	275	303	330	358	385	413	440	468	495
555	167	222	278	305	333	361	389	416	444	472	500
560	168	224	280	308	336	364	392	420	448	476	504
565	170	226	283	311	339	367	396	424	452	480	509
570	171	228	285	314	342	371	399	428	456	485	513
575	173	230	288	316	345	374	403	431	460	489	518
580	174	232	290	319	348	377	406	435	464	493	522
585	176	234	293	322	351	380	410	439	468	497	527
590	177	236	295	325	354	384	413	443	472	502	531
595	179	238	298	327	357	387	417	446	476	506	536
600	180	240	300	330	360	390	420	450	480	510	540
605	182	242	303	333	363	393	424	454	484	514	545
610	183	244	305	336	366	397	427	458	488	519	549
615	185	246	308	338	369	400	431	461	492	523	554
620	186	248	310	341	372	403	434	465	496	527	558
625	188	250	313	344	375	406	438	469	500	531	563
630	189	252	315	347	378	410	441	473	504	536	567
635	191	254	318	349	381	413	445	476	508	540	572
640	192	256	320	352	384	416	448	480	512	544	576
645	194	258	323	355	387	419	452	484	516	548	581
650	195	260	325	358	390	423	455	488	520	553	585
655	197	262	328	360	393	426	459	491	524	557	590
660	198	264	330	363	396	429	462	495	528	561	594
665	200	266	333	366	399	432	466	499	532	565	599
670	201	268	335	369	402	436	469	503	536	570	603
675	203	270	338	371	405	439	473	506	540	574	608
680	204	272	340	374	408	442	476	510	544	578	612
685	206	274	343	377	411	445	480	514	548	582	617
690	207	276	345	380	414	449	483	518	552	587	621

(continued)

Weight	30%	40%	50%	55%	60%	65%	70%	75%	80%	85%	90%
700	210	280	350	385	420	455	490	525	560	595	630
705	212	282	353	388	423	458	494	529	564	599	635
710	213	284	355	391	426	462	497	533	568	604	639
715	215	286	358	393	429	465	501	536	572	608	644
720	216	288	360	396	432	468	504	540	576	612	648
725	218	290	363	399	435	471	508	544	580	616	653
730	219	292	365	402	438	475	511	548	584	621	657
735	221	294	368	404	441	478	515	551	588	625	662
740	222	296	370	407	444	481	518	555	592	629	666
745	224	298	373	410	447	484	522	559	596	633	671
750	225	300	375	413	450	488	525	563	600	638	675
755	227	302	378	415	453	491	529	566	604	642	680
760	228	304	380	418	456	494	532	570	608	646	684
765	230	306	383	421	459	497	536	574	612	650	689
770	231	308	385	424	462	501	539	578	616	655	693
775	233	310	388	426	465	504	543	581	620	659	698
780	234	312	390	429	468	507	546	585	624	663	702
785	236	314	393	432	471	510	550	589	628	667	707
790	237	316	395	435	474	514	553	593	632	672	711
795	239	318	398	437	477	517	557	596	636	676	716
800	240	320	400	440	480	520	560	600	640	680	720
805	242	322	403	443	483	523	564	604	644	684	725
810	243	324	405	446	486	527	567	608	648	689	729
815	245	326	408	448	489	530	571	611	652	693	734
820	246	328	410	451	492	533	574	615	656	697	738
825	248	330	413	454	495	536	578	619	660	701	743
830	249	332	415	457	498	540	581	623	664	706	747
835	251	334	418	459	501	543	585	626	668	710	752
840	252	336	420	462	504	546	588	630	672	714	756
845	254	338	423	465	507	549	592	634	676	718	761
850	255	340	425	468	510	553	595	638	680	723	765
855	257	342	428	470	513	556	599	641	684	727	770
860	258	344	430	473	516	559	602	645	688	731	774
865	260	346	433	476	519	562	606	649	692	735	779
870	261	348	435	479	522	566	609	653	696	740	783
875	263	350	438	481	525	569	613	656	700	744	788
880	264	352	440	484	528	572	616	660	704	748	792
885	266	354	443	487	531	575	620	664	708	752	797

(continued)

(continued)

Weight	30%	40%	50%	55%	60%	65%	70%	75%	80%	85%	90%
890	267	356	445	490	534	579	623	668	712	757	801
895	269	358	448	492	537	582	627	671	716	761	806
900	270	360	450	495	540	585	630	675	720	765	810
905	272	362	453	498	543	588	634	679	724	769	815
910	273	364	455	501	546	592	637	683	728	774	819
915	275	366	458	503	549	595	641	686	732	778	824
920	276	368	460	506	552	598	644	690	736	782	828
925	278	370	463	509	555	601	648	694	740	786	833
930	279	372	465	512	558	605	651	698	744	791	837
935	281	374	468	514	561	608	655	701	748	795	842
940	282	376	470	517	564	611	658	705	752	799	846
945	284	378	473	520	567	614	662	709	756	803	851
950	285	380	475	523	570	618	665	713	760	808	855
955	287	382	478	525	573	621	669	716	764	812	860
960	288	384	480	528	576	624	672	720	768	816	864
965	290	386	483	531	579	627	676	724	772	820	869
970	291	388	485	534	582	631	679	728	776	825	873
975	293	390	488	536	585	634	683	731	780	829	878
980	294	392	490	539	588	637	686	735	784	833	882
985	296	394	493	542	591	640	690	739	788	837	887
990	297	396	495	545	594	644	693	743	792	842	891
995	299	398	498	547	597	647	697	746	796	846	896
1000	300	400	500	550	600	650	700	750	800	850	900

APPENDIX **C**

One Rep Maximum (I-RM) Conversion

Pounds	10	9	8	7	6	5	4	3	2
5	7	6	6	6	6	6	6	5	5
10	13	13	13	12	12	11	11	11	11
15	20	19	19	18	18	17	17	16	16
20	27	26	25	24	24	23	22	22	21
25	33	32	31	30	29	29	28	27	26
30	40	39	38	36	35	34	33	32	32
35	47	45	44	42	41	40	39	38	37
40	53	52	50	48	47	46	44	43	42
45	60	58	56	55	53	51	50	49	47
50	67	65	63	61	59	57	56	54	53
55	73	71	69	67	65	63	61	59	58
60	80	77	75	73	71	69	67	65	63
65	87	84	81	79	76	74	72	70	68
70	93	90	88	85	82	80	78	76	74
75	100	97	94	91	88	86	83	81	79
80	107	103	100	97	94	91	89	86	84
85	113	110	106	103	100	97	94	92	89
90	120	116	113	109	106	103	100	97	95
95	127	123	119	115	112	109	106	103	100
100	133	129	125	121	118	114	111	108	105
105	140	135	131	127	124	120	117	114	111

(continued)

(continued)

Pounds	10	9	8	7	6	5	4	3	2
110	147	142	138	133	129	126	122	119	116
115	153	148	144	139	135	131	128	124	121
120	160	155	150	145	141	137	133	130	126
125	167	161	156	152	147	143	139	135	132
130	173	168	163	158	153	149	144	141	137
135	180	174	169	164	159	154	150	146	142
140	187	181	175	170	165	160	156	151	147
145	193	187	181	176	171	166	161	157	153
150	200	194	188	182	176	171	167	162	158
155	207	200	194	188	182	177	172	168	163
160	213	206	200	194	188	183	178	173	168
165	220	213	206	200	194	189	183	178	174
170	227	219	213	206	200	194	189	184	179
175	233	226	219	212	206	200	194	189	184
180	240	232	225	218	212	206	200	195	189
185	247	239	231	224	218	211	206	200	195
190	253	245	238	230	224	217	211	205	200
195	260	252	244	236	229	223	217	211	205
200	267	258	250	242	235	229	222	216	211
205	273	265	256	248	241	234	228	222	216
210	280	271	263	255	247	240	233	227	221
215	287	277	269	261	253	246	239	232	226
220	293	284	275	267	259	251	244	238	232
225	300	290	281	273	265	257	250	243	237
230	307	297	288	279	271	263	256	249	242
235	313	303	294	285	276	269	261	254	247
240	320	310	300	291	282	274	267	259	253
245	327	316	306	297	288	280	272	265	258
250	333	323	313	303	294	286	278	270	263
255	340	329	319	309	300	291	283	276	268
260	347	335	325	315	306	297	289	281	274
265	353	342	331	321	312	303	294	286	279
270	360	348	338	327	318	309	300	292	284
275	367	355	344	333	324	314	306	297	289
280	373	361	350	339	329	320	311	303	295
285	380	368	356	345	335	326	317	308	300
290	387	374	363	352	341	331	322	314	305
295	393	381	369	358	347	337	328	319	311
300	400	387	375	364	353	343	333	324	316

(continued)

Pounds	10	9	8	7	6	5	4	3	2
305	407	394	381	370	359	349	339	330	321
310	413	400	388	376	365	354	344	335	326
315	420	406	394	382	371	360	350	341	332
320	427	413	400	388	376	366	356	346	337
325	433	419	406	394	382	371	361	351	342
330	440	426	413	400	388	377	367	357	347
335	447	432	419	406	394	383	372	362	353
340	453	439	425	412	400	389	378	368	358
345	460	445	431	418	406	394	383	373	363
350	467	452	438	424	412	400	389	378	368
355	473	458	444	430	418	406	394	384	374
360	480	465	450	436	424	411	400	389	379
365	487	471	456	442	429	417	406	395	384
370	493	477	463	448	435	423	411	400	389
375	500	484	469	455	441	429	417	405	395
380	507	490	475	461	447	434	422	411	400
385	513	497	481	467	453	440	428	416	405
390	520	503	488	473	459	446	433	422	411
395	527	510	494	479	465	451	439	427	416
400	533	516	500	485	471	457	444	432	421
405	540	523	506	491	476	463	450	438	426
410	547	529	513	497	482	469	456	443	432
415	553	535	519	503	488	474	461	449	437
420	560	542	525	509	494	480	467	454	442
425	567	548	531	515	500	486	472	459	447
430	573	555	538	521	506	491	478	465	453
435	580	561	544	527	512	497	483	470	458
440	587	568	550	533	518	503	489	476	463
445	593	574	556	539	524	509	494	481	468
450	600	581	563	545	529	514	500	486	474
455	607	587	569	552	535	520	506	492	479
460	613	594	575	558	541	526	511	497	484
465	620	600	581	564	547	531	517	503	489
470	627	606	588	570	553	537	522	508	495
475	633	613	594	576	559	543	528	514	500
480	640	619	600	582	565	549	533	519	505
485	647	626	606	588	571	554	539	524	511
490	653	632	613	594	576	560	544	530	516

(*continued*)

(continued)

Pounds	10	9	8	7	6	5	4	3	2
495	660	639	619	600	582	566	550	535	521
500	667	645	625	606	588	571	556	541	526
505	673	652	631	612	594	577	561	546	532
510	680	658	638	618	600	583	567	551	537
515	687	665	644	624	606	589	572	557	542
520	693	671	650	630	612	594	578	562	547
525	700	677	656	636	618	600	583	568	553
530	707	684	663	642	624	606	589	573	558
535	713	690	669	648	629	611	594	578	563
540	720	697	675	655	635	617	600	584	568
545	727	703	681	661	641	623	606	589	574
550	733	710	688	667	647	629	611	595	579
555	740	716	694	673	653	634	617	600	584
560	747	723	700	679	659	640	622	605	589
565	753	729	706	685	665	646	628	611	595
570	760	735	713	691	671	651	633	616	600
575	767	742	719	697	676	657	639	622	605
580	773	748	725	703	682	663	644	627	611
585	780	755	731	709	688	669	650	632	616
590	787	761	738	715	694	674	656	638	621
595	793	768	744	721	700	680	661	643	626
600	800	774	750	727	706	686	667	649	632
605	807	781	756	733	712	691	672	654	637
610	813	787	763	739	718	697	678	659	642
615	820	794	769	745	724	703	683	665	647
620	827	800	775	752	729	709	689	670	653
625	833	806	781	758	735	714	694	676	658
630	840	813	788	764	741	720	700	681	663
635	847	819	794	770	747	726	706	686	668
640	853	826	800	776	753	731	711	692	674
645	860	832	806	782	759	737	717	697	679
650	867	839	813	788	765	743	722	703	684
655	873	845	819	794	771	749	728	708	689
660	880	852	825	800	776	754	733	714	695
665	887	858	831	806	782	760	739	719	700
670	893	865	838	812	788	766	744	724	705
675	900	871	844	818	794	771	750	730	711
680	907	877	850	824	800	777	756	735	716
685	913	884	856	830	806	783	761	741	721

(continued)									
Pounds	**10**	**9**	**8**	**7**	**6**	**5**	**4**	**3**	**2**
690	920	890	863	836	812	789	767	746	726
695	927	897	869	842	818	794	772	751	732
700	933	903	875	848	824	800	778	757	737
705	940	910	881	855	829	806	783	762	742
710	947	916	888	861	835	811	789	768	747
715	953	923	894	867	841	817	794	773	753
720	960	929	900	873	847	823	800	778	758
725	967	935	906	879	853	829	806	784	763
730	973	942	913	885	859	834	811	789	768
735	980	948	919	891	865	840	817	795	774
740	987	955	925	897	871	846	822	800	779
745	993	961	931	903	876	851	828	805	784
750	1000	968	938	909	882	857	833	811	789
755	1007	974	944	915	888	863	839	816	795
760	1013	981	950	921	894	869	844	822	800
765	1020	987	956	927	900	874	850	827	805
770	1027	994	963	933	906	880	856	832	811
775	1033	1000	969	939	912	886	861	838	816
780	1040	1006	975	945	918	891	867	843	821
785	1047	1013	981	952	924	897	872	849	826
790	1053	1019	988	958	929	903	878	854	832
795	1060	1026	994	964	935	909	883	859	837
800	1067	1032	1000	970	941	914	889	865	842
805	1073	1039	1006	976	947	920	894	870	847
810	1080	1045	1013	982	953	926	900	876	853
815	1087	1052	1019	988	959	931	906	881	858
820	1093	1058	1025	994	965	937	911	886	863
825	1100	1065	1031	1000	971	943	917	892	868
830	1107	1071	1038	1006	976	949	922	897	874
835	1113	1077	1044	1012	982	954	928	903	879
840	1120	1084	1050	1018	988	960	933	908	884
845	1127	1090	1056	1024	994	966	939	914	889
850	1133	1097	1063	1030	1000	971	944	919	895
855	1140	1103	1069	1036	1006	977	950	924	900
900	1200	1161	1125	1091	1059	1029	1000	973	947
905	1207	1168	1131	1097	1065	1034	1006	978	953
910	1213	1174	1138	1103	1071	1040	1011	984	958
915	1220	1181	1144	1109	1076	1046	1017	989	963

(continued)

(continued)

Pounds	10	9	8	7	6	5	4	3	2
920	1227	1187	1150	1115	1082	1051	1022	995	968
925	1233	1194	1156	1121	1088	1057	1028	1000	974
930	1240	1200	1163	1127	1094	1063	1033	1005	979
935	1247	1206	1169	1133	1100	1069	1039	1011	984
940	1253	1213	1175	1139	1106	1074	1044	1016	989
945	1260	1219	1181	1145	1112	1080	1050	1022	995
950	1267	1226	1188	1152	1118	1086	1056	1027	1000
955	1273	1232	1194	1158	1124	1091	1061	1032	1005
960	1280	1239	1200	1164	1129	1097	1067	1038	1011
965	1287	1245	1206	1170	1135	1103	1072	1043	1016
970	1293	1252	1213	1176	1141	1109	1078	1049	1021
975	1300	1258	1219	1182	1147	1114	1083	1054	1026
980	1307	1265	1225	1188	1153	1120	1089	1059	1032
985	1313	1271	1231	1194	1159	1126	1094	1065	1037
990	1320	1277	1238	1200	1165	1131	1100	1070	1042
995	1327	1284	1244	1206	1171	1137	1106	1076	1047
1000	1333	1290	1250	1212	1176	1143	1111	1081	1053

APPENDIX **D**

Summary of Ergogenic Aids and Related Substances*

Type of Supplement	Common Uses (Claims)	Typical Dosage**	Considerations Rating as Ergogenic Aid (1 to 5)***
5-hydroxytryptophan (5-HTP)	Used to increase serotonin levels in the brain to reduce appetite and carbohydrate craving; promote sleep; reduce depression	25 mg/day; studies used as much as 900 mg/day	Used instead of the amino acid tryptophan (illegal in U.S.); potential association with fatal eosinophilia-myalgia syndrome needs clarification via additional research (1) **Rating : 3**
Acetyl-L-carnitine (see also Carnitine)	Used to enhance brain function and reduce depression in elderly; antioxidant	1,000 mg/day	May benefit certain types of dementia; more research needed (2,3) **Rating : 3**
Alpha-ketoglutarate	Used to prevent muscle protein breakdown during periods of stress such as recovery from surgery; anticatabolic	10–25 g/day	Can be converted to the amino acids glutamate and glutamine; some support for medical use as an anticatabolic; use as sports supplement needs more study; effective dosage likely impractical; similar to glutamine, may benefit athletes involved in heavy training (4,5) **Rating : 1**
Alpha-ketoisocaproate (KIC)	Precursor for the BCAA leucine; claims are made for prevention of muscle protein catabolism and reduction of fatigue during exercise	15–20 g/day	May have medical applications; unlikely to provide any ergogenic benefit beyond BCAA supplementation; it is primarily converted to leucine; effective dosage likely impractical (6) **Rating : 1**
Alpha-linolenic acid (also see DHA and EPA)	Increases omega-3 fatty acid intake; usual sources are flax oil, walnut oil, canola oil, and soybean oil	Not taken separately	Not equivalent to omega-3 fatty acids in fish oils; can be converted to the longer "fish oil" omega-3 fatty acids, but conversion may be too inefficient to meet needs for EPA and DHA (7,8) **Rating : 1**

(continued)

(continued)

Type of Supplement	Common Uses (Claims)	Typical Dosage**	Considerations Rating as Ergogenic Aid (1 to 5)***
Androstenedione	Precursor for testosterone; intended to increase testosterone; enhance muscle protein synthesis	50–150 mg/day (used in research)	Claims not consistently supported by research; may ↑ estrogen in men more than testosterone; no evidence for ↑ protein synthesis; may produce positive urine test for nandrolone (9–11) **Rating : 2**
Arginine	↑ growth hormone; promotes muscle protein synthesis; enhances nitric oxide synthesis and relaxation of smooth muscle in blood vessels	1–10 g/day	Significance of ↑ growth hormone is questionable except for disease conditions; good potential for reducing the risk of heart attack and possibly stroke (12,13) **Rating : 2.5**
Aspartate salts (potassium magnesium aspartate or PMA)	Delay fatigue and increase endurance time to exhaustion	7–13 g of PMA divided into 2 or 3 doses	Large dose needed; research results mixed; benefit more likely in untrained people than in trained individuals (14,15) **Rating : 2.5**
Beta-carotene	Antioxidant; prevention of exercise-induced muscle soreness; enhanced recovery from exercise stress	5–20 mg/day	Additional research is needed to understand possible health risks vs benefits of beta-carotene supplementation (16,17). Safe Upper Level set by Expert Group on Vitamins & Minerals (UK) is 7 mg/day (18) **Rating : 1**
Branched-chain amino acids (BCAA) (leucine, isoleucine and valine)	Suppress muscle protein degradation; enhance exercise recovery; reduce perception of fatigue during endurance exercise	3–6 g/day at least half leucine; split pre- and post-exercise	Some research (but not all) indicates prevention of muscle protein breakdown as well as reduced fatigue by inhibiting tryptophan uptake into the brain (19–21) **Rating : 3.5**
Beta-hydroxy-beta-methylbutyrate (HMB)	Typically used to reduce protein degradation and promote muscle protein accretion during resistance training	3 g/day in combination with intense resistance exercise	Research results equivocal; may benefit untrained individuals more than trained; possibly effective for enhancing recovery of damaged muscle; apparently safe (22–26) **Rating : 3**
Bromelain	Complex of proteolytic enzymes extracted from the base of pineapple plants; used to aid protein digestion or as an anti-inflammatory agent	Variable; dependent on specific preparation	Digestive aid function questionable; some of this enzyme escapes digestion and affects eicosanoids in a way that can reduce inflammation (27–31) **Rating : 3**
Caffeine	Stimulates central nervous system; improves reaction time, alertness, concentration; enhances mobilization of fat from fat cells; improves endurance performance	3–6 mg/kg body weight	Claims are supported by research; diuretic effect increases urine production at rest, but not during exercise; combination with ephedrine sources like ephedra (ma huang) may increase risk of adverse reactions (32–34) **Rating : 4**
Carnitine (L-carnitine) (also see Acetyl-L-carnitine)	Enhances utilization of fat (fatty acids) as an energy source and improves endurance by decreased reliance on carbohydrate (muscle glycogen)	2–6 g/day	Some studies support claims, however others do not; potential benefit likely depends on dosage, length of time taking supplement, and type of performance being tested (35–39) **Rating : 3**
Casein	Principal protein of milk and primary protein component of cheese; used as a component of protein supplements	Depends on dietary protein intake and body weight	Casein has a lower biological value than whey protein, but casein has been shown to support more sustained protein synthesis due to more gradual digestion and absorption (40,41) Depends

(continued)

Type of Supplement	Common Uses (Claims)	Typical Dosage**	Considerations Rating as Ergogenic Aid (1 to 5)***
Chitosan	A form of chitin extracted from the shells of crustaceans; used as a "fat blocker" to reduce absorption of dietary fat and cholesterol	1–4 g/day	Can help to reduce absorption of dietary cholesterol but apparently it does not bind enough fat to assist in weight loss (42–44) Rating : 2–3
Cholecystokinin (CCK)	CCK supplements are taken to stimulate satiety and reduce food intake	Effective oral dose unknown	Injected CCK can decrease appetite and food intake; it is thought that oral supplements of this peptide hormone are ineffective because the peptide is likely digested, however no human studies have been conducted (45) Rating : ?
Chondroitin sulfate (see also Glucosamine)	Promote joint health and treat osteoarthritis; usually combined with glucosamine sulfate	400–500 mg/day, usually combined with glucosamine	Perhaps the most thoroughly studied nutraceutical, generally shown to enhance joint health (46–49) Rating : 3–4
Chromium picolinate	Enhances loss of body fat and maintenance of lean tissue; maintains chromium status and normal insulin sensitivity	35–200 mcg/day of elemental chromium	Body composition claims not supported by research; chromium is an essential trace element needed for normal insulin function; the picolinate form is somewhat controversial due to mutagenic effects at high doses in isolated cell and animal studies (50) Rating : 1–2
Chromium nicotinate (chromium + niacin) Chromium chloride	Used to enhance loss of body fat with maintenance of lean tissue; maintain chromium status and normal insulin sensitivity	35–200 mcg/day of elemental chromium	Body composition claims not supported by research; chromium is an essential trace element needed for normal insulin function; these forms of chromium may be preferable to the picolinate form as a source of chromium in a dietary supplement (50) Rating : 1–2
Chrysin	Used by men to reduce the production of estrogen and increase testosterone levels	125–250 mg	Limited human research does not support a testosterone-stimulating effect of chrysin when consumed at typical doses (51) Rating : ?
Citrus aurantium— bitter orange (source of synephrine)	Used as a thermogenic to increase resting energy expenditure and enhance fat loss; contains synephrine, octamine, and tyramine	300–975 mg/day (with synephrine content from 2–20 mg)	Can increase blood pressure, especially in combination with stimulants like caffeine; interacts with several drugs; safety and effectiveness for human use requires further study; concentration of active components can vary among products (52–54) Rating : ?
Coenzyme Q-10 (ubiquinone)	Used to enhance energy metabolism and exercise performance; also used for various medical purposes	60–150 mg/day divided into 2–3 doses per day	Does not clearly affect exercise performance in normal healthy people; may benefit some disease conditions, but can have negative interactions with several drugs (55,56) Depends
Cola nut	Herbal source of caffeine		See: Caffeine
Conjugated linoleic acid (CLA)	Used for fat loss and cancer prevention; most common food sources are milk and beef fat	1–8 g/day	This is a trans fatty acid that is likely beneficial to health; effectiveness in fat loss and cancer prevention requires further research (57,58) Rating : 3

(continued)

(continued)

Type of Supplement	Common Uses (Claims)	Typical Dosage**	Considerations Rating as Ergogenic Aid (1 to 5)***
Creatine	Used to enhance high-intensity exercise performance	2–25 g/day	Generally effective for enhancing maximal power/strength exercise performance; apparently safe for short-term use; safety of long term-use and use by children and adolescents not known (59,60) Rating : 4–5
DHA (docosahexaenoic acid) (also see Alpha-linolenic acid and EPA)	Long chain omega-3 fatty acid found in fish oils and some algae oils; used to reduce the risk of cardiovascular disease and age-related macular degeneration, protect brain function, and reduce plasma triglycerides	200–400 mg/day; typically taken combined with EPA in fish or algae oil	DHA is the major fatty acid in the brain and the retina; deficiency may adversely affect mental function and vision; excess intake may suppress immune function and increase risk of internal bleeding; supplementation combined with "blood thinner" drugs requires medical supervision; potential health benefits depend on a person's essential fatty acid status (7,8) Rating : 2
DHEA (dehydroepiandros-terone)	Used to increase levels of steroid hormones that may increase protein synthesis; slow changes associated with aging	50–200 mg	Unlikely to enhance muscle mass and strength gains; potential benefits and risks require additional clarification; use only with medical supervision; some preparations can give positive drug test (61–64) Rating : 1–2
EPA (eicosahexaenoic acid) (also see Alpha-linolenic acid and DHA)	Long chain omega-3 fatty acid found in fish oils and some algae oils; used to reduce the risk of cardiovascular disease	200–500 mg/day; typically taken combined with DHA in fish or algae oil	EPA has important functions and can be elongated to DHA; supplementation combined with "blood thinner" drugs requires medical supervision; potential health benefits depend on a person's essential fatty acid status (7,8) Rating : 2
Ephedra (ma huang)	Used for weight loss (usually combined with a source of caffeine), enhancing athletic performance, and treatment of allergies and asthma	8 mg ephedrine alkaloids taken up to 3 times a day	Causes slight increase resting metabolic rate; banned substance for sports competition; may be unsafe for some people, especially during exercise and when combined with caffeine; illegal in the United States for sale as dietary supplements (65) Rating : 3–4
Ginkgo biloba (leaf extract standardized to 24% ginkgo flavanoid glycosides and 6% terpenes)	Major use is to enhance mental function in elderly who have limited blood circulation to the brain	40–80 mg of extract taken up to 3 times a day	Evidence for enhanced mental function is inconsistent; do not use during pregnancy, lactation; those on medication and those managing blood disorders should avoid use without medical supervision, however, this concern warrants further study (66–68) Depends
Glucosamine	Used to treat joint problems such as those associated with osteoarthritis and to prevent development of age-related joint problems; commonly taken in combination with chondroitin	1,500 mg/day divided into 3 daily doses of 500 mg each	Generally considered safe and potentially effective for adjunctive treatment of osteoarthritis (69) Rating : 3–4
Glutamine	Used for a variety of purposes, such as gastrointestinal support, prevention of muscle wasting, post-exercise recovery, immune system support	2–20 grams/day	Nonessential amino acid produced by muscle protein catabolism; used by gastrointestinal tract and immune system as energy source; supplementation beneficial for some conditions (70,71) Rating : 3–4

(continued)

Type of Supplement	Common Uses (Claims)	Typical Dosage**	Considerations Rating as Ergogenic Aid (1 to 5)***
Green tea extract	Used for weight control and general health promotion; has replaced ephedra as key ingredient in many weight loss products	100–600 mg standardized to 50% catechins	Potentially beneficial for intended uses; can interact with many drugs; avoid use with medications without medical supervision (72,73) Rating : 3
HMB (hydroxymethyl-butyrate or beta-hydroxy beta-methyl-butyrate)	Used to reduce protein degradation and promote muscle protein accretion during resistance training	1–3 g/day	Likely beneficial and apparently safe; possibly effective for enhancing recovery of exercise-damaged muscle (25,26) Rating : 3–4
HCA (hydroxycitric acid) (Garcinia Cambogia is a natural source of HCA)	Used for weight loss by inhibiting fatty acid synthesis, enhancing fat oxidation, and reducing appetite	250–1,500 mg HCA/day	Some research supports appetite control and enhanced fat oxidation effects; possibly enhances endurance; fat loss not supported by all studies (74–78) Rating : 2–3
Inositol	Lipotropic substance used to enhance liver handling of increased fatty acid levels during weight loss	1,000 mg	Human research is lacking to support the claims; may be beneficial in combination with other lipotropic substances; potential benefit to some mental disorders (79,80) Rating : 1–2
Iron	Essential for normal oxygen delivery to cells, energy production in cells, liver metabolism of toxins, etc.	Variable, depends on iron status	Iron supplementation can enhance exercise performance in individuals with anemic and nonanemic iron deficiency; medical assessment of iron status and supervision of iron supplementation is advisable (81) Rating : 5 (if iron deficient)
Leucine (L-leucine) (see Branched-chain amino acids)			
Lipoic acid (alpha lipoic acid)	Used as an antioxidant and by people with diabetes to lower blood glucose and prevent complications	100–800 mg/day	Some research supports antioxidant claims; fairly high doses are likely required to benefit diabetes (82,83)
Ma huang (see Ephedra)			
Medium-chain triglycerides (MCTs)	Used to facilitate weight loss and to enhance endurance performance	20–85 g/day	Possible weight loss benefit requires substitution of MCT for other dietary fat which is generally impractical; enhancement of endurance performance is unlikely (84,85) Rating : 1–2
Potassium magnesium aspartate (PMA) (see Aspartate salts)			
Pyruvate (pyruvic acid)	Used as a weight loss aid and to enhance endurance performance	7–50 g/day (doses used in research)	Claims are not consistently supported by research; very large amounts were used in studies showing benefit, which often caused intestinal distress (86) Rating : 2–3
Sodium bicarbonate	Enhance performance of high-intensity exercise that is highly dependent on anaerobic glycolysis (lactic acid system)	300 mg/kg body weight taken ~90 minutes prior to exercise	Potential for gastrointestinal distress such as nausea and/or diarrhea; correct dosing important for safety; familiarization with use of lower doses in training suggested (87) Rating : 4.5

(continued)

(continued)

Type of Supplement	Common Uses (Claims)	Typical Dosage**	Considerations Rating as Ergogenic Aid (1 to 5)***
Sodium chloride	Enhances endurance exercise performance that lasts long enough to significantly deplete body sodium through sweat loss (generally longer than 4 or 5 hours)	Highly variable; depends on individual sweat rate and sodium loss in sweat	Sweat rates and sodium loss in sweat can vary greatly among athletes. Very heavy training can cause losses as much as 10,000 mg of sodium per day (~5 teaspoons of salt); muscle cramping can result from sodium depletion and those who tend to cramp typically have greater sodium losses in sweat (88) Rating : 5
Sodium citrate	Enhances performance of high-intensity exercise that is highly dependent on anaerobic glycolysis (lactic acid system); also, see Sodium bicarbonate	500 mg/kg body weight taken ~ 120 minutes prior to exercise	Potential for gastrointestinal distress such as nausea and/or diarrhea; correct dosing important for safety; familiarization with use of lower doses in training suggested; higher dose needed than with sodium bicarbonate (87) Rating : 4
Taurine	Used for management of diabetes, heart problems, and miscellaneous other health problems	3–6 g/day	Nonessential amino acid that is synthesized in the body and is not essential in the diet; some evidence for benefits to heart problems and hypertension; limited research to support ergogenic claims in athletes (89,90) Rating : 2–3
Valine (see Branched-chain amino acids)			
Vanadyl sulfate	Used to enhance control of blood sugar level and enhance muscle development with strength training	Tolerable upper intake level for adults is 1.8 mg/day	Requirement for this mineral element is unknown; claims of benefit in healthy adults are not consistently supported by current research; effects on insulin sensitivity warrant further study (91,92) Rating : 1–2

*The information in this table is for instructional purposes only to describe the major purported uses of these components of dietary supplements. Many of these substances are powerful chemicals and should be used only with medical guidance and proper dosage. Caution is especially important for anyone using medication, for children, and for women during pregnancy and lactation.

**Typical dosages are based on current popular use and/or doses used in research. Safety issues may exist for some of these doses even for nutrients. For many ergogenic aids, it is best to consult with a health-care professional for dosage concerns related to an individual's goals and specific health status.

*** Ratings of potential for efficacy for some or all of the claims based on current research perspectives and a certain amount of unavoidable subjective judgment: 5 = Very Good, 4 = Good, 3 = Fair, 2 = Poor, 1 = Very Poor, ? = Not Known, Depends = Depends on conditions and purpose of use

REFERENCES

1. Shaw K, Turner J, Del Mar C. Tryptophan and 5-hydroxytryptophan for depression. *Cochrane Database Syst Rev* 2001;(3):CD003198.
2. Pettegrew JW, Levine J, McClure RJ. Acetyl-L-carnitine physical-chemical, metabolic, and therapeutic properties: relevance for its mode of action in Alzheimer's disease and geriatric depression. *Mol Psychiatry* 2000;5:616–32.
3. Hudson S, Tabet N. Acetyl-L-carnitine for dementia. *Cochrane Database Syst Rev* 2003;(2):CD003158.
4. Smith DJ, Norris SR. Changes in glutamine and glutamate concentrations for tracking training tolerance. *Med Sci Sports Exerc* 2000;32:684–9.
5. Castell L. Glutamine supplementation in vitro and in vivo, in exercise and in immunodepression. *Sports Med* 2003;33:323–45.
6. Matthews DE, Harkin R, Battezzati A et al. Splanchnic bed utilization of enteral alpha-ketoisocaproate in humans. *Metabolism* 1999;48:1555–63.
7. Gerster H. Can adults adequately convert alpha-linolenic acid (18:3n-3) to eicosapentaenoic acid (20:5n-3) and docosahexaenoic acid (22:6n-3)? *Int J Vitam Nutr Res* 1998;68:159–73.

8. Food and Nutrition Board, Institute of Medicine. Dietary Reference Intakes for Energy, Carbohydrate, Fiber, Fat, Fatty Acids, Cholesterol, Protein, and Amino Acids. Washington, DC: National Academy Press; 2005.

9. Catlin DH, Leder BZ, Ahrens B et al. Trace contamination of over-the-counter androstenedione and positive urine test results for a nandrolone metabolite. *J Am Med Assoc* 2000;284:2618–21.

10. Leder BZ, Longcope C, Catlin DH et al. Oral androstenedione administration and serum testosterone concentrations in young men. *J Am Med Assoc* 2000;283:779–82.

11. Leder BZ, Catlin DH, Longcope C et al. Metabolism of orally administered androstenedione in young men. *J Clin Endocrinol Metab* 2001;86:3654–58.

12. Wu G, Meininger CJ. Regulation of nitric oxide synthesis by dietary factors. *Ann Rev Nutr* 2002;22:61–86.

13. Wu G, Meininger CJ. Arginine nutrition and cardiovascular function. *J Nutr* 2000;130:2626–29.

14. Bucci L. Nutrients as Ergogenic Aids for Sports and Exercise. Boca Raton: CRC Press; 1993.

15. Spruce N, Titchenal A. An Evaluation of Popular Fitness-Enhancing Supplements, A Fitness Professional's Desk Reference. Strongsville, Ohio: Evergreen Communications; 2001.

16. Pryor WA, Stahl W, Rock CL. Beta carotene: from biochemistry to clinical trials. *Nutr Rev* 2000;58:39–53.

17. Cook N, Lee IM, Manson J et al. Effects of 12 years of beta-carotene supplementation on cancer incidence in the Physician's Health Study (PHS). *Am J Epidemiol* 1999;149:270–9

18. Expert Group on Vitamins and Minerals of the Food Standards Agency, United Kingdom. Safe Upper Levels for Vitamins and Minerals. 2003. Available at: http://www.foodstandards.gov.uk/multimedia/pdfs/vitmin2003.pdf.

19. Mittleman KD, Ricci MR, Bailey SP. Branched-chain amino acids prolong exercise during heat stress in men and women. *Med Sci Sports Exerc* 1998;30:83–91.

20. Blomstrand E. Amino acids and central fatigue. *Amino Acids* 2001;20:25–34.

21. Davis JM, Alderson NL, Welsh RS. Serotonin and central nervous system fatigue: nutritional considerations. *Am J Clin Nutr* 2000;72:573S-78S.

22. Slater GJ, Jenkins D. Beta-hydroxy-beta-methylbutyrate (HMB) supplementation and the promotion of muscle growth and strength. *Sports Med* 2000;30:105–16.

23. Panton LB, Rathmacher JA, Baier S et al. Nutritional supplementation of the leucine metabolite beta-hydroxy-beta-methylbutyrate (hmb) during resistance training. *Nutrition* 2000;16:734–9

24. Nissen S, Sharp RL, Panton L et al. Beta-hydroxy-beta-methylbutyrate (HMB) supplementation in humans is safe and may decrease cardiovascular risk factors. *J Nutr* 2000;130:1937–45.

25. Alon T, Bagchi D, Preuss HG. Supplementing with beta-hydroxy-beta-methylbutyrate (HMB) to build and maintain muscle mass: a review. *Res Commun Mol Pathol Pharmacol* 2002;111:139–51.

26. Crowe MJ, O'Connor DM, Lukins JE. The effects of beta-hydroxy-beta-methylbutyrate (HMB) and HMB/creatine supplementation on indices of health in highly trained athletes. *Int J Sport Nutr Exerc Metabol* 2003;13:184–97.

27. Miller, JM. The absorption of proteolytic enzymes from the gastrointestinal tract. *Clin Med* 1968;75:35–9.

28. Taussig SJ, Batkin S. Bromelain, the enzyme complex of pineapple (Ananas comosus) and its clinical application. An update. *J Ethnopharmacol* 1988;22:191–203.

29. Batkin S, Taussig SJ, Szekerezes J. Antimetastatic effect of bromelain with or without its proteolytic and anticoagulant activity. *J Cancer Res Clin Oncol* 1988;114:507–8.

30. Taussig SJ. The mechanism of the physiological action of bromelain. *Med Hypotheses* 1980;6:99–104.

31. Taussig SJ, Yokoyama MM, Chinen A et al. Bromelain: a proteolytic enzyme and its clinical application. A review. *Hiroshima J Med Sci* 1975;24:185–93.

32. Committee on Military Nutrition Research, Food and Nutrition Board. Caffeine for the Sustainment of Mental Task Performance: Formulations for Military Operations. Washington, DC: National Academy Press; 2001.

33. Spiller GA. Basic Metabolism and Physiological Effects of the Methylxanthines. In Spiller GA. Caffeine. Boca Raton, FL: CRC Press; 1998. p 225–32.

34. Laramine RJ. Caffeine as an Ergogenic Aid. In Spiller GA. Caffeine. Boca Raton, FL: CRC Press; 1998. p 233–50.

35. Soop M, Bjorkman O, Cederblad G et al. Influence of carnitine supplementation on muscle substrate and carnitine metabolism during exercise. *J Appl Physiol* 1988;64:2394–9.

36. Cerretelli P, Marconi C. L-carnitine supplementation in humans. The effects on physical performance. *Int J Sports Med* 1990;11:1–14.

37. Siliprandi N. Carnitine and Physical Exercise. In Benzi G, Packer L, Siliprandi N. Biochemical Aspects of Physical Exercise. Amsterdam: Elsevier; 1986. p 197.

38. Otto RM, Shores KVM, Perez HR. Effect of L-carnitine supplementation on endurance exercise. *Med Sci Sports Exerc* 1987;19:S68.

39. Shores Kv, Otto RM, Wygand JW et al. Effect of L-carnitine supplementation on maximal oxygen consumption and free fatty acid serum levels. *Med Sci Sports Exerc* 1987;19:S68.

40. Miller GD, Jarvis JK, McBean LD. Handbook of Dairy Foods and Nutrition, 2nd ed. Boca Raton, FL: CRC Press; 2000.

41. Boirie Y, Dangin M, Gachon P et al. Slow and fast dietary proteins differently modulate postprandial protein accretion. *Proceed Nat Acad Sci USA* 1997;94:14930–5.

42. Pittler MH, Abbot NC, Harkness EF et al. Randomized, double-blind trial of chitosan for body weight reduction. *Eur J Clin Nutr* 1999;53:379–81.

43. Gades MD, Stern JS. Chitosan supplementation and fecal fat excretion in men. *Obesity Res* 2003;11:683–8.

44. Bokura H, Kobayashi S. Chitosan decreases total cholesterol in women: a randomized, double-blind, placebo-controlled trial. *Eur J Clin Nutr* 2003;57:721–5.

45. Matson CA, Ritter RC. Long-term CCK-leptin synergy suggests a role for CCK in the regulation of body weight. *Am J Physiol* 1999;276:R1038–45.

46. Hungerford MW, Valaik D. Chondroprotective agents: glucosamine and chondroitin. *Foot Ankle Clin* 2003;8:201–19.

47. Towheed TE. Current status of glucosamine therapy in osteoarthritis. *Arthritis Rheum* 2003;49:601–04.

48. Keller L. Glucosamine for arthritis. *Adv Nurse Pract* 2003;11:19–21, 100.

49. Hungerford DS, Jones LC. Glucosamine and chondroitin sulfate are effective in the management of osteoarthritis. *J Arthroplasty* 2003;18:5–9.

50. Vincent JB. The potential value and toxicity of chromium picolinate as a nutritional supplement, weight loss agent and muscle development agent. *Sports Med* 2003;33:213–30.

51. Gambelunghe C, Rossi R, Sommavilla M et al. Effects of chrysin on urinary testosterone levels in human males. *J Med Food* 2003;6:387–90.

52. Calapai G, Firenzuoli F, Saitta A et al. Antiobesity and cardiovascular toxic effects of citrus aurantium extracts in the rat: a preliminary report. *Fitoterapia* 1999;70:586–92.

53. Keogh AM, Baron DW. Sympathomimetic abuse and coronary artery spasm. *Br Med J* 1985;291:940.

54. Haaz S, Fontaine KR, Cutter G et al. Citrus aurantium and synephrine alkaloids in the treatment of overweight and obesity: an update. *Obesity Rev* 2006;7:79–88.

55. Greenberg S, Fishman WH. Coenzyme Q 10: a new drug for cardiovascular disease. *J Clin Pharmacol* 1990;30:596–608.

56. Heck AM, DeWitt BA, Lukes AL. Potential interactions between alternative therapies and warfarin. *Am J Health Syst Pharm* 2000;57:1221–7.

57. Belury M. Not all trans-fatty acids are alike: what consumers may lose when we oversimplify nutrition facts. *J Am Diet Assoc* 2002;102:1606–7.

58. Belury MA. Dietary conjugated linoleic acid in health: physiological effects and mechanisms of action. *Ann Rev Nutr* 2002;22:505–31.

59. Kreider RB. Effects of creatine supplementation on performance and training adaptations. *Mole Cell Biochem* 2003;244:89–94.

60. Farquhar WB, Zambraski EJ. Effects of creatine use on the athlete's kidney. *Curr Sports Med Rep* 2002;1:103–6.

61. Legrain S, Girard L. Pharmacology and therapeutic effects of dehydroepiandrosterone in older subjects. *Drugs Aging* 2003;20:949–67.

62. Racchi M, Balduzzi C, Corsini E. Dehydroepiandrosterone (DHEA) and the aging brain: flipping a coin in the "fountain of youth". *CNS Drug Rev* 2003;9:21–40.

63. Delbeke FT, Van Eenoo P, Van Thuyne W et al. Prohormones and sport. *J Steroid Biochem Mole Biol* 2002;83:245–51.

64. Nissen SL, Sharp RL. Effect of dietary supplements on lean mass and strength gains with resistance exercise: a meta-analysis. *J Appl Physiol* 2003;94:651–9.

65. Shekelle PG, Hardy ML, Morton SC et al. Efficacy and safety of ephedra and ephedrine for weight loss and athletic performance: a meta-analysis. *J Am Med Assoc* 2003;289:1537–45.

66. Ponto LL, Schultz SK. Ginkgo biloba extract: review of CNS effects. *Ann Clin Psychiatry* 2003;15:109–19.

67. Bone KM. Potential interaction of Ginkgo biloba leaf with antiplatelet or anticoagulant drugs: What is the evidence? *Mole Nutr Food Res* 2008;52:764–771.

68. Birks J, Grimley Evans J. Ginkgo biloba for cognitive impairment and dementia. *Cochrane Database System Rev* 2007;18(2):CD003120.

69. Hungerford DS, Jones LC. Glucosamine and chondroitin sulfate are effective in the management of osteoarthritis. *J Arthroplasty* 2003;18:5–9.

70. Wernerman J. Glutamine and acute illness. *Curr Opin Crit Care* 2003;9:279–85.

71. Smith DJ, Norris SR. Changes in glutamine and glutamate concentrations for tracking training tolerance. *Med Sci Sports Exerc* 2000;32:684–9.

72. Dulloo AG, Duret C, Rohrer D et al. Efficacy of a green tea extract rich in catechin polyphenols and caffeine in increasing 24-h energy expenditure and fat oxidation in humans. *Am J Clin Nutr* 1999;70:1040–5.

73. Wang HK. The therapeutic potential of flavonoids. *Expert Opin Invest Drugs* 2000;9:2103–19.

74. Westerterp-Plantenga MS, Kovacs EM. The effect of (−)-hydroxycitrate on energy intake and satiety in overweight humans. *Int J Obesity Related Metab Disorders* 2002;26:870–2.

75. Tomita K, Okuhara Y, Shigematsu N et al. (−)-hydroxycitrate ingestion increases fat oxidation during moderate intensity exercise in untrained men. *Biosci Biotechnol Biochem* 2003;67:1999–2001.

76. Ohia SE, Opere CA, LeDay AM et al. Safety and mechanism of appetite suppression by a novel hydroxycitric acid extract (HCA-SX). *Mole Cell Biochem* 2002;238:89–103.

77. Lim K, Ryu S, Ohishi Y et al. Short-term (−)-hydroxycitrate ingestion increases fat oxidation during exercise in athletes. *J Nutr Sci Vitaminol Tokyo* 2002;48:128–33.

78. Heymsfield SB, Allison DB, Vasselli JR et al. Garcinia cambogia (hydroxycitric acid) as a potential antiobesity agent: a randomized controlled trial. *J Am Med Assoc* 1998;280:1596–600.

79. Benjamin J, Levine J, Fux M et al. Double-blind, placebo-controlled, crossover trial of inositol treatment for panic disorder. *Am J Psychiatry* 1996;152:1084–86.

80. Levine J, Barak Y, Gonzalves M et al. Double-blind, controlled trial of inositol treatment of depression. *Am J Psychiatry* 1995;152:792–4.

81. Hinton PS, Sinclair LM. Iron supplementation maintains ventilatory threshold and improves energetic efficiency in iron-deficient nonanemic athletes. *Eur J Clin Nutr* 2007;61:30–9.

82. Lynch MA. Lipoic acid confers protection against oxidative injury in non-neuronal and neuronal tissue. *Nutr Neurosci* 2001;4:419–38.

83. Packer L, Kraemer K, Rimbach G. Molecular aspects of lipoic acid in the prevention of diabetes complications. *Nutrition* 2001;17:888–95.

84. St-Onge MP, Jones PJ. Physiological effects of medium-chain triglycerides: potential agents in the prevention of obesity. *J Nutr* 2002;132:329–32.

85. Berning JR. The role of medium-chain triglycerides in exercise. *Int J Sport Nutr* 1996;6:121–33.

86. Sukala WR. Pyruvate: beyond the marketing hype. *Int J Sport Nutr* 1998;8:241–9.

87. Requena B, Zabala M, Padial P et al. Sodium bicarbonate and sodium citrate: ergogenic aids? *J Strength Cond Res* 2005;19:213–24.

88. Stofan JR, Zachwieja JJ, Horswill CA et al. Sweat and sodium losses in NCAA football players: a precursor to heat cramps? *Int J Sport Nutr Exerc Metab* 2005;15:641–52.

89. Lourenco R, Camilo ME. Taurine: a conditionally essential amino acid in humans? An overview in health and disease. *Nutrition Hospitalaria* 2002;17:262–70.

90. Schuller-Levis GB, Park E. Taurine: new implications for an old amino acid. *FEMS Microbiol Lett* 2003;226:195–202.

91. Fawcett JP, Farquhar SJ, Walker RJ et al. The effect of oral vanadyl sulfate on body composition and performance in weight-training athletes. *Int J Sport Nutr* 1996;6:382–90.

92. Mukherjee B, Patra B, Mahapatra S et al. Vanadium–an element of atypical biological significance. *Toxicol Lett* 2004;150:135–43.

Glossary

A

A-Band: The region of the sarcomere where myosin filaments are predominantly seen with minor overlap of the actin filaments.

Abduction: A movement in the frontal plane away from the midline of the body.

Acceleration: An ability to rapidly increase movement velocity.

Achilles Tendonitis: Irritation and inflammation of the Achilles tendon.

Acidosis: The accumulation of excessive hydrogen that causes increased acidity of the blood and muscle.

Actin: One of the two major myofilaments, actin is the "thin" filament that acts along with myosin to produce muscular contraction.

Action Potential: Nerve impulse that allows neurons to transmit information.

Active Flexibility: Designed to improve soft tissue extensibility in all planes of motion by employing the neurophysiological principle of reciprocal inhibition. Active flexibility utilizes agonists and synergists to actively move a limb through a range of motion, while the functional antagonists are being stretched. Active flexibility incorporates neuromuscular stretching and active-isolated stretching.

Active-Isolated Stretching: Stretching technique that uses agonists and synergists to dynamically move the joint through a range of motion.

Acute Variables: Important components that specify how each exercise is to be performed.

Adaptation: The human body's ability to adapt or adjust its functional capacity to meet the demands placed upon it.

Adduction: Movement in the frontal plane back toward the midline of the body.

Adenosine Triphospate (ATP): Energy storage and transfer unit within the cells of the body.

Adequate Intake (AI): A recommended average daily nutrient intake level, based on observed (or experimentally determined) approximations or estimates of nutrient intake that are assumed to be adequate for a group (or groups) of healthy people. This measure is used when an RDA cannot be determined.

Aerobic: Activities requiring oxygen.

Afferent Neurons: (Also known as sensory neurons) They gather incoming sensory information from the environment and deliver it to the central nervous system.

Agility: The ability to change direction or orientation of the body based on internal or external information quickly and accurately without significant loss of speed.

Agonist: Muscles that are the primary movers in a joint motion. Also known as prime movers.

Alarm Reaction Stage: The first stage of the GAS syndrome, the initial reaction to a stressor.

All-Or-None Principle: When a muscle fiber is stimulated to contract, the entire fiber contracts completely.

Altered Reciprocal Inhibition: The concept of muscle inhibition, caused by a tight agonist, which inhibits its functional antagonist.

Amenorrhea: Abnormal suppression or absence of menstruation.

Amortization Phase: The electromechanical delay a muscle experiences in the transition from eccentric (reducing force and storing energy) to concentric (producing force) muscle action.

Anaerobic: Activities that do not require oxygen.

Anaerobic Threshold: The point during high-intensity activity when the body can no longer meet its demand for oxygen and anaerobic metabolism predominates; also called lactate threshold.

Anatomical Locations: Refers to terms that describe locations on the body.

Annual Plan: Organizes the training program over a one-year period that provides the athlete with a blueprint (or map) of how the OPT™ training program will progress over the long term, month by month, to meet the desired goal.

Annulus Fibrosus: The outer, fibrous, ring-like portion of an intervertebral disc.

Antagonist: Muscles that act in direct opposition to agonists (prime movers).

Anterior Oblique Sub-System: Stabilization system consisting of the internal and external oblique muscles, the adductor complex, and hip external rotators and is necessary for functional activities involving the trunk, and upper and lower extremities. This system not only produces rotational and flexion movements, but is also instrumental in stabilizing the lumbo-pelvic-hip complex.

Anterior: Refers to a position on the front or towards the front of the body.

Anticipation: Recognizing certain stimuli and preparing the appropriate response pattern in advance.

Antioxidants: A substance, such as vitamin E, vitamin C, or beta-carotene, thought to protect body cells from the damaging effects of oxidation.

Aortic Semilunar Valve: Controls blood flow from the left ventricle to the aorta going to the entire body.

Appendicular Skeleton: The portion of the skeletal system that includes the upper and lower extremities.

Arthritis: Chronic inflammation of the joints.

Arthrokinematics: The motions of joints in the body.

Articulation: Junctions of bones, muscles and connective tissue where movement occurs. Also known as a joint.

Arteries: Vessels that transport blood away from the heart.

Arterioles: Medium-sized arteries that further divide into smaller arteries.

Arthrokinetic Dysfunction: The biomechanical dysfunction in two articular partners that lead to abnormal joint movement (arthrokinematics) and proprioception.

Arthrokinetic Inhibition: The neuromuscular phenomenon that occurs when a joint dysfunction inhibits the muscles that surround the joint.

Atherosclerosis: Clogging, narrowing, and hardening of the body's large arteries and medium-sized blood vessels. Atherosclerosis can lead to stroke, heart attack, eye problems and kidney problems.

Arthrokinematics: Joint motion.

Atrium: A smaller chamber located superiorly on either side of the heart.

Atrioventricular Valves: Allow for proper blood flow from the atria to the ventricles.

Atrophy: The loss in muscle fiber size.

Augmented Feedback: Information provided by some external source such as a fitness professional, videotape or a heart rate monitor.

Autogenic Inhibition: The process when neural impulses sensing tension are greater than the impulses causing muscle contraction. Stimulation of the Golgi Tendon Organ overrides the muscle spindle.

Axial Skeleton: The portion of the skeletal system that consists of the skull, rib cage and vertebral column.

Axon: A cylindrical projection from the cell body that transmits nervous impulses to other neurons or effector sites.

B

Backside Mechanics: Proper alignment of the rear leg and pelvis during sprinting, which includes ankle plantarflexion, knee extension, hip extension and neutral pelvis.

Balance: The ability to sustain or return the body's center of mass or line of gravity over its base of support.

Ball-and-Socket Joint: Most mobile joints that allow motion in all three planes. Examples would include the shoulder and hip.

Basal Ganglia: A portion of the lower brain that is instrumental in the initiation and control of repetitive voluntary movements such as walking and running.

Bicuspid (mitral) Valve: Two cusps control the blood flow from the left atrium to the left ventricle.

Bioenergetics: The study of energy in the human body.

Bioenergetic Continuum: Three main pathways utilized by the kinetic chain to produce ATP.

Biomechanics: Applies the principles of physics to quantitatively study how forces interact within a living body.

Bipenniform Muscle Fibers: Muscle fibers that are arranged with short, oblique fibers that extend from both sides of a long tendon. An example would be the rectus femoris.

Body Mass Index: Body composition assessment used for determining if one's weight is appropriate for height and is determined by dividing one's body weight (in kilograms) by their height (in meters squared).

Blood Vessels: Form a closed circuit of hollow tubes that allow blood to be transported to and from the heart.

Bracing: The act of "stiffening" or "tightening" the muscles of the midsection (Global Core Stabilizers).

Brain Stem: The link between the sensory and motor nerves coming from the brain to the body and vice versa.

C

Calories: The energy contained in food, measured in kilocalories. A unit of measurement of heat. The amount of heat needed to raise the temperature of water from 14.5° C to 15.5° C.

Cancer: Any of various types of malignant neoplasms, most of which invade surrounding tissues; may metastasize to several sites and are likely to recur after attempted removal and to cause death of the patient unless adequately treated.

Capillaries: Arterioles that branch out into a multitude of microscopic vessels.

Carbohydrate: Organic compounds of carbon, hydrogen, and oxygen, which include starches, cellulose, and sugars, and are an important source of energy. All carbohydrates are eventually broken down in the body to glucose, a simple sugar.

Cardiac Muscle: Heart muscle.

Cardiac Output (Q): Heart rate × stroke volume, the overall performance of the heart.

Cardiorespiratory (CR) System: The combination of the cardiovascular and respiratory systems that provide the tissues of the kinetic chain with oxygen, nutrients, protective agents, and a means to remove waste by-products.

Cardiorespiratory Training: Any physical activity that involves and places stress on the cardiorespiratory system.

Cardiorespiratory Training: Training that involves and places a stress on the cardiorespiratory system.

Cardiovascular Control Center (CVC): Directs impulses that will either increase or decrease cardiac output and peripheral resistance based upon feedback from all structures involved.

Cardiovascular System: The system composed of the heart, blood vessels, and blood.

Casein: The predominant phosphoprotein that accounts for nearly 80% of proteins in milk and cheese.

Cell Body: The portion of the neuron that contains the nucleus, lysosomes, mitochondria, and a Golgi complex.

Central Controller: Controls heart rate, left ventricular contractibility and arterial blood pressure by manipulating the sympathetic and parasympathetic nervous systems.

Central Nervous System: The portion of the nervous system that consists of the brain and spinal cord.

Cerebellum: A portion of the lower-brain that compares sensory information from the body and the external environment with motor information from the cerebral cortex to ensure smooth coordinated movement.

Cerebral Cortex: A portion of the brain that consists of the frontal lobe, parietal lobe, occipital lobe, and temporal lobe.

Cervical Spine: The area of your spine containing the seven vertebrae that compose the neck.

Chemoreceptors: Sensory receptors that respond to chemical interaction (smell and taste).

Circuit Training System: This consists of a series of exercise that an individual performs one after another with minimal rest.

Clean & Jerk: The second of the two Olympic lifts and is considered the double movement. The clean is the phase involving the lifting of the barbell from the floor to the shoulders and the jerk is the explosive lifting of the barbell from shoulders to overhead.

Co-contraction: Muscles contract together in a force couple.

Collagen: A protein that is found in connective tissue that provides tensile strength. Collagen, unlike elastin, is not very elastic.

Compound-Sets: Involve the performance of two exercises for antagonistic muscles. For example, a set of bench press, followed by cable rows (Chest/Back).

Concentric: When a muscle exerts more force than is being placed upon it, the muscle will shorten. Also known as acceleration or force production.

Conduction Passageway: Consists of all the structures that air travels before entering the respiratory passageway.

Condyles: Projections protruding from the bone to which muscles, tendons and ligaments can attach. Also known as a process, epicondyle, tubercle and trochanter.

Condyloid Joint: A joint where the condyle of one bone fits into the elliptical cavity of another bone to form the joint. An example would include the knee joint.

Contralateral: Refers to a position on the opposite side of the body.

Controlled Instability: Training environment that is as unstable as can safely be controlled by an individual.

Controlled Instability: A training environment that is as unstable, but can be SAFELY controlled.

Core: The center of the body and the beginning point for movement. The core is considered as the lumbo-pelvic-hip complex that operates as an integrated functional unit providing intersegmental stability, deceleration and force production during athletic activities.

Core Stability: Neuromuscular efficiency of the lumbo-pelvic-hip complex

Core Strength: The ability of the lumbo-pelvic-hip complex musculature to control an individual's constantly changing center of gravity.

Coronal Plane: An imaginary plane that bisects the body to create front and back halves. Also known as the Frontal Plane.

Corrective Exercise Training: A specialized form of training designed to correct muscle imbalances, joint dysfunctions, neuromuscular deficits and postural distortion patterns that the athlete may have developed during the season.

Corrective Flexibility: Designed to correct common postural dysfunctions, muscle imbalances and joint dysfunctions incorporating self-myofascial release, static stretching and neuromuscular stretching.

Creatine Phosphate: A high-energy phosphate molecule that is stored in cells and can be used to re-synthesize ATP immediately.

Cumulative Injury Cycle: A cycle whereby and "injury" will induce inflammation, muscle spasm, adhesions, altered neuromuscular control and muscle imbalances.

D

Davis' Law: States that soft tissue models along the line of stress.

Decelerate: When the muscle is exerting less force than is being placed upon it, the muscle lengthens. Also known as an eccentric muscle action or force reduction.

Deconditioned: Refers to a state in which a person has muscle imbalances, decreased flexibility and/or a lack of core and joint stability.

Deep Longitudinal Sub-system (DLS): Stabilization system consisting of the erector spinae, thoracolumbar fascia, sacrotuberous ligament, biceps femoris and peroncus longus, which provides a longitudinal means of reciprocal force transmission from the trunk to the ground.

Dendrites: A portion of the neuron that is responsible for gathering information from other structures.

Depression: A flattened or indented portion of bone, which could be a muscle attachment site. Also known as a fossa.

Diabetes: Chronic metabolic disorder, caused by insulin deficiency, which impairs carbohydrate usage and enhances usages of fats and protein.

Dietary Supplement: A substance that completes or makes an addition to daily dietary intake.

Diffusion: The process of getting oxygen from the environment to the tissues of the body.

Distal: Refers to a position furthest from the center of the body or point of reference.

Dorsal: Refers to a position on the back or towards the back of the body.

Dorsiflexion: Flexion at the ankle, moving the front of the foot upward.

Drawing-in Maneuver: Activation of the transverse abdominis, multifidus, pelvic floor muscles and diaphragm to provide core stabilization.

Drive Phase: A distinct phase during the stride cycle when the foot is in contact with the ground.

Dynamic Functional Flexibility: Multiplanar soft tissue extensibility with optimal neuromuscular efficiency throughout the full range of motion.

Dynamic Joint Stabilization: The ability of the stabilizing muscles of a joint to produce optimum stabilization during functional, multiplanar movements.

Dynamic Range of Motion: The combination of flexibility and neuromuscular efficiency.

Dynamic Stretching: Uses the force production of a muscle and the body's momentum to take a joint through the full available range of motion.

E

Eccentric: When the muscle is exerting less force than is being placed upon it, the muscle lengthens. Also known as deceleration, or force reduction.

Effectors: Any structure innervated by the nervous system, including organs, glands, muscle tissue, connective tissue, blood vessels, bone marrow, etc.

Efferent Neurons: Neurons that transmit nerve impulses from the brain and/or spinal cord to the effector sites such as muscles or glands. Also known as motor neurons.

Eicosanoid: Signaling molecules made by oxygenation of twenty-carbon essential fatty acids (EFAs). They exert complex control over many bodily systems, mainly in inflammation or immunity, and as messengers in the central nervous system.

Elasticity: The spring-like behavior of connective tissue that enables the tissue to return to its original shape or size when forces are removed.

Elastin: A protein that is found in connective tissue that has elastic properties.

Endocrine System: The system of glands in the human body that are responsible for producing hormones.

Endomysium: The deepest layer of connective tissue that surrounds individual muscle fibers.

Endurance Strength: The ability to produce and maintain force over prolonged periods of time.

Energy: The capacity to do work.

Energy-Utilizing: When energy is gathered from an energy-yielding source by some storage unit (ATP) and then transferred to a site that can utilize this energy.

Epicondyle: Projections protruding from the bone to which muscles, tendons and ligaments can attach. Also known as a condyle, process, tubercle and trochanter.

Epidemiology: Study of the cause and distribution of diseases in human populations.

Epimysium: A layer of connective tissue that is underneath the fascia, and surrounds the muscle.

Equilibrium: A condition of balance between opposed forces, influences or actions.

Ergogenic aid: Something that aids (enhances) athletic performance.

Ergolytic: Something that impairs performance.

Erythrocytes: Red blood cells.

Estimated Average Requirement (EAR): The average daily nutrient intake level that is estimated to meet the requirement of half the healthy individuals who are in a particular life stage and gender group.

Eversion: A movement where the inferior calcaneus moves laterally.

Excess Post-exercise Oxygen Consumption (EPOC): The state where the body's metabolism is elevated following exercise.

Excitation-Contraction Coupling: The process of neural stimulation creating a muscle contraction.

Exercise Order: Refers to the order that the exercises are performed during a workout.

Exercise Selection: The process of choosing exercises for program design.

Exhaustion: The result of prolonged stress or stress that is intolerable to a client.

Exhaustion Stage: The third stage of the GAS syndrome, when prolonged stress or stress that is intolerable to a client will cause distress.

Explosive Strength: The ability to develop a sharp rise in force production once a movement pattern has been initiated.

Expiratory: Exhalation

Extensibility: Capability to be elongated or stretched.

Extension: A straightening movement where the relative angle between two adjacent segments increases.

External Feedback: Information provided by some external source such as a Sports Performance Professional, videotape or a heart rate monitor.

F

Fan-Shaped Muscle: A muscular fiber arrangement that has muscle fibers span out from a narrow attachment at one end to a broad attachment at the other end. An example would be the pectoralis major.

Fascia: A connective tissue that binds muscles into separate groups.

Fascicle: A grouping of muscle fibers that house myofibrils.

Fast Twitch Fibers: Muscle fibers that can also be characterized by the term Type IIA and IIB. These fibers contain less capillaries, mitochondria and myoglobin. These fibers fatigue faster than Type I fibers.

Fats: One of the three main classes of foods and a source of energy in the body. Fats help the body use some vitamins and keep the skin healthy. They also serve as energy stores for the body. In food, there are two types of fats: saturated and unsaturated.

Feedback: The utilization of sensory information and sensorimotor integration to aid the human movement system in the development of permanent neural representations of motor patterns.

"Fight or Flight": A physiological response stating that animals/humans react to threats with a general discharge of the sympathetic nervous system, priming the animal/human for fighting or fleeing.

Flat Bones: A classification of bone that is involved in protection and provides attachment sites for muscles. Examples include the sternum and scapulae.

Flexibility: Ability of the human movement system to have optimum range of motion (ROM) as well as neuromuscular control throughout that ROM in order to prevent injury and enhance functional efficiency.

Flexibility Training: Physical training of the body that integrates various stretches in all three planes of motion in order to produce the maximum extensibility of tissues.

Flexion: A bending movement where the relative angle between two adjacent segments decreases.

Flow: A state of consciousness where one becomes totally absorbed in what one is doing to the exclusion of all other thoughts and emotions.

Force: The interaction between two entities or bodies that result in either the acceleration or deceleration of an object.

Force-Couples: The synergistic action of muscles to produce movement around a joint.

Force Velocity Curve: The ability of muscles to produce force with increasing velocity.

Formed Elements: Refers to the cellular component of blood that includes erythrocytes, leukocytes and thrombocytes.

Fossa: A depression or indented portion of bone, which could be a muscle attachment site. Also known as a depression.

Frequency: The number of training sessions in a given time frame.

Frontside Mechanics: Proper alignment of the lead leg and pelvis during sprinting, which includes ankle dorsiflexion, knee flexion, hip flexion and neutral pelvis.

Frontal Lobe: A portion of the cerebral cortex that contains structures necessary for the planning and control of voluntary movement.

Frontal Plane: Bisects the body into front and back halves with frontal plane motion occurring around an anterior-posterior axis.

Fructose: Known as fruit sugar; a member of the simple sugars carbohydrate group found in fruits, honey and syrups, and certain vegetables.

Functional Efficiency: The ability of the neuromuscular system to monitor and manipulate movement during functional tasks using the least amount of energy, creating the least amount of stress of the kinetic chain.

Functional Flexibility: Designed to improve multiplanar soft tissue extensibility and provide optimum neuromuscular control throughout that full range of motion, while performing functional movements that utilize the body's muscles to control the speed, direction and intensity of the stretch.

Functional Strength: The ability of the neuromuscular system to contract eccentrically, isometrically and concentrically in all three planes of motion.

Fusiform: A muscular fiber arrangement that has a full muscle belly that tapers off at both ends. An example would include the biceps brachii.

G

General Adaptation Syndrome (GAS): The human movement system's ability to adapt to stresses placed upon it.

General Warm-up: Consists of movements that do not necessarily have any movement specificity to the actual activity to be preformed.

Genu Valgum: Inward or medial curving of the knee; knock-knee.

Glenohumeral Joint: Shoulder joint formed by the articulation between the head of the humerus and the lateral scapula.

Gliding Joint: A non-axial joint that moves back and forth or side to side. Examples would include the carpals of the hand and the facet joints.

Global Core Stabilizers: Muscles that attach from the pelvis to the spine and act to transfer loads between the upper extremity and lower extremity and provide stability between the pelvis and spine.

Global Muscular Systems: Responsible predominantly for movement and consist of more superficial musculature that originate from the pelvis to the rib cage, the lower extremities or both.

Gluconeogenesis: A metabolic pathway that results in the generation of glucose from non-carbohydrate carbon substrates such as pyruvate, lactate, glycerol and glucogenic amino acids.

Glycemic Index: A ranking of carbohydrate-containing foods, based on the food's effect on blood sugar compared with a standard reference food's effect.

Glycogen: The complex carbohydrate molecule used to store carbohydrates in the liver and muscle cells. When carbohydrate energy is needed, glycogen is converted into glucose for use by the muscle cells.

Golgi Afferents: High threshold, slowly adapting sensory receptors located in ligaments and menisci. These receptors are mechanically sensitive to tensile loads and are most sensitive at the end ranges of motion.

Golgi Tendon Organs: Located within the musculotendinous junction and are sensitive to changes in muscular tension, and rate of tension change.

Goniometric Assessment: Technique measuring angular measurement, and joint range of motion.

Gravity: The attraction between earth and the objects on earth.

Ground Reaction Force (GRF): The equal and opposite force that is exerted back onto the body every step that is taken.

H

Heart Rate (HR): The rate at which the heart pumps.

Hemoglobin: Oxygen-carrying component of red blood cells and also gives it its red color.

High Ankle Sprain: A syndesmotic sprain involving the distal tibiofibular joint just proximal to the ankle.

High Glycemic Carbohydrates: Carbohydrates that break down rapidly during digestion, releasing glucose rapidly into the bloodstream.

High-load Speed Strength: The muscles' ability to contract with high force at high speed with a heavy resistance and quantified by power output.

Hinge Joint: A uniaxial joint that allows movement in one plane of motion. Examples would include the elbow and ankle.

Hip Hinge: The spine remaining stiff and neutral while movement occurs about the hip joint.

Homeostasis: The ability or tendency of an organism or a cell to maintain internal equilibrium by adjusting its physiological processes.

Horizontal Loading: Performing all sets of an exercise or a body part before moving on to the next exercise or body part.

Human Movement Science: The study of functional anatomy, functional biomechanics, motion learning and motor control.

Hypercholesterolemia: Chronic high levels of cholesterol in the bloodstream.

Hyperglycemia: Abnormally high blood sugar.

Hyperlipidemia: Elevated levels of blood fats (e.g., triglycerides, cholesterol).

Hypertension: Raised systemic arterial blood pressure, which, if sustained at a high enough level, is likely to induce cardiovascular or end-organ damage.

Hypertrophy: Enlargement of skeletal muscle fibers in response to overcoming force from high volumes of tension.

Hypertrophy Training: The third phase of the OPT™ Model.

Hyponatremia: Abnormally low levels of blood sodium.

H-Zone: The area of the sarcomere where only myosin filaments are present.

I

I-Band: The area of the sarcomere that only actin filaments are present.

Inferior: Refers to a position below a reference point.

Inner Unit: Provides intersegmental stabilization of the lumbo-pelvic-hip complex and generally consists of the transverse abdominus, multifidus, internal oblique and pelvic floor musculature.

Insertion: The part of a muscle by which it is attached to the part to be moved — compare to origin.

Inspiratory: Inhalation.

Insulin: A protein hormone released by the pancreas that helps glucose move out of the blood and into the cells in the body, where the glucose can be used as energy and nourishment.

Integrated Flexibility Training: A multifaceted approach integrating various flexibility techniques to achieve optimum soft tissue extensibility in all planes of motion.

Integrated Functional Unit: Muscle synergies.

Integrated Performance Paradigm: This paradigm states that in order to move with precision, forces must be reduced (eccentrically), stabilized (isometrically) and then produced (concentrically).

Integrative (Function of Nervous System): The ability of the nervous system to analyze and interpret the sensory information to allow for proper decision making to produce the appropriate response.

Integrated Training: A comprehensive approach that attempts to improve all components necessary for an athlete to perform at the highest level and prevent injury.

Intensity: The level of demand that a given activity places on the body. A level of muscular activity quantified by power output.

Internal Feedback: The process whereby sensory information is utilized to reactively monitor movement and the environment.

Internal Rotation: Rotation of a joint toward the middle of the body.

Interneurons: Transmit nerve impulses from one neuron to another.

Interval Training: Training at different intensities for certain periods of time in a given workout.

Inter-muscular Coordination: The ability of the entire human movement system and each muscular subsystem to work interdependently to improve movement efficiency.

Intervertebral Foramen: The lateral opening through which spinal nerve roots exit on each side of the spinal column; formed by the bony and soft tissues at each spinal joint.

Intra-muscular Coordination: The ability of the neuromuscular system to allow optimal levels of motor unit recruitment and synchronization within a muscle.

Intrapulmonary Pressure: Pressure within the thoracic cavity.

Inversion: A movement where the inferior calcaneus moves medially.

Ipsilateral: Refers to a position on the same side of the body.

Isometric: When a muscle is exerting force equal to the force being placed upon it. Also known as dynamic stabilization.

Irregular Bones: A classification of bone that has its own unique shape and function, which does not fit the characteristics of the other categories. Examples include the vertebrae and pelvic bones.

J

Joint: Junctions of bones, muscles and connective tissue where movement occurs. Also known as an articulation.

Joint mechanoreceptors: Receptors located in joints throughout the fibrous capsule and ligaments. These receptors signal joint position, movement and pressure changes.

Joint Mobility: The ability of a joint to move through its natural, effective range of motion and is further characterized as the balance of strength and flexibility regulating contrasting motions around a joint (i.e., flexion and extension).

Joint Motion: Movement in a plane occurs about an axis running perpendicular to the plane.

Joint Stiffness: Resistance to unwanted movement.

K

Kinesthesia: The conscious awareness of joint movement and joint position sense that results from proprioceptive input sent to the central nervous system.

Kinetic: Force.

Kinetic Chain: The combination and interrelation of the nervous, muscular and skeletal systems.

Knee Valgus: Femur internally rotated, and tibia externally rotated; knock-knee.

Knowledge of Performance (KP): A method of feedback that provides information about the quality of the movement pattern performed.

Knowledge of Results (KR): A method of feedback after the completion of a movement to inform the client about the outcome of their performance.

Kyphosis: Exaggerated outward curvature of the thoracic region of the spinal column resulting in a rounded upper back.

L

Lactic Acid: An acid produced by glucose-burning cells when these cells have an insufficient supply of oxygen.

Lateral: Refers to a position relatively farther away from the midline of the body or toward the outside of the body.

Lateral Ankle Sprain: Any of the lateral ligaments, including the anterior talofibular ligament (ATFL), calcaneofibular ligament (CFL) and posterior talofibular ligament (PTFL) that may be injured, often caused by forced plantar flexion and inversion of the ankle during landing on an unstable or uneven surface.

Lateral Flexion: The bending of the spine (cervical, thoracic and/or lumbar) from side to side.

Lateral Sub-system: Stabilization system comprised of the gluteus medius, tensor fascia latae, adductor complex and the quadratus lumborum and is responsible for frontal plane and pelvo-femoral stability.

Law of Acceleration: Acceleration of an object is directly proportional to the size of the force causing it, in the same direction as the force and inversely proportional to the size of the object.

Law of Action-Reaction: Every force produced by one object onto another produces an opposite force of equal magnitude.

Law of Gravitation: Two bodies have an attraction to each other that is directly proportional to their masses and inversely proportional to the square of their distance from each other.

Law of Thermodynamics: Weight reduction can only take place when there is more energy burned than consumed.

Length-Tension Relationship: Refers to the resting length of a muscle and the tension the muscle can produce at this resting length.

Leukocytes: White blood cells.

Ligament: Primary connective tissue that connects bone-to-bone to provide stability, proprioception, guide and limit joint motion.

Limit Strength: The maximum force a muscle can produce in a single contraction.

Linear speed: The ability to move the body in one intended direction as fast as possible.

Load: The amount of weight prescribed to an exercise set.

Local Core Stabilizers: Muscles that attach directly to the vertebrae and are primarily responsible for intervertebral/intersegmental stability and work to limit excessive compressive, shear and rotational forces between spinal segments.

Local Musculature System: Consists of muscles that are predominantly involved in joint support or stabilization.

Long Bones: A characteristic of bone that has a long cylindrical body with irregular or widened bony ends. Examples include the clavicle and humerus.

Longitudinal Muscle Fiber: A muscle fiber arrangement, that's fibers run parallel to the line of pull. An example would include the sartorius.

Lordosis: Low back rounding.

Low-load Speed Strength: The muscles' ability to contract with high force at high speed with low resistance and is quantified by power output.

Lower-brain: The portion of the brain that includes the brain stem, the basal ganglia and the cerebellum.

Lower-extremity Postural Distortion: An individual who had increased lower extremity proration.

Lumbar Spine: The portion of the spine, commonly referred to as the small of the back. The lumbar portion of the spine is located between the thorax (chest) and the pelvis.

Lumbo-Pelvic-Hip Complex: Involves the anatomical structures of the lumbar, thoracic and cervical spine, the pelvic girdle and the hip joint.

Lumbo-Pelvic-Hip Postural Distortion: Altered joint mechanics in an individual that lead to increased lumbar extension and decreased hip extension.

M

Maximal Oxygen Consumption (VO$_2$ max): The highest rate of oxygen transport and utilization achieved at maximal physical exertion.

Maximal Power Training: The sixth phase of the OPT™ Model.

Maximal Speed: The maximal running speed one is able to attain.

Maximum Strength: The maximum force an individual's muscle can produce in a single voluntary effort, regardless of the rate of force production.

Maximal Strength Training: The fourth phase of the OPT™ Model.

Mechanical Specificity: The specific muscular exercises using different weights and movements that are performed to increase strength or endurance in certain body parts. Refers to the weight and movements placed on the body.

Mechanoreceptors: Sensory receptors that respond to mechanical forces. Specialized neural receptors embedded in connective tissue that converts mechanical distortions of the tissue into neural codes to be conveyed to the central nervous system.

Mediastinum: The area where the heart is positioned obliquely in the center of the chest or thoracic cavity lying between the spine posteriorly and the sternum anteriorly and flanked by the lungs

Medial: Refers to a position relatively closer to the midline of the body.

Medial Ankle Sprain: Ankle sprains involving the deltoid ligament of the ankle, and may include avulsion fractures of the tibia or other foot bones.

Metabolic Specificity: The specific muscular exercises using different levels of energy that are performed to increase endurance, strength or power. Refers to the energy demand required for a specific activity.

Metabolism: Chemical reactions that transform energy in the cells of the body into mechanical work.

Metatarsal Stress Fracture: Fractures that occur to the metatarsals; the long bones of the foot between the phalanges (the toes) and the tarsals.

Mineral: An inorganic element, such as calcium, iron, potassium, sodium or zinc, that is essential to the nutrition of humans, animals and plants.

Mitochondria: The mitochondria are the principal energy source of the cell. Mitochondria convert nutrients into energy as well as doing many other specialized tasks.

M-Line: The portion of the sarcomere where the myosin filaments connect with very thin filaments called titin and create an anchor for the structures of the sarcomere.

Mode: Type of exercise performed.

Momentum: The product of the size of the object (mass) and its velocity (speed with which it is moving).

Monthly Plan: The monthly plan details the specific days of each workout, showing the athlete exactly what phase of the OPT™ model (the type of training) will be required each day of the week.

Mortise: A common name for the talocrual (ankle) joint because of the similarity of shape of the talocrual joint and a carpenter's mortise.

Motor Behavior: The collective study of motor control, motor learning and motor development. Motor response to internal and external environmental stimuli.

Motor Control: The study of posture and movements with the involved structures and mechanisms used by the central nervous system to assimilate and integrate sensory information with previous experiences. How the central nervous system integrates internal and external sensory information with previous experiences to produce a motor response.

Motor Development: The change in motor behavior over time throughout the lifespan.

Motor (Function of Nervous System): The neuromuscular response to sensory information.

Motor Learning: The integration of motor control processes with practice and experience that lead to relatively permanent changes in the capacity to produce skilled movements.

Motor Neurons: Neurons that transmit nerve impulses from the brain and/or spinal cord to the effector sites such as muscles or glands. Also known as efferent neurons.

Motor Unit: A motor neuron and the muscle fibers that it innervates.

Multipenniform: Muscles that have multiple tendons with obliquely running muscle fibers.

Multiple-set System: The system consists of performing multiple sets of the same exercise.

Multisensory Condition: Training environment that provides heightened stimulation to proprioceptors and mechanoreceptors.

Muscle Action Spectrum: The range of muscle actions that include concentric, eccentric and isometric actions.

Muscle Imbalance: Alteration of muscle length surrounding a joint.

Muscle Fiber Arrangement: Refers to the manner in which the fibers are situated in relation to the tendon.

Muscle Fiber Recruitment: Refers to the recruitment pattern of muscle fiber/motor units in response to creating force for a specific movement.

Muscle Spindles: Microscopic intrafusal fibers that are sensitive to change in length and rate of length change.

Muscular Endurance: The ability of the body to produce low levels of force and maintain them for extended periods of time.

Muscle Hypertrophy: Characterized by the increase in the cross sectional area of individual muscle fibers and is believed to result from an increase in the myofibril proteins.

Muscle Synergies: The ability of muscles to work as an integrated functional unit.

Multi-directional Speed: Being able to create speed in any direction or body orientation (forward, backward, lateral, diagonal, etc).

Myofibrils: A portion of muscle that contains myofilaments.

Myofilaments: The contractile components of muscle, actin and myosin.

Myosin: One of the two major myofilaments known as the "thick" filament that works with actin to produce muscular contraction.

Myotatic Stretch Reflex: When a muscle is stretched very quickly, the muscle spindle contracts, which in turn stimulates the primary afferent fibers that causes the extrafusal fibers to fire, and tension increases in the muscle.

N

Nervous System: A conglomeration of billions of cells specifically designed to provide a communication network within the human body.

Neural Adaptation: An adaptation to strength training where muscles are under the direct command of the nervous system.

Neuromuscular Efficiency: The ability of the central nervous system (CNS) to allow agonists, antagonists, synergists and stabilizers to work interdependently during dynamic athletic activities.

Neuromuscular Junction: The point where the neuron meets the muscle, to allow the action potential to continue its impulse.

Neuromuscular Specificity: The specific muscular exercises using different speeds and styles that are performed to increase neuromuscular efficiency. Refers to the speed of contraction and exercise selection.

Neuromuscular Stretching (NMS): Stretching technique that involves passively moving the limb until the first resistance barrier is noted. The individual then applies an agonistic contraction of 25% maximal resistance lasting 7–15 seconds. After relaxation of the brief isometric contraction, the limb is moved into the newly created range of motion, with assistance from the individual, and held for 20–30 seconds. This is repeated three times.

Neuron: The functional unit of the nervous system.

Neurotransmitters: Chemical messengers that cross the neuromuscular junction to trigger the appropriate receptor sites.

Neutral Spine: The natural position of the spine when all three curves of the spine—cervical, thoracic and lumbar, are present and in good alignment. This is the safest position to perform movement.

Nocioceptors: Sensory receptors that respond to mechanical deformation and pain.

Nucleus Pulposus: A semi-fluid mass of fine white and elastic fibers that form the central portion of an intervertebral disc.

O

Obesity: The condition of subcutaneous fat exceeding the amount of lean body mass.

Objective Information: Measurable data about a client's physical state such as body composition, movement and cardiovascular ability.

Obstructive Lung Disease: The condition of altered air flow through the lungs, generally caused by airway obstruction, due to mucous production.

Occipital Lobe: A portion of the cerebral cortex that deals with vision.

Optimum Performance Training: A systematic, integrated and functional training program that simultaneously improves and individuals biomotor abilities and builds high levels of functional strength, neuromuscular efficiency and dynamic flexibility.

Optimal Strength: The ideal level of strength that an individual needs to perform functional activities.

Origin: The more fixed, central, or larger attachment of a muscle compared to insertion.

Osteoarthritis: Arthritis in which cartilage becomes soft, frayed or thins out, due to trauma or other conditions.

Osteopenia: A decrease in the calcification or density of bone as well as reduced bone mass.

Osteoporosis: Condition in which there is a decrease in bone mass and density as well as an increase in the space between bones, resulting in porosity and fragility.

Overtraining: Excessive frequency, volume or intensity of training, resulting in fatigue (which is due also to a lack of proper rest and recovery).

Oxygen Uptake: The usage of oxygen by the body.

P

Paciniform Afferents: Large, cylindrical, thinly encapsulated, multi-cellular end-organ structures. These receptors are widely distributed around the joint capsule and surrounding periarticular tissue that are mechanically sensitive to local compression and tensile loading, especially at extreme ranges of motion. These receptors are associated with the detection of acceleration, deceleration or sudden changes in the deformation of the mechanoreceptors.

Parietal Lobe: A portion of the cerebral cortex that is involved with sensory information.

Pattern Overload: Repetitive physical activity that moves through the same patterns of motion, placing the same stresses on the body over a period of time.

Perception: The integrating of sensory information with past experiences or memories.

Periodization: Division of a training program into smaller, progressive stages. Also defined as: to categorize training cycles into discrete blocks, namely the microcycle, mesocycle and the macrocycle. It can also refer to the athletic cycle, the Olympic cycle and the multi-year cycle.

Perimysium: The connective tissue that surrounds fascicles.

Peripheral Arterial Disease: A condition characterized by narrowing of the major arteries that are responsible for supplying blood to the lower extremities.

Peripheral Heat Action System (PHA): A variation of circuit training that alternates upper body and lower body exercises throughout the circuit.

Peripheral Nervous System: 12 cranial and 31 pairs of spinal nerves that provide a connection for the nervous system to activate different bodily organs and relay information from the bodily organs back to the brain, providing a constant update of the relation between the body and the environment.

Patellofemoral Pain: Pain in the knee region that is provoked or accentuated by actions that involve motion at the patellofemoral joint and/or increase pressure of patella against the femoral condyles.

Patellofemoral Syndrome: Vague discomfort of the inner knee area and may be caused by abnormal tracking of the patella within the femoral trochlea.

Photoreceptors: Sensory receptors that respond to light (vision).

Physical Activity Readiness Questionnaire (PAR-Q): A questionnaire that has been designed to help qualify a person for low-to-moderate-to-high activity levels.

Pivot Joint: Allows movement in predominantly the transverse plane; examples would include the atlantoaxial joint at the base of the skull and between the radioulnar joint.

Plane of Motion: Refers to the plane (sagittal, frontal and/or transverse) in which the exercise is performed.

Plantar Fasciitis: An inflamed and irritated plantar fascia.

Plantarflexion: Ankle extension such that the toes are pointed toward the ground.

Plasma: Aqueous liquid-like component of blood.

Plasticity: The unrecoverable or permanent elongation of soft tissue.

Plyometric Training: Exercises that utilize quick, powerful movements involving an eccentric contraction immediately followed by an explosive concentric contraction.

Posterior: Refers to a position on the back or towards the back of the body.

Posterior Pelvic Tilt: A movement in which the pelvis rotates backward.

Posterior Oblique Sub-system: Stabilization system made up of both the gluteus maximus and latissimus dorsi and is responsible for sacroiliac stabilization. This system is also of prime importance for rotational activities.

Postural Distortion Patterns: Predictable patterns of muscle imbalances.

Postural Equilibrium: The ability to efficiently maintain balance throughout the body segments.

Posture: Position and bearing of the body for alignment and function of the kinetic chain.

Power: The ability to exert maximal force in the shortest amount of time.

Power Endurance: The repetitive execution of explosive movement.

Power Training: The fifth phase of the OPT™ Model.

Pre-Programmed: Activation of muscles in healthy people that occurs automatically and independently of other muscles prior to movement.

Principle of Individualization: Refers to the uniqueness of a program to the client for whom it is designed.

Principle of Overload: Implies that there must be a training stimulus provided that exceeds the current capabilities of the human movement system to elicit the optimal physical, physiological and performance adaptations.

Principle of Progression: Refers to the intentional manner in which a program is designed to progress according to the physiological capabilities of the human movement system and the goals of the client.

Principle of Specificity: The human movement system will specifically adapt to the type of demand placed upon it. Also known as the SAID principle.

Principle of Variation: A planned training program with progressive and systematic variations to the training.

Processes: Projections protruding from the bone to which muscles, tendons and ligaments can attach. Also known as condyle, epicondyle, tubercle and trochanter.

Program Design: A purposeful system or plan put together to help an individual achieve a specific goal.

Pronation: A multi-planar, synchronized joint motion that occurs with eccentric muscle function.

Proprioception: The cumulative neural input to the central nervous system from all mechanoreceptors that sense position and limb movement.

Proprioceptively Enriched Environment: An environment that challenges the internal balance and stabilization mechanisms of the body.

Protein: Amino acids linked by peptide bonds, which consist of carbon, hydrogren, nitrogen, oxygen and usually sulfur that have several essential biological compounds.

Proximal: Refers to a position nearest the center of the body or point of reference.

Pulmonary Arteries: Deoxygenated blood is pumped from the right ventricle to the lungs through these arteries.

Pulmonary Capillaries: Surround the alveolar sacs. As oxygen fills the sacs it is diffused across the capillary membranes and into the alveolar sacs.

Pulmonary Semilunar Valve: Controls blood flow from the right ventricle to the pulmonary arteries going to the lungs.

Pulmonary Ventilation: The actual process of moving air in and out of the body.

Pyramid System: Involves a triangle or step approach that either progress up in weight with each set or decreases weight with each set.

Pyruvate: A by-product of anaerobic gylcolysis.

Q

Q-angle: The angle formed by lines representing the pull of the quadriceps muscle and the axis of the patellar tendon.

Quadrilateral Muscle Fiber: An arrangement of muscle fibers that are usually flat and four-sided. An example would include the rhomboid.

Quickness: The ability to react and change body position with maximum rate of force production, in all planes of motion, from all body positions, during functional activities. Also defined as the ability to execute movement skill in a comparatively brief amount of time.

R

Range of Motion: Refers to the range that the body or bodily segments move during and exercise.

Rate Coding: Muscular force can be amplified by increasing the rate of incoming impulses from the motor neuron after all prospective motor units have been activated.

Rate of Force Production: Ability of muscles to exert maximal force output in a minimal amount of time.

Reciprocal Inhibition: Muscles on one side of a joint relaxing to accommodate contraction of antagonist muscles on the other side of that joint.

Reaction Time: The time elapsed between the athlete's recognizing the need to act and initiating the appropriate action.

Reactive Strength: The ability of the neuromuscular system to switch from an eccentric contraction to a concentric contraction quickly and efficiently.

Reactive Training: Exercises that utilize quick, powerful movements involving an eccentric contraction immediately followed by an explosive concentric contraction.

Recommended Daily Allowance (RDA): The average daily nutrient intake level that is sufficient to meet the nutrient requirement of nearly all (97% to 98%) healthy individuals who are in a particular life stage and gender group.

Recovery Phase: A distinct phase during the stride cycle when the leg swings from the hip while the foot clears the ground.

Recreation: A client's physical activities outside of their work environment.

Recruitment: An impulse transmitted simultaneously over an increasing number of nerve fibers pulling in increasingly more muscle fibers for the task. This is sensitive to the stretch intensity and the number of fibers recruited.

Relative Flexibility: When the body seeks the path of least resistance during functional movement patterns.

Relative Strength: The maximum force that an individual can generate per unit of body weight, regardless of the time of force development.

Repetition: One complete movement of a particular exercise.

Repetition Tempo: The speed with which each repetition is performed.

Resistance Development Stage: The second stage of the GAS syndrome, when the body increases its functional capacity to adapt to the stressor.

Respiratory Exchange Ratio (RER): The ratio of CO_2 produced to O_2 consumed measured at the cellular level.

Respiratory Passageway: Collects the channeled air coming from the conducting passageway.

Respiratory Pump: Moves air in and out of the body.

Respiratory Quotient: The amount of carbon dioxide (CO_2) expired divided by the amount of oxygen (O_2) consumed, measured during rest or at steady state of exercise using a metabolic analyzer.

Respiratory System: The system of the body responsible for taking in oxygen, excreting carbon dioxide and regulating the relative composition of the blood.

Rest Interval: The time taken to recuperate between sets and/or exercises.

Restrictive Lung Disease: The condition of a fibrous lung tissue, which results in a decreased ability to expand the lungs.

Rheumatoid Arthritis: Arthritis primarily affecting connective tissues, in which there is a thickening of articular soft tissue, and extension of synovial tissue over articular cartilages that have become eroded.

Roll: The joint motion that depicts the rolling of one joint surface on another. Examples would include that of the femoral condyles over the tibial condyles during a squat.

Root Cause Analysis: A method of asking questions on a step-by-step basis to discover the initial cause of a fault.

Rotary Motion: Movement of an object or segment around a fixed axis in a curved path.

Ruffini Afferents: Large, encapsulated, multi-cellular end-organ structures located within the collagenous network of the joint's fibrous capsule. These receptors are mechanically sensitive to tissue stresses that are activated during extremes of extension and rotation.

S

Sacroiliac Joint: The joint connecting the tail bone (sacrum) and pelvic bone (ilium).

Sacroiliac Joint Dysfunction: Dysfunction of the sacroiliac joint due to trauma or degenerative changes.

Saddle Joint: One bone is shaped as a saddle, the other bone is shaped as the rider. The only example is in the carpometacarpal joint in the thumb.

Sagittal Plane: An imaginary plane that bisects the body into right and left halves. Sagittal plane motion occurs around a frontal axis.

Sarcomere: The functional unit of muscle, repeating sections of actin and myosin.

Sarcolemma: A plasma membrane that surrounds muscle fibers.

Sarcopenia: A decrease in muscle fiber numbers.

Sarcoplasm: Cell components that contain glycogen, fats, minerals and oxygen that are found in the sarcolemma.

Self-myofascial Release: A flexibility technique that focuses on the neural and fascial systems in the body. Self-myofascial release concentrates on alleviating myofascial trigger points and areas of hyperirritability located within a band of muscle. This form of stretching incorporates the concept of autogenic inhibition to improve soft tissue extensibility.

Self-organization: This theory, which is based on the dynamic pattern perspective, provides the body with the ability to overcome changes that are placed upon it.

Self-talk: The inner and outer dialog that forms our thoughts and shared ideas.

Semilunar Valves: Allow for proper blood flow from the ventricles to the aorta and pulmonary arteries.

Sensation: The process whereby sensory information is received by the receptor and transferred to the spinal cord for either reflexive motor behavior and/or to higher cortical areas for processing.

Sensorimotor Integration: The ability of the nervous system to gather and interpret sensory information to anticipate, select and execute the proper motor response.

Sensors: Provide feedback from the effectors to the central controller and cardiovascular control system. They include baroreceptors, chemoreceptors and muscle afferents.

Sensory Feedback: The process whereby sensory information is utilized to reactively monitor movement and the environment.

Sensory Information: The data that the central nervous system receives from sensory receptors to determine such things as the body's position in space, limb orientation as well as information to the environment, temperature, texture, etc.

Sensory Neurons: Neurons that gather incoming sensory information from the environment delivered to the central nervous system. Also known as afferent neurons.

Serotonin: A neurotransmitter in the modulation of anger, aggression, body temperature, mood, sleep, sexuality, appetite and metabolism.

Set: A group of consecutive repetitions.

Short Bones: A classification of bone that appears cubical in shape. Examples include the carpals and tarsals.

Single-set System: The individual performs one set of each exercise, usually 8–12 repetitions at a slow, controlled tempo.

Skeletal System: The portion of the human movement system that comprises the bones of the body.

Skin Fold Caliper: An instrument with two adjustable legs to measure thickness of a skin fold.

Slide: The joint motion that depicts the sliding of a joint surface across another. Examples would include the tibial condyles moving across the femoral condyles during a knee extension.

Sliding Filament Theory: The proposed process of the contraction of the filaments within the sarcomere takes place.

Slow Twitch Fibers: Another term for Type I muscle fibers, fibers that are characterized by a higher amount of capillaries, mitochondria and myoglobin. These fibers are usually found to have a higher endurance capacity than fast twitch fibers.

Specific Adaptations to Imposed Demands (SAID) Principle: Principle that states the body will adapt to the specific demands placed upon it.

Snatch: The first of the two Olympic lifts and is sometimes described as a single movement as the weight is pulled from the floor with two hands and explosively lifted to arm's length overhead with no pauses.

Specific Warm-up: Consists of movements that more closely mimic those of the actual activity.

Speed: In the context of athletics, speed is best defined as the "rate of performance" of an activity. The ability to achieve high velocity of movement.

Speed Strength: The ability of the neuromuscular system to produce the greatest possible force in the shortest possible time.

Split Routine System: A system that incorporates training individual's body parts with a high volume on separate days.

Spin: Joint motion that depicts the rotation of one joint surface on another. Examples would include the head of the radius rotating on the end of the humerus during pronation and supination of the forearm.

Sprain: A partial or complete tear of a ligament.

Stability: The ability of the body to maintain postural equilibrium and support joints during movement.

Stabilizer: Muscles that support or stabilize the body while the prime movers and the synergists perform the movement patterns.

Stabilization Endurance: The ability of the stabilization mechanisms of the human movement system to sustain proper levels of stabilization to allow for prolonged neuromuscular efficiency.

Stabilization Endurance Training: The name of the first phase of the OPT™ Model.

Stabilization Strength: Ability of the stabilizing muscles to provide dynamic joint stabilization and postural equilibrium during functional activities.

Starting Strength: The ability to produce high levels of force at the beginning of a movement.

Static Stretching: Combines low force and long duration movements utilizing the neurophysiological principles of autogenic inhibition to improve soft tissue extensibility, allowing for relaxation and concomitant elongation of muscle. Static stretching requires holding the stretch at the first point of tension or resistance barrier for 30 seconds.

Strength: The ability of the neuromuscular system to produce internal tension in order to overcome an external force.

Strength Endurance: The ability of the body to repeatedly produce high levels of force, over prolonged periods of time.

Strength Endurance Training: The second phase of the OPT™ Model.

Stretch-Shortening Cycle: An active stretch (eccentric contraction) of a muscle followed by an immediate shortening (concentric contraction) of that same muscle. Also defined as the process of the forced, rapid lengthening of a muscle immediately followed by a shortening, creating a release of energy.

Stride Length: The distance covered with each stride.

Stride Rate: The amount of time needed to complete a stride cycle.

Stroke Volume (SV): The amount of blood that is pumped out with each contraction of a ventricle.

Structural Efficiency: The alignment of the musculoskeletal system, which allows our center of gravity to be maintained over a base of support.

Subacromial Impingement Syndrome (SAIS): A common diagnosis broadly defined as compression of the structures (tendons) that run beneath the coracoacromial arch, most often from a decrease in the subacromial space. The impinged structures include the supraspinatus and infraspinatus tendons, the subacromial bursa and the long head of the biceps tendon.

Subjective Information: Information that is provided by a client regarding personal history such as occupation, lifestyle and medical history.

Sucrose: Often referred to as table sugar, it is a molecule made up of glucose and fructose.

Sulcus: A groove in a bone that allows a soft structure to pass through.

Superior: Refers to a position above a reference point.

Superset System: Utilizes two exercises performed in rapid succession of one another.

Supination: A multi-planar, synchronized joint motion that occurs with concentric muscle function.

Supine: Lying on one's back.

Support Phase: A distinct phase during the stride cycle where the runner's weight is carried by the entire foot.

Synarthrosis Joint: A joint without any joint cavity and fibrous connective tissue. Examples would include the sutures of the skull and the symphysis pubis.

Syndesmosis: A joint where two bones are joined by a ligament or membrane. An example is the distal tibiofibular joint.

Synergist: Muscles that assist prime movers during functional movement patterns.

Synergistic Dominance: When synergists compensate for a weak or inhibited prime mover in an attempt to maintain force production and functional movement patterns.

Synovial Joints: This type of joint is characterized by the absence of fibrous or cartilaginous tissue connecting the bones. Examples would include the ball-and-socket joint, the hinge joint and the saddle joint.

T

Temporal Lobe: A portion of the cerebral cortex that deals with hearing.

Tendon: Connective tissue that attaches muscle to bone and provides an anchor for muscles to exert force.

Tendonitis: An inflammation in a tendon or the tendon covering.

Thoracic Spine: The twelve vertebrae in mid-torso that are attached to the rib cage.

Time: The length of time an individual is engaged in a given activity.

Tolerable Upper Level (TUL): The highest average daily nutrient intake level likely to pose no risk of adverse health effects to almost all individuals in a particular life stage and gender group. As intake increases above the TUL, the potential risk of adverse health effects increases.

Torque: The ability of any force to cause rotation around an axis. A force that produces rotation. Common unit of torque is the Newton-Meter, or N.m.

Total Response Time: The total summation of time it takes to execute a reactionary movement.

Training Duration: The time frame of a workout or the time spent in one phase of training.

Training Frequency: The number of training sessions that are conducted over a given period.

Training Intensity: An individual's level of effort compared to their maximum effort.

Training Plan: The specific outline, created by a health and fitness professional to meet a client's goals, that details the form of training, length of time, future changes and specific exercises to be performed.

Training Volume: The total amount of work performed within a specified time period.

Transverse Plane: An imaginary plane that bisects the body to create upper and lower halves. Transverse plane motion occurs around a longitudinal or a vertical axis.

Transfer-of-Training Effect: The more similar the exercise is to the actual activity, the greater the carryover into real-life settings.

Tricuspid Valve: Controls the blood flow from the right atrium from the right ventricle.

Tri-sets System: A system very similar to supersets, the difference being three exercises back-to-back-to-back-with little to no rest in between.

Trochanter: Projections protruding from the bone to which muscles, tendons and ligaments can attach. Also known as a condyle, process, tubercle and epicondyle.

Trochlea: A groove in front of the femur where the patella moves as the knee bends and straightens.

Tubercle: Projections protruding from the bone to which muscles, tendons and ligaments can attach. Also known as a condyle, process, epicondyle and trochanter.

Type: The type or mode of physical activity that an individual is engaged in.

U

Unipenniform Muscle Fiber: Muscle fibers that are arranged with short, oblique fibers that extend from one side of a long tendon. An example would include the tibialis posterior.

Upper-extremity Postural Distortion: An individual, who exhibits a forward head, rounded shoulder posture.

Universal Athletic Position: Standing in a quarter squat with flat feet, hands in front, hips back, knees over the shoulders, shoulders over the knees and neutral spine.

V

Veins: Vessels that transport blood back to the heart.

Ventilation: The actual process of moving air in and out of the body.

Ventral: Refers to a position on the front or towards the front of the body.

Ventricles: Larger chambers located inferiorly on either side of the heart.

Venules: Vessels that collect blood from the capillaries.

Vertical Loading: A variation of circuit training alternating body parts trained from set to set, starting from the upper extremity and moving to the lower extremity.

Viscoelasticity: The fluid-like property of connective tissue that allows slow deformation with an imperfect recovery after the deforming forces are removed.

Vitamin: Any of various fat-soluble or water-soluble organic substances essential in minute amounts for normal growth and activity of the body and obtained naturally from plant and animal foods.

VO_2 Max: The highest volume of oxygen a person can consume during exercise. Often used as a predictor of potential in endurance sports.

Volume: The total amount of weight lifted in a session or week and quantified by repetitions times weight.

W

Weekly Plan: Training plan of specific workouts that spans one week to show which exercises are required each day of the week.

Whey protein: The collection of globular proteins that can be isolated from whey, a by-product of cheese manufactured from cow's milk. Whey has the highest biological value (BV) of any known protein.

Wobble Board: A piece of training equipment used to develop physical balance. It is often used for rehabilitation purposes, although it can be very useful to improve proprioception and dynamic joint stability.

Wolff's Law: The principle that every change in the form and the function of a bone or in the function of the bone alone, leads to changes in its internal architecture and in its external form.

Work Capacity: The ability to endure high workloads within various intensities and durations utilizing a range of energy systems and displaying the ability to recover for the next bout of exercise.

Index

Page numbers followed by f indicate figure; those followed by t indicate table.